THE NORMAN EMPIRE

THE
NORMAN EMPIRE

BY

JOHN LE PATOUREL

OXFORD
AT THE CLARENDON PRESS
1976

Oxford University Press, Walton Street, Oxford, OX2 6DP

OXFORD LONDON GLASGOW NEW YORK
TORONTO MELBOURNE WELLINGTON CAPE TOWN
IBADAN NAIROBI DAR ES SALAAM LUSAKA ADDIS ABABA
KUALA LUMPUR SINGAPORE JAKARTA HONG KONG TOKYO
DELHI BOMBAY CALCUTTA MADRAS KARACHI

ISBN 0 19 822525 3

© Oxford University Press 1976

Printed in Great Britain
at the University Press, Oxford
by Vivian Ridler
Printer to the University

PREFACE

THIS book is an essay in reinterpretation. Its theme is the complex but coherent political structure which the Normans built up in Northern France and Britain during the eleventh and early twelfth centuries. This political structure can be seen to have had a beginning, times of expansion, consolidation, and disintegration, and an end. It was the political reality of its day rather than the kingdom of the English or the duchy of the Normans; and after it had come to its end the elements of which it had been composed were reassembled with others into a new and historically distinct political structure, the 'empire' of the Angevin kings. It is a relatively clearly defined historical phenomenon, though like all such phenomena it cannot be treated as entirely self-contained. Dividing lines are never sharp and exclusive; and all argument on continuity or discontinuity between one historical phase or subject and another must be treated as a matter of more or less, for both are present at all moments of change. The states which the Normans created in Mediterranean lands are not involved; for although these may be treated as part of the Norman 'expansion', and although they may have sent back ideas and wealth to Normandy, even to England, and there were certainly personal relationships between them, no medieval political organization could have spanned the distances from Rouen and Winchester to Palermo and Antioch.

The book is of necessity based principally upon the work of others and my dependence will be evident on every page, with a particularly heavy debt to the publications of Douglas, Lemarignier, Musset, and Yver among living historians. Nothing of this sort could be undertaken if the discovery, publication, and interpretation of the evidence had not reached an advanced stage and there were not already many detailed studies as well as general surveys. In fact, so much work has been done on the evidence and there is so much of it that to try to see and to understand all would delay conclusions of any sort indefinitely. There are bound to be omissions, conscious and unconscious. Moreover, an attempt to look at relatively familiar events, situations, and personalities in a less familiar way, to see the political structure which the Norman kings built up not as an episode in 'English history' or in the provincial history of France but as a historical reality in its own right, inevitably raises many more questions than can be answered immediately. On many subjects treated in this book I have been conscious of the further investigations that would have to be undertaken and the articles and theses written before my conclusions could be regarded as reasonably firmly grounded; yet the formulation of a question or a hypothesis is a necessary stage in understanding, and the best that could happen is that these first and second thoughts should stir up others to refine and restate them.

No doubt the title is provocative. The argument for it is given in chapter 9. I have tried to be consistent in the form of proper names, though this is difficult. Place-names are given wherever possible in their modern form and in their own language. In the case of personal names, forenames are given in their modern English equivalent where it exists, and 'sur-names' that are identifiable place-names are given as other place-names, with the particle in the appropriate language—thus, 'Henry of Winchester' but 'William de Rouen'. This cannot be done wholly consistently, since to speak of 'William de Varenne' rather than 'William de Warenne', for example, would only introduce obscurity; yet if the convention so far as it can be followed tends to emphasize the 'French' element in Normanno-English affairs during the time of the Norman kings, that is no disadvantage. I have used the form 'fitz-', as in 'William fitzOsbern', where this has been customary among historians. The words *comté*, *vicomté* and *vicomte* have been left untranslated in a French context, as their English equivalents can be misleading when used of the eleventh and twelfth centuries. *Comes* has been rendered as 'count' in a French context and 'earl' in an English one, though the relationship between these terms is delicate. Likewise, although neither was established or in any way 'official' before the middle of the twelfth century, the titles 'duke of Normandy' and 'duke of Brittany' have sometimes been used for convenience. References are given in abbreviated form in the footnotes but the works cited are fully identified in the bibliography.

I have incurred many obligations in writing this book. Professor R. H. C. Davis and Professor J. C. Holt each read a complete draft and offered comments from which I have greatly profited. On particular points I owe much to discussion or consultation with Professor C. N. L. Brooke, Professor C. R. Cheney, Dr. Pierre Chaplais, Sir Charles Clay, Dr. Sally Harvey, Professor C. Warren Hollister, Professor P. H. Sawyer (who has also read the proofs), and Professor Jean Yver. They may not agree with what I have finally written and they are certainly not responsible for it; but the book owes much to their kindness. Dr Marjorie Chibnall has put me greatly in her debt, principally by checking the index in typescript, and N. E. J. Le P. was very helpful with the proofs and the index in an earlier stage. The generous treatment given to me by the University of Leeds, particularly in the last few years, gave me my opportunity; and the courteous helpfulness of the librarians in the Brotherton Library has eased many difficulties. Nor can I forget at this time the almost unbelievably good fortune that made me a pupil of Sir Goronwy Edwards, Sir Maurice Powicke, and Professor V. H. Galbraith; for although they have had nothing directly to do with this book my debt to them is incalculable. H. E. J. Le P., besides providing the conditions which alone make work of this kind possible, has helped as critic and in many practical ways. The book is for her.

1976   J. Le P.

CONTENTS

PART I

CHRONOLOGY

1. The Beginning

THE origins of the great complex of lands and lordships over which King Henry Beauclerc exercised varying degrees of power and authority early in the twelfth century lie in the establishment of a body of Northmen in the lower Seine Valley some two centuries earlier. Although there had been Viking raids over northern France for several decades already, and perhaps a few scattered settlements, it was the agreement between Charles the Simple, king of the western Franks, and Rollo (as he is known to history), the Norse leader of a mainly Danish army, which enabled these Northmen to provide themselves with a base in northern France, to adapt themselves in course of time to the conditions of the country in which they found themselves, and ultimately to create a stable political structure. The traditional date of the agreement, 911, may well be correct, or at least approximately so; but its terms are far from certain for no text has survived (if there ever was one) nor any contemporary account that could be regarded as complete. All that can be said with any assurance is that King Charles granted a certain territory around the city of Rouen to Rollo and his followers, or acquiesced in their seizure of it, that they for their part agreed to accept Christianity after their fashion,[1] and that it was from this agreement and this territorial nucleus that the duchy of Normandy was eventually formed.

The territorial formation of the duchy is generally represented as having been achieved in three stages. The first of these stages is marked by the agreement of 911, which is understood to have conveyed to the Northmen what was later Upper Normandy; the second by a 'grant' made on behalf of King Rudolf in 924 of a territory identified with the Bessin and the Hiémois; and the third by a final 'grant', made by the same king in 933, which is interpreted as ceding the Cotentin and the Avranchin.[2] The implication that the Northmen obtained

[1] Douglas, 'Rollo of Normandy', pp. 417–29.
[2] e.g. Douglas, ibid., pp. 429–32; Prentout, *Étude critique sur Dudon*, pp. 199–203; Musset, 'Naissance de la Normandie', pp. 97–9.

the land of Normandy by a series of royal acts, each conveying a defined territory, has been greatly strengthened in recent years by the impressive argument that has been built up for deriving much of the authority of the Norman dukes of the later eleventh and twelfth centuries from Carolingian sources. In so far as certain ducal powers and prerogatives of that time are to be identified with the functions of Carolingian counts acting as royal officers, the case can be said to have been made and it would be almost impossible to challenge; but in so far as this is taken to imply direct continuity, a lawful transmission of authority in specific areas from the king of the Western Franks to Rollo and his successors within a recognized governmental framework, it is very much more doubtful.[1] Among the arguments brought forward for such continuity, in addition to the chronicler Flodoard's statements and the form in which he makes them,[2] are the correspondence between the boundaries of the duchy in their final form and those of the ecclesiastical province of Rouen (itself a continuation of the late Roman *Lugdunensis Secunda*), the survival of the Carolingian *pagi* (or counties) in Normandy, not simply as geographical terms but as administrative units (though in a form, naturally, very different from their Carolingian constitution), and the extent to which the frontiers of the later duchy respect the boundaries of the *pagi* included within it—so that Normandy could be regarded territorially and to some extent governmentally as a block of Carolingian *pagi* taken over by the Northmen with

[1] The thesis of continuity has been magisterially expounded by Yver in 'Premières institutions', an article which embodies a great deal of research by the author, by L. Musset, and others. When it was written, however, the thesis had already been challenged by M. de Bouard in a paper entitled 'De la Neustrie carolingienne à la Normandie féodale; continuité ou discontinuité?'. The fundamental problem seems to be one of transmission. The 'continuity' theory seems to make it necessary for the powers of a Carolingian count to have been taken over and exercised by Rollo and his immediate successors at once and more or less intact. This is a process which cannot be demonstrated and, in the conditions of the early tenth century, is scarcely credible. On the other hand, if there was a decisive break, by what means and at what point in time were these powers, certainly exercised by the duke in the late eleventh century, actually assumed? The compromise theory, suggested below, of a recovery of such powers by the Norman dukes at some point before the end of the eleventh century, is no more demonstrable; and whether it is more credible must be a matter of judgment (below, p. 13 and ch. 8).

[2] Below, pp. 6, 8, 281–2; cf. Lemarignier, *Hommage en marche* pp. 14–19 etc.

their boundaries and their administrative structure largely intact, the duchy being in fact constituted by means that could be regarded as lawful and fixed in its definitive frontiers no later than 933. However, the little we can know of the early history of the Scandinavian settlement in northern France suggests that war and conquest were quite as important in the territorial formation of Normandy as legitimate royal grant. It also suggests that this process took longer, was more complex and less tidy in its ultimate outcome, than the customary interpretation of the three 'grants' of 911, 924, and 933 would imply.

There can be little doubt that King Charles the Simple, in making the agreement of 911, hoped to provide a breakwater against further raiding and plundering of his kingdom, at any rate from the north, by securing the conversion of these Northmen to Christianity and giving them lands of their own to defend[1]—integrating them, that is to say, so far as it was possible to do this by a single act, into the Frankish populations among whom they were settling. But there were always at least two possible interpretations of the agreement of 911 and those of 924 and 933: a Frankish interpretation of territory formally granted to a leader of the Northmen, as any 'honour' might be granted by the king to one of his *fideles*, and a Viking interpretation of territory seized by them, their seizure being acquiesced in and perhaps in some way legitimized by royal act. What store these Northmen set by such legitimation at the time it is difficult to say; certainly there is nothing to suggest that they were satisfied with the 'grant' of 911, or even with all three 'grants' together; indeed, they seem to have looked upon the land they had acquired not 'as a land for peaceful settlement so much as a base of operations for future wars'.[2]

That at any rate is how they treated it, for they were on the march again within little more than a decade of the agreement of 911. In the year 923 they joined another body of Vikings operating in the Loire Valley on a raid into the Beauvaisis;[3]

---

[1] Diploma of King Charles the Simple, 918: 'Donavimus . . . illam abbatiam . . . praeter partem ipsius abbatiae quam annuimus Normannis Sequanensibus, videlicet Rolloni suisque comitibus, pro tutela regni': *Recueil des actes de Charles III le Simple*, no. xcii (p. 211); Douglas, 'Rollo of Normandy', p. 426.

[2] Stenton, 'The Scandinavian Colonies', p. 12.

[3] Lauer, *Robert Ier et Raoul de Bourgogne*, pp. 24–7; Flodoard, *Annales*,

two years later they penetrated as far as Arras and Noyon;[1] in 926 they were in Artois again and raiding the country as far as the county of Porcien.[2] Eventually their way was blocked in this easterly direction by the count of Flanders;[3] but by that time they had already turned to the west where raiding appeared to be more profitable. When a temporary peace was made with them in 924, on the authority of King Rudolf, a territory described by Flodoard as 'Maine and the Bessin' was ceded to them.[4] In the usual interpretation of this concession, 'Maine' has been amended to the Hiémois on the ground that there is no other record of the Northmen having possession of Maine in the tenth century whereas they must have acquired the Hiémois at about this time.[5] Flodoard may indeed have made a slip here; but it is perhaps equally likely that his statement was correct and that, in the confusion of the time, the Northmen were trying to occupy a territory of which they failed to obtain effective possession.

Later, in 933, when Rollo's successor William Longsword performed an act that was interpreted as homage to King Rudolf, he obtained from the King, in Flodoard's phrase again, 'the land of the Bretons by the sea coast'.[6] This has been understood to mean the Cotentin and the Avranchin,[7] because those districts had been surrendered by King Charles the Bald to Salomon, king of the Bretons, in 867,[8] because they were all that was needed to make up the historic Normandy, and they are certainly 'by the sea coast'. But since the king of the West

pp. 15–19. On the raids of the years 923–6 see generally E. Joranson, *The Danegeld in France*, pp. 163–74.

[1] Lauer, *Robert Ier et Raoul de Bourgogne*, pp. 37–40; Douglas, 'Rollo of Normandy', p. 434.

[2] Lauer, *Robert Ier et Raoul de Bourgogne*, pp. 43–4.

[3] Below, p. 19 n. 1.

[4] 'Nordmanni cum Francis pacem ineunt . . . absente rege Rodulfo: ejus tamen consensu terra illis aucta, Cinomannis et Baiocae pacto eis pacis concessae': Flodoard, *Annales*, p. 24.

[5] Lemarignier, *Hommage en marche*, p. 10 (note 2).

[6] 'Willelmus princeps Nordmannorum eidem regi [Rodulfo] se committit; cui etiam rex dat terram Brittonum in ora maritima sitam'; Flodoard, *Annales*, p. 55.

[7] Prentout, *Étude critique sur Dudon*, pp. 202, 291; Douglas, 'Rollo of Normandy', pp. 430–2.

[8] Prentout, *Étude critique sur Dudon*, pp. 284–7; Musset, 'Naissance de la Normandie', p. 96. On the Breton expansion in the ninth century, perhaps as far as the Orne and the Mayenne, Chanteux, 'Le Toponyme "Bretteville" en Normandie'; Boussard, 'Les destinées de la Neustrie', pp. 15 (note 2), 27.

Franks can have had little effective authority in this part of his kingdom during the early tenth century,[1] it is not at all un-likely that something more comprehensive and less precise was intended. Between 907 and 919 Brittany had been overrun by bands of Northmen operating in and from the Loire Valley, and these had actually received from Robert, count of the march of Brittany, a 'grant' of 'Brittany which they had devas-tated together with the county of Nantes'.[2] By that time most of the leading men in Brittany had fled the country and it looked as though another 'Normandy' might be established in the far west; but since the Bretons who stayed behind rose against the Northmen in 931 and eventually succeeded in driving them out,[3] it is not at all impossible that the 'grant' of the 'land of the Bretons' to William Longsword in 933 had been intended to assist them by setting one lot of Vikings against another. It is at any rate certain that the Northmen of the Seine were raiding and plundering Brittany for some time after this. In 944 they invaded the country and were settling on lands in the neigh-bourhood of Dol;[4] about 960 and in the following years they were pillaging the country as far as Nantes;[5] and as late as 1013–14 Duke Richard II received with honour two Vikings who, after raiding northern France at his invitation, arrived at Rouen with the booty from yet another sack of Dol.[6] If the assertion of Dudo de Saint-Quentin that King Charles the Simple gave Brittany to Rollo for plunder and sustenance is to be dismissed as one of his fables,[7] it is easy to understand how

[1] 'Reges enim Franciae omnino adnullati et adnihilati erant, nullaque fortitudo, nullus vigor defensionis in eis erat'; *Chron. Nantes*, p. 81.

[2] 'Robertus comes Nordmannos qui Ligerim fluvium occupaverant per quinque menses obsedit, acceptisque ab eis obsidibus, Britanniam ipsis, quam vastaverant, cum Namnetico pago concessit; quique fidem Xρisti coeperunt suscipere'; Flodoard, *Annales*, p. 6. The parallel, even to some of the wording, between this and Flo-doard's reference to the agreement between Charles the Simple and the Northmen of the Seine is worth noting (cf. below, p. 8 n. 6).

[3] *Chron. Nantes*, pp. 80–96; Flodoard, *Annales*, pp. 50, 68, 74; Durtelle de Saint-Sauveur, *Histoire de Bretagne*, i. 80–2.

[4] Flodoard, *Annales*, p. 94; Lauer, *Louis IV d'Outremer*, pp. 116–18; Durtelle de Saint-Sauveur, *Histoire de Bretagne*, i. 102.

[5] *Chron. Nantes*, pp. 111–12.

[6] William de Jumièges, *Gesta*, pp. 85–6; Douglas, 'Rise of Normandy', p. 108.

[7] 'Dedit itaque rex filiam suam Gislam nomine, uxorem illi duci, terramque determinatam in alodo et in fundo, a flumine Eptae usque ad mare, totamque Britanniam de qua posset vivere'; Dudo, *De Moribus*, p. 169; Prentout, *Étude critique sur Dudon*, pp. 203–5.

a Norman tradition to that effect might grow up, quite apart from the politics of Dudo's own day and the recently discovered numismatic evidence to suggest that William Longsword could be styled 'duke of the Bretons'.[1]

To the south, the Northmen raided the country around Chartres both before the agreement of 911 and during the 'Norman War' of 961–6 as well as on other occasions;[2] but in this direction their opportunities were more limited, for along much of the line that eventually became the Norman frontier in this sector there was a broad belt of difficult hill country and forest, and here their activities would directly confront the interests of the duke of the Franks. Hugh the Great was frequently in conflict with them and in 943 was actually in possession of Évreux.[3]

This narrative of the activities of the Northmen of the Seine in the decades following the agreement of 911 hardly suggests that they had accepted a defined territory and settled down to cultivate it, whatever Dudo might say. The dukes of Normandy may in the end have created a duchy with boundaries that came nearer to the modern idea of a frontier than most of their fellow territorial princes in Francia could achieve;[4] yet it seems unlikely that this was done simply by taking over a group of existing administrative units and perpetuating them. If the Carolingian *pagi* had been treated in this way, one would expect the territories ceded to the Northmen to be defined in terms of *pagi* and the frontier of the later duchy to follow their boundaries, and it has indeed been claimed that this is so.[5] But if the evidence can be made to support this interpretation, it can also be read differently. Though Flodoard describes the subject of the 'grant' of 911 as 'certain maritime *pagi*, with the city of Rouen which they [the Northmen] had almost destroyed and others dependent upon it',[6] these 'maritime *pagi*' can only be

---

[1] Dolley and Yvon, 'A Group of Tenth-Century Coins found at Mont Saint-Michel', esp. pp. 7–11.

[2] Lot, *Les derniers Carolingiens*, pp. 346–57; Douglas, 'Rise of Normandy', p. 107.

[3] Lauer, *Louis IV d'Outremer*, pp. 99–100.

[4] Lemarignier, *Hommage en marche*, pp. 11–14.

[5] Ibid., pp. 9–19.

[6] 'De Nordmannorum quoque mitigatione atque conversione valde laboravit [i.e. the archbishop of Reims]; donec, tandem post bellum quod Rotbertus comes contra eos Carnotenus gessit, fidem Christi suscipere coeperunt, concessis sibi maritimis quibusdam pagis cum Rothomagensi quam pene deleverant

identified by inference, by saying that since the frontier of this part of Normandy, when there is clear evidence of it, included the territory of certain *pagi* therefore the 'grant' must have been concerned with those particular *pagi*; and in fact this frontier, to the east and the south, did not respect the boundaries of the *pagi*. It did not exactly follow the eastern boundary of the *pagus Tellauus* (Talou);[1] it actually bisected both the *pagus Vilcassinus* (Vexin) and the *pagus Madriacensis* (Méresais);[2] and though it did eventually settle on the line of the river Avre, which had divided the *pagus Ebroicinus* (Évreux) from the *pagus Durocassinus* (Dreux) it only did so after a century of fluctuation.[3] As a whole it can only represent the line on which the king and the count of Flanders were able to halt the advance of the Northmen in these directions. In the west, where Flodoard's description of the territory ceded to William Longsword is quite vague, the persistent attempts of the Northmen of the Seine to settle the country around Dol likewise suggest that the ultimate frontier on the River Couesnon owed as much to the balance of military forces as to the existence of an earlier boundary of the *pagus Abrincatinus* (Avranchin).[4] The great Breton victory at Trans near Pontorson in 939 may have had something to do with it;[5] but even in the eleventh century Duke Robert I is said to have founded a castle at 'Carrucas' which, if the site is to be identified with the modern village of Cherrueix (as it must be, it seems),[6] is some miles to the west of the Couesnon.

urbe et aliis eidem [*or* et isdem] subjectis'; Flodoard, 'Historia Remensis Ecclesiae', p. 577. It is worth noting that Flodoard should write of certain *pagi* as 'subject to' Rouen (if that is the reading), as though there had been at that time an administrative unit consisting of a group of *pagi* centred on that city; and it would be interesting to know what he had in mind. It has been taken for granted here, and elsewhere in this chapter, that when Flodoard uses the word *pagus* he means the Carolingian unit of that name, or what it had become in his time.

[1] Lemarignier, *Hommage en marche*, pp. 34–9.

[2] Ibid., pp. 38–55. On the map at the end of Lemarignier's book the northern tributary of the River Eure should have been named 'Avre'.

[3] Musset, 'Les plus anciennes chartes normandes de l'abbaye de Bourgueil', pp. 36–47.

[4] Boussard, 'Le comté de Mortain au xiᵉ siècle', pp. 255–6.

[5] Flodoard, *Annales*, p. 74. Cf. *Chron. Nantes*, p. 91 (note 2); Durtelle de Saint-Sauveur, *Histoire de Bretagne*, i. 81–2.

[6] 'Non longe a fluvio Coisnon castrum stabilivit, quod Carrucas vocavit, ad munimen videlicet Normannici limitis'; William de Jumièges, *Gesta*, pp. 105–6. Robert de Torigni, in an interpolation, adds 'id est Carues' (ibid., p. 235). Cf. Yver, 'Châteaux forts en Normandie', p. 39.

The southern frontier, even if it eventually respected the boundaries of the *pagi* for much of its length, was not stabilized as a whole until later still. Alençon, though on the right bank of the Sarthe where it formed the boundary between the *pagus Sagensis* (Séois) and the *pagus Cenomannicus* (Maine), was fortified by the family of Bellême which was not Norman in origin and whose principal estates lay outside Normandy by any definition. The place only became Norman after it had been taken by Duke Robert I from William de Bellême;[1] and even then it had to be recaptured by William the Conqueror, this time from the count of Anjou. This was probably in 1051, when William went on to take Domfront and to annex the surrounding district of the Passais (hitherto part of the *pagus Cenomannicus* or Maine)—a territorial addition to his duchy that was by no means negligible.[2] And it was precisely along this southern frontier of the duchy and in the west that the dukes organized a region that had more of the characteristics of a 'march' than anything elsewhere in Normandy.[3]

Finally, the correlation so often observed between the frontiers of the duchy and the boundaries of the ecclesiastical province of Rouen may not have been as significant a factor in the determination of those frontiers as it has seemed to historians. The diocese of Rouen itself extended over the whole of the ancient *pagus* of the Vexin, while the Norman hold upon the eastern half of that *pagus*, the Vexin Français, was at most very temporary. Similarly the diocese of Séez included the *comté* of Mortagne and the lordship of Bellême, which were only attached to Normandy as possessions of families which also held land in the duchy; and though, like Norman ambitions in the Vexin Français, this created a possibility of ultimate inclusion in the duchy that possibility was not realized; whereas the Passais, though annexed by William the Conqueror in the middle of the eleventh century, remained ecclesiastically in the non-Norman diocese of Le Mans.[4]

It seems, indeed, anachronistic to look too soon in the history of Normandy for a stable linear frontier, clearly defined. Such

[1] White, 'The First House of Bellême', pp. 77–8.
[2] Douglas, *William the Conqueror*, pp. 59–61.
[3] Musset, 'Observations sur l'histoire et la signification de la frontière normande'.
[4] Lemarignier, *Hommage en marche*, pp. 39–55, 63–5.

a frontier could hardly come into being before governmental administration on either side of it had attained a certain level of sophistication. This point might be said to have been reached when the *coutume* of Normandy had 'crystallized', when it was internally consistent, distinct from other *coutumes* and clearly territorialized.[1] To bring it to this state could only be the work of the ducal courts and it was not achieved much before the end of the eleventh century. Indeed, if one is looking for a clear point of reference, a territorial definition of the duchy of Normandy in relation to which political fluctuations and boundaries for other purposes (such as ecclesiastical administration) can be described, the limits of the *coutume*—which can be precisely determined, which must have coincided with the limits of effective ducal government when they were established, and which were stable[2]—are probably the most satisfactory.[3]

It is almost certainly assuming too much to speak as though a legal frontier had been fixed by the 'grants' of 911, 924, and 933, even if it is admitted that such a frontier might or might not have been effective in detail at different times.[4] Legality can usually be found if it is sought for, and no doubt the kings of the Franks in the early tenth century were anxious in their own interests to cast a mantle of legality over the territorial acquisitions of these Northmen, as they were anxious to limit them. The Northmen for their part were forcing their way into Francia by violence; willing to accept the legitimation of their conquests when it suited them and so far as they understood it, and prepared to allow their leaders to accept the position of vassal or *fidelis* as then conceived for such advantages as it might offer;

---

[1] Below, p. 264.

[2] Génestal, 'Formation et développement de la Coutume de Normandie', pp. 40–2; Lemarignier, *Hommage en marche*, chs. i and ii. There are maps of the Norman dioceses in Powicke, *Loss of Normandy*, facing p. 424 (from *Magni Rotuli Scaccarii Normanniae*, ed. Stapleton, i., facing p. ix), and in Douglas, *William the Conqueror*, pp. 454–5; of the *pagi* in Longnon, *Atlas historique*, plate VII; of the limits of the *coutume* in Klimrath, 'Études sur les coutumes', and in Lemarignier, *Hommage en marche*, facing p. 180 (with discussion in ch. 2). The three sets of boundaries are put together in Map 2.

[3] The Vexin Français, for example, was governed by *coutumes* of the Parisian group; while Mortagne and Bellême were in the *ressort* of the *coutume* of Grand Perche; Lemarignier, *Hommage en marche*, pp. 23, 61; Klimrath, *Études sur les coutumes*, pp. 32–3.

[4] e.g. Musset, 'Les plus anciennes chartes normandes de l'abbaye de Bourgueil', pp. 41–4.

but yielding ultimately to no restraint other than superior force
or overstretched resources. Norman expansion began as it went
on; its origins were the origins of Normandy itself; war and
conquest had a very large part in it; but the limits of the duchy
formed in the course of this expansion were fixed as the internal
political structure of Normandy developed—they were not determined at the outset.

The form of Norman expansion was consistent from its earliest
days in another important respect. Colonization followed conquest. There may have been some scattered Viking settlements
within the territory of the future Normandy before the agreement of 911;[1] a substantial settlement almost certainly took
place immediately after that agreement;[2] and fresh bands of
raiders and settlers were arriving through most of the tenth
century.[3] The Scandinavian colonization of Normandy was not,
therefore, a simple, single operation, but a long and complex
process; even so it is clear that the regions intensively colonized
by people of Scandinavian origin amounted to very much less
than the whole of the territory dominated by them.[4] From the
first, that is to say, the Normans were an aristocratic minority
in the lands they ruled. Yet their devastations extended throughout the land that became Normandy, affecting regions which
they came to control, though hardly to colonize save as an
aristocracy, as well as those settled more intensively. So far as
can be seen, bishoprics, monasteries, and native Frankish
landowners suffered throughout the extent of the later duchy,
and in some parts far beyond it.[5] The earliest Normandy was
a robber state owing its evident prosperity largely to plunder
and to activities in which raiding and trading were not always

---

[1] Musset, 'Naissance de la Normandie', p. 101.

[2] Dudo, *De Moribus*, p. 171.

[3] Below, pp. 283-4.

[4] Musset, 'Naissance de la Normandie', pp. 101-6. There is a useful map on
p. 104.

[5] There are gaps in the lists of bishops of Lisieux (832-990), Avranches (862-
990), Séez (910-936); there are obscurities at Bayeux, and the bishops of Coutances
resided at Rouen from the early tenth century until *c.* 1025: Douglas, 'Rollo of
Normandy', p. 433; de Bouard, 'De la Neustrie carolingienne à la Normandie
féodale', p. 5; Le Patourel, 'Geoffrey of Montbray', pp. 134-5; Musset, 'Naissance de la Normandie', p. 119. No monastery survived as such and no leading
Norman family traced its ancestry back to the ninth century, in contrast to some
neighbouring lands: Musset, 'Les domaines de l'époque franque', pp. 43-4, and
cf. below, p. 289.

clearly distinguished.[1] Richer of Reims, who was writing in the last years of the tenth century and who constantly refers to the Northmen as *piratae*, and to Rollo and William Longsword as *princeps* or *dux piratarum*, still uses the same expression of Duke Richard I at the time of his death in 996, within a year or two of the moment when Richer was writing.[2]

It was not, perhaps, entirely inappropriate even then, though at that time a great change was coming over Normandy. The fact that Rollo and his leading men had come to an agreement with the church in Rouen that enabled the archbishop to return to his city and some monks of Saint-Ouen to their abbey,[3] together with the fact, as it must be, that many native Frankish people, if not their more important landowners, had survived certainly in the parts of Normandy that were dominated rather than colonized by the Northmen, meant that these Northmen must accommodate themselves eventually to the environment into which they had come and to the political and social conditions that were developing in the principalities growing up around them. The process of adaptation seems to have taken place in the later part of the tenth and the earlier part of the eleventh centuries.[4] In that time the Northmen of the Seine lost contact with the Scandinavian world and turned to Francia. When the change had been accomplished their language was 'French' and their law belonged to the family of regional *coutumes* that was taking shape in northern and western France; the successors of Rollo had converted themselves from Viking chieftains into territorial princes, assuming the powers of Carolingian counts while retaining some elements of their original authority as Viking chieftains; and as their administration developed they may have reconstituted in some measure the ancient *pagi* as administrative units, taking as their model those which had been disrupted least.[5]

---

[1] Above, pp. 5–8; cf. Musset, 'Naissance de la Normandie', pp. 106–8.

[2] Richer, *Historiae*, i. 64, 100, 104 (Rollo); 156, 168, 172 (William Longsword); ii. 328 (Richard I); and *passim*.

[3] Musset, 'Les domaines de l'époque franque', p. 44; 'Naissance de la Normandie', pp. 119–20.

[4] Douglas dates the beginning, if only the beginning, of the change from 965, ('Rise of Normandy', pp. 107–8); Musset regards it as largely completed by about 1020 ('Réflexions d'un historien sur les origines du droit normand', p. 364).

[5] On these changes and the problems connected with them, see below, pp. 280 ff.

As all this was going on in Normandy, the descendants or successors of the Carolingian counts in Francia generally were
building feudal principalities out of their counties, first making
their positions hereditary, then exercising on their own account
and for their own profit rights and powers which they had
hitherto exercised as royal officers, then adding *comté* to *comté*
by marriage, inheritance, conquest, or feudal or quasi-feudal
subjection. The principalities so formed were inevitably competitive and so aggressive; for in the absence of an effective
central authority each must dominate or be dominated. However different Normandy may have been in origin, and however
important these differences of origin would be in its development, it had to live in this environment, among principalities
that were fast becoming feudal—if the feudalism of the twelfth
century is taken as the standard. Like its neighbours, Normandy
might have to be aggressive simply to survive and it would have
to adopt their methods.[1]

In the early history of Normandy and Norman expansion,
then, we may distinguish a 'Viking' phase, when Rollo and his
immediate successors and followers formed a robber state living
largely on plunder both within the bounds of what later became
their duchy and beyond, and a later 'feudal' phase, when the
means by which the dukes controlled their duchy and extended
their dominion and exploitation beyond it were more like those
of contemporary feudal princes elsewhere in Francia. The distinction is more a matter of ways and means than of objectives
and results, and at many points the two phases overlap. This is
particularly clear in Brittany, where the Northmen had been
raiding and trying to settle during the 'Viking' phase, before
it was even clear what the territorial extent of Normandy would
be; and there is hardly a break between this early interest and
the point at which it began to take on a form more characteristic
of the second, the 'feudal' phase. Duke Richard II was im-
plicated in a Viking raid on Brittany as late as 1013–14;[2] but
already in the last decade of the tenth century the rivalry
between the counts of Rennes and the counts of Nantes for
predominance in Brittany moved Geoffrey Bérenger, count of

[1] This transformation of Normandy and the means by which it was accomplished
are more fully analysed in chapter 8.
[2] Above, p. 7.

Rennes, to seek the friendship and support of the duke of Normandy. In 996, or soon after, Geoffrey married Hawise, sister of Duke Richard II, and a little later Duke Richard married Geoffrey's sister Judith. This double marriage, or the understandings that must have accompanied it, created a relationship between the two families which had some at least of the characteristics of that between lord and vassal. Duke Richard acted as guardian of Geoffrey's two sons and also of Brittany during Geoffrey's pilgrimage to Rome. After Geoffrey's death on the return journey this relationship persisted, and Richard made use of it to obtain Breton auxiliaries in his war with the count of Blois (*c.* 1013–14). It is possible that Alan III, Geoffrey's son and successor, was trying to extricate himself from this position of dependence when war broke out between him and Duke Robert of Normandy about the year 1030; at all events, that war was only brought to an end when Alan did homage and promised service. He was one of those who were entrusted with the care of the young William when Robert in turn set off on a pilgrimage, and met his death in 1040 apparently while discharging his duty as guardian.[1]

William the Conqueror was hardly in a position to exercise any authority over the ruling family in Brittany during his minority or during the years when he was establishing himself in his own duchy; but though there are many mysteries surrounding his intervention in Brittany, probably in 1064, there are several suggestive points in the accounts we have of it. Fighting was then going on between Conan II, Alan's son and heir and at that moment more or less undisputed 'duke' of Brittany, and a group of seigneurs of the neighbourhood of Dol and Dinan led by Rivallon (Rhiwallon) de Combour. According to one story, Rivallon appealed to William who then intervened on his behalf;[2] according to William de Poitiers, Duke William invaded Brittany to enforce his suzerainty over Conan,[3] taking advantage of the rebellion. However it was, Conan defeated the rebels and William retired; but the incident as

[1] Douglas, *William the Conqueror*, pp. 29, 37–40; de la Borderie, *Histoire de Bretagne*, iii. 3, 8–10; Lemarignier, *Hommage en marche*, pp. 115–19.

[2] Le Baud, *Histoire de Bretagne*, quoted by Foreville in William de Poitiers, *Gesta*, pp. 110–11, note 4.

[3] William de Poitiers, *Gesta*, p. 106; cf. William de Jumièges, *Gesta* (interp. Robert de Torigni), p. 272.

variously presented to us reveals not only that the suzerainty of the duke of Normandy over the duke of Brittany could still be asserted, but also that William had direct relations with certain barons of eastern Brittany, some of whom seem to have possessed lands in Normandy.[1] It is perhaps significant that the men from Brittany who received the most extensive lands in England after 1066 were the sons of Eudo de Penthièvre, Conan's uncle, who had been effectively duke during Conan's minority, who resented his exclusion from power when Conan came of age and, though reconciled in 1062, continued to nurse a grievance and a sense of rivalry.[2] It looks very much as though William was taking such opportunities as were offered to him to re-establish, after the break during his minority, what he may well have regarded as the traditional dominance of the dukes of Normandy over the ruling family in Brittany; and was strengthening this by building up a clientage among the barons of eastern Brittany, making them his direct vassals for lands first in Normandy and later in England.

The dukes of Normandy were developing interests in other neighbouring lands as well during the early eleventh century. To the south lay the vast *comté* of Maine and the relatively small *comté* or *pagus* of the Vexin. The Vexin had been cut in two along the line of the River Epte, apparently by the original Norman settlement of 911. The western part of it, the 'Vexin Normand', lying between the Andelle and the Epte, had been incorporated into the duchy; the eastern part, the 'Vexin Français', lying between the Epte and the Oise, was held directly of the king by a line of 'counts of the Vexin', though it remained ecclesiastically in the diocese of Rouen.[3] According to Orderic, King Henry I of France conveyed the suzerainty of the Vexin Français to Duke Robert I in gratitude for assistance during the early troubles of his reign. Count Drew (*c.* 1027–35) accepted the arrangement, did homage to Robert, and married Godgifu who, with her brother Edward (the Confessor), was then a ducal protégée; he was frequently at Robert's court and

[1] Musset, 'Aux origines de la féodalité normande'; Fauroux, *Recueil*, nos. 159–62 (pp. 347–52). On the incident in general, Douglas, *William the Conqueror*, pp. 178–9; Lemarignier, *Hommage en marche*, pp. 119–20; de la Borderie, *Histoire de Bretagne*, iii. 16–20.

[2] De la Borderie, *Histoire de Bretagne*, iii. 25; below, pp. 74–5.

[3] Lemarignier, *Hommage en marche*, pp. 39–41, 47 ff.

accompanied him to the Holy Land, where both died.[1] There are difficulties in this story;[2] but Walter de Mantes, Drew's son and successor (his brother was Ralph, earl of Hereford), may have been William's vassal later on. At all events, William was able very quickly to frustrate Walter's attempt to make himself count of Maine in 1062.[3]

The origin of the Norman interest in Maine may well have been defensive. The duke had been in no position to challenge the suzerainty which the counts of Anjou had imposed upon the counts of Maine almost from the beginning of the eleventh century; but Count Geoffrey Martel of Anjou, after the citizens of Le Mans had driven out their young Count Herbert II and admitted him to the city, went on to attack the Bellême family by occupying Alençon (on the Norman bank of the Sarthe) and Domfront. Of these two places, Domfront lay some way into the *comté* of Maine; but William might well think that, in the hands of the count of Anjou, it would prove a threat to the western part of Normandy where the duke's authority was hardly consolidated even yet. He could not ignore the challenge; he captured both places and with Domfront went on to annex the district of the Passais. Largely as a result of this campaign the great family of Bellême, whose possessions stretched from 'France' through Maine into Normandy and whose heiress eventually married Roger II de Montgomery, was brought firmly into the vassalage of Duke William.[4]

After his victory at Mortemer in 1054, when he defeated an invasion of his duchy led by the king and the count of Anjou, William took the offensive. At some point he had advanced down the River Varennes from Domfront and fortified Ambrières. In the course of fighting off an attack upon this fortification, he secured the person and then the homage of Geoffrey de Mayenne, one of the principal barons of Maine. It was the technique which Fulk Nerra had employed in the Touraine; though, for the time, William did not advance further, nor did

---

[1] Orderic Vitalis, *H.E.* (ed. Le Prévost), iii. 223–4; (ed. Chibnall), iv. 74–6; Dhondt, 'Les relations entre la France et la Normandie sous Henri Ier', pp. 465–9. [2] Lemarignier, *Hommage en marche*, pp. 40–2.
[3] Douglas, *William the Conqueror*, pp. 73–4, 144, 174, (235).
[4] Douglas, *William the Conqueror*, pp. 59–61; Latouche, *Maine*, pp. 29–31; Boussard, 'La seigneurie de Bellême', pp. 52–3; Lemarignier, *Hommage en marche*, pp. 63, 65–6.

he shake the hold which Count Geoffrey Martel of Anjou had fastened upon Maine.[1] Later, however, and probably between 1058 and 1060, William came to an agreement with the exiled Count Herbert of Maine whereby the count, having done homage to him, was to marry one of William's daughters, and William's eldest son Robert was to marry Herbert's daughter Margaret. If Herbert should die without male heir William would succeed him in all his lands and possessions. Herbert died in 1062. In his last years, when his oppressor Geoffrey Martel was dead, he seems to have recovered some of his authority in his own *comté*, giving William the opportunity to make good his claim. Though a group of Manceaux barons invited Walter de Mantes (count of the Vexin), who had a claim through his wife, to take over the *comté*, William quickly disposed of them both, entered Le Mans in triumph, and went on to capture Mayenne (1063).[2] Orderic seems to say that the chief barons of Maine did homage to William.[3] If this was so, he became the effective lord and ruler of the *comté*. There is no record of extensive dispossessions, though castles were surrendered to him. He seems to have acquired enough property in Le Mans and perhaps elsewhere in Maine to need the services of a seneschal there for its administration;[4] and when the Angevin bishop of Le Mans, Vougrin, died in 1065 he was succeeded by Arnold, a Norman.[5] For all this, however, the overriding suzerainty of the count of Anjou was not disputed. William made his son Robert the nominal count of Maine, and Robert and his fiancée are said to have done homage to Count Geoffrey le Barbu at Alençon;[6] though with the *comté* of Anjou involved in a long succession-crisis William might well feel that his conquest was reasonably secure.

In the tenth century, the aggression of the Northmen to the

---

[1] Douglas, *William the Conqueror*, pp. 70–2; Latouche, *Maine*, pp. 31–2, 61.

[2] Douglas, *William the Conqueror*, pp. 73, 173–4; Latouche, *Maine*, pp. 32–5; David, *Robert Curthose*, pp. 7–10.

[3] Orderic Vitalis, *H.E.* (ed. Le Prévost), ii. 103–4; (ed. Chibnall), ii. 118. Neither William de Poitiers (*Gesta*, pp. 90–2) nor William de Jumièges (*Gesta*, pp. 130–1) make it clear, when speaking of the submission of the Manceaux, whether they are referring to the citizens of Le Mans or the barons and people of the *comté* generally.

[4] Latouche, *Maine*, p. 36 (note 3).

[5] Ibid., pp. 35, 79.

[6] Ibid., p. 35; David, *Robert Curthose*, pp. 9–10.

north-east had eventually been barred by the counts of Flanders.[1] Since then the south-western part of the counts' possessions and overlordships had disintegrated into a number of more or less autonomous principalities. Among these were the *comtés* of Boulogne and Guînes, whose counts still acknowledged the suzerainty of the counts of Flanders, and the *comté* of Pontieu, the suzerainty of which had been recovered by the king of France. Between Normandy and Flanders, therefore, there were now a number of small feudal units which might seem to offer a tempting field for Norman 'expansion', particularly as the count of Flanders was turning his attention more and more to the imperial lands north and east of the Scheldt. But Count Baldwin V (1035–67) was a powerful prince who, during the minority of King Philip I, administered the kingdom of France as *regni procurator et bajulus*.

William's first opportunity came in Pontieu. A sister of Count Enguerrand II had married William, count of Arques, Duke William's uncle; and when Count William revolted in 1052 Enguerrand joined the French force which invaded Normandy in the next year to relieve Count William's great stronghold at Arques. Enguerrand was killed in a skirmish at Saint-Aubin and his brother Guy succeeded him. To avenge him, Guy joined the army which invaded Normandy in 1054 and which was destroyed at Mortemer. He was taken prisoner[2] and, according to the death-bed speech which Orderic put into the mouth of William the Conqueror,[3] was only released after two years' detention and after he had done homage and had engaged himself to provide the service of 100 knights every year. Whether or not the details of this speech are to be accepted, that some such relationship existed is shown by Guy's surrender of Harold Godwinson to William on the occasion of Harold's landing in Pontieu;[4] for the time being, at any rate, the count of Pontieu had been brought into the Norman vassalage. It was

---

[1] On early Flanders, e.g. Pirenne, *Histoire de Belgique*, i. 57–60, 103–32; and for the contest between Normandy and Flanders for Pontieu in the early tenth century, Dhondt, *Les origines de la Flandre et de l'Artois*, pp. 40–5, 49–50.

[2] On these events, Douglas, *William the Conqueror*, pp. 62–9 (388–90). For the early counts of Pontieu, Brunel, *Recueil des actes des comtes de Pontieu*, pp. iii–vi; *Carmen de Hastingae Proelio*, pp. 130–1.

[3] Orderic Vitalis, *H.E.* (ed. Le Prévost), iii. 233–8; (ed. Chibnall), iv. 86–8.

[4] Douglas, *William the Conqueror*, pp. 175–7; *Bayeux Tapestry*, pp. 163–6, plates 8–16.

from a port in the *comté* that William and his army sailed in 1066, and Count Guy may have sailed with them.[1]

Beyond Pontieu lay Boulogne, whose count already had close ties with Normandy and England. The *comté*, originally a Carolingian *pagus*, had been cut in two by the formation of the *comté* of Guînes; but, by compensation as it were, the count had inherited the *comté* of Lens and acquired suzerainty over the *comté* of Saint-Pol. He was a very independent vassal of the count of Flanders; and the extent and the geographical position of his lands gave him some importance in the politics of the mid eleventh century.[2] Count Eustace II succeeded to his father in or about the year 1047. His first wife was Godgifu, a sister of Edward the Confessor and widow of Drew, count of the Vexin (d. 1035), by whom she was already the mother of Ralph, earl of Hereford. Eustace took a prominent (though not very glorious) part in the Hastings campaign; and this suggests, though it does no more than suggest, that he was already a vassal in some sense of Duke William. The suggestion is perhaps strengthened by the statement of William de Poitiers that he had sent one of his sons to Normandy as a hostage for his fidelity.[3] However this may be, there can be no doubt of his position after 1066;[4] and it is perhaps unlikely that there had been no anticipation of this.

The circumstances of Duke William's marriage to Matilda, daughter of Baldwin V, count of Flanders, have given rise to a great deal of discussion.[5] In this context, its most important effect was to secure the benevolent neutrality of the powerful Count Baldwin in 1066 and make it possible for his men to join William's army and to share in the spoils of England;[6] but if William of Malmesbury is to be believed, Baldwin already held something like a money-fief of Duke William and actually supplied troops for the expedition.[7] Looking to the future,

---

[1] Douglas, ' "Companions of the Conqueror" ', pp. 139, 147.

[2] On the early history of the *comté* of Boulogne, J. Dhondt, 'Les seigneuries [du Pas-de-Calais] du ixe au xiiie siècles', pp. 34 ff.

[3] 'Eustachius comes Boloniae . . . filium de fide ante bellum [Hastings] in Normannia obsidem dederat'; William de Poitiers, *Gesta*, p. 264.

[4] Round, *Studies in Peerage*, pp. 147 ff.

[5] Douglas, *William the Conqueror*, pp. 76–8.

[6] Dept, *Influences anglaise et française*, p. 18; George, 'The Contribution of Flanders to the Conquest of England'; Douglas, *William the Conqueror*, pp. 266–7.

[7] Malmesbury, *Gesta Regum*, ii. 478; Lyon, *From Fief to Indenture*, pp. 32–3.

however, the possibilities inherent in William and Matilda's marriage are sufficiently indicated by the fact that a grandson of theirs[1] eventually became count of Flanders, however briefly and insecurely.

At the same time as the dukes of Normandy were securing a foothold in the surrounding continental lands, and some of their barons were conquering principalities for themselves in South Italy, both duke and barons were acquiring interests across the Channel in England. During the tenth century, it seems that Vikings raiding England found useful bases, sometimes a refuge and often a market for their booty, in Normandy; and towards the end of the century this was giving rise to so much ill-feeling between Æthelred, king of the English, and Richard I, duke of the Normans, that the pope intervened and arranged a treaty between them (991).[2] This could be regarded as marking the end of the 'Viking' phase in 'Anglo-Norman' relations. The treaty was followed up, in 1002, by the marriage of Emma, Duke Richard's daughter, to King Æthelred himself. This marriage was the origin of Norman interest in England in the 'post-Viking' or 'feudal' phase—dynastically, because it was the son of Æthelred and Emma, Edward the Confessor, descendant of the Norman dukes through his mother and more than half Norman by upbringing, who succeeded to the kingdom in 1042;[3] and he, perhaps in 1051, is said to have designated his second cousin, William of Normandy, to succeed him.[4] It may be that Edward had, at that time, already promised the succession to Svein Estrithson of Denmark, and that in 1054 it was decided to recall Edward the Ætheling from his exile in Hungary, no doubt with a view to the succession; but the

[1] William Clito, son of Robert Curthose. Many of his contemporaries thought that he should have been duke of Normandy; and if he had been that he would assuredly have claimed England as well.

[2] Stenton, *A.-S.E.*, pp. 370–1; Douglas, *William the Conqueror*, pp. 159–60; Musset, 'Relations et échanges d'influences', pp. 74–5.

[3] For the circumstances, Barlow, *Edward the Confessor*, pp. 48 ff.

[4] Douglas, 'Edward the Confessor, Duke William of Normandy, and the English Succession'; Oleson, 'Edward the Confessor's Promise of the Throne to Duke William of Normandy'; Barlow, 'Edward the Confessor's Early Life, Character and Attitudes', pp. 240–51; Körner, *The Battle of Hastings, England, and Europe*, pp. 158–95; Barlow, *Edward the Confessor*, pp. 106–9; Brown, *Normans and the Norman Conquest*, pp. 121–4. Although opinions differ widely on the reasons for the designation and on its significance, few have rejected it altogether. The evidence comes almost entirely from the Norman side.

Ætheling, when he came in 1057, died before he could see the king,[1] though he left a son, Edgar, to represent what was perhaps the best claim on purely hereditary grounds. It may also be that, at the very end of his life, the Confessor agreed to sanction the succession of Harold Godwinson;[2] but none of this was likely to affect Duke William's own view of his rights, based on kinship and 'designation'.

Emma's marriage was also the origin of other Norman interests in England; for when she came to England she naturally brought Norman attendants with her, and in due course places had to be found for them.[3] The best-known of these followers was a certain Hugh, the administrator of her property in Devonshire;[4] but there were others as well. Edward the Confessor, though he made no clean sweep of his predecessor's household priests and officers, brought in some of his own both when he came to England and later.[5] Many of these were Norman: Ulf, who was made bishop of Dorchester in 1049; William, who became bishop of London in 1051; Peter, who was given land in Berkshire and Somerset, but who had to wait for his bishopric (Lichfield) until 1072; Osbern, who received part of the immensely valuable church of Bosham, but who likewise was not given his bishopric (Exeter) until 1072. In addition, Robert Champart, successively prior of Saint-Ouen and abbot of Jumièges (1037), was a friend of Edward's who came to England with him and received first the bishopric of London and later the archbishopric of Canterbury.[6] Ralph ('Ralph the Timid'), son of King Edward's sister Godgifu and the count of the Vexin, received an earldom of Hereford and, with two Normans who were probably his followers, Richard son of Scrob and Osbern 'Pentecost', began the building of castles there which attracted a good deal of attention and

---

[1] Barlow, *Edward the Confessor*, pp. 214–19.

[2] Barlow, *ubi supra*, pp. 243–55; cf. Beckerman, 'Succession in Normandy, 1087, and in England, 1066', pp. 259–60.

[3] Ritchie, *The Normans in England before Edward the Confessor*, pp. 10, 14–16.

[4] A.-S.C., 1003, CDE (p. 86); Florence of Worcester, *Chronicon*, i. 156.

[5] Apart from the men of Norman origin who are known to have received lands and offices in Edward the Confessor's England, there is a clear statement in the *Vita Edwardi*, p. 17. Cf. Brown, *Normans and the Norman Conquest*, pp. 113–19.

[6] Barlow, *English Church*, pp. 44, 81–2, 85–6, 156–8, 190–1; *Edward the Confessor*, pp. 50–1, 86–7, 104–5, 190–2.

hostility;[1] and Robert 'of Rhuddlan' who, after serving his military apprenticeship in Edward's household, went back to Normandy to return again as an energetic commander in the company of his cousin, Hugh d'Avranches, earl of Chester.[2] Not all the foreigners who obtained lands and offices in England at this time were Norman. Two of the most notable, Robert 'fitzWimarch' and Ralph 'the Staller' were Bretons,[3] and some of the bishops were Lotharingians (Herman of Ramsbury, Giso of Wells, and Walter of Hereford).[4] This list is not exhaustive, and it is difficult in any case to form a clear idea of the extent of the influx. That Edward should bring to England a number of servants, friends, relations, and followers who would expect to receive lands and places in his kingdom was quite natural, and we cannot tell how many may have forced themselves upon him; yet it is unlikely that he ever tried, save possibly during the short period of Earl Godwin's exile, to govern England through officers and magnates of Norman origin as a matter of policy.[5] Nevertheless, those who came to England in Edward's reign were showing the way. They represented what might have been the beginning of a peaceful penetration of England. Their presence meant that there would be a great deal of coming and going between the kingdom and the duchy,[6] and that not only the duke but the leaders of the Norman aristocracy were in a position to learn much about the wealth and the possibilities

[1] Stenton, *A.-S.E.*, p. 561; Douglas, *William the Conqueror*, pp. 166–8; Round, *Feudal England*, pp. 320–6; Barlow, *Edward the Confessor*, pp. 93–4.

[2] Barlow, *Edward the Confessor*, pp. 176, 191; below, pp. 312–3.

[3] *Complete Peerage*, ix. 568–74; Stenton, *A.-S.E.*, pp. 419–20; Douglas, *William the Conqueror*, pp. 231–2, 290; Barlow, *Edward the Confessor*, pp. 164–5, 191. William de Poitiers describes Robert fitzWimarch as a Norman (*Gesta*, p. 170, and see editor's note).

[4] Barlow, *English Church*, pp. 156–8.   [5] Cf. Stenton, *A.-S.E.*, pp. 419–20.

[6] The design of the Confessor's church at Westminster was closely based upon Norman models (Barlow, *Edward the Confessor*, pp. 229–32 and references there given). It is possible that Caen stone was already being imported into this country. Zarnecki states that the capitals of the tower arch in Sompting Church, Sussex, are of this material; and though he apparently changed his mind on the significance of this for their dating (*Romanesque Sculpture at Lincoln Cathedral*, p. 22 (note 2), and '1066 and Architectural Sculpture', p. 91), they seem to be pre-Conquest in style; cf. A. W. Clapham, 'Sompting Church', p. 407; H. M. and J. Taylor, *Anglo-Saxon Architecture*, ii. 561–2. English manuscripts were being taken to Normandy and copied there (Alexander, *Norman Illumination at Mont-Saint-Michel*, pp. vii–viii, 237–9 and *passim*) and the paintings in them are probably the source of the very 'Anglo-Saxon-looking' motifs that appear in some early Norman sculpture.

which England had to offer. Perhaps those who were already in England confidently expected William to succeed to the throne; they would at least enable him to be speedily informed about any developments in the country.[1]

There were still other forms of Norman penetration into England before 1066. Emma was probably responsible for Æthelred's intention to give important lands in East Sussex to the ducal abbey of Fécamp and for Cnut's fulfilment of that intention. It is likely that Fécamp also obtained rights in Steyning during the Confessor's reign, if not actual possession of the place. King Edward gave lands in Essex to the abbey of Saint-Ouen and Ottery in Devonshire to Rouen Cathedral.[2] The merchants of Rouen, already established in London, seem to have increased their privileges, and so presumably their activity, there during the Confessor's reign.[3]

Yet, in spite of William's 'designation' and the extent of the Norman interest in England, it was not likely that Edward's inheritance would fall into the hands of a Norman duke without effort on his part. There were indeed precedents for an invasion of England from Normandy. Cnut had married Emma, Æthelred's widow, not simply to render his conquest more acceptable to English people, but also to maintain good relations with the duke of Normandy who, until 1026, was still Emma's brother Duke Richard II, and thus to render any enterprise on behalf of the æthelings Edward and Alfred, who were maintained at the Norman court, less likely. When Robert I became duke, however, the Norman attitude (if indeed it had

---

[1] Traditionally it was William fitzOsbern who persuaded the Norman barons that an invasion of England was practicable (Douglas, *William the Conqueror*, p. 184). He and his brother Osbern were related both to Edward the Confessor and to William through their descent from Arfast, a brother of the Duchess Gunnor, Edward's grandmother and William's great-grandmother (Douglas, 'The Ancestors of William fitzOsbern'). Osbern was one of Edward's chaplains and possessed a part of the vast estates attached to the church of Bosham on Chichester Harbour (Barlow, *English Church*, pp. 134, 190–1), the port from which the Bayeux Tapestry shows Harold Godwinson setting sail for Normandy in 1064. Robert 'of Rhuddlan' is another obvious source of information about England (above, p. 23) and there were others.

[2] Matthew, *Norman Monasteries*, pp. 19–26, 143–9.

[3] Page, *London*, pp. 137–8; IV Æthelred, c. 2 (Robertson, *Laws*, p. 73); *Regesta*, iii, No. 729 (p. 269); Delisle-Berger, *Recueil*, i, No. xiv (p. 20). The reference to 'tempore Edwardi regis' in Duke Henry's charter may, however, be no more than a general indication of times before the Norman Conquest. On the early merchants of Rouen in general, Deck, 'Les marchands de Rouen sous les Ducs'.

been influenced by Emma's remarriage) changed. Robert himself was credited with an attempt at an invasion of England,[1] and he showed his support of the æthelings not only by giving them an honoured place at his court but by marrying their sister Godgifu to the count of the Vexin. Both æthelings, separately it would seem, attempted to exploit any confusion that might arise after Cnut's death by invading England; but although Edward won a battle at Southampton neither made any impression and Alfred was captured and done to death.[2] When Harthacnut associated Edward with him in the government of his kingdom[3] and Edward succeeded him in 1042, this phase of the Norman interest in England reached its fulfilment.

If it was to develop further, opposition could be expected from Scandinavia, where Cnut's successors in Norway and Denmark had their claims to England; though their own rivalries prevented any attempt to realize those claims until 1066.[4] There were also candidates for the succession in England who would surely offer some opposition to a Norman pretender. Edward the Ætheling's son Edgar might have been young still in 1066, though preparations (soon abandoned) were made to have him proclaimed in London during October–November.[5] At what point the rival ambitions of Harold Godwinson and his brother Tostig began to take shape it is impossible to say; but the Northumbrian rebellion against Tostig in 1065 and his exile, whatever Harold's part in this may have been, left Harold in a very strong position by the end of the year.[6] Duke William, moreover, though he had survived his troubled minority and was taking every opportunity to extend his power and possessions, would have been in no position to launch an expedition across the sea before 1060, the year in which the king of France, Henry I, and the count of Anjou, Geoffrey Martel, both died. Thereafter everything seemed to go in his favour: the king of France a minor in the guardianship of William's father-in-law the count of Flanders; a long-disputed succession in Anjou;

[1] William de Jumièges, *Gesta*, pp. 109–10.
[2] Ibid., pp. 120–2; William de Poitiers, *Gesta*, pp. 4–10; A.-S.C., 1036 CD (pp. 103–4).
[3] Barlow, *Edward the Confessor*, pp. 48–53.
[4] Stenton, *A.-S.E.*, pp. 417–22.
[5] Douglas, *William the Conqueror*, pp. 204–5.
[6] Barlow, *Edward the Confessor*, pp. 219–39, 296–300.

the circumstances, whatever they were, that brought Harold to Normandy in 1064 and led to his taking an oath to William there; the opportunity which this gave to William to justify his cause to the Church and to aristocratic opinion generally; even the set of the wind in the early autumn of 1066 that brought Harold Hardrada to England first, so that Harold Godwinson was in York when William landed in Sussex.

At first sight there seems no parallel, in the early Norman expansion, to this build-up of Norman dynastic and other interests in a country later to be conquered or otherwise subordinated, certainly not on such a scale. Yet the history of the Norman subjection of Brittany, not fully realized until the twelfth century, seems to be one of the gradual substantiation of claims which were at first quite undefined, while William's dealings with certain barons in the eastern part of the country has an analogy with some forms of pre-Conquest Norman penetration into England. Similarly with Maine. When William received Gervase du Château-du-Loir, the bishop of Le Mans exiled by Count Geoffrey Martel of Anjou,[1] and loaded him with 'gold and silver, castles and most lavish gifts',[2] he was not simply giving succour to a refugee but advancing a stage in the process of bringing the great family of Bellême, of which Bishop Gervase was an important member, into his vassalage; and the Bellême family had very extensive lands in Maine. This, with William's capture of Domfront and his fortification of Ambrières, by which he was able to secure the homage of a leading Manceau baron, Geoffrey de Mayenne, can be described not unreasonably as a 'pre-conquest' penetration of the *comté*. Thus the conquest of England was not simply a violent climax to a long period of close relations between the rulers of Normandy and England and between their peoples; conquest and pre-conquest penetration were alike an activity (if on an unprecedented scale) in which the Normans were already well practised on the Continent.

Moreover, the subjection of their continental neighbours was as much a part of the preparation for the conquest of England

[1] Halphen, *Comté d'Anjou*, pp. 69–76; Latouche, *Maine*, pp. 26–30. This is the beginning of the confrontation of Anjou and Normandy over Maine.

[2] 'Willelmus comes . . . dedit ei aurum et argentum, castella fortia et dona largissima': *Actus Pontificum Cenomannis*, p. 366.

as their early relations with that country. According to Guy d'Amiens there were men from 'France', Maine, Brittany, and even from South Italy as well as Normans in William's invasion army;[1] William de Poitiers adds men from Aquitaine among those from France in the wider sense[2] and Orderic Burgundians and Angevins;[3] there can be little doubt that there were Flemings as well.[4] Many must have come as adventurers pure and simple; some as mercenaries; some may have responded to the appeal that William could make as a loyal son of the Church, resolved to rid England of a perjured usurper; but many must also have felt obligations to William in varying degree as the result of the suzerainties that he and his predecessors had been spreading over their neighbours in northern France. From the beginning of the tenth century to 1066 and beyond, though the mode of activity might change as circumstances changed, the progress of Norman conquest, domination, and colonization was a continuous and consistent process.

[1] *Carmen de Hastingae Proelio*, pp. 16–18 (ll. 250–60). Cf. also p. 26 (ll. 413–14) and p. 32 (ll. 485–6).

[2] William de Poitiers, *Gesta*, p. 192. The vicomte of Thouars, Aimeri IV, led a contingent from Poitou (Richard, *Comtes de Poitou*, i. 298–9). It was he who advised William to take the crown of England (William de Poitiers, *Gesta*, pp. 196, 216–18).

[3] At various points in his narrative of the Conquest, Orderic Vitalis mentions French, Bretons, Poitevins, Burgundians, men from Maine, Aquitaine, and Anjou; *H.E.* (ed. Le Prévost), ii. 125, 148, 198; (ed. Chibnall), ii. 144, 174, 234. Körner's destructive criticism of the chroniclers' references to the presence of men from parts of France other than Normandy in the invasion army is too narrowly based to be accepted as more than cautionary (*The Battle of Hastings, England, and Europe*, pp. 220–55).

[4] Above, p. 20 nn. 6 and 7.

2. The Conquest and Colonization of England

In England the whole operation which is generally known as 'the Norman Conquest' went through two phases, a military phase and a colonizing phase. They overlapped chronologically, but it is as well to treat them separately. The military phase is well known and may be dealt with quite briefly: the colonizing phase, since it is less familiar but is nevertheless one of the most important elements in the formation of the Norman complex of lands and lordships, requires more extended treatment.

The battle of Hastings destroyed the ruling family in England; the battle and the march on London together gave William military control of south-eastern England and the first submission of the surviving English leaders; his coronation according to the English rite in Edward the Confessor's Westminster Abbey enabled him to claim the allegiance of all who had acknowledged Edward and Harold as king. But this was far from being the end of the matter. While William was celebrating his triumph in Normandy from March to December 1067, there were attacks upon Norman strongholds in Herefordshire and in Kent, though these were repulsed without undue difficulty by the commanders he had left in England; and when he returned he had to deal with resistance in the west country and in the north. But the real crisis came in 1069, when a Danish force appeared in the Humber. Most of the surviving English leaders joined them; no doubt the king of Scots was preparing to do the same; and the situation was complicated by simultaneous risings in the south-west and in the west Midlands. Leaving minor matters to be dealt with by his lieutenants, William recovered York, where his castles had been taken; he then systematically devastated Yorkshire and after that Cheshire and Staffordshire. When he had broken up the last large-scale resistance in the Fens, secured the departure of the Danish army, and imprisoned Earl Morcar of Northumbria (Earl Edwin of Mercia was killed in an obscure scuffle), and when, in

1072, he had secured his position in the north by his agreement with the king of Scots at Abernethy, the broad military decision could hardly be challenged.[1]

As the Normans moved over the country they plundered it: 'they ravaged all that they overran'.[2] William made haste to seize Harold's treasure;[3] Englishmen who had survived Hastings and who submitted to William offered him tribute and hostages 'and afterwards bought their lands'.[4] Tribute was also taken from English towns that were within the Conqueror's reach;[5] and still 'he laid taxes on the people very severely',[6] even before he returned to Normandy in March 1067. William de Poitiers gives an ecstatic account of the triumphal parade through his duchy. King William had brought with him, he says, as much gold as he could have obtained from the enslavement of the Three Gauls; gold and silver were sent to Rome; treasures from English monasteries were distributed among the churches of his native Normandy in acknowledgement of the efficacy of their prayers; there were enormous feasts wherever he went and his countrymen were amazed at the gorgeous robes and the royal display of precious metal.[7] But in addition to impressing his own people, William was able to pay off such of his mercenaries as wished to be released,[8] and reward those of his followers who, like Aimeri de Thouars,[9] did not accept land in England but are not likely to have gone empty away.

The group of intimate barons, whom William had commissioned to consolidate the Norman hold upon south-eastern England and to extend it while he was in Normandy from March to December 1067,[10] were also accused of oppressing

---

[1] The most recent full description of these events is by Douglas in *William the Conqueror*, pp. 181–227.

[2] A.-S.C., 1066, D (p. 144).   [3] William de Poitiers, *Gesta*, p. 222.

[4] A.-S.C., 1066, E (p. 142); William de Poitiers, *Gesta*, p. 224.

[5] William de Poitiers, ibid.   [6] A.-S.C., 1066, D (p. 145).

[7] William de Poitiers, *Gesta*, pp. 222–8, 242–6, 254–62. Cf. A.-S.C., 1067, E (p. 146)—'in this year the king went overseas and took with him hostages and money'; and Douglas, *William the Conqueror*, pp. 207–10.

[8] William de Poitiers, *Gesta*, p. 244.

[9] Ibid., p. 196; Douglas, '"Companions of the Conqueror"', p. 135.

[10] Odo de Bayeux based on Dover, William fitzOsbern based on Winchester (cf. Barlow, 'Guenta'), Hugh de Grandmesnil, Hugh de Montfort, and William de Warenne: William de Poitiers, *Gesta*, pp. 238–42; Orderic Vitalis, *H.E.* (ed. Le Prévost), ii. 166–7; (ed. Chibnall), ii. 194–6; A.-S.C., 1066, D (p. 145). Humphrey de Tilleul is said to have been entrusted with Hastings Castle 'from the day of its

and plundering the English;[1] and when William returned he again 'imposed a heavy tax upon the wretched people'.[2] In the spring of 1070 it is said that he raided the English monasteries, taking not only their own treasures but the money which wealthy Englishmen had deposited in them for safety.[3] When an Anglo-Danish force captured the Norman castles in York early in 1069 they found 'an incalculable treasure' there,[4] a treasure that could only have been accumulated in the space of a very few months.

England was a wealthy country in terms of gold and silver, even after the Danes had taken what they could. William de Poitiers says that it was richer than France; and although one must expect him to exaggerate things of this kind, there seems to be some support for his opinion.[5] King William and his Normans set out, systematically as it would appear, to possess themselves of this wealth. Plundering on this scale was exceptional, particularly as a great deal of it must have taken place before William could know that the English would offer prolonged resistance. But just as William and his followers plundered the treasure of England and the wealth which the land produced, so, in the end, they took the land itself. Conquest and plunder were followed by colonization and exploitation.

It is possible to imagine circumstances, however unlikely, in which William might have succeeded to the English throne peaceably, as Edward himself had done in 1041–2; and if this had happened, no doubt there would have been a further influx of Norman ecclesiastics and Norman laymen seeking places in their lord's new kingdom, as in the years after 1042 though on a much larger scale. This would have had a considerable effect

---

foundation', Orderic Vitalis, *H.E.* (ed. Le Prévost), ii. 186; (ed. Chibnall), ii. 220. Odo de Bayeux and Hugh de Montfort were operating beyond the Thames when Eustace de Boulogne made his attack on Dover (William de Poitiers, *Gesta*, p. 266).

[1] Orderic Vitalis, *H.E.* (ed. Le Prévost), ii. 171–2; (ed. Chibnall), ii. 202; A.-S.C., 1066, D (p. 145).

[2] A.-S.C., 1067, D (p. 146).

[3] A.-S.C., 1070, D E (pp. 150–1); Florence of Worcester, *Chronicon*, ii. 4–5. The plundering of Ely may have been due to special circumstances, but the account of it gives some indication of the wealth to be found in English monasteries at that time: *Liber Eliensis*, p. 194; cf. Clapham, *English Romanesque Architecture*, i. 141.

[4] A.-S.C., 1069, D (p. 150).

[5] William de Poitiers, *Gesta*, p. 254; Sawyer, 'Wealth of England'.

on the country, though not perhaps an overwhelming effect.[1] However, not only was William's accession violent, but the English resisted and for some years continued to resist; and because William was, after his coronation, the lawful king in England for his own people, for the Church, for most relevant European authorities outside Scandinavia, and even for some Englishmen, resistance to him could be treated as rebellion. Therefore all who had fought against him at Hastings and all who resisted subsequently, even if they were the tenants of English monasteries which had accepted William, were rebels; they forfeited their lands if not their lives as well when they came into his power, and their heirs were disinherited;[2] and since those who submitted 'afterwards bought their lands',[3] or, at the least, accepted William's lordship over them, this meant that in principle all English land sooner or later passed through his hands.

Even if he had wanted to do so, William could not have kept it all for himself and his family. Those who had taken part in 'the English War', who had guarded Normandy in his absence or who had some other claim on his gratitude, would look to him for reward; all who had invested themselves, their men and their wealth in his expedition would demand their dividends. Indeed, apart from the pressure that such men could bring to bear upon him, the only way that William could profitably utilize what he had won was to plant men whom he trusted on the land, the warrior aristocracy of Normandy that he had bound to himself[4] and the men from other lands whom he could call upon or whom he had attracted to his service; and he would do this so that they could build up new forces to hold his conquest, to exploit it and if possible to extend it. The changes in Britain that can be attributed to the Norman Conquest follow directly from the nature and the extent of the foreign influx that accompanied it.

Some idea of the extent of the Norman settlement in

---

[1] The style of the Confessor's Westminster Abbey and the castles that were constructed in the west Midlands during his reign would have been regarded as the beginning of 'Norman influence' on the country.

[2] For the tenants of the English monasteries, *Regesta*, i. No. 40 (App. No. vi); Stenton, *A.-S.E.*, pp. 590–1. For the treatment of the English as it was believed, a hundred years later, to have been, *Dialogus*, pp. 53–4.

[3] A.-S.C., 1066, E (p. 142). [4] Below, pp. 286–90.

England—it is convenient for brevity to speak of the immigrants as Normans, though there was a considerable number of Bretons, Flemings, and other 'Frenchmen' among them—can be obtained from Domesday Book; but it must be remembered that this great record enables us to measure the extent of a man's landed possessions only by the values assigned to them, that it supplies very little information about lands beyond Offa's Dyke in the west or the Ribble and the Tees in the north, none about the cities of London and Winchester, and that it cannot, clearly, tell us what happened after it was compiled. Bearing in mind these limitations, it has been calculated that, in 1086, King William and his immediate family held about 20 per cent of the land of England; the immigrant lay barons, including the king's two half-brothers (the bishop of Bayeux and Robert de Mortain), about 48 per cent; the Church about 26 per cent; and the few surviving pre-Conquest landowners, themselves not all of English origin, little more than 5 per cent.[1] In just about 20 years, that is to say, there had been an almost complete change in the landowners of England. The English lay aristocracy had been virtually exterminated.[2]

The Norman baronage which replaced it, however, could not exploit all its lands directly. Like the king himself, and for similar reasons, baronial landholders had to settle men on part of their estates; and Domesday records the names of many who were their sub-tenants, with a few who were sub-sub-tenants. Some bear English names, and these seem to be the survivors of the body of English landowners retaining a fraction of their former estates as a tenancy.[3] Others bear Norman names; and where it is possible to identify such tenants they can often be seen to have had some connection with their lord before they came to England. Likely instances of this can be recognized at once when the tenant-in-chief was not a Norman (the Breton colony that gathered on the estates of Count Alan in Yorkshire and Lincolnshire,[4] for example, or the Flemings holding of Drew de la

---

[1] Corbett, 'The Development of the Duchy of Normandy and the Norman Conquest of England', pp. 506–11. As quoted above, the percentages are given in very rough figures. For some refinements, Lennard, *Rural England*, pp. 25–30.

[2] Stenton, 'English Families'.   [3] Ibid., esp. pp. 7–8.

[4] *E.Y.C.*, iv, p. ix; v (*Honour of Richmond*), *passim* (cf. Ellis, 'Biographical Notes on Yorkshire Tenants named in Domesday Book', *Y.A.J.*, v. 299, 308, 321, 323–4, 327–8); Stenton, *English Feudalism*, pp. 25–7.

Beuvrière in Holderness) ;[1] but there are also several cases where the tenants of a Norman lord on his English estates can be shown to have come from places very near to his chief seat in Normandy.[2] Among the tenants of Robert Malet, whose seat was at Graville-Sainte-Honorine, now a suburb of Le Havre, were men with names derived from Claville, Colleville, Conteville, and Émalleville, all places near by; or among the tenants of Richard fitzGilbert or his son whose seat was at Orbec were Roger d'Abernon, Ralph de la Cressonnière, Picot de Friardel, Roger d'Orbec, Roger de Saint-Germain, whose names suggest that they came from places in or very near to Orbec. Neighbours were not necessarily vassals; but the subsequent relationship suggests that they often may have been, and in some cases this is certain. William Pantoul was certainly a vassal of Roger de Montgomery in Normandy before he became one of his principal tenants in Shropshire; the Clères family had been tenants of the Tosny family in Normandy before the Conquest, and in the twelfth century Ralph de Clères is found holding lands in Yorkshire which had belonged to Berengar de Tosny at the time of Domesday.[3] Ilbert de Lacy had almost certainly been a tenant of the bishop of Bayeux in Normandy before he became his tenant in the south Midlands; and it is quite likely that the Scorchebofe (Écorchebœuf) and Reineville families had been tenants of Lacy in Normandy before they renewed the relationship in Yorkshire.[4] In some cases a vassal was also bound to his lord by ties of kindred. Ribald, who held Middleham of Count Alan, was his brother;[5] Robert 'of Rhuddlan', the energetic second-in-command of Hugh d'Avranches, earl of Chester, and his tenant in Cheshire, North Wales and elsewhere, was a kinsman.[6]

These facts and probabilities become significant when they are put into relation with some statements made by the chroniclers. Orderic, for example, describes Gilbert d'Auffai as fighting in the principal engagements of 'the English War' 'with

---

[1] D.B., i. 323 b 1–325 a 1; cf. *V.C.H. Yorkshire*, ii. 171–2.
[2] In general, Loyd, *Anglo-Norman Families*, pp. 139–40 and *passim*.
[3] On these relationships, Douglas, *William the Conqueror*, pp. 95–6, 270; Loyd, *Anglo-Norman Families, passim*; Clay, *Early Yorkshire Families*, pp. 20–1.
[4] Wightman, *Lacy Family*, pp. 14–15, 55–6, 215–20; cf. Loyd, *Anglo-Norman Families*, pp. 84, 96.   [5] *E.Y.C.* v (*Honour of Richmond*, ii), 298.
[6] Tait, *Domesday Survey of Cheshire*, pp. 45–7.

his men about him'.[1] Lambert d'Ardre tells the story of a young follower of Count Eustace de Boulogne, who presumably accompanied his lord to England in 1066 and who, having been brought by the count to the attention of King William, served the king with such distinction that he was rewarded, not only with the usual 'daily pay' and gifts, but with a considerable estate in East Anglia; and the lands which made up this estate can be identified with those which he held of the Count of Boulogne in 1086.[2] Eadmer describes the bishop of Bayeux as exercising such power in Kent during the first few years after Hastings that no one could resist him; and many of the bishop's tenants there at the time of Domesday bore the names of places near to Bayeux.[3] It looks very much as though he had been leading something that was more like a private army than a detachment of royal forces; and this was almost certainly true of William fitzOsbern, for some of those he settled on the Welsh Border had most likely crossed the Channel under his leadership; he found a way of attracting knights to his service in such numbers as to cause King William some concern and he was able to accomplish a great deal in a very short time in England before his death in 1071.[4] The same might well be true, also, of the 'no little force' with which Brian de Bretagne met the sons of Harold in 1069,[5] or the 'militiae multitudo' that accompanied Hugh fitzBaldric about Yorkshire in the 1070s.[6]

All this suggests very strongly, as might be supposed on general grounds,[7] that the men who became tenants-in-chief in England, when they decided to take part in their duke's great adventure, had summoned their tenants and neighbours to join them, and that the groups so formed were fighting units, held together by some form of personal engagement. Such units seem to be clearly indicated in Orderic's description of Gilbert

---

[1] 'Coetibus suis stipatus', Orderic Vitalis, *H.E.* (ed. Le Prévost), iii. 44; (ed. Chibnall), iii. 254.

[2] Lambert d'Ardre, *Chronicon*, p. 253; Round, *Feudal England*, pp. 462–4, and *Studies in Peerage*, pp. 156–7.

[3] Eadmer, *Historia Novorum*, p. 17; Douglas, *Domesday Monachorum*, pp. 28–31 and *passim*.

[4] Lloyd, *History of Wales*, ii. 373–6; Wightman, 'The Palatine Earldom of William FitzOsbern', pp. 11–12, 17; *V.C.H. Herefordshire*, i. 274–80; Nelson, *The Normans in South Wales*, pp. 29–33.

[5] A.-S.C., 1069, D (p. 149).   [6] Stenton, *English Feudalism*, p. 137, note 1.

[7] Cf. Stenton, *A.-S.E.*, pp. 584–5.

d'Auffai's troop;[1] one such unit may even be shown in action on the Bayeux Tapestry in the scene where 'Odo episcopus baculum tenens confortat pueros',[2] if 'puer' here has the sense of 'vassal'. Very likely it was such units that provided the cohesion and the discipline in the army of invasion.[3] Then, just as William distributed a great deal of the land he had won to his immediate followers, they, in turn, distributed part of their winnings to their kinsmen, vassals, and other followers, and for the same reasons. For, just as the king needed trustworthy vassals to guard his castles and his lands in England or Normandy when his affairs occupied him in the other country, so men like William de Warenne, father and son, Roger de Montgomery or Hugh d'Avranches and many others needed established knights and vassals to keep their castles and their lands when their own affairs or those of the king took them from one country to the other.[4] And as the great men had followed William's leadership in search of a fortune, or one greater than they already had, so lesser men followed their lords with similar motives. Lands in England had thus to be found for a thrusting 'gentry', some of whom quickly rose to baronial rank, in addition to those who had already achieved that status before 1066 or in the primary distribution of English estates.

The English Church was treated in much the same way as the land of England.[5] From William's coronation until the death of William Rufus there were twenty-seven elections or nominations to English bishoprics. Of the men who took office, nineteen were certainly Norman in the sense that we can be reasonably sure that they were born in the duchy, or had served as a monk or priest or held some ecclesiastical office there. Four more were probably so. Of the remaining four, one was possibly Norman, two were Lotharingians (one a royal chaplain), and one had come from Tours (also a royal chaplain). Not one man who we can now be certain was an Englishman obtained

---

[1] Above, pp. 33–4.   [2] *Bayeux Tapestry*, plates 67–8.

[3] Cf. Hollister, *Military Organization of Norman England*, p. 89.

[4] That such men, with interests of their own as well as the king's service to consider, adopted a manner of living very similar to his, is well shown by the career of William II de Warenne (below, pp. 295–6).

[5] This seems to have been the view of Orderic Vitalis, to judge by the passage on ecclesiastical appointments following immediately upon his account of some of the principal grants of English lands to Norman laymen: *H.E.* (ed. Le Prévost), ii. 225–6; (ed. Chibnall), ii. 268–70.

an English bishopric during these two reigns.[1] It is difficult to say just how far the Normans were interested in the middle ranks of the ecclesiastical hierarchy in England. The cathedral constitutions established at Lincoln, York, and Salisbury by Bishop Remigius, Archbishop Thomas I, and St. Osmund respectively represent the continental type of organization to which the Norman cathedrals were rapidly approximating even if it was not completely established in them in every respect.[2] It is not surprising therefore that a fair proportion of the early deans, treasurers, precentors, chancellors, and archdeacons seem to bear Norman names, though little is known of them as men.[3] Almost half the chapter at London was Norman in the time of Bishop Maurice.[4] As for the monasteries, several of the principal houses in England had a succession of Norman superiors until the middle of the twelfth century,[5] and altogether the number of foreign abbots and priors was very considerable.[6] Norman priors were appointed at Canterbury, Rochester and Winchester;[7] there was a considerable Norman element at Canterbury under Archbishop Lanfranc[8] and at some other English monasteries, whether or not they were the seat of a bishop.[9] It is a commonplace that the arrival of Norman or French superiors brought profound changes into the life and

---

[1] Note on *The Provenance of the Bishops of English Sees*, below, pp. 49–51.

[2] For the assimilation of English cathedral constitutions and diocesan organization to those of Normandy, below, pp. 249–50.

[3] When Archbishop Anselm was consecrated in 1093, the four York dignitaries who accompanied Archbishop Thomas were Hugh the dean, Ranulf the treasurer, Durand the archdeacon, and Gilbert the precentor—not a likely collection of English names (Hugh the Chantor, *History of the Church of York*, p. 7). It may be possible to offer a rather more firmly based impression of the proportion of Norman to English dignitaries during the time of the Norman kings when the new edition of Le Neve's *Fasti 1066–1300* is complete; though the terms of reference of that work do not seem to include the systematic collection of such evidence as there may be for the provenance of the men concerned. The first volume to be published of the series relating to this time contains a useful bibliography of modern works containing *fasti* (*St. Paul's, London*, pp. 100–1).

[4] Brooke, 'Composition of the Chapter of St. Paul's, 1086–1163', pp. 121–2. There seems to have been a similar proportion at Salisbury (*V.C.H. Wiltshire*, iii. 158).

[5] *Heads of Religious Houses*, pp. 2–3, gives instances.

[6] Ibid., *passim*; Knowles, *Monastic Order*, pp. 111–13 and App. vii (p. 704).

[7] *Heads of Religious Houses*, pp. 33, 63, 80.

[8] Southern, *Saint Anselm and his Biographer*, pp. 246–8.

[9] Knowles, *Monastic Order*, pp. 113, 126–7. The chapter is entitled 'The Norman Plantation'. Cf. Dodwell, *The Canterbury School of Illumination*, pp. 7–8.

economy of the houses they ruled; and paradoxically, as it were, the almost peculiarly English institution of the monastic cathedral was not only perpetuated but even extended by the Normans, a reflection no doubt of the strength of the monastic element in the Norman Church of the mid eleventh century.[1]

Moreover, most of the greater churches in Normandy received benefits directly from the conquest of England in addition to their share of William's initial distribution of loot. Some twenty-three Norman and seven other French monasteries are recorded in Domesday Book as holding manors in England, estates with values ranging from the princely 200 pounds a year of Fécamp to the humble 2 pounds a year of Saint-Pierre-sur-Dives.[2] The canons of Bayeux, Lisieux, and Coutances had also acquired lands in England by 1086;[3] the canons of Rouen had retained what they already possessed in 1066 and added to it;[4] Évreux, Séez, and Avranches obtained property in England a little later.[5] The English lands of the bishops of Bayeux, Coutances, Lisieux, and Évreux were held, it seems, in their personal capacity.[6] To such estates must be added the many English churches that were given to Norman and French monasteries. It appears that the barons of the Conquest generation preferred to make an offering of their new-found wealth both in lands and churches to monasteries with which they had some connection in France rather than to establish new houses in England, not because they lacked the means, but because their ties with their places of origin must still have been very strong and because, in many cases, they must have been deeply committed already to the many monasteries of baronial foundation that were struggling into existence in Normandy in the fifties and sixties of the eleventh century. Such new foundations, since the competition for landed endowment in Normandy must already have been quite serious, would have been glad

---

[1] Knowles, *Monastic Order*, pp. 129–34.

[2] Ibid., App. vi (p. 703).

[3] D.B., i. 31 b 1; 196 a 1 (Bayeux); 68 b 1 (Lisieux); 79 a 1 (Coutances). Cf. Matthews, *Norman Monasteries*, pp. 13, 43, 72, 74.

[4] D.B., i. 104 a 2; Matthews, *Norman Monasteries*, pp. 24–5, 31.

[5] Matthews, *Norman Monasteries*, pp. 13, note 4; 43, note 1; 74.

[6] For the holdings of the bishops, Ellis, *General Introduction*, i. 376–7; ii. 292 (Bayeux); i. 400, 428; ii. 305 (Coutances); i. 424, 447; ii. 349 (Lisieux). The estate of the bishop of Évreux was relatively small: D.B., ii. 388 b. For Coutances, cf. Le Patourel, 'Geoffrey of Montbray', pp. 152–3.

to receive any addition to their resources, however difficult it might be to exploit.[1] When the Normans did found monasteries in England during the early years after Hastings, these were often put under the direction of, or actually colonized from, monasteries in France.[2]

Whatever can be said of any policy that the Norman kings may have had in their treatment of the Church in England,[3] or the opportunities which William's conquest of England ultimately gave to the reformers on the Continent to extend their ideas to this country, the appointment of Normans to ecclesiastical posts in England meant that Norman churchmen were given opportunities for promotion and advancement that were therefore denied to English clerks and monks; and these appointments, together with the gifts of English lands and churches to Norman cathedrals and monasteries, meant also that the twenty-six per cent of English land which was held by the Church at the time of Domesday was very largely in Norman hands. There was, on a small scale, a precedent for this. William's conquest of the *comté* of Maine was followed by the appointment of two successive Norman bishops and a Norman archdeacon of Le Mans, with a Norman abbot of Saint-Vincent.[4]

Normans took over the land and the Church; they also took a share, perhaps a large share, in English trade. Domesday Book records the presence of Frenchmen, often in considerable numbers, in seven English boroughs,[5] and they can certainly

[1] Matthews, *Norman Monasteries*, ch. ii; Knowles and Hadcock, *Religious Houses*, pp. 83–95. For monasteries founded in Normandy between 1050 and 1070, Knowles, *Monastic Order*, App. v (pp. 701–2) and below, pp. 297–9.

[2] e.g. Battle colonized from Marmoutier, Chester colonized from Bec, Shrewsbury from Saint-Martin-de-Séez. Blyth was a priory of La-Sainte-Trinité-de-Rouen; Pembroke of Saint-Martin-de-Séez; Holy Trinity, York, of Marmoutier etc. The great Warenne foundation at Lewes was colonized from Cluny; Bermondsey, Much Wenlock, and Pontefract from La Charité, etc. Knowles and Hadcock, *Religious Houses*, pp. 59, 62, 76, 52, 56, 58, 97, 96, 97 (respectively) and *passim*.

[3] Douglas, quoting Eadmer, 'to sustain in England the same usages and laws which he and his ancestors had been wont to observe in Normandy'; *William the Conqueror*, pp. 323–4.

[4] Latouche, *Maine*, pp. 79–80 (cf. Douglas, *William the Conqueror*, p. 339). Maurice, bishop of London, had been archdeacon of Le Mans; William de Saint-Calais, bishop of Durham, had been abbot of Saint-Vincent.

[5] Stephenson, *Borough and Town*, p. 75; Cambridge, D.B., i. 189 a 1; Hereford, 179 a 1; Norwich, D.B., ii. 118; Shrewsbury, D.B., i. 252 a 1; Southampton, 52 a 1; Wallingford, 56 a 2; York, 298 a 1.

be inferred in two more.¹ In London, which is omitted from the Survey, but where the men of Rouen had enjoyed trading privileges for some time,² there is later evidence of a considerable influx of Norman merchants;³ and it would be hard to believe that there were none in Winchester, also omitted from Domesday, where William found and continued a royal treasury.⁴ In some cases their settlement seems to represent a new extension of the town; and in most cases they seem to have enjoyed a privileged position, paying less in gafol or geld than the native townsmen.⁵ 'The English burgesses of Shrewsbury say that it is very hard on them that they should pay the whole amount of the geld as they did in the time of King Edward, although the earl's castle has taken the site of 51 *masurae* and another 50 *masurae* are waste, 43 French burgesses occupy *masurae* which paid geld in the time of King Edward and the earl has given 39 burgesses, who formerly paid geld with the others and in the same way, to the abbey which he is founding there. In all there are 200 less 7 *masurae* which do not pay geld.'⁶ It would also be hard to believe that none of the burgesses in the little boroughs that were coming into existence or were deliberately founded beside the new baronial castles was French.⁷ The monks in the castle priories often were.⁸ Orderic, speaking of the years about 1070, says that English and Normans were living peacefully together in boroughs, towns, and

---

¹ Stephenson, *Borough and Town*, pp. 75, 195–7, 199–200; Nottingham, D.B., i. 280 a 1; Northampton, 219 a 1.   ² Above, p. 24, n. 3.

³ *Materials for the History of Thomas Becket*, iv. 81.

⁴ The Surveys of Winchester, made c. 1110 and in 1148 (D.B., 1816, iv. (*Additamenta*) pp. 529–62; cf. Round's introduction in *V.C.H. Hampshire*, i. 527–37, and the section on Winchester, ibid., v. 21–2) contain enough foreign names, with a high proportion that are specifically Norman, to indicate a substantial French settlement, even when all due allowance for the nature of such evidence has been made. Through the kindness of Mr. Biddle and Professor Barlow I have been allowed to see parts of the forthcoming *Winchester in the Early Middle Ages. An Edition and Discussion of the Winton Domesday*, ed. M. Biddle (*Winchester Stndies*, i) in proof. The surveys are re-edited by F. Barlow and the personal names analysed by O. von Feilitzen.

⁵ Stephenson, *Borough and Town*, pp. 93–4.

⁶ D.B., i. 252 a 1. The figures are as given in D.B.

⁷ Stephenson, *Borough and Town*, p. 75, gives a list of these castle-boroughs, but in no case are the burgesses specifically described as French. However, the spread of the 'laws of Breteuil' from Hereford, where they are associated with the French colony, to Rhuddlan etc. (Bateson, 'Laws of Breteuil') is suggestive.

⁸ Matthews, *Norman Monasteries*, pp. 54–8.

cities, and that French merchants could be seen in villages and market towns.[1] There seems indeed to have been a 'mercantile' colonization of England as there was a baronial and an ecclesiastical colonization. No doubt the merchants of Normandy were hoping to organize and to profit by the development of trade in England; certainly to have a share in it.

Thus Domesday Book, with other evidence, enables us to form some idea of the extent of the Norman colonization of England after the first generation or so. It shows this colonization to have been, at least up to that point, essentially aristocratic, ecclesiastical, and mercantile; but the indications given in Domesday of the way in which it had been brought about are fragmentary and indirect. Yet the nature of this colonization can only be understood if it is studied to some extent as an activity in progress. To do this as it should be done would require a vast amount of detailed genealogical work; but there is one point which can be made in general terms and which is immediately relevant.

It is that the process by which the Normans took possession of the land of England, the Church in England, and, to some extent, English trading potential was not complete by 1086 but extended over several decades. The Anglo-Saxon Chronicle says that when William returned to England from Normandy, in December 1067, 'he gave away every man's land'.[2] He cannot have given it all away at that time, unless it was by anticipation, for his powers did not then extend far beyond the south-eastern corner of the country. It is possible that some grants were made before he went to Normandy in March.[3] The men whom William left in England during his absence at that time to consolidate and extend his hold on the country may have been given licence to take some English lands for themselves;

---

[1] Orderic Vitalis, *H.E.* (ed. Le Prévost), ii. 214–15; (ed. Chibnall), ii. 256. The words Orderic uses are 'in burgis, castris et urbibus' and 'vicos aliquot aut fora urbana'. Domesday also records the presence of a certain number of anonymous Frenchmen in the English countryside (Ellis, *General Introduction*, ii. 317–18, s.v. 'Francigenae').

[2] A.-S.C., 1067 E (p. 146). The practice of giving lands 'to be conquered' was common enough in fourteenth-century France.

[3] William de Poitiers says that Eustace de Boulogne forfeited the fiefs that he had received from King William after his attack on Dover in 1067. He does not say directly that these fiefs were in England, though this may perhaps be presumed (*Gesta*, pp. 266–8; quoted by Davis, 'The Norman Conquest', p. 282).

at least it seems that they did so.[1] Those to whom he had entrusted the safeguarding of his duchy during the Hastings campaign are not likely to have been given their English lands before December 1067;[2] and they would still have to secure possession of them. There is much to suggest that the greater estates in the Midlands did not begin to take shape before the death of Earl Edwin of Mercia in 1070–1,[3] though some grants may have been made earlier. Gerbod probably received Chester in 1070,[4] though he can have done little to organize the earldom before he returned to Flanders; Roger de Montgomery seems to have obtained his lands in Shropshire, if not the earl's title, in 1071;[5] and though Florence of Worcester says that William fitzOsbern was made earl of Hereford in 1067, there are many reasons for thinking that he did not take possession of the county before 1069.[6] The personal history of Hugh de Grandmesnil, similarly, is against any likelihood that he could have begun the organization of his Midland estate centred on Leicester before the 1070s.[7] In the north, it has been argued that the great compact estates of Ilbert de Lacy at Pontefract, Roger de Bully at Tickhill, Alan de Bretagne at Richmond, and perhaps William de Warenne at Conisburgh, were being put together in the 1080s.[8] We have Domesday's explicit statement that Robert de Brus did not receive his Yorkshire estates until 'after the Book of Winchester was written';[9] and, although the evidence is less direct, Robert de Rumilly's honour of Skipton was probably assembled in the reign of William Rufus.[10] That this matter of chronology is not a simple one, however, is shown by the claim of William de

---

[1] Douglas, *William the Conqueror*, p. 207; Orderic Vitalis, *H.E.* (ed. Le Prévost), ii. 166–7, 171–3; (ed. Chibnall), ii. 194–6, 202–4; Eadmer, *Historia Novorum*, p. 17.

[2] e.g., Roger de Montgomery: Mason, 'Roger de Montgomery and his sons', p. 2; *Complete Peerage*, xi. 684–5.

[3] This is the natural conclusion to be drawn from Orderic's description of William's distribution of English lands, *H.E.* (ed. Le Prévost), ii. 218–24; (ed. Chibnall), ii. 260–6.

[4] Barraclough, 'Earldom and County Palatine of Chester', pp. 26–7; Douglas, *William the Conqueror*, p. 267.

[5] Mason, 'Roger de Montgomery and his sons', pp. 3–4.

[6] Wightman, 'The Palatine Earldom of William fitzOsbern', pp. 11–12.

[7] *V.C.H. Leicestershire*, i. 290–1.   [8] Wightman, *Lacy Family*, pp. 20–8.

[9] 'Hic est feodum Rotberti de Bruis quod fuit datum postquam liber de Wintonia scriptum fuit'; D.B., i. 332 b 1.

[10] *E.Y.C.*, vii (*Honour of Skipton*), 1–4.

Percy, at the time of Domesday, that he had held Bolton in Yorkshire while William Malet was sheriff, that is in 1068–9. Bolton Percy is not far from York. He may have obtained the manor in the first distribution of lands after King William took possession of the city in 1068 and he probably lost it in the troubles of the following year.[1]

In any case, great estates were not created and organized in a day. It seems to have taken Ilbert de Lacy a good dozen years to organize his castlery of Pontefract,[2] while the build-up of a great family fortune took much longer. William I de Warenne, who had already acquired a considerable estate in Normandy before 1066, most likely took or was granted the rape of Lewes in 1067; some at least of his lands in Norfolk cannot have been acquired before 1070; he had obtained Conisburgh in Yorkshire before 1086, but perhaps not very long before that date; his lands in Surrey, which eventually provided a title, were given to him most likely in 1088; while it was his son, William II de Warenne, who added Wakefield in Yorkshire and Saint-Saëns in Normandy to this vast accumulation during the reign of Henry Beauclerc.[3] New fortunes were to be made even then. It seems that the Ballon family and Robert fitzHamon both owed the foundation of their estates to William Rufus;[4] and Orderic has a famous passage about the men whom Henry 'raised from the dust': Geoffrey of Clinton, Ralph Basset, Hugh of Buckland, William Trussebut, Hamon de Falaise, and others;[5] though he does not mention in this connection men like Ranulf and William le Meschin,[6] Nigel d'Aubigny,[7] Brian fitzCount,[8] or even Stephen of Blois[9] who, though hardly raised from the dust, were mightily advanced by King Henry. Some of these later fortunes, it is true, were made in part out of the

---

[1] D.B., i. 374 a 1.　　　　　　　　　　　[2] Wightman, *Lacy Family*, ch. 1.

[3] *E.Y.C.*, viii (*Honour of Warenne*), 2–9, 178. For the date at which he acquired Conisburgh, cf. Wightman, *Lacy Family*, p. 28; the Surrey lands, *V.C.H. Surrey*, i. 340–1; Lewes and the lands in East Anglia, Mason, *William the First and the Sussex Rapes*, pp. 15–16.

[4] Round, *Studies in Peerage*, pp. 189 ff.; *Complete Peerage*, v. 683.

[5] Orderic Vitalis, *H.E.* (ed. Le Prévost), iv. 164–7; cf. Le Patourel, *Normandy and England*, pp. 30–1, 33 (for Geoffrey of Clinton and Ralph Basset); *E.Y.C.*, x (*Trussebut Fee*), 5 (for William Trussebut).

[6] *Complete Peerage*, iii. 166; *E.Y.C.*, vii. 4–6.

[7] Greenway, *Charters of the Honour of Mowbray*, pp. i–xxvi.

[8] *D.N.B.*, s.v. 'FitzCount, Brian'; Davis, 'Henry of Blois and Brian fitzCount'.

[9] Davis, *King Stephen*, pp. 7–12.

lands of Norman families which had ruined themselves in one way or another; but this does not invalidate the conclusion that England was a land of opportunity still for pushing, ambitious, and acquisitive Normans in the early twelfth century.

Furthermore, not all the men of Norman origin in the middle ranks of the feudal hierarchy in England had 'come over with the Conqueror' any more than all their lords had done. If the honour of Skipton was not organized until the reign of William Rufus, the Sandervilles, who may well have been tenants of the lord of the honour in Normandy already, could not have been his tenants in Yorkshire before then.[1] As with the tenants-in-chief, the settlement of the sub-tenants was a long process, made longer by the fact that it took some time to organize a great estate. It was this secondary settlement, moreover, that brought final disaster to English landowners. The greater Norman tenants-in-chief dispossessed the greater English landowners; but many Englishmen of the second rank, who might have survived as tenants of the Norman magnates, were dispossessed by their Norman followers. Thus, just as Domesday Book does not represent the end of the process of Norman settlement, a process that continued well into the twelfth century, so it does not indicate the extent of English dispossession. For example, the unusually large number of Anglo-Scandinavian sub-tenants on Ilbert de Lacy's lands in Yorkshire, as recorded in Domesday Book, has often been remarked upon; but their survival is now explained by the indications there are that the organization of the honour of Pontefract had not gone very far by 1086, and many of them disappeared even as sub-tenants of this honour not long after.[2] This does not mean that the humbler English were driven completely from the land as their betters were. The new French lords might rearrange or concentrate the units of property, but would not disrupt the agricultural or pastoral routine if they could avoid it, for an estate

[1] e.g. Loyd, *Anglo-Norman Families*, pp. 94–5; *E.Y.C.*, vii (*Honour of Skipton*), 98, note 6. Likewise if, as Dr. Wightman argues, the honour of Pontefract was still in process of organization in the 1080s and 1090s, it follows that the Norman sub-tenants (Reineville, Scorchebofe), who had probably been Lacy tenants in Normandy before 1066, cannot have obtained their Yorkshire lands until then (Loyd, ubi supra, pp. 139, 96, 84; Wightman, *Lacy Family*, p. 217). It seems that several of the fiefs held of the honour of Boulogne by families connected with the count in France were created after 1086 (Round, *Studies in Peerage*, pp. 158–61).

[2] Wightman, *Lacy Family*, pp. 40–3; cf. *V.C.H. Yorkshire*, ii. 162–4.

was only of value to them as a going and productive concern. Some English families did survive; there was some intermarriage between English and Norman; and no doubt the survival rate was relatively higher in the towns.[1] But it does mean that the survivors of the lesser English landowning class could not hope to retain more than a fraction of their former lands, and then only as tenants of some Norman lord. They were being pushed further and further down the tenurial and social scale until some as yet undetermined point in the twelfth century;[2] and it means that there could be one, two, and sometimes three superimposed French lords who possessed a profitable interest in one English estate, with the Norman king on top of them all.[3]

The Norman hold upon the English Church and its property was scarcely relaxed in the course of Henry's reign. Among the bishops[4] there were now a certain number who, though bearing Norman names and coming from families of Norman origin may well have been born in England; but they must have been regarded as Norman in their time, for Eadmer certainly thought that English clerks and monks had a poor chance of promotion in their own country.[5] Likewise, it seems to be only from the ten years or so after Henry's death that the succession of Norman abbots in the greater English monasteries seems to falter.[6] In terms of property, grants of English lands and churches to Norman monasteries did not cease either. Saint-Georges-de-Boscherville and Aumale, for example, were re-founded as Benedictine houses in 1114 and 1120 respectively, and appear to have received their English properties at the time

[1] Stenton, in 'English Families', says most of what there is to be said at present about English survival. Clay gives some examples from Yorkshire in *E.Y.C.*, x pp. xi–xii, and in *Early Yorkshire Families*. Cf. Southern, *Medieval Humanism*, pp. 225–7. For intermarriage between Norman and English, below, pp. 254–5.

[2] Stenton suggests that the English reached their lowest point between 1080 and 1120 ('English Families', p. 8). Good examples of the process of degradation are given in Wightman, *Lacy Family*, pp. 40–3; Stenton, *English Feudalism*, p. 116; *V.C.H. Nottinghamshire*, i. 229–30; Lennard, *Rural England*, p. 24.

[3] e.g. a certain Humphrey held Steeple Aston (Oxfordshire) of Adam (de Ryes), who held it of the bishop of Bayeux (*V.C.H. Oxfordshire*, i. 380; D.B., i. 156 a 2. Stenton (*William the Conqueror*, p. 447) quotes a case where there were four.

[4] See note on *The Provenance of the Bishops of English Sees* at the end of this chapter.

[5] *Historia Novorum*, p. 224. Æthelwulf of Carlisle seems to be the only bishop appointed in Henry's reign who could be regarded as English in any fuller sense, and he is hard to document.

[6] *Heads of Religious Houses*, p. 3.

of the refoundation.[1] Lessay also received its very extensive properties in England, the gift of Robert de la Haye, in Henry's reign.[2] It should be remembered that these endowments were cumulative, adding to the total possessions of the Norman monasteries in England, for gifts to ecclesiastical communities were made in principle for ever;[3] whereas the later acquisitions of Norman laymen in England, though they show that Norman fortunes were still to be made in this country, often simply represented, at least so far as their tenants were concerned, the substitution of one Norman lord for another.

The early part of the twelfth century is not a time when the internal development of English towns is well documented. This makes it difficult to form any clear idea of the fortunes of the Norman or French colonies which Domesday records in several of them; though there are a few small indications to show that, at least, they were not simply absorbed into the mass of the English townsfolk—the continuance of different legal rules in the 'French borough' and the 'English borough' at Nottingham,[4] the possible survival into the thirteenth century of customs derived from the 'laws of Breteuil' at Hereford and Shrewsbury;[5] while at Norwich it seems that the French borough so flourished that the urban centre moved from its earlier position in Tombland to the newer settlement in what was later known as Mancroft.[6] Similarly, the continued recourse to these 'laws of Breteuil' by Norman barons founding boroughs beside their castles in the west of England and the Welsh Marches implies that there may often have been Norman immigrants among their first burgesses;[7] just as the explanation offered by an anonymous biographer for the presence of Archbishop Thomas

---

[1] Knowles, *Monastic Order*, p. 702; Knowles and Hadcock, *Religious Houses*, pp. 83–4; *Abbayes et prieurés*, pp. 34, 49–50; *Regesta*, ii, Nos. 1012, 1099, 1100, 1694 (pp. 106, 127, 249; 324–6, 372–3).

[2] *Cal. Docs. France*, Nos. 921–3; *Regesta*, ii, No. 1441 (pp. 196, 353–4).

[3] No doubt ecclesiastical institutions did lose, sell, or exchange properties from time to time; but the principle holds nevertheless.

[4] Stevenson, *Records of the Borough of Nottingham*, i. 124–6, 185–9. Cf. Pollock and Maitland, *H.E.L.*, i. 647; ii. 279.

[5] Bateson, 'Laws of Breteuil', *E.H.R.*, xv. 302–18. The claim that the customs of the Norman immigrants eventually spread to all the burgages of the towns in which these 'laws' can be traced may be exaggerated (cf. Hemmeon, *Burgage Tenure*, p. 167), but there seems to have been at least some survival.

[6] Hudson, *Records of the City of Norwich*, i, pp. vii–xi.

[7] Bateson, 'Laws of Breteuil', *passim*.

Becket's Norman parents in London, that they had come to reside in the city with a number of merchants from Rouen and Caen, suggests, though the chronology is uncertain, that such people were still finding a place in England during Henry's reign.[1] The fixing of the English terminal of the royal transfretations to and from Normandy at Southampton and Portsmouth, as it seems, together with the movement of funds to and from the principal royal treasury in England at Winchester, must have involved the continued residence of a number of Normans in those towns.[2]

Such thin evidence, however, does no more than indicate that the Normans had indeed secured a share in England's commercial potential in accordance with the intention implied by the Domesday colonies. No doubt the fact that they would have had to compete with so many other continental merchants for England's foreign trade,[3] and the likelihood that there could hardly be an unlimited surplus of merchants in the Norman towns anxious to improve their prospects in the promised land across the Channel, meant that the Normans' part in English commerce could never be as overwhelming as their expropriation of the English aristocracy or their dominance of the English Church. But they certainly had a share, and kept it throughout the time of the Norman kings.

The colonization of England that accompanied and followed the military operations was thus not simply a matter of paying the debts that William the Conqueror owed to those who had assisted him in his great venture; it was a long and complicated process, far from complete when Domesday Book recorded the stage it had reached in 1086, and continuing far into the twelfth century. If William's claim to be the lawful king of the English after his coronation is accepted, if Englishmen who refused to acknowledge him are regarded as rebelling against their rightful king rather than as continuing to resist the invader, and if attention is concentrated on the manner in which the Normans generally stepped into the shoes of their English *antecessores*, taking over rights, obligations, and traditions, it is easy to think of this vast process of colonization as a lawful,

---

[1] *Materials for the History of Thomas Becket*, iv. 81.
[2] Below, p. 175.
[3] Poole, *Domesday Book to Magna Carta*, pp. 88–95.

even an orderly affair, with William in control all the time.[1] Certainly the machinery existed for reallocating the land of England in an orderly manner;[2] in many cases Anglo-Saxon units of property were preserved not only in outline but in detail; there can be no doubt that the shire courts had some part to play in the process; and indeed the tenurial revolution never got out of hand or degenerated into a wild scramble; but the process started with the great violence of the invasion and the battle of Hastings, the campaigns in the west and the devastation of the north, and it would not be surprising if it continued with the innumerable petty violences of Norman barons taking what they thought had been allotted to them or taking what they could. They had the power; and because a legal theory was found to cover the vast change of land-ownership that took place it does not follow that it was achieved justly.

Very little direct evidence of the actual process of redistribution in England has been preserved. If William made grants to laymen by charter, very few have survived;[3] and the chroniclers, save one, are curiously silent about it. The exception among the chroniclers is Orderic; and he has some claim to impartiality in this matter for he was born in England, of a French father and an English mother, and claimed to be an Englishman though he lived all his thinking life in a Norman monastery which had profited very considerably from the conquest of England. He constantly returns to the theme of the violence and brigandage prevalent in England during the years after 1066. 'England . . . lay open to foreign robbers, supporters of the victorious William, and presents a melancholy subject for the sensitive historian.'[4] His complaints, moreover, are supported by Domesday, in the occasional glimpses it affords of the activities of men like the bishop of Bayeux,[5] Eustace 'the

---

[1] Stenton, *A.-S.E.*, p. 618; Douglas, *William the Conqueror*, pp. 270 ff. Both writers allow for occasional violence but both stress the mantle of legality thrown over the territorial revolution that took place in England.

[2] Davis, 'The Norman Conquest', pp. 282–4.

[3] Brown, *Normans and the Norman Conquest*, pp. 228–30.

[4] Orderic Vitalis, *H.E.* (ed. Le Prévost), ii. 162; (ed. Chibnall), ii. 190 (the quotation is taken from Forester's translation). For other references to this theme, ibid. (ed. Le Prévost), ii. 223, 226–32, 265; iii. 44; (ed. Chibnall), ii. 266, 270–8, 318–20; iii. 254–6.

[5] e.g. *V.C.H. Essex*, i. 342–3; *V.C.H. Kent*, iii. 188–90. Cf. *Domesday Monachorum*, pp. 30–3; Eadmer, *Historia Novorum*, p. 17.

Sheriff',[1] Turold 'of Rochester',[2] or more generally in the *clamores* and *invasiones* recorded in certain counties.[3] Whatever else this great survey may have been intended to achieve, it was a 'final' sorting out of many disputes, a legalization of many injustices with rough justice, an ultimate court of appeal, for there could be no appeal against Domesday. It is clear that the Norman colonization of Wales, where also units of property with the rights and obligations attached to them were often preserved, was carried out very largely by violence, for in this case some record of the process has survived.[4] Is there any reason to suppose that the same men at much the same time acted in a wholly different manner in England?

[1] *V.C.H. Huntingdonshire*, i. 333–4. On *invasiones* cf. ibid., pp. 315–16.

[2] *V.C.H. Essex*, i. 342–3, and more generally, ibid., pp. 354–6. The history of Ramsey Abbey suggests an early phase of land-grabbing only gradually brought to order (Raftis, *Estates of Ramsey Abbey*, pp. 23–33).

[3] Domesday occasionally disguises a dispute by entering the property under the name of both claimants (e.g. Round, *Feudal England*, pp. 21–7).

[4] Below, pp. 63–4, 312–15.

Note on the Provenance of the Bishops elected to English Sees, 1066–1144

In the following list, the letter N denotes a man known to have been born in Normandy, to have been a monk or priest or to have held some ecclesiastical office there; F, origin similarly defined in some part of France other than Normandy; L, similarly in Lotharingia; E, similarly in England; U, unknown. C indicates a royal clerk or chaplain. A query indicates that the origin is less certain or less direct, the evidence being derived from name, membership of a family of Norman origin, or circumstance. No reference is given where there is an entry in the *D.N.B.* adequate for these purposes. For the royal clerks, *Regesta*, i, pp. xviii–xxi; ii, pp. ix–xi; iii, pp. xi–xiii. Dates of nomination, election, consecration, or translation (or the earliest if more than one are known) are taken from *Handbook of British Chronology*, pp. 202–66 and Le Neve, *Fasti 1066–1300*, vols. i and ii.

CANTERBURY. Lanfranc (1070), N; Anselm (1093), N; Ralph d'Écure (1114), N;[1] William de Corbeil (1123), F;[2] Theobald (1138), N.

CARLISLE. Æthelwulf (Athelwold, Adelulf, etc.) (1133), ?E.[3]

CHICHESTER.[4] Stigand (1070), C ?N;[5] Godfrey (1088), U; Ralph Luffa (1091), C ?N; Seffrid (1125), N.[6]

[1] Translated from Rochester. For his name, Mayr-Harting, *Bishops of Chichester*, p. 4.

[2] *D.N.B.*, s.v. 'Corbeil'. Bethell, 'William of Corbeil and the Canterbury York Dispute', pp. 145–55, states that nothing is known of his origin; but he began his career as a clerk of Ranulf Flambard, bishop of Durham (Simeon of Durham, *Historia Regum* in *Opera*, ii. 268–9).

[3] Formerly prior of Nostell. Evidence is quoted in *V.C.H. Cumberland*, ii. 12 that he held land in Yorkshire. Robert of Torigni speaks of him as King Henry's confessor (*Chronica*, p. 123). On his identity see also Wightman, 'Henry I and the Foundation of Nostell Priory', p. 59, note 1. Other accounts in Prescott, *Register of Wetherhal Priory*, App. B., pp. 478–89, and Le Neve, *Fasti 1066–1300*, ii. 19, 21, do not give any further information on his origin.

[4] For the early post-Conquest bishops of Chichester, Mayr-Harting, *Bishops of Chichester*, pp. 1–7. This writer thinks that the shadowy Bishop William, placed between Godfrey and Ralph Luffa in *Handbook of British Chronology* (p. 216), did not exist.

[5] No direct evidence of origin. His name could be Anglo-Scandinavian or Norman, but opinion favours a Norman origin (Darlington, *Vita Wulfstani*, p. xliv, note 1; Stenton, 'The Scandinavian Colonies', p. 7).

[6] Monk of Séez; half-brother of Ralph d'Écure (Rochester, Canterbury).

DURHAM. Walcher (1071), L; William de Saint-Calais (1080), N;[1] Ranulf Flambard (1099), C N; Geoffrey Rufus (1133), ?C ?N.[2] [William Cumin (1141–4), ?E];[3] William de Sainte-Barbe (1143), ?N.[4]

ELMHAM–THETFORD–NORWICH. Herfast (1070), C N; William de Beaufour (1085), C ?N;[5] Herbert Losinga (1090–1), C N;[6] Everard (1121), C ?N.[7]

ELY. Hervey (1108), C F;[8] Nigel (1133), ?N.[9]

EXETER. Osbern fitzOsbern (1072), C N; William Warelwast (1107), C N; Robert Warelwast (1138), ?N.[10]

HEREFORD. Robert Losinga (1079), C L; Gerard (1096), C N; Reinhelm (1102), U;[11] Geoffrey de Clive (1115), C U;[12] Richard de Capella (1121), C ?N; Robert de Béthune (1131), F.

LICHFIELD–CHESTER–COVENTRY. Peter (1072), C N;[13] Robert de Limési (1085), C N;[14] Robert Peche (1121), C U (?N);[15] Roger of Clinton (1129), ?N.[16]

LINCOLN. Remigius (1067), N; Robert Bloet (1093), C N; Alexander (1123), ?N.[17]

---

[1] *D.N.B.*, s.v. 'Carilef'.

[2] Chancellor to King Henry; *D.N.B.*, s.v. 'Rufus, Geoffrey'; *Regesta*, ii, pp. ix–x.

[3] Chancellor to David, king of Scots. Said to be English by birth though of French origin (Ritchie, *Normans in Scotland*, pp. 281–2; cf. Le Neve, *Fasti 1066–1300*, ii. 105).

[4] Name presumably from the priory of Sainte-Barbe-en-Auge (Calvados). For some references, Clay, 'Notes on the Early Deans of York', pp. 364–6.

[5] Le Neve, *Fasti 1066–1300*, ii. 55, 67; *D.N.B.*, s.v. 'Beaufeu, William de'.

[6] Cf. Dodwell, 'Foundations of Norwich Cathedral', pp. 3–4.

[7] *D.N.B.*, s.v. 'Eborard'. Identity uncertain: he has been identified with a son of Roger de Montgomery and with Everard 'de Calna', an archdeacon in the diocese of Salisbury (Landon, 'Everard bishop of Norwich'; Le Neve, *Fasti 1066–1300*, i. 61; ii. 55–6). The names of his relations, a brother Arthur, and nephews Reginald, Adam, Nigel, Richard, Herbert, Peter, Walter, suggest Norman rather than English origins.   [8] A Breton: translated from Bangor.

[9] Cf. Kealey, *Roger of Salisbury*, pp. 274–6.

[10] A nephew of William Warelwast (*Letters of John of Salisbury*, p. 9, note 1) who is described as 'a Norman by birth'.

[11] Chancellor of Queen Matilda (*Regesta*, ii, p. xi).

[12] Florence of Worcester, *Chronicon*, ii. 68.

[13] Barlow, *English Church*, p. 157.

[14] Described by Robert de Torigni as 'Robertus Normannus de Limesia' (*Chronica*, p. 121). Cf. A.-S.C., 1085 E (p. 161); Loyd, *Anglo-Norman Families*, p. 54.

[15] 'Ex capella regis Henrici ad episcopatum datus'; Malmesbury, *Gesta Pontificum*, p. 310.

[16] Nephew of Geoffrey of Clinton (Malmesbury, *Gesta Pontificum*, p. 311). On Geoffrey, Le Patourel, *Normandy and England*, pp. 30–1, and references there given.

[17] Cf. Kealey, *Roger of Salisbury*, pp. 274–5.

LONDON. Hugh d'Orival (1075), ?N;[1] Maurice (1085), C N; Richard de Beaumais (1108), C N;[2] Gilbert (1127), F; [Anselm (1136–8)];[3] Robert 'de Sigillo' (1141), U (?N).[4]

ROCHESTER. Arnost (1075), N;[5] Gundulf (1077), N; Ralph d'Écure (1108), N;[6] Ernulf (1114), N; John I (1125), U;[7] John II de Séez (1137), ?N;[7] Ascelin (1142), U (?N).[8]

SALISBURY. Osmund (1078), C ?N;[9] Roger (1102), C N;[10] [Philip d'Harcourt (1140), N];[11] Jocelin de Bohun (1142), ?N.[12]

WELLS–BATH. John de Villula (1088), C F; Godfrey (1123), 'German';[13] Robert (1136), E (F).[14]

WINCHESTER. Walkelin (1070), C N; William Giffard (1100), C N; Henry de Blois (1129), F.

WORCESTER. Samson (1096), C N; Theulf (1113), C N;[15] Simon (1125), ?L.[16]

YORK. Thomas I (1070), C N; Gerard (1100), C N;[17] Thomas II (1108), C ?N; Thurstan (1114), C N; William fitzHerbert (1141), C ?E.[18]

[1] The only indication seems to be his name—from Orival, dept. Seine-Maritime, arr. Rouen?   [2] Loyd, *Anglo-Norman Families*, pp. 13–14.

[3] Nephew of Archbishop Anselm (Canterbury), Le Neve, *Fasti 1066–1300*, i. 1. For his career, Williamson, *The Letters of Osbert of Clare*, pp. 191–200.

[4] Keeper of the seal to King Henry, *Regesta*, ii, p. x. Cf. Gibbs, *Early Charters of St. Paul's*, p. xxxiii.   [5] A monk of Bec (Florence of Worcester, *Chronicon*, ii. 8).

[6] Later archbishop of Canterbury.

[7] On both Johns, Saltman, 'John II, bishop of Rochester'.

[8] Formerly sacrist of Christ Church Canterbury and prior of Dover. Also called Anselm (*Heads of Religious Houses*, p. 87).

[9] Origin unknown, but circumstantial evidence points to Normandy (Edwards, *English Secular Cathedrals*, p. 13; Douglas, 'The Norman Episcopate', pp. 107–13).

[10] 'Abrincensis aeclesiae presbyterum nomine rogerum' at the time of his election (Ker, *English Manuscripts in the Century after the Norman Conquest*, plate 9a).

[11] Previously archdeacon of Évreux and subsequently bishop of Bayeux (*Gallia Christiana*, xi. cols. 360–4; *Regesta*, iii, p. x).

[12] On his career and relationship to the Bohun family, Knowles, *Episcopal Colleagues*, pp. 17–22.

[13] Chancellor to Queen Adela of Louvain. 'Godefridus natione quidem Theutonicus' ('Historia de primordiis episcopatus Somersetensis', in *Ecclesiastical Documents*, p. 22); Bethell, 'English Black Monks and Episcopal Elections', pp. 683–4.

[14] 'Flandrensis genere sed est natus in partibus Angliae' (Florence of Worcester, *Chronicon*, ii. 95).

[15] Formerly canon of Bayeux, Le Neve, *Fasti 1066–1300*, ii. 99.

[16] The queen's chancellor. Origin unknown; but he was nominated while he and the king were in Normandy, at the same time as Seffrid of Chichester (Florence of Worcester, *Chronicon*, ii. 79; Bethell, 'English Black Monks and Episcopal Elections', pp. 683–4).   [17] Translated from Hereford.

[18] Probably born in England, but of French origin. A kinsman of King Stephen and of Bishop Henry de Blois (Winchester) (Poole, 'The Appointment and Deposition of St. William', pp. 273–7).

3. Further Expansion

THE kingdom which William conquered between 1066 and 1072 was in some ways very advanced for its time. Its government has an appearance of maturity that few of its continental contemporaries could show; and the seemingly patriotic sentiments expressed in the Anglo-Saxon Chronicle when describing certain events in Edward the Confessor's reign give a surprising impression of national solidarity. Yet this kingdom was not a clearly defined unit, politically or territorially. Its people could not look back to such formal political unity, even, as those of the kingdom of the Western Franks might do; there was no mould into which the ingredients of an England were being poured, no ideal of England in the minds of men to be remembered or striven for; and it was this very lack of definition in the kingdom of the English as it was on the day that King Edward was alive and dead that provides one of the reasons why the Norman Conquest would be more than a conquest of 'England'. For, in its early stages, the formation of the kingdom had been a synthesis. A part of Britain had been settled by Anglo-Saxon peoples from the continental mainland in a large number of small units; and these, by a process of political cannibalism, became a smaller number of larger units. Left to itself, this process could well have continued to the point at which one Anglo-Saxon kingdom dominated and absorbed not only all the others but all the British and Scandinavian kingdoms and principalities within the island of Britain as well, if it did not extend its dominion still further afield. Such a point had not been reached when the Normans came, though it could perhaps already be envisaged—and this was their opportunity.

During the seventh and eighth centuries the strong kings of one or other of the Anglo-Saxon kingdoms had often exercised a hegemony over the others, or most of them; and this hegemony, combined with vague memories of Roman government, seems to have been acknowledged by giving to the king who exercised it the title of 'Bretwalda', now usually interpreted as 'ruler of Britain'; while his authority over the client kingdoms was

described by Bede as an 'imperium'.[1] In the early part of the
ninth century this hegemony was exercised by King Ecgbert
of Wessex, and eventually it was his kingdom which formed the
nucleus of the much larger kingdom of the mid eleventh
century; but this had only been possible because he and his
successors were able to intensify the old hegemony by suppressing some of the client kingdoms and annexing their
peoples and territories to Wessex, and also to treat the accumulation of lands as it grew from generation to generation as an
impartible inheritance.[2] Ecgbert himself conquered and annexed Kent, Surrey, and Sussex, which came to be regarded as
an integral part of the kingdom of the West Saxons. He also
conquered Cornwall, which was subjected to West-Saxon
colonization during the following century or so and gradually
brought into the West-Saxon ecclesiastical and political organization.[3] The hegemony of the older kind that he exercised
over Mercia and Northumbria proved temporary.

It was this enlarged and strengthened Wessex which faced
the Scandinavian attacks and settlements of the ninth and tenth
centuries. One important consequence of these settlements was
that they replaced the Anglo-Saxon rivals of Wessex, which had
often dominated her in the past, by a disunited collection of
Danish kingdoms and earldoms, making it relatively easy for
the West-Saxon kings to overcome them, once King Alfred had
set a limit to their conquests and established himself and his
monarchy as the leader and protector of all who would resist the
invaders.[4] On the foundation of this achievement King Edward
the Elder, apparently using a mixture of force and negotiation,
was able to subdue and annex all the Danish states south of the
Humber; and he annexed the south-western half of Mercia,
which had not been dominated by the Danes, at the same time.[5]

---

[1] Stenton, *A.-S.E.*, pp. 33–5, 201–11; John, *Orbis Britanniae*, pp. 6 ff.; cf.
Deanesly, 'Roman Traditionalist Influence among the Anglo-Saxons'.

[2] Le Patourel, 'The Norman Succession', pp. 240–2; and on the royal lands,
John, *Orbis Britanniae*, pp. 37–44.

[3] Hencken, *Archaeology of Cornwall and Scilly*, pp. 247–57; Finberg, 'Sherborne,
Glastonbury, and the Expansion of Wessex'; Taylor, *Celtic Christianity of Cornwall*,
pp. 64–9, 89, 120–1.

[4] A.-S.C., 886 (p. 52), 893 (p. 54), 900 (p. 58); Hodgkin, *History of the Anglo-
Saxons*, ii. 602–3, 647–52.

[5] On the annexation of 'English' Mercia, Stenton, *A.-S.E.*, pp. 257, 320, 325–6;
Wainwright, 'Æthelflæd Lady of the Mercians', esp. pp. 67–9.

After this Wessex, 'English' Mercia, with Danish East Anglia and the land of the Five Boroughs, were governed as one political unit; though both Mercian law and Danish law long survived as regional customs.[1] The integration of these lands south of the Humber was advanced, though not completed, by a certain amount of West-Saxon colonization which King Edward promoted,[2] by the great courts of magnates held by King Æthelstan and his immediate successors,[3] by the organization of a system of local government with quite a high degree of uniformity throughout Wessex, Mercia, and the southern Danelaw,[4] and by the monastic movement of the mid tenth century which, under royal patronage and protection, not only brought the power of the West-Saxon kings firmly into English and Danish Mercia but tended to exalt their authority to match their extended dominion,[5] in much the same way as the slightly later renaissance of the Church in Normandy exalted that of the duke.[6]

King Edward the Elder must have contemplated the conquest of the Danish kingdom of York quite early in his reign, for he sent a raiding force into the country in 909 and annihilated a counter-invasion in the following year. This had the effect of so weakening the Northumbrian Danes that they could neither support their countrymen south of the Humber against the attacks of King Edward and his sister, Æthelflæd, the 'Lady of the Mercians', nor defend themselves against the Norse adventurer from Ireland who made himself king of York in 919 and who, no doubt to secure recognition, was prepared to acknowledge Edward's overlordship in 920. The tension between the incoming Norse and the Danes who had been settled around York for over a generation provided yet another

[1] Below, p. 264.

[2] Stenton, *A.-S.E.*, pp. 318–19; 'The Danes in England', pp. 208–9, 211; Whitelock, 'Dealings of the Kings of England with Northumbria', p. 81. The boroughs established by Edward and Æthelflæd must have served as centres of English colonization in the areas of Danish settlement as well as instruments of conquest.

[3] Stenton, *A.-S.E.*, pp. 345–8.

[4] Blair, *Introduction to Anglo-Saxon England*, pp. 222–44.

[5] Knowles, *Monastic Order*, pp. 31 ff. The king's part is emphasized by John, *Orbis Britanniae*, pp. 154–80, and cf. Fisher, 'The Anti-Monastic Reaction', pp. 261–7. On Edgar's coronation of 973, John, op. cit. pp. 56–60, 276–89 and works there quoted.

[6] Cf. below, pp. 238–9 246 ff., 296 ff.

condition that helped Æthelstan to conquer the kingdom in 927
and to suppress the monarchy. It is true that the Norse kings of
Dublin were able to recover the kingdom for a few months from
time to time after his death, and Eric Bloodaxe from Norway to
make himself king on two occasions; but this revival of Norse
rule was episodic. It was not recognized by the West-Saxon
kings, and King Eadred's eviction of Eric in 954 was final.[1]

The Danes of York had not penetrated to any extent into
that part of the older English kingdom of Northumbria that lay
to the north of the Tees, though they must have exercised some
form of lordship over the native dynasty of reeves who ruled
there as the successors (and very probably the descendants) of
the earlier Northumbrian kings. This overlordship had passed,
at least from time to time, to the kings of Wessex even before
their final conquest of the Scandinavian kingdom of York.[2]
After that conquest, the whole of the ancient, pre-Danish
kingdom of Northumbria east of the Pennines was treated by
the West-Saxon kings as two earldoms within their kingdom,
one to the north of the Tees and the other (representing the
Scandinavian kingdom of York) between the Tees and the
Humber. The earldom to the north remained in the hands of
the descendants of the ancient line of reeves; but a man drawn
from somewhere well to the south of the Humber was generally
set over the southern earldom. Sometimes the two earldoms
were united, either under the northern earl who then held both
earldoms, or under a southern earl who would recognize the
contemporary representative of the ancient line as a fairly
independent subordinate north of the Tees.[3]

Yet, although some of these earls of Northumbria were
drawn from the south, and the West-Saxon kings endeavoured
to secure the appointment of archbishops of York who at least
had some connection with the south,[4] it is difficult to say just
how far Northumbria was being integrated with the remainder
of the kingdom of the English. The monastic movement of the
tenth century had had virtually no impact north of the River

---

[1] Stenton, *A.-S.E.*, ch. x.
[2] A.-S.C., 920 (pp. 67–8), 927 D (pp. 68–9), 954 DE (p. 73); Stenton, *A.-S.E.*,
pp. 330, 336, 357–8.
[3] Whitelock, 'Dealings of the Kings of England with Northumbria'; cf. Stenton,
A.-S.E., pp. 411–12.
[4] Whitelock, ubi supra.

Welland,[1] and the later West-Saxon kings were hardly ever seen beyond that river on a peaceful errand. The Northumbrian peoples kept their own laws[2] and for some time their languages; they had their own individual blend of Briton, English, Dane, and Norse in their ethnical make-up; they looked across the North Sea rather than across the Humber. On the other hand, a Danish dynasty securely established in England might well have commanded the loyalty of their chief men; Edward the Confessor's demesne lands in Yorkshire, outside the city of York, were of relatively small extent (less than a quarter of Earl Morcar's in 1066);[3] but it is perhaps more remarkable that he had lands there at all. Some Yorkshire lands at least were assessed for geld in Edward's time.[4] The relationship between Northumbria and the king is perhaps accurately indicated by the incident of 1065. The Northumbrian magnates could insist on Tostig's exile and Morcar's appointment in his place and get their way; but they recognized that it was for King Edward to appoint their earl.[5] The authority of a West-Saxon king in Northumbria was indeed not much more than overlordship, and it was an overlordship which had to be exercised with tact, for there was always the possibility that the Northumbrians would throw in their lot with a Scandinavian invader, as they did in 1013, 1066, and 1069; yet it was an overlordship with some elements of direct rule, a potential which of itself might develop further.[6]

Through their increasing interest in Mercia and Northumbria, the West-Saxon kings found themselves ever more concerned with what had been the border problems of those kingdoms, quite apart from any theory there might be that a Bretwalda's authority extended, or should extend, over the

---

[1] Archbishop Oswald may have tried to introduce monks into Ripon (Knowles, *Monastic Order*, p. 52). If he did, which is doubtful, it was the only attempt, and that unsuccessful, to set up a monastery in the Benedictine sense in Northumbria between the time of the first Danish settlements and the Norman Conquest.

[2] Below, p. 264.

[3] *V.C.H. Yorkshire*, ii. 150.

[4] e.g. D.B. i., 317 b 1.

[5] Barlow, *Edward the Confessor*, pp. 233–9.

[6] Stenton, 'Danes in England', pp. 243–6; Brown, 'The Norman Conquest', pp. 116–18. The details of the manner in which the kings of the English handled Northumbria have been well set out in Whitelock, 'Dealings of the Kings of England with Northumbria'.

whole island of Britain. This brought them into direct contact with the kings of Wales and, in the north, with the kings of the Strathclyde Britons and the kings of the Scots.

The kingdoms of Wales have a history of 'empire-building' very similar to that of the Anglo-Saxon kingdoms; but since their kings retained the custom of partition, including even illegitimate sons, no 'empire' survived its creator. Anything like the steady build-up of the West-Saxon kingdom from King Ecgbert's time onwards was thus impossible in Wales, though successive 'empires' show a tendency to include an ever larger number of the normally independent kingdoms.[1] The struggles of the Welsh kings among themselves and against Scandinavian intruders in the ninth and tenth centuries inevitably drove them to seek allies or protectors among the Anglo-Saxon kings and enabled those kings to establish some form of supremacy over them. Already in 830 Ecgbert of Wessex, after he had defeated the Mercians, claimed to have reduced the Welsh to submission; and though this submission might be ephemeral, it was the first of many.[2] In the tenth century the overlordship of the West-Saxon kings might almost be regarded as established; for in addition to ceremonies which must at least have resembled the act of homage,[3] Welsh kings appear frequently as witnesses to the charters of Æthelstan, Eadred, and Eadwig, and were therefore, presumably, attending the court.[4]

Beyond Northumbria the dominant power was the kingdom of the Scots, formed in the mid ninth century by the union of the Scots of Argyll (intruders from Ireland) with the Picts north of the Forth–Clyde isthmus. The destruction by the Danes of the English kingdom of Northumbria which had once extended beyond the Forth in the north-east and to the Ayrshire coast in the north-west, enabled the Scots to acquire Lothian, and the British kings of Strathclyde to expand southwards as far, probably, as Stainmore; but both acknowledged,

[1] e.g. those of Rhodri Mawr, Hywel Dda, and Gruffydd ap Llywelyn (Lloyd, *History of Wales*, i. 323–7, 333–43; ii. 357–73).

[2] A.-S.C., 830 (p. 41). Cf. 853 (p. 43), 893 (p. 56); Lloyd, *History of Wales*, i. 325, 328–30; Stenton, *A.-S.E.*, p. 264.

[3] A.-S.C., 918 (p. 67), 927 D (pp. 68–9), 973 DE (pp. 76–7); Florence of Worcester, *Chronicon*, i. 142–3. Cf. Lloyd, *History of Wales*, i. 332–3, 335–8, 348–50; Stenton, *A.-S.E.*, pp. 326, 336–7, 363–5.

[4] Lloyd, *History of Wales*, i. 336, 348, 353. For relations between the Welsh princes and Mercia after Edgar's death, ibid., pp. 350–1.

from time to time, the overlordship of the West-Saxon kings in terms identical (at least as reported) with the periodic expressions of submission made by the Welsh kings.[1]

It is not altogether surprising, therefore, that high-sounding and even 'imperial' titles were attributed to the West-Saxon kings of the tenth century in their charters[2] and on their coins.[3] The meaning of these titles has been much discussed; but their appropriateness could hardly be gainsaid if 'imperial' is taken to imply no more than an overlordship over other kings and rulers, a hegemony, for the West-Saxon kings had achieved that in fact. Moreover, the position was not lost with the incapacity of Æthelred II or Cnut's conquest; for Cnut went north 'and the king of Scots surrendered to him and became his man, though he observed it but little time',[4] and King Malcolm III, who owed his throne in part to King Edward, visited him in 1059 and almost certainly acknowledged Edward's overlordship.[5] By this time the kings of the Scots had annexed the kingdom of the Strathclyde Britons; but this did not alter their relationship with the kings of the English. In the west, Edward could even intensify the traditional overlordship of the West-Saxon kings over the Welsh kings. Gruffydd ap Llywelyn, at the moment of his triumph, when almost the whole of Wales was under his control together with extensive lands on the English side of what had hitherto been the border, 'swore oaths that he would be a loyal and faithful under-king to King Edward';[6] and a few years later, when Gruffydd had been killed, Edward was able to 'entrust the country' to Gruffydd's half-brothers, Bleddyn and Rhiwallon, with the intention, apparently, that they should exercise the same authority in Wales as Gruffydd had done, but under Edward's

[1] A.-S.C., 920 (pp. 67–8), 927 D (pp. 68–9), 934 (p. 69), 937 (pp. 69–70), 945 (p. 72), 946 ABCD (p. 72), 973 DE (pp. 76–7); Florence of Worcester, *Chronicon*, i. 129, 131–4, 142–3; Anderson, *Early Sources*, i. 409, 449, 478–9; *Scottish Annals*, pp. 65, 67–79; Stenton, *A.-S.E.*, pp. 330, 335–6, 337–9, 354–5, 363–5.

[2] Loyn, 'The Imperial Style of the Tenth Century Anglo-Saxon Kings'; John, *Orbis Britanniae*, pp. 46–56.

[3] North, *English Hammered Coinage*, i. 93–4, 104.

[4] A.-S.C., 1027 DEF (p. 101); Anderson, *Early Sources*, i. 545–9; *Scottish Annals*, pp. 82–3; Stenton, *A.-S.E.*, pp. 412–13.

[5] Ritchie, *Normans in Scotland*, pp. 7–8, 385–8; Barlow, *Edward the Confessor*, pp. 202–3.

[6] A.-S.C., 1056 C (pp. 132–3); Lloyd, *History of Wales*, ii. 364–8; Barlow, *Edward the Confessor*, pp. 204–8.

overlordship.[1] It was not an empty boast, therefore, in King Edward's obituary, that

> He governed the Welshmen,
> Æthelred's son; ruled Britons and Scots,
> Angles and Saxons, his eager soldiers.
> All that the cold sea waves encompass
> Young and loyal yielded allegiance
> With all their heart to King Edward the noble.[2]

In the eleventh century, though more high-sounding titles were not entirely abandoned, 'king of the English' gradually came to be the accepted title or description of the successors to the West-Saxon kings.[3] Their kingdom could indeed hardly be defined in territorial terms. Though it is difficult to avoid doing so in practice, to call it the 'kingdom of England' is an anachronism,[4] unless it is very clear that 'England' did not mean then what it means today. Rule and dominion were exercised in varying degrees of intensity. Over the people living south of the Thames, in Ecgbert's West-Saxon kingdom, the king ruled directly; between the Thames and the Humber directly still, though with some limitations; between the Humber and the Tweed it was hardly more than an overlordship; beyond Tweed

---

[1] A.-S.C., 1063 DE (pp. 136–7); Florence of Worcester, *Chronicon*, i. 222; *Brut y Tywysogion, Peniarth MS. 20 Version, Translation*, pp. 15–16 (1068–9, 1073–5); *Red Book of Hergest Version*, pp. 27–9 (1069, 1075). Lloyd, *History of Wales*, ii. 372–3, suggests that Bleddyn and Rhiwallon were made kings of Gwynedd and Powys respectively, and is followed in this by other writers. But the texts can be read in the sense that they should rule the territories over which Gruffydd ap Llywelyn had ruled and do so jointly. They were the leaders in the resistance to the Normans, and seem to have acted together until Rhiwallon was killed in the battle of Mechain. If this interpretation is correct the policy that lay behind Henry II's treatment of the Lord Rhys in the twelfth century (below, pp. 211–3) was already taking shape in the eleventh.

[2] A.-S.C., 1065 CD (p. 139—the quotation is as in this translation). Cf. for example *Regularis Concordia*, p. 1, 'Gloriosus etenim Eadgar, Christi opitulante gratia Anglorum ceterarumque gentium intra ambitum Britannicae insulae degentium rex egregius', and Barlow, *Edward the Confessor*, pp. 135–8.

[3] One cannot speak of a royal style before the time of Henry II. Until his time, therefore, the titles attributed to kings in England have only a limited constitutional significance. They express what some people thought rather than an official assertion.

[4] The term is indeed used in MS. D of the A.-S.C. (a late eleventh-century MS.) under the year 1017—'to eall Engla landes rice'. But this is very exceptional. The corresponding phrase in MS. E is 'to eall Angel cynnes rice' (Earle and Plummer, *Two of the Saxon Chronicles Parallel*, i. 154–5). Blair discusses the point in *Introduction to Anglo-Saxon England*, pp. 11–13.

and Stainmore, as beyond Wye and Dee, it was certainly no more than overlordship, but it was also no less—and all these varying degrees of dominion over different peoples went to make up his 'kingdom'.[1] It had been formed by the expansion of the ninth-century kingdom of Wessex, by the vigorous empire-building of the West-Saxon kings; and it was fundamentally a West-Saxon 'empire' still, with its political and religious centre at Winchester[2] (even if Edward the Confessor had begun the move to Westminster), in some ways very like the contemporary 'empires' of the Norman dukes or the counts of Anjou.

In the middle of the eleventh century there were two conflicting tendencies in this kingdom. The experience of the previous three or four hundred years had been that overlordship tended to be intensified as kingship developed; client monarchies were degraded and ultimately suppressed and their peoples and their territories absorbed into those of their overlord. On that line of development no one could say, in 1066, where the boundary between the kingdom of the Scots and the kingdom of the English, for instance, would ultimately be drawn, or whether indeed it would not eventually disappear altogether and the kingdom of the Scots be absorbed into the kingdom of the English, as the kingdom of the Mercians had been absorbed into the kingdom of the West Saxons, as the kingdom of the Northumbrians was in process of being so absorbed, or as the kingdom of the Picts had been absorbed into the kingdom of the Scots; for these 'empires' were a stage in the formation of larger political units. On the other hand it is possible that in 1066 the lands ruled directly by the king of the English were entering upon a fresh cycle of disintegration and regrouping. The great earldoms of the Confessor's day were not yet territorial principalities on the continental model by any means, but they were beginning to show some continental characteristics.[3] The accession of Harold Godwinson in 1066 had something in common with that of Hugh Capet some eighty

[1] The point is well made by John in *Orbis Britanniae*, pp. 47–8.

[2] For an indication of the archaeological evidence that we may one day have for Winchester as a 'capital' of the pre-1066 kingdom of the English, Biddle, 'Excavations at Winchester, 1970: Ninth Interim Report', p. 125.

[3] Stenton, *A.-S.E.*, p. 539; Barlow, *Edward the Confessor*, pp. 168–9; Bullough, 'Anglo-Saxon Institutions and Early English Society'.

years before. In each case a 'principality' annexed the monarchy; and the consequences could have been much the same in England, if Harold had survived, as they were in France.[1]

It was as king of this kingdom, with its potential for expansion and progressive integration—or disintegration—that William of Normandy was crowned on Christmas Day, 1066. His kingship included not only the varying degrees of authority that he might exercise, as successor to the West-Saxon kings, over the peoples living in what is now England, but a superiority that might well develop into something more over the kings of the Scots and the kings of the Welsh; and he would be no less concerned to assert and establish this superiority, at the least, than he was to possess himself of all that his kingship might give him in England. He had to decide very quickly how this was to be done; for if, as seems likely, Bleddyn and Rhiwallon had been set up as kings of all Wales under Edward's suzerainty, their association with Eadric the Wild and then with Edwin and Morcar in resistance to the Normans could be regarded as an overt repudiation of any claim to lordship over the Welsh kingdoms that might be made by the new Norman king of the English;[2] and the reception of the English exiles by Malcolm, king of the Scots, and his raid into Yorkshire in 1070,[3] might well be interpreted in the same sense.

There seems to be no record of any formal assertion on William's part of lordship over the Welsh kings; but overlordship was implied in actions that were taken very soon after 1066. It is not known whether Bleddyn submitted to King William at the same time as his ally Eadric the Wild in 1070 (Rhiwallon had been killed a few months earlier in a purely

[1] Cf. Corbett, 'The Development of the Duchy of Normandy and the Norman Conquest of England', p. 482; Dhondt, *Principautés territoriales*, p. 146.

[2] A.-S.C., 1067 D (p. 146); Florence of Worcester, *Chronicon*, ii. 1–2; Lloyd, *History of Wales*, ii. 374–5; Orderic Vitalis, *H.E.* (ed. Le Prévost), ii. 182–4, 193, 198; (ed. Chibnall), ii. 214–18, 228, 234.

[3] A.-S.C., 1067 D (p. 146), 1068 DE (p. 149); Anderson, *Early Sources*, ii. 23–5; *Scottish Annals*, pp. 87–93. Orderic Vitalis, in *H.E.* (ed. Le Prévost), ii. 185; (ed. Chibnall), ii. 218, and Benoît de Sainte-Maure (extract in translation in Anderson, *Early Sources*, ii. 21) both say that Malcolm came to terms with William first in 1068; though they may be confusing this with 1072. The ecclesiastical primacy of the archbishop of York 'ad extremos Scotiae fines' was asserted some months before William's expedition of 1072 (Bishop and Chaplais, *Facsimiles of English Royal Writs*, plate xxix (text)).

Welsh dispute),[1] though it is possible that he did so. At all events the statement in Domesday Book that William fitz-Osbern had resettled certain Welshmen in Gwent in accordance with the customs of 'King Griffin', and this 'by licence of King William',[2] implies clearly that the Conqueror was claiming authority in a Welsh kingdom at least as early as 1070. There is evidence also that the son of William fitzOsbern was styled 'dominus Gwenti'.[3] If so it is not unlikely that fitzOsbern himself was similarly entitled, and both were vassals of the Norman king. By 1086 the position is clear. In the north Hugh d'Avranches held the country as far as the Clwyd, apparently as an appendage to his earldom of Chester;[4] his vassal and kinsman Robert 'of Rhuddlan' held Rhos and Rhufoniog 'in fee' of the king,[5] and the grant of a fief necessarily implies the assertion of lordship on the part of the grantor. Robert also held 'Nort Wales', which has been identified with the kingdom of Gwynedd, 'at farm for £40';[6] and in the south 'Riset de Wales', identified with Rhys ap Tewdwr king of Deheubarth, 'paid £40 to king William', a payment that has been interpreted with great probability as a 'farm' paid in respect of his kingdom,[7] as Robert 'of Rhuddlan' was paying £40 for Gwynedd. It is clear that King William was claiming the right to dispose of Welsh lands; that is, he was claiming, and indeed exercising, an overlordship at least as effective as that exercised by Edward the Confessor.[8]

---

[1] Florence of Worcester, *Chronicon*, ii. 7; Lloyd, *History of Wales*, ii. 375, 377.

[2] D.B., i. 162 a 1; Lloyd, 'Wales and the Coming of the Normans', pp. 144–5, 149; *History of Wales*, ii. 367, 375–6.

[3] Lloyd, *History of Wales*, ii. 375, note 54; Edwards, 'Normans and the Welsh March', p. 162 note 3.

[4] D.B., i. 268 b 2; 269 a 1; Tait, *Domesday Survey of Cheshire*, pp. 22–6; Lloyd, *History of Wales*, ii. 386–7.

[5] 'In feudo quod ipse Robertus tenet de Rege ROS et REWENIOV . . .', D.B., i. 269 a 2.

[6] 'Robertus de Roelent tenet de rege NORTWALES ad firmam pro xl libris, praeter illam terram quam rex ei dederat in feudo et praeter terras episcopatus', ibid. Gruffydd ap Cynan, king of Gwynedd, was imprisoned in Chester at the time when Domesday Book was compiled (Lloyd, *History of Wales*, ii. 385–8; Edwards, 'Normans and the Welsh March', pp. 161–2).

[7] 'Riset de Wales reddit regi W. xl. libras', D.B., i. 179 a 2; Edwards, 'Normans and the Welsh March', p. 161. On Round's doubts of the identification of 'Riset de Wales' with Rhys ap Tewdwr, see Nelson, *Normans in South Wales*, pp. 36–9.

[8] Cf. *Brut y Tywysogion, Peniarth MS. 20 Version, Translation*, p. 18 (1085–7); *Red Book of Hergest Version*, pp. 30–1 (1087).

He also established on the borderland of Wales three vigorous barons, William fitzOsbern as earl of Hereford, Roger de Montgomery as earl of Shrewsbury, and Hugh d'Avranches as earl of Chester. Each was given a large and compact fief on which he could settle his followers, massed and poised for conquest, men like Walter de Lassy (Lacy), Warin 'the Bold', and Robert 'of Rhuddlan'.[1] It is very possible that the grants of these earldoms included a licence to conquer lands in Wales.[2] Whether this is so or not, these men were in fact soon invading the Welsh kingdoms, certainly with William's acquiescence, most likely with his encouragement. It was not difficult for the Normans to gain an entry. The very nature of Welsh kingship meant that there were pretenders in almost every kingdom and a constant succession of dynastic wars. This gave the Normans the kind of opportunity that they had already taken in South Italy and would take again in Ireland. Thus when Caradog ap Gruffydd, king of Gwynllwg, defeated Maredudd ab Owain, king of Deheubarth, on the banks of the Rhymni in 1072, there were already 'Frenchmen' in his army;[3] while Gruffydd ap Cynan began his struggle to regain his ancestral kingdom of Gwynedd by going to Rhuddlan, where Robert was already established, and openly inviting his co-operation.[4] This was in 1073; it enabled Gruffydd to win his first victory; but it led straight to his kidnapping, his imprisonment, and the Norman conquest of Gwynedd which, though it proved to be transitory, might well have turned out differently.

The Normans, however, did not always wait to be invited. William fitzOsbern's invasion of Brycheiniog, the advance of Roger de Montgomery and his sons into Ceredigion and Dyfed, the conquest of Morgannwg by Robert fitzHamon, the later conquest of Brycheiniog by Bernard de Neufmarché, all appear to have been pure aggression.[5] But, however the thing started, the Normans made it their objective to remove the Welsh kings

[1] Orderic Vitalis, *H.E.* (ed. Le Prévost), ii. 218–21, 412–23; iii. 283–6; (ed. Chibnall), ii. 260–2; iii. 138–50; iv. 138–42. Cf. below, pp. 307–14.
[2] This is at least suggested by Orderic in the passages cited in the preceding note and by what actually happened.
[3] Lloyd, *History of Wales*, ii. 377; Nelson, *Normans in South Wales*, p. 35.
[4] Lloyd, *History of Wales*, ii. 380.
[5] Lloyd, 'Wales and the Coming of the Normans', p. 146; Lloyd, *History of Wales*, ii. 400–1, 402, 397; Davies, *Episcopal Acts*, i. 102–5, 108–9, 110–12, 107–8; Nelson, *Normans in South Wales*, pp. 31, 94, 103–9, 82–94.

and princes by warfare, kidnapping,[1] imprisonment,[2] exile,[3] marriage,[4] murder,[5] and any such means as came to hand, and then to step into their shoes. As in England the Norman barons stepped into the shoes of their English *antecessores*, taking over the rights and obligations that went with their lands, so in Wales they took over the rights and obligations of the Welsh kings and princes they replaced. The 'marcher lordships' thus created were essentially Welsh principalities in Norman hands; and the extraordinary 'liberties' of the marcher lords were secured by combining the prerogatives of a Welsh prince with the powers of a feudal lord.[6]

Nevertheless, however great their liberties, they were vassals of the king.[7] He could if necessary discipline them through their lands in England. When Henry broke and banished the sons of Roger de Montgomery, he redistributed their lands in Wales to an assortment of Welsh and Norman claimants; and thus both owed their titles as a matter of fact to him.[8] In this way, if no other, a number of Welsh princes found their relationship with the king taking on some feudal characteristics. Others, like the princes of Powys in the early years of Henry's reign, were as anxious to secure royal backing in their feuds and rivalries among themselves as they had been to enlist such Norman troops as they could attract to their service; and repeated royal intervention would have the same effect.[9] When a Welsh prince,

---

[1] e.g. the kidnapping of Gruffydd ap Cynan, Lloyd, *History of Wales*, ii. 385.

[2] In addition to Gruffydd ap Cynan, the imprisonment of Hywel ab Ithel was the prelude to the seizure of his territories of Rhos and Rhufoniog by Robert 'of Rhuddlan', ibid., pp. 383–4. Arnulf de Montgomery secured his hold upon Pembroke by imprisoning a son of Rhys ap Tewdwr (ibid., p. 401).

[3] e.g. Gruffydd ap Cynan's recurrent periods of exile.

[4] e.g. Gerald of Windsor's marriage to Nest, daughter of Rhys ap Tewdwr (Lloyd, *History of Wales*, ii. 416); conversely, Cadwgan ap Bleddyn married a daughter of Picot de Sai and obtained land on the Border thereby (ibid., p. 419).

[5] e.g. the murder of Hywel ap Gronw (ibid., pp. 415–16). In all this the Normans were doing no more to the Welsh than the Welsh were doing to one another.

[6] Edwards, 'Normans and the Welsh March', esp. pp. 169–75; Rees, *South Wales and the March*, pp. 26–7, 43–6, and *passim*.

[7] For a definition of the legal relationship of the lords marcher and the Welsh princes to the king of England in its developed form, Edwards, *Littere Wallie*, pp. xlvii–l.

[8] *Brut y Tywysogion, Peniarth MS. 20 Version, Translation*, pp. 22–5; *Red Book of Hergest Version*, pp. 40–7; Lloyd, *History of Wales*, ii. 412–15.

[9] *Brut y Tywysogion, Peniarth MS. 20 Version, Translation*, pp. 28–46, *Red Book of Hergest Version*, pp. 54–101; Lloyd, *History of Wales*, ii. 417–22.

such as Gruffydd ap Cynan of Gwynedd, seemed to be making himself too independent, a royal expedition brought him to homage and fealty—that is, to something like the status of a royal vassal.[1] The old overlordship which William the Conqueror had taken over from his West-Saxon predecessors was being feudalized.[2]

As in England, conquest was followed by colonization. Once established on their Welsh lands, the Norman barons created tenancies for their vassals and knights there. In some places, notably in southern Pembroke and in Gower, English and Flemish freemen were settled on the land in considerable numbers.[3] In each lordship of the colonized region, as it came to be organized, there was an Englishry, usually consisting of castle, borough, and manor and often settled with people of non-Welsh origin, and a Welshry still inhabited by Welsh people. The Englishry was in the plain, on the richer lands; it was organized in a fashion that resembled the Anglo-Norman manor as nearly as could be; it represented the direct exploitation of the land by and for the colonizers. The Welshry was usually on the highland, where many ancient usages long survived; it was exploited indirectly by the conquerors, through tribute, though there are many instances of Welsh nobles holding lands of Norman lords or of the king on much the same terms as the Normans held among themselves.[4]

Norman conquest and colonization affected the Church in Wales as it affected the Church in England; perhaps even more profoundly in the end, for the Normans completely reorganized the old quasi-monastic and tribal institutions into a Church with territorial dioceses, archdeaconries, rural deaneries, and parishes, firmly under the metropolitan jurisdiction of

[1] *Brut y Tywysogion*, *Peniarth MS. 20 Version*, *Translation*, pp. 37–8; *Red Book of Hergest Version*, pp. 78–83; cf. p. 64, n. 7.

[2] The political significance of this relationship in its feudal form is analysed below, ch. 6.

[3] Lloyd, *History of Wales*, ii. 424, 430, 475. There was an analogous though rather later plantation of Flemings in Clydesdale; Barrow, *Kingdom of the Scots*, pp. 289–90.

[4] On the process of settlement, Lloyd, *History of Wales*, ii. 423–46; Nelson, *Normans in South Wales*, pp. 91–3, 107–9, etc.; Rees, *South Wales and the March*, pp. 26–31 and *passim*. For Welsh princes accepting from the king lands previously held by Norman lords and apparently on the same terms, Davies, *Episcopal Acts*, i. 116.

Canterbury.[1] This did not happen all at once, but progressively, as the Norman colonization spread over the country; and if the new bishops and archdeacons did not bear French names as regularly as in England (the Welsh bishoprics were relatively poor), they none the less represented the new order of Canterbury and Rome. Norman exploitation showed itself more clearly in the seizure of the property of the older Welsh Church. Some of this was restored to the new or renewed foundations, some went to the priories which the Normans founded, often beside their castles and usually dependent upon their 'family' monasteries in France or upon the Normanized monasteries in England,[2] and some was lost to the Church for ever.[3] Apart from the four bishoprics, where the *clas* was converted into a cathedral chapter of more or less normal form, the ancient *clas* churches were mostly reduced to parochial status and in any case lost the greater part of their endowments; even dedications were often changed to the conventional saints of Western Christendom. It is true that the Welsh clergy were not transformed overnight and were not generally replaced by 'Frenchmen'; many ancient usages (the quasi-hereditary succession to some ecclesiastical offices, for example) persisted for some time; but the new order, besides profoundly changing the Church in Wales and giving many an opportunity of territorial and spiritual gain to Norman barons, provided the Norman and Angevin kings of England with a powerful weapon of political control in Wales.[4]

In England, the Normans had planted substantial colonies in a number of established towns as well as founding new boroughs;[5] in Wales, the boroughs they founded beside their castles seem to represent the first beginning of urban development in the country. There were not many of them before 1135; and not very much is known about such as there were or about

[1] For the Normans and the Church in Wales, Lloyd, *History of Wales*, ii. 447–59; Davies, *Episcopal Acts*, Introduction, *passim*.

[2] Convenient list in Williams, *Introduction to the History of Wales*, ii. 27.

[3] There seems to have been an analogous spoliation in Cornwall, Taylor, *Celtic Christianity of Cornwall*, pp. 108–11, 118.

[4] Compare the use of excommunication as a means of political control given to the kings of France for use in Flanders by the Treaty of Melun (1224), Petit-Dutaillis, *Étude sur la vie et le règne de Louis VIII*, pp. 100–1; Lucas, *Low Countries and the Hundred Years War*, pp. 361–2, 372–3.

[5] Above, pp. 38–40.

the people who came to live and work in them; but in Rhuddlan there were elements of industry and commerce already by
1086, and the burgesses had been given the 'laws of Breteuil',
taken directly from Hereford, where they were associated with a
French colony.¹ In these boroughs the Normans were perhaps
consciously doing no more than providing for the needs of those
who garrisoned their castles; but if trade were to develop in
Wales it would be under their control.

As in England, also, the process of colonization in Wales
extended over a considerable period, and was still in progress at
the end of King Henry's reign. By that time the greater part of
the country south of a line from Aberystwyth to Montgomery
was in Norman hands and the whole land was under the lordship of the Norman king. The marcher lords were clearly his
vassals and the position of the surviving Welsh princes was
being progressively assimilated to theirs. There was no move,
however, to incorporate Wales into the kingdom of the English,
and the Welsh kept their own laws; nevertheless, whether the
form of exploitation was direct or indirect, a large part of the
actual and potential wealth of the country was falling into
the hands of Normans or men of Norman origin.

William the Conqueror's expedition to Scotland in 1072 can
be interpreted in a number of different ways: as a simple
reaction to King Malcolm's reception of the English exiles and
his raid into Yorkshire of 1070; as an essential element in the
process of securing the Norman hold upon the north of England;
or as an assertion of his claim to the same superiority as had
been exercised over the kings of Scots and the kings of the
Strathclyde Britons by his West-Saxon predecessors, whether
or not he regarded Malcolm's acts as a direct challenge to that
superiority. The first two interpretations no doubt have some
truth in them so far as they go; but the third must have more to
it, for Malcolm offered no resistance to William's invading
army but 'came and made peace with the king William, and
gave hostages and became his man'.² It is even possible that

¹ Beresford, *New Towns*, pp. 339–43, 527–74. For Rhuddlan, D.B., i. 269 a 1;
Lloyd, *History of Wales*, ii. 386–7; Tait, *Domesday Survey of Cheshire*, pp. 238–41.
These foundations should probably be regarded as no more than 'potential towns'.
Cf. Miller, 'Medieval New Towns', and below, ch. 8.
² A.-S.C., 1072 DE (pp. 154–5). The quotation is taken from the translation
by Gomme.

Malcolm had accepted William's overlordship already in 1068.[1]

The relationship between the two kings and their successors which this act created persisted until the end of King Henry's reign, however precisely it is to be described. When, to punish a later raid of Malcolm's, Robert Curthose led a force into Scotland on behalf of his father in 1080, Malcolm seems to have reaffirmed the relationship;[2] and when, in 1091, William Rufus and Robert again led an army to Scotland in answer to yet another Scottish raid, Malcolm came to Rufus 'and became his man to the extent of such allegiance as he had done to his father, and confirmed it with an oath'.[3] Of Malcolm's immediate successors, Duncan II, Edgar, Alexander I, and David I, four of his sons who reigned in succession after him, all save David owed their thrones directly to the Norman king and his Norman troops. It is explicitly recorded of Duncan that he did homage to William Rufus;[4] Edgar made specific acknowledgement of his vassalage and Alexander's is clearly implied;[5] while David was certainly King Henry's vassal.[6] He had been married to the widow of the earl of Huntingdon and allowed to hold the earldom as a matter of policy;[7] and he apparently did not secure possession of 'Cumbria' which his brother Edgar had bequeathed to him without Norman assistance.[8] The Norman kings had converted the old relationship between the king of Scots and the kings of the English into a form with which they were familiar, and the language that was being used to describe it was the language of continental feudalism. It was, in fact,

[1] Above, p. 61, n. 3.

[2] Anderson, *Scottish Annals*, pp. 102–4; *Early Sources*, ii. 45–6; David, *Robert Curthose*, p. 31.

[3] A.-S.C., 1091 E (p. 169); Florence of Worcester, *Chronicon*, ii. 28; Anderson, *Scottish Annals*, pp. 104–8; *Early Sources*, ii. 48–9; David, *Robert Curthose*, pp. 66–8.

[4] A.-S.C., 1093 E (p. 170); Florence of Worcester, *Chronicon*, ii. 32.

[5] A.-S.C., 1097 E (p. 175); 1107 E (p. 181); Anderson, *Scottish Annals*, pp. 119, 128–9; *Early Sources*, ii. 99, 144; Duncan, 'Earliest Scottish Charters', pp. 103–4, 125–35.

[6] For a fuller discussion, below, pp. 208–10.

[7] That this was so might be supposed on general grounds; but these are strengthened by the fact that Matilda already had a son by her first marriage, Simon de Senlis II, who in fact held the earldom intermittently from 1136 and continuously from *c.* 1141 until his death in 1153 (cf. A.-S.C., 1114 H, p. 183). The earldom included interests in the neighbouring counties of Northampton, Bedford, and Cambridge.

[8] Anderson, *Scottish Annals*, p. 193; *Early Sources*, ii. 141, 166–7 (notes).

being intensified; certainly the Norman kings reacted immediately and effectively to any act of the king of Scots which they might regard as contravening the obligations which it placed upon him.[1]

As in Wales, the establishment of Norman overlordship was followed by Norman colonization; and at first it looked as though the colonization of Scotland might take much the same form as in Wales. In 1092 William Rufus seized Cumbria, driving out the man who was ruling the region in allegiance to the king of Scots, planted a castle at Carlisle, and settled knights and peasants in the neighbourhood. At some point Ranulf le Meschin, *vicomte* of Bayeux, was made lord of these settlers; but it seems that his position differed from that of the earls on the Welsh border during the Conqueror's reign, in that he was put in charge of an existing colony rather than given the opportunity to settle his own men there.[2] At all events neither he nor Robert de Montbrai, the energetic earl of Northumberland, seem to have made any attempt to carve out lordships for themselves further into Scotland. Perhaps this was because the kingdom of Scots was unitary, at least on the surface, whereas in Wales there were many kingdoms and they were small, disunited and unstable; perhaps it was because Ranulf and Robert and the other Norman barons in the North were too much occupied in securing what had been given to them on the English side of the Border; perhaps geography was already against them.

Yet, like the Welsh kings and princes (and rulers in south Italy earlier in the eleventh century), Malcolm's successors were often glad to make use of Norman troops in their own domestic warfare. Both Duncan and Edgar had set off from England to win their crowns at the head of an Anglo-Norman force supplied by the Norman king, and Duncan's utter dependence upon this force was shown by the immediate collapse of his power when the Scots forced him to dismiss it.[3] When Donald Bane, the last representative of the Celtic rule of succession in Scotland, supported the rebellion of Robert de

---

[1] e.g. the invasions of 1072, 1080, 1091. The significance of this feudal relationship is discussed below in ch. 6.

[2] A.-S.C., 1092 E (p. 169); Anderson, *Early Sources*, ii. 49; Barrow, *Kingdom of the Scots*, pp. 143–4.

[3] A.-S.C., 1093, 1094, 1097 E (pp. 170, 172, 175).

Montbrai in 1095,[1] he presumably had in mind the possibility of reciprocal services in Scotland; and, just before the Battle of the Standard, Robert de Brus is said to have reminded King David of the Norman assistance he had received when he had to put down a rebellion in Moray in 1130—as well as to secure possession of 'Cumbria' during his brother Alexander's reign.[2] But, unlike the Welsh, though the Scottish kings made use of Norman troops they never seem to have lost control of them completely.

The Norman colonization of Scotland, when it came, was effected in a way quite different from their colonization of Wales and, though considerable, was relatively less extensive. All four of Malcolm's sons had spent a considerable time at the court of the Norman king before they succeeded to the throne. Their experiences at that court and their employment of Norman troops had given them at least the opportunity to see how the Normans organized their affairs. It cannot have failed to strike them that the Norman kings had a control of their aristocracy through homage and fealty and a military power through knights and castles which the traditional social and political institutions of Scotland could never give them. David, moreover, as earl of Huntingdon, had been a great 'Norman baron' himself; in this capacity, as well as that of 'the queen's brother', he had attended the court of King Henry;[3] he was the lord of barons and knights who no doubt would have been behind him if there had been any difficulty when he inherited the throne of Scotland, and he had even furnished himself with a household of continental type before he became king.[4] It must have been very clear to him, even if it had not been clear to his brothers, that to realize the potential of his kingdom, even to preserve such independence as it might have already or might win in the future, still more to cut a figure in this new feudal world dominated by 'France', he must bring the government of Scotland into line.

The 'Normanization' of Scotland, so far as it went, began

---

[1] Ritchie, *Normans in Scotland*, pp. 64–5.

[2] Anderson, *Scottish Annals*, pp. 192–4; Ritchie, *Normans in Scotland*, pp. 230–5.

[3] *Regesta*, ii, Nos. 1062, 1102, 1108, 1180, 1241, 1247, 1248, 1249, 1285, 1301, 1334, 1359, 1391, 1398, 1400.

[4] Lawrie, *Early Scottish Charters*, Nos. xxxii, xxxv, xlvi, liii; cf. Ritchie, *Normans in Scotland*, pp. 142–59; Barrow, *Feudal Britain*, pp. 134–6.

with the Church. Before the end of the eleventh century Benedictine monks had come from Canterbury at the request of St. Margaret and had been established, probably at Dunfermline. In Alexander's reign Augustinians were settled at Scone, Tironensians at Selkirk, and the first bishop with a Norman name elected at St. Andrews.[1] But whatever anticipations there may have been, it was under David, chiefly, that the great change was made in ecclesiastical as in other matters.[2] The old Celtic organization was abandoned, as in Wales; a system of territorial dioceses was set up, and a considerable number of monasteries of the normal western European kind were founded. Many of the first dignitaries and the first monks came from France or the Normanized monasteries of England; but because the change was not imposed by Norman conquerors but brought about by kings who, however Norman they may have been in outlook, were of the native dynasty, the Church in Scotland was able to avoid that obedience to York which the Church in Wales had had to yield to Canterbury, though it had to fight for its independence. Church and monarchy were so closely interrelated that the Normanization of the Church may be regarded almost as part of the transformation of the Scottish monarchy, which was likewise changed in an Anglo-Norman sense. The rule of succession was normalized; the royal household remodelled in imitation of the household of the Norman kings; a royal seal, again imitated from theirs, was introduced; a local administration very like that of Anglo-Norman England was gradually formed; and when King David instituted a Scottish coinage, the design of his coins was based on the coins of Henry I and Stephen.[3]

Feudalism came with the planting of Norman families in Scotland, partly on the lands of the Celtic Church, mostly in David's own lordships of Cumbria and Lothian.[4] Among the famous names were the Brus, who were lords of Guisborough, Cleveland, and other lands in Yorkshire and came almost certainly from Brix in the Cotentin; the Morevilles, also from

---

[1] Easson, *Medieval Religious Houses, Scotland*, pp. 4–5, 51, 60, 83, 167–72. Ritchie, *Normans in Scotland*, pp. 170–1, 197–8.

[2] Generally, Barrow, *Feudal Britain*, pp. 136–40; *Kingdom of the Scots*, pp. 165–87.

[3] Barrow, *Feudal Britain*, pp. 141–4; *Regesta Regum Scottorum*, i. 27–56; Stewart, *The Scottish Coinage*, pp. 1–7.

[4] In general, Barrow, *Kingdom of the Scots*, pp. 315–28.

the Cotentin and already established on lands in David's honour of Huntingdon; the de Sules, ultimately from Soules again in the Cotentin, but immediately holding lands in Oxfordshire, Kent, Northamptonshire, and in the Avranchin; the fitzAlans, originally from Dol-de-Bretagne on the borders of Normandy and Brittany and established by King Henry in Norfolk and Shropshire, the ancestors of the Stewarts.[1] There were others, and they began to build their castles and parcel out their fiefs among their clients; but the scale of this influx, at all events in David's reign, should not be exaggerated. It hardly affected the country north of the Forth; and even in the south the actual number of immigrants was still not very great.[2] Yet, whatever the magnitude of the operation, the Scottish kings of the early twelfth century were doing what the Norman dukes themselves had done in their duchy during the eleventh,[3] and basically what the Norman kings were doing with the lands they had won in England—they were bringing in new men whose relationship to them would be that of vassal to lord and who would owe substantial advancement to them, and they were doing this to enlarge their own military and political strength, to increase the hold they had on their country, and to make themselves felt beyond it. With the traditional organization of Scotland alone they could never have stood up to the Norman kings. Their best protection was to accept Norman suzerainty and to reorganize their country on the Anglo-Norman model, including the settlement of Anglo-Norman barons on Scottish lands. Yet even though this settlement had been made by the Scottish kings for their own purposes, and however limited it might have been in extent, such as it was it meant that families of French origin, with broad estates already in England and often in France as well which in general they would continue to hold and for which they would continue to be the vassals of the Norman kings, could now extend their fortunes into Scotland as others were doing by rather different methods in Wales. By the suzerainty of the Norman king and the Normanization of the Scottish monarchy and the Scottish

[1] In addition to Barrow, ibid., Ritchie, *Normans in Scotland*, pp. 147–8 (Brus), 187–8, note 3 (de Sules), 278–81 (fitzAlan-Stewart, with Round, *Studies in Peerage*, pp. 120–31 and *passim*); Loyd, *Anglo-Norman Families*, pp. 49–50 (Morville).

[2] Barrow, *Kingdom of the Scots*, pp. 279–83.

[3] Below, pp. 286–7.

Church, Scotland also was brought into the field of Norman expansion and colonization.

The conquest of England led naturally to the extension of Norman overlordship and Norman colonization into Wales and Scotland because the kings of the English had traditionally exercised some form of superiority over the rulers of those countries; less directly perhaps, but no less certainly, it led to an extension of Norman suzerainty and Norman interests on the continental mainland. In part it was a matter of resources. Already, before 1066, the dukes had established their interests and often their suzerainty in principalities bordering upon Normandy;[1] after the Conquest, the far greater wealth of the Norman kings in money and in men could be expected to make it easier for them to continue this activity if they were minded to do so. In part it was a matter of defence. The king of France, the count of Anjou, even the count of Flanders, were bound to seize any opportunity that came their way to weaken what must have seemed to them the overwhelming power of the Norman kings, and this could only be done by attacking Normandy. Against their pressure the Norman kings could strengthen the duchy with a network of castles, as they did;[2] but it would also be a great advantage if they could build up an outer defence in the form of a belt of client principalities. In part, also, they were committed already. Men from principalities bordering upon Normandy had joined the invasion army of 1066,[3] and some of them had received great estates in England like the Normans themselves. This inevitably gave the Norman kings an interest in their continental homelands and bound up the affairs of England and northern France in such a way that action to defend the Norman king's authority in England, for example, might often involve action in France as well;[4] and this, when it was successful, could lead to further extension of power and influence there.

Much of this is well shown in their relations with Brittany. There were certainly Bretons in William's army at Hastings.

[1] Above, pp. 14–21, 26–7.
[2] Yver, 'Châteaux forts en Normandie', *passim*; Brown, Colvin, and Taylor, *King's Works*, i. 35; below, pp. 83, 131, 305–6.   [3] Above, pp. 26–7.
[4] e.g. as in the case of Ralph de Gael and Robert de Bellême, below, pp. 74–5, 84–5.

What their strength was it would be difficult to estimate; but the Bretons who received lands in England after the battle seem to have formed the largest non-Norman element in the foreign aristocracy which established itself in the country. The estates acquired by the sons of Eudo de Penthièvre were among the largest given to any of William's followers. Brian, the second son, received vast lands in the south-west; Alan 'Rufus', the third son, the huge complex in Yorkshire, Lincolnshire, and in many other counties that came to be known as 'the honour of Richmond'. Brian did not remain in England for many years and his lands there were lost to the family when he departed; but Richmond passed, after the death of Alan 'Rufus', to his younger brother Alan 'Niger',· and from him to the youngest brother Stephen, who eventually inherited the family lands in Brittany (Penthièvre, Tréguier, Guingamp, etc.) as well, and thereafter held the English and the Breton lands together until his death (c. 1135).[1]

Besides this family there were other Bretons who received lands in England, only less extensive. Judhael 'of Totnes' had a large fief in the south-west; Geoffrey 'de Wirce' (La Guerche, near Rennes) another in the Midlands; Oger 'the Breton' and others had large estates in Lincolnshire, Tihel de Helléan in Essex. In fact Bretons were to be found in almost every part of the country;[2] and in addition to those who received English land after 1066 there were some who had established themselves in England during the Confessor's reign. Among these latter was Ralph de Gael, who inherited the lands in East Anglia and the title of earl that had been held by his father, Ralph 'the Staller', and who held these with the very considerable seigniory of Gael in eastern Brittany.[3]

In 1075 he started a rebellion against King William in England, associating Roger de Breteuil, the earl of Hereford, with him, and implicating Waltheof, the son of Earl Siward of Northumbria, as well as a number of his Breton compatriots.[4]

---

[1] Cf. above, pp. 15–16. On the relationship of Eudo de Penthièvre to the dukes of Brittany, *E.Y.C.*, iv (*Honour of Richmond*, i), 84; and on the lands given to his sons in England, ibid., pp. 85–9 and Jeulin, 'Un grand "honneur" anglais'.

[2] Stenton, *English Feudalism*, pp. 25–7; Douglas, *William the Conqueror*, pp. 267–8.

[3] *Complete Peerage*, ix. 568–74; de la Borderie, *Histoire de Bretagne*, iii. 68–9 and the map at the end of the volume.

[4] Douglas, *William the Conqueror*, pp. 231–5.

The rebellion was easily put down; King William did not even find it necessary to return to England from Normandy; but Ralph made his escape and returned to his lands in Brittany where he joined a revolt against Duke Hoel, the successor to Duke Conan II. The leaders of this rebellion were Geoffrey Grenonat, who was a relative and a potential rival of the duke and whose lands lay very near to those of Ralph de Gael, the same Eudo de Penthièvre who could not forget that he had exercised the ducal power during the minority of Conan II and whose sons were so richly possessioned in England, and a concentration of seigneurs whose interests also lay in eastern Brittany.[1] Ralph and Geoffrey established themselves in Dol. When, therefore, King William came up and laid siege to the place he was not simply pursuing an 'English' rebel to his continental lair, he was probably also taking this opportunity to reassert the hold he had had upon the seigneurs of eastern Brittany,[2] and he was bringing assistance to the reigning duke whom he may well have considered to be his vassal. Though William had to abandon the siege when the king of France intervened, and was thus prevented from taking his vengeance upon Ralph de Gael and, at least for the time, from strengthening his hold upon Brittany, Duke Hoel for his part eventually triumphed over the Breton rebellion, whether or not William's action had helped him to achieve this result.[3]

Alan Fergent, Hoel's son and successor, married William's daughter Constance[4] and some years later brought a Breton contingent to join King Henry's army at Tinchebrai.[5] This at least suggests the possibility that he was in some sense King

[1] De la Borderie, *Histoire de Bretagne*, pp. 24–7.

[2] Above, pp. 15–16.

[3] De la Borderie, *Histoire de Bretagne*, iii. 27–8. Ralph de Gael kept his Breton lordship, and his son obtained the honour of Breteuil in Normandy during Henry's reign (*Complete Peerage*, ix. 574).

[4] French writers have credited William with a campaign in Brittany in 1086 to enforce his suzerainty there, a campaign which was concluded by a *foedus amicitiae* between him and Duke Alan Fergent and the marriage of Duke Alan to William's daughter Constance (de la Borderie, *Histoire de Bretagne*, iii. 30–1; Lemarignier, *Hommage en marche*, pp. 120–1). This is based chiefly on Orderic's narrative, *H.E.* (ed. Le Prévost), ii. 290–2; (ed. Chibnall), ii. 350–2. But Douglas has treated it as a confusion with William's campaign of 1076 (*William the Conqueror*, pp. 401–7). At all events, there can be no doubt of Alan's marriage with Constance.

[5] Lemarignier, *Hommage en marche*, pp. 120–1; David, *Robert Curthose*, pp. 173–6.

Henry's vassal;[1] but all doubts on this score were resolved in 1113 when King Louis VI 'conceded the whole of Brittany' to Henry; and Orderic adds that Henry had betrothed a (natural) daughter to Duke Alan's son and successor Conan, and that Alan (who had retired from the government of the duchy the previous year)[2] had already done homage 'to the king of the English'.[3] Conan, who may therefore be presumed to have been King Henry's vassal, brought military assistance to him in the campaigns of 1116–20; and although he later joined King Louis on his expedition into Auvergne he did nothing to deny the Norman king's suzerainty as long as Henry lived.[4]

The Norman conquest and colonization of England, therefore, involving as it did the grant of large estates in the country to Breton lords, made it all the more necessary for the Norman kings to maintain and develop the suzerainty over the rulers of Brittany which their ducal predecessors had initiated, and at the same time it enlarged the means they possessed to do this. A similar development can be seen in their relations with the count of Boulogne. Count Eustace II had himself taken part in the Hastings campaign; and although there is a suggestion that he was already William's vassal, this is not certain and it may not have been clear at the time.[5] In spite of what looks very like an attempt to make good the claim that he might himself make to the English throne while William was away in Normandy during the year 1067, Eustace was at some point given the huge estate in England that came to be known as the 'honour of Boulogne', with its 120 knights' fees. The effects of the relationship which this created can be seen clearly in the time of King Henry. The successor of Eustace II as count of Boulogne and lord of the honour of Boulogne in England was his son by a second marriage, Eustace III (c. 1093–c. 1120). To him Henry gave in marriage Mary, a daughter of the king of Scots and

---

[1] An illegitimate son of Alan's, known to English historians as Brian fitzCount, was brought up by King Henry, whom he served during the later part of his reign as a prominent baron and officer (above, p. 42, n. 8).

[2] De la Borderie, *Histoire de Bretagne*, iii. 35.

[3] The two kings met at Gisors in March 1113—Suger, *Vita Ludovici Grossi Regis*, pp. 170–2; Luchaire, *Louis VI le Gros*, No. 158 (p. 81). The terms of the agreement are reported by Orderic Vitalis, *H.E.* (ed. Le Prévost), iv. 307–8, who also gives the information about Alan Fergent's homage and the betrothal of Henry's daughter to Conan.

[4] Jeulin, 'L'hommage de Bretagne', pp. 412–13.　　　　[5] Above, p. 20.

sister of his own queen—no doubt a perfectly conscious act of policy. The son of the marriage died young; consequently, when Eustace III retired from the world about the year 1120, his inheritance fell to his daughter Matilda, in whose marriage King Henry naturally had a considerable interest. The husband Henry found for her was his nephew Stephen of Blois; and since he had already given Stephen the *comté* of Mortain and other lands in Normandy, with the honours of Eye and Lancaster in England, Stephen acquired a commanding position on both sides of the Channel. Whether or not Henry understood the possible consequences of his prodigal advancement of Stephen, his suzerainty over the count of Boulogne had been intensified to the point where he could virtually control the succession to a continental *comté* which, with its important sea-port and its proximity both to England and to the powerful *comté* of Flanders, had considerable significance in the politics of the time.[1]

The count of Pontieu, on the other hand, had more certainly been William's vassal in 1066. It is possible that Count Guy, like the count of Boulogne, took part personally in the Hastings campaign.[2] If he did so, he apparently acquired no lands in England in return for his service; but Agnes, his daughter and heiress, married Robert de Bellême, who inherited all the vast Montgomery–Bellême lands in Normandy and beyond, most of the family's possessions in England and Wales, and finally, through her, became count of Pontieu.[3] His rebellion against King Henry in 1102 cost him his lands on the English side of the Channel, though he retained at least some of the Norman estates until Henry arrested and imprisoned him in 1112. Some time between 1106 and 1111 he had resigned Pontieu (of which he had taken possession on the death of Agnes in 1103) to his son William Talvas, to whom Henry restored the Norman lands in 1119.[4]

[1] Round, *Studies in Peerage*, pp. 147 ff.; Davis, *King Stephen*, pp. 7–10. For Henry's part in the marriages, Florence of Worcester, *Chronicon*, ii. 51; Malmesbury, *Historia Novella*, p. 57.
[2] Above, pp. 19–20.
[3] *Complete Peerage*, xi. 689–96.
[4] Ibid., xi. 697; Orderic Vitalis, *H.E.* (ed. Le Prévost), iv. 347–8. The restoration of the Norman lands did not include Bellême, which Henry had given to Rotrou de Perche (Lemarignier, *Hommage en marche*, p. 64), and Henry confiscated the other lands again in 1135—Orderic Vitalis, *H.E.* (ed. Le Prévost), v. 46–7.

William Talvas, in turn, resigned the *comté* of Pontieu to his younger son Guy (II) between 1126 and 1129, though he retained the Norman lands (which Henry confiscated in 1135, though some must have been recovered after Henry's death) and the title 'count of Pontieu'. Until the death of Count Guy II in 1147, charters of the counts relating to lands and rights in Pontieu were issued in his name and those relating to the Norman lands in the name of Count William.[1] Until the act of 1126–9, therefore, the count of Pontieu claimed or possessed extensive lands in Normandy and must have been King Henry's vassal for them; but this act cannot have been regarded as a definitive partition, for, quite apart from Count William's retention of the title 'count of Pontieu' and his occasional confirmation of Count Guy's grants in the *comté*,[2] Guy must also have retained an interest in the Norman lands. He consented to William's grants to his abbey of Perseigne[3] (near Alençon, though in the diocese of Le Mans), and as late as 1166 his son and successor in Pontieu joined Count William (then described as count of Séez) in the surrender of the castles of Alençon and La Roche Mabille to King Henry II.[4] Certainly until the death of Henry Beauclerc, therefore, the counts of Pontieu must have been vassals of the Norman king; though in this case it cannot be said that King Henry did more than hold the position which his father had already acquired.

Given his interest in Boulogne, however, and his growing interest in Flanders, it may not have seemed necessary to do more. It is possible that Baldwin V, count of Flanders, whose daughter had married William the Conqueror, was already the pensioner of the Norman duke in 1066; it is likely that there were Flemings in William's army of invasion and it is certain that a number of Flemings obtained broad lands in England after the Conquest.[5] Since William had opposed the seizure of the *comté* by Robert le Frison,[6] his relations with Flanders were

---

[1] Brunel, *Recueil des actes des comtes de Pontieu*, pp. v–vi and *passim*. Brunel describes Guy as William's eldest son; but in a charter of *c.* 1145 William's other son, John d'Alençon, describes himself as 'filius comitis primogenitus' (ibid., p. 56).

[2] Ibid., pp. 36, 44.　　　　　　　　　　　　　　　　　　　[3] Ibid., p. 53.

[4] Robert de Torigni, *Chronica*, p. 227.

[5] Above, p. 20; Douglas, *William the Conqueror*, pp. 266–7.

[6] Opinions differ on the interpretation to be put on the expedition of William fitzOsbern in 1071; e.g. Douglas, *William the Conqueror*, pp. 224–5; Verlinden, *Robert Ier le Frison*, pp. 61–3.

strained while Robert was count (1071–93);[1] but in 1093 this Robert, or perhaps his son Count Robert II who succeeded in that year, sought an alliance with William Rufus against the king of France.[2] In 1101 this was followed up by a formal agreement (*conventio*) between King Henry and Count Robert II.[3] Politically this agreement was a treaty of alliance directed against Robert Curthose, duke of Normandy, if only by implication; but it had important feudal characteristics. In return for an annuity of 500 pounds sterling *in feudo*, Count Robert undertook to serve King Henry with 1000 knights in England or Normandy, or 500 in Maine, *sicut suum amicum et de quo feudum tenet*.[4] This agreement was renewed in 1110, when Henry was fully in control of Normandy and Robert Curthose his prisoner. The relationship was then expressed in the same terms, though the service was reduced to 500 knights in England or Normandy, 250 in Maine, and the annuity to 400 marks of silver.[5] If the total *servitium debitum* of England at this time was 'around 5000 knights',[6] these figures are significant.

It may be that the alliance which Henry and the count of Flanders entered into could be expressed only in these feudal terms under the conditions of the beginning of the twelfth century, that this was the form in which such an alliance would then have to be made; and it would certainly be too much to claim that this agreement made the count of Flanders a vassal of the Norman king in any substantial sense.[7] The count was a powerful prince who was already the very independent vassal of the king of France and of the emperor. In relation to England,

[1] Verlinden, ibid., pp. 107–12.   [2] Ibid., pp. 78, 112.

[3] William of Malmesbury (*Gesta Regum*, ii. 478–9) has a story that it was Count Robert who made the initial approach and that he was brusquely rebuffed by Henry. If anything of the sort actually happened, Henry quickly changed his mind, and the date of the agreement, 10 March 1101 (*Regesta*, ii, No. 515, p. 7) is significant (below, pp. 185–6).

[4] *Diplomatic Documents*, i. 1–4; important commentary by Ganshof, 'Note sur le premier traité anglo-flamand de Douvres'. Cf. Lyon, *From Fief to Indenture*, pp. 34–5 (where the agreement is still assigned to the year 1103, now abandoned) and Hollister, *Military Organization of Norman England*, pp. 187–9.

[5] *Diplomatic Documents*, i. 5–8.

[6] Hollister, *Military Organization of Norman England*, p. 188.

[7] The text of the agreement employs the formula of liege homage; 'Robertus comes Flandrie . . . juvabit eum [King Henry] ad tenendum et ad defendendum regnum Anglie contra omnes homines qui vivere et mori possint'; but qualifies it not only by reference to the defence of England etc., but also with the saving clause, 'salva fidelitate Philippi regis Francorum', *Diplomatic Documents*, i. 1.

moreover, his interests were conflicting. Economic ties might already make it difficult for him to break with the country completely at any time,[1] and the annuity, if it had been paid regularly, would have been a very considerable element even in a wealthy count's revenue.[2] On the other hand, England and Normandy together made a very formidable neighbour, and the temptation to add his weight from time to time to any difficulties that Henry might have on the Continent proved irresistible to the ruler of Flanders. Thus Count Robert II[3] joined the alliance led by the king of France in 1111, the very next year after the renewal of his agreement with King Henry, and Baldwin VII did the same in 1116;[4] but it seems quite possible that the next count, Charles the Good, renewed the agreement with Henry once more.[5] Henry naturally took a considerable interest in the succession crisis that followed Charles's murder in 1127. If he thought of making a claim to the *comté* himself, his more immediate concern must have been to prevent his nephew, William Clito, son of Robert Curthose and the French king's candidate, from establishing himself in Flanders.[6] When the agreements of 1101 and 1110 were

[1] There is little evidence of a substantial trade between England and Flanders before the twelfth century (Grierson, 'Relations between England and Flanders before the Norman Conquest', pp. 104–6), but it is well-attested by 1127 (Galbert of Bruges, *Murder of Charles the Good*, pp. 25–6, 113–14).

[2] The only evidence that the payments were actually made in the time of Henry I seems to be Galbert's story that William d'Ypres took £500 of English money from the treasure of Count Charles after the murder in 1127 (*Murder of Charles the Good*, pp. 190–1) and the Hyde Chronicler's statement that Henry 'restaurat...annuos redditus ex Anglia' in 1120 (*Liber Monasterii de Hyda*, p. 320). Nor has any indication been found that the military service stipulated in the agreements of 1101 and 1110 was ever performed, unless it is somehow represented by Stephen's 'Flemish mercenaries' (*D.N.B.*, s.v. 'William of Ypres'; Davis, *King Stephen*, pp. 21, 27, 64, 69, etc.) or by a phrase in a charter probably given by Count Robert II, 'me contra Nortmannos anglico regi ferentem auxilium' (Vercauteren-De Smet, 'Étude sur les rapports politiques de l'Angleterre et de la Flandre'). No Flemish troops are mentioned as present at Tinchebrai, where they might most obviously have been expected to be (David, *Robert Curthose*, pp. 173–4, 245–8; Davis, 'The Battle of Tinchebrai: a Correction'; Ganshof, 'Note sur le premier traité anglo-flamand de Douvres', p. 257; Dept, 'Les marchands flamands et le roi d'Angleterre', pp. 304–5).

[3] On Robert II's relations with William Rufus and Henry, Vercauteren-De Smet, ubi supra.   [4] Below, p. 82.

[5] Galbert de Bruges, *Murder of Charles the Good*, p. 312; Malmesbury, *Gesta Regum*, ii. 479. The Hyde Chronicler is specific (*Liber Monasterii de Hyda*, p. 320).

[6] Henry was the youngest son of William the Conqueror and Matilda of Flanders; William Clito the only son of their eldest son Robert Curthose.

renewed in almost identical terms early in the reign of Henry II (1163), it was stated in the formal document that Count Thierry d'Alsace (1128–68), the ultimately successful candidate in the turmoil of 1127–8, had done homage to King Henry, grandfather of the then King Henry.[1] Put into conjunction with the statements of Galbert de Bruges,[2] this must mean that he had renewed the agreement, yet again, soon after he became count; and it also provides specific evidence that the agreement was accompanied by an act of homage.

It was on their southern frontier that the Norman dukes and kings had to meet the opposition to their growing power and where advance would be most difficult. The opposition had manifested itself as early as the 1050s, when the king of France decided to withdraw the support he had hitherto given to Duke William and to ally himself with the duke's rival, the count of Anjou.[3] Thereafter king and count generally acted together, using every opportunity to weaken what must have seemed to them the dangerous power of the Norman rulers. After the campaign of Mortemer in 1054, however, the king of France made no serious attempt to take the offensive against the Anglo-Norman colossus until the time of Louis VI. There was a period of desultory warfare from 1111 to 1113. At the end of it the advantage lay wholly with Henry. The count of Flanders, who had joined in, was killed; Fulk of Anjou had to do homage for Maine and betroth his daughter to Henry's son and heir; Robert de Bellême was taken prisoner by Henry, not entirely honourably, and the king of France had to recognize Henry's suzerainty over Brittany, Maine, and the seigniory of Bellême.[4] Henry had to meet the same alliance again in 1116, re-formed at least nominally in support of the claim which William Clito, the son of his imprisoned brother Robert Curthose, could make to Normandy, and joined by a certain number of barons in Normandy itself. In the end Henry was as successful as before.

---

[1] *Diplomatic Documents*, i. 11: 'Et quia comes Teodoricus hominium fecerat regi Henrico avo istius regis Henrici, comes Philippus fecit hominium isti regi Henrico'.

[2] Galbert says that Count Thierry 'went to the kings of France and England to receive from them fiefs and royal gifts' (*feoda et donaria regalia*): *Murder of Charles the Good*, p. 312. For the Latin text, Galbert de Bruges, *Histoire du meurtre de Charles le Bon*, p. 176.

[3] On this 'diplomatic revolution', Douglas, *William the Conqueror*, pp. 61–71.

[4] Above, p. 76, n. 3.

Count Baldwin VII of Flanders was mortally wounded in 1118; the count of Anjou made peace separately and his daughter was married to William Ætheling in June 1119; King Louis was defeated in a skirmish with Henry at Brémule two months later and had to accept the homage of William Ætheling for Normandy in 1120. Henry's triumph, however, was shattered by the White Ship disaster in that same year. This gave Louis an opportunity to take up the cause of William Clito once more, joined yet again by the count of Anjou and barons in Normandy. This time the Norman rebels were defeated at Bourgtheroulde. Henry, by marrying his daughter, the widowed Empress Matilda, to Geoffrey son and heir of Count Fulk and by then the effective ruler of Anjou, detached the count of Anjou from his alliance with the king of France, put an end to the old rivalry between Normandy and Anjou over Maine, and provided his own solution to the problem of the succession. King Louis's last throw was to make William Clito count of Flanders after the murder of Count Charles the Good. In this matter Henry was favoured by simple good fortune, for the Clito was mortally wounded while he was still in the process of establishing himself in the *comté*.[1] Such a summary may well make Henry's success seem too easy: there were many occasions when the situation in France must have caused him acute anxiety if not despair.

The natural battlefield between the king of France and the duke of Normandy was the Vexin, an ancient *pagus* divided early in the tenth century into the 'Vexin Normand' and the 'Vexin Français' at the River Epte. During the middle decades of the eleventh century the Norman dukes seemed to be extending their interests into the Vexin Français, as though to round off their duchy by taking the other half of the *pagus*. They were proceeding in the usual way, fastening a form of suzerainty over the counts of the Vexin (as the counts established in the Vexin Français were styled),[2] and putting no obstacle in the way of their own vassals when they extended their possessions into that country, as the 'Beaumont' family did when

---

[1] On these events, e.g. Ramsay, *Foundations of England*, ii. 268–72, 277–91, 299–311; Chartrou, *L'Anjou*, pp. 5–25; Poole, *Domesday Book to Magna Carta*, pp. 121–30.

[2] Above, pp. 16–17.

Roger de Beaumont married the heiress of the *comté* of Meulan.[1] But no king of France could tolerate the strengthening of Norman interests so near to Paris for long; and when Simon de Crépy, count of the Vexin, retired from the world in 1077 the king hastened to annex this part of the *pagus*, so that the Royal Domain and the duchy of Normandy came to have a common frontier. When the French garrison of Mantes made a raid into Normandy in 1087, William the Conqueror retaliated immediately. His counter-raid could have been intended to be no more than punitive; it is more likely that he was seizing an occasion to recover his position in the Vexin Français. During the sack of Mantes he received the wound from which he died.[2]

The Conqueror had failed, in the end, to fasten his lordship securely over the whole of the Vexin, and the king of France followed up his own success by taking Gisors, on the west bank of the Epte, from Robert Curthose; but William Rufus made two further attempts to conquer the Vexin Français after he had taken over the government of Normandy. Though the count of Meulan and other seigneurs, notably the lord of La Roche Guyon, gave their active support, Rufus was no more successful than his father had been.[3] Yet Robert count of Meulan continued to hold his lands in the Vexin Français, as well as his estates in Normandy and England, and survived to be one of Henry's most intimate and active barons and counsellors.[4] Through him and his son Waleran, Norman interest in this territory was kept alive; though the great barrier of castles which Rufus and Henry constructed on the line of the River Epte[5] could be interpreted as an admission on their part that this, and not the River Oise, would be their frontier over against the Royal Domain. The king of France for his part pushed on, and having secured the Vexin Français made a serious effort to take the Vexin Normand as well. Much of the sporadic fighting between King Louis VI and King Henry took

[1] Douglas, *William the Conqueror*, pp. 86–7, 357; *Complete Peerage*, vii. 520–6; Le Patourel, *Norman Barons*, pp. 12–16, 30, note 13.

[2] Douglas, *William the Conqueror*, pp. 235, 357–8.

[3] Poole, *Domesday Book to Magna Carta*, pp. 111–12; Lemarignier, *Hommage en marche*, pp. 42–3; Pépin, *Gisors et la vallée de l'Epte*, pp. 13–14; Orderic Vitalis, *H.E.* (ed. Le Prévost), iv. 19–26.

[4] He was probably the first earl of Leicester (*Complete Peerage*, vii. 523–6).

[5] Pépin, *Gisors et la vallée de l'Epte*, p. 14 and the map on p. 17; Lemarignier, *Hommage en marche*, pp. 44–5.

place there; and the battle at Brémule[1] was fought perilously
near to the Andelle and not twenty miles from Rouen itself.
This is the one area in which the Norman kings made no
progress and even retreated in the years from 1066 to 1135; and
though the Vexin was but a small country it was vital to the
defence of Normandy—as Richard Cœur-de-Lion understood
very well when he built his Château-Gaillard.

A little to the south and west, however, the cumulation of
lands by the great border families still offered opportunities for
the extension of Norman interests and power. In 1118 the lord
of Montfort l'Amaury in the Île-de-France, Amauri III, inherited the *comté* of Évreux. Though his family already had
many connections with Normandy, this could well have looked
more like an extension of 'French' interests into the duchy than
the reverse; and when Henry refused him investiture Amauri
joined the king of France in his war against the Norman king.
After a good deal of fighting and destruction, Amauri accepted
Henry's terms, which were that he should have the *comté* but not
the castle of Évreux. Though Amauri joined the later rebellion
of 1123–4, he and his successors kept the *comté* which, for the
next sixty years, they held with Montfort and other lands in
'France'; and as it was the largest single element in their
possessions it tended to make the family 'more Norman than
French'.[2]

Further west, the great seigniory of Bellême had been held
by a vassal of the Norman kings since Mabel de Bellême, the
wife of Roger de Montgomery, inherited the lands from her
uncle, Yves de Bellême (d. 1070). Robert de Bellême, Roger's
son and ultimately heir to all his possessions on both sides of the
Channel, seems to have transferred his allegiance to the king of
France after Henry had driven him from his English and Welsh
lands in 1102. This led to his joining King Louis in the war of

---

[1] Brémule, now no more than a farm, is marked on the Michelin map, sheet 55,
on the main road from Rouen to Paris, 5 km. S.-E. of Fleury-sur-Andelle.

[2] Rhein, *La seigneurie de Montfort-en-Iveline*, pp. 38–62, 94–6; *Complete Peerage*, vii,
App. D (pp. 708–17); Lemarignier, *Hommage en marche*, pp. 59–60. Simon de
Montfort, Amauri's son and his next successor but one, divided his inheritance,
assigning Évreux to his elder son Amauri and Montfort, with the other 'French'
lands, to a younger son Simon. Of these two, Amauri married Mabel, one of the
co-heiresses of William earl of Gloucester, and their son at least had the title 'earl
of Gloucester'; Simon's son and grandson, his namesakes, were earls of Leicester
(*Complete Peerage*, v. 689–93; vii. ubi supra and pp. 520, 536–47).

1111 and his arrest and capture by King Henry.[1] When Henry had secured an acknowledgement of his suzerainty over Bellême from King Louis in 1113,[2] he gave the seigniory to Rotrou, count of Perche, whose lands beyond Normandy already included the *comté* of Mortagne and the seigniory of Nogent-le-Rotrou. As a result of this addition to his possessions, Count Rotrou changed his style to 'count of Perche and lord of Bellême'.[3] He had enjoyed Henry's support as an opponent of Robert de Bellême and had been given one of Henry's illegitimate daughters in marriage, with 'lands and wealth' in England.[4] Whatever obligations he may have had to other lords, he remained the faithful vassal of the Norman kings until 1141.[5]

The vast *comté* of Maine occupied a position between the *comté* of Anjou and the duchy of Normandy analogous to that of the Vexin between the Royal Domain and the duchy. Duke William had conquered the *comté* in 1063, given the comital title to his eldest son Robert Curthose and secured the allegiance, or so it seemed then, of the people of Le Mans and the Manceaux barons. There were Manceaux in his invading army of 1066 and among those who obtained lands across the Channel;[6] and this strengthened Norman interest in Maine as it did elsewhere. But the overriding suzerainty of the count of Anjou, established earlier in the century, had not been disputed, and the count naturally looked for any opportunity to make this suzerainty effective. This, with the apparent hostility of the Manceaux to Norman rule, meant that the Norman kings' control of the *comté* was never very secure. William managed to retain it to the end of his life, though he had to fight for it on more than one occasion; Robert Curthose, when he became count in fact as

---

[1] Above, pp. 17, 77–8; *Complete Peerage*, xi. 683–96.
[2] Above, p. 76 n. 3.
[3] Lemarignier, *Hommage en marche*, pp. 60–5.
[4] Orderic Vitalis, *H.E.* (ed. Le Prévost), iv. 187; v. 3–4. For Henry's 'marriage policy', Hollister and Keefe, 'Making of the Angevin Empire', p. 5.
[5] Below, p. 100.
[6] Above, pp. 17–18, 26–7. For the Chaworth family, *Cal. Docs. France*, p. xlviii. The Ballon family appears to have settled on the Welsh Border during the time of William Rufus (Round, *Studies in Peerage*, pp. 189–206). Norman ecclesiastics obtained preferment in Manceaux churches (above, p. 38), and the abbeys of La Couture and Saint-Vincent at Le Mans received property in England (*Cal. Docs. France*, pp. 364–9; Knowles and Hadcock, *Religious Houses*, p. 52).

well as in name after 1087, let it go.[1] A local baron, Hélie de la Flèche, who had a claim derived from his marriage to a daughter of Count Herbert Éveille-Chien, established himself as count of Maine in 1092; and though he was dispossessed of the county from 1098 to 1100 by William Rufus (who was here, as in the Vexin, pursuing Norman interests on the Continent as the effective duke of Normandy), he recovered it and held it until he died in 1110.[2] During the last years of his life he seems to have tried to balance the competing pressures of Anjou and Normandy. The military assistance he brought to King Henry in his Norman campaign of 1105, and again spectacularly at Tinchebrai in the following year,[3] suggests that he regarded himself or felt bound to act as the vassal of the Norman king; but at the same time he engaged his daughter and heir to Geoffrey Martel, the son of Count Fulk le Réchin of Anjou by his second wife, and then, when Geoffrey died in 1106, to Count Fulk le Jeune, le Réchin's son by his third wife and eventually his successor. The marriage took place in 1109; and when Fulk le Jeune succeeded to Anjou in the following year the union of the two *comtés*, after a century of effort on the part of his predecessors, seemed assured.[4]

But this prospect did not extinguish the Norman interest in Maine by any means. When Hélie de la Flèche died in 1110, and Fulk le Jeune, who had already succeeded to his father as count of Anjou, became count of Maine in right of his wife, Henry demanded homage for the *comté*. Fulk refused, and Henry made war on him, a war that was soon confused with the larger conflict of these years between Henry and King Louis VI of France. Fulk was forced to give in and to do homage for Maine (Henry's suzerainty over the *comté* was recognized by King Louis at the same time)[5] and to engage his daughter Matilda to Henry's son and heir, William Ætheling.[6] Henry could regard the relationship thus created with satisfaction until about 1117,

---

[1] Halphen, *Comté d'Anjou*, pp. 180–7; Latouche, *Maine*, pp. 35–44; David, *Robert Curthose*, pp. 13–15, 32–5, 68–75; Douglas, *William the Conqueror*, pp. 223–4, 228–9, 234–5, 242, 401–7.

[2] Halphen, *Comté d'Anjou*, pp. 187–90; Latouche, *Maine*, pp. 45–53.

[3] Latouche, ibid.; for Tinchebrai, David, *Robert Curthose*, pp. 171–6, 245–8.

[4] Halphen, *Comté d'Anjou*, pp. 189–90; Latouche, *Maine*, pp. 52–3; Chartrou, *L'Anjou*, pp. 1–5.

[5] Treaty of 1113, above, p. 76.

[6] Chartrou, *L'Anjou*, pp. 5–7; Poole, *Domesday Book to Magna Carta*, pp. 122–4.

when Fulk again joined the king of France in his war against the Norman king. But as before he made his own peace with Henry. Matilda and William Ætheling were married at Lisieux in 1119 (William was by now recognized as Henry's heir in both kingdom and duchy), Maine was assigned to Matilda as her dowry, and Fulk, who was on the point of making a pilgrimage to the Holy Land, is said to have commended Anjou itself to Henry's care, to be William's if he should fail to return.[1]

All these arrangements collapsed with the death of William Ætheling in the White Ship disaster of the next year. When Count Fulk returned safely from his pilgrimage he changed sides yet again. For some years it must have seemed that Norman suzerainty over Maine was no more than a memory; but when Henry, as part of his solution to the problem of the succession to the Norman lands, negotiated the marriage of his daughter and heiress, the widowed Empress Matilda, to Geoffrey Plantegenêt, Count Fulk's heir, Maine was included in a grandiose plan which would bring all the lands and suzerainties of the counts of Anjou into the Norman complex of lands and lordships—at least that would be its effect from Henry's point of view.[2] The eighty-year conflict between the dukes of Normandy and the counts of Anjou for possession of Maine would end in a Norman take-over.

At first sight, perhaps, Norman expansion after the conquest of England had not been so spectacular in northern France as in Britain. William the Conqueror and his sons had had to give ground in the Vexin, a very dangerous development even though all hope of recovery had by no means been lost; but they had intensified their suzerainty over the dukes of Brittany and the counts of Boulogne, they had established a relationship

---

[1] Malmesbury, *Gesta Regum*, ii. 495.

[2] Cf. above, p. 82, and Le Patourel, 'The Norman Succession', pp. 245–6. Count Fulk would no doubt have seen the marriage differently, as the triumphant climax to his and his predecessors' efforts to solve 'the Norman problem'. It was, after all, his son who was marrying the Norman heiress, at a time when descent in the male line was coming to be regarded more and more as the criterion of family identity. Cf. Duby, 'La noblesse dans la France médiévale', pp. 8–9. The note of triumph in Jean de Marmoutier's account of the reception of Geoffrey and Matilda in Angers after their marriage ('Historia Gaufredi ducis', in *Chron. des comtes d'Anjou*, p. 181) is in marked contrast to Anglo-Norman views on the marriage.

with the counts of Flanders which was at least expressed in feudal terms, and their interests seemed to be extending beyond the duchy into the country between the Seine and the headwaters of the Sarthe. These were important gains. If Henry's plan for the succession had gone smoothly there would have been no visible limit to what his successors might achieve.

4. The End[1]

DURING the last ten years of his reign, Henry Beauclerc ruled England and Normandy directly, and he was overlord in some sense[2] of the king of Scots, of the surviving Welsh kings and princes and the Norman barons who were creating lordships for themselves in Wales, of the duke of Brittany, and the counts of Flanders, Boulogne, Pontieu, and Perche. Though his suzerainty over Maine had been in question, there was at least a prospect that the *comté* would eventually be added to the Norman complex together with the lands and suzerainties of the counts of Anjou. Only in the Vexin had the Norman kings been forced to retreat.

During the ten years that followed Henry's death in 1135 this great complex of lands and lordships collapsed. By the mid 1140s England and Normandy were ruled by two men, each of whom had sons to succeed him and whose families had been rivals in France for several generations already; and though all the links between the two countries had certainly not been broken it must have seemed unlikely that the relationship which had existed between them in Henry's day could be re-established. At that time, neither the king of England nor the duke of Normandy was able to maintain the suzerainties over neighbouring countries that Henry had exercised. More than that, the duke of Normandy had had to give up places long considered to be part of his duchy to the king of France, and the king of England had virtually had to surrender the northern part of his kingdom to the king of Scots.

---

[1] The first draft of this chapter was adapted as a paper, under the title 'What did not happen in Stephen's Reign', which was read before a meeting of Midland Medievalists at the University of Birmingham in May 1972 and printed with some slight development in *History*, lviii (1973), 1–17. The chapter was then rewritten and later revised, with some changes of mind, or at least of emphasis. I am grateful to Professor R. H. C. Davis for allowing me to use the article in this way and for the opportunities he has given me to test my ideas, as well as for his helpful criticism.

[2] The sense in which King Henry was overlord of these princes is discussed below in ch. 6.

The union of England and Normandy, which was the foundation of Henry's dominion, broke on the problem of the succession. Henry had clearly intended his only legitimate son, William
Ætheling, to succeed him in all his lands and lordships.[1] William
had been designated as the future king of the English in 1116
and the barons had done homage to him as such; they had
already done homage to him as the future duke of the Normans
in the previous year and he had himself done homage for the
duchy to the king of France in 1120; and when he married the
daughter of the count of Anjou in 1119, the *comté* of Maine was
her dowry. All this was brought to nothing when William
perished in the wreck of the White Ship. As Henry's second wife
bore him no children, he decided in the end to designate his
newly widowed daughter Matilda as his heir in England and
Normandy; and since she would have little chance of succeeding unless she were remarried he secretly negotiated her marriage to Geoffrey Plantegenêt, heir to the count of Anjou. On all
political calculations there was a great deal to be said for this
marriage. Geoffrey must have seemed a promising youth and
the union ought to bring the long rivalry between Normandy
and Anjou to an end, a rivalry which, if it continued, would
certainly make it very difficult for Matilda to hold Normandy—
it had been difficult enough for Henry. There were indeed
personal and other problems: a disparity in age between the
spouses; Matilda, having been the wife of an emperor, might
well feel disparaged at being married to the heir of a count;
and their early quarrels were almost disastrous. It is difficult
to say just how unpopular the marriage was with the Norman
barons at the time, for when they accepted Stephen they had to
find reasons for going back on their oath to Matilda; though
Orderic certainly suggests that there was a deep-seated enmity
between the Normans and the Angevins[2]—which would hardly
be surprising after three-quarters of a century of intermittent
warfare.

However much, relatively, Stephen may have owed to the
unpopularity of Matilda and her husband, to his own speed of

[1] On Henry's arrangements for the succession, Le Patourel, 'The Norman
Succession', pp. 244–6, and below, pp. 187–90.

[2] e.g. 'Unde omnes . . . hostili odio Hilibecci despective cognominati sunt':
Orderic Vitalis, *H.E.* (ed. Le Prévost), v. 67. Cf. ibid., pp. 69, 73.

movement and the efficiency with which he followed the procedure Henry had adopted thirty-five years before (immediate seizure of the treasury at Winchester, quick agreement with the Londoners, and promises all round), or to the cooperation of his younger brother, Bishop Henry of Winchester, his coup in December 1135 was brilliantly successful.[1] It gave him almost unquestioned possession of England; and when a group of barons who had been discussing the succession in Normandy and who had already offered to submit to Stephen's elder brother Theobald heard what had happened, they abandoned Theobald at once and accepted Stephen.[2] Moreover, though he was soon up against the difficulties that any new ruler might have to face in the twelfth century, it seems that Stephen was able to take over Henry's governmental organization both in the kingdom and in the duchy and to make it work for him without any immediate dislocation.[3] So far as anyone could see, Stephen had successfully gathered up the inheritance that Henry had intended for Matilda and his grandson. The troubles that followed were not so much those of an incompetent king as the incidents of a civil war following a disputed succession; and in that war of succession both sides were fighting for the whole of Henry's inheritance, Normandy and England together and all that went with them, not simply one or the other.

Geoffrey and Matilda, though they had allowed themselves to be forestalled and outmanœuvred by Stephen, had no intention of abandoning their rights. They were in a sense doubly involved; for in addition to the claims to the Norman inheritance which they could make on behalf of their son or of themselves, Stephen's coup had its place in two long-term continental disputes. One was the struggle between the counts of Anjou and the dukes of Normandy, immediately for control of the intervening *comté* of Maine but ultimately for the predominance that that would bring to the successful party, and such a contest

---

[1] For recent accounts of the beginnings of Stephen's reign, though concerned primarily with England, Davis, *King Stephen*, pp. 13 ff.; Cronne, *Reign of King Stephen*, pp. 26 ff.

[2] Le Patourel, 'The Norman Succession', p. 247.

[3] In England, Cronne, *Reign of King Stephen*, pp. 186 ff.; Morris, *Medieval English Sheriff*, pp. 104–9; in Normandy, Haskins, *Norman Institutions*, pp. 124–8; in general, Le Patourel, 'What did not happen in Stephen's Reign', pp. 3–5.

could only end with the invasion of one by the other.[1] Beside
this was the even older rivalry between the counts of Anjou and
the counts of Blois, who had been building up their 'empires' in
competition with one another in the Loire Valley and the
marches of Brittany.[2] It is possible that Geoffrey and Matilda
thought that Henry's designation would be sufficient or, if there
was to be a fight, that it would be in terms of the old Anjou–
Normandy and Anjou–Blois wars; at all events it appears that
they had done nothing, either since their marriage or since the
birth of their son, to build up a body of support among Henry's
chief bishops and barons when Stephen's coup confronted them
with a merging of the two struggles, for a member of the Blois
family was now effectively the ruler of Normandy and had England and Boulogne behind him as well. Geoffrey's chief concern,
during Henry's last years, was with the castles which he said
Henry had promised him, presumably as a base for taking
possession of Normandy after Henry's death; but he had not
been able to obtain these either.[3]

At the beginning of what was to be the 'War of the Norman
Succession', therefore, Stephen was in possession. It was for
him to hold on to what he had won by his dash and his good
luck and if possible to improve upon the position that Henry
had won for himself beyond kingdom and duchy. Geoffrey and
Matilda would have to drive him out. They started from a
position of considerable disadvantage. They had nothing to set
against the support which Stephen was able to attract, initially
as the greatest of the Anglo-Norman barons who was also the
count of Boulogne, and then as crowned and anointed king.
Nor had they anything to balance Stephen's possession of the
whole of Henry's treasure that was deposited in England at the
time of his death and probably the greater part of what was
then deposited in Normandy,[4] or his Flemish mercenaries or the

[1] Above, chs. 1 and 3.
[2] Halphen, *Comté d'Anjou*, pp. 13–53, 149–51 etc.; Dhondt, *Principautés territoriales*,
pp. 142–5 etc.; Guillot, *Comte d'Anjou*, pp. 1–126; Lex, 'Eudes comte de Blois', pp.
191–241; and, for the rivalry in Brittany, Lemarignier, *Hommage en marche*, p. 116.
[3] Orderic Vitalis, *H.E.* (ed. Le Prévost), v. 45–6; Robert de Torigni, *Chronica*,
pp. 125, 128.
[4] For the organization of Henry's treasure, below, pp. 145–55. One of Stephen's
first acts had been to secure the treasury at Winchester (Malmesbury, *Historia
Novella*, pp. 15, 17; *Gesta Stephani*, pp. 5, 30). Henry, on his deathbed, commanded
his son Robert, earl of Gloucester, to use 60,000 pounds from the treasure which had

ecclesiastical support which his brother the bishop of Winchester could organize for him. The Norman and English bishops accepted Stephen to a man and the pope confirmed the archbishop's action in crowning him. Certainly there were those who refused their allegiance or who found occasion for rebellion—Hugh Bigod, Robert of Bampton, and Baldwin de Reviers in England;[1] William Talvas (son of Robert de Bellême and titular count of Pontieu, who had recently been deprived of Séez, Alençon, and his other Norman possessions by King Henry), Amauri de Montfort (count of Évreux), Roger de Tosny, Rabel de Tancarville (one of Henry's chamberlains), the *vicomte* Guigan Algason, and others in Normandy;[2] but Geoffrey and Matilda either made no attempt or were unable to organize them into the nucleus of a party. Even Earl Robert of Gloucester, Matilda's half-brother, decided to give his allegiance initially to Stephen, whether or not it was sincerely given.[3]

Geoffrey and Matilda, in fact, had to start almost from nothing, with no assets other than Henry's designation, a claim to legitimacy, and such resources as the Angevin lands could provide. Whatever military ability they could find in themselves or attract to their service, their progress initially was bound to be slow; but to begin with neither side did very well. Stephen failed to exploit his initial advantage. His treatment of the first rebels in England may have been civilized but was hardly such as to command respect in the early twelfth century; the visit to Normandy in 1137, intended presumably to be the

lately come from England and was in his custody at Falaise to pay off his household servants and mercenaries (Orderic Vitalis, *H.E.* (ed. Le Prévost), v. 50; Robert de Torigni, *Chronica*, p. 129). Whatever remained after this order had been carried out, if it was carried out, would presumably have been at Stephen's command as long as Robert was in his allegiance. The treasury at Rouen must certainly have come into Stephen's possession, for Henry's treasurers remained in office (Haskins, *Norman Institutions*, p. 126). Henry of Huntingdon's account of Stephen's visit to Normandy in 1137 gives the impression that he was not hampered by lack of money there whatever other troubles he met (Huntingdon, *Historia Anglorum*, p. 260), and he must have relied to some extent on the cash that was available in the duchy (cf. Prestwich, 'War and Finance', pp. 38–42).

[1] Ramsay, *Foundations*, ii. 353–5 etc.; Davis, *King Stephen*, pp. 17–20, 24–6, 41.
[2] Chartrou, *L'Anjou*, pp. 39–41, 49–51; Orderic Vitalis, *H.E.* (ed. Le Prévost), v. 56–9, 64–5, 67–8, 81; Ramsay, *Foundations*, ii. 361.
[3] Malmesbury, *Historia Novella*, pp. 17–18; Patterson, 'William of Malmesbury's Robert of Gloucester'.

occasion of a formal assumption of the government of the duchy and to initiate a regular division of his time and activity between kingdom and duchy, turned into a disaster because the quarrels between the Normans and the Flemings in his army prevented him from taking any effective action against Geoffrey and Matilda; the arrest of the bishops of Salisbury, Ely, and Lincoln, whatever the justification for it, was bound to cause a scandal, if only for the manner in which it was carried out; while to allow Matilda to proceed to Bristol in 1139 when he had her in his grasp at Arundel was hardly the act of a realist.

On their side, Geoffrey and Matilda were no more effective. At the moment of Henry's death they were in Anjou. As soon as they heard the news, Geoffrey sent Matilda into Normandy where she was received by the *vicomte* Guigan Algason into the castles which were in his charge, Argentan, Domfront, and Exmes. Geoffrey followed immediately, taking over Alençon, Séez, and the other Norman castles of William Talvas.[1] But there was no general rising on their behalf—indeed, this first expedition seems to have done little but excite hostility in the duchy—and no indication that they made any attempt to secure Henry's treasure stored in Rouen or other Norman castles. Perhaps this was beyond practical possibility; at all events, their first moves gave them no more than a foothold in Normandy and no prospect of a welcome there. For five years indeed their campaigns in the duchy were no more than raids which accomplished very little; the initial support which Earl Robert gave to Stephen and his many months of inactivity after he had decided to support his half-sister and her husband were no help, though his decision when it came gave them access to Caen and Bayeux; and the fact that England did not immediately rise to her support when Matilda (with Earl Robert though without Geoffrey) landed in 1139, any more than Normandy had done in 1136, must have been very discouraging.[2] Even the king of Scots, whose repeated invasions of the north of England, though largely self-interested, might have created a useful 'second front', had been defeated at the Battle of the Standard.

---

[1] Chartrou, *L'Anjou*, pp. 39–40.
[2] On affairs in Normandy between 1135 and 1141, Ramsay, *Foundations*, ii. 346–7, 359–63, 376–7; Haskins, *Norman Institutions*, pp. 124–8; Chartrou, *L'Anjou*, pp. 36–41, 49–59.

The critical point came in 1141 with the capture of King Stephen at the Battle of Lincoln, an engagement which, in relation to the main issue, was a side-show. Geoffrey at once entered Normandy and summoned the barons who were in the duchy to deliver their castles and to refrain from any hostile action. A little later these barons met together under the leadership, apparently, of the archbishop of Rouen, and again offered kingdom and duchy to Stephen's elder brother, Theobald of Blois. When he declined they could see no alternative but to make what terms they could with Geoffrey, though the archbishop himself remained faithful to Stephen as long as that was possible.[1] It was at this point that Geoffrey's conquest of Normandy really began. In this same year Falaise capitulated; the elderly and ailing bishop of Lisieux, at one time the head of Henry's administration of Normandy, surrendered his cathedral city and submitted; the count of Meulan, hitherto one of Stephen's most prominent supporters and advisers, also came to terms with Geoffrey, for his principal Norman possessions, situated in the valley of the Risle, were immediately threatened; and the count of Perche likewise abandoned Stephen. Within a few months Geoffrey had the whole of central Normandy from the Seine to the Orne. His campaigns of 1142 and 1143 gave him all the west as well as the Pays de Caux in the east. He entered the city of Rouen in January 1144 and by the summer of that year he had obtained recognition from the king of France and was using the ducal title. Arques, the very last Norman stronghold to submit, surrendered a year later. Geoffrey had conquered Normandy.[2]

In England, Stephen's capture and imprisonment led to no such decisive result; partly because of Matilda's impolitic behaviour and partly because Earl Robert of Gloucester was himself captured in the rout of Winchester a few months later. Nothing more conclusive could then be devised than a simple

---

[1] Orderic Vitalis, *H.E.* (ed. Le Prévost), v. 130–3. That all this concerned England as much as Normandy is shown by the facts, if Orderic has got them right, that these barons offered Theobald the kingdom as well as the duchy and that one of the first to negotiate with Geoffrey was Robert earl of Leicester, whose interests lay more immediately in England than in Normandy.

[2] For Geoffrey's conquest of Normandy, Ramsay, *Foundations*, ii. 414–16, 431–2; Haskins, *Norman Institutions*, pp. 128–30; Chartrou, *L'Anjou*, pp. 59–66; Davis, *King Stephen*, pp. 68, 78–9.

exchange of prisoners, king for earl. Thereafter, though he did not lack opportunities, Stephen was never able to defeat or to win over all Matilda's supporters in England or to reduce all their castles, notwithstanding the slow but steady decline of their strength in the country during the remainder of the 1140s. Geoffrey, to whom Matilda and Earl Robert appealed in 1142, preferred to complete his conquest of Normandy and to deal with his own rebellious barons in Anjou[1] rather than risk an expedition to England. It was a wise decision; but it meant that England could not be won in his lifetime, short of some lucky accident. Earl Robert died in 1147; Matilda returned to Normandy for good in 1148; and her son Henry, though he visited England in 1142–3, in 1146–7, and again in 1149–50,[2] made no impression on the country in those years. The position then was that Stephen seemed unshakeably in possession of the throne of England, even though there were parts of his kingdom which he did not control; while Geoffrey was firmly and completely in possession of Normandy. Since neither side had any real prospect of realizing its objectives in full, whatever attitudes they might adopt, and certainly not between 1142 and 1152, it was a stalemate; and this stalemate meant division and collapse; for England and Normandy, the union of which had been the foundation of the great political edifice of the Norman kings, were now put asunder. The two countries were under different and mutually hostile rulers, neither of whom had any reason at that time to think that he would not be able to transmit what he then held, at the least, to a son of his, certainly not before the bishops in England finally refused to crown Stephen's son Eustace.

Under these conditions of disputed succession and then partition, it was hardly to be expected that Stephen and Geoffrey would be able to maintain the suzerainties which William the Conqueror and his sons had established over neighbouring principalities. Both in Britain and in Northern France the Normans were in retreat during Stephen's nineteen long winters.

The king of Scots, as soon as he heard of Stephen's coup, invaded England. Stephen went north with an army at once.

---

[1] Chartrou, *L'Anjou*, pp. 33–4, 62.
[2] Poole, 'Henry Plantagenet's Early Visits to England'; *Gesta Stephani*, introduction, pp. xvi–xvii, xxii–xxiii.

When the two kings met, David refused to do homage on account of the oath he had taken to Matilda. However, he allowed his son Henry to do homage and to receive from Stephen 'Carlisle', Doncaster, the earldom of Huntingdon, and a promise that his claim to Northumbria would be borne in mind.[1] It represented a weaker relationship between the two kings than that which had existed between David and Henry and something of a compromise. King David was able to profit by the opportunity which Stephen's accession gave to him; for though he surrendered a few places that he had captured in the English borderland, he secured control of the Cumbrian lands which he regarded as his by right and which had been taken from his father by William Rufus, and his son and heir had succeeded to his Midland earldom. Stephen, on his part, though he had to recognize that the king of Scots was not his man, was now lord of the heir to the Scottish throne.

David, however, was anxious to do more for Matilda's cause and his own. He threatened an invasion in 1137, came over the Border early in 1138, and led the great expedition a month or two later that was utterly defeated at the Battle of the Standard. Notwithstanding all this, when peace was made at Durham in April 1139, Stephen not only restored what he had given to Earl Henry in 1136 but added the earldom of Northumbria, except for Bamburgh, Newcastle, and the lands of St. Cuthbert of Durham and of St. Andrew of Hexham.[2] Coming after King David's defeat at the Standard this represented either extraordinary weakness on Stephen's part, unlikely even for him, or, more probably, the price he was willing to pay for such hold over the ruler of Scotland as the homage of the king of Scots's heir might give him; and his anxiety that Earl Henry should spend some time at his court supports this second interpretation.

Nevertheless David joined Matilda in her brief triumph during the year 1141 and was involved with her in the rout of Winchester. Stephen naturally confiscated Earl Henry's lands in England, though he was only able to make this effective in the earldom of Huntingdon and probably in Doncaster. David retained control, *de facto*, of a large part of the north of England from which Stephen could not dislodge him. A remark of

---

[1] Anderson, *Scottish Annals*, pp. 170–4; *Early Sources*, ii. 196–7.
[2] Anderson, *Scottish Annals*, pp. 176–216; *Early Sources*, ii. 197–200.

William of Newburgh and David's interest in the dispute over the election to the bishopric of Durham after the death of Bishop Geoffrey Rufus both suggest that his domination, in the east, extended as far as the Tees;[1] while in the west it reached to the Ribble and even beyond.[2] But as a result of the confiscation even his son was no longer Stephen's man. Given the relationship that had existed between the kings of Scots and the kings of the English for so long, this was an anomalous and therefore an unstable situation; but for as long as it lasted, that is until after the end of Stephen's reign, the traditional relationship between the kings was destroyed, and the king of Scots was not only independent in his own kingdom but in control of a large part of the north of England as well.

The Welsh reaction to Norman conquest and colonization had begun in Henry's time with the conquests of Gruffydd ap Cynan in North Wales; but to Henry the emergence of a strong prince in Wales might not be entirely unwelcome so long as his own overlordship was acknowledged.[3] That Stephen succeeded initially to the overlordship that Henry had exercised over the marcher lords is evident, and this must have extended in principle to the surviving Welsh princes; but as the parties in the struggle for the succession became more clearly defined the marcher lords tended to follow their natural leader, the earl of Gloucester, in allegiance to Matilda and her son. This put up a barrier which effectively denied Stephen access to Wales, for he never succeeded in taking their great strongholds, Bristol, Gloucester, Hereford, and Chester. If the proposal for an expedition into North Wales, which was made by Earl Ranulf of Chester during his brief period of allegiance to Stephen in 1146, was seriously intended, it seems to have been Stephen's only opportunity after 1139 to make his presence felt in Wales; and it came to nothing.[4] With the king unable to intervene in person, and the marcher lords unable to devote themselves to

[1] William of Newburgh, *Historia*, p. 70; evidence on the Durham dispute conveniently collected in Anderson, *Scottish Annals*, pp. 217–19.

[2] Barrow, 'King David I and the Honour of Lancaster', pp. 85–9; *Regesta Regum Scottorum*, i. 111–12.

[3] For Gruffydd ap Cynan, above, pp. 63–5; Lloyd, *History of Wales*, ii. 462–9.

[4] *Gesta Stephani*, pp. 121–3, 128–33; Cronne, *Reign of King Stephen*, pp. 103–8; Davis, *King Stephen*, pp. 93–5.

their affairs in Wales without constantly looking over their shoulders at what was going on in England and Normandy, many Welsh princes took the opportunity to recover their lands and their independence; but it is too much to call such success as they achieved a 'national revival'.[1] The movement was quite unco-ordinated. The Welsh were fighting one another as much as they were fighting the Anglo-Norman colonists;[2] and Miles of Gloucester and the earl of Gloucester were not seriously disturbed in their hold upon Brycheiniog and Morgannwg. Yet, for the time being, the overlordship which the Norman kings had exercised over the rulers of Wales, Welsh and Norman alike, was ended;[3] and any possibility there may have been in Henry's time that the progressive Norman conquest and colonization of the country would continue uninterruptedly until the whole of Wales was brought under the same subjection as the South no longer existed.

After his loss of Normandy, and even before, there was little chance that Stephen would be able to maintain Henry's overlordships on the continent. As far as can be seen, he had no influence in Brittany. Alan III, lord of the great honour of Richmond and styled earl of Richmond from 1136, seems to have had few interests in the duchy[4] and was loyal to Stephen until his death in 1146. The then duke of Brittany, Conan III, Alan's distant cousin, was more closely related to Geoffrey Plantegenêt and was a friend and ally of his.[5] Likewise, in the absence of any specific evidence one way or the other, it can only be regarded as highly improbable that the count of Flanders, particularly a Thierry d'Alsace, would have renewed the money fief with Stephen.[6] The possibility has always to be

---

[1] Lloyd, *History of Wales*, ii. 462–80.

[2] e.g. the conquest of Ceredigion by the sons of Gruffydd ap Rhys of Deheubarth from the sons of Gruffydd ap Cynan of Gwynedd.

[3] Hugh de Mortimer may have been an exception (below, p. 105, n. 3).

[4] His father, Count Stephen, had divided his lands between his three sons, giving Penthièvre to the eldest, Geoffrey Boterel II who was an adherent of Matilda, Richmond to the second, Alan (III), and Tréguier and Guingamp to the youngest, Henry; but Alan must have had interests actual or potential in Brittany for he retired there in 1145, died there in the following year, was buried in the abbey of Bégard (*E.Y.C.*, iv (*Honour of Richmond*, i), 84, 87–93) and his son certainly had an interest in the duchy.

[5] De la Borderie, *Histoire de Bretagne*, iii. 39–40; *E.Y.C.*, iv (*Honour of Richmond*, i), 84; Chartrou, *L'Anjou*, pp. 287–8.

[6] Stephen, at the time of his accession, was count of Boulogne in right of his

considered that Stephen's 'Flemish mercenaries' represented in some way the service due from the count of Flanders for his pension; but this seems unlikely. These mercenaries would presumably have been called 'Flemings', even if they had come very largely from Stephen's own *comté* of Boulogne; and if William d'Ypres was indeed their commander, he was no friend of Count Thierry, who had defeated his attempt to make himself count of Flanders in the succession war of 1127–8 and had banished him from the *comté*.[1] It goes without saying that Stephen could exercise no authority in the lands to the south of Normandy, at least after 1141. He had secured the support of Rotrou count of Perche with a grant of Moulins-la-Marche in 1137; but after Stephen's capture at Lincoln, Rotrou was one of the first to go over to Geoffrey, having nursed a grievance against Stephen for some months previously; and Waleran, count of Meulan, soon followed his example. William Talvas and Amauri de Montfort had apparently been Geoffrey's partisans from the first.[2] The one exception to Stephen's general lack of authority on the Continent after 1141 was Boulogne; for he remained count in right of his wife until he invested their eldest son Eustace with the *comté* (*c.* 1147); and when Eustace died in 1153 he was succeeded by his younger brother William, who may have been under age at the time.[3]

On Geoffrey's side, though his conquest of Normandy would give him a claim to King Henry's continental overlordships, it is not likely that he raised the matter in institutional form. He was unquestionably count of Maine, for he had inherited the *comté* from his mother before his conquest of Normandy.[4] The count of Flanders, Thierry d'Alsace, was his brother-in-law.

wife, and as such he was traditionally the vassal of the count of Flanders (*Histoire des territoires ayant formé le département du Pas-de-Calais*, pp. 63, 71). This relationship had been virtually ineffective for some time (Ganshof, 'Note sur le premier traité anglo-flamand de Douvres', p. 257); but, according to Orderic Vitalis, Henry had made Stephen do homage to Count Thierry in 1128 (*H.E.* (ed. Le Prévost), iv. 484).

[1] On Stephen's Flemish mercenaries and William d'Ypres, above, p. 80 n. 2; Ramsay, *Foundations*, ii. 361; Dept, 'Les marchands flamands et le roi d'Angleterre', pp. 304–5.

[2] Orderic Vitalis, *H.E.* (ed. Le Prévost), v. 83, 130–1; Robert de Torigni, *Chronica*, p. 142; Orderic, ibid., pp. 56–7, 68.

[3] *E.Y.C.*, viii (*Honour of Warenne*), 13–15; cf. Round, *Studies in Peerage*, pp. 167–72.

[4] Latouche, *Maine*, pp. 52–3; Chartrou, *L'Anjou*, pp. 4–7, 24.

He seems to have been friendly, for he brought a large force to assist Geoffrey in his conquest of Normandy, though only after Geoffrey had entered Rouen and almost the whole of the duchy had been won;[1] but he could hardly have been a vassal in any sense, for Geoffrey was in no position to renew the pension which King Henry had undertaken to pay to the count of Flanders and so to receive Count Thierry's homage.[2] Similarly Geoffrey had a family relationship, but apparently no more, with the duke of Brittany, for Conan III was his first cousin. He was on sufficiently good terms with the duke to bring military assistance when Conan was trying to put down the rebellious Robert de Vitré.[3] His relations with the cross-border families may well have been more of a feudal kind; for William Talvas (titular count of Pontieu) and Amauri de Montfort who had supported him from the first, and Waleran de Meulan and Rotrou de Perche who came over in 1141, all held important fiefs in Normandy, and William Talvas had lands in Maine as well.[4] But Geoffrey had to give way even further than Henry had done in the Vexin; for the price of recognition as duke of Normandy by King Louis VII was the complete abandonment of the Vexin Normand, either wholly in 1144 or in two instalments, one then and one in 1151.[5] Since Norman claims to the Vexin Français had had to be given up some time before, this represented a very big concession, bringing the king of France through the fortified line of the Epte to the Andelle, dangerously close to Rouen itself, and giving up territory which had been regarded as part of Normandy from the first.[6]

In Britain, Matilda had the support of the marcher lords in Wales and their allegiance, but seems to have had no relationship with the independent Welsh princes. She also had the support of the king of Scots. The oath of 1127 was apparently an

---

[1] Robert de Torigni, *Chronica*, pp. 148–9; Chartrou, *L'Anjou*, pp. 64–5, 73.

[2] When the 'money-fief' was reinstituted in 1163, the act stated that Count Thierry had done homage to 'King Henry, grandfather of the present King Henry', but refers to no other precedent for the act of homage which Thierry's son performed on that occasion (*Diplomatic Documents*, i. 11).

[3] De la Borderie, *Histoire de Bretagne*, iii. 39–40.

[4] Above, pp. 84–5. For the lands of William Talvas in Maine, Orderic Vitalis, *H.E.* (ed. Le Prévost), v. 47.

[5] Lemarignier, *Hommage en marche*, p. 45, note 53.

[6] Above, pp. 16, 82–4.

oath of fealty as well as an oath to support her succession;[1] but what degree of feudal relationship this was understood to create it is hard to say. Moreover, King David's support was clearly interested. His intervention had secured for him a large part of the north of England; and he took the occasion of the knighting of the young Henry fitzEmpress at Carlisle in 1149 to exact a promise from him that, 'if he became king of England', he would recognize David's possession of Northumberland. At the same time Henry must have accepted the agreement between David and Earl Ranulf of Chester that left the king of Scots in possession of Cumbria—and all this without any suggestion of homage then or at some later date, at least in the accounts of their meeting that we have.[2] Whatever the outcome of the civil war in England and Normandy, King David intended to keep as much as possible of the territory he had won, and to keep it, as this would have been expressed later, 'in full sovereignty'.

Thus England and Normandy, under different and mutually hostile governments, had been mutilated in their territory, and the suzerainty which the Norman kings had exercised in varying degrees over the rulers of lands beyond kingdom and duchy had mostly gone. Quite apart from any loss of effectiveness in the government of England and any temporary disruption in the government of Normandy, it was a far-reaching collapse.

The significance of this collapse has been largely concealed by Henry II's very successful propaganda and by the extent to which he was able to reconstruct the relationship between Normandy and England as it had been in the time of his grandfather. The propaganda began with his christening—'Henry' after his maternal grandfather rather than 'Fulk' or 'Geoffrey' in the tradition of his paternal ancestors. It continued with his insistence on his hereditary right to England and Normandy through his mother,[3] and in the use of the sobriquet 'fitz-Empress'[4] which he can have done nothing to discourage. His

---

[1] Round, *Geoffrey de Mandeville*, pp. 31–3. Huntingdon (*Historia Anglorum*, p. 256) refers retrospectively to the oath that Stephen among others took as 'sacramentum fidelitatis'.

[2] Anderson, *Scottish Annals*, pp. 221–3; *Gesta Stephani*, pp. 142–3.

[3] e.g. 'Henricus filius filie Regis Henrici rectus heres Anglie et Normannie' (1141); *Regesta*, iii, No. 635.

[4] e.g. Ritchie, *Normans in Scotland*, pp. 354–5.

treatment of Stephen as a usurper,[1] whose reign established no rights or precedents and must be ignored, with his parade of respect for 'the customs of his grandfather',[2] was all designed to emphasize continuity, to minimize the change which had taken place. And certainly there was some basis for his claims and attitudes, though they could be, had been, and may still be disputed.

The fact that much of the relationship between Normandy and England, as it had existed in the time of Henry Beauclerc, had survived or could be revived greatly helped Henry fitzEmpress to reconstruct it, and also the relationship between the Norman kings and the vassal princes, albeit in a different context and with important modifications. Enough had survived of Henry Beauclerc's machinery of government in kingdom and duchy for it to be set going again, if indeed it had ever completely stopped. Thus the two exchequers, as financial institutions and as instruments for the administration of the king's delegated justice, the justices sent out to supplement the judicial work of local officers and ultimately to supersede it, had not been so destroyed that they could not be reactivated immediately after 1154. Indeed the fact that Henry had so much to build on here no doubt explains the great difference in administrative sophistication between England and Normandy on the one hand, and Brittany, Anjou, and Aquitaine on the other, during the later part of the twelfth century, a difference which might well have been gradually reduced if Henry's empire had survived in the form it then took. Henry himself would certainly have maintained that the relationship between the king and the ecclesiastical authorities which his grandfather had established was continued in his own time.[3]

By no means all the links between the two countries that had been created by those barons who had built up great estates extending into both kingdom and duchy, by Norman cathedral

---

[1] 'Tempore regis Stephani, ablatoris mei', Delisle–Berger, *Recueil*, No. 682 (p. 306); quoted by King, 'King Stephen and the Anglo-Norman Aristocracy', p. 181, note 8, where it is happily translated as 'King Stephen my Usurper'. This must be a play on the oft-repeated words 'regis Henrici avi mei', as in the next note.

[2] e.g. 'Ista recordatio vel recognitio cujusdam partis consuetudinum et libertatum et dignitatum antecessorum suorum, videlicet Henrici avi sui'; Constitutions of Clarendon (Stubbs, *Select Charters*, p. 163).

[3] As in the Constitutions of Clarendon (ibid., pp. 163–7).

chapters and monasteries which had acquired lands and churches in England, and by ambitious Norman and other continental churchmen who had obtained preferment across the Channel, had been irremediably broken. It might have been expected that as Geoffrey conquered Normandy and Stephen gradually recovered control of England after 1141, the men who held 'cross-Channel' estates would be forced to choose between the two allegiances; and certainly there were those who lost their lands in Normandy on account of their fidelity to Stephen or in England on account of their allegiance to Geoffrey and Matilda;[1] but although a systematic investigation would almost certainly produce many more examples than are now readily available, it is doubtful whether it will ever be possible to produce a statistically valid estimate of the number of estates so affected or of the number of barons who were able, wholly or in part, to avoid such losses.

There were indeed several circumstances that tended to make the dilemma of these men less acute than that which faced their descendants in the thirteenth century. Although Stephen seemed to be gaining ground steadily in the late 1140s, he never in fact recovered control of the whole of his kingdom. He was never able to dispossess the earl of Chester of all his English lands,[2] or Robert earl of Gloucester (or, apparently, William his son and successor),[3] or Hugh Bigod earl of Norfolk,[4] or even a man of less consequence such as William de Moion (Mohun) of Dunster whose estates were mostly in Somerset and the Cotentin.[5] So far as can be seen, these men (all except the earl of Chester) kept their Norman lands and at least the essential core of their English estates throughout the civil war. There were many ways in which they could defend themselves; by military force; by

---

[1] e.g. lands in Normandy lost: Ranulf, earl of Chester (*Regesta*, iii, Nos. 58, 178, 180); Warenne (ibid., No. 272); Stephen's *comté* of Mortain (ibid.); Lacy (ibid., No. 58; cf. Wightman, *Lacy Family*, pp. 74, 76–80, 185–9, 218–20); Paynel (Les Moutiers Hubert, *E.Y.C.*, vi (*Paynel Fee*), 5, 7); Mowbray (Greenway, *Charters of the Honour of Mowbray*, p. xxvi); lands in England lost: Reginald de Saint-Valéry (*Regesta*, iii, No. 329); earldom of Huntingdon (Henry of Scotland, *Regesta Regum Scottorum*, i. 102–5); Brian fitzCount (Davis, 'Henry of Blois and Brian fitzCount', p. 302).

[2] By implication, Cronne, 'Ranulf de Gernons'; Davis, 'King Stephen and the Earl of Chester Revised'.

[3] Davis, *King Stephen*, pp. 37–8, etc.; *Complete Peerage*, v. 683–7.

[4] *Complete Peerage*, ix. 579–83.

[5] *Complete Peerage*, ix. 18–19; xii (1), 37–9; *Gesta Stephani*, pp. 54–5, 85.

agreements with neighbours who might otherwise welcome an opportunity to enrich themselves at the expense of a baron of the opposing allegiance;[1] by seeking the privileges of a crusader (the Second Crusade came at a very opportune moment for several hard-pressed Anglo-Norman barons);[2] or even by keeping out of the way.[3] It may have been possible on occasion to make family arrangements. Robert earl of Leicester, the greater part of whose possessions lay in England though he had an important fief in Normandy, remained faithful or at least avoided giving offence to Stephen until 1153; while his twin brother, the count of Meulan, who was in the converse situation, went over to Geoffrey in 1141. Earl Robert's action at Worcester in 1151 and the apparent ease (and certain profit) with which he came to terms with Duke Henry in 1153 suggest that he and his brother were able to look after one another's interests in their respective countries until Henry's succession to Normandy and England seemed assured.[4]

More important, however, than any of these circumstances or devices that might enable some barons to avoid dispossession and thus limit the divisive force of competing allegiances was what appears to have been the underlying assumption on both sides. Although we can now say that Stephen had virtually no

---

[1] e.g. the well-known *conventio* between the earls of Leicester and Chester (Stenton, *English Feudalism*, pp. 248–57, 286–8; and generally, Davis, *King Stephen*, pp. 111–14).

[2] e.g. William de Warenne, *Complete Peerage*, xii (1), 496–7; Roger de Mowbray, ibid., ix. 370; Waleran de Meulan, ibid., xii (2), 833, who probably also made a pilgrimage to Compostela, ibid., pp. 833, 836. William le Gros, Count of Aumale and lord of Holderness, took the crusader's vow, but was unable to make the journey and commuted it by founding Meaux Abbey in 1150, ibid., i. 353.

[3] Hugh de Mortimer, who is thought to have remained loyal to Stephen or at least to have given no offence, though his lands were in territory mostly dominated by the Angevins, seems to have spent much of the 1140s campaigning in Wales, *Complete Peerage*, ix. 266–9 (esp. p. 268, note j); Lloyd, *History of Wales*, ii. 477, 479, 495–6, 501; *Regesta*, iii, Nos. 180, 437. It cannot be shown that the Norman lands were held continuously, but his son had them, *Complete Peerage*, ix. 269–72.

[4] In 1141, as Geoffrey threatened the valley of the Risle in which their ancestral lands lay (these lands were then held by the count of Meulan though Earl Robert's lordship of Breteuil was not far away), Robert, who was in Normandy at the time, negotiated a truce on his own behalf and that of his brother (Orderic Vitalis, *H.E.* (ed. Le Prévost), v. 131–2), and the count of Meulan himself came to terms with Geoffrey not long after (Robert de Torigni, *Chronica*, p. 142). Earl Robert's action at Worcester is described in Davis, *King Stephen*, pp. 113–14, and his agreement with Duke Henry given in *Regesta*, iii, Nos. 438–9. Cf. *Complete Peerage*, vii. 527–30; xii (2), 829–38.

chance of recovering Normandy after 1144, even if he did not recognize Geoffrey's conquest,[1] and although Geoffrey refused to be diverted into a campaign for the conquest of England, yet each acted as though he or his successor would one day reconstruct the dominions of Henry Beauclerc. In 1146, most probably, Stephen gave the castle and city of Lincoln to Ranulf earl of Chester 'until the king should restore the earl's land in Normandy with all his castles';[2] while Duke Henry, on the other side, confirmed an arrangement whereby Reginald de Saint-Valéry and his son assigned to Fontevrault an annuity of twenty pounds of Rouen money from the revenues of the port of Dieppe until 'with God's help, they should have recovered their hereditary rights in England'.[3] The most revealing document, however, if it is interpreted rightly, is one which records the grant made by the bishop of Bayeux to Robert earl of Gloucester of land which the earl of Chester held of the church of Bayeux, saving the services due to that church, until an heir should present himself whom the duke of the Normans would recognize as the rightful heir of Ranulf earl of Chester; and when this happened that heir should hold the land of the church of Bayeux and of the bishop in chief. This document is dated September 1146.[4] It seems that Duke Geoffrey, or possibly the bishop himself, had seized the lands which the earl of Chester held of the church of Bayeux in Normandy, presumably at the time of the earl's brief reconciliation with Stephen, but that this seizure was not intended to be a disinheritance. Whatever offence the earl had committed against the duke when he came to terms with Stephen did not carry that penalty. It was not treason as that was later understood; for the land which the earl held of the bishop had been seized by his immediate lord the bishop, or by Duke Geoffrey and returned to him, and it was intended that it should eventually be restored to the earl's heir.[5]

---

[1] Grant to the earl of Chester, 'donec idem rex fecerit ei terram suam Normannie et omnia castella sua habere' (*Regesta*, iii, No. 178). Stephen's son Eustace joined the king of France in an attack upon Normandy as late as 1152 (Robert de Torigni, *Chronica*, p. 165). For what it may be worth as evidence in this connection, Stephen continued to use a seal bearing the ducal title to the end of his life (*Regesta*, iii, pp. xv–xvii; iv. 4 and plates I and II).

[2] See preceding note.

[3] *Regesta*, iii, No. 329. [4] Ibid., No. 58.

[5] Cf. Pollock and Maitland, *H.E.L.*, i. 351–2, 461–2; ii. 505–6; Powicke, *Loss of Normandy*, pp. 286–90.

During Stephen's reign, and in the restorations and con-
firmations by which Duke Henry smoothed his way to the
throne of England, the strictly hereditary character of fiefs
seems to be recognized more explicitly than hitherto. It has been
suggested that the nobility was taking the opportunity afforded
by the disputed succession to obtain some assurance against the
practices by which the Norman kings had exploited uncertainties in the rules of inheritance for their own profit as well
as confiscating lands for rebellion; that these practices, particularly under Henry Beauclerc, had led to 'endless family feuds
over the inheritance of land' and ultimately to the troubles of
Stephen's reign; and that it was the experience of these troubles
that persuaded Henry II and his successors to accept a fully
hereditary nobility in England.[1] But just as the civil war was
concerned with more than baronial disputes and royal high-
handedness, so the whole question of the heritability of fiefs,
certainly where there was no adult and capable son ready to step
immediately into his father's shoes, is perhaps more complex
than this interpretation might suggest;[2] and the progressive
definition and standardization of rights of inheritance (whatever
part politics may have played in the process) was a phenomenon
that was certainly not confined to England in the twelfth century.
Count Geoffrey and his immediate predecessors in Anjou were
finding that they were not able to grant, resume, and re-
distribute fiefs with the freedom that earlier counts had enjoyed; and, with the proliferation of private castles among other
general causes, the hereditary tenure of fiefs was in fact growing
more and more secure.[3]

Duke Henry had perhaps had more direct experience of his
father's struggles in Anjou than of the conflict in England. For
his part he had to win support and make concessions if he was
to gain what he believed to be his right; and he himself based
his claim to England and Normandy on heredity. When a baron
claimed lands in both countries by hereditary or by any other
right (and no family claim based on rights once held, however
remotely in the past, was ever forgotten), recognition of his

[1] Davis, 'What happened in Stephen's Reign', pp. 5–12.
[2] Holt, 'Politics and Property in Early Medieval England'.
[3] Halphen, *Comté d'Anjou*, pp. 112–13, 152–75; Chartrou, *L'Anjou*, pp. 26–35
(esp. Berlai, pp. 27–8), 69–76; Guillot, *Comte d'Anjou*, i. 346–52.

claim for any reason meant the confirmation or the reconstruction, occasionally even the enlargement, of a 'cross-Channel' estate.[1] Thus even when we know that a family had lost lands in one country or the other for its allegiance to Stephen or Henry (or his father and mother), or where we cannot readily find evidence to show specifically whether it had done so or not whatever the presumption might be, we can certainly say that a great many of the 'cross-Channel' estates existing before 1141 survived or were reconstructed in 1153 and the following years,[2] with all that that implied. This is the important thing, whether it was achieved through the operation of a progressively defined law of inheritance[3] or by the working of political conditions; and once England and Normandy were again under a single ruler there was no reason why individual 'cross-Channel' holdings should not continue to be created.[4] Stephen had not made any general seizure of the English possessions of Norman monasteries and cathedrals, or so it seems;[5] and they certainly continued to hold their lands and churches in England, and even to acquire additional property, after his reign as before. Men of French origin still obtained important positions in the English Church.[6]

[1] e.g. *Regesta*, iii, Nos. 44, 180, 272, 438–9, 582, 653.

[2] e.g. Aumale, *Complete Peerage*, i. 351–3; Clare (earl of Pembroke), ibid., x. 348–53; Trussebut, *E.Y.C.*, x (*Trussebut Fee*), 5–9; Paynel, *E.Y.C.*, vi (*Paynel Fee*), 5–8, 18–20, 32–3 and pedigree; Bigod, *Complete Peerage*, ix. 580 and note (c); Mowbray, ibid., 367–74; Roumare, ibid., vii. 667–71, and Cazel, 'Norman and Wessex Charters of the Roumare Family', pp. 77–8, 82; Beaumont (the earl of Leicester and the count of Meulan), *Complete Peerage*, vii. 527–30 and xii (2), 829–38, and *V.C.H. Dorset*, iii. 55. Generally, Powicke, *Loss of Normandy*, pp. 328–58.

[3] The rule of primogeniture in England (Pollock and Maitland, *H.E.L.*, ii. 262–74) and the *droit d'aînesse* in Normandy with its rule that fiefs as such were impartible (Génestal, 'Formation du droit d'aînesse'). Presumably a case involving lands in the two countries could only be decided in the highest form of the *curia regis*, that which was held in the presence of the king himself and so common to both.

[4] After the partition of *c.* 1090, the 'Hertford' line of the Clare family apparently had no lands in Normandy until the second earl of Hertford (d. 1173) married Matilda heiress of the lordship of Saint-Hilaire, and his son Richard, the third earl, inherited this and acquired a moiety of the Giffard lands (*Complete Peerage*, vi. 498–501; Ward, 'Estates of the Clare Family', unpublished Ph.D. thesis, London, 1962, pp. 12, 65, 67, and pedigree. I am indebted to Dr. Ward for permission to quote her thesis). Conversely, the Norman branch of the Stuteville family seems to have held no more in England than a relatively small estate in Hampshire until Robert d'Estouteville (whose father d. 1177) married Leonia, daughter of Edward of Salisbury, and his brother also acquired lands across the Channel (*E.Y.C.*, ix (*Stuteville Fee*), 41–54). [5] Matthew, *Norman Monasteries*, p. 72.

[6] But not so exclusively as hitherto (below, p. 115).

The barons and the churchmen, for their part, if they had been called upon to rationalize their natural desire to keep their property and their prospects, would have done so in much the same terms as they would have done in the years 1087–91 or 1100–1. They regarded the civil war as a dispute over the succession to the rule of a single political entity.[1] They acted in what seemed to them to be their best interests within that conception,[2] and they were in fact largely successful in protecting their interests during the time of troubles or recovering them when a settlement had been reached. So far as England and Normandy were concerned, they could regard the reign of Henry fitzEmpress as a continuation of the reign of Henry Beauclerc; and for many it would seem as though nothing fundamental had been changed. That is why the consequences of the French conquest of Normandy would come as such a shock to the Anglo-Norman barons, and to many lesser men, when no settlement between the king of France and the king of England was possible that would allow them to hold lands in both countries.

The material existed likewise for reconstructing the suzerainty which Henry Beauclerc had exercised over neighbouring princes. Stephen had not been able to make effective the lordship over the princes and marcher lords in Wales that he had inherited from Henry, but the Church in Wales remained firmly under the jurisdiction of Canterbury throughout the reign.[3] This in itself had important political implications;[4] and

---

[1] The point is developed below, ch. 6.

[2] For the view that the barons were more concerned to keep what they already possessed than to use the lack of governance as an opportunity to grab more and to create principalities for themselves: King, 'King Stephen and the Anglo-Norman Aristocracy'.

[3] The campaign for making St. David's an archbishopric can be regarded as the ecclesiastical counterpart of the secular Welsh reaction to Norman colonization, but it did not get very far. Bishop Bernard of St. David's, its leader, was succeeded by David fitzGerald (1148) who, though partly Welsh himself, was consecrated by Archbishop Theobald and professed obedience to him 'in the fullest terms'. The same is true of Meurig (1140) of Bangor (who also swore fealty to King Stephen); Uchtryd (1140) and Nicholas (1148) of Llandaff; Gilbert (1143) and Geoffrey (1140) of St. Asaph: Lloyd, *History of Wales*, ii. 447–59, 480–6; Davies, *Episcopal Acts*, i. 64–9, 190–208 and *passim*; Saltman, *Theobald Archbishop of Canterbury*, pp. 92–5, 105–6, 110–14, 119–20.

[4] Above, pp. 65–6. There is a nice analogy in the hold which the king of France endeavoured to maintain over the Breton bishops after he had had to recognize the suzerainty of Henry Beauclerc over Brittany in 1113; Luchaire, *Louis VI le Gros*, pp. cvii–cviii; Durtelle de Saint-Sauveur, *Histoire de Bretagne*, i. 119.

once the marcher lords and the king were no longer at logger-
heads with one another both would be able to recover what
they had lost. The fact that the main result of the Welsh reaction during the first half of the twelfth century was the predominance of Gwynedd in the north and Deheubarth in the
south would make it on the whole easier for Stephen's more
secure successor to obtain the homage of the rulers of such
principalities in return for recognition of their superiorities
over other princes.[1] In Scotland the Church was not subject
to York as the Church in Wales was subject to Canterbury.
With the support of the kings of Scots it was fighting (in the
end successfully) for its identity and its independence; and the
political implications of ecclesiastical obedience or independence
are no less clear in Scotland than in Wales.[2] But there were
families which would wish to retain their possessions on both
sides of the Border,[3] and, when there was a strong king in England there was much to be said for the kind of relationship
which had existed between King David and King Henry, even
from the Scottish king's own point of view. Nationalist sentiments of the nineteenth and twentieth centuries should not be
projected into the twelfth.

Likewise, though Stephen might find it impossible to exercise
the suzerainty over continental principalities that Henry had
established, there were still connections which would ease the
task of Henry fitzEmpress in re-establishing these overlordships
when circumstances were more favourable. Thus whatever interests the earl of Richmond, Alan III, had in Brittany were in
no danger from Geoffrey after he had conquered Normandy.
Alan therefore risked nothing by his steadfast allegiance to
Stephen. In 1145 he retired to Brittany and died there.[4] His son
Conan, though he was a minor at the time of his father's death
and, we must suppose, had been taken to Brittany with him,
seems to have succeeded to the earldom of Richmond before
1154.[5] Through his mother he had a strong claim to the duchy

---

[1] Below, pp. 212-3.

[2] *Concilia Scotiae*, i., pp. xxiv–xl, where the documents are printed or cited. For
a recent account, without references, Dickinson, *Scotland from the Earliest Times to
1603*, ch. 15.

[3] Barrow, *Kingdom of the Scots*, esp. pp. 320-8; cf. Barrow, *Robert Bruce*, pp.
28–30.   [4] *E.Y.C.*, iv (*Honour of Richmond*, i), 89–91.

[5] Ibid., p. 92. In a charter to be dated 1150–4, Archbishop Theobald con-

of Brittany, a claim which King Henry II must have helped him to realize.[1] When the earl of Richmond and the duke of Brittany were one and the same person the king of England was presented with a splendid opportunity to make his domination of the duchy really effective; and Henry took full advantage of that opportunity.[2] Similarly, Geoffrey's personal relationship with the count of Flanders would assist his son, once he was king of England, to re-establish the feudal relationship which Henry Beauclerc had had with earlier counts. In 1163 the money-fief was reinstituted and Philip, the son and heir of Count Thierry d'Alsace, did homage.[3]

Yet, with all these elements of continuity there were great and fundamental changes, such as mark the end of one political structure and the beginning of another. That there should be both continuity and fundamental change need cause no surprise. Much that was characteristic of Anglo-Saxon England was incorporated into the new Norman structure after the Conquest, yet no one would deny that the Norman Conquest brought changes on such a scale that historians, for their purposes, can treat the Anglo-Saxon polity as ending in 1066 and the Norman as beginning at that date—so with the change from Romano-British to Saxon, from Romano-Gaulish to Frankish, from Frankish to Norman, not to mention all the great revolutions in the history of the world of which anything much is known. Each new political structure is built on the

firmed the gift of a rent of 20s. which 'Comes Conanus' had made to the hospital of St. Peter in York (*E.Y.C.*, i, No. 185, pp. 155–6). The fact that Conan is here styled 'comes' is not in itself conclusive evidence that he had already succeeded to the earldom, for members of the ducal family in Brittany were normally given that title (*E.Y.C.*, iv (*Honour of Richmond*), 97–101); but the fact that Conan was contributing a rent, presumably assigned on lands in Yorkshire, to an institution in York, creates a presumption in favour of it.

[1] Conan led the expedition of 1156 which defeated his step-father, Eudo de Porhoët, from England; and as he was by then certainly Henry's vassal for Richmond and his success or failure in Brittany was a matter of such importance to Henry, it is hard to believe that Henry had no hand in it (cf. Robert de Torigni, *Chronica*, p. 190).

[2] De la Borderie, *Histoire de Bretagne*, iii. 269–73, writes very much as a Breton patriot when he describes Henry's seizure of Brittany, and his treatment is virtually reproduced by Durtelle de Saint-Sauveur in *Histoire de Bretagne*, i. 119–21. See also Pocquet du Haut-Jussé, 'Les Plantagenets et la Bretagne', pp. 3–14; *E.Y.C.*, iv (*Honour of Richmond*, i), 30–73, 92–3.

[3] *Diplomatic Documents*, i. 8–12.

ruins of the old, may incorporate a great deal of its fabric, but is
no less a new construction.

To begin with, Henry, though styled 'fitzEmpress' and claiming to be the rightful heir of Henry Beauclerc, was descended
in the direct male line from the counts of Anjou; and therefore,
as family identity was understood in his time, his accession to
the throne of England, like his father's recognition as duke of
Normandy, represented a change of dynasty,[1] and one that
could be brought about only by force. It is true that Stephen
may well have given up hope of establishing a dynasty in England after the death of Eustace in 1153, perhaps even after the
bishops had finally refused to crown him, and the 'Treaty of
Winchester' settled the matter; yet things might very well have
turned out differently if his surviving but younger son William
had been the man his father was in 1135, or if Henry had suc-
cumbed to the forces ranged against him in 1152.[2] There can
be no question but that Geoffrey had had to conquer Normandy; and his son Henry had, in effect, to conquer England.
Henry had made no impression whatever on the country until
he was already duke of Normandy, count *de facto* of Anjou,
Maine, and Touraine, and had married the duchess, in her own
right, of Aquitaine; and though his campaign of 1153 in England has not impressed itself upon historians in the way that
William's campaign of 1066 has done, because the final pitched
battle was prevented by barons anxious to avoid a fight to the
finish,[3] there was nothing to suggest that Stephen would have
agreed to disinherit his son William, with all the other provisions of the 'Treaty of Winchester', if Henry had not shown
his military strength very plainly. Furthermore, whatever precedents and surviving links there were to build on, Henry only
re-established his grandfather's suzerainty over the king of Scots,[4]

---

[1] Le Patourel, 'The Plantagenet Dominions', pp. 290–6; above, p. 87, n. 2.

[2] It may be that ideas of legitimacy and the strength of Henry's claims had
gained more force by 1153 than this remark would seem to imply, or that the support which Henry had won by this time, irrespective of principle, was already very
powerful. But no one can say what a determined resistance might have achieved.
In 1152 opinion in Normandy apparently did not rate Henry's prospects at all
highly (King, 'King Stephen and the Anglo-Norman Aristocracy', p. 184, quoting
Robert de Torigni, *Chronica*, pp. 165–6).

[3] Below, p. 200.

[4] Agreement with King Malcolm IV, 1157 (*Regesta Regum Scottorum*, i. 9–10;
Anderson, *Early Sources*, ii. 235–6; *Scottish Annals*, pp. 239–40, 242).

the Welsh princes,[1] or the duke of Brittany,[2] by force or the threat of it; and it was no doubt the fact that he had already made himself the ruler of England and Normandy, with so much else besides, that persuaded the count of Flanders to re-institute the *conventio* of 1101 and 1110.[3] Henry might claim that he was his grandfather's rightful heir; but he had to re-construct his grandfather's inheritance piece by piece; and as he did so he added it, with his own acquisitions, piece by piece, to the 'empire' which his Angevin ancestors had been building up in and about the Loire Valley. This 'empire' had as its origin and nucleus all that remained at the beginning of the tenth century of the ancient *pagus* of the Andegavi, the lords of which gradually recovered the whole of it, extended their pos-sessions into Aquitaine, took the Touraine from the counts of Blois, Maine from its own counts in the face of strong Norman competition, and ultimately, through the marriage of the heir of the count of Anjou to the heiress of the Norman lands and lordships, secured a claim to the whole of the Norman inheri-tance. With Normandy acquired in 1144, Aquitaine could be added in 1152–3, England in 1153–4, the overlordships in the course of the next few years, and additions made subsequently even to this already enormous assemblage.[4]

What is often known as the 'Angevin Empire' was therefore not a continuation of the Norman complex, but a new construc-tion built partly, but only partly, on its ruins. Family interests, ecclesiastical and other ties between England and Normandy, continued or were restored; perhaps even a notion of political union between the two countries that was proof against dynastic accidents remained;[5] the suzerainties exercised over neighbour-ing princes by the Norman kings were re-established; but all in a different context. The Angevin accumulation of lands and

---

[1] Lloyd, *History of Wales*, ii. 496–500, 505–7; Ralph de Diceto, *Ymagines Histo-riarum*, p. 311.

[2] Above, p. 111, n. 2.   [3] Ibid. and n. 3.

[4] Outline in Le Patourel, 'The Plantagenet Dominions', pp. 290–4; but since that was written a new dimension has been brought into the early development of Anjou by Guillot in his work *Le comte d'Anjou*.

[5] Suggested by the testament of Geoffrey Plantegenêt as reported by William of Newburgh, *Historia*, i. 112–13 (it is reported differently, though not incon-sistently in this respect, by Robert de Torigni, *Chronica*, p. 163), and by the settle-ment of 1169 which gave England and Normandy to the Young Henry (Poole, *Domesday Book to Magna Carta*, pp. 212–13, 329–30).

lordships was far more extensive than the Norman assemblage had ever been. Its political centre of gravity was nearer to the Loire than to the English Channel; and the counts of Anjou, in their expansion, had formed different traditions of government. They had, for example, developed the practice of associating the eldest son in the business of government while his father was still alive, and this might involve a partition within the family in prospect, if not always realized in the event;[1] in contrast to William the Conqueror's obstinate refusal to give his eldest son Robert anything more than a purely nominal part in the government[2] and the Norman kings' efforts to transmit their lands and lordships as an undivided inheritance.[3] Under the Norman kings there was a considerable degree of assimilation between the laws of England and the laws of Normandy, and between the institutions of government in the two countries; under the Angevins there was vastly less 'movement' of custom and institutions between one 'dominion' and another. In part, this was almost a matter of chronology. At the time of the Norman Conquest, neither English law nor Norman law had 'crystallized' sufficiently to preclude assimilation under a common government; but by the middle of the twelfth century customs had been standardized and territorialized sufficiently, through the workings of the courts, for there to be hardly any assimilation as between Angevin and Norman custom after Count Geoffrey's conquest of Normandy, and still less as between these and Henry's other lands after 1154.[4] It was also

---

[1] Fulk le Réchin associated first his eldest son Geoffrey Martel, and then, after Geoffrey's death in 1106, his second son Fulk in the government of his lands, and Fulk succeeded him. Fulk 'le Jeune', as this Fulk was known, associated his son Geoffrey Plantegenêt, possibly at the time of his marriage with Matilda, at all events some little time before he set off for Jerusalem in 1129 (Halphen, *Comté d'Anjou*, pp. 173–5; Chartrou, *L'Anjou*, pp. 1–4, 22–4). Geoffrey's grant of Normandy to his eldest son Henry in 1150 may be regarded as a continuation of this practice, with slightly varied formula; for since, according to William of Newburgh's version of Geoffrey's testament, Henry was only to have the paternal inheritance consisting of Anjou, Maine, and Touraine until he had secured the maternal inheritance of Normandy and England, it would seem that Geoffrey had intended that he and Henry should rule in partnership as long as he lived, Geoffrey in Anjou etc. and Henry in Normandy, and that his lands should be divided between his two elder sons after his death (see preceding note and *Regesta*, iii, pp. xxxii–xxxiii).   [2] Below, pp. 141–2, 181–2; David, *Robert Curthose*, pp. 17 ff.
[3] Below, pp. 179–90.
[4] The 'assimilation' and 'crystallization' of customs is discussed below in ch. 7. It is true that rules of inheritance for feudal tenures were extended from Nor.

a matter of colonization, or the lack of it. There was no Angevin
colonization of Normandy after 1144, or of Aquitaine after
1152, or of England after 1154 that was in any way comparable
with the Norman colonization of England in the eleventh and
early twelfth centuries. There was no general displacement of
landowners in England by men from the *pays* of the Loire after
Henry had made himself king in succession to Stephen. Frenchmen were indeed appointed to English bishoprics and some important abbacies after 1154; but they no longer had the virtual
monopoly of such offices that they had enjoyed before 1135,[1]
and 'Englishmen' could now be appointed to continental
bishoprics.[2] The traffic was no longer in one direction only, but
flowed in both directions and at a much lower density—the
kind of interchange of personnel that would naturally be expected as between lands that were associated as the Angevin
lands were associated after 1154. A comparison between the
Angevin conquest of the Touraine in the early eleventh century,
where there was both some degree of aristocratic colonization
and some degree of assimilation of custom,[3] with the Angevin
conquest of Normandy just a hundred years later, when there
was hardly any of either, illustrates the point.

Whereas, therefore, the itinerant Norman kings, with their
household and court, tended to assimilate the customs and
institutions of the countries they governed, bringing those

mandy into Brittany by the 'assise au conte Geoffroy' (*Très Ancienne Coutume de
Bretagne*, ed. Planiol, pp. 319–25; cf. Pocquet du Haut-Jussé, 'Les Plantagenets et
la Bretagne', p. 21) and also into Aquitaine (Poumarède, *Les Successions dans le
sud-ouest de la France*, pp. 69–72 etc.), that certain institutions introduced into
Aquitaine (Renouard, 'Essai sur le rôle de l'empire angevin') and into Brittany
(Pocquet du Haut-Jussé, ubi supra, pp. 21–2) seem to bear a family resemblance to
their counterparts in Normandy etc., and that the Angevin kings could, very
occasionally, legislate for all their lands together (below p. 275). None the less, it
was under their rule that a clear conception of a law of England, a *coutume* of
Normandy, a *coutume* of Anjou, of Brittany, of Poitou, etc. developed, and also a
firm rule that each land should be governed according to its own laws and
customs.

[1] *Heads of Religious Houses*, pp. 2–3.
[2] e.g. John of Salisbury (bishop of Chartres, 1176–80) and John of Canterbury
or 'aux Bellesmains' (bishop of Poitiers, 1162–81, archbishop of Lyon, 1181–93):
D.N.B., s.vv. 'John of Salisbury', 'Belmeis or Belesmains, John'; Webb, *John of
Salisbury*, pp. 1–21 etc.; Clay, 'Early Treasurers of York', pp. 11–16.
[3] Boussard, 'L'Éviction des tenants de Thibaut de Blois par Geoffroy Martel';
Yver, 'Les caractères originaux du groupe de coutumes de l'ouest de la France',
pp. 4–9.

countries into more integral union, the Angevins moved among more self-sufficient 'provincial' administrations and governed each according to its own native laws and customs. Count Geoffrey is indeed said to have advised his son not to attempt to transfer custom from one land to another, and he certainly set an example in his government of Normandy from 1144 to 1150.[1] There was a purely practical consideration that contributed to this difference. Henry Beauclerc had only to divide his time between Normandy and England, with occasional incursions into Wales; Henry fitzEmpress had to distribute his time between Aquitaine, Anjou with its annexes, Normandy, and England, with incursions into Brittany, Wales, and Ireland. Under the later conditions, if the king wished to keep some personal control over the affairs of each of his lands and was not prepared to entrust any of them fully to a relative or vassal, it was clearly necessary that each country should have the means to look after itself to a very much greater extent; hence the development of the vice-regal seneschals in Anjou, Normandy, Aquitaine and Brittany, and the vice-regal justiciar in England and later in Ireland (officials whose origins lay as much in the continental lands as in England), together with the further growth of delegated jurisdiction and financial administration in all these lands under the direction of seneschal or justiciar.[2] Moreover, though William the Conqueror and Henry Beauclerc, while king, had not done homage to the king of France, Geoffrey did so in 1144 when he had substantially completed his conquest of Normandy, and his son Henry fitzEmpress likewise shortly after he became duke; and even after he had become king he was prepared to do homage for all his continental lands.[3]

For all the elements of continuity that may be discerned, therefore, elements of continuity which certainly have their place in later political constructions, the war of succession between Stephen on the one hand and Geoffrey Plantegenêt, Matilda, and their son Henry on the other, marks a real break. For the purposes of dividing the past into the subjects and periods without which it is unintelligible to mortals, the Norman

[1] Below, pp. 275–6.
[2] Le Patourel, 'The Plantagenet Dominions', pp. 296–8.
[3] Below, p. 220.

'empire'[1] and the greater Angevin 'empire' are distinct historical units. The one had come to an end by 1145; and the other, though constructed in part on the ruins of the first, had a different origin, grew into a far larger structure, was held together on rather different principles, and was ruled by a different dynasty.

[1] The argument for the use of this term is set out below, ch. 9.

PART II

ANALYSIS

5. The Practical Problems of Government

WHEN William the Conqueror took possession of the kingdom of the English he had been duke of Normandy effectively for almost twenty years, in name for thirty-one. It would not occur to him that his new acquisition might make it necessary for him to give up his powers and responsibilities as duke in his home country any more than his earlier conquest of the neighbouring *comté* of Maine had done. He had simply added a great new source of wealth and power to those he possessed already, not exchanged one position for another. Therefore, from the moment of his coronation in Westminster Abbey on Christmas Day 1066 until his death in a suburb of his city of Rouen in September 1087 he had to provide for the government and the exploitation of the two countries, Normandy and England, as well as to maintain the other lordships that he had been building up. The same was true of his son and successor, William Rufus, from the autumn of 1096 when he took possession of Normandy as security for the loan he had just made to the duke, his brother Robert Curthose, until his death in the New Forest in August 1100; and it was true also of Henry Beauclerc from the time when he took possession of Normandy after the battle of Tinchebrai (September 1106) until his death at Lyons-la-Forêt in December 1135, and of Stephen of Blois from his accession in December 1135–January 1136 until the moment, some time between February 1141 and the summer of 1145, when he must have realized that he no longer had any effective power or authority in the duchy even though he may not have given up all hope of recovering the position he had lost.[1] If, therefore, we reckon the years between the end of 1066 and the early months of 1144, that is from the coronation of William the Conqueror to the assumption of the ducal title by Geoffrey of Anjou, England and Normandy were ruled together by one man for all but 15 out of the 77; and even during those 15 years

[1] Above, pp. 95, 106 n. 1.

the two rulers were brothers, William Rufus and Robert Curthose from 1087 to 1096 and Henry Beauclerc and Robert
Curthose from 1100 until 1106, each trying to oust the other
and to reunite his father's inheritance in his own hands.[1]
Whatever ideas these rulers or their advisers may have had
about the nature of royal and ducal authority, and whatever
intentions or policies they may have pursued in the maintenance
and the expansion of their interests beyond kingdom and
duchy, they were faced as a matter of fact with the problem of
ruling the peoples of two lands which were separated geographically by the English Channel, and of preserving and if
possible extending the superiorities which William the Conqueror had established over rulers and their vassals beyond
Normandy and England. It is best to try to discover how
William and his successors dealt with this problem in practice
before discussing how they may have rationalized their actions
and how they looked upon this vast complex of assets and responsibilities—whether they regarded it as forming an integral
unity in any sense, and, if a unity, what kind of a unity it could
have been.

Their task was to establish and maintain a degree of authority
over widely dispersed peoples of differing languages, having different customs, and still in different stages of political development, and over a very considerable extent of territory, from
the Lowlands of Scotland to the marches of Normandy and
Maine, from Wales and Brittany to the vulnerable Seine Valley
and the approaches to Flanders. In the eleventh century there
was more than one way in which this could be done. After his
conquest of England, Cnut had attempted to govern Denmark
through a viceroy acting as guardian of his son Harthacnut,
and later by making Harthacnut king of Denmark under his
own overriding authority. When he eventually brought Norway
to submission, he at first gave the viceroyalty to a native earl,
and then sent his son Svein to rule the country under the
guardianship of Svein's mother Ælfgifu of Northampton.[2]
William the Conqueror may have thought of something similar
for the conquered *comté* of Maine when he gave the title of count

---

[1] The situation during these periods of fraternal rule is discussed below, ch. 6;
and Henry's determination, quite early in his life, to reunite his father's inheritance
in his own hands in ch. 9.   [2] Stenton, *A.-S.E.*, pp. 393–400.

to his young son Robert Curthose;[1] but if he did so the idea was never given any substance. In England the West-Saxon kings were still so far from integrating the conquered kingdom of Northumbria into their dominion that the earls, at least under Edward the Confessor, who hardly ventured beyond the ancient kingdom of Wessex while he was king, might reasonably be described as regional viceroys.[2] With these precedents to hand it could well have crossed William's mind at some point, after the battle of Hastings or before, that he might settle in England, like Cnut, and govern Normandy through one of his sons or some great baron whom he could trust, or stay at home, like Edward the Confessor, and set up a viceroyalty of some kind in England.

Instead, he met the problem in quite a different way. There are even indications that he consciously rejected the idea of viceroyalty. The great earldoms of pre-Conquest England, so far as they may be regarded as viceroyalties, were allowed to lapse and something quite different put in their place; moreover, there is nothing to suggest that Robert Curthose was ever more than nominally count of Maine even after he had come of age, and he was denied any effective authority in Normandy during his father's lifetime.[3] Before 1066 the Norman dukes had not attempted to rule their duchy from a fixed seat of government. Although the evidence does not enable us to follow them in their movements, it is quite clear from the few charters which state the place at which they were given and from the evidence of the chronicles that the dukes and such governmental organization as they had (other than purely local institutions) were itinerant.[4] After 1066 it is equally clear that the Norman kings continued this life of movement, though the much ampler documentation of the time still does not enable us

[1] David, *Robert Curthose*, pp. 7–14.
[2] Whitelock, 'Dealings of the Kings of England with Northumbria', pp. 76–88; Barlow, *Edward the Confessor*, pp. 168–9; Stenton, *A.-S.E.*, pp. 539–40.
[3] Below, p. 141.
[4] Ducal charters before 1066 were dated at Argentel, Bayeux, Bonneville-sur-Touques (3), Brionne, Caen, Courdemanche, Domfront, Fécamp (3), La Hougue (2), Le Bec, Rouen (9), Saint-Léger de Préaux, Senlis, Troarn, Vitry-aux-Loges (Fauroux, *Recueil*, *passim*), but only 28 of the 142 charters in this collection have a place-date. There is some indication that Fécamp and Rouen had a special place in the ducal itinerary (Musset, 'Gouvernés et Gouvernants', p. 463; Fauroux, *Recueil*, p. 65), but as favoured residences rather than as seats of government in the modern sense.

to plot their itinerary in any detail. The post-Conquest charters and chronicles do, however, provide a good deal of information of a general kind about their movements, and, supplemented with a little imagination perhaps, give some idea how their government worked. For this purpose the years from 1106 to 1135, when Henry Beauclerc was firmly established in England and Normandy, are particularly instructive.

During these years Henry divided his time, as between Normandy and England, in the proportion of nearly five to three,[1] visiting England eight times.[2] Nine whole years, each from January to December, were spent in Normandy, four wholly in England.[3] He made two expeditions into Wales;[4] otherwise his lordship over neighbouring principalities was maintained by other means.[5] It is on the whole rather more difficult to follow Henry's movements while he was in Normandy than while he was in England;[6] but it is at least clear that during those years he visited almost every corner of his duchy at some point, from Barfleur and Dieppe to Verneuil and Alençon, from Gisors to Falaise. The kingdom was similarly treated; although the greater part of the time he spent in England as king was passed in the territory bounded by a line drawn from London to Portsmouth, then by Salisbury, Bath, Gloucester, Northampton to Huntingdon and back to London. There seems to be only one certain occasion when he was seen north of York.[7]

There is one half-year in which we can obtain some impression of his movements in rather greater detail, that is during the months from Christmas 1122 until the middle of June 1123.

'The king spent Christmas [1122] at Dunstable, and from thence went to Berkhampsted ... From thence the king went to Woodstock, a remarkable place where the king had provided for men and beasts

---

[1] Approximately 210 months in Normandy, 140 in England. On this paragraph generally, see the *Table of Transfretations* at the end of this chapter, and below, pp. 330–1.

[2] 1107–8, 1109–11, 1113–14, 1115–16, 1120–3, 1126–7, 1129–30, 1131–3.

[3] 1112, 1117, 1118, 1119, 1124, 1125, 1128, 1134, and 1135 in Normandy; 1110, 1121, 1122, 1132 in England.

[4] In 1114 and 1121.

[5] Below, pp. 159–63.

[6] Nothing comparable to the Anglo-Saxon Chronicle and the chronicles related to it has survived from ducal Normandy.

[7] Farrer, 'Outline Itinerary of King Henry I'; *Regesta*, ii, pp. xxix–xxxi; Map 1.

to live together . . .'[1] 'Then, soon after, the king . . . ordered his bishops and abbots and thegns all to come and meet him for his council meeting on Candlemas Day [2 February 1123] at Gloucester, and they did so . . . The king gave the bishopric of Bath to the queen's chancellor . . . This took place at Woodstock on the day of the Annunciation of St. Mary [25 March]. Then soon after that the king went to Winchester and was there all Eastertide [Easter Day, 15 April] . . . Then the king went from there to Portsmouth and stayed there all over Whitsun week [3–10 June]. Then as soon as he had a wind he went over to Normandy.'[2]

The repeated use of the phrases 'Then the king . . .' and 'From thence . . .' suggest that these are consecutive movements, or at least that the chroniclers have mentioned the principal stopping-places by name.

These quotations indicate the scale and the pace of the king's movement and suggest that it is worth investigating further. There seems to have been no single or simple reason for it. In part it was tradition, in part necessity, in part policy. One of the traditional elements amounted almost to ritual. The Anglo-Saxon Chronicle[3] and William of Malmesbury[4] both say that William the Conqueror was accustomed to spend Christmas at Gloucester, Easter at Winchester, and Whitsun at Westminster whenever he was in England; and there, in a great assembly of bishops and magnates with visitors from abroad, he wore his crown in great solemnity, the *Laudes* were sung in his presence and all the supernatural element in his authority reaffirmed.[5] Malmesbury adds that Rufus continued the practice; and there is just enough evidence of actual assemblies to confirm that such a programme could have been regarded as normal between 1066 and 1100. Malmesbury also says that Henry abandoned these ceremonies. At the beginning of his reign Henry had given an order that the convents of Westminster, Winchester, and Gloucester should have their full allowance at all feasts when he wore his crown in their churches, as they had been accustomed to do;[6] and for the first ten years

---

[1] Huntingdon, *Historia Anglorum*, p. 244; A.-S.C., 1123, E (p. 188).
[2] A.-S.C., 1123, E (pp. 188–90). [3] A.-S.C., 1087, E (p. 164).
[4] Malmesbury, *Gesta Regum*, ii. 335.
[5] Douglas, *William the Conqueror*, pp. 249–50.
[6] *Regesta*, ii, No. 490 (p. 2); Richardson and Sayles, *Governance of Medieval England*, p. 217, note 2.

of his rule in England he did at least celebrate the principal feasts at some great ecclesiastical centre even if the routine was varied somewhat. After that it can only be said that he spent some of the great feasts at ecclesiastical centres; others might be spent at places like Brampton or Woodstock where hunting was probably the chief activity of the court.[1] What Malmesbury probably meant was that Henry gave up the regular crown-wearings during the course of his reign, though he certainly did not abandon the practice altogether. No such regularity can be traced in Normandy. There may have been a tradition that the court would be at Fécamp for Easter[2] and Henry is known to have spent Christmas on one occasion at Bayeux.[3] There is some evidence that the king wore his crown when he was in the duchy; and a form of the *Laudes* was sung before him there.[4]

Ecclesiastical affairs in a stricter sense also took the king from place to place. He sometimes attended the dedication-ceremonies of important churches as, for example, the Conqueror attended the dedication of Bayeux Cathedral in 1077,[5] Rufus that of Battle in 1094,[6] and Henry those of St. Albans in 1116, Séez in 1126, and both Canterbury and Rochester in 1130.[7] Whoever decided where ecclesiastical synods were to be held, William and his sons were directly concerned. If Henry did not always preside over them in person as his father had done, he maintained the same watchful control. While the archbishop of Canterbury held a synod at Westminster in 1127 the king stayed in London, kept himself informed of the proceedings and confirmed the decrees.[8] Similarly, the Norman kings kept a tight hold upon elections to bishoprics and to the principal abbacies. Generally speaking, appointments were made or sanctioned by Henry while he was in the country in which the office would be held; though in 1125 he appointed bishops

---

[1] For Henry's later practice in this respect, A.-S.C., 1111 (p. 182), 1114 (p. 183), 1116 (p. 185), 1121 (p. 187), 1122 (ibid.), 1123 (p. 188), 1127 (p. 192)—all MS. E.

[2] e.g. Musset, 'Gouvernés et gouvernants', p. 463; below, ch. 7, p. 237 n. 1.

[3] *Regesta*, ii, No. 1212 (p. 148).   [4] Below, pp. 239–41.

[5] *Regesta*, i, p. xxii, No. 98 (p. 26).   [6] A.-S.C., 1094, E (p. 171).

[7] A.-S.C., 1116, E (p. 185); 1130 E (p. 196); Huntingdon, *Historia Anglorum*, p. 252; Orderic Vitalis, *H.E.* (ed. Le Prévost), iv. 471.

[8] Douglas, *William the Conqueror*, pp. 331–5; Florence of Worcester, *Chronicon*, ii. 85–8. Cf. below, pp. 247–8.

to Worcester and Chichester while he and the elect were in Normandy.[1]

Walter Map, writing half a century later, praised Henry for his accessibility to his subjects and the firm control he exercised over his barons and his officers; and he associated these virtues of his rule with the careful planning of his itinerary by which it could be known, so he said, just where the king and court would be at any particular moment and how long they would be there.[2] However accessible Henry may or may not have been to the humble and the oppressed, it must undoubtedly have been convenient to barons, prelates, and ecclesiastical communities, or their influential advocates and their messengers, not only to know just where the king was to be found but to be able to approach him in their own country without too much delay. The occasion of a royal visit, if it did not happen very often, would certainly be seized upon by a monastery to secure the confirmation of their title-deeds or some extension of their possessions and liberties, as the monks of Saint-Évroult did when Henry stayed at the monastery for a day or two in 1113. Even then, Henry could only give orders that a document should be prepared while he was at Saint-Évroult, though he was no doubt paying for his board and lodging in this way; the draft had to be taken to him at Rouen where the charter embodying the confirmation of the monks' possessions was dated.[3] Few ecclesiastical bodies, however, would wait for an occasion like this unless the king was upon them fairly regularly, as would be the case with the monks of Westminster or Winchester or the canons of Rouen; and, however they were secured, charters could in fact be issued at almost any distance from the beneficiary in the course of the royal itinerary—a charter for the cathedral-priory of Durham, for instance, is dated at Lyons-la-Forêt[4] and charters for the hospital of Saint-Jean-de-Falaise are dated at Clarendon and Winchester.[5] Thus, while the

---

[1] Florence of Worcester, *Chronicon*, ii. 79.

[2] Walter Map, *De Nugis Curialium*, pp. 219–20, 234–6; *Translation*, pp. 242, 258–9.

[3] Orderic Vitalis, *H.E.* (ed. Le Prévost), iv. 301–3; v. 196–9; *Regesta*, ii, No. 1019 (p. 108).

[4] *Regesta*, ii, No. 1586 (pp. 226–7); Chaplais, 'Seals and Original Charters of Henry I', p. 266.

[5] *Regesta*, ii, Nos. 1742, 1764 (pp. 258, 263); Chaplais, ubi supra, p. 267.

majority of surviving charters for English beneficiaries are certainly dated at some place in England, and correspondingly in Normandy for Norman beneficiaries, suggesting that it was generally convenient to approach the king while he was reasonably near at hand and to secure the document before he crossed the sea, this was not formally necessary.

Walter Map connected Henry's control of his barons and officers with the regularity of his movements.[1] In an age when communications were such that local officers had necessarily to be given a good deal of freedom and private castles were increasing in number, it would have been difficult to keep a continuous hold upon them, and upon barons or prelates who had liberties which amounted to powers of local government, if the king had never come into their regions. Certainly he could summon them to his court and, in case of disobedience, confiscate their possessions; but such action might well lead to just the kind of disorder that he would wish to avoid.[2] On more strictly political matters, an interview with the king of France would take Henry to the immediate vicinity of Gisors, for it had become a point of diplomatic protocol that the two kings should meet, when they did meet, at that point on the frontier between their lands, and the king would still be involved personally in a diplomatic move of any consequence. Gisors was also the natural place at which to meet Pope Calixtus II in 1119 when the pope had been holding a council at Reims.[3] Yet, with such knowledge as we have, it is often impossible to say just why the king should be at a particular place at a particular time. Why, for instance, should Henry have summoned a great assembly to Gloucester in 1123 when both the monastery and the borough had been burnt less than a year before?[4] The main business on this occasion seems to have been the Canterbury election; and as some were anxious that the new archbishop should not be a monk[5] it may have seemed advisable to hold the council at a distance from the cathedral-monastery; but there were many places in England that would have satisfied

---

[1] Walter Map, *De Nugis Curialium*, pp. 235–6; *Translation*, pp. 258–9.
[2] As when Henry had to discipline Robert de Bellême in 1102.
[3] Lemarignier, *Hommage en marche*, p. 91.
[4] A.-S.C., 1122, 1123, E (pp. 187–9).
[5] Bethell, 'English Black Monks and episcopal elections', pp. 673–4 and *passim*.

that condition more conveniently, it might be thought, than burnt-out Gloucester.[1]

There must also have been some relationship between the king's itinerary and the problem of supplying the household and the court with food, fodder, and accommodation. The survival in Domesday of a payment called the 'farm of one night' or 'of one day'[2] suggests that there had been a time when the king and his entourage relied upon the products of the royal estates, moving simply from one to another, or one group to another, at any rate in the ancient kingdom of Wessex. In Henry's reign this time must have been long in the past; but though it is clear that supplies were brought to the household from wherever they could be obtained,[3] a great deal must have been purchased locally wherever the king might be and some even taken directly from the produce of such royal estates as lay conveniently at hand.[4] Whatever the proportion may have been between these different sources, however, the presence of the court must have affected local stocks—and prices—very greatly. Walter Map says that there was never any lack of food or other supplies in Henry's court, and he attributed this again to the detailed planning of Henry's itinerary which made it possible for merchants to congregate wherever the court might be.[5] According to Eadmer and William of Malmesbury, Henry also

[1] The extent of the disaster may well have been exaggerated as such reports often were, and timber buildings could presumably be replaced relatively quickly. All the same it is interesting, to say the least, that the place could be got ready for a royal visit in less than a year.

[2] Round, *Feudal England*, pp. 109–15; Poole, *Exchequer in the Twelfth Century*, pp. 26–30; Stenton, *A.-S.E.*, pp. 474–6; *V.C.H. Dorset*, iii. 27–30; *V.C.H. Wiltshire*, ii. 61–2.

[3] In the *Pipe Roll of 31 Henry I*, the sheriffs of London are recorded as claiming allowance for herring, grease (?), oil, and nuts and their transport to Woodstock, for the purchase and transport of wine and the purchase of pepper, cummin, ginger, and of towels, basins, and wine-vessels for the king's use (p. 144; cf. Farrer, 'Outline Itinerary of King Henry I', p. 555). The king was at Woodstock early in the year 1130.

[4] In the same pipe roll, the sheriff of Oxford is recorded as claiming allowance for the loss of farm in respect of the multure of a mill which the king's bakers had kept fully employed for 80 days, and also for mowing the king's meadow and carrying the hay to Stonesfield and Woodstock (*Pipe Roll 31 Henry I*, p. 1; Farrer, ubi supra). The demesne lands were widely distributed both in England and in Normandy (e.g. Corbett, 'Development of the Duchy of Normandy and the Norman Conquest of England', pp. 508–9; Delisle, 'Revenus publics', *B.É.C.*, xi. 401–10 etc.).

[5] Walter Map, *De Nugis Curialium*, ubi supra.

restrained the officers of his household from misusing his right of purveyance, so that the effect of the court upon the countryside through which it passed would not amount to devastation as it is said to have done when William Rufus was king.[1] Even so, with all the planning and the restraint imaginable, it would clearly put an intolerable strain upon any community if the king, his household, and his court settled in its midst for any length of time.

One obviously unplannable reason for movement was the need to meet rebellion or foreign invasion or the threat of them. Baronial rebellion took Henry to Tickhill and Bridgnorth in 1102,[2] and he was very much concerned with it while he was in Normandy from 1123 to 1126 when the record of his movement as we have it is largely a progress from one siege to another.[3] Invasion of Normandy by the king of France and the count of Anjou in the interests of William Clito (who was also supported by a number of barons in Normandy) took Henry to the duchy in 1111 and 1116 and kept him there for some time on both occasions. But while William of Malmesbury duly notes that Normandy was the country in which Henry chiefly resided and that it was the principal cause of his wars,[4] the periods of his residence in the duchy were not all occasioned by war or the threat of it. He may have thought it wise to be in Normandy at the time of the accession of King Louis VI in 1108; but he must have made his decision to cross the Channel, and may even have made the crossing itself, before King Philip died; and though there was some trouble in the Vexin while he was there this can hardly have been the reason for this stay in the duchy.[5] Conditions were generally peaceful when he was in Normandy in 1114–15 and in 1133–5. On the latter occasion his difficulties with his son-in-law must have occupied him a good deal, it is true, and William Talvas had to be disciplined; but these difficulties did not involve him in open war. In any case, if he should be regarded as being 'based' in Normandy, on the ground that he gave rather more of his time and attention to the duchy than to the kingdom after 1106, his visits to

---

[1] Eadmer, *Historia Novorum*, pp. 192–3; Malmesbury, *Gesta Regum*, ii. 487; cf. A.-S.C., 1097, E (p. 175).   [2] e.g. Ramsay, *Foundations*, ii. 240–3.
[3] Ibid., pp. 299–302.   [4] Malmesbury, *Gesta Regum*, ii. 487–8.
[5] A.-S.C., 1108, E (p. 181) seems to exaggerate the trouble. Cf. Lemarignier, *Hommage en marche*, p. 44.

England could not normally have been made specifically to meet trouble there; for the country was unusually calm during his reign and faced no serious threat from outside. Henry's two expeditions into Wales seem to have been decided upon and organized in England and did not involve him in a Channel crossing for the purpose;[1] though in 1135, just before he died, he is said to have tried repeatedly to return to England when the Welsh were causing him anxiety.[2] No expedition into Scotland was called for during his reign. One military consideration which could have influenced his itinerary constantly was his preoccupation with his castles. Robert de Torigni describes Henry as a great castle-builder in Normandy and, although his personal involvement across the Channel is not so well recorded, he seems to have done almost as much in England.[3] During his one recorded visit to the far north in 1122 he gave orders for additional military works at Carlisle;[4] and it may well be that one reason for this extension of his normal itinerary was precisely to inspect the Border fortifications.

The king, however, was human. He could not work all the time and he certainly did not try to do so. For recreation he had his hunting-lodges. His devotion to the chase would explain his frequent and often lengthy visits to places like Woodstock or Brampton in England;[5] while in Normandy the reasons that so often took him to his castles at Argentan, Lyons-la-Forêt, or Rouen must have included their proximity to ducal forests.[6] Yet the king was perhaps never completely off duty. He was accompanied even on such occasions by bishops and barons and household officers, and the affairs of his dominions would

---

[1] The expedition of 1114 was mounted nearly a year after Henry's crossing from Normandy in July 1113 and just before he returned to the duchy again; that of 1121 took place in June and he had been in England since the previous November.

[2] Orderic Vitalis, *H.E.* (ed. Le Prévost), v. 45–7.

[3] William de Jumièges, *Gesta*, pp. 309–10 (interp. Robert de Torigni); Robert de Torigni, *Chronica*, pp. 106–7, 126; Brown, Colvin, and Taylor, *King's Works*, i. 34–40.   [4] Ibid., ii. 595.   [5] Ibid., ii. 901–2, 1009–1010.

[6] e.g. Orderic Vitalis, *H.E.* (ed. Le Prévost), v. 49. For an indication of the extent and location of the royal forests in England, see the maps in Bazeley, 'Extent of the English Forest in the Thirteenth Century', facing pp. 140 and 160 and the list on pp. 160–3. Cf. for the north, Holt, *The Northerners*, map at end; and for a study of the English forests specifically in the time of Henry Beauclerc, Cronne, 'The Royal Forest in the Reign of Henry I'. In Normandy, Delisle, 'Revenus publics', *B.É.C.*, xi. 437–51; Strayer, *Administration of Normandy under Saint Louis*, pp. 69–70 and references there given.

not always respect office hours. Indeed, our knowledge of the times he spent in his hunting-lodges comes mostly from the record of governmental business that was done while he was there.

Even such a superficial analysis of his itinerary seems to show, therefore, that the king moved about his kingdom and his duchy and further afield not because he had to do so in order to keep his household and court supplied with necessities, or not primarily so, nor even because government from a fixed capital was impracticable. It was a mode of governing, a way of maintaining his authority as far as it could be made to extend and exploiting the wealth that went with it, as an alternative to government by viceroys. Regents[1] of a kind he had to have; but they were no more than supplementary to his itineration. Rather than an anxious debate on the problem of ruling kingdom and duchy together, it is perhaps more likely that it never occurred to William the Conqueror that his conquest of England would oblige him to change his mode of government. All he had to do was to extend his itinerary to take in his conquest. William Rufus and Henry did the same when they took possession of Normandy in 1096 and 1106 respectively. The very flexibility of this manner of ruling was its strength; and it was the more effective because, at this stage in the growth of governmental institutions in the West, most of what we should now classify as the 'central government' of the Norman kings itinerated with them.

The first and by far the most important component of their 'central government' was the king himself, and his personal character counted for more than any other single political fact in all his dominions. The relative effectiveness of a Henry Beauclerc and a Robert Curthose shows this at once. But he could not govern alone and he did not travel alone. A part of the company that moved round with him was formed by a body known as his household.[2] It is very difficult to define as an institution. Clearly the king, like any important person, had

---

[1] The terms 'regent' and 'viceroy' are used in this chapter in their dictionary sense, viz. regent, 'one appointed to administer a kingdom during the minority, absence, or incapacity of the sovereign'; viceroy, 'one who acts as the governor of a country, province, etc. in the name and by the authority of the supreme ruler' (*Shorter Oxford English Dictionary*).

[2] For what follows on the household, the fundamental text is the 'Constitutio Domus Regis' (most convenient edition in *Dialogus*, pp. 128–35), and for general commentary, White, 'Household of the Norman Kings'.

to have an elaborate domestic service, a number of cooks, butlers, larderers, chamberlains, and, since he was so often on the move, constables to look after the horses, a bearer of the king's bed, a tent-keeper, carters, sumpter-men, bakers to go ahead and prepare for the king's coming, marshals to find lodgings and so on. Some at least of the men so described must have been always and continually with the king, itinerating with him and ministering to his personal needs; but among them there were already groups which, though domestic in origin and still essentially domestic in character, were developing into embryonic departments of state with important governmental functions. The king had a seal and a chancellor to look after it. This seal must always have been kept near him for it authenticated his mandates and grants wherever he might be when they were issued and whichever of his lands they might concern. There was no question of a seal for England and a seal for Normandy. The chancellor had a keeper of the seal (or master of the writing office) under him and a body of clerks, the whole forming the beginnings of a chancery, the king's secretariat, but still a part of his domestic household.[1] Likewise, since such money and valuables as the king carried about with him were looked after by his chamberlains in his chamber, this formed another embryonic department with more than a purely domestic significance; for money was often paid directly to the king and constantly had to be spent by him and his household, and such transactions could have considerable administrative and even political importance.[2] The constables and

[1] On the proto-chancery of the Norman kings, *Regesta*, i, pp. xvi–xxi; ii, pp. ix–xi and below, ch. 7, pp. 232–3, 243–5.

[2] White, in 'Financial Administration under Henry I', speaks of the *camera curie*, after the treasury organization had hived off, as dealing with 'what may be called the Privy Purse expenses and those of the Household' (p. 57); but Richardson and Sayles (*Governance of Medieval England*, p. 228 and ch. xii) show that the chamber was 'the great spending department' and the 'real centre of financial control' in the later twelfth century, and Tout thought that Henry II's chamber was essentially the same as that of his grandfather (*Chapters*, i. 100). It is clear that even when the exchequers had been fully established, much of the royal financial business did not pass through them, and so was not recorded on their rolls (for England, Tout, *Chapters*, i. 83–6; for Normandy, Delisle, 'Revenus publics', *B.É.C.*, x. 277–8); and if that was so then, the business of the chamber must have been even more comprehensive before the exchequers were developed. Haskins (*Norman Institutions*, p. 41) specifies the revenues that do not figure on the Norman exchequer rolls.

marshals were primarily concerned with the king's horses and his hunting and in keeping some order among the vast concourse of people that formed the court. It would seem natural to look to them for commanders of the armies that were raised from time to time; but their part in the military organization during the twelfth century is hard to define.[1]

In Henry's time and before, however, there were a number of men who bore the titles of household offices but who cannot have been with the king all the time, perhaps not even much of the time. The 'Constitutio Domus Regis',[2] the document which provides most of the information we have concerning the household of the Norman kings, seems to distinguish between those members who took all their meals with the household, and who were therefore presumably always 'in attendance', and those who spent part of the time 'eating out', away from the household. It is perfectly understandable that some larderers and marshals should be out and about from time to time in the course of their purely domestic duties: it is not so easy to see immediately why this should also apply to some stewards and chamberlains. The fundamental reason seems to be that the Norman kings, and the Norman dukes certainly before them, liked to have men 'of their own class' to serve them,[3] and that such men were glad to attend their sovereign at least from time to time and certainly on great ceremonial occasions. Consequently men who were great barons, men whom the king might employ as justices and military leaders, were often also stewards, chamberlains, butlers, or constables. To such men their household office might well be, and certainly soon became, no more than a title of honour, attached eventually to no function beyond some symbolic service at a coronation. In Henry's time and before there could well be more than one man holding

---

[1] The higher commands in the army seem to have been filled by important personages *ad hoc*, and many subordinate commanders seem to have been barons leading their tenants (Hollister, *Military Organization of Norman England*, pp. 86–9). The household constables are not to be confused with the constables of castles; and eminent men may well have accepted the office of constable in the household without expecting thereby to undertake any active function beyond the household.

[2] *Dialogus*, pp. 128–35.

[3] Round, *King's Serjeants*, pp. 5–9. Cf. Barlow, *Edward the Confessor*, pp. 165–6. In Normandy before 1066 men like William fitzOsbern and Ralph de Tancarville had held household offices.

these offices at any one time; and there would be others, bearing the same title and not always easy to distinguish from them, who were performing the more properly domestic work appropriate to the office. The great men holding positions in the household still attended the king from time to time, for their presence is attested as witnesses to royal charters. To this extent they were still part of the itinerant household. At other times they would be doing the king's work in England or in Normandy or attending to their own affairs. Such men were Aubrey de Vere, sheriff and justice in England and chamberlain; Henry de la Pommeraye, baron of the exchequer in Normandy and constable; Geoffrey of Clinton, who was steward, justice, and baron of the exchequer acting in both countries—all in Henry's time and all lords of great estates which would certainly demand some of their time and attention.[1]

The household, therefore, both in its domestic and in this larger sense, formed a considerable part of the king's administration in itself. The position in the early twelfth century seems to have been the result of two complementary processes, one by which domestic members of a ruler's household were sent out to do his work elsewhere and one by which men who were of importance in the country at large were drawn into the household organization. It is true that the men who were justices and auditors and barons as well as being chamberlains and stewards and constables can only have been members of the household in a certain sense; nevertheless, it is likely that their membership of the household, however nominal it might be, was looked upon by them as a source of honour and a means of advancement and by the king as one useful method of holding his administration together. For the household was still his household, personal to him. There could not be an 'English' household or a 'Norman' household when one member of the royal family ruled over both countries, only a king's household;[2]

---

[1] For biographical notes and references, Le Patourel, *Normandy and England*, pp. 30–2.

[2] The unity of the king's household, when one man ruled over both kingdom and duchy, is affirmed by White in 'Household of the Norman Kings', pp. 127–8; though some remarks of his in *Complete Peerage*, x, Appendix F, seem curiously inconsistent. The fact that the lands, or the principal lands, of a baron holding household office could be in one country or the other might tend to bring him to court more frequently when the king was in the country where those lands lay; but it is very doubtful if there was any such office, for example, as 'chamberlain

and that household existed to serve the king, not England or Normandy in any direct sense. The household of William the Conqueror after 1066 was a direct continuation of his household in Normandy before the Conquest. We cannot imagine him dismissing his servants on the morrow of Hastings and finding a new lot, or leaving his ducal household in Normandy to perpetuate itself there and providing himself with a second household for England; and there is nothing to indicate that he did either. On the contrary, a sufficient number of men are recorded as serving William both as duke and as king to demonstrate this continuity, notably William fitzOsbern, steward; Hugh d'Ivry, butler; Herfast, a ducal chaplain whom William as king made his chancellor; Gerald, a steward; Hugh de Montfort, constable; Ralph de Tancarville, chamberlain.[1] William certainly employed such Englishmen as could be of use to him, but they were few and they do not seem to have survived long in his service. After 1087 William Rufus and Robert Curthose each had his own household, formed, as to its nucleus at least, while they were still princes; but each, when they became king and duke respectively, took over some members of his father's

of England' or 'of Normandy' in the time of the Norman kings. Aubrey de Vere, who was given the 'master-chamberlainship of all England' according to the presumably genuine text of a writ of 1133, held lands in Normandy as well as in England and attended the king in Normandy after this writ had been issued. Similarly William de Tancarville and his son Rabel, hereditary chamberlains and generally associated with the duchy, held lands in England as well as in Normandy; and of the surviving acts of King Henry attested by William twice as many are dated in England as in Normandy: Le Patourel, *Normandy and England*, pp. 11 (note 25), 30, 37–8.

[1] In general, Le Patourel, ibid., pp. 10–11. For William fitzOsbern, Haskins, *Norman Institutions*, p. 58, note 289; Douglas, 'Ancestors of William fitzOsbern', pp. 75–9; Fauroux, *Recueil*, p. 62, note 286 (his father Osbern was seneschal, and on one occasion William attested as *pincerna*, ibid., No. 126, p. 297). A 'Hugo pincerna' or 'botillarius' attests charters both before and after 1066: Fauroux, *Recueil*, Nos. 116 (p. 279), 137 (p. 314), 138 (p. 315), 156 (p. 342), 188 (p. 371), 230 (p. 442), 233 (p. 449); *Regesta*, i, Nos. 48 (p. 13), 55 (p. 15), 56 (ibid.), 150 (p. 41). Some of these attestations at least must have been made by Hugh d'Ivry (cf. Fauroux, *Recueil*, pp. 61–2; *Regesta*, i, p. xxvii; and White, 'Household of the Norman Kings', pp. 141–3). Herfast, according to William of Malmesbury (Malmesbury, *Gesta Pontificum*, p. 150), had been one of William's chaplains for some time before he was made chancellor (Fauroux, *Recueil*, p. 41; *Regesta*, i, p. xvi). Orderic states that Hugh de Montfort was already a constable at the time of the battle of Hastings: Orderic Vitalis, *H.E.* (ed. Le Prévost), ii. 148; (ed. Chibnall), ii. 174; cf. White, 'Constables under the Norman Kings', p. 113. For Ralph de Tancarville, *Complete Peerage*, x, Appendix F, pp. 49–50.

household.[1] Henry had almost certainly formed a large part of his permanent household before he became king, though he subsequently added elements from the households of both his brothers.[2] Wherever the king might be, however, he and those who were members of the household in one sense or another were joined by a number of people who could hardly be described as members of the household in any sense whatever. The number and the identity of these people varied greatly from time to time; but whether there were few or many, and whoever might be involved, the concourse that attended the king at any point constituted his court.[3] Some idea of the identity of those present on any particular occasion may be obtained from a chronicler's statement[4] or from the names of persons figuring as witnesses to

[1] Almost nothing is known of Robert's and Rufus's establishments before 1087. It is clear that Robert had a following (Orderic Vitalis, *H.E.* (ed. Le Prévost), ii. 294–6, 377–82; (ed. Chibnall), ii. 356–8, iii. 96–102; William de Jumièges, *Gesta*, interp. Robert de Torigni, p. 268) and failed to persuade his father to give him the means to strengthen it; and this and Orderic's narrative imply that he had a household, however elementary, separated from that of the king. Orderic's statements (*H.E.* (ed. Le Prévost), ii. 391; (ed. Chibnall), iii. 114) could be taken as implying that Rufus and Henry were similarly endowed at some point before 1087. Rufus took Robert Bloet with him to England (Orderic Vitalis, *H.E.* (ed. Le Prévost), iv. 11–12), presumably as a chaplain, but Robert had been one of the Conqueror's chaplains (ibid. and *Regesta*, i, pp. xvii–xviii). For Rufus's and Robert's households after 1087, *Regesta*, i, pp. xviii, xxi, xxii–xxvii; Haskins, *Norman Institutions*, pp. 74–7. Besides Robert Bloet, Gerard, who was made chancellor by William the Conqueror, continued to serve William Rufus for a while (Galbraith, 'Girard the Chancellor'); while William de Tancarville and Roger d'Ivry, respectively a chamberlain and a butler under the Conqueror, joined Robert Curthose (*Complete Peerage*, x, Appendix F, pp. 51–2; *Regesta*, i, Nos. 308, 324).

[2] According to William of Malmesbury, Roger the future bishop of Salisbury and Henry's chief minister in England, had served him as steward or treasurer before 1100 (*Historia Novella*, pp. 37–8). For other possibilities, below, pp. 346–7. William Giffard, who had been made chancellor by William Rufus, was not immediately replaced after Henry's accession (*Regesta*, ii, p. ix); a Herbert and also William de Warelwast, with others no doubt, seem to have served as chaplains both to Rufus and to Henry (ibid., pp. x–xi); four stewards and some of the constables likewise (ibid., pp. xi–xii, xv–xvi); while William de Tancarville, who had served both William the Conqueror and Robert Curthose as chamberlain, joined Henry after Tinchebrai (Le Patourel, *Normandy and England*, pp. 11–12, 37–8).

[3] There can be little doubt that Walter Map's description of the court of Henry II in his own day applies in general terms to the court of the Norman kings. See in particular the first chapter of his book, where he insists on the extreme variation in the composition of the court (*De Nugis Curialium*, p. 1, *Translation*, p. 1).

[4] e.g. A.-S.C., 1085, E (p. 161) (William's 'deep speech' at Gloucester); 1087,

royal charters;[1] but though it is possible to list the categories
of persons whom one could expect to meet at King Henry's
court—a king of Scots, a Welsh prince, bishops, abbots, earls
and counts, barons and knights, merchants and a more or less
respectable trail of hangers-on, besides members of the household in all senses of the term—it is probably impossible to produce an attendance-list for any particular occasion or even to
say whether the presence of certain persons was necessary or
appropriate to certain occasions or to certain things that the
court might do.

Whoever might or might not be present, however, and wherever it might be, there could only be one royal court in this
sense. There could not be a *curia regis* for England and a *curia
ducis* for Normandy,[2] or even two forms of the *curia regis*, one for
England and the other for Normandy, differing in personnel or
function. There was but one royal household and it was the
nucleus of the royal court; and among the persons who might
attend the king, and who were not members of the household
in any sense, the bishops of English sees were frequently in
attendance in Normandy and the bishops of Norman sees in
England, barons with the title of an English earldom or of a
continental *comté* might attend the king at any point in his
itinerary[3]—they were all (by Henry's time) of continental

E (p. 164) (William's crown-wearings as described in his obituary); 1114, E
(pp. 183–4) (a possible indication of the court on the move, prelates and nobility
present when the bishop of Rochester was appointed); 1123, E (p. 188) (summons
to a council at Gloucester); 1127, E (pp. 192–3) (Christmas court of 1126 at
Windsor).

[1] e.g. Stephen's Easter court at Westminster and Oxford, 1136 (*Regesta*, iii,
Nos. 944, 46, 271, pp. 347–8, 16–17, 96–7; Round, *Geoffrey de Mandeville*, pp. 16–24,
262–6). Some of Henry's charters are dated 'in concilio', e.g. *Regesta*, ii, Nos. 918
(p. 87), 919 (pp. 87–8), 1091 (pp. 124–5), 1715 (p. 253); and the long lists of witnesses to Nos. 544 (pp. 12–13), 547 (pp. 13–14), 548 (p. 14), etc. also seem to
represent at least some part of the court. But while it is probable that the men whose
names are given were as a general rule actually present at the court, a short list of
witnesses is no evidence of a small attendance. For this point as it applies to the
Old English witan, e.g. Whitelock, review of Oleson, *The Witenagemot in the Reign
of Edward the Confessor*, *E.H.R.*, lxxi (1956), pp. 640–2; to the pre-Conquest Norman
curia, e.g. Fauroux, *Recueil*, No. 115 (p. 278), in which the witnesses could hardly
represent the 'primates curiae meae' before whom the case was heard. Similarly, a
charter of Henry I dated at Rouen 'praesente magno procerum conventu' has only
five named witnesses including the king himself (*Regesta*, ii, No. 809, p. 64), though
it does add 'with many others'.   [2] Below, p. 240 n. 4.

[3] e.g. *Regesta*, ii, Nos. 833 (p. 70), 919 (p. 87), 956 (p. 95), 1091 (pp. 124–5),
1124 (p. 131), 1204 (p. 146), 1215 (p. 148), 1425–6 (p. 192), 1466 (pp. 201–2),

origin and mostly held important lands on both sides of the Channel. When the court was in England it is certain that the bishops of English sees predominated, and it is probable that magnates whose principal lands lay in England did the same; conversely when the court was in Normandy; but this was a matter of convenience rather than of principle and only a particular instance of the general rule that the court tended to attract to it for the time being the important men of any region it passed through.[1] There can be no doubt that there was direct continuity between the court of the Norman kings and their court as Norman dukes, as there was continuity in their household before and after 1066. It is true that in the first few years of William the Conqueror's reign some important Englishmen are found at his court, or at least witnessing his charters; and it has been held that their presence constitutes a link between the pre-Conquest English witan and the post-Conquest court.[2] It is indeed possible that they were able to give information to William and his court about conditions in England and about English customs and institutions; but as they were replaced in their offices by Normans they disappear as a group from the court, which was fundamentally the same whether it met in Normandy or in England.[3]

1547 (p. 217), 1740 (p. 258), 1764 (p. 263), 1896 (p. 288), 1908 (p. 290). These generalizations should probably be qualified for the time of William the Conqueror (Douglas, *William the Conqueror*, p. 335), when the English episcopate was hardly in a settled state; but cf., e.g. *Regesta*, i, Nos. 26 (p. 8), 125 (pp. 32–3), 146a (pp. 39–40), 150 (pp. 41–2), 168 (p. 46).

[1] Cf. Musset, 'Gouvernés et gouvernants', pp. 462–3.

[2] e.g. Stenton, *William the Conqueror*, pp. 412–14; *A.-S.E.*, pp. 614–15; Douglas, *William the Conqueror*, pp. 284–5.

[3] The English witan and the ducal *curia* were very similar as assemblies, and neither was so clearly defined that any attempt at a brief comparison between them in constitutional terms would be profitable. What probably happened was that William's *curia* took in a few notable Englishmen for as long as they held their earldoms, bishoprics, or other offices; but as they were replaced by Normans the court reverted to an almost exclusively Norman composition. The witness-lists of pre-Conquest ducal charters are analysed in Fauroux, *Recueil*, pp. 58–63, and commented upon by Musset in 'Gouvernés et gouvernants', pp. 461–3. In so far as the composition of the court can be deduced from these witness-lists (above, p. 138 n. 1), it appears that the higher clergy were giving way before the rising feudal aristocracy in the years before 1066. The bishops and abbots are certainly found in charters issued on great occasions after 1066 on both sides of the Channel, and conceivably this may owe something to English precedent; but the witness-lists in ducal charters such as Fauroux, *Recueil*, Nos. 159 (pp. 344–8) and 219 (pp. 415–17), are very much like those of comparable post-Conquest royal charters.

Its essential function was to magnify the king's authority and to provide a vehicle for its expression. The divine origin of this authority and the royal majesty were made manifest in the great courts held on the chief festivals of the Church, when the king wore his crown 'and was very dignified'. Matters of general importance, whether they were concerned with ecclesiastical or secular affairs would be discussed;[1] partly because the king could not make up his mind without advice on all the problems that were likely to be brought before him, and partly perhaps to associate powerful men in his decisions and so facilitate their execution. Or it might serve as a court of law, for cases with important legal implications and for cases which involved important people or institutions—cases which in practice could only be settled by the king acting with advice or by men acting under his commission; and such cases were creating and defining the law as it concerned the barons and the greater churches.[2] But the business of the court was not all high seriousness. There was certainly feasting and relaxation, hunting and story-telling, no doubt a great deal of gossip and some buffoonery, all—though the men involved may not have been conscious of it—serving to promote and to maintain the solidarity of the dominant and exploiting group.[3]

Like the household in its most extended form, the court was itinerant not in the sense that it moved about with the king as a body, but in the sense that he was never alone and that those who were with him in any place and at any time constituted his court; and, whether it was enlarged into a great 'council' by a formal summons to prelates and magnates and others[4] or was reduced to the domestic household with one or two bishops or barons who might count as the king's personal friends, it was an integral part of the itinerant government.

---

[1] e.g. the assembly at Westminster of bishops, abbots, nobles, and others that discussed the question of investitures and in which King Henry ratified his agreement with Anselm and appointed bishops to vacant sees in England and Normandy (Eadmer, *Historia Novorum*, p. 186; Florence of Worcester, *Chronicon*, ii. 55–7; A.-S.C., 1107, E (pp. 180–1), and the series of assemblies held by Henry in Normandy after Tinchebrai when he reorganized the government of Normandy (Orderic Vitalis, *H.E.* (ed. Le Prévost), iv. 233–4, 269).

[2] e.g. *Regesta*, ii, Nos. 880 (pp. 79–80), 918 (p. 87); A.-S.C., 1096, E (p. 173)—in England; *Regesta*, ii, Nos. 1570 (p. 222), 1579 (p. 225), 1593 (p. 228)—in Normandy. Cf. Stenton, *English Feudalism*, pp. 31–8.

[3] Cf. Below, ch. 9.   [4] e.g. A.-S.C., 1123, E (p. 188).

Those who had business at the court, whether they were obliged to attend by reason of their tenure or for some other cause, or whether they sought favours or redress for themselves or their clients, had to seek it out wherever it might be or wait until it came to them.

No doubt it is simply because so much of the work of the king's government was done by men who were members of his household or his court, either accompanying him on his travels or out doing his work in one country or the other, that no clearly defined institution of regency evolved in the early twelfth century, even though the ruler's absences from England or Normandy might last for three or four years at a time.[1] William the Conqueror, as he set off on his great adventure in 1066, designated his son Robert as his heir and left him in Normandy under the guardianship of the Duchess Matilda assisted by a council of prelates and barons; and it is most likely that Matilda continued to act as regent in Normandy on most occasions when William was in England until her death in 1083.[2] By that time Robert was in rebellion against his father, and there is nothing to show who was in charge in Normandy during the last years that William spent in England—unless it was William Rufus, to whom he may have been thinking of transferring the inheritance.[3] On the English side, when William left the country in March 1067, the military conquest of the kingdom was far from complete, and William fitzOsbern and Odo of Bayeux, who were left there with a supporting group of barons, should probably be regarded as military commanders left to consolidate and continue the work of conquest rather than as regents in the ordinary sense.[4] In 1075, at the time of the rebellion of the earls,

[1] William the Conqueror's longest known absences from Normandy after 1066 (December 1067 to the end of 1071) and from England (1076 to 1080) both lasted about four years. After 1106, Henry was in Normandy on one occasion for over 3 years (1123–6) and on another for over four and a half years (1116–20). His longest stay in England between 1106 and 1135 lasted just over two and a half years (1120–3). See the *Table of Transfretations* at the end of this chapter.

[2] William de Poitiers, *Gesta*, pp. 260–1; Orderic Vitalis, *H.E.* (ed. Le Prévost), ii. 177–8, 188, 234, 236; (ed. Chibnall), ii. 208–10, 222, 280, 284; Douglas, *William the Conqueror*, pp. 185, 236; David, *Robert Curthose*, pp. 12–16. So far as can be judged from *Regesta*, i, Matilda witnessed relatively few of William's charters that are dated or likely to have been given in England.

[3] Le Patourel, 'The Norman Succession', pp. 232–4.

[4] A.-S.C., 1066, D (p. 145); Florence of Worcester, *Chronicon*, ii. 1; Orderic Vitalis, *H.E.* (ed. Le Prévost), ii. 166–7; (ed. Chibnall), ii. 194–6.

Archbishop Lanfranc was clearly acting as regent, and during William's long absence from 1076 to 1080 Odo of Bayeux, the king's half-brother, probably performed similar functions; but though the bishop of Coutances and others also acted for the king from time to time it is impossible to establish a succession of regents in England during William's absences or to have any confidence that a formal appointment was always made.[1]

It is much the same under William Rufus. In England he used a changing group of ministers, no one of whom can be singled out individually as regent;[2] in Normandy, for whose government he was responsible from the autumn of 1096, there seems to be no evidence at all. It is just possible that his brother Henry acted for him in the duchy;[3] but he cannot have done this all the time, for he was in the fatal hunting-party in the New Forest. After 1106, Henry's queen Matilda seems generally to have acted as regent in England, perhaps as guardian of their son William; and William acted on his own after her death (May 1119) until he joined his father in Normandy a year later.[4] After William was lost in the White Ship disaster, Henry was apparently content to leave England in the charge of Roger bishop of Salisbury; though whether this was as regent in any formal sense, or as the head of an administration which was capable of carrying on for a year or two without king or regent, it is difficult to say.[5] Henry's provisions for a regency in Nor-

[1] Stenton, *A.-S.E.*, pp. 601–2; West, *Justiciarship in England*, pp. 2–10.

[2] Ibid., pp. 10–13. According to the Annals of Winchester, Rufus crossed the sea in 1097 'and committed the kingdom' to Bishop Walkelin of Winchester and Ranulf Flambard (*Annales Monastici*, ii. 39).

[3] From 1094, certainly, Rufus and Henry worked together in opposition to Robert. Rufus put Henry in charge of the campaign of 1095 in Normandy and gave him a command in the Vexin campaign of 1097. When Rufus took possession of Normandy in 1096, he 'gave' Henry the Cotentin (of which he was almost certainly already in possession), and the Bessin apart from the towns of Bayeux and Caen, in addition to the other lands and interests that Henry already had in the duchy. A sentence in Robert de Torigni's interpolations in the *Gesta* of William de Jumièges (p. 275), though not unambiguous, can be read in the sense that Rufus gave Henry a large part in the building of his new and important castle at Gisors (below, pp. 341–5).

[4] West, *Justiciarship in England*, pp. 14–15.

[5] Ibid., pp. 15–23. When the Anglo-Saxon Chronicle (1123, E, p. 190) says that King Henry 'went over to Normandy and committed all England to the care and government of Bishop Roger of Salisbury', it certainly suggests a formal regency, though the statement is isolated. On Roger's position in the government of England, in addition to West, ubi supra, Le Patourel, *Normandy and England*, p. 35, and Kealey, *Roger of Salisbury*, esp. ch. 2 and Appendix 2.

mandy, if he made any, are quite mysterious. There seems nothing to indicate that either of the two men whom he might have been expected to use in that capacity, his nephew Stephen of Blois or his illegitimate son Robert of Gloucester, did in fact act as regent. John bishop of Lisieux appears to have occupied a position very similar in relation to the administration of Normandy to that which Roger of Salisbury held in England;[1] and it is possible that with him in charge Henry thought it unnecessary to find a royal or almost royal regent for the duchy, and that this formed a precedent for Roger of Salisbury's position in England after 1120. On the whole, Henry's absences from Normandy were shorter than his absences from England,[2] and he may have intended that they should be no longer than they needed to be; but the only positive evidence that the bishop of Lisieux acted formally as regent in Normandy is what appears to be an association of ideas in Orderic's mind when he mentions Henry's settlement of Normandy after Tinchebrai in the same sentence as the appointment of John to the bishopric.[3]

On the death of King Henry, the chief barons then in Normandy formed themselves into a kind of council of regency which appointed William de Warenne to govern Rouen and the Pays de Caux and William de Roumare, Hugh de Gournay, and others to defend the frontiers, evidently those to the south and west.[4] This council also invited Theobald of Blois to be their ruler; but when the news of Stephen's success in England was brought to them they quickly accepted him as duke as well as king,[5] and since it must have been clear that he would hardly be able to visit Normandy for a few months at least[6] it is probable that they continued to act as a provisional council of regency and that the bishop of Lisieux remained in the position he had held under Henry.[7] When Stephen returned to England after his six months in Normandy during the year 1137, he left William de Roumare, Roger de Saint-Sauveur, 'and others' as 'justiciars'

[1] Haskins, *Norman Institutions*, pp. 88–99; Le Patourel, *Normandy and England*, pp. 32–3.
[2] *Table of Transfretations* at the end of this chapter.
[3] Orderic Vitalis, *H.E.* (ed. Le Prévost), iv. 273–4.
[4] Ibid., v. 52.   [5] Ibid., 54–6.
[6] Stephen was in fact in Normandy within fifteen months of his coronation.
[7] The bishop of Lisieux is rather conspicuously absent from the witness-lists in the charters issued at Stephen's Easter court of 1136 (above, p. 138 n. 1); but he was with Stephen in Normandy in 1137 (*Regesta*, iii, No. 298, pp. 112–13).

in the duchy. Whatever kind of scheme this represented,[1] Orderic's account of the events of 1141 in Normandy strongly suggests that there was then no effective regent in the duchy, for the bishop of Lisieux and the principal barons all made their peace with Geoffrey of Anjou individually.[2] In England, since Roger of Salisbury evidently continued to exercise the powers Henry had given him until he was broken by Stephen in 1139, it can only be assumed that he acted during the time that Stephen spent in Normandy as he had done in Henry's absences during his later years.[3] If Stephen had been able to continue Henry's manner of governing, it is likely that his queen, yet another Matilda, would often have acted as regent in England. She certainly showed her competence in 1141.

It is difficult to know what to make of all this. Perhaps the very fact that the regency as an institution is so obscure is an indication of the extent to which the Norman kings relied upon their own personal action exercised through itineration. Contemporary writers who were concerned to record events in a regular chronological sequence certainly pay far more attention to the king's coming and going than to the identity of those he left in charge when he crossed the Channel.[4] Yet the position

---

[1] Orderic Vitalis, *H.E.* (ed. Le Prévost), v. 91–2. Roger's commission could have been restricted to the Cotentin (Delisle, *Histoire de Saint-Sauveur-le-Vicomte*, pp. 28–9), but that of William de Roumare seems to have been of general application (Haskins, *Norman Institutions*, pp. 92, 127). Orderic's description of their commission, for what it may be worth, is interesting and anticipates that of later justiciars and seneschals: 'illis praecipiens facere quod ipse praesens agere non poterat, justitiam videlicet discolis inferre, et pacem inermi populo procurare'. But their administration did not last very long. Roger was ambushed and killed by Angevin adherents in the Cotentin very soon after his appointment (Orderic Vitalis, *H.E.* (ed. Le Prévost), v. 104–5) and William had deserted or had been relieved of his post by 1140, for, with the earl of Chester, he seized Lincoln Castle in December of that year (*Complete Peerage*, vii. 668).

[2] Orderic Vitalis, *H.E.* (ed. Le Prévost), v. 130–3.

[3] West, *Justiciarship in England*, pp. 23–6.

[4] The Anglo-Saxon Chronicle, for example, apart from referring to Odo of Bayeux and William fitzOsbern who 'stayed behind and built castles far and wide throughout this country' when William the Conqueror returned to Normandy in 1067 (1066, D, p. 145), mentions a regent left in charge of England during the king's absence on one occasion only between 1066 and 1144. That was when he committed 'the care and government' of the country to Roger of Salisbury in 1123 (above, p. 142 note 5). It was the first occasion on which Henry had crossed to Normandy since the deaths of Queen Matilda and William Ætheling; and the fact that the Chronicle makes a point of it may mark a stage in the evolution of Roger's position (cf. West, *Justiciarship in England*, pp. 16 ff.).

of William the Conqueror's Queen Matilda in Normandy and Henry's Queen Matilda in England alone shows that the Norman kings would leave responsibility, certainly on occasion, in the hands of a dignified personage for what was intended to be a relatively short time, and such a person can only be called a regent. One important circumstance perhaps is that the Norman kings did not have enough suitable relatives for all the occasions when a regent might be needed, and therefore had to rely upon bishops or barons, often in a group, or an administrator like the bishop of Salisbury or the bishop of Lisieux. This must have had something to do with the evolution of the later office of justiciar in England and seneschal in the continental lands of the Angevin kings.

Yet even though so much of the work of government in kingdom and duchy could be done directly by the itinerant king with his household and court, the fact that his itinerary had been so greatly extended by the conquest of England must inevitably mean that the chief centres in both countries—Fécamp, Rouen, Caen, Bayeux; Winchester, London, Gloucester, Oxford—would see less of the king-duke than they had seen of duke or king hitherto, and something had to replace his formerly more frequent presence. Since he was not represented in either country by a viceroy, and not regularly by a regent, some means had to be found to deal with the more routine work of government, particularly in matters of finance and justice, whether he were absent or present—when he was absent because of the delays which would necessarily follow if every problem had to be referred to him abroad or wait until he returned, and when he was present because he was always a bird of passage, always on the move. It may even be that, with the standards that the Norman kings set themselves, the government of England and Normandy together provided more work than any ruler with nothing but an unprofessionalized household and court could possibly deal with.

Since king and duke had been itinerant before 1066, there was something to build on both in England and in Normandy. This is seen most clearly, though still not very clearly, in matters of finance. Both countries were wealthy in the eleventh century,[1]

---

[1] England: Sawyer, 'Wealth of England' and, e.g., William de Poitiers, *Gesta*, pp. 252–4. Normandy: Musset, 'Conditions financières d'une réussite

and the rulers of each had found the means to exploit this wealth[1]—for their financial systems, such as they were, did not exist to provide a public service but to enable king or duke to live and rule as he wished to do.[2] In England the chief sources of the king's revenue were his own lands, the ancient food-rents now largely commuted, the profits of his control of the coinage, and, save when it had to be used to ransom the country from the Danes, the geld.[3] In Normandy the duke had his demesne lands and his forests, with revenues from markets and fairs; he had a monopoly of the coinage, some of the profits of which he commuted to a direct triennial tax, the *monnéage* or *fouage*; and he seems to have preserved some, at least, of the taxes of a public character which derived from Carolingian administration, notably the very profitable tolls which could be levied on the movement of merchandise.[4] What proportion of these revenues was collected in the form of money or converted into money in the course of collection is uncertain in either country; but both royal and ducal officers must have been accustomed to handling relatively large sums of money and their systems of collection were much the same, at least in principle. Regular revenues (from land, tolls, fairs, etc.) were farmed by permanent local officers (chiefly sheriffs in England, *vicomtes* in Normandy) in large units, and having made local payments on the order of king or duke they remitted the balance to a royal or ducal treasury. Extraordinary revenues (the geld in England, sundry casual profits in Normandy) were gathered by collectors

architecturale', and earlier papers by the same writer there cited and summarized in 'Naissance de la Normandie', pp. 106–8, 126; Douglas, *William the Conqueror*, pp. 133–6.

[1] As shown in England, e.g., by their power to collect the geld, in Normandy by the mounting of the invasion of England in 1066.

[2] It is true that there were levies in both countries which had or had once had a public character, the geld in England and vestigial payments such as *bernage* and *graverie* in Normandy (works of L. Musset cited in Yver, 'Premières institutions', p. 339, note 96); but once collected all revenues were at the king's or the duke's disposal.

[3] Loyn, *Anglo-Saxon England and the Norman Conquest*, pp. 122–8, 303–14; below, pp. 326–7.

[4] Haskins, *Norman Institutions*, pp. 39–40; Musset, 'A-t-il existé en Normandie au xie siècle une aristocratie d'argent?'; 'Recherches sur quelques survivances de la fiscalité ducale'; 'Que peut-on savoir de la fiscalité publique en Normandie à l'époque ducale?'; 'Sur les mutations de la monnaie ducale normande au xie siècle'; Yver, 'Premières institutions', pp. 337–43. An important work on *monnéage* is expected from Professor T. N. Bisson.

apparently appointed *ad hoc*. In Normandy these were paid directly into the ducal *camera*.[1]

In both countries the ruler's itinerant treasury, his chamber, was part of his household establishment and provided for current needs. Besides cash, it contained other objects of value including, in all probability, records.[2] If there had ever been a time when king or duke carried all his cash and valuables about with him, that time was already long past. In England the kings had at one time deposited some of their treasure in monasteries, which combined supernatural with some physical security; but by the eleventh century there was a treasury or depository at Winchester, apparently located in the royal residence there rather than in any of the monasteries of the city and thus requiring royal servants to administer it.[3] In Normandy there seem to have been no such places that we can now identify with certainty, though we can be sure that they existed.[4] Even these meagre facts imply a relatively sophisticated financial service in both countries. They imply some organizational relationship

---

[1] England: Jolliffe, *Constitutional History of Medieval England*, pp. 128–9; Barlow, *Edward the Confessor*, pp. 185–7; *V.C.H. Dorset*, iii. 116–17; *V.C.H. Wiltshire*, ii. 170–1 (the evidence for the method of collecting the geld comes from the Conqueror's reign but with strong indications of pre-Conquest antecedents). Normandy: Haskins, *Norman Institutions*, pp. 40–5.

[2] In Normandy it must be supposed that the *camera* included an itinerant or household element, whatever else it may have been (below); in England this is clear and is illustrated by the famous story of the box in the Confessor's chamber (e.g. Barlow, *English Church*, p. 123).

[3] Jolliffe, *Constitutional History of Medieval England*, pp. 129–30; Larson, *King's Household*, pp. 130–3; Poole, *Exchequer in the Twelfth Century*, p. 35. For the deposit of royal treasure in monasteries, see also Chaplais, 'The Anglo-Saxon Chancery: From the Diploma to the Writ', p. 165.

[4] The distinction made in a charter of Duke Richard II between the extraordinary or occasional revenues which were handled by the ducal *camera* and the regular revenues which were not seems to imply the existence of a non-household treasury or treasuries already in the early eleventh century; and this could only be in some fixed place or places (Haskins, *Norman Institutions*, pp. 40–1). Breteuil ('Rescolium', canton Nonancourt, dept. Eure) is mentioned in a ducal charter of *c.* 1015–25 as a place where 'res fisci colligebantur vel congregabantur' (Fauroux, *Recueil*, No. 29, p. 117; Yver, 'Premières institutions', pp. 337–8; Adigard des Gautries, 'Les noms de lieux de l'Eure', p. 52). If so small a place (*viculus*) so near the frontier served as some kind of treasury, there must have been others in such centres as Fécamp (where an enormous hoard of coins was found in 1963: Dumas-Dubourg, *Le Trésor de Fécamp*, pp. 3–5, 15–16), Rouen, etc. One of Duke William's charters was 'made' 'apud Bajocas in camera Guilelmi ducis' (Fauroux, *Recueil*, No. 227, p. 437). Although not unambiguous, this seems to refer to a structure and therefore to a ducal treasury of some sort.

between itinerant and localized treasuries; they imply some central machinery for the collection of non-routine revenues, particularly as the sums involved could be very large and such quantities of cash could be handled only in fixed treasuries;[1] they imply a system of record-keeping, for which indeed there is some evidence.[2] However, unless the word used in Normandy for the ducal treasury (*camera*) was still being used in something like its Carolingian sense to indicate the whole treasury organization, as well as in its quasi-domestic sense[3] (and there was certainly a *princeps camerae* as well as ducal chamberlains),[4] it is difficult to give a clear picture of the pre-Conquest royal or ducal financial services as a whole, though it is impossible to visualize the handling of the geld in England or the mounting of William's great expedition of 1066 without a financial organization of some sophistication.

Whatever form this organization took in either country at the time of the Conquest, however, a ruler who aspired to govern the two together would have to develop his financial administration in each very considerably. In England, William to begin with would naturally take over the organization he found there. His biographer indicates that one of the first things he did after the battle of Hastings was to take possession of Harold's treasure.[5] Presumably this happened when, according to Guy d'Amiens, he sent a detachment to secure the submission of Winchester while he himself was still approaching London.[6]

---

[1] In England the geld was taken by the collectors to Winchester (above, p. 147 n. 1, and Galbraith, *Making of Domesday Book*, p. 88); in Normandy it was the non-routine revenues that were paid directly into the ducal *camera* (Haskins, *Norman Institutions*, p. 41). But there was nothing like the geld in Normandy.

[2] Normandy: Haskins, *Norman Institutions*, p. 44; England: Harvey, 'Domesday Book and its Predecessors', esp. pp. 755–63.

[3] Cf. Ganshof, 'Charlemagne et les institutions de la monarchie franque', pp. 361, 383; Yver, 'Premières institutions', pp. 338–9.

[4] 'Camerarii': Fauroux, *Recueil*, Nos. 123 (p. 293), 137 (p. 314), 138 (p. 315), 184 (p. 367), 185 (p. 368), 191 (p. 374), 198 (p. 386), 219 (p. 417), 220 (p. 419, Rodulfus and Ragnulfus), 227 (p. 437), 231 (p. 445, Hunfridus, p. 446, Radulfus), 233 (p. 449). The fullest indications we have of the nature of the Norman ducal *camera* before 1066 come from a charter of Richard II for Fécamp and one of duke Robert for Saint-Bénigne of Dijon (ibid., Nos. 34 and 86, pp. 130, 227; Haskins, *Norman Institutions*, pp. 40–1; Yver, 'Premières institutions', pp. 338–9).

[5] William de Poitiers, *Gesta*, p. 222.

[6] *Carmen de Hastingae Proelio*, p. 41; Freeman, *Norman Conquest*, iii. 540–1. Orderic Vitalis states that while the campaign in the North was in progress, William sent to Winchester for the crown and the royal insignia and plate (*H.E.*

Clearly he would not abandon any source of revenue that Edward had enjoyed, nor did he have any machinery for collection that would be an improvement on the system of shires and sheriffs; but as conquerors he and his successors were able to increase the worth of England to its ruler, and to do so on a prodigious scale. They could double the value of the royal lands, extract money from the towns under various pretexts, take huge sums from men who had been granted fiefs in the country as reliefs or as payments for favours and facilities of all kinds, make royal justice itself a source of revenue—not to mention the loot that the Conqueror had taken in the course of the conquest itself.[1] William is said to have been generous to the monasteries of his native land, to have spent a good deal on his personal adornment, and to have paid off promptly the mercenaries he had engaged in 'the English War';[2] but the long-term result of the much more intense exploitation to which the Norman kings could subject England must have been a great increase in the treasure flowing in and out of the Winchester treasury.[3] In Normandy the conquest of England would not in itself change the sources from which the ducal revenues were derived; but the duchy was greatly enriched by it and this would certainly increase the amount of those revenues.[4]

All this was happening just when the government of the two countries by an itinerant king meant that the officers of his household could not give more than about half the time to the management of the finances of either that they or their predecessors had hitherto given to this work. The result could

---

(ed. Le Prévost), ii. 196; (ed. Chibnall), ii. 232) and that he celebrated Easter there in 1068 and 1069 (ibid. (ed. Le Prévost), ii. 181, 188; (ed. Chibnall), ii. 214, 222). The Anglo-Saxon Chronicle adds 1070 (1069, D, p. 150). All these statements suggest that whatever treasury organization there was at Winchester before 1066 continued to function through the invasion and that William took it over as a going concern.

[1] Above, pp. 29–30, below, pp. 326–9.
[2] William de Poitiers, *Gesta*, pp. 222–6, 256–62; Orderic Vitalis, *H.E.* (ed. Le Prévost), ii. 187; (ed. Chibnall), ii. 220.
[3] e.g. the description of the Winchester treasury as it was when William Rufus took possession of it: 'it was impossible for anyone to describe how much was accumulated there in gold and silver and vessels and costly robes and jewels, and many other precious things that are hard to recount' (A.-S.C., 1087, E, p. 166). Henry of Huntingdon (*Historia Anglorum*, p. 211) says that there were 60,000 pounds of silver in addition to the gold and jewels, plate and robes.
[4] Below, pp. 331–4.

only be an enormous development of those parts of the financial organization in both countries which were already detached or were in process of detachment from the household; for even the most elementary royal store-houses or depositories, unless they were in monasteries, would require staffing, and the most natural source of such staff was the household.

That such an expansion actually took place can be seen most clearly in England, where the treasury at Winchester came to take a very important place not only in the administrative structure but even in the political events of the time—William Rufus, Henry, and Stephen each found that to secure possession of it was an essential part of the process of making himself king. Some of the men who administered it can now be identified. They were called 'chamberlains',[1] a term which implies that they or their predecessors were once part of the domestic, itinerant household, and that the fixed store-houses or treasuries had indeed been originally staffed from the household, though the men who administered them were now clearly detached from it. These chamberlains probably had a considerable part in the production of Domesday Book, supplying essential information from their own records[2] and having custody of the written survey when it had been completed. The point had certainly been reached when the king could not keep all his records beside him but needed a record office; and the natural place for his records was the treasury. Moreover, it kept its own accounts[3] and evidently occupied premises so substantial that it could be convenient for the king's court to hear cases there.[4] It was the most important treasury in England, though there may well have been others.[5]

There was a very similar development in Normandy. Whatever may have been the case before 1066, there was certainly

[1] For the chamberlains of the treasury in England, White, 'Financial Administration under Henry I', pp. 56–78, and 'Household of the Norman Kings', pp. 130–1.

[2] Harvey, 'Domesday Book and its Predecessors', pp. 755–63.

[3] *Pipe Roll 31 Henry I*, p. 130.

[4] *Regesta*, ii, No. 1000 (p. 104); cf. Poole, *Exchequer in the Twelfth Century*, pp. 34–5, note 2.

[5] There seems to have been a safe-deposit of some kind at Portchester for treasure in transit between Normandy and England in the time of Henry II, and at least some evidence of its existence already in his grandfather's time (Round, in *V.C.H. Hampshire*, i. 432; Haskins, *Norman Institutions*, p. 113).

an important treasury at Rouen after that date. The treasure which William Rufus found at Winchester in 1087 was paralleled by the treasure which Robert Curthose found in Rouen;[1] and though each brother executed his father's dying wishes in the matter of charitable bequests in his country, each retained sufficient means to secure the support he needed immediately and for other current needs; and the Rouen treasury must have had to find William the Conqueror's legacy to his youngest son Henry as well. There was certainly more than one treasury in Normandy by the end of Henry's reign, in the sense of a place where money was deposited; though the Rouen treasury probably held the same pre-eminence in the duchy as the Winchester treasury held in England. In 1135, if not before, a considerable sum of money was being kept at Falaise,[2] and some of it,

[1] Florence of Worcester, *Chronicon*, ii. 20–1; Orderic Vitalis, *H.E.* (ed. Le Prévost), iii. 244, 266–7; (ed. Chibnall), iv. 94–6, 118. Although the chroniclers do not say specifically that the treasure which William left in Normandy and Robert found there was kept in a treasury at Rouen, this seems to follow from Orderic's story that Henry hastened (*festinavit*) from his father's bedside to have the money bequeathed to him counted out (ubi supra) and from Robert of Torigni's precise statement that Robert returned immediately to Rouen when he heard of his father's death (William de Jumièges, *Gesta*, p. 268). The story of the Monk of Caen that William ordered the officers of his chamber (*ministri camere sue*) to bring out the precious objects in the royal treasuries (*in thesauris regalibus*) so that he might express his will concerning them, with Orderic's story of Henry and his legacy, illustrates the distinction between the itinerant household treasury (the chamber, then presumably at or near Saint-Gervais where the king lay) and the fixed treasury (presumably at the palace in the city from which William had been removed on account of the noise); but that is perhaps putting more upon their words than they will bear ('De Obitu Willelmi', in William de Jumièges, *Gesta*, p. 146; *English Historical Documents*, ii. 279, but cf. below, p. 183 n. 1; Orderic Vitalis, ubi supra). It is, however, worth noting that Henry, in Orderic's story, as soon as he had taken possession of his money, at once found a secure place of deposit and trustworthy keepers (Orderic Vitalis, ubi supra). Orderic's language here is non-technical; but it is clear that what he is describing is Henry's establishment of a fixed treasury, with treasurers, from which his moving household would be supplied with cash. For the treasury at Rouen in the time of Henry I, Haskins, *Norman Institutions*, p. 107. The charter which Haskins prints (ibid., p. 295, no. 3) and which is dated 'in thalamo regis apud Rothomagum' is unfortunately ambiguous in this context, for the word 'thalamus' could as well mean 'chamber' as 'treasury' (in the sense of a permanent, fixed treasury), though the second is perhaps the more likely.

[2] When the dying Henry ordered his son Robert earl of Gloucester to take £60,000 from the treasure in his custody at Falaise ('de thesauro quem idem servabat Falesie') and to pay off his household servants and mercenaries, an important treasury in the castle there is implied (Orderic Vitalis, *H.E.* (ed. Le Prévost), v. 50); though there is no evidence to support Haskins's statement that it represented 'the bulk of his treasure' then in Normandy (*Norman Institutions*, p. 107).

according to Robert de Torigni, had recently been brought over from England[1]—an interestingly specific instance of that movement of funds from one treasury to another and one country to another that must have been going on all the time to serve the king's needs wherever he might be.[2] In Normandy, however, the men who administered the king's treasure there seem to have been styled 'treasurers' rather than 'chamberlains'.[3] It is doubtful if this has much significance, since the two terms could be used interchangeably at the time;[4] unless it be taken as further evidence of the existence of fixed treasuries separated from the ducal household in Normandy before 1066.

Although there was almost certainly some system of auditing the accounts of local officers and other collectors before 1066, both in the kingdom and in the duchy, there is little to show how it operated. The accounts of the king's or the duke's officers may have been examined by the chamberlains in the household, as the men ultimately responsible for seeing to it that the king had money when he needed it.[5] If the king had insisted on taking part personally in the operation after the Conquest it would have had to continue in the household; and if, in such circumstances, an attempt had been made to hold auditing sessions regularly, it would have meant making the king's officers and other accountants, including the sheriffs with their sacks of silver pennies, cross the Channel constantly, with all the dangers and lack of control which that would necessarily involve. Otherwise their accounts could have been examined only irregularly on the occasions when the king happened to be in their country. Quite apart from the problem of dealing in a household organization with the much greater sums and the larger number of persons involved when

---

[1] *Chronica*, p. 129.

[2] It is tempting to suppose that money had been brought to Falaise in anticipation of possible trouble with William Talvas or Henry's son-in-law, Geoffrey count of Anjou (cf. below, ch. 7, p. 228).

[3] Haskins, *Norman Institutions*, pp. 106–10. The question whether there was one chief treasurer over the whole system, or a treasurer for England and a treasurer for Normandy, or some other arrangement, is discussed below (p. 229 n. 1).

[4] White, 'Financial Administration under Henry I', pp. 68–9.

[5] In England, before the Conquest, it is reasonable to suppose that the sheriffs accounted with a royal chamberlain, at any rate for the revenues that were not farmed; but there is little evidence (Morris, *Medieval English Sheriff*, p. 31).

the revenues of the two countries together had to be audited, neither possibility seems satisfactory now, and it can hardly have seemed satisfactory then.

However, it would have been impossible in any case to put the clock back and to make the king's officers and other accountants pay all the money due to the king into his moving chamber when they must already have been accustomed to paying a considerable proportion of it into fixed treasuries in either country; and since accounting and auditing could not be entirely disassociated from collection, the fact that fixed treasuries existed in both countries already determined that there would have to be an auditing operation in each, distinct from the household and functioning without the king's necessary presence. The institution that was devised or which evolved to meet these conditions came to be known as the 'exchequer'. We cannot tell how or when it was invented, or who was responsible; but some time before the end of Henry's reign there appears to have been a fully developed exchequer functioning both in England and in Normandy.[1]

The name was taken from a chequered cloth that was laid on the table standing between the auditors and the accountants. On this cloth counters could be moved up and down to represent the arithmetical processes and the calculations could be followed by everyone present. Almost certainly it was to make this collective computation possible, as much as the difficulty of calculating in Roman figures or the presumed illiteracy of any of the accountants, that explains the use of a form of abacus in this way. It was an important innovation; but far more important was the other element in the exchequer, that is the appointment of commissions to audit accounts, and the appointment of such commissions periodically to hold the audit in predetermined places and on the same dates, regularly in each year. The exchequer in either country was in fact the meeting of a committee of the king's court, including a few

[1] England: Round, *Commune of London*, ch. 4; *Dialogus*, introduction to the edition by Hughes, Crump, and Johnson, 1902; Poole, *Exchequer in the Twelfth Century, passim; Pipe Roll 31 Henry I.* Normandy: Haskins, *Norman Institutions*, pp. 88–112. The suggestion that some of the ideas on which the exchequers were based came from meetings in England between Roger, bishop of Salisbury, and John, the future bishop of Lisieux, during the years 1103–7 was made by Round in 'Bernard the King's Scribe', pp. 427–8 and taken up by Poole, op. cit., pp. 58–9.

men holding household offices.[1] Since two such commissions were appointed, one for each country, the accounting process was entirely independent of the movements of king and household; and officials and debtors knew that they would be called to account with complete regularity wherever the court might be. It seems that two sessions of each commission were held in the year from the beginning, one at Easter and one at Michaelmas, that is, they met at the same time in each country.[2]

It is perhaps conceivable that there could have been only one such commission, proceeding from the one *curia regis*, meeting in the two countries alternately; but it probably made for efficiency to have two, for this would enable each commission to build upon the accounting traditions of the country in which it worked. We know that this was done; for Round could show that the English system of assaying the money brought in went back at least to the time of Domesday and most likely beyond,[3] and Haskins that the units of ducal revenue in Normandy, the farms of *vicomtés* and *prévôtés*, certainly existed before 1066.[4] This meant that practice would vary in detail as between the two exchequers, though they drew their authority from the same source and the principles of their working were the same.

[1] The little that can be known about the identity of the persons who served on these commissions is discussed below (pp. 224–8).

[2] The direct evidence for the holding of these audit sessions in Henry's reign on broadly the same lines as the comparatively well-known procedures of his grandson's time lies principally in the one surviving English pipe roll of the reign (*Pipe Roll 31 Henry I*) and in the document which Round discovered showing that there were 'barons of the exchequer' in Normandy at the same time (Round, 'Bernard the King's Scribe', pp. 425–6). Haskins, who made this document the foundation of his discussion, also found details of procedure in the Norman exchequer of the later twelfth century that can be traced back to Henry's time and even to the time of William the Conqueror (*Norman Institutions*, pp. 41–4, 88–9 etc., 105–6). For the Easter and Michaelmas sessions in the early part of the century, Morris, *Medieval English Sheriff*, p. 95; *Pipe Roll 31 Henry I*, pp. xv–xx; Haskins, *Norman Institutions*, pp. 107, 176–8. Barlow suggests that the custom of holding the Easter court at Winchester may originally have had something to do with the accounting procedures (*Edward the Confessor*, p. 186). It is not clear why these dates were chosen. Possibly they bear some relation to the dates when the farm and other renders were due and these in turn to the seasonal rhythm of agriculture; but auditing dates, as they came to be settled in the different principalities of France show such a wide variety (and in the late thirteenth century the accounts of the constable of Bordeaux, for example, were audited by an *ad hoc* commission when he went out of office) that it is difficult to be confident of such a relationship.

[3] *Commune of London*, pp. 65–9; cf. his introduction to the Hampshire section of Domesday Book in *V.C.H. Hampshire*, i. 415.

[4] *Norman Institutions*, pp. 41–4, 105–6.

Each exchequer produced a written record of its operations for the year. In England this record is known as the Great Roll of the Pipe. The earliest surviving example relates to the year ending Michaelmas 1130. It is so mature a document, so much like those of the almost unbroken series that begins in the second year of Henry II, that it is impossible to believe that it was the first to be produced.[1] The exchequer in England must have existed in recognizable form for some time before 1130. No similar roll for Normandy survives of a date earlier than 1180; but a roll for 1136 is said to have been in existence still in the eighteenth century.[2] Whether the Norman exchequer derived from England or the English exchequer derived from Normandy is a question that has been much debated. No decisive conclusion has been reached and indeed the discussion seems to have little significance; for if one had a lead over the other it must have been very short and both were created by the same authority to meet the same need. It was precisely the conjunction of the two countries under an energetic but itinerant ruler who was determined to exploit them both for all they were worth that made something like the two exchequers necessary.[3]

There were analogous developments in the administration of justice and for similar reasons. In both countries the long process whereby the ancient communal and private courts were ultimately to be superseded by a comprehensive royal judicial system was already beginning in the eleventh century. In Normandy it was based partly upon a special authority claimed by the duke as such, considerably extended by the responsibility he assumed for enforcing the Truce of God and the probably deliberate confusion of this responsibility with the maintenance of the duke's peace, and partly upon a lengthening list of pleas which he asserted to be particularly his own, together with his growing ability to make ducal justice effective. At first, no doubt, his interest in these pleas, which came to be

---

[1] *Pipe Roll 31 Henry I.* I am indebted to Professor J. C. Holt for pointing out to me that this Pipe Roll, like all its successors, contains items outstanding from earlier years, some of which he thinks are datable to 1120–1. This is a more specific reason for thinking that this roll is a lone survivor of a series that started many years earlier.

[2] Haskins, *Norman Institutions*, p. 105.

[3] See *Note on the Evolution of Financial Organization* at the end of this chapter (pp. 173–4).

known as the 'pleas of the sword'[1] (analogous to the 'pleas of the crown' in England) was primarily financial, the penalties so far as they were in money and property would be his whatever court actually dealt with the case; but more and more he was able to insist that they should be heard in his own court or in a court appointed by him. This meant that he was taking the initiative, increasingly, in the repression of disorder;[2] while, as relations between him and the Norman aristocracy took on more and more of a feudal character, as more monasteries were founded in quick succession, each with a growing endowment in land and profitable rights, and as the duchy grew more prosperous, more litigants sought the ultimate authority of the duke's court. Already by 1066 these developments were bringing more work to it than it could handle in its ordinary meetings, and the hearing of individual cases was being delegated to men commissioned by the duke.[3]

The conquest of England increased the amount of work which came to what would now be called the 'king's court' to an enormous extent. It was not simply that the territories over which William and his successors would have to keep the peace had been greatly extended, but the Norman colonization of England in itself, besides other conditions arising out of the conquest, gave occasion to a very great deal of litigation;[4] while in Normandy the increased wealth of barons and churches would have a similar if less spectacular effect—and all this was happening (as in financial matters) just when the king and his court had to divide their time between the two countries. It is true that anxious or determined litigants might have a more urgent and personal reason for pursuing the court in its wanderings than men who had to render an account, and this pursuit would always be necessary for those who insisted on bringing their causes to the king in person; but in general the fact that he was by so much the less accessible than either king or duke

---

[1] There is an early instance of the use of the term 'pleas of the sword', apparently not later than 1150, in *Regesta*, iii, No. 381 (p. 147); Haskins, *Norman Institutions*, pp. 152–3, 160–1, 187–9, and *passim*. It is clear that the fact existed long before the earliest known use of the term.

[2] On the development of ducal jurisdiction in Normandy, below, pp. 265–6.

[3] Haskins, *Norman Institutions*, pp. 55–8; Fauroux, *Recueil*, No. 209 (pp. 398–9).

[4] Douglas, *William the Conqueror*, pp. 306–8; 'Odo, Lanfranc, and the Domesday Survey', pp. 54–7.

had been hitherto, together with the increasing demands which were being made upon him, meant inevitably that he must delegate more.

It is possible that there were precedents for this in England as well as in Normandy, for the kings of the English had been enlarging the share which they took in the actual administration of justice as the Norman dukes were doing. But they were doing this under different conditions and probably much more slowly, chiefly because the courts of the shire and hundred, for all the influence that was coming to be exercised over them by the king's reeves and local magnates, had generally preserved more of their communal form than their counterparts in Normandy and were still regarded as the normal source of justice.[1] Their survival, however, was of positive assistance to William and his successors; for they provided ready-made courts and local assemblies in which the king's commissioners and justices could sit, could be advised of local custom, could carry out enquiries and hear pleas under the king's authority, applying native or feudal custom as the occasion demanded.[2] It should certainly be no matter for surprise that the Norman kings took pains to preserve these courts in England although there was nothing comparable in Normandy at the time, and although it meant that there would be many differences between local government in England and local government in Normandy under their rule.[3]

The delegation of royal and what had been ducal justice did indeed develop to such an extent that by the end of Henry's reign something that can reasonably be called a royal judicial system can be discerned, evolved to meet the needs of a cross-Channel monarchy. At its head the king's court itself, the court over which the king presided in person, remained available to litigants in their own country from time to time and at all times to those who were prepared to travel and if necessary to take their pleas across the sea, with all that that might cost them in local testimony to fact and custom. But for matters which did not require the king's personal attention or presence, and yet came within his growing sphere of jurisdiction, there was now increasingly elaborate provision. Such matters must have

---

[1] Below, p. 266.   [2] Douglas, *William the Conqueror*, pp. 305–9.
[3] Below, pp. 257–60.

formed by far the greater part of all the judicial work that came to the king's court in one way or another, and it was the part that was increasing all the time. For there was a clear practical limit to the amount of judicial work which the king could deal with personally, however anxious he might be to carry out this part of his royal function; consequently all the expansion of judicial activity in his name, the growing list of pleas of the crown and of the sword, the increasing responsibility he was assuming for keeping the peace, all the cases which were not out of the ordinary in some way or other, must of necessity be handled by delegation. To meet this need, a recognizable if not very clearly defined body of men was formed, bishops, barons, and men holding household offices, and these men were taking over more and more of the king's judicial work. They were not 'professional' lawyers and some of them may not have acted in this way very frequently or over a very long period of their lives; others were serving so often that they seem to have formed something like a permanent tribunal in England and in Normandy, a group of justices presided over by a chief justice or justiciar. As a body, the men who formed this tribunal were probably identical with the 'barons of the exchequer'; in fact it is likely that they thought of themselves as meeting on certain occasions to audit accounts and on other occasions to hear pleas—if indeed they distinguished very clearly between the two activities.[1] What is important is that in each country there was now a central court in fact, even if it had never been formally constituted, which was doing justice in the king's name whether he could attend in person or not.[2]

The same men were appointed as the itinerant justices whom the king was sending out both in his kingdom and in his duchy, to supplement the work of the 'central court' by taking his justice to the shires and the *vicomtés*. He was also experimenting with local justices who did not move around but dealt with royal pleas in a shire or group of shires in England, in a *vicomté* or other local unit in Normandy. The courts which they held, whether they were sitting in what would otherwise be

[1] Below, pp. 224, 227–8.
[2] England: Pollock and Maitland, *H.E.L.*, i. 109; Richardson and Sayles, *Governance of Medieval England*, pp. 174–6, 188; Stenton, *English Justice*, pp. 58–60; Poole, *Exchequer in the Twelfth Century*, pp. 174–7. Normandy: Haskins, *Norman Institutions*, pp. 88–105.

a shire court or a baronial court, were as much the king's courts as the central body itself; they were indeed simply extensions of it, described as *curia regis* in Normandy as well as in England; for the justices, besides being drawn from the group of royal justices that was forming centrally, were administering the king's justice and acting in his name.[1] The whole judicial organization, under the general supervision of a chief justice or justiciar in each country, had long passed the point at which the delegation of royal or ducal justice was an occasional, *ad hoc* affair. It was now a matter of routine and rapidly being institutionalized. The duke's justice, already developing in Normandy before 1066, had been stimulated by the need which the conquest of England and the extension of the itinerary created, and by the opportunities which the surviving local institutions of that country offered, to take the initiative and eventually to compete whether consciously or not with baronial and other courts. In the end, over a very long term of years, it would supersede them all, reaping the financial and the political profits; and the law of the king's courts would become the common law of England and the 'coutume de Normandie'.

Thus both in their financial and in their judicial administration the Norman kings found it necessary to supplement the direct rule of their itinerant selves, household and court, with institutions which seem to have been built on the customs and traditions of each country. These institutions were to have an enormous importance in the later development of government, particularly in England; but in the eleventh and early twelfth centuries they formed only a part of the solution to the problem of governing kingdom and duchy together—they were still only supplementary to the itinerant king-household-court. Moreover the itinerant and the localized provision for the rule of England and Normandy together did not of itself solve the whole of the problem of government which faced the Norman kings. William the Conqueror both as duke and as king, following in the footsteps of his ancestors, had established some form of

[1] England: Stenton, *English Justice*, pp. 60–8; Richardson and Sayles, *Governance of Medieval England*, pp. 175–88; Cronne, 'The Office of Local Justiciar in England under the Norman Kings'. Normandy: Haskins, *Norman Institutions*, pp. 99–104; Delisle, *Histoire de Saint-Sauveur-le-Vicomte*, pièces justificatives, Nos. 36, 42 (pp. 40, 46–7).

lordship over a number of neighbouring princes.[1] This over-lordship had to be maintained and if possible strengthened and extended, if only because rights once established must not be allowed to lapse.

The problem in relation to the 'vassal principalities' was not that of providing an administration, for the native rulers were left to manage their internal affairs, but of maintaining and consolidating a relationship. This might not be very difficult in practice, for in every case both sides stood to gain at least something from it. On the king's side, these overlordships gave him prestige and they contributed to the defence of the lands he ruled directly. For prestige, his lordship over the king of Scots, whatever its precise character at any given time, made him a 'king of kings'; and it could be argued that the same was true of his lordship over the surviving Welsh princes.[2] In both cases his overlordship provided cover for Norman expansion and protection for Norman colonists in those countries, and above all it gave him security on the northern and western boundaries of his kingdom. Whether or not William the Conqueror could have destroyed the Scottish kingdom or occupied the whole of Wales if he had put his mind to it, in fact he adopted his usual stance as the lawful successor of Edward the Confessor and demanded no more, initially, than the rights and superiorities that the Confessor had enjoyed, though translated into terms that the Normans could understand. This left him with two land frontiers in Britain, the best protection for which would undoubtedly be the extension of his influence and authority beyond them.

There were analogous reasons for maintaining the continental overlordships. Brittany, like Wales, was a weak and disunited country, whose troubles might well spill over into Normandy—a possibility which was the more dangerous, at least in the eleventh century, because the western part of Normandy had hardly yet been fully integrated into the duchy. Flanders, by

---

[1] The terms 'principality' and 'prince' are here used as general terms to cover the kingdom of the Scots, the Welsh kingdoms or principalities, the various duchies, *comtés*, and lordships that were involved in France, and their rulers. The facts of Norman overlordship are given above in chapter 3, pp. 61–88, and some discussion of the characteristics of this overlordship below in chapter 6, pp. 206–18.

[2] For the kingly character of the Welsh princes, Edwards, 'The Normans and the Welsh March', pp. 169–75.

contrast, was relatively very strong and had blocked Norman expansion in a north-easterly direction in the tenth century. It was clearly advantageous to have client principalities (Pontieu, Boulogne) between Normandy and Flanders and if possible some form of lordship over the counts of Flanders themselves. The need to dominate the Vexin Français, the *comté* of Maine, and the seigneuries that lay between them, scarcely needs explaining. Paris is not very far from Rouen, and the natural line of attack for the king of France was down the Seine valley or through the *comté* of Évreux; while the counts of Anjou must attack through Maine and the Bellême lands. Moreover, the overlordships which the Norman dukes and kings did establish facilitated the raising of troops, particularly mercenary troops and particularly in Brittany and Flanders.

When considering the advantages which the vassal princes, for their part, might see in the relationship, it is important to avoid modern nationalist assumptions. Even the kings of Scots, at least those who followed Malcolm III, most probably regarded their association with the Norman kings as conferring prestige upon them rather than as compromising their independence. It certainly gave solid advantages: military assistance of an up-to-date kind against rivals and rebels in their own country, the opportunity to modernize their monarchy and to develop their own royal authority, security in the south which would enable them, in due course, to face the problem of the Highlands. The 'dukes' of Brittany at this time were but counts of Rennes or Cornouailles, claiming, but not always able to exercise, authority over the other Breton counts and seigneurs.[1] An understanding with their powerful Norman neighbours, and even a measure of protection for the time being, was necessary if they were to hold their own against internal competitors, or external rivals such as the counts of Anjou. To a count of Boulogne, the lands he acquired in England would be a very considerable addition to his wealth; and to a count of Flanders the promised annuity would be an item in his revenue that would be by no means negligible. Even the Welsh princes were using Norman troops when they could and competing for such favours as they might obtain from the king; and Hélie de la Flèche, when he established himself as

[1] Briefly, in Waquet, *Histoire de la Bretagne*, pp. 35–9.

count of Maine, could only survive the competing pressures of Normandy and Anjou by yielding in some measure to both of them.[1]

Mutually advantageous relationships of this kind could be kept in repair without a great deal of activity. Such action as there was seems to have been adapted to each individual case and to have followed no readily discernible pattern. In Scotland, once Edgar had been established on the throne, his experience and that of his brothers as hostages or guests at the Norman court, and what might almost be described as their education there, counted for a great deal. They must have seen that if they could furnish themselves with something of the Norman military apparatus of knights and castles this would not only raise the effectiveness and so the status of the monarchy in their own country but give them what hope they might ultimately have of holding their own against their mighty neighbour; while David I, by continuing to hold the earldom of Huntingdon after he had become king, left a valuable pledge in King Henry's hands. In Wales, with the constant rivalries and disputes among the still independent princes, the continuous pressure of the marcher lords needed only to be reinforced by an occasional royal expedition. The campaigns of the Norman kings in Wales were regarded at the time as somewhat ineffective, and have been so regarded by historians, no doubt because they did not win victories of a conventional kind; but it is very likely that nothing more than a military demonstration was needed or intended.[2] On the Continent the Norman kings must often have relied upon such hold as fiefs in England or Normandy gave them over seigneurs beyond the duchy, certainly in the case of the counts of Boulogne, Pontieu, and Perche, the lords of Montfort l'Amaury and other 'cross-border' families. On the evidence, the full recognition of the vassalage of the duke of Brittany in 1113 seems like an almost incidental result of Henry's war against the king of France and the count of Anjou; but Brittany at this time was unlikely to be completely independent of both Normandy and Anjou, and Henry for the time being was victorious. As for his suzerainty

---

[1] In general, above, pp. 61–88.
[2] Particularly if, as in 1114, that was enough to reinstate or reinforce the relationship (Lloyd, *History of Wales*, ii. 463–4).

over Maine, once direct control of the *comté* had been lost this was vital to the ruler of Normandy and constantly challenged. It could only be held, so far as it was held, by war, diplomacy, and the apparatus of dynastic marriages; but the maintenance of an interest in Maine was a large part of the whole defence of the Norman lands and lordships.

There is one final element in the practical working of the Norman kings' government that was vital in their time and which has to be included in any credible description of their government. The English Channel lay across their lands and lordships, dividing them geographically into two parts which, if not equal in territorial extent, were at least of equal concern to their rulers. Any king who aspired to rule England and Normandy directly and to maintain the overlordships he had established beyond them by sharing out his time and itinerating with household and court among them, had to organize a ferry service that was reasonably quick and reliable and was not subject to undue delay by reason of weather or other incalculable causes. If conveying the king and all who moved around with him across the sea was treated as something of an emergency, to be improvised on each occasion and avoided if possible, the efficiency of his rule—given the form of government that the Norman kings had adopted—would be hardly adequate to hold their lands and lordships together. In fact, they had to over-come the obstacle which this stretch of sea presented; and the historian, before he accepts the argument that they were indeed trying to rule their lands and maintain their overlordships as a single political entity and to do so basically by itineration, has to satisfy himself that they appreciated the problem and had mastered it so far as was necessary for their purposes. There is perhaps just enough evidence[1] to show that they achieved this.

---

[1] The evidence for the royal transfretations, and indeed for much of the royal itinerary during the period of the Norman kings, is to be found mainly in the Anglo-Saxon Chronicle and its related texts, Florence of Worcester (*Chronicon*), Henry of Huntingdon (*Historia Anglorum*), and Simeon of Durham (*Historia Regum*, in *Opera*, ii). Save during William the Conqueror's reign, these annalistic English chroniclers together record the king's comings and goings with fair regularity. The Norman chronicles are generally less informative on this matter and the charters, save on one point, rarely do more than help to fix a probable port of arrival or departure. The following account of the royal transfretations, and the table at the end of the chapter, is based on the evidence of these texts together with the incidental references in the other chronicles of the time and the general

In the first place, it can be shown that the Norman kings crossed and re-crossed the sea at quite frequent intervals. William the Conqueror probably made the crossing some seventeen times in the twenty-one years between his coronation at Westminster and his death in a suburb of Rouen;[1] William Rufus five times in the rather less than four years between September 1096, when he took possession of Normandy, and his death in the New Forest on 2 August 1100; but he had been sufficiently interested in Normandy to make the crossing another five times already between his coronation in 1087 and that last interview with his brother Robert in 1096. Henry crossed sixteen times between the battle of Tinchebrai and his death at Lyons-la-Forêt in 1135; but he too had made the crossing three and possibly five times between his coronation in England and his victory in Normandy. Stephen paid but one visit to Normandy as king, crossing and re-crossing in the year 1137. Altogether there were some fifty royal transfretations (counting each journey in either direction as one) between December 1066 and the summer of 1144 when Geoffrey Plantegenêt assumed the title duke of the Normans, that is an average of about one in every eighteen months. This includes the years when kingdom and duchy were ruled separately (or at least nominally so)[2] by two brothers, but reckons only the journeys of the king. Naturally the intervals between transfretations varied considerably in length. After 1066, William the Conqueror seems to have had one spell of about four years at a stretch in each country; the longest period that Henry spent continuously in either after 1106 was about four-and-a-

guidance of Farrer, 'Outline Itinerary of King Henry I', the itineraries in *Regesta*, i and ii, and Douglas, *William the Conqueror*, from which most references can be obtained. Attention has, however, been restricted to the royal voyages, and those only between 1066 and 1144, and no attempt has been made to carry out an exhaustive search in all possible sources of information or to study navigation in the English Channel generally during the eleventh and twelfth centuries. The subject deserves a much more thorough treatment. In Norman times the organization of the royal transfretations was as important a part of the mechanism of government as the working of the treasuries or the royal secretariat.

[1] After William's return to England from Normandy in December 1067 there are many uncertainties in his itinerary. The figure given above seems the most probable—*Handbook of British Chronology*, p. 31; Stenton, *A.-S.E.*, p. 601; Douglas, *William the Conqueror*, pp. 451–3 and *passim*.

[2] It is questionable how far Robert Curthose was ever a completely free and independent ruler in Normandy (chs. 4 and 6).

half years in Normandy (1116–20), his longest spell in England after that date lasting little more than two-and-a-half years (1120–3); while William Rufus crossed three times in one year (1099). With such a number of crossings[1] to be undertaken and organized, it would suggest gross inefficiency if no elements of routine showed themselves, while any evidence of such routine or regularity would be a useful indication of the degree to which the Norman kings regarded this operation as part of the normal mechanics of government.

The amount of organization needed on any one occasion would depend upon the number of persons to be conveyed with the king and the amount of gear and general cargo that would have to be transported with them. This varied from the armies which William the Conqueror brought to England in 1066[2] and 1085,[3] or which Henry took from England to Normandy in 1106, 1116, and 1123,[4] with household and court, to the few companions which William Rufus took with him, perhaps in a single ship, when he made his emergency crossing during a summer storm in 1099.[5] The number of ships employed can only be guessed, for we know neither their normal complement nor the total number of persons transported on any one occasion. Orderic thought that there were 300 souls in all on board the White Ship when she foundered and that it was the irresponsibility of the company rather than their numbers that

---

[1] See table at the end of this chapter (pp. 175–6).

[2] For estimates, Douglas, *William the Conqueror*, pp. 189–90, 198–200.

[3] 'William . . . went to England with a larger force of mounted men and infantry from France and Brittany than had ever come to this country, so that people wondered how this country could maintain all that army'; A.-S.C., 1085, E (p. 161); cf. Florence of Worcester, *Chronicon*, ii. 18.

[4] The occasions were the Tinchebrai campaign, the period of warfare in Normandy culminating in the battle of Brémule, and the rebellion of Norman nobles in favour of William Clito. On all these occasions there seem to have been troops from England in Henry's army (respectively, Huntingdon, *Historia Anglorum*, p. 235; Orderic Vitalis, *H.E.* (ed. Le Prévost), iv. 316, 333, 458. The precise meaning of the term 'Angli' may be doubtful in this context (Hollister, *Military Organization of Norman England*, pp. 250–3), but at least it should mean men brought from England whatever their racial origins.

[5] The story of Rufus's crossing in 1099 evidently grew in the telling. It seems clear that the number of men accompanying him was very small (William de Jumièges, *Gesta*, interp. Robert de Torigni, p. 276); but only Orderic actually says that no more than one ship was used, and that an old one (*H.E.* (ed. Le Prévost), iv. 58). Huntingdon uses the plural (*Historia Anglorum*, p. 231; cf. Malmesbury, *Gesta Regum*, ii. 373).

caused the disaster.[1] Whether or not this figure is credible,[2] circumstances suggest that she must have been one of the larger ships of her time. When Henry was waiting to embark in 1133, probably at Portsmouth, one ship dragged her anchors and fouled seven others.[3] He is not known to have had more than household, court, and bodyguard with him on that occasion; but the clear implication of the accounts of the incident that we have is that these eight ships did not make up the whole fleet and that there were almost certainly more. It seems that there was already a royal ship, the *esnecca*, and a steersman, or master-steersman, who owed the service of producing her when required and commanding her.[4] We can only suppose that when the master-steersman received notice of the king's intention to make the crossing, it was his business to impress shipping along the coast from which the king was sailing, as the admiral did in the fourteenth century.[5] If Henry arranged his itinerary some time in advance,[6] the master-steersman could at least be given plenty of time to do this, so that the king is not likely to have been delayed at the port simply because the ships were not ready; while the existence of a ship devoted primarily to conveying the king to and fro between Normandy and England suggests that there was a nucleus of experienced pilots and sailors who knew the tides and passages between the ports he was most likely to use.

The ports which the Norman kings did use, so far as they can be identified, afford in themselves some evidence of increasing

---

[1] Orderic Vitalis, *H.E.* (ed. Le Prévost), iv. 411–14.

[2] At least the figure he gives for the number of rowers, 50, is quite plausible, for there appear to have been between 40 and 52 rowers in the Skuldelev longship and ships of this type were used in the eleventh century (Crumlin-Pedersen, 'The Viking Ships of Roskilde', p. 9).

[3] Florence of Worcester, *Chronicon*, ii. 93–4.

[4] Orderic Vitalis, *H.E.* (ed. Le Prévost), iv. 411; Haskins, *Norman Institutions*, pp. 121–2.

[5] The only reference to this operation in the time of the Norman kings that has so far been found is contained in Orderic's narrative of the White Ship disaster: 'Henricus rex, in Normannia rebus post multos labores optime dispositis, decrevit transfretare . . . Unde classem continuo jussit praeparari, et copiosam omnis dignitatis militiam secum comitari . . . Ingenti classe in portu qui Barbaflot dicitur, praeparata, et nobili legione in comitatu regis Austro flante aggregata, vii⁰ kalendas decembris, prima statione noctis, rex et comites ejus naves intraverunt, et carbasa sursum levata ventis in pelago commiserunt et mane Angliam . . . amplexati sunt' (*H.E.* (ed. Le Prévost), iv. 409–11).

[6] Above, pp. 127–8.

organization and routine. Under William the Conqueror and
William Rufus there seems to be no regularity, apart from an
apparent preference for the shorter crossings, as though they
were employing the services owed by the towns later grouped
together as the Cinque Ports;[1] but under Henry it looks as
though the terminal on the English side was coming to be fixed
at Portsmouth-Southampton,[2] and if this is so it must bear some
relation to the growing importance of the treasury at Winchester. It is even possible that there was already some installation at Portchester for treasure in transit between Winchester
and the Norman treasuries.[3] The evidence is by no means so
clear on the Norman side, but only Barfleur and the growing
port of Dieppe are mentioned in Henry's time. Increasingly
stabilized routes suggest an increasingly high degree of organization.

The ships themselves are likely to have been very similar to
those shown on the Bayeux Tapestry, which, whatever its exact
date and origin, is near enough contemporary and sufficiently
representational for these purposes.[4] They could carry cargo[5]
and horses[6] as well as human passengers, and means had been
found to get the horses on and off without undue difficulty.[7]

---

[1] e.g. Dover, D.B., i. 1 a 1; Sandwich, D.B., i. 3 a 1; Romney, D.B., i. 4 b 1 and
10 b 2. For the early history of the Cinque Ports, Murray, *Constitutional History of the
Cinque Ports*, chs. 1 and 2.
[2] See *Table of Royal Transfretations, 1066–1144*, at the end of this chapter
(pp, 175–6).   [3] Above, p. 150 n. 5.
[4] *Bayeux Tapestry*, plates 5–8, 30, 36–9, 42–5; cf. Crumlin-Pedersen, 'The Viking
Ships of Roskilde' and, in greater detail, with O. Olsen, 'The Skuldelev ships'.
That the ships used by the Norman kings were closely related to the Viking ships
is shown not only by the correspondence between representations on the Bayeux
Tapestry and archaeological finds in Scandinavia, but by the use of the 'Latin'
word *esnecca* (Danish and Norwegian, *snekke*, Icelandic, *snekkja*) to denote the
Anglo-Norman royal ship. The Tapestry seems to show only the longships and their
tenders, but broader cargo vessels must have been used as well.
[5] *Bayeux Tapestry*, plates 40, 41. The White Ship in 1120 carried the king's
treasure and some casks of wine as well as its crew, marines, and passengers:
Orderic Vitalis, *H.E.* (ed. Le Prévost), iv. 412–13, 419.
[6] *Bayeux Tapestry*, plates 42–5. It seems to have been customary in the eleventh
century for royal envoys to take their horses with them across the Channel, as a
modern tourist takes his car; and the charge at Dover for the horse was 3*d.* in
winter and 2*d.* in summer (D.B., i. 1 a 1. I owe this reference to Dr. Sally Harvey).
[7] They are shown disembarking on *Bayeux Tapestry*, plate 45; and that this was
a practical method is demonstrated in Sawyer, *Age of the Vikings*, p. 77 and plate IX.
The Tapestry does not show how they were put on the ships (cf. plate 42; Crumlin-
Pedersen, 'The Viking Ships of Roskilde', p. 9 and illustration No. 10).

The ships could be beached;[1] and indeed when a large fleet
had to be used there was probably no alternative, though some
form of quay may have been used for ships carrying important
personages or when the number of ships was small.[2] Both oars
and sails were used, and this is important; for it meant that
the fleet need not be becalmed if the wind dropped to nothing
in mid Channel and also that the ships would be able to
negotiate the entrances to harbours, which frequently involved
several changes of course in confined waters, without delay
and with less chance of fouling one another.[3] It is unlikely that
they could sail into the wind at all, though they could probably
make progress with a side wind.[4] The turn of the eleventh and
twelfth centuries is regarded by historical climatologists as a
period of 'climatic optimum' in these latitudes, which would
mean prevailing westerlies and a relative infrequency of really
bad storms in the Channel,[5] conditions which would at least
keep the number of occasions when a crossing was impossible to
a minimum. This, however, is a relative matter, for the weather
can disrupt Channel traffic for a matter of hours even today;
and the chroniclers certainly do record occasions when the
king had to wait for the weather.[6] It must not be thought that
a twelfth-century ship could sail from a port in England to a
port in Normandy on the shortest and most direct course, like
a modern ferry. The direction and strength of the tide would
have been as important as the direction and strength of the
wind, which underlines the importance of having experienced

[1] *Bayeux Tapestry*, plates 42, 45.

[2] Some form of harbour installation seems to be shown in *Bayeux Tapestry*, plate
30; and it would have been a simple matter to construct a quay at Barfleur if the
twelfth-century place for embarkation and disembarkation was in the same creek
as the present fishing harbour—the obvious place for it.

[3] See *Note on the Use of Oars* at the end of this chapter (pp. 177–8).

[4] Their navigational capabilities cannot have been very different from those of
the Viking ships (Sawyer, *Age of the Vikings*, ch. 4, esp. p. 75). Above, p. 167 n. 4.

[5] Lamb, *The Changing Climate*, pp. 7, 174. I am indebted to Dr. J. G. Lock-
wood of the Geography Department, University of Leeds, for discussing this point
with me.

[6] The most famous example is the hold-up of William's invasion fleet at Saint-
Valéry in 1066; but in that case a large army had to be landed in good order on a
hostile shore and conditions had to be perfect, as in 1944. Rufus was held up for
some weeks at Hastings in 1094 (A.-S.C., 1094, E, p. 171) and in both directions
three years later (ibid., 1097, E, pp. 174–5); Henry for an unstated period of time
in 1114 (ibid., 1114, E, H, pp. 183–4). There is no need to multiply examples: the
use that was made of the time is more important.

crews; for even though the discovery of a portable sundial of this period at Canterbury[1] suggests that some primitive navigational aids may already have been available, the pilots of Henry's time must have relied much more on rule-of-thumb.[2] Mention of overnight crossings[3] suggests the use of the stars for navigation, though it may also indicate a desire to approach the opposite coast in daylight. The time and probably the date of departure were almost certainly determined by the tides and the wind; but everything suggests that the voyage itself lasted no more than a matter of hours.[4]

There must have been plenty of ships and plenty of experienced sailors in the Channel during the eleventh and twelfth centuries. This hardly needs demonstrating for the Straits of Dover and the adjacent waters;[5] and in the far west the very close contact between the Cornish and the Breton peninsulas could only have been maintained, as it was maintained, by a constant traffic of small boats between them.[6] As far as the middle section is concerned, the accounts we have of the invasion of Robert Curthose in 1101 show that each side had a good knowledge of the other's movements on the opposite shore, and that, since Robert's sailors were able to seduce the crews of the ships that Henry had sent to destroy or disable the transports assembled at Le Tréport, and even persuade them to pilot the invading fleet past Pevensey, where Henry's army was waiting, into Portsmouth, seamen on either side of that part

---

[1] Binns, 'Sun Navigation in the Viking Age and the Canterbury Portable Sundial', pp. 23–34.

[2] If one could be sure of the exact date of sailing and both departure and arrival ports, it might be possible to work out a probable course with the retrospective astronomical information that is now available. But all the necessary data are not found together for any one transfretation in the time of the Norman kings. I am very much indebted to Mr. Alan Binns, of the University of Hull, for discussing this matter with me.

[3] e.g. the crossing in 1066, Rufus's crossing to Normandy in 1099 (Orderic Vitalis, *H.E.* (ed. Le Prévost), iv. 58), and Henry's crossing to England in 1120 (ibid., p. 411). The idea of embarking in the evening and landing next morning must have seemed credible to Orderic, who had himself crossed the Channel at least three times.

[4] In a letter to me Mr. Binns worked out a hypothetical course from Portsmouth to Dieppe, assuming that the ships could make 5 knots and take full advantage of the tides. Such a voyage would take about 16 hours, and a similar voyage from Portsmouth to Barfleur about 10 hours.

[5] e.g. the entry for Dover in Domesday Book (i., 1 a 1).

[6] Fleuriot, 'Breton et cornique à la fin du moyen âge', p. 705.

of the Channel could understand one another pretty well—which again argues frequent contact.[1]

The means existed, therefore, for the Norman kings to incorporate the Channel crossing into the general organization of their itinerary. That they did so is curiously indicated by the use made of the words 'transfretatio' and 'transitus', in addition to the evidence already discussed. Some seventeen of Henry's charters are dated 'in transitu' or 'in transfretatione', and they are so dated at Arques, Dieppe, Bishops Waltham, Eling, Fareham, Romsey, Portsmouth, Southampton, Westbourne, and Winchester.[2] Not all these places are on the coast or are possible places for embarkation or for landing. The 'transfretatio' therefore was not simply the actual sea voyage, but was rather a stage in the royal progress that might last for days or even weeks, when the king's intention to make the crossing had been announced, preparations were being made, and the business of the court would be arranged with the eventual sea-crossing in mind.[3] The time that might have to be spent waiting for wind and tide to be right was not spent idly.[4] If the king was at Eling or Romsey or Winchester some of his time would be occupied, no doubt, in the New Forest, but a good deal of it

[1] David, *Robert Curthose*, pp. 130–1; Hollister, 'The Anglo-Norman Civil War: 1101', pp. 325–6.

[2] *Regesta*, ii, Nos. 682 (Romsey, 'in transitu regis', p. 40), 987 (Winchester, 'in transitu regis', p. 101), 988 (Bishops Waltham, 'in transitu regis in Normanniam', p. 101), 1068 (Westbourne, Sussex, about 5 miles NE. of Portsmouth, 'in transitu', p. 109), 1152 (Southampton, 'in transitu regis', p. 137), 1494 (Portsmouth, 'in transfretatione', p. 207), 1498, 1499, 1500, 1501, 1502 (Eling, Hampshire, 3 miles west of Southampton across the estuary of the River Test, 'in transitu', pp. 208–9), 1693, 1694, 1695 (Arques-la-Bataille, 6 km. inland from Dieppe, 'in transitu', pp. 248–9), 1697 (Dieppe, 'in transitu', p. 249), 1777 (Fareham 'apud Ferneham in transfretatione Regis', p. 266), 1782 (Westbourne, 'apud Burnam in transfretatione mea', p. 267).

[3] The entry in A.-S.C., 1114, E (pp. 183–4) seems to exemplify this interpretation. 'In this same year the king went towards the sea and meant to cross over but the weather prevented him'. He then summoned the abbot of Peterborough, and on 15 September at Westbourne, apparently in an assembly, forced him to take the bishopric of Rochester. On 21 September at Rowner (Hampshire, 2 miles north of Gosport), the king appointed John, a monk of Séez, to Peterborough; 'and on the same day . . . went on board ship at Portsmouth'. This narrative is to be connected with the group of documents dated at Westbourne and attributed to the year 1114 (*Regesta*, ii, Nos. 1060–72, pp. 117–20), of which one is further dated 13 September 1114 (No. 1070, p. 120) and another 'in transitu' (No. 1068, p. 119).

[4] Florence of Worcester, *Chronicon*, ii. 93–4: 'The king, having gone to the coast for the purpose of crossing the sea, delayed his departure though the wind was often fair for the voyage.'

was certainly employed on matters of state. We know of this because of the charters and writs that were dated on these occasions,[1] and most of them must have claimed the king's attention to some extent. In 1094 Rufus is said to have waited about six weeks for the weather at Hastings; but the chronicler who reports this also says that during that time he had Battle Abbey consecrated and dealt with the case of the bishop of Norwich; and Henry's period of waiting in 1114 seems to have been fully occupied.[2] Apart from normal periods of rest and the few hours during which he was actually at sea, the king was probably not inactive at any time during a 'transfretatio'. The time was not lost, and business could be adjusted to any special conditions that this particular phase in the royal itinerary might impose.

If the king chose to plan his itinerary some way ahead, as Henry did, there was no reason why the need to cross the Channel, even frequently, should interfere with the course of his affairs to any appreciable extent. That being so, he could enjoy all the advantages which transport by water had over transport by land for conveying men and goods in bulk before the invention of the steam engine. He had ships suited to his purposes such that, given the general pace of life and events in the early twelfth century, they were not likely to be unduly affected by wind and weather.[3] Moreover, their safety record seems to have been good. The dreadful political consequences of the foundering of the White Ship have exaggerated its importance as a purely maritime disaster in the minds of historians. One ship was lost out of a possible twenty or thirty on one occasion, and there were some fifty such occasions. No doubt there were

[1] The references given above (p. 170 n. 2) are restricted to those in which the terms 'in transitu' or 'in transfretatione' are actually used; but there are a great many other charters and writs, not so dated, which can reasonably be attributed to the same or similar occasions, e.g. *Regesta*, ii, Nos. 1496–1509 (pp. 208–10), 1692–8 (pp. 248–9); though it should perhaps be remembered that their present association is editorial.

[2] A.-S.C., 1094, E (p. 171); above, p. 170 n. 3.

[3] That they were not even subject to the delays of enforced sailing in convoy is implied by statements that the main fleet left Barfleur some time in advance of the White Ship in 1120 (though she tried to catch up), and that Henry's first thought, when the White Ship did not show up at the landing in England next day, was that she must have put in at some other port along the coast (Simeon of Durham, *Historia Regum*, in *Opera*, ii. 259). The conditions under which William's invasion fleet had to cross the sea were quite different.

many other mishaps; but whereas a chronicler can report fully
an incident in which one ship dragged its anchors and fouled
seven others in port, without loss of life or personal injury,[1] no
other accidents were deemed worthy of mention. There is sufficient evidence to show that the business and the movements of
the court were arranged on the assumption that the crossing
would have to be undertaken every so often, and that the
crossing itself was so far organized that it could be treated as
a matter of routine. It may even be that the English Channel,
set in the midst of the lands and lordships of the Norman kings,
served to bind those lands and lordships together, as the
Mediterranean and the Irish Seas have served in other times
and contexts, and that its existence was of positive assistance
to those who were trying to establish a Normanno-English
kingdom astride the English Channel. Whatever objections
there may be to the idea of such a kingdom, the existence of
the Channel cannot be one of them.

[1] Florence of Worcester, *Chronicon*, ii. 93–4. Admittedly the incident was attributed to an earthquake.

Note on the Evolution of Financial Organization

(p. 155 note 3)

THE whole process of evolution suggested here was certainly not peculiar to Normandy and England: (1) at first the ruler takes all his treasure about with him in his 'chamber'; (2) as it grows he deposits part, temporarily or on a semi-permanent basis, in monasteries which are responsible for its safe-keeping etc.; (3) later he begins to deposit treasure in buildings of his own, and therefore has to find staff for its administration; (4) this staff is 'seconded' from his household and eventually separates from it, forming (5) a treasury organization that supersedes the monastic treasuries though for some purposes (e.g. archives) there was a considerable overlap, and finally, (6) he takes the auditing of accounts out of the household organization likewise and entrusts it to a committee of the *curia*. At some time before 1146, the Capetian kings deposited such of their treasure as they did not need for current purposes with the Templars in Paris, who acted as the royal treasurers until the end of the thirteenth century. It is a special case of the use of monastic or quasi-monastic institutions for the keeping of royal treasure, and the financial expertise of the Templars seems to have delayed the development of the fully royal financial organization in France. When a commission of the court, the *curia in compotis*, was first appointed to examine accounts in the king's interest, it met at the Temple. It was only in 1295 that the king withdrew his treasure from the Temple and set up his own treasury, and the full organization of Treasury, Chambre des Comptes as the auditing body and the Chambre aux Deniers to keep the accounts of the household begins to appear (Lot and Fawtier, *Histoire des institutions françaises*, ii. *Institutions royales*, pp. 196–200, 240). In Flanders a central fixed treasury was located at Bruges early in the twelfth century (Lyon and Verhulst, *Medieval Finance*, pp. 13–15, 56–7) and later in the century a central auditing body, the *ratiocinatores supremi*, was formed. This may even have used a chequer-board for collective computation (ibid., pp. 38–9). The different stages were reached at different dates in different countries. In the duchies of Brittany and Burgundy the ducal finances were still managed within the household organization at the end of the thirteenth century, and the dukes still took a personal part in the auditing (Jones, *Ducal Brittany*, pp. 23–5; cf. Pocquet du Haut-Jussé, 'Le plus ancien rôle des comptes du duché, 1262'; Richard, 'Les Institutions ducales dans le duché de Bourgogne', in Lot and Fawtier, *Histoire des institutions françaises*, i. *Institutions seigneuriales*, pp. 229–34, and *Les Ducs de Bourgogne*, pp. 412–27, 441–7).

Since the count of Flanders was wealthy and in firm control of his territories, and the county itself almost certainly in advance, economically, of England and Normandy, the relative precocity of the Norman kings' financial organization must owe a great deal to the necessities imposed upon them by the government of the two countries together and by their extended itinerary.

Table of Royal Transfretations, 1066–1144

		Normandy		*England*
WILLIAM I				
Sept.	1066	Saint-Valéry	→	Pevensey
Feb./Mar.	1067	Dieppe (??)	←	Pevensey
Dec.	1067	Dieppe	→	Winchelsea

From this point the dates of William's transfretations are uncertain and the ports he used unknown. It is probable that he was on the Continent from winter 1071/2 to spring 1072, in 1073, 1074–5, 1076–80, 1081–2, 1083–1083/4, 1084–5, and 1086 until his death in a suburb of Rouen in September 1087. William Rufus was in Normandy at the time of his father's death.

		Normandy		*England*
WILLIAM II				
Sept.	1087	Touques	→	Portsmouth (??)
Feb.	1091	Le Tréport (??)	←	Dover (??) or Hastings (??)
Aug.	1091	—	→	—
Mar.	1094	Le Tréport (??)	←	Hastings
Dec.	1094	Wissant	→	Dover
Sept.	1096	—	←	Hastings
Apr.	1097	—	→	Arundel
Nov.	1097	—	←	—
Apr.	1099	—	→	—
July	1099	Touques	←	Southampton (?)
Sept.	1099	—	→	—

William Rufus was killed in the New Forest, 2 August 1100. His brother Henry was in England at the time.

HENRY I				
Apr.	1105	Barfleur	←	Portsmouth/Southampton (?)
Aug.	1105	—	→	—
July	1106	—	←	—
Mar./Apr.	1107	—	→	—
July/Aug.	1108	—	←	Portsmouth (?)
June	1109	—	→	—
Aug.	1111	Dieppe (??)	←	Portsmouth (?)
July	1113	—	→	—
Sept.	1114	—	←	Portsmouth
July	1115	—	→	—
Apr.	1116	—	←	Portsmouth (??)
Nov.	1120	Barfleur	→	Southampton (?)
June	1123	—	←	Portsmouth
Sept.	1126	Dieppe (??)	→	—

HENRY I (*cont.*)

Aug.	1127	—	←	Portsmouth/Southampton (?)
July	1129	—	→	—
Sept.	1130	—	←	Portsmouth
July	1131	Dieppe	→	Portsmouth (??)
Aug.	1133	—	←	Portsmouth (?)

Henry died at Lyons-la-Forêt, not far from Rouen, 1 December 1135. Orderic Vitalis credits him with a brief visit to Normandy in 1104, but this is not confirmed by any other writer. Robert Curthose crossed from Le Tréport to Portsmouth in 1101: it is not known by what route he returned.

STEPHEN

| Mar. | 1137 | La Hougue | ← | Portsmouth (??) |
| Dec. | 1137 | — | → | Portsmouth (?) |

No query   = direct evidence.
One query   = good evidence short of a specific statement.
Two queries = some evidence, usually circumstantial.
—   = no evidence.

This table is illustrative only. For the evidence on which it is based and the possibilities of gathering fuller and more accurate information, above pp. 163 note 1, 170 note 2.

Note on the Use of Oars
(p. 168, note 3)

T H E use to which oars were put is very clearly shown in the representation of Harold's voyage of 1064 on the Bayeux Tapestry
(*Bayeux Tapestry*, plates 5–8), where they are shown as employed at
the beginning and the end of the journey. In Orderic's description
of Rufus's voyage of 1099, the word used when the king gave the
order to cast off is 'remigare' (*H.E.* (ed. Le Prévost), iv. 58). Orderic
also states that the White Ship was rowed on to her rock, an important statement since the rock can probably be identified. Robert
de Torigni, in his interpolations to William de Jumièges (*Gesta*,
p. 281), describes the disaster as taking place 'inter Barbae fluvium
et Hantoniam in quodam maris loco periculoso, qui ab incolis
Cataras dicitur'; and Walter Map states that King Henry's son was
drowned 'in Raso Barbari fluctu' (*De Nugis Curialium*, p. 236). The
'Raz de Barfleur' is marked on the modern chart (Admiralty Chart,
France, North Coast, Cape Barfleur to Courseulles, 1919) opposite
the village of Gatteville, anciently 'Catteville', which suggests that
Torigni's 'Cataras' could represent 'Catte raz', perhaps an older or
alternative name for the Raz de Barfleur (cf. Orderic Vitalis, *H.E.*
(ed. Le Prévost), iv. 413, note 3). If so, the rock now called Quillebœuf, which begins to uncover at about half-tide, is an obvious
candidate. According to the chart it dries 12 feet, the vertical rise
and fall of the tide at this point being in the region of 25 feet
at the springs (*France*, iv, *Ports and Communications*; Geographical
Handbook Series, Naval Intelligence Division, 1942, pp. 3–4), and
Orderic describes the rock on which the White Ship struck as
'ingenti saxo quod quotidie fluctu recedente detegitur et rursus
accessu maris cooperitur' (ed. Le Prévost, iv. 413), a description
which fits Quillebœuf very well. If, in 1120, the main fleet left
Barfleur at High Water or soon after (as it would probably do, so
that the fleet could use the tide at least as far as the cape and clear
Barfleur before the rocks outside became too dangerous), and if the
White Ship cast off after the main fleet as Orderic's narrative
indicates, and all were on the natural course to Southampton, the
White Ship would be passing Quillebœuf when the tide had already
fallen some way; and if further the night was fine and calm, as
Orderic and others say it was, the rock might not be visible though
just below the surface (there was no moon). In these circumstances

it might not have needed a drunken crew to put the White Ship on it. Assuming these identifications, the story shows that oars were used not only to negotiate the passages between the rocks immediately outside Barfleur harbour but at least until the ships reached the open sea, a practice which, apart from making generally for safety, would minimize delays on leaving and entering port.

Since so much in this argument hangs on Orderic's narrative (*H.E.* (ed. Le Prévost), iv. 409–20), and some details in it can be shown to be wrong (ibid., p. 409, note 2, and p. 414, note 1), it is worth remarking that he makes a point of saying that, having personally no relative to mourn, he was moved solely by *pietas* and *diligentia* in recording the details of the disaster.

6. Unity

THE way in which the Norman kings ruled their lands and lordships, by itinerating with their household through Normandy and England, holding their court wherever they made stay and keeping their hold on the 'vassal principalities' through the feudal relationship, suggests that they had at least achieved a functional unity in the government of the lands which, in varying degrees, lay under their domination. Such a functional unity is scarcely conceivable if the union of England and Normandy was regarded as simply personal to the Norman kings; the question whether it led to, or was accompanied by, a more integral political union, any assimilation of customs and institutions, ultimately any fusion of the peoples, has therefore to be considered.

Since the attitude of the ruling family to its rights and possessions, as expressed in the mode of succession adopted, is an important consideration in the discussion of the integrity of a political unit in the early Middle Ages, it is best to begin by asking if there was any rule of succession in the family of the Norman dukes and kings, and if so how it operated. In spite of the conclusions which seem to follow from William the Conqueror's partition of 1087, and the fact that Normandy and England were under different rulers from 1087 until 1096 and again from 1100 to 1106, there are good reasons for supposing that the family thought of its possessions, both in terms of property and in terms of authority so far as the two can be distinguished, as constituting an indivisible inheritance.[1]

So far back as we can see it at all clearly, the rule in Normandy was one of non-partition, whatever might be added to the ducal possessions from one generation to another. Thus the possessions of Rollo, which seem to have been more extensive at his death than they were immediately after the original 'grant'

[1] Parts of the following discussion on the indivisibility of the Norman inheritance are set out more fully in Le Patourel, 'The Norman Succession'. Most of the documentation of that article is assumed here. I am grateful to the Editor of the *English Historical Review* for permission to use the article in this way.

of 911, descended intact to William Longsword; and those of William, who certainly added what later became the western part of the duchy to the lands he had inherited from his father, descended undivided to Richard I in spite of all the difficulties that followed from William's assassination in 942. Dudo de Saint-Quentin, writing before the end of Duke Richard II's reign,[1] and William de Jumièges following him, represent both Rollo and William Longsword as designating a son of his, in the presence of the magnates, to succeed him in all his rights and possessions; while Dudo makes Richard I, whom he must have known personally, designate his son Richard as his successor and require his other sons to do homage to Richard for the lands he would assign to them. Richard II, in 1026, likewise designated his son and namesake to be his successor; and though he provided for a younger and clearly very demanding son Robert by giving him the *pagus* of the Hiémois, this was done on condition that Robert did homage to the heir for his 'apanage', thus preserving the ultimate unity of the inheritance. In the next year, it is true, Richard III died in somewhat suspicious circumstances, and Robert made himself duke, disposing of Richard's son Nicholas by putting him into a monastery; but when Robert in turn had to make provision for the succession as he set out on his perilous journey to the Holy Land, he designated his young son William to be his heir should he fail to return. William, in spite of his youth, his illegitimate birth, and the ambitions of some of his kinsmen, did in fact succeed not only to the whole duchy as Robert had ruled it but also to the rights which Robert had acquired over Brittany and the Vexin (Français).[2]

Up to the time of William the Conqueror, therefore, the tradition and practice of the Norman ducal family had been to treat the duchy, with the additions to their possessions and rights which the dukes were able to make from time to time, as impartible; and this was how William himself treated his first major acquisition. When he conquered the neighbouring *comté* of Maine in 1063 he affianced his eldest son Robert, still a child, to the infant heiress of the *comté*, and the couple are said to have done homage for the *comté* to Geoffrey le

[1] Prentout, *Étude critique*, pp. 13–15.
[2] Le Patourel, 'The Norman Succession', pp. 234–6.

Barbu, count of Anjou. Although Robert could at that time be no more than nominally count of Maine, the title was occasionally attributed to him and it must have been intended that he should eventually be count in substance, as indeed he was.[1] At the very same time, however, he was recorded in a charter as giving his consent, with his parents, to certain gifts and was there described as 'Robert, their son, whom they had chosen to govern the *regnum* after their deaths'. There can be no doubt that the word *regnum* included Normandy and may well have embraced all the rights of government held at that time by Duke William, both within the duchy and beyond it. In any case, since Robert had been given the title 'count of Maine', the intention must have been that he should succeed to duchy and *comté* together, to William's acquisition as well as to his inheritance, and his two younger brothers then living were ignored.[2]

But it might well be thought that England would be a different proposition, being a kingdom, being so much larger than Normandy in territorial extent, greater no doubt in population and almost certainly in wealth, and separated from the duchy by the English Channel; it cannot perhaps be taken for granted that it would be treated like a French *comté* just over the hills. The evidence for William's intentions respecting England is not as specific as could be wished; but so far as it goes it seems clear enough.

Robert had certainly been designated as William's heir in general terms before 1066, and this designation seems to have been reaffirmed at some date between the conquest of England and Robert's quarrel with his father, though the terms of the renewed designation are nowhere precisely stated.[3] The quarrel

---

[1] It is difficult to know just what was given to Robert in 1063, and it is possible to argue that it was no more than a designation or the promise of a designation as future count of Maine. The titles attributed to him in charters are analysed by David in *Robert Curthose*, pp. 10, note 34, and 13, note 46. One solitary document, dated 1076, refers to him as though he were effectively count of Maine before 1087 (ibid., p. 10, note 35). It is perhaps significant that no mention is made of his withdrawing into Maine or making any effort to exploit his position as count at the time of his quarrel with his father; and if he then complained that he had nothing wherewith to maintain his following, as Orderic reports (*H.E.* (ed. Le Prévost), ii. 378–9; (ed. Chibnall), iii. 98), he cannot have then been enjoying such revenues and patronage as the *comté* might afford to its Norman conquerors. It should be remembered that the Norman hold upon Maine was never very secure.

[2] Le Patourel, 'The Norman Succession', pp. 232–3.

[3] David, *Robert Curthose*, pp. 11–12, 15, and references there given. Orderic's

itself seems to have arisen over Robert's demand for the immediate possession and rule of Normandy or some other part of William's dominions, that is an effective vice-royalty in fact rather than his ultimate expectations.[1] When, however, William of Malmesbury is describing the succession as it actually turned out in 1087, he says that Robert 'lost England and only just retained Normandy', a remark which certainly implies that some people regarded Robert as William's heir in England.[2] Robert de Torigni likewise puts into Robert's mouth the boast that 'if I were in Alexandria the English would wait for me and would not dare to make anyone king before I returned';[3] and, if Orderic can be believed on the point, Malcolm King of Scots had recognized Robert as heir to the suzerainty which William the Conqueror had exercised over him, and Malcolm would have thought of William as primarily king of the English.[4] Similarly Lanfranc's reluctance to crown Rufus in 1087, as described by Eadmer, may well have been due to a long-standing expectation on the archbishop's part that he would eventually be called upon to crown Robert, not William Rufus.[5] At the time of William's death, however, Robert was in rebellion against his father. He did not come to the royal bedside; and the anonymous tract 'De Obitu Willelmi', for what it may be worth, strongly suggests that the king had already resolved to disinherit Robert completely and to convey the whole inheritance to Robert's younger brother William Rufus. According to this tract it was the archbishop of Rouen and others in

reference to the two designations, before and after 1066 (ed. Le Prévost, ii. 294; ed. Chibnall, ii. 356) states that William commanded his barons (*optimates*) to do homage and swear fealty to Robert as his heir on both occasions. It is perhaps worth remembering that on the second occasion many if not most of these barons would already be in possession of large estates in England; and the implications would presumably not have been lost upon them if they had been asked to recognize Robert as his father's heir in the continental lands only, with the expectation that England would go to a brother.

[1] Le Patourel, op. cit. p. 233   [2] Malmesbury, *Gesta Regum*, ii. 332.
[3] William de Jumièges, *Gesta*, p. 268 (interp. Torigni).
[4] Orderic Vitalis, *H.E.* (ed. Le Prévost), iii. 394–6; (ed. Chibnall), iv. 268–70; cf. David, *Robert Curthose*, pp. 67–8. Orderic's story may seem the less plausible in that he makes Malcolm accept Robert as heir because *primogenitus* (cf. Orderic Vitalis, *H.E.* (ed. Chibnall), ii, introduction, pp. xxxvi–xxxvii); but it is supported by A.-S.C., 1091, E (p. 169), and by Florence of Worcester, *Chronicon*, ii. 28, who make it clear that Robert negotiated with Malcolm on Rufus's behalf and successfully, which in itself suggests some relationship or understanding between them.
[5] Eadmer, *Historia Novorum*, p. 25.

attendance upon him who persuaded William, when he was perhaps too weak to resist, to show some forgiveness to his rebellious son, to compromise and to divide the inheritance; but William's own intention seems to have been to transmit his lands and rights, whole and entire, to one son or the other.[1] In this he was simply endeavouring to continue the practice

[1] Le Patourel, 'The Norman Succession', pp. 231–4. In this article some emphasis was placed on the account of William's death and last dispositions given in the tract 'De Obitu Willelmi'. Since it was published, L. J. Engels has shown that the passage concerned, and indeed much of the tract as a whole, is taken almost word for word from the *Vita Hludowici Imperatoris* ('De obitu Willelmi ducis Normannorum regisque Anglorum: Texte, modèles, valeur et origine'). It is a nice point to decide how much credence should be given to a text which, though it uses the words and phrases of another and lifts whole passages *verbatim*, yet makes the changes and omissions necessary for its own purpose. However, the conclusion that the partition which William made on his deathbed was forced upon him is supported by other writers (e.g., Malmesbury, *Gesta Regum*, ii. 337), and to that extent the evidence that he originally intended an undivided succession is confirmed. I am very much indebted to Mrs. Marjorie Chibnall for drawing my attention to Engels's work.

The article on 'The Norman Succession' also took no account of the fact that the earliest statement of the distinction between *propres* and *acquêts* in any lawbook occurs in the *Leges Henrici Primi* (70. 21; ed. Downer, pp. 224–5), written about thirty years after William's death. This does not say, however, that the *acquêts* must go to someone other than the eldest son, only that they may do so; and William had already signified that Robert should have Maine as well as Normandy. There is therefore no reason in terms of this distinction why he should not originally have intended him to have England as well. Holt, in 'Politics and Property in Early Medieval England', pp. 45–8, thinks that the evidence for Robert's designation as heir to England is insufficient, and that Maine could have been regarded in 1087 as *héritage* rather than as an *acquêt*. It must be a matter of opinion; and the case in favour of Robert's designation in the first place to the whole of William's inheritance is given above. As for Maine, if Flodoard was right and Maine had been 'granted' to the Normans in 924 (above, p. 6), there is nothing to show that they secured possession of the *comté* then or at any other time before 1063. The arrangement by which Duke William was made Count Herbert's successor, failing a direct heir, was probably concluded between 1058 and 1060, in any case before Herbert's death in 1062 (cf. above, p. 18). After that date, William had a claim to the *comté* as he had a claim to England in 1066, but both could be realized only by force. The comparison is explicitly made by William de Poitiers (*Gesta*, p. 86).

Beckerman, in 'Succession in Normandy, 1087, and in England, 1066', has stated the case for thinking that William, in consenting to the partition on his deathbed, was acting in accordance with the custom which gave a particular sanctity to a *post obitum* gift. It may be so; but this suggestion hardly affects the discussion of William's original intentions in the matter. In any case William's '*post obitum* gift', if respected in the short run, was disregarded in the long run. The whole question of the place of law and custom in this discussion is very difficult; but no speculations on William's intentions or the law or custom that may have influenced or determined his action affect such conclusions as may be drawn from the course of events between 1087 and 1106.

of his forefathers. Nor was there anything in the traditions of the country he had conquered to cause him to think differently. The kingdom of the West Saxons had grown into a kingdom of the English very largely because its kings had not divided their lands and authority, and the acquisitions of each generation had thus accumulated to form the much larger kingdom of the eleventh century. On the Continent, too, there was a distinct movement among royal and princely families away from partition towards a unitary succession—a very important element in the development of the European state-system.[1]

The partition which William made in 1087, therefore, giving England to William Rufus and allowing Robert to have Normandy and Maine (Henry, the youngest, was given no territory, only a large sum of money), was uncharacteristic and almost certainly against his real wishes and the tradition of his family. Neither, evidently, did it accord with the ideas of his sons; for though each brother hastened to secure what had been assigned to him in 1087, each was very soon doing all he could to reunite the whole of his father's inheritance into his own hands.

Rufus had no sooner established himself on the English throne than he had to meet a rising of the greater part, or so it seems, of the Norman baronage in favour of Robert. Though Robert may have been rather slow to take advantage of the opportunity thus offered to him, he did eventually prepare an expedition. William Rufus, however, was able to destroy Robert's fleet before it reached the English coast and to break up the opposition in England at the cost of a couple of sieges. Robert's failure to make a landing in England made it possible for Rufus to consider his own ambitions;[2] and he at once went over to the offensive, buying the support of the chief barons holding lands in eastern Normandy and following this up with an expedition under his own command early in 1091. He was so far successful, more by corruption than fighting, that when peace was made between the brothers Rufus secured a very substantial foothold in the duchy, with a number of castles, a port both in the east and in the west, and an agreement that if either brother should

---

[1] Le Patourel, 'The Norman Succession', pp. 236–42; cf. above, pp. 52–60.

[2] Malmesbury (*Gesta Regum*, ii. 359) says that William Rufus was ambitious and suggests, though not explicitly, what the object of his ambition was.

die without lawful heir (neither was then married) the other should inherit his lands. Rufus undertook to assist Robert to re-establish his authority in Maine and in Normandy; and he must have interpreted this as giving him a right to share in the rule of the continental lands, for he and Robert caused a formal state-ment of the ducal rights in Normandy to be recorded—pre-sumably for their mutual guidance and protection.[1] It amounted very nearly to a condominium, at least in Normandy. Within four years of the Conqueror's death his lands had been reunited under two of his sons who had apparently agreed to rule together and who had certainly made provision for more complete reunion under whichever of them survived the other.

But though Robert accompanied his brother on the Scottish expedition of 1091, to Rufus's very considerable advantage it seems, Rufus himself did little to help Robert in the ensuing years. This drove Robert to denounce the agreement in 1093, giving Rufus any excuse he may have needed to prepare for the seizure of Normandy with his own personal blend of diplomacy, bribery, and force. There were expeditions to Normandy both in 1094 and in 1095; but a military solution was rendered un-necessary when Robert resolved to take part in the First Crusade and pledged his duchy to Rufus for a loan of the 10,000 marks of silver which he needed for the enterprise. When Rufus took possession in September 1096 the Conqueror's inheritance was effectively reconstituted, even if Rufus was never duke *en titre*: and no doubt it would have remained so if Robert had decided to take a principality in the east, or had met the fate of his grandfather there, or even, perhaps, if he had returned with the money he had raised in South Italy for the redemption of his duchy to find Rufus alive and in possession.[2]

A very similar course of events ensued after the sudden death of William Rufus in August 1100 had given Henry the oppor-tunity to seize the throne of England.[3] Robert arrived back in Normandy a few weeks later, in time to recover his duchy

---

[1] Haskins, *Norman Institutions*, pp. 277–84. For examples of joint-rule in practice, Orderic Vitalis, *H.E.* (ed. Le Prévost), iii. 377–9, 394–6; (ed. Chibnall), iv. 250–2, 268–70.

[2] For these events, David, *Robert Curthose*, pp. 42–123.

[3] On Robert's invasion of 1101 and the 'Treaty of Alton', David, *Robert Curthose*, pp. 120–37; Hollister, 'The Anglo-Norman Civil War'.

without having to repay the loan but too late to obstruct Henry in England. His claim to England had not been passed over in silence however; it had considerable support both there and in Normandy and might well have been made effective if Robert had been a different sort of person. He succeeded in landing a force in England during the summer of 1101 and in giving Henry some cause for anxiety; but allowed himself to be bought off with promises of a pension and of the surrender of all that Henry then held in Normandy except Domfront.[1] Robert renounced his claim to England and released Henry from the homage he had done for his Norman lands.[2] As in 1091 it was agreed that if either brother died without lawful heir the other should inherit his lands; but this provision did not have the significance it had had on the earlier occasion, for both brothers were now married and Henry's queen was pregnant. Robert's heir was not born until October 1102,[3] but from the autumn of 1100 there was always the possibility that there would be such an heir. It is probably more important that there seems to be no record of any renunciation by Henry of his possible claims to Normandy to balance Robert's renunciation of his claim to England. Henry's agreement with the count of Flanders earlier in the year was no doubt made primarily for the defence of England; but it also envisaged the possibility that the count would bring military assistance to Henry in Normandy or in Maine as well as in England—in itself important evidence of the way that Henry's mind was working.[4] It is quite likely, indeed, that just as Robert had evidently determined almost from the moment of his return to drive Henry out of England, so Henry intended from the first to dispossess his brother of Normandy as soon as an opportunity presented itself; and he had the advantage that he already possessed a large part of the

[1] Henry at that point held a large part of western Normandy (below, pp. 342–6).

[2] It is not known when Henry did this homage, possibly in 1088 when he received the Cotentin from Robert. In his denunciation of Henry for the continued imprisonment of his brother Robert, King Louis VI asserted as late as 1119 that Robert was Henry's lord (Orderic Vitalis, *H.E.* (ed. Le Prévost), iv. 376).

[3] David, *Robert Curthose*, pp. 123, 146–7 (there seem to be difficulties involved in the chronology of Robert's return journey); Hollister, 'The Anglo-Norman Civil War', p. 330.

[4] Above, p. 79. For the date, 10 March 1101, *Regesta*, ii, No. 515 (p. 7). Ganshof also argues that the treaty was directed primarily against Robert Curthose ('Note sur le premier traité anglo-flamand de Douvres').

duchy at the moment of his seizure of the kingdom.[1] At all events, once he had dealt with Robert de Bellême and his brothers, he began to build up support in Normandy by much the same methods as Rufus had employed; and the two campaigns of 1105 and 1106, culminating in the battle of Tinchebrai, were sufficient to give him the whole of Normandy. He secured the person of his brother and kept him in prison for the remainder of his long life.[2]

These events make it hard to believe that William the Conqueror's partition of 1087 had ever been accepted by his family. Robert could well have believed that he was the rightful heir to England as well as to Normandy and Maine and to all the overlordships which his father had won; but all three brothers had rights of some kind, and rights of any kind were to be cherished and to be realized when possible. Rufus had brought Normandy effectively under his rule; and though in law he only had the duchy in pawn this could well have been a stage on the way to definitive possession. Henry in the end had won Normandy by conquest, whatever his justification may have been, dispossessing and removing his brother; and he ruled kingdom and duchy together for all but thirty years.

His own views on the succession were quite clear. He had only one legitimate son surviving, William, to whom Orderic gave the title 'Ætheling'; and it might seem that he need only let events take their course. But the tradition in the family of the Norman dukes and kings required formal designation and Henry took no chances. He had designated William as his heir in Normandy in 1115[3] and in England in 1116,[4] and had required the chief men then in either country to do homage to him on those occasions; he had arranged for William to do homage to the king of France for Normandy in 1120, though he

---

[1] It is by no means certain that Henry honoured his promise of 1101 to give up the lands he then held in Normandy apart from Domfront (David, *Robert Curthose*, pp. 134–5, 157). Certainly he was able to land an army unopposed at Barfleur in 1105 and progress through the Cotentin without hindrance. Henry of Huntingdon says directly that the lands which Henry held in Normandy enabled him to dispossess Robert of the whole duchy (Huntingdon, *Historia Anglorum*, p. 211).

[2] On Henry's conquest of Normandy, David, *Robert Curthose*, pp. 138–76.

[3] A.-S.C., 1115, E (p. 184); *Regesta*, ii, No. 1074 (pp. 120–1); Huntingdon, *Historia Anglorum*, p. 239; Simeon of Durham, *Opera*, ii. 258 (confused with William's homage to King Louis in 1120).

[4] Florence of Worcester, *Chronicon*, ii. 69.

himself, as William of Malmesbury points out, had refused to do this;[1] he had betrothed William to the daughter of the count of Anjou, with Maine as her dowry, as early as 1113, and when the marriage took place in 1119 William became count of Maine.[2] Each country was provided for by a separate act, and most of the chroniclers who mention the matter at all speak of the designation in one country only;[3] but the fact that Henry seemed to think of everything suggests that the series of ceremonies was intended to constitute a designation to the whole of his lands and lordships as he himself held them, with an assurance of acceptance by all concerned; and William of Malmesbury, at least, clearly saw it in this way.[4]

When the disaster of 1120 made it necessary for Henry to start again he had a very much more difficult problem to solve. His queen had died two years earlier; and though he re-married immediately after his son's death the second marriage produced no children. He could not recognize Robert's son, William 'Clito', though many felt that William was now the rightful heir,[5] for to do so would deny his own rights to Normandy and England; it was apparently no longer possible to designate one of his illegitimate children, as his grandfather had done, though Robert earl of Gloucester, apart from his bastardy, might have made an acceptable king;[6] and if he considered his other nephew Stephen of Blois, to whom in other respects he had shown great favour, he rejected him.[7] It was only after the

---

[1] Lemarignier, *Hommage en marche*, pp. 91–2; Malmesbury, *Gesta Regum*, ii. 496.

[2] Chartrou, *L'Anjou*, pp. 6–7, 13.

[3] e.g. A.-S.C., 1115, E (p. 184), Normandy; Henry of Huntingdon (Huntingdon, *Historia Anglorum*, p. 239), Normandy (homage of the barons, 1115), though in the 'De Contemptu Mundi' he uses vaguer expressions which might be taken to refer to Henry's inheritance as a whole (ibid., pp. 303–4); Eadmer (*Historia Novorum*, p. 237), England 1116; Florence of Worcester (*Chronicon*, ii. 69), England; Orderic Vitalis (*H.E.* (ed. Le Prévost), iv. 416), England.

[4] Malmesbury, *Gesta Regum*, ii. 495–6.

[5] e.g. Huntingdon, *Historia Anglorum* ('De Contemptu Mundi'), pp. 304–5. There was a considerable movement in his favour in Normandy, 1123–4.

[6] Henry had made him and Stephen of Blois the wealthiest of his barons (Patterson, *Earldom of Gloucester Charters*, p. 3).

[7] On Henry's 'build-up' of Stephen, Davis, *King Stephen*, pp. 7–10, 14–15 (and note 3). After the *coup* of 1135, a story was put about that Henry had disinherited Matilda in his last moments and designated Stephen; but this was clearly invented to salve the conscience of those who had taken the oath to Matilda and who had now accepted Stephen. The story is discussed by Round in *Geoffrey de Mandeville*, p. 6, by Chartrou in *L'Anjou*, pp. 42–3, and by Davis, ubi supra, pp· 15–16.

death of his son-in-law, the Emperor Henry V, that what seemed to him a possible solution presented itself. He brought home his widowed daughter Matilda, secured an oath of fealty to her as heir to England and Normandy from the magnates assembled at the Christmas court of 1126–7,[1] and negotiated her marriage to the heir of the count of Anjou— thus detaching one of William Clito's chief supporters, resolving finally (as he would hope) the old feud between Normandy and Anjou, and making secure provision for Maine. It is interesting that Henry should have preferred to other possible solutions the very uncertain chance that Matilda would be accepted as his successor when it came to the point, in principle as a woman or in fact as a personality, particularly as he can have known little of the character of the husband he chose for her; but in all this he never seems to have questioned for an instant the assumption that the succession was his to determine, that it was unitary and that there would be no partition. When a ruling family regards its lands and its dominions as an indivisible inheritance, and has done so for some generations, a long step has been taken towards the political unification of those lands. If more evidence were needed that this stage had been reached in the Norman lands and lordships it is provided almost paradoxically by Stephen's irregular succession. For Orderic has a story, written into his history very shortly after the event, that when the death of Henry Beauclerc became known in Normandy a group of barons met at Le Neubourg and were about to offer their submission to Theobald of Blois, Stephen's elder brother, when a messenger brought the news of Stephen's successful coup in England. They then resolved unanimously 'to serve under one lord on account of the *honores* which they held in both countries', and abandoned Theobald.[2] Whether this story is true in detail or not (Robert de Torigni has a similar story which, though differing in some points, has the same implication),[3] it is at least clear that Stephen's acceptance in England carried Normandy with it, that is, kingdom and duchy were treated as forming an indivisible entity for purposes of the succession even when a man

[1] Round, *Geoffrey de Mandeville*, pp. 29–32; Chartrou, *L'Anjou*, pp. 18–20.
[2] Orderic Vitalis, *H.E.* (ed. Le Prévost), v. 54–6.
[3] Robert de Torigni, *Chronica*, pp. 128–9.

with so questionable a title as Stephen succeeded.[1] Moreover, the inheritance also included the overlordships. The slow intensification of the dukes' and the kings' suzerainty over the dukes of Brittany was a continuous process from the early eleventh century to the time of Henry Beauclerc, as was the lordship which kings of the English exercised over the kings of the Scots and the Welsh princes.[2] Each ruler inherited such rights of overlordship as an integral part of his royal or ducal inheritance.

The dynastic interests of the royal family were supported by those of the aristocracy. The dispossession of the English landowning class had been so complete that Henry's baronage was composed almost exclusively of men born and brought up in Normandy or of Norman parentage, with a few from Brittany, Flanders, and other neighbouring principalities in northern France. Those who had taken estates in England, however, did not abandon the lands or expectations they might have in Normandy, even though their acquisitions in England were often so very much greater in extent and value. These acquisitions in England were added to inherited lands and acquisitions in France. Thus William fitzOsbern added the lordship of the Isle of Wight and the earldom of Hereford to the honours of Pacy and Breteuil which he had inherited in Normandy;[3] Roger de Montgomery added Arundel and the earldom of Shrewsbury to his Norman inheritance, that is the lordship of Montgommery, the *vicomté* of the Hiémois and to the inheritance of his first wife Mabel de Bellême;[4] William de Warenne added vast lands in Sussex, Norfolk, and Yorkshire to Mortemer and the estates centred on Bellencombre in Normandy which he had already acquired before 1066;[5] and Robert 'de Beaumont' obtained extensive lands in the Midlands of England and subsequently inherited the ancestral lands of his family in the Risle valley from his father and the *comté* of Meulan in the Vexin Français from his mother, as Hugh

---

[1] On Henry's succession problem, Le Patourel, 'The Norman Succession', pp. 244–7.

[2] Below, pp. 207–10.

[3] *Complete Peerage*, vi. 447–9; Douglas, *William the Conqueror*, pp. 89–90.

[4] *Complete Peerage*, xi. 682–7.

[5] *Complete Peerage*, xii (1), 491–5; *E.Y.C.*, viii. 1–7; Loyd, 'The Origin of the Family of Warenne'.

d'Avranches acquired most of the enormous territory that came to be attached to the earldom of Chester and later inherited the *vicomté* of Avranches and other lands in Normandy.[1]

Thus one important consequence of the Norman conquest of England was the creation of a number of 'cross-Channel' estates which would in themselves inevitably tend to bind the two countries together. It is true that in many of these families a partition was made at the death of the first holder, giving the Norman lands to the eldest surviving son and the English lands to a younger, apparently making what came to be the customary distinction between *propres* and *acquêts*.[2] If such a partition had been obligatory upon the Norman colonists in England, and if every family had managed to produce two or more sons who survived to manhood sound in mind and body, none of these cross-Channel estates could have endured beyond the lifetime of the men who formed them, for the families would have split at once into a Norman branch and an English branch. That did indeed happen in some cases, as with the de Courcy family for example;[3] but it clearly could not happen in all cases, and if it was certainly usual for fiefs to pass from father to son when the succession was direct and conditions normal, it is doubtful if there were established rules of inheritance in the ranks of feudal society that provided for remoter contingencies at this time.[4]

---

[1] *Complete Peerage*, vii. 521–6; iii. 164–5; Musset, 'Naissance de la Normandie' (*Documents*), pp. 94–8.

[2] Of those just mentioned, this was done with the lands of William fitzOsbern (*Complete Peerage*, vi. 449) and Roger de Montgomery (ibid., xi. 688, 690–1). In terms of inheritance and acquisitions it was done also with the lands of Robert 'de Beaumont', though his inheritance included lands in England as well as in Normandy, all of which went to the elder of his twin sons (ibid., vii. 526, note 'c'); but of the two sons of William I de Warenne, whose lands in Normandy appear to have been as much acquisitions as his lands in England, the elder seems to have had the English lands and the younger the lands of his mother in Flanders—it is not certain what happened to the Norman lands immediately but they went with the English lands to the elder son eventually (*E.Y.C.*, viii (*Honour of Warenne*), 6–9, 44, 73, 80–1). Both Chester and Avranches descended to Richard, apparently the only son of Hugh d'Avranches (*Complete Peerage*, iii. 165). In at least one case the Norman inheritance went to a second son and the English acquisitions to the eldest (estate of Henry 'de Beaumont', first earl of Warwick; ibid., xii (2), 357–60 and Appendix A (3)). [3] Le Patourel, *Normandy and England*, pp. 33–4.

[4] Pollock and Maitland, *H.E.L.*, ii. 266–7. In Normandy the *coutume* came to insist on partition. The integrity of fiefs must be respected; but with that proviso they should be distributed among the sons as far as they would go, the eldest son having the first choice (ibid., pp. 265–6; Génestal, 'Formation du droit d'aînesse'). In the case of the succession to Roger de Montgomery (d. 1094), the eldest

Nor can there have been any idea that the English lands and the Norman lands, as such, ought to be separated in principle. The king often had a hand in family settlements. The division of the lands of William fitzOsbern, for example, giving the paternal inheritance in Normandy to his elder son and the English acquisitions to his younger son, is said to have been the act of William the Conqueror and might be quoted in favour of such an idea;[1] but William Rufus accepted a relief of 3,000 pounds from Robert de Bellême that Robert might add his deceased younger brother's English lands to his own enormous Norman inheritance,[2] and Henry confirmed the family settlement which divided the lands of Robert (I), count of Meulan and earl of Leicester, between his twin sons, giving to Waleran (the elder twin) the English lands of his grandfather as well as his father's inheritance in Normandy, and his father's English acquisitions to the younger, but providing that if either were to die or be incompetent to hold the lands his share should pass to his brother.[3] The arrangement by which Henry allowed Ranulf le Meschin, *vicomte* of Bayeux, to succeed to the lands of his cousin Richard d'Avranches, earl of Chester, in 1120, perpetuated one cross-Channel estate and merged it into another at the moment when it could have been broken up into its English and Norman components if such had been the royal policy; for if Henry apparently insisted that Ranulf should give up other English possessions that he already had, Ranulf acquired thereby the much vaster lands of the earldom of

surviving son took the inheritance of his father in Normandy, having already succeeded to the very considerable inheritance of his mother there, the second surviving son the acquisitions in England, leaving three other sons who had no part in the inheritance though there would have been plenty of fiefs to go round. Two of these three acquired lands for themselves (Roger le Poitevin and Arnulf de Montgomery); but the third, Philip 'Grammaticus', and Everard, Roger's son by his second wife, got nothing, though apparently sound in mind and body. In England primogeniture became the rule; but neither this nor the Norman 'droit d'aînesse' governed the succession to Roger de Montgomery though he had vast lands on both sides of the Channel. The whole matter of the developing rules of inheritance has been taken a great deal further by Holt in 'Politics and Property in Early Medieval England'.

[1] Orderic Vitalis, *H.E.* (ed. Le Prévost), ii. 236; (ed. Chibnall), ii. 282-4. There was a third son Ralph who had been a monk from boyhood (*Complete Peerage*, vi. 449, note 'c').

[2] *Complete Peerage*, xi. 691-2.

[3] White, 'The Career of Waleran, Count of Meulan and Earl of Worcester', p. 20.

Chester as well as the *vicomté* of Avranches, and he kept his lands in the Bessin.[1]

Moreover, lands which had once been partitioned might be brought together again later on. The succession of Robert de Bellême to the English lands of his younger brother Hugh in 1098 meant, among other things, that the inheritance of his father, Roger de Montgomery, had been reunited after the partition four years earlier. There even seems to have been a notion that lands which had once been identified with an ancestor should be kept together, or brought together again if separated. A family relationship, even a distant one, could provide a claim, the successful prosecution of which might depend as much on circumstances as upon law and custom. This would explain the repudiation by Ranulf aux Grenons, earl of Chester, of his father's surrender of the lands about Carlisle. It would also explain the extraordinary attempt by Earl Robert II of Leicester to re-create the vast estate of William fitzOsbern on no firmer hereditary basis, it seems, than his marriage to fitzOsbern's great-grand-daughter. He was not entirely successful in this enterprise; but he managed to build up a great cross-Channel estate for himself in the process, when his inheritance, according to the family settlement, had consisted only of his father's English lands.[2]

If there was only one heir, or one heir recognized, there would be no partition in any case; and any rule there may have been permitting or prescribing different treatment for inheritance and acquisitions would no longer apply to the assemblage of estates involved, for all would henceforth be inheritance.[3] In fact, many cross-Channel estates remained intact or substantially intact for one reason or another through several generations, in some cases to the separation of England and Normandy in the thirteenth century.[4] Moreover, there was nothing to prevent

---

[1] *Complete Peerage*, iii. 166; Holt, 'Politics and Property in Early Medieval England', pp. 51–2.

[2] The story can be pieced together from *Complete Peerage*, vi. 447–51; vii. 527–30; ix. 574.   [3] Cf. Holt, ubi supra, p. 13.

[4] As examples of cross-Channel estates which survived as such through most or all of the twelfth century, the following may be quoted: the lands of the Bigod earls of Norfolk (*Complete Peerage*, ix. 580, note 'c'); of the Mohun family (*Complete Peerage*, ix. 17–19; xii (1), 36–9); of the counts of Aumale (ibid., i. 350–4); Boulogne (the 'honour of Boulogne' in England escheated in 1159, but the counts obtained other lands in England, Round, *Studies in Peerage*, ch. iii), and Eu (*Complete Peerage*,

new ones from being created at any time. Of the men whom King Henry is said to have 'raised from the dust' with offices and lands in England, Geoffrey of Clinton, Ralph Basset, and William Trussebut are known to have had lands in Normandy which they did not give up;[1] while many of those who were favoured by Henry but who could hardly be said to have been 'raised from the dust', men like Ranulf le Meschin,[2] Stephen of Blois,[3] and Henry's own illegitimate son Robert earl of Gloucester,[4] acquired enormous interests on both sides of the Channel.

It would be impossible to present this matter statistically on the basis of the knowledge we have at present, to say for example what proportion of the families whose estates as a whole exceeded a certain value had lands and interests in both countries at a given date, and therefore to estimate how important this 'cross-Channel' element was in the baronage at large either in terms of the value of their lands or of numbers of land-holders. A great deal more work could profitably be done on the subject than has yet been done;[5] though it is likely that the obscurities and ambiguities of so much of the evidence, where it exists, would for ever make firm, quantitative estimates impossible.[6] Even at this stage, however, it can be said that examples of cross-Channel estates and interests at almost all levels can be quoted;[7] that as they are sought for more are found; and that as they continued to be formed throughout the period of the Norman kings and there was no political, social, or

v. 151–65); of the earls of Chester (ibid., iii. 164–9); of the families of Mortimer of Wigmore (ibid., ix. 266–73), Mowbray (ibid., ix. 367–74 and Greenway, *Charters of the Honour of Mowbray*, pp. xvii–xxxii), and Lacy (Wightman, *Lacy Family*, ch. vii). The way in which a huge cross-Channel accumulation could be brought together by inheritance and the incidents of family history is well shown by the Breton family which held the honour of Richmond (*E.Y.C.* (*Honour of Richmond*, i), 84–93). In general cf. also Powicke, *Loss of Normandy*, pp. 328–58.

[1] Orderic Vitalis, *H.E.* (ed. Le Prévost), iv. 164–7; *E.Y.C.*, x (*Trussebut Fee*), 5–12; Le Patourel, *Normandy and England*, pp. 30–3.

[2] *Complete Peerage*, iii. 166.   [3] Davis, *King Stephen*, pp. 7–10, 14–15.

[4] *Complete Peerage*, v. 683–6; Patterson, *Earldom of Gloucester Charters*, p. 3.

[5] The great English genealogists have shown much more interest, perhaps naturally, in the details and the descent of the English than of the Norman lands.

[6] It is often difficult to be sure that the names of all the legitimate sons of a family have survived or to be certain of their order of seniority.

[7] Evidence of a humbler cross-Channel estate than most of those already quoted is given by Round in 'Bernard the King's Scribe', pp. 425–6 and Southern, *Medieval Humanism*, pp. 225–7.

economic force working against them—indeed the gradual establishment of the principle of strict heredity with the insistence on the non-partibility of fiefs in Normandy and the rule of primogeniture in England working strongly for their perpetuation[1]—one can trust the impression that they were in sufficient number to be entirely characteristic of the Norman lands and lordships. Given the general rule that marriages in baronial families were made within the aristocratic group so that family interrelationships reinforced feudal and other relationships,[2] it is clear that there were certainly enough families with interests both in England and Normandy to make the whole of Henry's baronage one homogeneous, aristocratic community. There could be no opposition between a 'Norman baronage' and an 'English baronage'; for if there were families whose effective interests, at any given moment, were restricted to one locality or region, as there certainly were, they would have been connected in some way with others whose interests extended very much further; and there was no reason why the fortunes of individual families should not change quite dramatically at any time by marriage, inheritance, or royal favour. All men who at any time had interests in England and Normandy would be concerned for the political union of the two countries.

The concern of the more highly-placed churchmen and some others would not be very different. Until the middle of Stephen's reign, at the earliest, men whose origin by birth or education or both lay in northern France had a near monopoly of the bishoprics and the greater abbacies of England.[3] Both they and their patrons, certainly their potential successors, would wish to keep this way of advancement open; and though it might be supposed that the king would find some advantage in promoting at least a few English clerks, Henry is said to have been strongly prejudiced against them.[4] The cathedrals and the monasteries of Normandy, nearly all of which had lands of greater or less importance in England, were in much the same position as the barons with cross-Channel interests. At the very least they would find it easier to enjoy what their possessions in

---

[1] Pollock and Maitland, *H.E.L.*, ii. 262–74; Davis, 'What happened in Stephen's Reign'; above, p. 191. [2] Below, ch. 9.
[3] Above, pp. 49–51. [4] Eadmer, *Historia Novorum*, p. 224.

England were worth to them if the two countries were under one ruler.

Furthermore, the interests of this aristocratic community extended into neighbouring principalities and reinforced the Norman kings' overlordship there. When the Marcher lords set about their conquests in Wales, it meant that a William fitzOsbern or a Roger de Montgomery was adding principalities in Wales to the huge estates he already held in England and Normandy; and, allowing for family vicissitudes, such interests would persist. The acceptance of fiefs in Scotland, somewhat later, by men of Norman or Breton origin settled in England would have a similar effect; for if it might be difficult to show, on presently accessible evidence, that the first few actually held lands in France at the time when they took up new possessions in Scotland they certainly had interests across the Channel.[1] Robert de Bellême, for a few years, held vast lands in England and Normandy, lands beyond the Norman frontier into 'France', principalities and lordships in Wales, and he was count of Pontieu in right of his wife;[2] Waleran de Meulan took his title from lands in the Vexin Français, had properties in Paris and lands beyond the city, inherited the family estates in Normandy with some of those in England, and was created earl of Worcester.[3] Ralph de Gael, earl of Norfolk, retained his lands in Brittany after he had been driven from England, and his son recovered most of his lands in Normandy.[4]

The interests of the baronage, indeed, corresponded very closely with those of the king-duke. A man who had wealth and patronage both in England and in Normandy, and even interests in the lands beyond, would carry a great deal more weight than one whose lands and interests were confined to one corner of kingdom or duchy. The greatest of these Norman barons must indeed have lived lives very like those of their lord the king; for where an outline itinerary of one of them can be compiled, as it could be for a William II de Warenne for example, it shows the same continual movement, the same frequent journeys across the Channel, partly on the king's

---

[1] Above, pp. 71–2; below, pp. 294 n. 1, 346.
[2] Le Patourel, *Norman Barons*, pp. 19–20, 31, notes 16–18.
[3] Ibid., pp. 15–16, 30, note 13.
[4] *Complete Peerage*, ix. 573–4.

business but partly also, there can be no doubt, upon his own.[1] Such men, and indeed all with interests actual or potential in kingdom and duchy, must have been every bit as much concerned for their continuing unity under one ruler as the royal family itself. Their part in the troubles of 1087 to 1096 and of 1100 to 1106, as distinct from that of the royal family, shows this very clearly. There is a well-known passage in Orderic's *History* in which he describes the predicament of men with possessions on both sides of the Channel when, in 1087, they found kingdom and duchy under different rulers, even though they were brothers;[2] and it seems that the great majority of these men[3] decided in the first instance that the only solution was to eliminate one of them. At first Rufus was to be deposed. Only Orderic claims to know the barons' reasons for preferring Robert. These were that he was the elder, that he was the more pliable, and that they had already sworn allegiance to him.[4] The first may be a reflection, in part at least, of Orderic's own views about primogeniture;[5] the second, though implied by other writers, is hard to take seriously since the greater landholders had so much to lose from insecurity and disorder and so much to gain from firm leadership; but the third is important, for Orderic is here consistent with his own earlier statements that the barons had accepted the Conqueror's designation and had sworn fealty to Robert as his heir after as well as before 1066,[6] that is, when many of them already had great possessions both in England and in Normandy and could presumably foresee the difficulties which a divided succession would create. Robert, however, let them down; and partly for that reason and partly because of Rufus's success in dealing with the rising in England they swung over

[1] Below, pp. 295–6, n. 3.
[2] Orderic Vitalis, *H.E.* (ed. Le Prévost), iii. 268–9; (ed. Chibnall), iv. 120–4.
[3] 'The most powerful Frenchmen' (A.-S.C., 1088, E, p. 166); 'pars etenim nobiliorum favebat regi Willelmo, sed minima, pars vero altera favebat Rotberto comiti Normannorum et maxima' (Florence of Worcester, *Chronicon*, ii. 21); 'Normannos pene omnes' (Malmesbury, *Gesta Regum*, ii. 361); Orderic Vitalis (ubi supra) describes a meeting of 'optimates utriusque regni'.
[4] Orderic, ubi supra.
[5] Orderic Vitalis, *H.E.* (ed. Chibnall), ii. pp. xxxvi–xxxvii.
[6] References collected and discussed in David, *Robert Curthose*, pp. 11–12, 15. Some of these barons must also, however, have sworn fealty to William Rufus at the time of his coronation.

massively to him when he landed in Normandy early in 1091.
If Malmesbury is to be believed it was they who then brought
about the settlement within a few weeks, for they were not yet
prepared to see Robert ousted completely.[1] Those who had
opposed Rufus obtained pardons from him and the restoration
of lands he had confiscated after his successful siege of Rochester;[2] and though Rufus was clearly unchallenged in England
and in a very strong position in Normandy the agreement
between the brothers must have been intended, among other
things, to make it possible for the barons to 'serve two masters'
and so to avoid the losses which a fight to the finish or a complete division in the rule of the two countries would inevitably
entail. No doubt such an arrangement[3] was doomed from the
start by its inherent difficulties and would in any case have to
contend with Robert's incompetence and Rufus's ambition, so
that the more radical solution involving the elimination of one
brother or the other was likely to be reached sooner or later.
Yet it was an interesting experiment, made at a time when the
political and social implications of the Norman conquest and
colonization of England were only beginning to be understood.

The events that followed Henry's seizure of the throne of
England in 1100 show the same forces at work. Henry was
successful because he was prepared to act decisively, because he
had already built up a party of barons who were ready to link
their fortunes with his,[4] and because the accident in the New
Forest occurred when it was not known when, or perhaps even
if, Robert would return safely to Normandy. Therefore, as soon
as it was seen that his *coup* was immediately successful, churchmen and barons, including 'cross-Channel' barons who were
then in Normandy, rallied to him, encouraged no doubt by the
promises he was prepared to make;[5] but almost as soon as
Robert reappeared in Normandy many of these same men took

[1] Malmesbury, *Gesta Regum*, ii. 363: 'Pauci quibus sanius consilium, consu-
lentes suis commodis quod utrobique possessiones haberent, mediatores pacis
fuere.' David, *Robert Curthose*, 59–61, 65–6. David suggests that Bishop William
de Saint-Calais may have had a leading part in these negotiations.

[2] For the confiscations, A.-S.C., 1088, E (p. 168); Huntingdon, *Historia
Anglorum*, p. 215; cf. Orderic Vitalis, *H.E.* (ed. Le Prévost), iii. 274, 277, 279–80;
(ed. Chibnall), iv. 128, 132, 134. For the restorations, A.-S.C., 1091, E (p. 169);
Florence of Worcester, *Chronicon*, ii. 27.

[3] For the terms, above, pp. 184–5.   [4] Below, ch. 9.

[5] Orderic Vitalis, *H.E.* (ed. Le Prévost), iv. 92–5.

up his claim to the kingdom as well as to the duchy.¹ On this occasion the greater barons seem to have been rather more equally divided between the brothers, though on no principle that can be seen.² Those who supported Robert were supporting the reunion of William the Conqueror's lands and lordships under his rule; those who remained faithful to Henry must have intended the same for him,³ and there can be no doubt that Henry himself was determined from the first to take over Normandy as soon as he felt sufficiently secure in England.⁴

Once again, according to the English accounts at any rate,⁵ it was the greater barons who prevented a judgement by battle after Robert's invasion and brought about an arrangement between the brothers. Henry's weaker position, as compared with that of Rufus in 1091, is shown by the concessions he had to make. The principal terms of the so-called 'Treaty of Alton' could well have brought about a complete and possibly permanent separation between England and Normandy if they had been honoured; but the barons had secured a provision for the mutual pardon by the brothers of each others' adherents and the restoration of confiscated estates on each side.⁶ With this provision they might again hope that it would be possible for them to 'serve two masters', to be Henry's vassals for their

¹ Ibid., pp. 103–10; A.-S.C., 1101, E (p. 177); Florence of Worcester, *Chronicon*, ii. 48; Huntingdon, *Historia Anglorum*, p. 233; Malmesbury, *Gesta Regum*, ii. 470–1. Several transferred their allegiance openly as soon as Robert landed in England (Orderic Vitalis, *H.E.* (ed. Le Prévost), iv. 110).

² Orderic again says that those who supported Robert did so because they thought that his rule would be milder (ed. Le Prévost, iv. 103) and that Robert claimed England on grounds of primogeniture (ibid., 113). Malmesbury alleges personal and even trivial reasons (*Gesta Regum*, ii. 471). Hollister analyses in detail the support given to each brother in 'The Anglo-Norman Civil War', pp. 317–22.

³ Orderic says that Henry's supporters 'ad illum transferre ducatum Normannie decreverunt' (ed. Le Prévost, iv. 106).   ⁴ Above, pp. 185–6.

⁵ A.-S.C., 1101, E (p. 177); Florence of Worcester, *Chronicon*, ii. 49; Huntingdon, *Historia Anglorum*, p. 233; Malmesbury, *Gesta Regum*, ii. 472. Orderic has a different story, making the barons in the two armies eager for a fight and attributing the peace to Henry's initiative in seeking a personal interview with Robert (ed. Le Prévost, iv. 113–14). David, *Robert Curthose*, pp. 133–4, gives good reasons for preferring the version of the English writers, and the extract printed by Hollister ('The Anglo-Norman Civil War', pp. 328, 334) supports the idea of an agreement reached through baronial mediation.

⁶ A.-S.C., 1101, E (p. 177); Florence of Worcester, *Chronicon*, ii. 49. For the difficulties in Orderic's rather different account of the treaty (ed. Le Prévost, iv. 114–15), David, *Robert Curthose*, pp. 134–6; Hollister, 'The Anglo-Norman Civil War', pp. 330–1.

lands in England and Robert's vassals for their lands in Normandy, thus preserving the unity of the Norman baronial community. Such double allegiance was certainly not unknown to men of the time,[1] and in some circumstances it might cause no trouble; but in this case it could hardly fail to do so. To be workable, such an arrangement would have had to be followed up by a series of contracts defining the obligations of each 'cross-Channel' baron to the two brothers respectively, on the lines of the agreement between Henry and the count of Flanders as it defined their relations with the king of France;[2] but this would have required a degree of co-operation between king and duke which is scarcely conceivable, and Henry, for his part, soon made it clear that he was bent upon breaking those whom he regarded as traitors, that is, those who had been Robert's leading supporters.[3] His action against them and the expulsion of such men as Robert de Bellême from England could only exacerbate the disorders in Normandy which would be Henry's reason or excuse for taking over the duchy. Thus, as in the 1090s, only the radical solution, the elimination of one brother or the other, would do.

When next Normandy and England seemed to be falling apart, it was the barons again, according to Orderic, who tried to dissuade Stephen from provoking a pitched battle with Geoffrey of Anjou in 1137, even before the troubles broke out in his army;[4] and in 1153, when all seemed set for the final conflict between King Stephen and Duke Henry, it was they who prevented the engagement and secured an agreement between the two contestants for the inheritance of King Henry Beauclerc.[5] So far at least as maintaining the unity of that inheritance was concerned, their interests coincided with those of the royal family through all the years of the Norman kings. If those who took possession of estates in Britain on such an enormous scale during the Conqueror's reign or later did indeed envisage the possibility of a partition such as was made in 1087 or a division such as came about in 1100 or in the 1140s, they must have hoped that they would be able to cope with the

---

[1] Below, p. 214.
[2] *Diplomatic Documents*, i. 1–8.
[3] David, ubi supra, pp. 138 ff.; Hollister, ubi supra, pp. 331–3.
[4] Orderic Vitalis, *H.E.* (ed. Le Prévost), v. 84.
[5] Davis, *King Stephen*, pp. 118–21.

situation somehow if it arose. When they were faced with it their sympathies were at first divided too, for reasons at which we may guess but which we can probably never know; but they supported one rival or the other as claimant to the whole,[1] and when a battle seemed imminent in which they could have little to gain (for in the aftermath confiscations were likely to go to 'new men'), they tried to reach an accommodation which would enable them to keep their estates and their interests in kingdom and duchy and beyond, even under two rulers. That such an accommodation was not likely to work for very long in practice may not have been very clear at the outset; though when it became so most of them rallied (for a consideration no doubt) to the more competent brother and so restored the integrity of the Conqueror's inheritance in full. Under 'two masters' or one, the barons regarded the Norman lands and lordships as a unity and saw that it was greatly in their interest to maintain that unity.[2]

There were other elements of unity in the Norman lands and lordships besides the practical necessities of government, the notion of the indivisibility of its inheritance which the royal family held, and the interests of the barons and churchmen in matters of property and politics. *Vis-à-vis* other rulers, the Norman complex must certainly have appeared as a unit of military power, for the resources of England and Normandy were equally at the command of the Norman kings and to some extent those also of the countries over which they exercised some form of overlordship. There were Englishmen in the armies that William the Conqueror took to Maine in 1073 and 1081[3] and in the army which faced Robert Curthose at Gerberoi in 1079–80;[4] conversely, when he strengthened the

---

[1] There seems to be no specific evidence that this is true of Rufus's supporters in 1088—but they must have known something of the king's character and ambition.

[2] It might almost be said that the aristocracy stepped in to maintain the integrity of what they regarded as a political unit when the ruling dynasty, through the incidents of personal or family history, had compromised it. Compare, for example, the action of the Breton aristocracy in 1378–9 (Jones, *Ducal Brittany*, pp. 85–7) and that of the estates of Béarn in 1391 (Tucoo-Chala, *La Vicomté de Béarn*, pp. 89–93).

[3] Hollister, *Military Organization of Norman England*, pp. 117–18; Douglas, *William the Conqueror*, p. 242.

[4] Hollister, *Military Organization of Norman England*, pp. 250–1. As Hollister points out, there is an ambiguity in the use of the word *Angli* by chroniclers writing in the first half of the twelfth century; but at the least it must mean men of whatever origin with an interest in England.

defences of his kingdom to meet the Danish threat in 1085 he brought over a larger body of men from France and Normandy 'than had ever come to this country'.[1] According to Orderic, Rufus had men from France, Burgundy, Flanders, Brittany, and Normandy with him when he recovered Maine in 1098[2] and he speaks as though there were Englishmen and men from Aquitaine among the forces that Rufus had taken into the Vexin in 1097–8.[3] Henry had men from Normandy, England, Maine, and Brittany in his army at Tinchebrai;[4] English, Norman, and Breton troops in the campaigns he fought in Normandy and on the marches from 1116 to 1120,[5] and also, apparently, when he was putting down the Norman rebels in 1123–4.[6] There was a Scottish contingent, led by King Alexander, as well as Welsh and Anglo-Norman troops in the army he led into North Wales in 1114; and when Owain ap Cadwgan, king of Powys, accompanied him to France later in the same year the Welsh prince presumably did not go unattended.[7]

The Norman kings could clearly demand the fulfilment of military obligations by their vassals and others both in Normandy and in England, and their relationship with the vassal princes seems to have given them the right to call for some military service from them—by contract in the case of the count of Flanders, though there seems to be no record that the service he undertook to give was ever performed in Henry's day. It would be difficult now to determine whether Count Hélie of Maine or Duke Alan Fergent of Brittany brought their troops to Henry at Tinchebrai, or King Alexander his army to North Wales in 1114, specifically as allies, mercenaries, or vassals, and it may well be that these capacities were not clearly distinguished as a basis for military service in the early twelfth century. An element of vassalage certainly entered into the motives that produced their action, but it seems that mercenaries (or troops

---

[1] 'Rex Willelmus de tota Gallia solidariis, pedonibus et sagittariis multis millibus conductis et nonnullis de Normannia sumptis . . . Angliam rediit' (Florence of Worcester, *Chronicon*, ii. 18); 'a larger force of mounted men and infantry from France and Brittany than had ever come to this country' (A.-S.C., 1085, E, p. 161).

[2] Orderic Vitalis, *H.E.* (ed. Le Prévost), iv. 44–5.

[3] Ibid., pp. 19–26.

[4] David, *Robert Curthose*, pp. 174–5 and Appendix F; Hollister, *Military Organization of Norman England*, pp. 123, 128, note 1.

[5] Orderic Vitalis, *H.E.* (ed. Le Prévost), iv. 316, 333.

[6] Ibid., p. 458.   [7] Lloyd, *History of Wales*, ii. 421–2, 463–4.

serving for pay, whether or not they were also under some obligation to serve) formed a large and perhaps the largest element in the Norman armies, taking the military effort as a whole. There was a very considerable mercenary element in the armies that William the Conqueror used in England from 1066 to 1070 and in the force he brought to England in 1085; Orderic makes it plain that the impressive array of 'nationalities' in the army that Rufus led into Maine in 1098 had been brought together by the pay he offered; Henry used Breton mercenaries so regularly as to suggest that his suzerainty over the duchy was important to him chiefly for what it could do to ensure a supply of such troops; Stephen had his Flemish mercenaries—and it is clear that there were men from England and Normandy serving for pay besides those from the 'vassal' principalities.[1]

Military power thus depended to a great extent already upon financial strength, particularly upon the wealth of Normandy and England and the ability of the Norman kings to mobilize that wealth. The continual complaints of the chroniclers writing in England of the 'very severe taxes' that were laid upon the people of that country are well known and seem the more impressive because the annalistic form of several of their chronicles enabled them to report such levies year after year;[2] while the exactions attributed to Ranulf Flambard and Rufus's demands upon Archbishop Anselm and Bishop Walkelin of Winchester are among the familiar stories of his reign. The fact that the Norman chroniclers say much less about this suggests that the duchy was not subjected to such exploitation; but, though no Norman exchequer roll has survived to provide direct evidence for the time of the Norman kings, we can be sure that ducal rights in matters of revenue were enforced to the limit of legality and probably beyond.[3] It is unlikely that the vassal princes made a significant contribution in money to the king-duke's total resources, though tribute was occasionally

---

[1] In general, Prestwich, 'War and Finance', Hollister, *Military Organization of Norman England*, ch. vi. For English mercenaries specifically, Orderic Vitalis, *H.E.* (ed. Le Prévost), iv. 316.

[2] e.g. A.-S.C., 1090, 1096, 1097, 1098, 1104, 1105, 1110, 1116, 1117, 1118, 1124, E (pp. 168, 174, 175, 179, 182, 185, 186, 191); Huntingdon, *Historia Anglorum*, p. 240.

[3] e.g. Orderic Vitalis, *H.E.* (ed. Le Prévost), iv. 439–40.

received from the Welsh princes;[1] and the fact that even a token amount was received should not be forgotten.

The military potential of the Norman kings was thus based on the resources of all their lands and lordships. The weight of the burden varied from one to another, but all were involved. It is unlikely that the king ever attempted to bring together in one concentration all the forces that he could call upon, or that such a concentration was at all feasible or would have been manageable if achieved. Their military strength lay in the fact that they had so many sources on which they could draw, and that they could call out men from whichever of their lands or lordships might be most convenient or practicable in any given situation. Thus when speed was essential, as Rufus conceived it to be in Maine when Hélie de la Flèche seemed to be recovering his *comté* in 1099, the king relied upon such troops as he could raise quickly as he passed through his continental lands, though he was in England when the crisis broke;[2] when Henry felt that there was hardly anyone in Normandy whom he could trust, he employed paid troops from England and Brittany; for an expedition into North Wales he could add a force from Scotland to his Anglo-Norman army; while for really big affairs like William's operations in England from 1066 to 1070, Rufus's conquest of Maine in 1098 or Henry's campaign in Normandy that culminated in Tinchebrai, all that existing obligations or money could produce in practice was put into action.[3] It was this potential which any body of rebels, or the king of France, or the count of Anjou, or any other opponent had to face.

The unity among their lands and lordships which this implies may also be seen in the Norman kings' defence of them, for nothing was treated as expendable. The fact that they relied heavily upon a network of castles in England for internal security, and in some measure for defence against attack from outside, is a commonplace;[4] but this is equally true of their rule

---

[1] Whether the 40 pounds recorded in Domesday as paid by 'Riset de Wales' (identified as Rhys ap Tewdwr, king of Deheubarth) to King William should be regarded as tribute is a matter that could be discussed (above, p. 62), though the Welsh probably thought of it as such. Gruffydd ap Cynan, king of Gwynedd, had to pay Henry 'a heavy fine' in 1114 and Maredudd ap Bleddyn, king of Powys, 10,000 cattle in 1121 (Lloyd, *History of Wales*, ii. 464–5).

[2] Ramsay, *Foundations of England*, ii. 219–20, quotes the chronicle accounts.

[3] Above, pp. 202–3.

[4] In general, Brown, Colvin, and Taylor, *King's Works*, i. 21–32. There were at

on the Continent. Well before 1066 the dukes had begun to build castles not only in the eastern part of Normandy, where they mostly resided, but also in the west, which still had to be brought firmly under their control.[1] Both William Rufus and Henry continued to build on an enormous scale, both for internal security as at Rouen, Caen, or Coutances, and for the defence of the duchy as a whole, as particularly in the valley of the Epte, covering Rouen.[2] Their active warfare shows a similarly comprehensive purpose. Douglas has argued that events in England, Maine, Flanders, Brittany, Scotland, and even in the Vexin during the years from 1069 to 1077 presented William the Conqueror with strategic problems that could hardly be disentangled;[3] and much the same could be said of Rufus's warfare in Normandy, on the borders of England and Scotland, in Wales, and later in Maine and the Vexin; while it was the ultimate success of the two Williams in their treatment of Scotland that enabled Henry to concentrate upon the dangerous situation that faced him in Normandy without having to look continually over his shoulder to see what might be going on in the north of England. For this situation resembled that which confronted Stephen, at least in principle, and it was as critical. Robert Curthose's son, William Clito, had a very good claim to Normandy; and when he was of an age to put forward this claim seriously he was supported, in their own interests no doubt, by the king of France and more spasmodically by the counts of Flanders and Anjou, as well as by a considerable body of opinion in the Norman baronage—and after 1120 Henry had lost his own son William. The Clito attacked Normandy first, for it was immediately accessible to him. Henry's defence, as it turned out, was effective; but there can be little doubt that if William Clito had been more successful in Normandy he would have gone on to claim England. Henry, that is to say, was not simply defending Normandy in those long spells he spent in the

least fifty castles in England by 1087; but the difficulties of calculating the number at any given time are indicated by Brown in *The Normans and the Norman Conquest*, pp. 234-9, as well as many other important matters concerning them.

  [1] Yver, 'Châteaux forts en Normandie', pp. 34-59.
  [2] Robert de Torigni, *Chronica*, pp. 106-7, 126 (and in William de Jumièges, *Gesta*, p. 309); Brown, Colvin, and Taylor, *King's Works*, i. 35; Pépin, *Gisors et la vallée de l'Epte*, pp. 13-17, 30-1. For the Normans' use of the castle generally, below, pp. 308-18.   [3] Douglas, *William the Conqueror*, pp. 222-44.

duchy between 1116 and 1128; he was in the front line of the defence of his lands and lordships as a whole. It is very likely that if Stephen had been able to defeat Geoffrey and Matilda in battle while he was in Normandy during the year 1137 his subsequent difficulties in England would have been far less serious; but by that time his suzerainty over the king of Scots had been repudiated and the north of England was far from secure. The defence of the Norman lands and lordships was indivisible.

The fact that Scotland, Wales, Brittany, Maine, and the other 'vassal principalities' were involved in the defence of England and Normandy, that succession to the kingdom of the English or to the duchy of the Normans seemed to include such rights of suzerainty over these principalities as the last king or duke had held, and that the interests of barons and churchmen also extended into them, suggests that these overlordships should be regarded as an integral part of the authority and power of the Norman kings, that the effective political unit was not simply England and Normandy but the whole of 'the Norman lands and lordships'. It is a suggestion that needs to be examined carefully, for at first sight it was not so. It is customary to see a continuous line of development leading from Pictish, Scottish, and British tribes to an autonomous kingdom of the Scots; from a confusion of Welsh tribes, combining and re-assorting themselves in bewildering fashion, to the almost united principality of the thirteenth century; from a similar confusion of *comtés* and *seigneuries* in Brittany (the ruins, it is true, of what had once been a kingdom of a sort) to the quasi-independent duchy of the fourteenth and fifteenth centuries. But these political groupings were involved in another line of development which was being pursued at the same time, the growth of the kingdoms of the West Saxons and the Western Franks which, in their different ways, could, and in some cases did lead to their absorption into much larger units. The fact that there were two such lines of development in progress simultaneously shows that the ultimate emergence of the national kingdoms in the form they took at the end of the Middle Ages should not be regarded as predestined; the question, indeed, is whether the association of these countries in the Norman lands and lordships represented yet a third possibility.

In formal terms, as distinct from the exercise of power from time to time, the question whether the Norman lands and the lands over which the Norman kings exercised some overlordship attained an integral unity as a whole will hang on the nature of the relationship that was being formed between the Norman kings on the one hand and these kings and princes on the other.

Perhaps the most important thing about these relationships is that they were neither uniform nor stable. They were expressed in feudal terms, but feudal relationships were themselves changing and evolving at this time. Homage and fealty had not always been distinguished nor associated necessarily with the tenure of a fief, though they came to be so, and the benefits and obligations implied by the tenure of a fief, and the conditions of such tenure, were subject to progressive definition.[1] Thus, although the acts of submission made by the kings of Scots and the kings of the Welsh to the kings of the English before 1066 were almost certainly identical with acts which would be accepted as acts of homage by students of Frankish institutions, such acts did not then carry the same implications, personal or political, on either side of the Channel, as similar acts in the twelfth century or later. This condition of change and evolution in these relationships has in fact a far greater significance than the precise form of any one of them at any particular moment, if that indeed could be defined. They varied, naturally, with personalities and circumstances, but they were also evolving institutionally and in a direction favourable to the overlord.

This can be seen very clearly in the case of Scotland. The origin of the relationship lies in the acts of subordination repeatedly performed by kings of Scots to the kings of the West Saxons who were growing into kings of the English. Whether these acts should be interpreted as a symbol of deference to a

[1] Dumas, 'Encore la question, "Fidèles ou Vassaux?"', pp. 192–229, 357–61, 370–2, etc.; Ganshof, 'Les relations féodo-vassaliques aux temps post-carolingiens'. This idea of evolving feudal relationships as applied to the relations between rulers of peoples and territories is the foundation of Lemarignier's study of the vassalage of the dukes of Normandy *vis-à-vis* the kings of France (*Hommage en marche*). Its application here to the relations between the kings of Scots and the kings and princes of Wales on the one hand and the kings of England on the other, with the idea that a 'kingdom of Britain' or a 'kingdom of Britain and Northern France' might have been created during the Middle Ages, should be regarded as a preliminary essay only.

'basileus of all Britain'[1] or simply as an acknowledgment of hegemony based on military power, or something of both, they became traditional and were therefore acquiring an institutional basis. On the other hand, the homage which King Malcolm III did to William the Conqueror at Abernethy has all the marks of what came to be classified on the Continent as an 'hommage de paix'.[2] In terms of creating a permanent relationship it might not mean very much, though it included the giving of hostages and it seemed to translate the older relationship into terms which the Normans could understand; for William almost certainly thought of himself as succeeding to the position that Edward the Confessor had held—as he understood it. In 1091, in a similar situation, Malcolm would only do homage to William Rufus 'in the same manner as he had done to his father',[3] and in 1093 at Gloucester he seemed to be arguing for an 'hommage en marche' which carried an implication of equality between the parties.[4] Up to this point at least, the relationship seems to have been essentially personal. There is little evidence as yet that it was bound up with the kingdom of the Scots or with any lands held in England by the king of the Scots.[5]

The relationship on the one hand between Malcolm's sons, who followed him successively on the throne, and Rufus and

[1] e.g. Barlow, *Edward the Confessor*, pp. 135–8; Ritchie, *Normans in Scotland*, pp. 385–8; and above, pp. 57–9.

[2] Anderson, *Early Sources*, ii. 34–6; *Scottish Annals*, p. 95. It could hardly have been ordinary homage, for William was well into Malcolm's territory when the Scottish king came to meet him. On 'hommage de paix', Lemarignier, *Hommage en marche*, pp. 81–3 and e.g. 117–19.

[3] Anderson, *Early Sources*, ii. 48–9; *Scottish Annals*, pp. 104–8. On the other hand, the Abingdon chronicler thought that Malcolm gave hostages to Robert Curthose when he was acting for his father in 1080, 'ut regno Angliae principatus Scotiae subactus foret', and prefaced his account of Robert's expedition with the observation that 'Rex Scotiae Malchomus subesse regi Willelmo eo tempore detrectabat' (*Chronicon Monasterii de Abingdon*, ii. 9–10; cf. Anderson, *Scottish Annals*, pp. 103–4).

[4] Malcolm refused to do right (*rectitudinem facere*) to King William: 'nisi in regnorum suorum confiniis, ubi reges Scottorum erant soliti rectitudinem facere regibus Anglorum, et secundum judicium primatum utriusque regni' (Florence of Worcester, *Chronicon*, ii. 31). This does not refer directly to homage but rather to some form of 'law of the march'; but in this context the principle is the same.

[5] On the lands held in England by the Scottish kings, Ritchie, *Normans in Scotland*, pp. 385–8; Moore, *Lands of the Scottish Kings in England, passim*; *Complete Peerage*, vi. 641–4. But Lothian may still have been regarded as part of the kingdom of the English at this time, Earle and Plummer, *Two Saxon Chronicles Parallel*, ii. 195, 267–8, 280.

Henry on the other, was different for a number of reasons. King Edgar declared, in a solemn charter, that he 'possessed all the land of Lothian and the kingdom of Scotia by gift of my lord William, king of the English, and by paternal inheritance'.[1] This certainly looks like an unequivocal acknowledgment that the Scottish kingdom was held as a fief of the king of the English in the fullest sense, that the homage of the Scottish king was or had become 'real' and not merely personal; though the term 'paterna hereditate' may represent a qualification of this and the phrase 'dono domini mei Willelmi' could conceivably mean no more than that Edgar owed his throne as a matter of historical fact to the timely assistance of William Rufus, though King William was still his lord. All the same, the statement introduces a tenurial element into the relationship; and this was strengthened when David I, who as earl of Huntingdon must already have done homage to King Henry, succeeded to the Scottish throne in 1124 and did not give up the earldom.[2] It could now be argued, as King David's successors did argue in the thirteenth century,[3] that the king of Scots was the vassal of the king of the English only for the lands he held in England, or what was deemed to be England, not for his kingdom or as king of Scots; and that this opinion was already current in the twelfth century is shown by Hugh the Chantor's statement that the archbishop of York thought it advisable to controvert it in the papal *curia* when claiming metropolitan rights over the Scottish Church.[4] Nevertheless, even if it had been clear that the king of Scots owed homage only for his English lands and not for his kingdom, the situation could still have been exploited by the Norman kings; for if after 1124, when David I succeeded to the throne of Scotland, the earl of Huntingdon did homage, the king of Scots was certainly involved in whatever act or ceremony was performed.[5] In the fourteenth century

---

[1] Duncan, 'The Earliest Scottish Charters', pp. 103–7.

[2] *Complete Peerage*, vi. 641.

[3] e.g. Stones, *Anglo-Scottish Relations*, pp. 38–41.

[4] Hugh the Chantor, *History of the Church of York*, p. 126: 'Set archiepiscopus noster et secreto et palam in curia ostendit Scociam de regno Anglie esse, et regem Scottorum de Scocia hominem esse regis Anglie: quod debuit dominus papa sic esse credidit'.

[5] I have found no direct evidence that David ever did homage to Henry after he had succeeded to the Scottish throne in 1124; but it is very possible that he did so when he was in England in 1126–7. Henry had been in Normandy since June

still, when such distinctions of capacity were a good deal clearer than they were in the twelfth, the king of England found it impossible to ensure that his obligations as duke of Aquitaine would not affect his interests as king of England; and one of the main reasons why the kings of France did not seem unduly anxious to drive 'the English' out of France completely during that century may well have been that the hold which the king of France had over the king of England by reason of his duchy of Aquitaine was still considered too valuable to be sacrificed to the ideal of a more unified kingdom.[1] However, in the case of the Scottish kings, the question was settled for the time being in 1174, when King William the Lion was forced to do liege homage 'for Scotia and for all his other lands', and to record this in a formal treaty.[2] What the political implications of this might ultimately have been was shown in the 1290s when, after a similar act of homage, appeals were taken from the Scottish courts to those of the king of England; and this could well have been a stage in the incorporation of Scotland into some form of 'kingdom of Britain'— if King Edward I had played his cards better.[3]

1123, returning in September 1126 ('mense Septembri', Malmesbury, *Historia Novella*, p. 3; 'between the Nativity of St. Mary and Michaelmas', A.-S.C., 1126, E, p. 192; 'iii idus Septembris', Simeon of Durham, *Opera*, ii. 281, but under the year 1127); 'and then after Michaelmas David, king of Scots, came from Scotland into this country and King Henry received him with great honour, and he stayed all the year in this country' (A.-S.C., ubi supra). This apparent anxiety on David's part to meet Henry at the earliest possible opportunity after his own accession suggests that he came primarily to obtain recognition; and this, with the fact that he stayed so long in England on this occasion, and was acting as a royal justice in 1130 (Orderic Vitalis, *H.E.* (ed. Le Prévost), iii. 403–4; (ed. Chibnall), iv. 276; cf. Anderson, *Scottish Annals*, pp. 166–7), further suggests a renewal of homage in some form. When he refused to do homage to Stephen, the reason alleged was not that homage was not due but that he had taken an oath to support Matilda's succession (Anderson, *Scottish Annals*, pp. 170–2), and, unlike so many barons who took that oath, he remained faithful to it.

[1] Le Patourel, 'The Origins of the War', pp. 28–36.

[2] Stones, *Anglo-Scottish Relations*, pp. 1–5.

[3] Stones, ibid., pp. 63–7. The connection between liege homage and the idea of sovereignty (in the medieval sense), and the way in which it could be used by a suzerain to integrate a virtually independent principality more and more into the government of a kingdom, is well shown in the case of the king of France and the duchy of Aquitaine (e.g. Chaplais, 'La souveraineté du roi de France'), and Edward I was duke of Aquitaine. Moreover, this did not apply only to such principalities within 'the kingdom', for the expansion of France to the south-east was brought about by very similar means. Certainly, this idea of sovereignty was a good deal more developed at the end of the thirteenth century than it was in the

The lordship of the Norman kings over the rulers of Wales shows a similar intensification, though this was achieved in quite a different way. Wales was a land of small principalities or kingdoms, and the process by which it was eventually brought under the effective rule of the kings of England was complicated by the piecemeal conquest of some of these principalities by Norman barons. Under William the Conqueror the relationship between the king and those Welsh princes who had accepted his overlordship and who still held their principalities was probably much the same as it had been before 1066. The £40 which 'Riset de Wales' is recorded in Domesday as paying to the king has been interpreted as the farm paid by Rhys ap Tewdwr for his kingdom of Deheubarth, on the analogy of the farm of £40 which Robert 'of Rhuddlan' was paying for 'Nort Wales', that is the kingdom of Gwynedd; but it is likely that the Welsh thought of Rhys's 'farm' as tribute and that it did not in itself imply a higher degree of subjection than had been offered to William's Saxon predecessors. Some of the Norman conquerors themselves seem to have stepped into the shoes of the princes they displaced, both in relation to the Welsh inhabitants and in relation to the king. The 'farm' of £40 which Robert 'of Rhuddlan' was paying for the kingdom of Gwynedd in 1086 may have been a tribute imposed originally upon the Welsh prince Gruffydd ap Cynan or one of his predecessors;[1] and when Gruffydd was captured and imprisoned Robert either secured a grant of Gwynedd as 'land to be conquered' on condition of continuing the tribute or farm, or he set about the conquest on his own or Earl Hugh's initiative and secured recognition, on the same terms, of what he hoped to achieve—for his conquest of Gwynedd was far from complete at the time of Domesday.[2] Some of the conquests were said to be held of the king 'in fee', as Robert 'of Rhuddlan' held Rhos and Rhufoniog in 1086; but these must have been fiefs of a rather special kind, at least in the hands of their original Norman holders; for at that time they had never been in the king's hands for him to give, unless it was by some form of nominal surrender

early part of the twelfth; the argument here is that in the early stages of its development there were points in common between Britain and France as well as the differences that are more frequently pointed out.

[1] As suggested by Edwards in 'The Normans and the Welsh March', pp. 161–2.   [2] Below, pp. 312–4.

and grant. The only legal basis for such a grant, or for a grant as 'land to be conquered', was William's succession to the overlordship of Edward the Confessor; and the holders might well feel that they owed as much to their own strong right arms as to the king. Certainly they were his vassals already, before they started on their conquests in Wales; but there seems to be no evidence to show whether a new act of homage was required for licence to conquer lands in Wales or for recognition of their conquests.[1]

The situation developed considerably under Henry Beauclerc. The vigilance of the king and the ordinary course of events gradually brought the lords marcher more and more into a normal feudal relationship with him, however exceptional their position in their Welsh lands might be; while appeals to the king for favours or backing in their disputes among themselves, with spontaneous royal intervention from time to time, meant that the relationship between the king and the surviving Welsh princes was also beginning to take on feudal characteristics.[2] Tenures of a feudal kind were even beginning to appear as between Welshmen.[3] This gave a new significance to the policy already initiated, or so it seems, by Edward the Confessor in his dealings with Gruffydd ap Llywelyn and with Bleddyn and Rhiwallon who succeeded him,[4] whereby the king would recognize and support the supremacy which a leading Welsh prince established over his fellows provided that his own overriding suzerainty was acknowledged. When Henry's expedition of 1114 brought the rulers of Gwynedd and Powys to do homage and swear fealty,[5] the effect can only have been to give royal sanction and support to their conquests and overlordships so long as they remained faithful to him. The opportunity to develop this policy came when the Welsh reaction to the Norman invasion and colonization (a reaction that was chiefly evident under Stephen though it began earlier) resulted in the predominance of the two kingdoms, Gwynedd and Deheubarth. When Henry II made the Lord Rhys of Deheubarth (d. 1197) his 'justiciar in all Deheubarth' (1172),[6] his position is probably to be understood as analogous to that

---

[1] Above, pp. 61–4.   [2] Above, pp. 64–5.
[3] e.g. Lloyd, *History of Wales*, ii. 416.   [4] Above, pp. 58–9.
[5] A.-S.C., 1114, E H (p. 183); cf. Lloyd, *History of Wales*, ii. 421–2, 463–4.
[6] 'Iustus yn holl Deheubarth', *Brut y Tywysogion, Red Book of Hergest Version*, pp. 158–9; Lloyd, *History of Wales*, ii. 542–3.

assigned to the king of Connaught in Ireland by the Treaty of Windsor three years later.[1] If so, this would imply not only recognition of the place that the Lord Rhys had made for himself in Wales but that Henry was treating the authority he had won over subordinate princes as a delegation from himself. After the death of the Lord Rhys, leadership among the Welsh princes reverted to Gwynedd. Llywelyn ap Iorwerth (d. 1240), who not only brought the greater part of Wales under his rule or overlordship but endeavoured to give some institutional expression to the degree of unity thus achieved, did homage both to King John and to King Henry III:[2] and, although there were troubles, his normal position was that of a vassal of the king of England. The last logical step in the evolution of this relationship is represented by the Treaty of Montgomery of 1267. For fealty, homage, and 'the accustomed services', King Henry and his son Edward 'granted' to Llywelyn ap Gruffydd the 'principality of Wales' and the homages of the 'Welsh barons of Wales',[3] thus setting up a complete chain of feudal authority from the king to the humblest Welsh prince. The situation thus created could have led naturally to the peaceful integration of Wales into a wider political system with the king of England at its head; but Llywelyn's failure to do homage to King Edward I on his accession led to conquest and annexation which, in contrast to Scotland, proved permanent.

Thus, although these developments in Scotland and Wales did not reach their term under the Norman kings, and they had their ups and downs as one would expect, there were at least the beginnings of a progressive definition of the relationship between the Norman kings on the one hand and the kings of Scots and the princes of Wales on the other, a definition in a feudal sense leading to the gradual intensification of the authority and powers of the suzerain.

---

[1] 'Scilicet quod Henricus rex Angliae concessit praedicto Roderico, ligio homini suo, regi Connactae, quamdiu ei fideliter serviet, quod sit rex sub eo, paratus ad servitium suum sicut homo suus; et quod terram suam teneat . . . reddendo ei tributum; et totam aliam terram et habitatores terrae habeat sub se *et justiciet*, ut tributum regi Angliae integre persolvant, et per manus ejus, et sua jura sibi conservent' (italics for emphasis). *Gesta Henrici*, i. 102 (substantially identical text in Roger of Howden, *Chronica*, ii. 84).

[2] Lloyd, *History of Wales*, ii. 616–17, 653–4, 682–7; Williams, *Introduction to the History of Wales*, ii. 78–9.

[3] Edwards, *Littere Wallie*, pp. 1–5 (and Introduction, pp. xxxvi–l).

The problem of determining how far the continental over-lordships of the Norman kings should be regarded as forming part of a political unity with their kingdom and duchy is more complex, for the dukes and counts concerned all owed homage to another lord as well, sometimes more than one. Such multiple homages were a commonplace,[1] and the resolution of the conflicts of allegiance which they could produce was one of the general political difficulties of the time.[2] In the case of such relationships with the Norman kings it would probably not have presented itself to contemporaries in so crude a form as a trial of strength; for long-established relationships were not forgotten, and though their effectiveness might be lost for a while it might also be recovered. Still, circumstances and personalities must usually have determined the outcome.

Perhaps the simplest case is that of the count of Boulogne. His *comté* had been formed out of territories which had once been held by the count of Flanders and he remained traditionally the count's vassal.[3] However precisely the new relationship between Count Eustace II and Duke William should be described as it existed just before 1066, there can be no doubt that he became King William's vassal for the vast lands he acquired in England after the Conquest; and whatever force the old relationship with the count of Flanders may have then retained, the fact that the count of Boulogne held the 'honour of Boulogne' in England enabled King Henry to arrange the marriage of Count Eustace III to suit his own policies; and when Eustace retired from the world in about 1120 Henry virtually controlled the succession to the *comté* as well as to the English honour. Indeed his action led to a union of the *comté* with the kingdom and the duchy of much the same kind as the union of England and Normandy after 1066.[4]

---

[1] Ganshof, *Feudalism* (1952), pp. 92–3 (*Qu'est-ce que la Féodalité?*, 1947, pp. 121–3); 'Les relations féodo-vassaliques aux temps post-carolingiens', pp. 111–14. Cf. Barlow, *Edward the Confessor*, pp. 64–5.

[2] e.g. the provisions in the agreement between King Henry Beauclerc and the count of Flanders safeguarding the count's obligations to the king of France (*Diplomatic Documents*, i. 1–8). The difficulty was eventually overcome in France by distinguishing between liege homage and ordinary homage, the king requiring liege homage from the principal seigneurs of the kingdom.

[3] Ganshof, 'La Flandre' in Lot and Fawtier, *Histoire des institutions françaises*, i. *Institutions seigneuriales*, pp. 344–9; above, pp. 99–100, n. 6.

[4] Above, pp. 76–7. Round (*Studies in Peerage*, pp. 155–63) shows how churches

Boulogne thus shows the same 'intensification of suzerainty' leading to the possibility of union as has been found in the case of the Scottish kingdom and the Welsh principalities. It also shows one of two potentially inconsistent feudal relationships coming out stronger than the other, for Count Eustace apparently did not follow either Robert II or Baldwin VII, successive counts of Flanders, in their fighting against Henry in Normandy.[1] A similar development can be seen in Brittany, though here the relationship was more complex. The duke of Brittany must have been regarded as the vassal of the king of France in some sense during the eleventh century,[2] though this can have had little practical effect. He had also entered into a relationship, which had feudal characteristics, with the dukes of Normandy before 1066. After that date repeated acts implying vassalage led to the comprehensive recognition of Henry's suzerainty in 1113.[3] Whether this should be regarded as substituting the suzerainty of the Norman king for that of the king of France or simply as inserting him between the Breton duke and the French king in the feudal hierarchy, Norman suzerainty had been 'intensified' here as elsewhere, and of the two originally somewhat remote allegiances that which bound the duke of Brittany to the Norman dukes and kings had proved the stronger.

In the case of Brittany, however, fiefs first in Normandy and later in England as well had been granted, not to the duke himself, but to other Breton lords.[4] The potential conflict of allegiance which this represented would presumably be avoided so long as the Norman king held his suzerainty over the Breton duke; but the fiefs held in England or Normandy by Bretons or men of Breton origin, whatever connections they still retained

and seigneurs of the Boulonnais obtained lands in eastern England, producing a situation on either side of the Straits of Dover very like that formed by the Norman Conquest on either side of the English Channel, though on a much smaller scale.

[1] At least there seems to be no indication that he did. There would surely have been repercussions in England if he had done so. In 1118 he was on his way to Jerusalem to prosecute a claim to the kingdom.

[2] King Philip's intervention in the fighting in Brittany during the year 1076 is hard to explain save on the basis of some belief in his suzerainty; and it was King Louis VI, according to Orderic, who 'granted' Brittany to Henry: 'Tunc Ludovicus Henrico . . . totamque concessit Britanniam. Fergannus etenim, Britonum princeps, homo regis Anglorum jam factus fuerat', Orderic Vitalis, *H.E.* (ed. Le Prévost), iv. 307–8. [3] Above, pp. 14–16, 73–6. [4] Above, pp. 74–5.

H

with their homeland,[1] would only increase the Norman kings' interest in Brittany, certainly in practical terms.[2] One of these grants, as it turned out, had even more momentous consequences. William the Conqueror had given the lands that came to form the great honour of Richmond to a junior branch of the Breton ducal family. When Earl Conan of Richmond inherited a claim to the duchy and was able to make it good, certainly with the acquiescence and most likely with the active assistance of King Henry II, the earl of Richmond and the duke of Brittany were one and the same man. The king was then presented with an opportunity which he did not neglect; and within a few years Brittany was in fact if not yet in theory under his direct rule.[3]

In all this, the position of the holders of 'cross-border' estates ought perhaps to be treated as a distinct element. There were several ways in which such estates could be created. A Norman baron might acquire lands beyond the frontier (e.g. Roger 'de Beaumont' who married the heiress of the count of Meulan)[4] or a 'foreign' lord might similarly acquire lands in Normandy (e.g. Amauri de Montfort who inherited the *comté* of Évreux from his maternal uncle).[5] That the political implications of such family events were well understood is shown by Henry's reaction to Amauri's claim to Évreux.[6] Or estates in the Norman lands might be given to 'foreign' lords (e.g. Breton lords in Normandy and England, Flemings in England, Welsh princes in England); or families settled in Normandy and England might acquire lands beyond the frontier—by conquest as in Wales, by invitation as in Scotland. In all cases this could represent an

[1] The Penthièvre family which obtained the honour of Richmond certainly retained interests in Brittany (*E.Y.C.*, iv (*Honour of Richmond*, i), 84–93). Ralph de Gael retained his great Breton estates after he had been deprived of those he held in East Anglia by William the Conqueror in 1075, and his son and namesake obtained the honour of Breteuil in Normandy as well (*Complete Peerage*, ix. 571–4). The descendants of Hascuit Musard (Staveley, Derbyshire), Eudo fitzSpirewic (Tattershall, Lincolnshire), and Tihel de Helléan (Helions Bumpstead, Essex), all of Breton origin, continued to hold their English estates through the twelfth century (Sanders, *English Baronies*, pp. 83, 88, 121).

[2] e.g. William the Conqueror's expeditions to Brittany in 1064 and 1076; above, pp. 15–16, 74–5.

[3] *E.Y.C.*, iv (*Honour of Richmond*, i), 84–93; Pocquet du Haut-Jussé, 'Les Plantagenets et la Bretagne'. [4] *Complete Peerage*, vii. 522–4.

[5] Ibid., pp. 709–14; Lemarignier, *Hommage en marche*, pp. 59–60.

[6] Above, p. 84.

extension of Norman interests and influence, and would do so as long as the centre was strong and the momentum of expansion maintained. If or when the tide turned, such cross-border links would work the other way. The whole subject deserves a much fuller investigation.

Thus, however the relationships between the vassal princes and the Norman kings are to be defined, and it may well be that clear definition at a given moment in time is scarcely possible, there seems to be a tendency for them to grow stronger.[1] Paradoxically, as it must seem, while the barons of England and Normandy, who could be said to owe their fiefs to royal or ducal grant, were strengthening their position by making their tenures more securely hereditary, the princes beyond kingdom and duchy who entered into feudal relations with him by quite a different process found that in their case it was the rights of the suzerain that were being strengthened. Since this could lead eventually to the suzerain undertaking the direct rule of their lands, it is clear that these overlordships cannot be left out of account as part of the bundle of rights and authorities, influences and possibilities that made up the Norman kings' 'lands and lordships'. The analogy with the development of the relationship between the 'territorial princes' and the kings of France is always at hand; and it is particularly relevant because Normandy was directly involved. If a certain authority over the king of Scots, the princes of Wales, the dukes of

---

[1] This did not happen in every case, though the examples cited show that it was always possible. The Norman kings actually lost ground in the small but strategically vital *pagus* of the Vexin (above, pp. 82–4) and no 'intensification of suzerainty' can be detected in their relations with the counts of Pontieu, though all vestiges of the feudal relationship were not lost (above, pp. 77–8). Henry's agreements with the count of Flanders should probably be regarded as treaties of alliance cast into the feudal form which often clothed such contracts in the eleventh and twelfth centuries. Yet even the feudal formalities could be made to show some reality; for when Count Robert II and Count Baldwin VII fought on the side of the king of France against Henry, they may have been invoking the clause in the agreement which enabled them to join the king of France in an invasion of Normandy with twenty knights to avoid losing the fief (the *comté* of Flanders) which they held of him. There seems to be no clear record, however, that they ever sent to Henry the 1,000 knights for which the agreement provided. Count Thierry, at all events, thought it worth while to renew the contract when he had secured the *comté* and actually did homage to Henry (above, pp. 78–81). Maine stands by itself in this context, though the *comté* would have been brought immediately under the direct rule of Henry's successor if his plans for the succession had matured (above, pp. 86–7).

Brittany, and so on is to be reckoned as part of the 'lands and lordships' of the Norman kings, then Normandy has to be reckoned as in some sense a part of the *regnum Francorum*; and in fact the relationship between the rulers of Normandy as such and the kings of France shows much the same course of evolution as that between the 'vassal princes' and the Norman kings.

There can be no doubt that the territory which later formed the duchy of Normandy was a part of the *regnum* of the Carolingian kings and their Capetian successors, and that the land of Normandy was regarded as having been granted to Rollo and his successors by the king of the Western Franks, however that 'grant' was interpreted at the time, in the eleventh and early twelfth centuries, or later, and whatever part such a grant may have formed in the settlement of the Northmen in Normandy as a matter of historical fact. In the time of William the Conqueror and his sons, therefore, Normandy was traditionally a part of the kingdom of which Henry I (of France), Philip I, and Louis VI were kings. Moreover, before 1066 the 'dukes of Normandy' had been vassals of the 'king of France' in the sense that can be given to the term at that time; although this was very different from the meaning that had been put into it by the time of King John of England. Such acts of the earlier dukes as can be interpreted as acts of homage made to the king had been performed on the borders of Normandy and 'France', that is 'on the march', with an implication of equality between the parties. There are indeed other incidents implying a lord–vassal relationship, in the contemporary sense, between king and duke;[1] and the action of King Henry of France during and just after the minority of William the Conqueror seems very like that of a suzerain protecting the interests of a vassal and in so doing protecting his own;[2] but when this attitude of the king turned abruptly to hostility in or about the year 1052[3] the

---

[1] Lemarignier, *Hommage en marche*, pp. 73–91; 'Les fidèles du roi de France'. The texts are collected in Lot, *Fidèles ou vassaux?*, pp. 177–200. For half a century suzerainty over the duke of the Normans passed from the king to the duke of the Franks (Lot, ibid., pp. 186–93; Douglas, 'Rise of Normandy', pp. 109–10), until the duke of the Franks became the king of the Franks in 987.

[2] Douglas, *William the Conqueror*, pp. 44–52, 59–61.

[3] Lot, *Fidèles ou vassaux?*, pp. 198–203; Douglas, *William the Conqueror*, pp. 61–4, etc.

situation changed radically. From then, for over a hundred years, no man while he ruled over both England and Normandy, neither William the Conqueror nor Henry Beauclerc nor Stephen,[1] certainly not William Rufus while he held the duchy in pawn, is known to have done homage to the king of France; and Henry, it seems, refused to do it when it was demanded of him.[2] If Robert Curthose did homage as duke or future duke of Normandy, which is possible but not certain, it is as likely that he did it when he was in rebellion against his father as at any time after 1087[3]—and he was never king of the English.

In practice, then, the suzerainty of the kings of France over the Norman kings as dukes of Normandy was hardly more than a memory or a tradition, an ineffective juridical concept, and certainly gave no authority or power of control. Yet it was never forgotten, and it had in it the same potential (with memories of earlier political association added) as the over-lordships of the Norman kings; and this potential, as the kings of France profited by such opportunities as came their way and as their general situation in their kingdom improved, enabled them eventually to make it more of a reality. King Philip I had been able to profit from the disputes between William the Conqueror and his eldest son and from the rivalries of Robert Curthose, William Rufus, and Henry Beauclerc to the extent that these family quarrels may have assisted his advance into the Vexin, with all that that meant for the defence of Normandy; and when Henry, in 1120, wished to make sure of his son's succession in Normandy and to parry the claim of Robert Curthose's son William Clito, he made William Ætheling do homage to King Louis VI, and for the first time the homage was

---

[1] Orderic Vitalis seems to suggest that Stephen did homage in 1137 (ed. Le Prévost, v. 81), but Lemarignier shows good reason for preferring other accounts which state that it was his son Eustace who did homage on that occasion (*Hommage en marche*, 93, note 70).

[2] According to Malmesbury, Henry refused 'pro culmine imperii' (*Gesta Regum*, ii. 496; Luchaire, *Louis VI le Gros*, No. 72, pp. 38–40; Dumas, 'Encore la question, Fidèles ou Vassaux?', pp. 351–3), though it was claimed on behalf of King Louis VI that Normandy had been granted to him as a fief (Suger, *Vita Ludovici Grossi*, p. 106; Lot, *Fidèles ou vassaux?*, pp. 201–2).

[3] Lot, *Fidèles ou vassaux?*, pp. 200–1; Lemarignier, *Hommage en marche*, p. 85, note 41. The participation of William fitzOsbern in the Cassel campaign of 1071, which some (including Lot, ubi supra, p. 200) have thought represented the performance by William of his feudal service to the king of France, may also be interpreted in other ways (above, p. 78, note 6).

recorded as homage for Normandy.[1] Stephen did the same with his son Eustace in 1137; and when Eustace repeated this homage in 1140 he further conformed to the rule that homage should be renewed at the accession of a new suzerain.[2] Though neither Henry nor Stephen did homage himself, and it would seem that the homage of their sons was performed primarily to strengthen their claim to the succession (there is no suggestion that the homage itself or the king's acceptance of it, even though it was for Normandy, gave them possession of the duchy), that homage was no longer indeterminate or simply personal, but 'real', and Normandy was the consideration for which it was done. The duchy was coming to be regarded as a fief in a fuller sense, and held of the king of France. The next step in this progression was taken in 1151 when Duke Henry (the future King Henry II), having been given Normandy by his father, did liege homage for the duchy and did it in Paris where his suzerain had his residence.[3] Homage was done on more than one occasion by Henry after he had become king of England, in contrast to the refusal of the Norman kings, and similarly by his sons; and though there was an opinion forming in Normandy which emphasized the equal status of the two parties implied by homage on the frontier, where in fact most of these later acts were performed, and though we cannot always be sure of the technicalities in such reports of these acts as we have,[4] the line of development lay through the difficult succession of 1199 and its consequences, the judgment of 1202 and the war that followed, to the conquest of Normandy by the king of France.

The only important respect in which the evolution of the relationship between the dukes of Normandy and the kings of France differed from that of the relationships between the 'vassal princes' beyond England and Normandy and the Norman kings is that, whereas it was never disputed at this time that Normandy was a part of the traditional kingdom of the Western Franks whatever the actual relationship between the duke and the king might be, the 'principalities' could not be said to form part of a pre-existing unit with England or Normandy—unless, to the north of the Channel, the 'Britannia'

---

[1] Lemarignier, *Hommage en marche*, pp. 91–2.   [2] Ibid., pp. 92–3.
[3] Lemarignier, *Hommage en marche*, pp. 93–5; Lot, *Fidèles ou vassaux?*, pp. 204–5.
[4] Lemarignier, pp. 92–111; Lot, 212–21.

of the Anglo-Saxons is to be given a political content similar to that of the 'regnum Francorum'[1] or, to the south, some reality given to a Carolingian 'maritime march' or series of marches along the coastal lands from the Scheldt to the Loire.[2] In other respects the analogy is clear and close and corresponds to the evolution and progressive definition of feudal relations in France and Britain during the eleventh and twelfth centuries. And just as, through these relationships, the 'vassal principalities' can be seen to be working generally towards a more integral unity with kingdom and duchy, so Normandy was eventually to be integrated with the kingdom of France. It can certainly be argued that the Norman kings resisted the intensification of the French kings' suzerainty over Normandy, which in any case was still in a very early stage; that they may have thought, if indeed they did think in this way, that the integrating effects of their rule in England and Normandy would withstand the centripetal pull of Paris and the king of France; nevertheless this traditional suzerainty, ignored, resisted, or denied, but never forgotten, introduces an important qualification into the notion of a progressive unification of the Norman lands and lordships, whether or not it was seen to be such at the time.

[1] John, *Orbis Britanniae*, pp. 1–63; Barlow, *Edward the Confessor*, pp. 135–8.
[2] Dhondt, *Principautés territoriales*, pp. 277–83; but cf. de Bouard, 'De la Neustrie carolingienne à la Normandie féodale', pp. 2–3.

7. Assimilation

WHEN the Norman kings extended their itinerant manner of ruling their duchy to kingdom and duchy together, and exercised such authority as they might have over neighbouring rulers through the lord–vassal relationship backed by force or the threat of it, they put into practice a form of government which would tend to unify their lands and lordships; for the higher levels of government, direct and indirect, would be common to them all. This tendency was reinforced by the interests of the royal family and of the aristocracy, and by what we may dimly discern to have been their political assumptions, as well as by the front they presented to other 'powers'. It remains to be asked whether there were also tendencies in the opposite direction; and, if so, whether the integrating or the dividing forces were likely to prove the stronger, whether indeed there were fundamental differences between the countries concerned that would for ever resist the integrating effects of a common government, however strong these might be; or whether, taking everything into consideration, it may be said that the Norman lands and lordships were moving towards an increasingly intimate political union.

After the conquest and the colonization of England the 'king-dukes' had found, as to some extent the kings and dukes had found before them, that it was not possible to handle all their financial and judicial business in Normandy and England through the itinerant household and the court that assembled wherever they might be. In order to achieve the efficient collection of revenue in both countries, and to do this for a king who divided his time between them, the two exchequers had been devised, one in England and one in Normandy. In England, those who sat at the exchequer would have to deal primarily with the sheriffs, and at least some elements of their procedure were based upon the procedures of the chamberlains of the Anglo-Saxon kings and their treasuries. In Normandy the exchequer had to deal primarily with *vicomtes* and *prévôts*, and rested upon an organization of the ducal finances which differed from that of the pre-Conquest kings in England. In each country the ruler had preserved or established certain sources of revenue, which naturally differed from one country to the other; and these differences persisted. No serious attempt seems to have been made, or perhaps could have been made, to standardize sources of revenue (except for those based upon feudal tenures) or methods of collection; indeed it might be expected that each of the two exchequers would soon build up bureaucratic traditions of its own which would tend not only to perpetuate but to intensify these differences.

Similarly, the king had had to extend the delegation of his judicial functions, as the dukes had already begun to do in Normandy; for the court which attended the king at different points in his itinerary could not deal with all the judicial business that men would have liked to bring to it or which it was imposing on them, any more than the itinerant chamber could deal with all the king's financial affairs. In England the men whom the king employed to do the judicial work, his justices, tended to act in the shire courts, which they converted into *curia regis* for the occasion, and in what seem rather to have been baronial courts in Normandy, which likewise they converted into *curia regis* for the occasion. These men were drawn from those who frequented the king's court in one capacity or another; they were in fact extending the jurisdiction of that court by dealing locally with business that it could not have coped with otherwise; and there seems to have been a tendency in Henry's time for such of these men as were more frequently employed in this way to form a group in each country under the bishop of Salisbury in England and the bishop of Lisieux in Normandy. Since each group would naturally have to take account of existing custom in its own country, it could be expected to build up its own practice and to become ever more clearly defined. Thus in judicial as in financial matters the development of the king's government could well lead to a departmentalization which would tend to perpetuate and to intensify the different traditions and customs of the two countries.[1]

Yet even at the time of Henry's death this departmentalization, if that is what was happening, was still in a very elementary stage; and it need not be assumed that delegated financial

[1] Above, pp. 145–59.

and judicial administration, as two distinct 'departments', would necessarily come together to make up an 'English' administration on one side of the Channel and a 'Norman' administration on the other, each growing ever more distinct from the itinerant element of the government and autonomous in itself. The Norman kings probably had no alternative to building on such administrative institutions as existed already in the two countries respectively in 1066; most medieval governments had to deal with customs and institutions that differed from one part of their lands to another; and as the barons of the exchequer and the justices were drawn from and frequently rejoined the king's court they could still have been serving to integrate rather than to divide. The exchequer and the courts do not seem to have been specialized as yet, either in personnel or in function. The term 'barons of the exchequer' could refer to men acting as judges or to men acting as auditors. Both senses are found in records relating to England during Henry's reign,[1] and the only known example of the use of the term in Normandy at this time occurs in the record of a plea.[2] Moreover, since the object of the audit was to decide judicially on problems arising in the course of the accounting rather than to secure the arithmetical accuracy of the accounts themselves,[3] the exchequers were certainly judicial as well as financial institutions —so far as they can be regarded as established institutions at this time rather than as the name of an accounting device used in periodic meetings of men who acted both as auditors and as justices.

But if it is difficult to distinguish clearly between the judicial and financial administration of the Norman kings at the higher levels, it is equally difficult to distinguish between their administration on one side of the Channel and the other. In terms

---

[1] e.g. Poole, *Exchequer in the Twelfth Century*, p. 39 and note 4; *Pipe Roll 31 Henry I*, pp. 96, 140.

[2] Round, 'Bernard the King's Scribe', pp. 425–6; Haskins, *Norman Institutions*, p. 88, note 18.

[3] This is what Richard fitzNeal says of Henry II's time: 'Assident inquam ad discernenda iura et dubia determinanda que frequenter ex incidentibus questionibus oriuntur. Non enim in ratiociniis sed in multiplicibus iudiciis excellens scaccarii scientia consistit.' *Dialogus*, ed. Johnson, p. 15. That this was also the case under Henry I is shown by an entry in the *Pipe Roll 31 Henry I*, p. 96. Cf. Morris, *Medieval English Sheriff*, pp. 94–5; Richardson and Sayles, *Governance of Medieval England*, p. 188.

of personnel, and taking as examples some of the more prominent of Henry's ministers rather than attempting a quasi-
statistical inquiry into the officers of the Norman kings, there
are some, it is true, who seem to have held office only in one
country or the other. Of these, Roger bishop of Salisbury and
John bishop of Lisieux, though neither held any clearly defined
office, are associated the one with England and the other with
Normandy and, so far as the evidence goes, acted officially only
in the country with which each was thus associated. Ralph
Basset acted as a justice in England, his son Richard as justice
and sheriff, Aubrey de Vere likewise as justice and sheriff,
William de Pont-de-l'Arche as sheriff and treasurer; while
Henry de la Pommeraye appears as a 'baron of the exchequer'
only in Normandy. On the other hand, Geoffrey of Clinton
served as a justice and a treasurer both in England and in Normandy; as a chamberlain he attended the king in both countries,
and if his landed fortune was made in the kingdom he did not
discard his hereditary estates in the duchy; Robert Mauduit
served in the treasuries of both countries; a Robert de Courcy
appears as a baron of the exchequer in Normandy and as a
justice in England, and a Robert de la Haye as baron of the
exchequer in Normandy and constable of Lincoln Castle.[1]

In fact, the evidence that would support any attempt to assign
men to a supposed 'English' or 'Norman' administration is not
at all strong. The charters, which are the principal source of
information in the time of the Norman kings, do not always
by any means give men the titles of the offices which they are
known to have held. There is only one surviving document of
this time which specifically names certain men acting as barons
of the exchequer on a particular occasion in Normandy;[2] none
for England, though there are two from which some names
might be deduced.[3] Thus the fact that a man appears in surviving records as exercising office in only one of the two countries
is far from proof that he did not act officially in the other. In
most cases such men can be shown to have attended the king

---

[1] The evidence for these statements is indicated in Le Patourel, *Normandy and
England*, pp. 30–8. On Roger of Salisbury, add Kealey, *Roger of Salisbury, passim.*
The careers of Henry's ministers form a subject that could profitably be taken a
good deal further.   [2] Above, p. 224 n. 2.

[3] *Regesta* ii, Nos. 1000, 1211; Richardson and Sayles, *Governance of Medieval
England*, pp. 176, 249.

and to have had interests in the country with which they were not so identified. Bishop Roger of Salisbury entered Henry's service in Normandy before 1100, and he attended the king in Normandy certainly on one occasion in the latter part of Henry's reign; the bishop of Lisieux attended the king in England more than once; the king chose the occasion of a transfretation to Normandy on which Aubrey de Vere accompanied him to issue the charter which recorded the grant of the office of his 'master chamberlain of all England', and Aubrey still had interests in the Cotentin and in Brittany.[1] Ralph and Richard Basset maintained their family property in Normandy; William de Pont-de-l'Arche, a busy servant of the king in England, attended him in Normandy, probably as chamberlain of the *camera curie*, and had other connections with the administration of the duchy; Henry de la Pommeraye attended the king in both countries, probably as constable, and had extensive landed interests in the West Country of England as well as in the Bessin. William de Tancarville (d. 1129), though he and his family are now associated with Normandy where their principal seat lay, attended the king as chamberlain in both countries, and had estates in England.[2] All these men were of Norman origin; they must have been personally acquainted with one another for they would meet at the greater sessions of the king's court if not elsewhere; and although offices were not strictly hereditary in Henry's time, there were certainly 'administrative families' prominent in his administration (the families of Roger of Salisbury, of John of Lisieux, the Bassets, the de Courcys, the Tancarvilles, and others): so that if an individual cannot be shown to have acted in an official capacity in both countries it often appears that close relatives did so between them. It could perhaps be argued that the use of the terms *justiciarii totius Angliae*[3] and *justitii Normanniae*[4] suggest a distinction between the personnel of judicial administration in the one country and the other; but there still seems to be no reason

---

[1] Le Patourel, *Normandy and England*, pp. 35, 32–3, 30 (respectively). The charter for Aubrey de Vere is calendared in *Regesta*, ii, No. 1777, reproduced in a seventeenth-century 'facsimile' in *Sir Christopher Hatton's Book of Seals*, plate I (text, No. 39, pp. 25–6) and discussed in Le Patourel, op. cit., p. 11, note 25.

[2] Le Patourel, op. cit., pp. 33, 36–7, 31–2, 37–8 (respectively).

[3] Richardson and Sayles, *Governance of Medieval England*, pp. 174–6.

[4] Haskins, *Norman Institutions*, pp. 99–100.

why a man should not act in both,[1] and in any case these terms seem rather to indicate a general as opposed to a localized commission in England or Normandy.[2] Thus, though the evidence is incomplete and ultimately perhaps inconclusive—for the fact that an individual can be shown to have held office in the two countries at the same time or at different times does not rule out the possibility that men were beginning to think of two distinct administrations, one for each country—the ministers who served Henry still look more like one body than two.[3] Furthermore, the process of detaching the financial and judicial institutions which seem to be localized in kingdom and duchy from the undifferentiated household-court was far from complete.[4] The staff of the treasuries seems to have been drawn originally from the household, and men like Robert Mauduit or Geoffrey of Clinton could still hold office in both.[5] The fact that some of those who were probably barons of the exchequer might also be justices or local officers as well as holding office in the itinerant household suggests that we have to imagine each session of the exchequer as held by an *ad hoc* rather than a permanent commission at this time, and that those who served as local or itinerant royal justices were appointed from and returned to a central pool, which can only have been the king's household and court. The only point that might seem to argue against this is that the exchequers of England and Normandy appear to have been held simultaneously, at Easter and Michaelmas,[6] so that one man could hardly serve in both at the same time; but there is no reason why he should not have served in one on one occasion and in the other on another occasion. When the records of the auditing sessions of the English and the Norman exchequers can be compared (and this is not before 1180), their general similarity, with differences

---

[1] Geoffrey of Clinton, at least, seems to have done so: Richardson and Sayles, *Governance of Medieval England*, pp. 175–7; Haskins, *Norman Institutions*, pp. 89–90; Le Patourel, *Normandy and England*, pp. 30–1.

[2] van Caenegem, *Birth of the Common Law*, p. 14.

[3] Cf. Haskins, *Norman Institutions*, pp. 113–14.

[4] Richardson shows that the process of 'departmentalization' still had some way to go at the end of the twelfth century: *Memoranda Roll 1 John*, pp. xi–xvi etc.

[5] Le Patourel, *Normandy and England*, pp. 30–1, 36; Haskins, *Norman Institutions*, pp. 113–14.

[6] *Pipe Roll 31 Henry I*, pp. xv–xx; Morris, *Medieval English Sheriff*, p. 95; Haskins, *Norman Institutions*, pp. 107, 176.

in detail, argues not only a common origin but a considerable period of at least overlapping membership.[1]

Since the localized offshoots of the household and court were still not clearly distinguished from the parent body in terms of personnel, it is hardly surprising that their functions were still not completely separated. As the king's revenues increased, the importance of the fixed treasuries grew in relation to that of the itinerant chamber; but it was still possible for money due to the king to be paid directly into the chamber and to be spent by it without ever going into one of the treasuries or passing through an exchequer audit.[2] Since the treasuries existed to serve the itinerant king, they had to work together; for money certainly had to be moved from place to place as he needed it. The money which was under the care of the earl of Gloucester at Falaise in 1135 'had recently been brought from England'.[3] probably against the possibility that the king's disciplining of William Talvas and others would require extensive military operations in that part of Normandy;[4] the treasure which was being conveyed to England in 1120 with the king was loaded on to the White Ship and apparently survived the wreck;[5] according to Orderic, the proceeds of Ranulf Flambard's exactions in England were transmitted to Rufus in Normandy.[6] Money due to the king in England could be paid into a Norman treasury and its receipt recorded on the English pipe roll.[7] Though there was apparently one minister who presided over the English exchequer and another who presided over the Norman exchequer, and though the auditing operations produced two sets of records, one in England and one in Normandy, the anomalous position of the treasurer in the *Constitutio Domus Regis*, seemingly half in the household and half out of it, is best explained by supposing that he still had an over-all responsibility for all the treasuries, fixed and itinerant, with, working

---

[1] Haskins, op. cit., pp. 176–8.

[2] Tout, *Chapters*, i. 84–5. The incompleteness of the English Pipe Rolls and the Norman Exchequer Rolls as statements of the king's revenue and expenditure in the twelfth century is demonstrated for England by Richardson and Sayles, *Governance of Medieval England*, pp. 216–17, 229–39 and for Normandy by Delisle in 'Revenus publics', *B.É.C.*, x. 277–8.

[3] Orderic Vitalis, *H.E.* (ed. Le Prévost), v. 50; Torigni, *Chronica*, p. 129.

[4] Chartrou, *L'Anjou*, pp. 37–8.

[5] Orderic Vitalis, *H.E.* (ed. Le Prévost), iv. 412–13, 419.   [6] ibid., p. 54.

[7] Haskins, *Norman Institutions*, pp. 107–8, 113; *Pipe Roll 31 Henry I*, pp. 7, 13, etc.

under him, chamberlains in the itinerant household and in the English treasuries, and treasurers in Normandy.[1]

However, to show that the localized institutions of government, the treasuries, the exchequers, and the groups of royal justices, had not yet differentiated themselves at all completely from the household and court, or as between England and Normandy, does not in itself tell us whether the government of the Norman kings was moving in the direction of progressive integration or the reverse. It simply indicates that, whatever the line of development that their emergence represents, they had not yet moved far along it and might not yet be irrevocably committed to it. Are we to suppose that with geographical separation, different local conditions, and the normal processes of bureaucratic evolution, these localized institutions would inevitably build up in course of time into two separate and more or less self-contained administrations, one for each country, the control of the itinerant king and the men who moved around with him becoming more and more remote? Or should we say rather that in 1066 two countries which, for all their earlier contacts and common experiences, were distinct in origin, in political tradition, and in other respects, had been brought together, that the degree of unity which the Norman kings had imposed on them was already a long step in the direction of integration and that local differences were likely to be smoothed out eventually by the working of a common government? It may be that a direct answer cannot be given to these questions,

[1] 'Magister camerarius par est dapifero in liberatione. Thesaurarius, ut magister camerarius, si in curia fuerit et servierit in thesauro' (*or* ut Thesaur'): *Dialogus*, ed. Johnson, p. 133 (cf. White, 'Financial Administration under Henry I', pp. 64–5). As the stewards received the same livery as the chancellor if they took their meals outside the household (ibid., pp. 129–30), the result of these equations is that the treasurer ranked with the chancellor and the stewards, officers who were still members of the itinerant household. Haskins thought that there was a treasurer for England and a treasurer for Normandy (*Norman Institutions*, pp. 108–10) and his opinion was elaborated by Tout (*Chapters*, i. 80–2) and followed, at least by implication, by others (Richardson and Sayles, *Governance of Medieval England*, pp. 224–5; Chrimes, *Introduction to the Administrative History of Medieval England*, pp. 27–9, though Chrimes mentions White's dissent in a footnote). White does not deal with the point directly in 'Financial Administration', though in an article published soon after it ('Treasurers in Normandy under Henry I') he put forward the evidence against Haskins's opinion and in favour of a single treasurer. The fact that the treasurer is treated by the *Constitutio* as a high-ranking member of the household, though with duties outside it, strongly supports the idea set out above—if *thesaurarius* in the passage quoted does indeed mean '*the* treasurer'.

or cannot be given yet; but one possible indication of the direction in which things were moving would be provided by an attempt to estimate the degree of assimilation between the institutions and societies of England and Normandy that was actually achieved under the rule of the Norman kings. The answer which such an approach offers may still be a little dusty; but it seems unlikely that anything better will emerge until a great deal more thought has been given to the problem.

In some respects the process went beyond assimilation to identity. Between 1066 and 1144 the king of the English and the duke of the Normans were normally[1] the same person. This was a time when king or duke ruled personally; he chose to rule his lands directly by itineration, and such governmental apparatus as he had at his disposal existed to serve him rather than to serve, in any direct sense, the people he ruled. It is natural for us to think of William or Henry as uniting in their persons two distinct dignities or offices, king and duke, and acting therefore in two different capacities. Yet there is little to show that they or their contemporaries thought consistently in this way. No contemporary treatise that would give a systematic analysis of their position seems to survive, if any was ever written;[2] and the indications of what men thought and the assumptions on which they spoke and acted have to be sought in the titles they attributed to their rulers or were assumed by them, in the ceremonial of kingship, in royal actions, and in the descriptions of these that we have.[3]

[1] Above, pp. 184–7, 196–201, for the degree to which the years 1087–96 and 1100–6 were regarded as abnormal.

[2] The only writer who might be quoted was formerly known as the 'Anonymous of York', now more usually as the 'Norman Anonymous'. In his treatise, 'De Consecratione pontificum et regum', he appears to claim for a *dux* or a *princeps* qualities and authority similar to those of a king (Williams, *The Norman Anonymous of 1100 A.D.*, pp. 52–5). Whether the writer had the duke of the Normans particularly in mind and, if so, this is evidence that he was writing in Normandy, particularly in the year 1100, is open to question, as will appear from the following discussion.

[3] Since writing the first draft of the following section on the relationship between the Norman kings' royal and 'ducal' capacities, and a contribution to a forthcoming volume of *Mélanges* to be presented to Professor Jean Yver, I have been privileged to read in typescript a paper by C. Warren Hollister on 'Normandy, France, and the Anglo-Norman *Regnum*' due to be published in *Speculum* during 1976. I am grateful to Professor Hollister for allowing me to do this. He and I had been working independently on very similar problems, though we approached them from rather different angles and have been looking for rather different conclusions. I have profited greatly from reading his paper, chiefly in clearing my mind on my

So far as titles are concerned, contemporary chroniclers writing in England refer to the king as *rex* simply, *rex Willelmus* (or *Henricus*) or *rex Anglorum*, whether they are describing his activities in England or in Normandy. Those writing in Normandy do the same; either because they gave him the higher title in courtesy or because they thought of him as acting as king in Normandy whatever his title might have been in any 'constitutional' sense. Occasionally, it is true, writers on either side of the Channel give the two titles, *rex Anglorum et dux Normannorum*, or some variant of the Norman title, but they seem to reserve that, on the whole, for rather special occasions. Generally speaking they use the term *regnum* for England. They often seem to be trying to avoid the word *ducatus* by referring to Normandy by name wherever possible; though very occasionally they may distinguish between *regnum* and *ducatus*. Moreover the term *regnum* could be used of Normandy,[1] and is occasionally used in a context in which it can only be understood to refer to the two countries together or even to the totality of the lands over which the king exercised some form of dominion, his whole sphere of authority.[2] The only writer who seems to be consciously searching for a term to express the relationship between the two countries as he saw it is the Hyde Chronicler, who speaks of *rex Norman-Anglorum, regnum Norman-Anglorum, principes Norman-Anglorum* and *ecclesia Norman-Anglorum*; and, although he is not wholly consistent in this, there can be little doubt that he uses these terms to signify the people or institutions of both Normandy and England, not simply the Norman and English people living in England. If he had in mind the earlier term (*rex*) *Angul-Saxonum*, his adaptation of it to the situation after 1066 is of great interest, though isolated.[3]

own approach and in the confidence gained from finding that we were in agreement on many important matters.

[1] Fauroux, *Recueil, index rerum*, s.v. *regnum* (p. 468).

[2] Ibid., No. 158 (p. 344) where the term as used in a charter of 1063 must be taken to include Maine; later examples, e.g. Orderic Vitalis, *H.E.* (ed. Le Prévost), iv. 329, 373, 402; v. 45. On the difficulties of the word *regnum* in a French context during the twelfth and thirteenth centuries, e.g. Wood, 'Regnum Francie'. The above generalizations on the usage of chroniclers writing between 1066 and 1144 are based on impressions gained from a rapid re-reading *ad hoc*, rather than any attempt at a systematic or statistical survey which, to judge from the evidence presented here, would not be worth the labour.

[3] 'Chronica Monasterii de Hida juxta Wintoniam', in *Liber Monasterii de Hyda*,

Nevertheless, it is not easy to see any clearly conceived or consistent distinction between a royal and a ducal capacity in literary usage; and the inconsistency, even the imprecision, of the titles used in the formal written acts of the Norman kings give a similar impression of a lack of definition or regularity in the use of titles at this time. Probably all the *acta* that were written in diploma form, and a considerable proportion of those in writ form, were drafted by or under the direction of the beneficiaries, and the titles attributed to the ruler in such documents can only be taken to be those regarded as appropriate in an individual scriptorium.[1] The fact that the king was prepared to acknowledge, by his *signum* or by having his seal affixed to them, documents which show no consistency in the titles attributed to him, indicates that nothing which could be regarded as a formal style expressing an official doctrine of the king's authority or claims to authority over various peoples, such as the chanceries of Henry II and his successors adopted, was being used in the charters and writs of the Norman kings. Since the distinction between king and duke is made in certain formal documents, however, such as those recording the primacy agreement of 1072,[2] in many acts in diploma form, and elsewhere as for example in Anselm's letters to King Henry,[3] it must be accepted that for some people at some moments the distinction did exist, however theoretical it may have been; although the most that can be said of 'official' usage is that in such royal writs as are thought to have been written by a royal scribe, and may therefore have been drafted in court or household, the simple *rex Anglorum* is almost invariably used, whether the document concerns English or Norman affairs and whether it was dated

pp. 283–321, *passim*. I am indebted to Professor Hollister for pointing out the relevance of this chronicle to me. For 'rex Angul-Saxonum', e.g. Barlow, *Edward the Confessor*, p. 136.

[1] Chaplais, 'The Anglo-Saxon Chancery'; 'Seals and Original Charters of Henry I', pp. 261–2, 270–1; Bishop and Chaplais, *Facsimiles*, p. xv. In Normandy before 1066 various titles were given to the dukes in their charters—*dux, marchio, marchisus, patricius, comes, consul, princeps, rector*—often two together (Fauroux, *Recueil*, pp. 49–50). For some post-Conquest examples, Musset, *Actes de Guillaume le Conquérant . . . pour les abbayes caennaises*, pp. 37–8; *Regesta, passim*.

[2] Bishop and Chaplais, *Facsimiles*, text facing plate xxix.

[3] Archbishop Anselm gives Henry the ducal title in two letters written immediately after Tinchebrai, though not apparently otherwise. Henry's letters to the archbishop always use the style *rex Anglorum* (*Anselmi Opera*, v, Nos. 402, 404, etc.).

in or addressed to persons or institutions in either country.[1] So far as it goes this may suggest that in the court itself the royal title was regarded as comprehending the ducal, though not to the extent that the royal *signum* or seal would be refused to formal documents bearing titles that expressed the distinction.

It might be supposed, however, that the titles engraved on the king's seal-matrix or on his coin-dies would have some official significance and give expression to his and his advisers' view of the nature and extent of his authority. William the Conqueror took over the practice of using a two-sided seal from Edward the Confessor, and on one side of it he is represented as throned in majesty (as Edward had been represented on both

---

[1] Chaplais believes that there is only one original writ of William the Conqueror that has been 'definitely identified as the work of a royal scribe'. It was given in favour of Westminster Abbey, concerns lands in England and, if it was issued as he thinks in the last year of the Conqueror's reign, was almost certainly written and sealed in Normandy (Chaplais, 'The Anglo-Saxon Chancery', p. 176; Bishop and Chaplais, *Facsimiles*, No. 27). Bishop and Chaplais identify eight of Rufus's writs, ibid., Nos. 6, 10, 13, 17, 18, 22, 23, and 29, as written by royal scribes. No. 13 is dated in Normandy and concerns land in England granted to Fécamp; No. 23 is also dated in Normandy and is concerned with liberties, presumably in England, granted to Thorney. All these writs use the style 'rex Angl(orum)'. A number of original writs attributed to Henry's chancery scribes are listed and described by Chaplais in 'Seals and Original Charters of Henry I', pp. 266–7, 271–5, and a few more reproduced in facsimile in Bishop, *Scriptores Regis*. All save one of these use the style 'rex Angl(orum)'. The exception (Chaplais, 'Seals and Original Charters of Henry I', pp. 265–8) uses the style '(Henricus rex Anglorum) et dux Normannorum' in a writ dated at Winchester in 1133 and concerning land in Normandy granted to the hospital at Falaise. It is probable that any style other than 'rex Anglorum' should be treated as anomalous in a Latin document produced by a royal scribe of the Norman kings, as, for example, in the curious 'charter', combining characteristics of the English writ and the continental diploma, issued in the name of William the Conqueror, very likely in Normandy and concerning lands in England granted to Fécamp, which uses the style 'patronus Normannorum et rex Anglorum', echoing the titles on William's seal (Chaplais, 'Une charte originale pour l'abbaye de Fécamp', pp. 93–104, 355–7). In the writs quoted in this note all the permutations of country in which the lands or rights concerned were situated, country in which the document was dated, and country with which the beneficiary was identified are represented, save (significantly) writs dated in either country concerning lands in Normandy granted to an English beneficiary; but it should be remembered that all are in fact titles to land or rights whether in the form of grant, confirmation, or precept, and that the administrative writ, the writ-mandate, has rarely survived from the time of the Norman kings, though it was certainly used then (for its evolution, Chaplais, *English Royal Documents*, pp. 4–6). There is plenty of evidence that the king was still concerned with the affairs of one country when he was physically present in the other (above, pp. 126–8).

sides of his seal) and on the other on horse-back. The inscription on the majesty side refers to his authority in England, that on the equestrian side to his authority in Normandy; but the two inscriptions are most naturally read as a single sentence, beginning with the equestrian or Norman side, '+ HOC NORMAN-NORVM WILLELMVM NOSCE PATRONVM SI' and continuing on the majesty side '+ HOC ANGLIS REGEM SIGNO FATEARIS EVNDEM'. It is a literary[1] rather than an official composition, but it seems intended to unite the two dignities rather than to differentiate between them; and for what significance it may have in this connection the Norman title is given first, yielding priority to William's ducal heritage rather than to his royal conquest. William Rufus also had a two-sided seal, with a representation of the king in majesty on one face and on horseback on the other, but with the same inscription, '+ WILLELMVS DEI GRACIA REX ANGLORVM', on each. There is no evidence of a second seal after 1096 on which a Norman title might have been displayed; no doubt because he was regarded as being no more than a 'caretaker' for his brother in the duchy, though he was effectively 'duke' in Normandy and ruled there as his father had done. His seal, however, associates the royal title with what came to be established as the ducal or seigniorial representation, and Henry's first two seals do the same; but at some point in his reign Henry adopted a third seal which has the inscription '+ HENRICVS DEI GRATIA DVX NORMANNORVM' on the equestrian side.[2] Both Stephen's seals had design and inscriptions similar to this third seal of Henry's, changing only the king's name.

These seals were used to authenticate documents relating to English and Norman affairs indifferently, whether they were dated in the one country or the other.[3] Both Henry and Stephen used more than one seal in the course of their reigns; but there is no reason to suppose that two or more were used concurrently and there was certainly never one seal for English

[1] It is indeed metrical in intention if not completely successfully so in fact. I owe assurance on this point to Mr R. H. Martin of the University of Leeds.

[2] Four seals have been attributed to Henry; but as Chaplais has shown that the traditional 'first' is a forgery ('Seals and Original Charters of Henry I', pp. 262–5), the traditional 'second', 'third', and 'fourth' have here been called first, second, and third.

[3] Chaplais also notes that in the case of charters for English beneficiaries the seal is placed with the majesty or the equestrian side uppermost indifferently: 'Une charte originale pour l'abbaye de Fécamp', p. 95.

affairs and another for Norman affairs. The distinction between the king's capacity as king of the English and his capacity as duke of the Normans, if it existed, would have been expressed on his seal, therefore, only in the design, which makes the distinction, when the two titles appear, by placing the English title (with an appropriate representation) on one face, and the Norman title (again with what could be considered an appropriate representation) on the other; but neither the inscriptions nor the representations were used with strict consistency or appropriateness. William Rufus and Henry both used the equestrian representation with the royal title; and at whatever date Henry's third seal (traditional 'fourth'), that which bore the ducal title, came into use it was some time after the battle of Tinchebrai, so that he had been using a seal without the Norman title for several years after he had formally assumed the government of the duchy;[1] and Stephen continued to use a seal with the ducal title long after he had lost all authority in Normandy.

The titles on the seals, therefore, like the titles in the text of royal *acta*, support only a negative conclusion. They provide no firm evidence for a clearly conceived and consistently applied distinction between a royal and a ducal capacity. The evidence of the coins is equally negative. The Norman kings took over the whole apparatus of the royal currency in England after 1066, making no substantial change other than that of substituting their own names for those of their pre-Conquest predecessors; but they kept to the same form, *Willelm* or *Henri rex* in place of *Eadward* or *Harold rex*, and like their predecessors

---

[1] Chaplais argues that the third seal (traditional 'fourth') was introduced early in 1121, and bore the ducal title because Henry had just lost his son and heir, William Ætheling, and the claims of his nephew, William Clito, had thus become very serious. It may be so; but if a seal could be changed in 1121 for political reasons it is very strange that the second seal (traditional 'third'), which does not bear the ducal title, should have been introduced, in Chaplais's opinion, 'at the beginning of 1107', that is at the very moment when Henry, in Normandy from July 1106 until March/April 1107, was assuming the government of the duchy (Haskins, *Norman Institutions*, pp. 86–7); and this was an event which had been long prepared and was accompanied by important assemblies in which Henry reorganized the government of the duchy. Furthermore, if the third seal had the political significance attributed to it, its use on a document to be dated 30 January 1121 was an almost unbelievably quick reaction, if not perhaps quite impossible, to the death of William Ætheling on the preceding 25 November (Chaplais, 'Seals and Original Charters of Henry I', pp. 264–5).

sometimes use the Latin form of the name and give a suggestion of the word *Anglorum*.[1] In Normandy the ducal coinage was in full decline during the eleventh century, a most mysterious phenomenon considering the amount of evidence there is for the use of money in the duchy.[2] No coins in the name of William or Henry are known to have been struck in Normandy during the eleventh or twelfth centuries, and the few surviving coins minted there after 1066 still preserve the name of a Duke Richard if they bear a recognizable name of the issuing authority at all.[3] In both countries, that is to say, the practice obtaining before the Conquest was continued in the time of the Norman kings. There never was a situation in which a common currency bearing the title *rex* in England and *dux* or *comes* in Normandy was being used; nor did a pre-existing currency bearing a Norman title that could be opposed to the royal title in England survive in the duchy.

The evidence of the coronations, on the other hand, suggests that these negative conclusions may have a positive side. William the Conqueror was crowned and anointed as king in Westminster Abbey.[4] The only important modification that was made in the traditional English rite for that occasion was that the archbishop of York asked the English people present, in their own language, whether they would have William as king, and the bishop of Coutances put the same question in French to the Normans.[5] Now the Normans who were there can only have been William's followers in the Hastings campaign, and

---

[1] Dolley, *The Norman Conquest and the English Coinage*, pp. 7–15; North, *English Hammered Coinage*, 128–52.

[2] Musset, 'A-t-il existé en Normandie au xı^e siècle une aristocratie d'argent?'; and 'La vie économique de l'abbaye de Fécamp sous l'abbatiat de Jean de Ravenne', esp. pp. 69–76.

[3] Dieudonné, 'La numismatique normande: les monnaies féodales', pp. 339–43; Poey d'Avant, *Monnaies féodales de la France*, i. 17–32.

[4] The only chronicler writing before 1144 who states specifically that William was crowned 'king of the English' is Orderic Vitalis (*H.E.* (ed. Le Prévost), ii. 156–7; (ed. Chibnall), ii. 182–4). He was writing this part of his history about 1125 (ed. Chibnall, ii. p. xv). However, in the coronation *ordo* that was most probably used on this occasion, the king was consecrated to rule over the *regnum anglorum uel saxonum*; and the revised *ordo* which was apparently composed in the Conqueror's reign introduces no greater modification than *regnum anglosaxonum* (Legg, *English Coronation Records*, p. 16; Legg, *Three Coronation Orders*, p. 55; Schramm, *History of the English Coronation*, pp. 28–9, 233–4).

[5] Douglas, *William the Conqueror*, pp. 206–7 and ch. 10; Schramm, *History of the English Coronation*, pp. 27 ff.

at that moment, whatever their expectations, they were land-holders in Normandy only. To this extent Normandy was involved in William's coronation; and William's triumphal progress through the duchy in 1067, particularly his royal display during the Easter festival at Fécamp, must have been intended not only to exhibit his new royalty but to reinforce that involvement.[1] There could have been no such involvement when William Rufus was crowned in 1087. Although Robert Curthose is reported to have returned to Rouen as soon as the news of his father's death reached him and then and there to have taken possession of the duchy, nothing is said of any ceremony of investiture.[2] Nor can there have been much involvement of Normandy at Henry's coronation in 1100, whatever his intentions at that moment may have been; yet although there is no record of any ceremony in Normandy during the six months he spent there after Tinchebrai, it seems clear that he manifested his royal power in the important assemblies he held then as his father had done in 1067. Indeed Orderic's statements that he ordained *regali sanctione* that the peace should be kept throughout Normandy and also that he maintained stern justice and was always ready to protect the Church and peaceful men of humble status seem almost to suggest the promises of the coronation oath.[3] According to the *Gesta Stephani* the archbishop of Canterbury consecrated and anointed Stephen *regem in Angliam et Normanniam*;[4] and this with the fact that the archbishop of Rouen and four of his suffragans were present at Stephen's first great court at Easter 1136[5] (they could hardly have been present at the coronation itself) and the statement of William of Malmesbury that Matilda was elected *Anglie Normannieque dominam* in 1141,[6] seems to take this involvement a long

---

[1] Douglas, *William the Conqueror*, pp. 207–10 and especially the accounts of William de Poitiers and Orderic Vitalis there quoted. On William's dispositions in Normandy on this occasion, below, pp. 239–40.

[2] William de Jumièges, *Gesta*, p. 268 (interp. Torigni); cf. David, *Robert Curthose*, p. 42.

[3] Orderic Vitalis, *H.E.* (ed. Le Prévost), iv. 233–4, 237, 269; Eadmer, *Historia Novorum*, p. 184 ('Normannia ergo sub regia pace disposita').   [4] *Gesta Stephani*, p. 8.

[5] Round, *Geoffrey de Mandeville*, pp. 262–6; *Regesta*, iii, Nos. 944, 46, 271. It is not easy to see why Schramm should think that their presence was intended to secure Stephen's recognition as 'duke of Normandy' (*History of the English Coronation*, p. 46); but it seems that Normandy was somehow involved, and deliberately so.

[6] Malmesbury, *Historia Novella*, p. 54. On the sense of the title 'domina' in this context, Round, *Geoffrey de Mandeville*, pp. 69–80.

step forward; but too much cannot be made of these titles, for the style used in the *Gesta Stephani* is isolated and Malmesbury says that Stephen was crowned *in regem Anglie*[1] simply.

Although the coronations of the Norman kings always took place in England and an English rite was used which has specific reference to the English people, the record we have of them suggests that they did in some way concern Normandy and the Norman people. Such concern would be very hard to define; but the negative point that there is no evidence of any separate investiture as duke of the Normans is significant because such a form of investiture did appear later under the Angevin kings when the relationship between the king's various 'capacities' was differently and more precisely understood.[2] It would clearly be going too far to say that William or Henry or Stephen was 'king of the English and of the Normans', and no contemporary so far as is known did say that, though the Hyde chronicler comes very near to it; but there is a good deal of evidence to confirm the idea contained in the phrase used by the author of the *Gesta Stephani*, that the Norman kings were kings 'in' Normandy as well as in England.

For all the emphasis that has been placed upon it, William took a relatively short step when he assumed royal status in 1066. In spite of the variety of titles attributed to the rulers of Normandy before the Conquest, their government had been scarcely less than royal. It can certainly be argued that more rights and prerogatives derived ultimately from Carolingian royalty had survived or been revived in the hands of the dukes of Normandy than most other princes in Western Francia had managed to preserve.[3] They had provided initiative and resources for the renaissance of the Church in their lands; they had founded or re-founded abbeys, brought in men to provide instruction in discipline and liturgy, taken a share in the re-establishment of the diocesan centres and retained a control

---

[1] Malmesbury, *Historia Novella*, p. 15.

[2] Schramm, *History of the English Coronation*, pp. 46–7; Kantorowicz, *Laudes Regiae*, pp. 170, 178. Professor Hollister has developed this point in his forthcoming article on 'Normandy, France and the Anglo-Norman *Regnum*' (due to appear in *Speculum*, 1976). See also below, pp. 242–3.

[3] Yver, 'Premières institutions', pp. 302–19 etc.; 'Le développement du pouvoir ducal en Normandie'; and 'Contribution à l'étude du développement de la compétence ducale en Normandie'; Musset, 'Naissance de la Normandie', pp. 112–13; Lemarignier, *Hommage en marche*, pp. 22–31.

over elections to bishoprics and abbacies and an important place in ecclesiastical councils—all of which cannot have failed to impart a substantial religious element to their authority in Normandy.[1] However their relationship with the king of France before 1066 should be defined, and although the king had some part in William's accession to the duchy and his survival during the troubles of his minority, he had no rights or property in Normandy itself and his confirmation was not deemed necessary in ducal *acta*.[2] It is even probable that Duke William had been acclaimed by name in *Laudes* sung at the great festivals in Rouen Cathedral and at Fécamp, an honour then reserved for potentates of the very highest rank;[3] and beyond his duchy he could be described as effectively king of all his land.[4] Little indeed had been lacking but the form—anointing, coronation, and the regular attribution of a royal title.

Their government in Normandy was certainly no less royal after 1066. Orderic's description of William the Conqueror's 'settlement' of Normandy in 1067 and Henry's in 1106–7, even, to some extent, the activity of William Rufus in the duchy when he took it over in 1096, certainly gives the impression that a royal government was being set up there. William, in 1067, 'laid down just laws, gave fair judgments to rich and poor alike, and appointed the best possible men as judges and officials in the provinces of Normandy. He took holy monasteries and their endowments under his protection, granting royal privileges (*regalibus privilegiis*) of exemption from unjust exactions. He sent out heralds to proclaim peace for all men'.[5] Henry 'ordained by

[1] Below, pp. 296–302.

[2] Musset, *ubi supra*. The king of France is, however, acknowledged in the opening protocol of what seems to be the 'official' text of the canons of the council of Lillebonne: 'Anno incarnationis . . . MLXXX, papatus domini Gregorii pape septimi octauo, Francorum rege regnante Philippo, Anglorum rege Willelmo gubernante Normanniam . . .' (Chaplais, 'Henry II's reissue of the canons of the council of Lillebonne', p. 629).

[3] Douglas, *William the Conqueror*, p. 154; Kantorowicz, *Laudes Regiae*, pp. 166–71; Wormald, 'An Eleventh-Century Copy of the Norman *Laudes Regiae*'. Kantorowicz thinks that the acclamation 'Guillelmo Normannorum duci' in the eleventh-century text of the Rouen litany is not conclusive proof that it antedates the Conquest. This begs all the questions.

[4] Fauroux, *Recueil*, No. 137 (p. 314); 'Qua de re, domnus abbas Albertus, tunc Majori Monasterio praesidens, . . . Willelmum Normannorum principem et ducem et, ut expressius dicatur quod difficile in aliis reperies, totius terrae suae regem . . . adiit'. Quoted by Musset, 'Gouvernés et gouvernants', p. 460.

[5] Orderic Vitalis, *H.E.* (ed. Le Prévost), ii. 177; (ed. Chibnall), ii. 208–9.

royal command (*regali sanctione*) that firm peace should be maintained throughout Normandy'; and Orderic specifically equates his rule in Normandy with his rule in England, saying that he restored order there after Tinchebrai 'with royal power' (*regali potestate*).[1] William Rufus, as soon as he had possession of Normandy, at once set about recovering his father's lands (*dominia*) and making appointments to vacant abbeys.[2]

Their relations with the Church in Normandy after the Conquest were a direct continuation of the relationship that existed before 1066. Their patronage of the monasteries, their part in elections to bishoprics and abbacies and in the holding of ecclesiastical councils shows no perceptible change other than that which was gradually brought about by the reforming movement within the Church itself. In this respect the innovations they made in England produced an almost complete assimilation of their relations with the Church, and their evolution, in the two countries.[3] Their court in Normandy, both when it met in their presence and when it exercised jurisdiction by delegation, was as much *curia regis* as it was in England;[4] their officers in Normandy are described as royal officers[5] and their actions there constantly spoken of as effected 'by royal command', 'by royal authority'.[6] The *Laudes* continued to be sung for them in Normandy as in England;[7] even the solemn crown-wearings on the great feasts of the Church, normally regarded

[1] Orderic Vitalis, *H.E.* (ed. Le Prévost), iv. 233–4, 237, 269; Eadmer, *Historia Novorum*, p. 184.

[2] Orderic Vitalis, ubi supra, pp. 18–19.

[3] Patronage, Orderic Vitalis, *H.E.* (ed. Le Prévost), ii. 177; (ed. Chibnall), ii. 208; appointments, ibid. (ed. Le Prévost), ii. 200–1; (ed. Chibnall), ii. 238 (William the Conqueror); ibid. (ed. Le Prévost), iv. 18–19 (William Rufus), 433–5, 448 (Henry); v. 124 (Stephen). Councils, e.g. Orderic's introduction to his text of the canons of the council of Lillebonne (ed. Le Prévost, ii. 315–16; ed. Chibnall, iii. 24). In general, Douglas, *William the Conqueror*, ch. 13 and below, pp. 296–302.

[4] e.g. Orderic Vitalis, *H.E.* (ed. Le Prévost), ii. 322; iv. 303, 459; (ed. Chibnall), iii. 34; Delisle, *Histoire du château de Saint-Sauveur-le-Vicomte*, pièces justificatives, pp. 40, 46; Haskins, *Norman Institutions*, pp. 90, 91, 95, 98, etc. The 'Consuetudines et Justicie', drawn up when Robert Curthose was duke, refer throughout to *curia domini Normanniae*, not *curia ducis* (Haskins, ibid., pp. 281–4).

[5] e.g. Orderic Vitalis, *H.E.* (ed. Le Prévost), ii. 316; iv. 305; (ed. Chibnall), iii. 26. In the first reference Orderic is giving the text of a formal document (cf. Chaplais, 'Henry II's reissue of the canons of the council of Lillebonne', p. 630).

[6] In addition to references above (pp. 239 n. 1, 240 n. 1) Orderic Vitalis, *H.E.* (ed. Le Prévost), ii. 237; iii. 192; (ed. Chibnall), ii. 284; iv. 44.

[7] Valin, *Le Duc de Normandie et sa cour*, p. 258 (No. III); Kantorowicz, *Laudes Regiae*, pp. 169–79.

as a particular feature of their rule in England,¹ may have taken place in Normandy as well. No chronicler shows such a detailed interest in stating the places where the Norman kings celebrated these great festivals when they were in Normandy as the Anglo-Saxon Chronicle and the related chronicles show in England; but some at least of them are known to have been kept at principal Norman churches;² and if the record of William the Conqueror's abbey of Saint-Étienne at Caen is correct in describing the crown which he bequeathed to the monks as *coronam qua in celebrioribus festivitatibus inter sacra missarum sollenpnia coronabatur*,³ then we may reasonably deduce that he had that crown with him in Normandy during at least the last year of his life and surely made some use of it there.

If some contemporaries, therefore, attributed two or sometimes three titles to the Norman kings (*rex* for England; *dux*, *comes*, *princeps*, *dominus*, etc. for Normandy; *princeps* for Maine), they do so with no consistency and show little other evidence that they had a clear conception of any distinction of capacities; though such distinctions were certainly being made in other contexts during the eleventh and twelfth centuries. It could be argued that the *Consuetudines et Justicie*, the sworn statement of ducal rights and prerogatives in Normandy that was drawn up for William Rufus and Robert Curthose in 1091, when they had agreed to rule their father's lands jointly, implies that William the Conqueror had had one body of rights and prerogatives in Normandy and another in England.⁴ William and Robert did not proceed to a corresponding inquiry in England; yet the differences thus implied between the two countries need

---

¹ e.g. Schramm, *History of the English Coronation*, pp. 31–2; Jolliffe, *Constitutional History of Medieval England*, pp. 176–7. Richardson and Sayles, *Governance of Medieval England*, pp. 405–12, argue that both the crown-wearings and the *Laudes* were known in England before the Conquest.

² Easter, 1067, Fécamp; Easter, 1075, Fécamp; Easter, 1083, Fécamp; Christmas, 1119, Bayeux; (Easter, 1124, Rouen): *Regesta*, i, pp. xxi–xxii; ii. pp. xxix–xxxi.

³ Musset, *Actes de Guillaume le Conquérant pour les abbayes caennaises*, pp. 132–4. Cf. *Regesta*, i, No. 397 (p. 100); ii, No. 601 (p. 24); Delisle-Berger, *Recueil*, i, No. clii (pp. 261–4). Repeated redemptions of the crown suggest recovery for an occasion, as for a crown-wearing. Cf. also Engels, 'De Obitu Willelmi: Texte, modèles, valeur et origine', p. 255. William clearly had more than one crown.

⁴ Haskins, *Norman Institutions*, pp. 281–4: 'Hec est iusticia quam rex Guillelmus qui regnum Anglie adquisivit habuit in Normannia.' The document throughout refers to the ruler of Normandy by the non-committal 'dominus Normanniae'.

have been no greater in principle than those between Wessex, Mercia, and the Danelaw within William's kingdom of England.[1] Most rulers of the time must have been accustomed to rights and prerogatives that differed from one part of their lands to another. Nor did the relationship of Normandy to the kingdom of France seriously affect the matter. Quite apart from the consideration that, as a matter of fact, no ruler of Normandy who was a king did homage to the king of France between 1066 and 1144,[2] kings who were vassals of other kings were certainly not unknown at that time—the Norman kings themselves were the lords of other kings.

The Norman kings could not put off the supernatural qualities of kingship when they crossed the sea from England to Normandy, as they were constantly doing, nor resume them on the return journey. If they were not to be formally styled 'king of the Normans', their kingship, derived from their English kingdom, extended to Normandy as many of the characteristics of their earlier rule as dukes in Normandy were extended to England.[3] Neither could their Angevin successors discard their royalty in their continental lands; but in France their kingly style was understood more clearly as a courtesy title[4] and they made the distinction between their rule in England and their rule in Normandy much more specific. For, living at a time when laws and customs were more stabilized and territorialized,

---

[1] e.g., 2 Cnut, cc. 12, 14, 15 (Robertson, *Laws*, pp. 180–1); *Leges Henrici Primi*, c. 6 (ed. Downer, pp. 96–8 and cf. pp. 44–5).

[2] Above, p. 219.

[3] The idea of the extension to Normandy of the king's royal authority is sometimes expressed in formal documents, e.g. 'Anglorum rege Willelmo gubernante Normanniam' (Chaplais, 'Henry II's Reissue of the Canons of the Council of Lillebonne', p. 629); 'principante in Normannia rege Anglorum Stephano' (cartulary copy of a charter of the archbishop of Rouen to Saint-Wandrille; Lot, *Études critiques sur l'abbaye de Saint-Wandrille*, p. 125, No. 70); 'Regnante Henrico rege Anglie' (cartulary copy of a private charter to Saint-Wandrille, ibid., p. 108, No. 52, and cf. p. 115, No. 60); 'Hec donatio . . . a domino nostro Henrico Anglorum rege in Normannia principante regali potestate statuta et confirmata' (charter of William II de Warenne granting lands and rents in England to the priory of Bellencombre in Normandy, *E.Y.C.*, viii. 81, No. 29). But there is no consistency, and sometimes the distinction between king and duke is clearly made, e.g. Lot, ubi supra, p. 121, No. 67; pp. 133, 137, No. 73. The transference to England of many characteristics of ducal rule in Normandy forms the subject of much of the present chapter.

[4] Professor Hollister quotes Richard de Poitiers, who enumerates the lands of Henry II and adds 'ob honorem tamen et reverentiam Regalis nominis Rex Anglorum vocatus est' (*Historiens de la France*, xii. 1877. 417).

they treated the laws and customs of each of their lands as proper to it, and could only generalize them to a very limited extent;[1] whereas the Normans, living when this process was at an early stage, could assimilate. In their time England and Normandy were normally ruled by one man who could not be divided in his person and who ruled both countries with the same royal authority.

The uniformity of the Norman king's rule in England and Normandy, and his itinerant manner of ruling, determined the mechanics of his government in many ways. Naturally he was served by one household, essentially the same body whether the king was in England or in Normandy and however those in attendance might vary and fluctuate from time to time and place to place;[2] and such a body would act in much the same way in both countries. Within the household the king had one chancellor, one keeper of his one seal and a body of clerks, making up an embryonic chancery. Few of the elements of this chancery had come from Normandy. The seal, with all its characteristics, except the equestrian representation and the ducal title, was English; and so in all probability was the office of chancellor, at least in the form it took after 1066. William no doubt employed some of the clerks who had served Edward the Confessor;[3] and through these survivors from the Confessor's reign he and his advisers learnt of the nature and the uses of the English sealed writ, which they adopted immediately;[4] and because there was but one seal and one chancery for England and Normandy this led to an important point of assimilation in governmental practice in the two countries.

In 1066 the English sealed writ was a relatively recent invention, certainly in the form it took at that time, and it was still in an early stage of its development.[5] During the preceding half-century or so the king in England had begun to send written and sealed notifications to the officers and suitors of the shire court that lands or other rights in their shire had changed hands, or that it was his will that certain persons or communities should have or be confirmed in their possession of

---

[1] Below, pp. 275–6.   [2] Above, pp. 132–7.   [3] *Regesta*, i, pp. xvi–xxi.
[4] A few writs issued in William's name and belonging to the first years of his reign were written in Old English, as those of Edward the Confessor had been.

[5] What follows on the writ and the chancery is based upon Chaplais, 'The Anglo-Saxon Chancery'.

lands or rights. This practice seems to have taken the place of an oral notification, possibly accompanied by a loose seal or other evidence of the authenticity of the message. The written and sealed notification, the writ, unlike the older diploma which it supplemented and ultimately superseded, was in the form of a letter, brief, matter-of-fact and written in the vernacular; for it had to convey information to the suitors of the shire courts. But it was also intended to serve as a title-deed, for though it was addressed to the persons attending the shire court it passed into the hands of the beneficiary to be kept by him—indeed it was often written by a scribe employed by him, and when this happened it may never have passed out of his hands except for the time needed to affix the royal seal. But since it bore that seal, which could not lawfully be attached to any document without the king's consent, it possessed an authenticity which the old English diploma could never have.

William had disposed of no such instrument in Normandy. He probably did not have a seal before he became king,[1] and the diplomas produced in the duchy before 1066 show little consistency of form.[2] Since they had been written by scribes employed by the beneficiaries, as the English diplomas were,[3] the fact that William took over the English writ for use in England could not immediately introduce any significant change in the instruments used in Normandy to give title to property. It would not have been appropriate to use the English form of writ for grants of land in Normandy to Norman beneficiaries because such beneficiaries would not immediately accept so unfamiliar a document as a title (they would certainly not have been able to draft one for themselves), and still more because the writ, in the state of evolution it had reached in 1066,

---

[1] This is a matter which has been long debated. Madame Fauroux (*Recueil*, pp. 45–7) seems inclined to accept the possibility of a ducal seal or seals before 1066; Chaplais appears to reject it in 'Une charte originale de Guillaume le Conquérant pour l'abbaye de Fécamp', p. 94. In 'The Anglo-Saxon Chancery', pp. 160–1, however, he makes the indisputable point that even if William had had some sort of seal before the Conquest it was not used for the same purpose as Edward the Confessor's great two-sided seal.

[2] Fauroux, *Recueil*, pp. 41 ff.

[3] Chaplais, 'Anglo-Saxon Chancery', pp. 162–6. Continental diplomas, however, including those produced in Normandy, often have autograph *signa*; whereas the *signa* in English diplomas, in Chaplais's opinion, are never autograph. Cf. Musset, *Les Actes de Guillaume le Conquérant pour les abbayes caennaises*, p. 38.

generally presupposed a shire court in which it would be published, and no such institution existed in Normandy.[1] In due course, however, through the growing knowledge of English ways which would be gained by Norman churches which received property in England, through the development of the writ itself (particularly the development of its use for administrative orders or mandates which would naturally be addressed to other persons besides the officers of the shire courts) and the change of language from English to Latin,[2] the writ came to be used as a vehicle for conveying the king's will just as regularly in Normandy as in England, certainly in Henry's reign;[3] and the old diploma gradually went out of use in both countries. In this respect governmental procedure in the two countries was completely assimilated in course of time.

Likewise, in spite of a 'membership' which had an even greater fluidity than that of the household, the court which assembled wherever the king made stay or which was summoned to attend him was fundamentally the same institution whether it was meeting in England or in Normandy; and though it may have gathered up a few English characteristics in the early years of William's reign in England, when surviving English magnates and bishops attended it, it was a direct continuation of William's court in Normandy before 1066. At its highest level, therefore, the *curia regis*, as a political, judicial, and social institution, was identical in the two countries, and its activity could hardly change in any significant manner as it moved from one to the other. In particular, with litigation and other matters that were brought before the king or initiated by him in either country, in so far as this involved matters of feudal

---

[1] On the shire courts in England and the vice-comital courts in Normandy, below, pp. 277–9.

[2] Chaplais, *English Royal Documents*, pp. 4–7; Bishop and Chaplais, *Facsimiles*, pp. xiii–xv; van Caenegem, *Birth of the Common Law*, pp. 31–2.

[3] *Regesta*, ii, *passim*. Chaplais ('Anglo-Saxon Chancery', p. 161) deduces from the fact that few of William the Conqueror's, and not many more of William Rufus's surviving writs concern Norman affairs, that these two rulers kept the administration of England and the administration of Normandy quite distinct. Apart from the many general arguments against such an idea, the time-lag in applying the writ to Normandy as a normal and regular instrument of government and administration seems to be adequately explained by the considerations set out above. Considering how alien the English writ must have seemed to the Normans it is more remarkable that it should have come into regular use for Norman affairs at all than that it should have taken some time to do so.

custom, its work would assist the assimilation of law and social structure in the two countries, certainly in their judicial organization.[1]

Assimilation of the same kind can be seen in the relations between the ruler and the Church in Normandy and in England. In general, certainly in practical terms, the relationship between duke or king and the ecclesiastical authorities had been much the same in the two countries before 1066. In both, the Church owed its resurrection from the troubles of the ninth and tenth centuries in large measure to the ruler,[2] and thus practical as well as theoretical considerations gave the rulers of the eleventh century a very great authority in what would later be regarded as specifically ecclesiastical matters, an authority which had been assumed not only by the pre-Conquest kings of the English but also by the Norman dukes in their duchy.[3] But there were differences in the way in which this authority had been exercised. In England, legislation on matters which would later be classified as ecclesiastical had been promulgated by the king in his witan (attended by bishops as well as high-ranking laymen) and hardly distinguished from legislation on other matters;[4] in Normandy, since the early 1040s, it had been largely the work of councils of the ecclesiastical province of Rouen, in which the duke and the barons had had an important part but which were still truly ecclesiastical assemblies.[5] In England there was certainly a concept of church law, though it was not very clearly defined and was little influenced as yet by the attempts that were then being made on the Continent to form an autonomous body of canon law.[6] Its administration, so far as this was by judicial action, was effected, along with the other business of those courts, by the

---

[1] Stenton, *English Feudalism*, pp. 29–41; below, pp. 260 ff.

[2] For Normandy, e.g. Musset, 'Naissance de la Normandie', pp. 118–22; for England, above, p. 54, and Barlow, *English Church*, pp. 31–5.

[3] Barlow, *Edward the Confessor*, pp. 179–80; Douglas, *William the Conqueror*, ch. 5; Haskins, *Norman Institutions*, pp. 30–9.

[4] Barlow, *English Church*, pp. 137–46.

[5] Prentout, *Histoire de Guillaume le Conquérant*, pp. 101–5; Douglas, *William the Conqueror*, pp. 130–2; Musset, 'Gouvernés et gouvernants', pp. 465–7. The published summary of a paper by Professor Foreville, 'Le synode de la province de Rouen aux xie et xiie siècles' (*R.H.D.*, li, 1973, pp. 566–7) promises important clarifications.

[6] Barlow, *English Church*, p. 139 etc.; Brooke, *English Church and the Papacy*, pp. 50–1.

bishop (assisted in some dioceses by an archdeacon) sitting with the earl or his deputy in the courts of the shire and hundred, and laymen probably had a considerable part in this administration and its profits.[1] In Normandy before the Conquest, where there were already one or two noteworthy ecclesiastical centres of legal study,[2] the bishops could not exercise the jurisdiction inherent in their office in any courts analogous to the English courts of shire and hundred, for there were no such courts there. The fact that this jurisdiction (*consuetudines episcopales, leges episcopales*) could be held in certain places by laymen and could be granted by them or the duke to monasteries (unless it was simply the profits that were being so granted), suggests that it had been subjected to a process of fragmentation very similar to that undergone by royal jurisdiction in post-Carolingian times; but the bishops and their archdeacons certainly did hold courts for such of this jurisdiction as was left to them.[3]

According to Eadmer, it was William's policy to 'maintain in England the usages and laws which his fathers and he were accustomed to have in Normandy'.[4] In the context, Eadmer was not distinguishing between secular and ecclesiastical matters, though he may be presumed to have had ecclesiastical matters particularly in mind; and William's dealings with the Church in England as we know them certainly bear out his general statement. In particular, William, or those who advised him, disapproved of the way in which ecclesiastical justice was administered in England; and he accordingly commanded that no layman should have any part in that jurisdiction and that bishops and archdeacons should administer it, not in the hundred courts, but in places which the bishop should appoint for the purpose, and do so not in accordance with the law administered in the hundred courts but in accordance with 'the canons and episcopal laws'.[5] It may well be that this order did

---

[1] Barlow, *English Church*, pp. 146–53; Morris, 'William I and the Church Courts', pp. 453–6; 3 Edgar c. 5 (Robertson, *Laws*, pp. 26–7).

[2] Knowles, *Monastic Order*, pp. 96–8; Brooke, *English Church and the Papacy*, pp. 57–60.

[3] Haskins, *Norman Institutions*, pp. 30–8; Lemarignier *et al.*, *Institutions ecclésiastiques* (Lot and Fawtier, *Histoire des institutions françaises*, iii), pp. 71–2; Lemarignier, *Étude sur les privilèges d'exemption*, ch. iv. For the early Norman archdeacons, Douglas, 'The Norman Episcopate', pp. 108–10.

[4] Eadmer, *Historia Novorum*, p. 9.　　　　　[5] Robertson, *Laws*, pp. 234–7.

not establish immediately a system of church courts entirely distinct from the secular courts in England;[1] but it was a long step in that direction, the terminology it uses is Norman, and the range of jurisdiction intended by the term 'leges episcopales' in William's writ is most likely to be that defined in the canons of the council of the Norman Church held at Lillebonne in 1080.[2] Furthermore, Lanfranc brought over from Le Bec a collection of papal decretals and canons of councils, of which he seems to have distributed copies to the bishops of English sees, so that their judgements in ecclesiastical causes could be given, as William complained they had not been given in the hundred courts, 'in accordance with the precepts of the sacred canons'.[3] Though William's writ was issued 'with the counsel of archbishops, bishops, abbots and of all the magnates of his kingdom', this was royal legislation on ecclesiastical matters; but the general reform of the English Church was carried out in church councils under royal authority as reform had been carried out under ducal and, after 1066, was being carried out by royal authority in Normandy. Such councils, very largely the means by which the Church in England had been reformed during the tenth century, had died out in England by the Confessor's time,[4] save in so far as the witan was attended by bishops and abbots as well as lay magnates and could deal with ecclesiastical as well as other matters. After the Conquest, councils of the Church were held in both countries in the same way and were concerned with much the same matters.[5]

Both in Normandy and in England the ruler had had a dominant part in the election of bishops and the more important abbots before the Conquest. As William the Conqueror filled episcopal vacancies in England by men of Norman (or at

---

[1] Morris, 'William I and the Church Courts'; van Caenegem, *Birth of the Common Law*, pp. 12–13, 15–16.

[2] Haskins, *Norman Institutions*, pp. 30–9; Orderic Vitalis, *H.E.* (ed. Le Prévost), ii. 315–23; (ed. Chibnall), iii. 24–34; Chaplais, 'Henry II's Reissue of the Canons of the Council of Lillebonne', pp. 629–32.

[3] Robertson, *Laws*, p. 234, para. 1; Brooke, *English Church and the Papacy*, pp. 57–83. Cf. Somerville, 'Lanfranc's Canonical Collection and Exeter'. For the rapid assimilation of England and the Continent in knowledge and application of the canon law, Mary Cheney, 'The Compromise of Avranches of 1172 and the Spread of Canon Law in England'.

[4] Barlow, *Edward the Confessor*, p. 179; Douglas, *William the Conqueror*, p. 331.

[5] Douglas, ibid., pp. 331–6.

least of continental) origin, the hierarchies in the two countries came to be closely assimilated not only in origin and on occasion by family relationship, but also by the type of man appointed.[1] In Normandy, before the Conquest, the bishops were characteristically drawn from aristocratic families and often from the ducal family itself;[2] in England, during the Confessor's reign, many had been promoted from the king's chapel.[3] After the Conquest men who had been royal or ducal chaplains are found as bishops in Normandy[4] as well as in England,[5] and men from aristocratic families or even claiming kinship with the king himself came to occupy sees in England[6] as they continued to do in Normandy.[7] If Edward the Confessor had been 'master' of the English Church in his day,[8] William's supremacy over it was a direct continuation of the supremacy he had exercised and still exercised over the Church in Normandy; and he brought to England likewise his attitude to reform and to the papal authority.[9] Even his support for Canterbury's claim to primacy over York may have owed as much to his desire for one ecclesiastical authority to deal with in England, such as he had in Normandy, as to any of the other reasons commonly given for it.[10]

Inevitably, assimilation in ecclesiastical matters went beyond the relations between the king and the hierarchy. In Normandy episcopal centres had remained or been revived in the old Roman cities even after the Viking destructions; in England there were several (Lichfield, Selsey, Sherborne, Elmham,

---

[1] Above, pp. 35–6, 49–51; below, pp. 338–9.

[2] Douglas, 'The Norman Episcopate', pp. 102–6; *William the Conqueror*, pp. 118–20.   [3] Barlow, *English Church*, pp. 99–110, 130–7, 156–8.

[4] e.g. Baldwin (1066) and Ouen (1113) of Évreux; Turold (1097) of Bayeux; Gilbert Maminot (1077) of Lisieux; Michael (1067) and Turgis (1094) of Avranches (*Regesta*, i, pp. xviii–xxi; ii, p. x; Douglas, *William the Conqueror*, pp. 319–20).   [5] Above, pp. 49–51.

[6] e.g. Osbern of Exeter; Robert de Limési and Roger of Clinton of Lichfield; Jocelin de Bohun of Salisbury; possibly Walkelin of Winchester and Gerard of Hereford and York; more certainly Henry de Blois of Winchester and St. William of York (above, pp. 49–51). Naturally a man with aristocratic or even royal connections could also be a royal chaplain.

[7] Douglas, *William the Conqueror*, pp. 319–20, and a forthcoming paper by Professor C. N. L. Brooke on the bishops of England and Normandy in the eleventh century (communication to Settimana di studio internazionale, vi, La Mendola, 1974) in which the importance of the monastic element in the episcopate of both countries is brought out.   [8] Barlow, *Edward the Confessor*, pp. 179–80.

[9] Douglas, *William the Conqueror*, pp. 336–43.   [10] Ibid., p. 322.

Dorchester, Wells) in relatively obscure places. These were now moved, in the space of twenty years or so, to important centres in accordance with continental tradition; and though this process had already begun under Edward with the removal of the see of Devon and Cornwall from Crediton to Exeter and was often inspired, at least in part, by the desire to improve the revenues of a poor see, it was predominantly a Norman operation and had the effect of assimilating diocesan centres in England to those in Normandy.[1] At the same time the constitution of the body of clerks that served a cathedral, and the administrative structure of the dioceses, were brought into line, if not directly modelled upon those of Rouen and Bayeux as was once thought, at least generally with those of the Norman sees.[2] Exceptionally, one almost peculiarly English institution, the cathedral served by a monastic community, was preserved and even extended by the Normans;[3] and in Normandy Séez was served by regular canons from 1129.[4]

The advent of Norman abbots and sometimes a number of Norman monks to English monasteries[5] brought about an analogous assimilation in the monasteries of the two countries. English monasteries, whatever the Normans might say, were not scandalously lax or backward on the eve of the Conquest; but they did not have the zeal, enthusiasm, and conviction, almost the aggressiveness, characteristic of a new movement, such as the Norman monasteries of that time possessed, nor their intellectual activity. Relative to the extent of the two countries, there were few active monastic foundations in England at the time of the Conquest, none north of Burton-on-Trent.[6] In

---

[1] e.g. Douglas, ibid., pp. 328–9.

[2] Brooke, 'Continental Influence on English Cathedral Chapters'; Edwards, *English Secular Cathedrals*, pp. 8–19 etc. For cathedral bodies and diocesan organization in England before 1066, ibid., and Darlington, 'Ecclesiastical Reform in the Late Old English Period', pp. 403–4; Barlow, *English Church*, pp. 239–42. Even if it cannot be said that the post-Conquest constitution of any English cathedral was modelled directly on that of any one Norman cathedral, it is clear that the Norman bishops devised constitutions for English cathedrals on the same general lines as those which were coming into being in Normandy (Douglas, 'The Norman Episcopate', pp. 107–14 and *William the Conqueror*, pp. 122–3).

[3] Edwards, *English Secular Cathedrals*, pp. 10–11; Douglas, *William the Conqueror*, p. 329.

[4] Douglas, 'The Norman Episcopate', p. 111; Edwards, *English Secular Cathedrals*, p. 14, note.

[5] Above, p. 35.   [6] Below, p. 302.

Normandy monasteries were being founded at such a rate that the conquest of England must have seemed to offer an almost providential source of monastic endowment. The dominant figure among the Norman monks was Lanfranc; and when he became archbishop of Canterbury he introduced into the cathedral priory a set of Constitutions which he himself had drawn up and which were based largely upon the customs of Le Bec. These were not generalized by any act of authority, but were adopted or taken as a model by other important houses in England. Nor did they introduce any strikingly new elements in monastic observance, being based ultimately on the same traditions as those of the English tenth-century reform;[1] but they set a standard, a Norman standard, for English monasteries; and beside this assimilation of the older houses, several of the new monasteries founded in England by the king or by Norman baronial families drew their first monks from, or were placed under the control of, an established continental house.[2]

The result was a Normanization of English monasteries, an assimilation between the monasticism of the two countries. The new abbots immediately set about to build or rebuild their monasteries in the style and on the ambitious scale of the buildings that were going up in Normandy, as the bishops were doing with their cathedrals. In time it would be possible to speak of an 'Anglo-Norman' school of Romanesque architecture, a common style of building extending from the north of England to the southern marches of Normandy, with motifs moving in both directions. The Norman abbots also brought with them the intellectual culture of Le Bec in its hey-day. They built libraries and stocked them with books.[3] In the illuminated manuscripts that were produced in England and Normandy during the time of the Norman kings the process of assimilation in

[1] Knowles, *Monastic Order*, esp. pp. 122–4; Knowles (ed.), *The Monastic Constitutions of Lanfranc, passim*.

[2] Examples in Knowles and Hadcock, *Religious Houses*, pp. 52–95, e.g., Blyth (Sainte-Trinité, Rouen), Boxgrove (Lessay), Battle (Marmoutier), etc. Chester and Shrewsbury were recolonized or colonized from Le Bec and Saint-Martin-de-Séez respectively (cf. above, pp. 37–8).

[3] Knowles, *Monastic Order*, pp. 119–26; Clapham, *Romanesque Architecture in Western Europe*, pp. 138–53. Characteristically, only some features spread into Scotland before the middle of the twelfth century (ibid., pp. 153–5). On the characteristics of Norman Romanesque, see also Musset, *Normandie romane*, i, pp. 11–24, etc.

style is complex; for Normandy already owed much to England in this respect and continued to be influenced after 1066. Yet, though the native styles remained strong in England, some new elements were brought in from the Continent and the general result by the beginning of the twelfth century, whatever happened later, was a remarkable degree of uniformity between the two countries.[1] Much the same could be said of sculpture, again with English influence in Normandy before the Conquest and elements of style moving in both directions after it.[2] English vernacular literature was not extinguished,[3] though it was driven underground by the requirements of the new Norman aristocracy and the Normanized Church; and what was not written in Latin was written in 'Anglo-Norman',[4] producing, in the course of the twelfth century, a not undistinguished body of literature.[5] It is certainly arguable that much was lost by the progressive submerging of native English styles and craftsmanship in art and literature by this massive influx of continental fashions; but for better or for worse it meant assimilation between England and Normandy in these respects. In one important matter at least the assimilation of monastic organization on either side of the Channel could hardly be reckoned an advantage; for English monasteries were brought into the military organization of the Norman kings by their assessment to knight service, as the Norman monasteries already were. To some extent this may have been due in the first instance to conditions that were quite temporary; but the arrangement was perpetuated, as such arrangements so often are.[6] In the final balance, however, it was Norman initiative, not always very scrupulous nor wholly admirable, and the Norman wealth it produced, that were providing the material basis for that great flowering of the

[1] Dodwell, *The Canterbury School of Illumination*, pp. 6–40, and *Painting in Europe, 800–1200*, pp. 85–9; Wormald, 'The Survival of Anglo-Saxon Illumination after the Norman Conquest'.

[2] Musset, *Normandie romane*, pp. 243–96; Zarnecki, *English Romanesque Sculpture, 1066–1140*, pp. 5–24, and '1066 and Architectural Sculpture'.

[3] Chambers, 'The Continuity of English Prose', pp. lxxxi–c.

[4] 'The traditional French spoken and written in Britain from the Norman Conquest on to approximately the last quarter of the fourteenth century', Pope, *The Anglo-Norman Element in our Vocabulary*, p. 1. Cf. Vising, *Anglo-Norman Language and Literature*, pp. 27–33.

[5] e.g. Poole, *Domesday Book to Magna Carta*, pp. 242–59; Darlington, *Anglo-Norman Historians*; Legge, 'La précocité de la littérature anglo-normande'.

[6] Knowles, *Monastic Order*, pp. 607–12; Haskins, *Norman Institutions*, pp. 8–14.

later twelfth century in which England and Normandy found themselves together in the mainstream of European culture. Whether that was preferable, so far as England was concerned, to a particular insular civilization must be a matter of opinion.

Just as the appointment of men of Norman origin and education to rule the bishoprics and the chief monasteries of England led to the Normanization of the Church in England, so the great distribution of the land of England to men of Norman and North-French origin led to some degree of assimilation in the social structures of England and Normandy. At the highest level of society there was an outright substitution of a North-French aristocracy for the English aristocracy of pre-Conquest times, which was exterminated or degraded by the Norman king and his followers; so that at this level the same group of men and often the very same families held the positions of greatest wealth and consequence on either side of the Channel. Yet it can no longer be said without qualification that 'William the Conqueror introduced feudalism into England', for there were many anticipations and partial anticipations of feudalism in England before 1066,[1] some Anglo-Saxon conditions of tenure survived the Conquest,[2] and the feudalism of Normandy itself in the 1060s has been found to have been less highly developed[3] than it was once thought to be.[4] But although we do not know the precise terms on which William gave estates in England to his followers (or the precise terms on which he had given lands to his vassals in Normandy for that matter), so that there is still room for a great deal of discussion on questions of rights of succession to dependent tenures, services due, and so on, yet there can be little doubt that generally speaking these terms, as between king and baron, reproduced those that William and his vassals were familiar with in Normandy, and that the processes of subinfeudation extended them. But it was not simply a matter of setting up a new aristocracy in England with conditions of tenure and a relationship with the king very similar to (if not identical with) that between Norman barons and the duke

---

[1] The question how far Anglo-Saxon precedents contributed to Anglo-Norman feudalism is discussed by Douglas in *William the Conqueror*, pp. 275–8, with references to the literature of the controversy to 1964.

[2] e.g. Douglas, 'The Norman Conquest and English Feudalism', pp. 137–9.

[3] Strayer, 'On the Early Norman Charters'; Douglas, *William the Conqueror*, ch. 4.   [4] As by Haskins, *Norman Institutions*, pp. 5–30.

before 1066. This Norman military aristocracy had been very largely the creation of the dukes.[1] The conquest of England provided an opportunity to extend the wealth and the membership of that aristocracy (for many Normans of relatively modest estate obtained vast possessions in England and so rose rapidly in the social scale),[2] and did so under conditions of conquest that gave to the Norman kings much greater opportunities of control than most contemporary rulers can ever have had. That control may often have faltered in practice; but such as it was it enabled the Norman kings to establish some degree of order and system in feudal tenures in England; and their own much greater wealth and power after 1066, together with the fact that so many of the families that held great estates in England also held great estates in Normandy, enabled them to extend much of this order and system to the duchy.[3] Thus, however many differences in detail there might be in services, terminology, and details of tenure between the two countries,[4] or between different parts of each,[5] due to pre-existing conditions or different circumstances, there can be no doubt that in matters of feudal tenures, with all their social and political implications, conditions in the two countries were for all practical purposes the same in 1135, with no greater differences between them than might be found within the bounds of either. With the overwhelming predominance among the greater landholders in England of families which were of Norman origin and which characteristically maintained their interests in the duchy, the upper levels of society in England and Normandy were completely assimilated, indeed merged into one community.

So far as can be seen, the greater Norman baronial families were already primarily concerned, in arranging their marriages, with dynastic ambition and considerations of property. Characteristically, therefore, they married within their own ranks.[6]

---

[1] Below, pp. 286–9. [2] Below, p. 296.

[3] Douglas, *William the Conqueror*, pp. 283–4; cf. Haskins, *Norman Institutions*, pp. 22–3; and for assimilation in law and custom generally, below.

[4] These are brought out by Stenton in *English Feudalism*, pp. 12–29.

[5] Ibid., pp. 24–9.

[6] A glance at a few entries in the *Complete Peerage* will demonstrate this, e.g., s.vv. Arundel, Aumale, Chester, Clare, Devon, Eu, Gloucester, Hereford, Leicester, Mowbray, Norfolk, Percy, Shrewsbury, Surrey, Tosny (of Flamstead), Warwick. Other points that seem to emerge are that the estate-building instinct was already

At the lower levels of the aristocracy, among Norman knights and feudal sub-tenants and the survivors of the English thegns, now reduced to tenant status and living as a general rule on a fraction of their former lands,[1] there may well have been a certain amount of intermarriage during the twelfth century—until Richard fitzNeal could make his famous remark that there had been so much intermarriage in England that men of Norman and English descent were becoming hard to distinguish; though he was careful to limit this to freemen.[2] That was late in the reign of Henry II. How far intermarriage in this class had been statistically significant during the reign of Henry Beauclerc or earlier it is very difficult to say.[3] In any case these speculations relate only to England; for although it was not quite unknown for an English family to possess land in Normandy,[4] there was certainly no English colonization of the duchy at this social level, or any other, to put beside the Norman colonization of England.

Lower down the social scale, this applies equally. The settlements of 'Frenchmen' in the larger English towns no doubt introduced a Norman element into them; though the slight indications that there are suggest that these colonies kept themselves pretty much to themselves for some time after their first

strong, that when members of these families married outside the close ranks of the Norman baronage it was often into families settled on land just beyond the borders of Normandy, and that among the families of this time those with the most interbaronial connections by marriage were Clare and Warenne. Stenton ('English Families and the Norman Conquest', pp. 5–6) could quote only two possible examples of marriage with an Englishwoman among men of this class.

[1] Stenton, ibid., pp. 6–8; Wightman, *Lacy Family*, pp. 40–3 etc.

[2] *Dialogus*, p. 53.

[3] The difficulty of forming any quantitative estimate is well shown by Sir Charles Clay's study of *Early Yorkshire Families*, centred on about a hundred families which held land in Yorkshire during the twelfth century and which can be shown to have descended in the male line (or with not more than one break) from the time of Henry I until that of Edward I or beyond. Not more than half a dozen marriages between a Norman and an Englishwoman or an Englishman and a Norman woman are cited; but, while there must certainly have been others among the twenty or so of those families which had an Englishman in their demonstrable ancestry, it is clear that the evidence does not permit any firm figures, even though it may not have been examined for this work with the point particularly in mind. So far as it goes, however, it does support the generalization offered above that such marriages took place between the luckier survivors of the English landed families and the second or third ranks of the Norman baronage rather than any group of higher rank.

[4] Southern, *Medieval Humanism*, pp. 225–7.

arrival.[1] The small boroughs that grew up beside the new Norman castles in England look very like the *bourgs* so often associated with castles in Normandy and may often have started with French settlers;[2] and it was under the Norman kings that the first permanent Jewish settlement was made in England— from Rouen and apparently confined to London at this time.[3]

At the level of the peasantry, of the men who tilled the soil and kept the flocks and herds, there can have been no mingling of peoples that was of any consequence at all. Yet although no one seems to have attempted a specific comparison between the condition of the peasantry in Normandy and England as it was during the eleventh century, there is no suggestion of any fundamental difference save in one respect;[4] and in that respect there was direct assimilation. At the time of the Conquest slavery and serfdom were virtually extinct in Normandy;[5] but slaves were common enough in England and there was a famous slave-trade through the port of Bristol. After the Conquest slavery died out in England.[6] Otherwise there was no occasion for extensive changes; for while Norman barons might often rearrange the units of which the Anglo-Saxon estates they took over were composed when constructing their castleries and honours, or entrust their exploitation to farmers,[7] they would not wilfully disrupt the agricultural or pastoral routine; for the value of their manors to them was as going and profitable concerns. There was no great revolution in English rural life.

The total result is complex and perhaps not very definite; but the structure of society in Normandy and in England must have seemed rather more uniform in 1135 than it had done on

---

[1] Above, pp. 38–40, 45.   [2] Above, p. 39; below, pp. 316–18.

[3] Roth, *History of the Jews in England*, pp. 4–10; Richardson, *The English Jewry under the Angevin Kings*, pp. 1–9.

[4] General accounts of conditions on one side of the Channel or the other: Loyn, *Anglo-Saxon England and the Norman Conquest*, pp. 188–95; 343–54; Delisle, *Études sur la classe agricole en Normandie*, pp. 1–26 etc.; Musset, 'Les domaines de l'époque franque', pp. 64–78. A brief comparison is indeed made by Stenton in *Anglo-Saxon England*, p. 472, but it amounts to very little and it has been overtaken by Musset's work. It would be easier to make if it were accepted that the 'régime domanial' had a long history in England as well as in Normandy, as argued by Aston in 'The Origins of the Manor in England'.

[5] Delisle, *Études sur la classe agricole en Normandie*, pp. 15–26.

[6] Loyn, *Anglo-Saxon England and the Norman Conquest*, pp. 349–53; Pollock and Maitland, *H.E.L.*, i. 35–7.

[7] Wightman, *Lacy Family*, pp. 28–31; Lennard, *Rural England*, pp. 105 ff.

the day that King Edward was alive and dead, whether looked at from above or below. At the highest level, the replacement of the aristocracy of Anglo-Saxon England by an extension of the new, military, and proto-feudal aristocracy of Normandy meant the formation of a single Norman–French aristocratic community in the two countries. At an intermediate level, there may have been a degree of mingling of the peoples in England only, though at what date this became significant is doubtful—the languages remained distinct and the contact with French that so enriched the English language seems to have happened later.[1] There was no English settlement in Normandy that mattered. At the lower levels there was no mingling on either side of the Channel; yet the gradual elimination of slavery in England and the tendency to put all the peasantry into a single class of *villani* produced at least a superficial appearance of similarity with the peasantry of Normandy. It was assimilation up to a point.

Another process of assimilation 'up to a point' may be seen in the sphere of local government. The chief local officers in Edward the Confessor's England had been the earl, the shire-reeve, and the bishop, for secular and ecclesiastical administration had not been so clearly distinguished as they were later to become. The earl generally held a number of shires and had something of the character of a regional viceroy; the shire-reeve had once been his deputy in the shire and was so still in theory, though he was becoming more and more a directly royal officer in practice, in fact 'the king's chief executive agent in every branch of local government'.[2] The institutions they worked through were the shire and the hundred (or wapentake in the regions of Scandinavian settlement) with their courts. These units were still conceived of more as bodies of people than as territorial divisions, and their courts as 'public' meetings which took decisions on matters of justice and administration, secular and ecclesiastical, rather than as courts administering justice in the name of the king. As a structure that was more or less uniform throughout the kingdom, these institutions had taken shape in the tenth century and they still retained their vigour

---

[1] Legge, 'Anglo-Norman and the Historian'; Wilson, 'English and French in England, 1100–1300'; Poole, *Domesday Book to Magna Carta*, pp. 252–4. The evidence is uncertain and confusing. Little of it refers to the time between 1066 and 1144.

[2] Stenton, *A.-S.E.*, p. 540.

in the eleventh, even if royal authority was growing and was seeking to use them more and more as a vehicle for its exercise, and the influence of local magnates must often have been at least as decisive as the opinions of the other suitors.[1] Although the frontier of Normandy in the eleventh century divided several ancient *pagi*, the duchy may be thought of for these purposes as though it consisted of a group of Carolingian *pagi* or counties, including some fragments of *pagi*, held in plurality by one count (the 'duke').[2] Throughout the tenth century there were no other counts in the 'duchy', though early in the eleventh a small number of men bearing the title of count do appear. The territorial designation that often goes with the title suggests that their sphere of authority was generally one of the ancient *pagi*, usually in a frontier region and including an important castle. They were all kinsmen of the duke.[3] Rather than the count, the true local representative and agent of the duke in Normandy was the *vicomte*. The evidence is not sufficient for us to say that Normandy in 1066 was divided for administrative purposes into a number of *pagi* or *comtés* of ancient origin, in each of which the chief local officer was a *vicomte* acting as the deputy of the duke considered as the count of all these *comtés*, and that where the duke appointed a member of his own family to represent him in one of these *comtés* the higher title of count was given,[4] but this seems to be the principle if it was not completely realized in practice. The *vicomte* was responsible for the collection of much of the ducal revenue in his *vicomté*, and he farmed it as the shire-reeve farmed the royal revenues in the English shire; he administered much of the duke's rights of justice in his locality and he had certain military functions; but there was a strong tendency towards heredity in the tenure of his office. The *vicomtes* seem all to have been of baronial rank and wealth; and while there is almost no evidence of the nature of the courts they held other than

---

[1] Stenton, *A.-S.E.*, pp. 289–98, 322–4, 538–42; Morris, *Medieval English Sheriff*, pp. 1–39; Blair, *Introduction to Anglo-Saxon England*, pp. 222–44; Bullough, 'Anglo-Saxon Institutions and Early English Society', pp. 655–8.

[2] Yver, 'Premières institutions', pp. 310, 315–16.

[3] Douglas, 'The Earliest Norman Counts'; Yver, 'Premières institutions', pp. 323–5.

[4] The members of the ruling family in Brittany were given the title 'comes' (*E.Y.C.*, iv, *Honour of Richmond*, i, 97–101), but it is doubtful if the title was derived in Normandy from membership of the ducal family (below, pp. 342–3 n. 5).

enumerations of the pleas they might hear in them it is most unlikely that these courts preserved anything like as much of the communal character of the Carolingian *mallus* from which they must ultimately have been derived as the English shire courts had preserved of their original constitution. In terms of those attending and the *vicomte*'s place in them, these courts must have been difficult to distinguish from feudal courts. The jurisdiction of the *vicomte* and the jurisdiction of the bishop seem clearly differentiated, at least in principle.[1]

After the Conquest the great viceregal earls disappeared in England and were replaced by men who were kinsmen or intimates of the king. Their sphere of activity was generally associated with one ancient shire[2] and an important castle, and usually situated in an outlying part of the kingdom. Their resemblance to the Norman counts is striking, the more so as it is difficult to see these creations either as constituting a comprehensive scheme of frontier defence or as part of a system of local government in either country.[3] The English shire-reeves, or sheriffs, who were not immediately displaced but replaced gradually like the bishops, were identified by the Normans with their *vicomtes* and soon took on many of their characteristics. With the change in the character of the earls, and the removal of the bishops and ecclesiastical administration from the hundred courts and ultimately from the shire courts, the sheriff became in the fullest sense the king's secular representative and agent in the English shires. There was a tendency to appoint men of baronial standing to shrievalties, a tendency for them to make their offices hereditary, a tendency to give them charge of the royal castle in each shire;[4] while the development

---

[1] Haskins, *Norman Institutions*, pp. 45–7; Douglas, *William the Conqueror*, pp. 139–43; Yver, 'Premières institutions', pp. 325–32, 345–7. For the *leges episcopales*, above, pp. 247–8.

[2] Though it did not necessarily coincide with a shire; e.g. Wightman, 'The Palatine Earldom of William fitzOsbern'.

[3] Douglas, *William the Conqueror*, pp. 294–6. Odo bishop of Bayeux and earl of Kent was William's half-brother; William fitzOsbern, Roger de Montgomery and Alan de Bretagne claimed descent from the ducal family and Hugh d'Avranches was distantly connected with it (Le Patourel, 'Norman Colonization of Britain', p. 420, note 38). The change in character of the English earldoms is very clearly shown by the maps in Freeman, *Norman Conquest*, ii, facing p. 585 and in Stenton, *William the Conqueror*, facing pp. 412, 414, 416.

[4] Morris, *Medieval English Sheriff*, pp. 41–74; Douglas, *William the Conqueror*, pp. 293–4, 296–9.

which had already begun to make the shire courts an instrument for the administration of royal justice was intensified by
a new conception of royal jurisdiction and expressed in Henry's
reign by the regular appointment of royal justices, local and
itinerant, to supplement the work of the sheriffs, as local and
itinerant justices were being appointed by that time in Normandy.[1] But at that point the process of assimilation stopped.
Under Henry many of the sheriffs were not the sons of his two
predecessors' sheriffs nor drawn from the established baronial
families; and at least part of the object of his well-known order
concerning the shire and hundred courts was to prevent the
sheriffs from treating the shire courts as their own, that is to
say from bringing them more and more into line with the
courts of the *vicomte* in Normandy.[2] The king and his advisers
had evidently come to understand how valuable the shire and
the hundred could be in their traditional English form, and how
useful the sheriffs could be as ministers rather than as barons
with administrative responsibilities, even though baronial
claims and ambitions could not always be resisted; but if Henry
ever thought of continuing the process of assimilation by reviving the communal character of the courts of the *vicomtes* in
Normandy he must have come sadly to the conclusion that their
decay had gone too far. Thus, in respect of local institutions,
though assimilation went quite a long way, residual points of
difference remained and these differences eventually proved to
be momentous; for the persistence of the shire with many of its
ancient characteristics is one of the most important elements in
English constitutional development, and the absence of any such
institution in Normandy or any part of France at this time must
always be taken into account when attempting to explain the
progress of the French monarchy towards absolutism.

It may well be that the same could be said, finally, of the
assimilation of law and custom in England and Normandy

---

[1] Morris, *Medieval English Sheriff*, pp. 100–3; above, pp. 158–9.

[2] Morris, op. cit., pp. 75–109. For the writ, Robertson, *Laws*, pp. 286–7: 'Sciatis
quod concedo et praecipio ut amodo comitatus mei et hundreda in illis locis et
eisdem terminis sedeant, sicut sederunt in tempore regis Eadwardi et non aliter.
Et nolo ut vicecomes meus propter aliquod necessarium suum, quod sibi pertineat,
faciat ea sedere aliter'. Later in the twelfth century it was necessary only to modify
the sheriff's office in England rather than to superimpose a new type of local
officer as in Normandy.

during the time of the Norman kings; though assurance on this matter will hardly be possible until legal historians have made a detailed and technical comparison of developments on either side of the Channel. There has been no lack of discussion on the origins of the legal institutions of the two countries; but generally they have been treated apart from one another,[1] and sub-nationalistic feelings have not been entirely foreign to the attempts that have been made from time to time to identify institutions with one country or the other. The fact that England and Normandy were ruled together under the Norman kings, and again from 1154 until 1204, is frequently mentioned in general terms; but the question how far this might tend towards the assimilation of law and custom as between the two countries has rarely been considered specifically.

In one or two respects indeed there was no need for assimilation for there was virtual identity already. The control which the Norman dukes had exercised over the mints in their duchy, for example, could easily be identified with the control which the kings of the English had over the coinage in their kingdom.[2] In some other respects, assimilation was direct and complete if not quite instantaneous. This would apply to the setting up of episcopal courts in England and the introduction of canon law as it was coming to be understood in Normandy and in Western Christendom generally. The ultimate effect of this was to withdraw ecclesiastical jurisdiction from the royal and communal courts in England, making a clear distinction between ecclesiastical and other jurisdiction such as already existed in Normandy, and to make possible a parallel development of canon law in the two countries.[3] It would apply similarly to the

---

[1] Maitland does indeed consider Norman and English law together (Pollock and Maitland, *H.E.L.*, chs. 2–4); but Maitland was writing before Haskins, Génestal, Yver, and others on the Norman side, and many historians on the English side have in recent times tended to minimize the effects of the Norman Conquest upon institutions in England. Van Caenegem, in *Royal Writs in England*, expressly excludes the Norman writs from consideration (pp. vi–vii), and considers them only in general terms in his Cambridge lectures on *The Birth of the Common Law*. Yver, in his masterly review of the *Royal Writs*, 'Le bref anglo-normand', indicates what could be done.

[2] Normandy: Lemarignier, *Hommage en marche*, pp. 25–6; Yver, 'Premières institutions', pp. 340–3; England: Dolley and Metcalf, 'The Reform of the English Coinage under Eadgar', pp. 136–68; Loyn, *Anglo-Saxon England and the Norman Conquest*, pp. 120–32.

[3] Above, p. 248.

introduction into England of the Norman institution of the forest, and the forest law that went with it;[1] and this meant assimilation to the point of identity in another big exception to the jurisdiction of the ordinary courts, a matter that affected a large number of people and vast tracts of country both in kingdom and duchy. Likewise, the Norman colonization of England, at a time when feudal tenures were still in process of development in Normandy and only to some degree anticipated in England, could only lead to a parallel development of the law relating to fiefs in the two countries. Some differences of detail would remain as between kingdom and duchy and as between different parts of each;[2] but the general similarity that appears in the course of the twelfth century in the personal and tenurial relationships between the king and the knightly class, in both countries, is more important than local differences of detail; and the common law and the *coutume de Normandie*, when their characteristics can be diagnosed and analysed, both show themselves to be strongly feudal in character.[3] Here again, there was at least assimilation.

Yet in spite of the very considerable changes which the introduction into England of a separate ecclesiastical jurisdiction, a forest law, a body of custom relating to feudal tenures, and other legal institutions of less importance (such as the judicial duel[4] and the *murdrum* fine,[5] though these exceptionally made a distinction between Norman and English) must involve, it seems to have been the intention of William the Conqueror

---

[1] On the extent of the forest, above, p. 131, n. 6. For the law of the forest, Yver, 'Premières institutions', p. 342; Petit-Dutaillis, *Studies Supplementary to Stubbs' Constitutional History*, i–ii (1923), 166–78; Lemarignier, *Hommage en marche*, pp. 24–5.   [2] Above, pp. 253–4.

[3] 'Feudal law did not become the law of the knightly, aristocratic class, nor the law of some parts of the country alone; it became the common law of England' (Simpson, *Introduction to the History of the Land Law*, p. 3). 'Le premier trait marquant de la Coutume normande est, certainement, la très forte empreinte qu'elle a subie de la structure féodale. Aucun pays occidental, — l'Angleterre mise à part ... — n'a été plus fortement et, il faut dire, plus logiquement, féodalisé que la Normandie' (Yver, 'Les caractères originaux de la coutume de Normandie', pp. 314–15).

[4] William's rule assumed that the Normans would wish to use their traditional method of proof in England, and made it optional for the English. Before 1066 England was exceptional among the countries of Western Europe in not using it (Robertson, *Laws*, pp. 232–3; van Caenegem, *Birth of the Common Law*, 65–6; Pollock and Maitland, *H.E.L.*, i. 39–40, 89–90; ii. 632–4 etc.

[5] Pollock and Maitland, *H.E.L.*, i. 89.

and his sons that English law should be maintained and that, in the kingdom, it should govern the Norman colonists where relevant as well as the surviving natives.[1] In practice this must have meant, so far as the Normans in England were concerned, that in their relations with the English and in the exploitation of their English estates, certainly in their relations with the customary tenants on their manors, they must observe English law and custom;[2] but all that concerned their relations with their feudal tenants, peers, and superiors as such would be regulated by a feudal custom which could not be very different from that which obtained in Normandy. It also meant the continuation of the courts of the shire, hundred, and wapentake, their English composition and procedure and the law they administered (though with ecclesiastical and forest matters withdrawn from them), and the survival of much local custom in the boroughs and elsewhere; but new feudal courts came in with feudal tenures,[3] new feudal pressures were brought to bear upon the older courts,[4] and a specifically royal jurisdiction was superimposed upon them all. William's conservative order that 'the laws of King Edward' should continue to be observed in England, with the additions he had made, could not guarantee English law against change in a Norman sense, for England now had a Norman monarchy, a Norman aristocracy and a predominantly Norman ecclesiastical hierarchy; it certainly could not guarantee it against being gradually pushed into the background by the new law that was being developed in the Norman king's courts.

A great deal, relatively, can be known about English law, or English laws, as it stood in the middle of the eleventh century, from the surviving texts of the legislation of the Anglo-Saxon

[1] William's charter to London (Robertson, *Laws*, p. 230), the laws attributed to him in the 'Ten Articles' (ibid., p. 240, c. 7) and the coronation charter of Henry I (ibid., p. 282, c. 13). Cf. Pollock and Maitland, *H.E.L.*, i. 88.

[2] This is strikingly shown in the accounts we have of the famous trial on Penenden Heath (Le Patourel, 'Reports of the trial on Penenden Heath', pp. 21–4, text A). In general, the Norman colonists took over English estates as going concerns, with the rights and obligations attached to them (e.g. Pollock and Maitland, *H.E.L.*, i. 92–3).

[3] There were private jurisdictions in England before the Conquest; and communal courts fell into private hands both before and after 1066; but there was also a jurisdiction that derived from the relationship of a lord to his tenants (e.g. Pollock and Maitland, *H.E.L.*, i. 530–32).

[4] Above, pp. 259–60.

kings, from charters and wills, from the Domesday survey, and from the various attempts that were made to set it down in writing by men of the early twelfth century who saw the great change beginning.[1] It was a body of Germanic custom as modified by ecclesiastical influences. It varied between the great divisions of Wessex, Mercia, and the Danelaw and also between much smaller units since, royal legislation apart, it must have been very largely formed in the shire courts.[2] Much less could be said of the law of Normandy at the same time; for the age of the capitularies was long past in the Frankish lands out of which the duchy had been formed, there was no Norman Domesday Book, surviving charters are relatively few, and no treatises on Norman law have survived from any time earlier than the later part of the twelfth century, if any were written. We can be sure, however, from later evidence, that it was basically Frankish in origin and substance, that Scandinavian influence upon it had been slight,[3] and that it had hardly 'crystallized' as yet in the sense that one could speak of a 'custom of Normandy', internally consistent, applied in a territory coinciding with the political extent of the duchy and clearly differentiated from neighbouring *coutumes*.[4] At the time of the Norman Conquest, therefore, the laws and customs of England and Normandy had much in common, ultimate Germanic origins modified by similar ecclesiastical influences (the chief distinction being that England lacked what may have survived of a Roman substratum and Carolingian legislation in northern France), so that really fundamental differences between them are hardly to be looked for; there was considerable local and

---

[1] e.g. Pollock and Maitland, *H.E.L.*, i. 97–107; *Leges Henrici Primi* (ed. Downer, introduction, pp. 5–7 etc.).

[2] e.g. *Leges Henrici Primi*, c. 6 (ed. Downer, pp. 96–9 and introduction, pp. 44–5).

[3] Though perhaps a little more than was thought until very recently (Musset, 'Place de la Normandie dans la géographie coutumière de l'ancienne France', p. 187).

[4] At the earliest, Norman law is thought to have 'crystallized' in the time of William the Conqueror. For the idea of 'crystallization' of the *coutumes*, Génestal, 'Formation et Développement de la Coutume de Normandie'; Yver, 'Caractères originaux du groupe de coutumes de l'Ouest', pp. 21–7; and 'Premières institutions', pp. 316–23. On early Norman law in general, these same works and cf. Musset, 'Réflexions d'un historien sur les origines du droit normand'. For local variations surviving in Normandy, Klimrath, *Études sur les coutumes*, pp. 62–4; though some of these *coutumes locales* may represent later developments.

regional variation within each country, and it may be added that in neither would existing law be likely to meet the needs of an aggressive feudal society led by a vigorous monarchy.

Beyond those matters in which the law in England was brought directly into conformity with the law in Normandy, assimilation began with the establishment of a single, overriding judicial authority as the duke became king and the duke's court became the king's court acting directly in both countries. By far the most important development in law and jurisdiction that took place in England and Normandy after the Conquest was the vast increase in the activity of this court. It may be that the conquest of England itself acted as a great stimulus to this activity, adding so much to the extent of the territory over which the peace had to be kept and providing a fertile source of litigation as Norman barons and churchmen took possession of the lands and rights of their English *antecessores*;[1] but it seems very likely that the initial impulse came from Normandy and that this expansion of royal justice would not have taken place if a concept of judicial organization that was different from anything hitherto known in England had not already been developed in Normandy.

It is now held that the dukes had preserved or recovered more of the rights of jurisdiction inherent in the Frankish monarchy than most of their fellow princes in northern Francia had done.[2] With the disintegration of Frankish royal power and authority and the transformation of the public courts (the *mallus*, analogous to the English shire court), rights of jurisdiction had degenerated into a species of private property, included in the general term *consuetudines*, which over most of France were falling into the hands of magnates and castellans.[3] In Normandy, however, the duke had kept or recovered a greater proportion of these *consuetudines* than neighbouring princes had succeeded in doing,[4] and he had a direct interest in extending rights which to him represented political power and wealth. When the Truce of God was proclaimed in Normandy it was proclaimed under

---

[1] Above, pp. 155–9.   [2] Above, p. 238 n. 3
[3] Lot, Pfister, Ganshof, *Les Destinées de l'Empire en Occident*, pp. 308–10, 579–80; Lemarignier, 'La Dislocation du "pagus" et le problème des "consuetudines" '.
[4] Yver, 'Contribution à l'étude du développement de la compétence ducale en Normandie', esp. pp. 147–59; 'Premières institutions', pp. 344–50; Lemarignier, *Hommage en marche*, pp. 26–31.

the duke's auspices and its enforcement was eventually confused, probably intentionally, with the maintenance of a duke's peace; save during William's minority, the duke had the power to enforce the judgements of his court, a fact which would attract litigants however powerful;[1] in Normandy the *vicomte's* courts were administering what were essentially the duke's rights of justice;[2] and although some monasteries and barons had the right to ducal *consuetudines*, the fact that this could in so many cases be traced directly to ducal grant was enabling the duke and his court to approach the doctrine that all judicial authority in the duchy was the duke's or derived from him.[3] It was not so much that the duke had some residual right to exercise a public justice as that he had a dominant share in what had generally become private justice, and such a jurisdiction was by its nature expansionist. Already the duke had had occasion to refer a case brought to him to a group of *fideles* (in this instance, his half-brother, three bishops, and an abbot) who heard it and gave judgement in his name.[4] In England, on the other hand, however much the part of the king, his officers, and local magnates in the administration of justice might be growing,[5] it was still thought of differently. The courts of the shire and the hundred still retained their communal or public character; the basis of their authority was still the customary law as interpreted by the suitors; and, what is more, they were still regarded as the normal source of justice, with resort to the king and his court as exceptional and to be used only when justice could not be obtained otherwise.[6] Thus there was a duke's justice in Normandy in a sense in which there was not a king's justice in England before 1066; the duke's justice already had ambitions to be the primary source of justice within its territory; and the effect of the conquest of England was to transfer this Norman idea of the administration of justice to the kingdom, where it

---

[1] De Bouard, 'Sur les origines de la trève de Dieu en Normandie'; Yver, 'Premières institutions', pp. 359–60. The duke possessed and exercised the power of banishment, Musset, 'Naissance de la Normandie', p. 108.

[2] Haskins, *Norman Institutions*, pp. 46–7; Yver, 'Premières institutions', pp. 345–7.

[3] Haskins, *Norman Institutions*, pp. 27–39; Yver, 'Premières institutions', esp. pp. 348–9; Lemarignier, *Hommage en marche*, pp. 26–9.

[4] Fauroux, *Recueil*, No. 209 (pp. 398–9).   [5] Above, pp. 257–8.

[6] Pollock and Maitland, *H.E.L.*, i. 40–4, 532–60; Barlow, *Edward the Confessor*, pp. 176–8; Jolliffe, *Constitutional History of Medieval England*, pp. 107–27.

superseded the native English practice and where it was presented with enormous opportunities.[1]

Given, then, the conditions of the two countries after 1066, there was a natural and very rapid expansion of royal jurisdiction in both. The practice of delegating this jurisdiction to groups of royal justices grew rapidly, at first *ad hoc*, then as a regular practice, either to justices sitting 'centrally' in each country and sitting and giving judgement in the king's name whether he could be physically present or not, or these same justices supplementing and gradually superseding local officers holding local courts, either in a specific region or on circuit. At least so far as the provision of courts for the exercise of this increasingly active royal jurisdiction was concerned, England and Normandy were treated in exactly the same way, with minor adjustments only to meet local conditions,[2] for the same authority, the king and his advisers, was operating in both.

This royal justice was not content, however, simply to provide courts whose judgements were backed by royal authority and the force of royal power. The king intervened directly at the solicitation of one of the parties to a dispute or in his own interest; and he did so by means of a distinctively English instrument, the sealed writ. It has been argued that in England the form of the writs used for this purpose was, to begin with, a peremptory order to satisfy the demands of the party which had the ear of the king at that moment; but often there was a qualification—action was only to be taken if the circumstances were as stated, or if it could be done justly; or it was prescribed that action should be taken on the basis of an inquiry. From these qualifications and the gradual emergence of fixed forms of writ corresponding to the forms of action as these themselves were progressively defined, there developed eventually the 'original writs' of the end of the twelfth century. Since this development was not towards a general all-purpose writ that would initiate a whole category of actions but towards a system in which a specific form of writ was required for each narrowly defined set of circumstances, it resulted in the 'formulary system'

[1] The ultimate origin of the common law of England, since it was the law of the king's courts, is this superimposing of the Norman duke's near monopoly of a justice that had become essentially private upon a judicial system which still preserved, in vigorous shape still, the institutions of a public form of justice, the shire and the hundred. [2] Above, pp. 157–9.

characteristic of English common law.[1] Although the evidence
is not so plentiful across the Channel (in part, perhaps, because
the use of any form of writ was hardly established there before
the time of Henry Beauclerc), it would support a similar interpretation, certainly in the light of the English analogies;[2] and the
result was the same. Procedures in Normandy as described in the
custumals of the beginning of the thirteenth century can as well be
described as based on a 'formulary system' as those in England.[3]

The royal judicial organization was also experimenting with
methods of proof, various forms of collective testimony on oath,
in place of the old ordeals, compurgations, and duels. The
principle of such testimony can be found on either side of the
Channel before the Conquest, but not in the specific form of the
inquest at the king's command.[4] This, however, appears very
quickly both in Normandy and in England after 1066, as an
administrative instrument for ascertaining and so protecting
royal rights[5] and as a royal procedure that could be allowed to
important personages or institutions as a favour or for a consideration. In this way it came to be used in matters with an
increasingly judicial content,[6] to provide decisive testimony

---

[1] van Caenegem, *Royal Writs in England*, pp. 107–346, 391–403 *passim*; *Birth of
the Common Law*, pp. 29–61.

[2] e.g. writs quoted in Haskins, *Norman Institutions*, p. 93, note 30 (early form of
writ *praecipe*); p. 98, No. 7 (early form of writ of right); p. 296, No. 5 (early form
of writ of *novel disseisin*); also p. 93, note 31; p. 101, No. 9; p. 102, Nos. 13, 14, and
the general remarks on pp. 104–5. To be compared with the forms given in van
Caenegem, *Royal Writs in England*, pp. 413–515.

[3] van Caenegem, *Birth of the Common Law*, pp. 57–9; Yver, 'Le bref anglo-
normand'.

[4] There is an important bibliographical note on this much-debated point in
van Caenegem, *Royal Writs*, p. 58; cf. Yver, 'Le bref anglo-normand', pp. 313–15.
The problem seems to be that whereas collective sworn testimony with the consent
of the parties is found in England before 1066, the inquest at the king's command is
not. The celebrated provision in 3 Æthelred c. 3 (Robertson, *Laws*, pp. 64–7), that
the twelve leading thegns with the reeve should swear that they would not accuse
any innocent man nor shield any guilty one, comes very near to it but is isolated.
In Normandy, on the other hand, where the tradition of the Frankish royal inquest
may well have been gathered up by the Norman rulers, there is no known instance
of its use before 1066. Cf. van Caenegem, *Birth of the Common Law*, pp. 72–9.

[5] e.g. the Domesday survey in England. In Normandy, the 'Consuetudines et
justicie' of 1091 ('sicut . . . fecerunt recordari et scribi per episcopos et barones suos',
Haskins, *Norman Institutions*, p. 281); or the Bayeux Inquest of 1133, ibid., pp. 201–
2; Gleason, *Ecclesiastical Barony*, pp. 25, 68–82.

[6] England: van Caenegem, *Royal Writs in England*, pp. 51–103, esp. p. 83; Yver,
'Le bref anglo-normand', p. 315. Normandy: Haskins, *Norman Institutions*, pp.
222–3: van Caenegem, *Birth of the Common Law*, pp. 133–4, note 34.

(*recognitio, veredictum*) in litigation, and eventually made available to all freemen who demanded it and paid the necessary fees. Again, so far as can be seen, the process of development was the same in the two countries, at least in the time of the Norman kings. After proof came judgement and punishment. Another major change was the substitution of the king's *misericordia*,[1] in principle arbitrary but which could easily develop into a flexible system of pecuniary penalties graduated according to the gravity of the offence and replacing the old tariffs of *wer* and *wīte* and *bōt* in England and the monetary compensations of the older Frankish law in Normandy. As with the inquest, it seems likely that the germ of the institution existed in the two countries before the Conquest and it appears in developed form in both soon after.

Although the surviving evidence for legal developments in Normandy during the time of the Norman kings is so much slighter than it is in England, there can be no doubt that these ideas and devices were being used, and used in the same way, in the two countries. Later, but not before the advent of the Angevin kings, the writs would become 'original writs', stereotyped in form and initiating proceedings in a court, usually a royal court, rather than attempting almost extrajudicially to settle a dispute by executive action; they would be associated with the royal inquest to produce the assizes, and both would be available, not as a royal favour but as of right to all freemen who could pay a standard and relatively small fee; the inquest in the form of the jury of indictment and presentment would be used by the justices to supplement powerfully the uncertain and more easily deflected private accusation and to bring offenders of all kinds into the royal courts, and the jury of trial emerge as an alternative to ordeals and duels.[2] The parallel development in the two countries seems natural and almost inevitable, for the prodigious enlargement of royal justice in both was the work of a single authority. King and duke were generally one person,

---

[1] For the *misericordia* and its antecedents in Normandy, Yver, 'Premières institutions', pp. 350–5. In England, ibid., p. 355, note 145; Pollock and Maitland, *H.E.L.*, i. 46–9, 105–7; ii. 513–15 and cf. *Leges Henrici Primi*, c. 13 (ed. Downer, pp. 116–19).

[2] England: e.g. Pollock and Maitland, *H.E.L.*, i. 136–53; van Caenegem, *Royal Writs in England*, pp. 195–346; Normandy: Haskins, *Norman Institutions*, pp. 187–9; ch. vi, esp. pp. 234–7; van Caenegem, *Birth of the Common Law*, pp. 57–9; Yver, 'Le bref anglo-normand'.

who was as royal in his duchy as in his kingdom (no question of appeals from his courts in Normandy to any higher court in France, no hesitation in using the royal prerogative of the inquest in the duchy); his courts were *curia regis* in Normandy as in England and the justices who acted in his name in kingdom and duchy were drawn from the same body of men. It is true that such changes in procedure do not explicitly change the substance of the law; yet they were bound to modify it in practice. If new means were found to protect old rights, such rights were likely to be more clearly defined at the least, and to that extent changed, as the introduction of the assize of *mort d'ancestor* in Henry II's time affected the law of inheritance.[1] The use of apparently identical procedures in England and in Normandy, as well as the fact that royal jurisdiction was starting on its way to supersede all other jurisdictions in both countries,[2] must have had a strongly assimilative effect on their laws and customs. For, in a time and a region of customary law and in the absence of comprehensive legislation such as was scarcely conceivable in the time of the Norman kings, the only way in which a body of law could be formed that was consistent over a given territory was by the action of courts working under the authority whose effective power extended over that same territory.[3] The Norman kings ruled over England and Normandy, and their courts operated in both countries; it would be surprising if the law that they were making were not the same, or very similar, on either side of the Channel.

Nevertheless there is a problem. Law in England and law in

---

[1] Thorne, 'English Feudalism and Estates in Land', pp. 203–4. Cf. Milsom, introduction to Pollock and Maitland, *H.E.L.*, Reissue of second edition, 1968, i. pp. xxxvi–xxxviii.

[2] In England the author of the *Leges Henrici Primi* is already saying, *c.* 1114–18, 'Preter hoc tremendum regie maiestatis titulamus imperium quod preese iugiter legibus ac salubriter frequentamus aduertendum' (ed. Downer, p. 96, c. 6, 2a), and 'Legis etiam Anglice trina partitio est . . . supersunt regis placita curie que usus et consuetudines suas una semper immobilitate seruat ubique' (ed. Downer, p. 108, c. 9, 10a). In Normandy the last clause of the canons of the council of Lillebonne seems to say that the king's court, by its judgement, determines the limits of other jurisdictions (Chaplais, 'Henry II's reissue of the canons of the council of Lillebonne', p. 632; Orderic Vitalis, *H.E.* (ed. Le Prévost), ii. 322–3; (ed. Chibnall), iii. 34). Cf. Yver, 'Premières institutions', pp. 348–63.

[3] e.g. Yver's description of 'crystallization' of the *coutume d'Anjou*—'Caractères originaux du groupe de coutumes de l'Ouest', pp. 21–7; or the description of the formation of the *coutumes* of the *châtellenies* in Poitou by Garaud in *Châtelains de Poitou*, pp. 109–10.

Normandy can hardly be compared in any detail, and the degree of assimilation measured, before the end of the twelfth century or later when the earliest custumals were written—the treatise that goes by the name of Glanvill (*c.* 1187–9) for England[1] and the two shorter and less sophisticated tracts (one of *c.* 1199 and the other of *c.* 1220) that were put together to form the *Très Ancien Coutumier* for Normandy.[2] There is no custumal for England and Normandy together; yet even a superficial reading of these works seems to confirm the impression already gained from the evidence of institutional and procedural developments, that the ancient laws and customs of England and Normandy were being refashioned by one single authority which was applying the same ideas and devices in the two countries. In all three treatises the predominance of the king's court and its usages is assumed; the inquest, the recognition, and the writ are described as employed in the same ways; there are the same possessory assizes and the same 'grand assize', though they may be known by slightly different names. The revived study of Roman law and the development of the canon law have had much the same effect both upon the writers of these treatises and upon the law they describe. They were not so much a direct source of rules and maxims (though this cannot be entirely excluded) as a stimulus and an education in orderly thinking about the law.[3]

Besides so much that the laws and customs of the two countries clearly had in common, however, there were also differences between them, differences both fundamental and superficial. For example, the *consuetudo Anglie* and the *consuetudo Normannie* could be opposed to one another on specific points in the records of the king's court that were kept in England at the turn of the twelfth and thirteenth centuries.[4] Primogeniture

---

[1] Glanvill, *Tractatus*, ed. Hall. Other editions are listed in this work.

[2] *Le Trés Ancien Coutumier de Normandie, Texte Latin.* Tardif shows that the French text, which he has also edited, is a translation.

[3] e.g. Pollock and Maitland, *H.E.L.*, i, ch. v and pp. 162–7; Glanvill, *Tractatus*, ed. Hall, introduction pp. xv–xviii, xxvii–xxix; Besnier, *Coutume de Normandie: histoire externe*, pp. 49–55, 63–9; Joüon des Longrais, *Henry II and his justiciars*.

[4] *Curia Regis Rolls*, i. 256; ii. 227. Many references to *consuetudo Anglie* or *consuetudo regni* were no doubt made in opposition to Roman or Canon law; but in the context of some such references in the Curia Regis rolls there must also have been the consciousness of a distinction from *consuetudo Normannie* (cf. Pollock and Maitland, *H.E.L.*, ii. 268).

in the English sense was never the rule in Normandy save in the Pays de Caux, nor was the *parage* of classical Norman custom the rule in England;[1] the principle that 'no one is bound to answer concerning any free tenement of his in the court of his lord unless there is a writ from the king or his chief justice', fundamental in England, is not found in Normandy;[2] and though the formulae of the writs which initiate the possessory assizes as given in Glanvill and the *Très Ancien Coutumier* correspond very closely, they differ in detail and these detailed differences sometimes have very important implications.[3]

It will not be possible to interpret this balance of common characteristics and points of difference and to say what it means, nor to decide how far the laws and customs of Normandy and England were moving towards identification in a single legal system for the two countries during the twelfth century or towards separation into two distinct if related systems, until a full and technical comparison, legal point by legal point, has been made between the law as described by Glanvill, the law described by the authors of the *Très Ancien Coutumier*, and the rules that may be inferred from such documents recording their application as there may be. Yet one or two preliminary suggestions may be made. It is not certain, for example, when the formulae of the original writs used for the 'assizes' as given in Glanvill and in the *Très Ancien Coutumier* are put beside one another, that like is being compared with like. It can presumably be taken that the writs quoted in Glanvill are quoted in the form they had reached in the last decade of Henry II's reign; but the texts of the writs quoted in the *Très Ancien Coutumier* occur in only the second part of that compilation, the part that dates from *c.* 1220, that is more than thirty years after Glanvill was writing and some sixteen years after the French conquest of the duchy, when the Norman exchequer of the thirteenth century (a continuation of the court of the seneschal and justices 'at the exchequer' and corresponding in the late

---

[1] Pollock and Maitland, *H.E.L.*, ii. 262–70, 274, 276–8, 289–94; Holt, 'Politics and Property in Early Medieval England', pp. 9–11, 44–5 and references there given; Wightman, *Lacy Family*, p. 218.

[2] Glanvill, *Tractatus*, xii. 2, 25 (ed. Hall, pp. 137, 148); Yver, 'Le bref anglo-normand', pp. 319–20; Haskins, *Norman Institutions*, p. 189; van Caenegem, *Royal Writs in England*, pp. 212–14 and *Birth of the Common Law*, p. 59.

[3] Yver, 'Le bref anglo-normand', pp. 319–28.

twelfth century to the court which was becoming the court of common pleas in England) was presided over by justices of the king of France appointed in his *parlement* and subject to appeal thereto.[1] Nevertheless, the result of such comparisons as have been made is curious. The writ of Novel Disseisin as quoted in Glanvill, for example, has shed all its 'executive'[2] characteristics and is a fully developed writ of summons, initiating an action in the king's courts; but the corresponding writ in the *Très Ancien Coutumier* is still in the 'praecipe' form,[3] so that even in 1220 it was less developed in this respect than the English writ. On the other hand, the writ in Glanvill specifies that the disseisin must have taken place since the king's last crossing into Normandy, a term which would naturally grow longer after 1204 and which did in fact lengthen progressively in England, making the action less and less purely possessory; whereas in Normandy the term was 'since last autumn or the autumn before' and this remained fixed, making the Norman action more possessory in character.[4] The full legal implications of points of this kind for any comparison between the development of English and Norman law in the twelfth century need fuller investigation.

There is another respect in which Glanvill and the *Très Ancien Coutumier* should not perhaps be taken at quite their face value. Both are concerned with actions in the king's courts; but the king's courts, though they were gaining ground all the time, were by no means the only courts operating in England and Normandy, even in secular matters. It is naturally impossible to estimate the proportion of judicial business that came before the traditional courts, public and private, and the king's courts respectively in the twelfth century, but it seems in every way likely that the older courts still had the greater part of the work over the two countries as a whole. Moreover, even the king's courts must administer customary law in matters not yet covered by their own new procedures, and they respected local custom where it was established.[5] Such custom varied not

---

[1] e.g. Besnier, *Coutume de Normandie: Histoire externe*, pp. 75–6.

[2] Glanvill, *Tractatus*, xiii, 33 (ed. Hall, p. 167). The word 'executive' is used in the sense in which it is employed by van Caenegem in *Royal Writs in England*.

[3] *Très Ancien Coutumier*, lxxiii. 2 (ed. Tardif, 1ère partie, p. 70).

[4] Yver, 'Le bref anglo-normand', pp. 322–6.

[5] For the relation between custom and the common law, Plucknett, *Concise History*, pp. 290–7 and e.g. Neilson, 'Custom and the Common Law in Kent'.

only as between Normandy and England but as between different parts of each country, and it would take centuries, even at the rate at which the 'law of the king's courts' was advancing in the twelfth century, for it to supersede all such custom with an all-embracing national system of law. To some extent also the actual proceedings in the royal courts must have been founded upon the concepts and terminology of the older courts,[1] and this in itself would introduce an element of variation as between the two countries. If the king's seneschal in Normandy, during the last decades of the twelfth century, issued writs in the king's name and his own, and had a chancery detached from the king's still itinerant chancery to produce them, as the justiciar in England appears to have had,[2] such variation might well enter the formulae of the original writs; though the same men could still serve as royal justices in both countries,[3] and a man like Richard of Ilchester, whose early administrative experience was in England, could act as a chief justiciar in Normandy as well as a justice in England.[4]

It is also likely that although the impetus towards centralizing the administration of justice came from Normandy, giving that country a start in the process, the survival of the shire courts in England provided an instrument for the exercise of royal justice to which there was no parallel in Normandy, enabling it to advance more swiftly in the kingdom than in the duchy. The shire court offered an established institution in which the royal justices could act and a public meeting in which royal policy could be proclaimed and explained; it moreover provided a ready-made unit for early royal inquests which in England were characteristically made by the 'men of the shire' or the 'men of the hundred', bodies that were already accustomed to expressing their collective mind; whereas in Normandy there is nothing to show that the courts of the *vicomte* could act in this way, and the corresponding unit for the royal inquest was the much vaguer entity, 'the men of the neighbourhood'.[5]

The suggestion that royal jurisdiction may have progressed

---

[1] Milsom, Introduction to Pollock and Maitland, *H.E.L.*, Reissue of second edition, 1968, i. pp. xxvii–xxviii.

[2] *Memoranda Roll, 1 John*, introduction by Richardson, pp. lxxv–lxxxvii and *passim.* [3] Haskins, *Norman Institutions*, p. 180.

[4] Ibid., p. 174, note 104; Delisle-Berger, *Recueil*, Introduction, pp. 431–4.

[5] Yver, 'Le bref anglo-normand', p. 315.

at a different rate in the two countries, notwithstanding the fact that the same men could act as justices in both, introduces a chronological element into the comparison. The new forms of procedure in the royal courts on which the common law of England and the *coutume* of the thirteenth century in Normandy would be founded were still tentative, experimental, *ad hoc*, before the accession of King Henry fitzEmpress in 1154. It was only after that date that they became fixed in their formulae and available to any free man who would pay for the writs, and the payment itself would be standardized. In so far as this long step could have been taken by legislative or quasi-legislative acts, such acts could have been framed separately for each country, with adjustments to its special circumstances. Henry and his sons could on occasion legislate for all their lands together, for their lands in groups, or for each one individually.[1]

The possibility that England and Normandy had to some extent been treated differently after the middle of the twelfth century, though by the same high authority, is supported by some quite general considerations. From the conquest of Normandy by Count Geoffrey of Anjou in 1144 until the accession of his son Henry to the throne of England ten years later, the two countries had been under the rule of two men descended from different and rival families; and Geoffrey is not only said to have advised his son against transferring customs from one country to another, but seems to have set an example in his own government of Anjou and Normandy from 1144 to 1150.[2] It is possible that he regarded himself as no more than a 'caretaker'

[1] The ordinance of the Saladin Tithe was promulgated at Le Mans, apparently for all Henry's lands (*Gesta Henrici*, ii. 30–3; Roger of Howden, *Chronica*, ii. 335–8); the Assize of Arms was promulgated in the same city for Henry's continental lands and in England for the kingdom (*Gesta Henrici*, i. 269–70, 278–80; Roger of Howden, *Chronica*, ii. 253, 260–3). Other enactments such as the Assizes of Clarendon and Northampton seem to apply only to England (*Gesta Henrici*, i. 107–11; Roger of Howden, *Chronica*, ii. 89–91, 248–52), Yver has studied the scanty indications there are of what must have been a considerable body of legislation in Normandy, and its relation to the English enactments, in 'Le "Très Ancien Coutumier" de Normandie, miroir de la législation ducale?'. Not all of it concerned Normandy alone. For the manner in which these assizes were promulgated in England, Pollock and Maitland, *H.E.L.*, i. 136–8; and for the texts, Holt, 'The Assizes of Henry II: The Texts'.
[2] Jean de Marmoutier, 'Historia Gaufredi Ducis', p. 224; quoted by Haskins, *Norman Institutions*, p. 155 and by Powicke, *Loss of Normandy*, pp. 18–19. The chronicler speaks specifically of Normandy and England. On Geoffrey's government of Normandy, Haskins, ibid., pp. 130–55; Chartrou, *L'Anjou*, pp. 107–62.

in Normandy: it is more likely that he was giving early expression to the understanding by rulers that law and customs were far more stabilized, generalized, and territorialized ('crystallized') in 1150 than they had been in 1066. At all events, the idea that law is territorial and that each land should be governed according to its own native laws and institutions when one prince ruled several became a fundamental principle of the Angevin 'empire'.[1] The same principle, as a principle, could certainly be deduced from the promises given by William the Conqueror and his son Henry that the 'laws of King Edward' should be maintained in England; but quite apart from the fact that law could not be 'frozen' in that way, the Norman colonization of England and the initiative of the Norman kings' court made it impossible to honour those promises in the long run.

It may therefore be possible, when the matter has been studied a good deal more fully, to explain the similarities between English law and Norman law in the early years of the thirteenth century by saying that both had been worked upon by a single authority using the same ideas and devices in each, and their differences by saying that this authority had to take account of local custom, that it found institutions in one country that enabled it to progress more quickly in that country and, above all, that when the Angevin kings took the really decisive steps, after 1154, they took them on the general assumption that while it was possible to make the same provision for more than one country it was better to proceed on the principle that each country had its own special conditions and that these should be taken into consideration.

It is unfortunate that we do not seem able to test this explanation from the records of the courts themselves.[2] From Richard I's reign rolls were being kept in England for the court held by the king's justices at Westminster ('the Bench', the court that would eventually be known as the Court of Common Pleas),

---

[1] For this principle in the dominions of the Angevin kings later on, Le Patourel, 'The Plantagenet Dominions', esp. pp. 302–6. When the justices of the king of England visited the Channel Islands in the fourteenth century, for example, they had to conduct their proceedings 'according to the law and custom of the Islands'; and that was a system of law which was not simply Norman in origin but was kept *au courant* with legal developments in what had then been French Normandy for over a century: Le Patourel, *Medieval Administration of the Channel Islands*, p. 95. Cf. pp. 52–60, and 'The Authorship of the Grand Coutumier de Normandie'.

[2] Unless this could be done, eventually, from chronicle or charter evidence.

the courts held by his justices itinerant, and, at least from John's first stay in England after his accession, the court held *coram rege*;[1] and it is entirely probable that similar rolls were being kept for the corresponding courts in Normandy, the court of the seneschal and justices sitting 'at the exchequer' in Caen or elsewhere, the courts of the justices itinerant, and the court held *coram rege* when the king was in the duchy; but no rolls have survived from the courts in Normandy of this time.[2] There is, however, more than a suggestion that a specifically Norman law was being fashioned by the judgements of the king's courts in Normandy when the author of the first part of the *Très Ancien Coutumier* speaks of certain changes which, certainly, he attributes to the personal command of the seneschal, but which are more likely to have been made in the court of the seneschal and justices.[3]

[1] Pollock and Maitland, *H.E.L.*, i. 169–71; Flower. *Introduction to the Curia Regis Rolls*, esp. pp. 19–20.

[2] Besnier, *Coutume de Normandie: Histoire externe*, p. 43, For the court *coram rege* in Normandy, e.g. *Curia Regis Rolls*, i. 257, 428, and for the courts of the seneschal and justices and of the justices itinerant there, Haskins, *Norman Institutions*, pp. 164–9, 178–81, 183–5, and 334–6. Although no rolls corresponding to the Curia Regis rolls and the assize rolls of England appear to have survived for Normandy, a number of final concords levied before the seneschal, justices, and barons at the Exchequer at Caen are enrolled on a 'Rotulus cartarum et cyrographorum Normannie' printed in *Rotuli Normanniae*, pp. 1–22 (for the nature of this roll, Richardson, introduction to *Memoranda Roll, 1 John*, pp. liv–lvii). Rolls were certainly kept of the 'assizes' in Normandy (*Très Ancien Coutumier*, xxv, 2; xxviii, 2; lxv, 1, 2: ed. Tardif, pp. 24, 25, 56–7). Parallel series of rolls had been kept by the English and the Norman exchequers apparently from the first (above, pp. 154–5); and in the early years of John's reign the chancery was keeping parallel series, for England and Normandy, of 'Fine' rolls and 'Close' rolls, both involved in the working of the exchequers. The roll printed in *Rotuli Normanniae*, pp. 37–44 is a Norman 'Fine' roll; those printed ibid., pp. 22–37, 45–98, 98–122, and *Memoranda Roll, 1 John*, pp. 97–8, are Norman 'Close' rolls. The parallel English series are included, respectively, in *Rotuli de Oblatis et Finibus* and *Rotuli de Liberate* (later *Rotuli Litterarum Clausarum*) (identification and description in Richardson's introduction to *Memoranda Roll, 1 John*, pp. xvi–xxxv). However, in the earliest Charter and Patent Rolls, which are chancery records proper, one series served, at least initially, for all the king's lands. In May 1204 King John was transporting his 'charters and rolls', from Caen to London (*Rotuli Litterarum Clausarum*, i. 3). For the records of the Norman exchequer after the French conquest of the duchy, in the form in which they have survived, Delisle, *Recueil de jugements de l'échiquier de Normandie au XIIIe siècle (1207–1270)* (mémoire, pp. 247–89). The English series of Pipe Rolls and Curia Regis rolls continued.

[3] *Très Ancien Coutumier*, lx–lxv (*Texte Latin*, ed. Tardif, pp. 51–7). Cf. Powicke, *Loss of Normandy*, pp. 62–3 and notes 132–3. It may be worth noting that the author of this first part of the custumal speaks of 'dux Normannie' and 'curia ducis' throughout, except in the last chapter, where the term 'curia domini Regis' is used. This part of the custumal was put together *c.* 1200.

Nothing, however, that took place after 1144 in any way diminishes the cogency of the evidence which shows the king's courts acting in the same way and employing the same ideas and devices in the two countries before that date; and this, so far as it went, was an assimilative force. Yet the question whether, in the most general sense, the lands and lordships of the Norman kings were moving towards an even closer integration in the last years of King Henry Beauclerc, or whether there were already factors which would bring their integration to a halt at some point or even put the process into reverse, still cannot be answered with any assurance. It can be said that the organization of the localized institutions of administration, the treasuries, exchequers, and delegated royal courts, had not reached the point at which normal bureaucratic tendencies must inevitably make them combine together in each country to form two complete and distinct administrations, one for Normandy and the other for England; though that is what happened late in the thirteenth century as between England and Gascony when the royal itinerary was ceasing to take in the continental lands.[1] It can also be said that king, household, and court were common to the two countries, as the aristocracy and the higher ranks of the ecclesiastical hierarchy formed a single society likewise common to both; and that there was a very considerable degree of assimilation as between the laws and institutions of the two countries, which seems to have been progressing still in 1135. Certainly, the relations between the Norman kings on the one hand and the kings of Scots, the Welsh princes, the dukes of Brittany, and the other vassal princes on the other, were growing closer, with the authority of the suzerain increasing steadily. Perhaps it is not too much to say that the forces making for an integrated and stable Normanno-English kingdom, bestriding the English Channel and extending well beyond the limits of kingdom and duchy as they were understood then, were at least as strong as those making for an eventual kingdom of England and kingdom of France; and it may be this, with the difference between the attitude of rulers to the laws and customs of their lands in the mid eleventh and the mid twelfth centuries, that distinguishes the Norman complex of lands and lordships from the Angevin complex that followed it.

[1] Le Patourel, 'Plantagenet Dominions', pp. 299–300, 303–6.

8. The Dynamic and the Mechanics of Norman Expansion

DURING the second half of the eleventh century and the early years of the twelfth, the Normans had made their presence felt over an astonishingly large portion of the accessible surface of the world. In northern France they had established some form of dominion over most neighbouring principalities. Across the Channel they had achieved a military conquest and an aristocratic colonization of England, a conquest and a similar colonization of a large part of Wales, their interest in Scotland was growing, and they may even have toyed with plans for a conquest of Ireland. They had established Norman rule in South Italy and Sicily; they had been involved in the wars in Spain; their activities had affected the fortunes of the papacy and the politics of Byzantium. They had played a special part in the First Crusade and had founded the Norman principality of Antioch.

Fortunately, no explanation of this extraordinary 'achievement',[1] taken as a whole, need be attempted here, for there was at least one fundamental difference between their activities, or the results of their activities, in the Mediterranean lands and in the north-west of Europe. For all the contacts and relationships that there may have been between the South Italian kingdom and the homeland in Normandy, there never was any integral political union between the two countries such as was formed between England and Normandy; and it may safely be said that there never could have been any such union. William the Conqueror and his sons ruled both England and Normandy, dividing their time between kingdom and duchy; a Count Roger or a King Roger could not rule simultaneously in Sicily and in Normandy; and although there was indeed a Norman aristocratic colonization of southern Italy, Sicily, and Antioch,[2] it is very doubtful if it reached anything like the same intensity as in England and it is certain that the Normans in the south

---

[1] Douglas, *The Norman Achievement*.   [2] Ibid., pp. 173–81.

could not maintain interests in Normandy to the same degree as their cousins who had possessed themselves of lands in England could do. What does need some explanation in this context is not so much the impulse that carried the Normans over the greater part of the world as it was known to them as the dynamic that built up the complex of lands and lordships over which Henry Beauclerc held dominion, the instruments with which such a complex could be built up at that time and what gave it its particular structure.

Since its chief architect was William the Conqueror, a convenient starting-point may be found in the conditions that enabled him to launch a successful conquest of 'the kingdom of the English', with all that was included in that term, and to lay the foundations of the relationship between Normandy and England which his son Henry developed. In any discussion of William's power and achievement some place must be found for sheer personality. That he was ambitious, ruthless, possessed of a ferocious energy and of great organizing ability, and was perhaps very lucky at certain critical moments in his career, hardly needs demonstration; but any argument founded upon these qualities is likely to be circular since they can only be deduced from the very actions that have to be explained. It is true that his obituary in the Anglo-Saxon Chronicle, written by one who had 'looked on him and lived at his court', lays great stress on his and his followers' 'greed';[1] and though a twentieth-century writer might use less simplistic terms, there can be no doubt about the insatiable acquisitiveness of the Normans at this time. But it may be that greed or acquisitiveness and the instinct for power are common characteristics of humanity, that given the opportunity to gratify their urges men are indeed acquisitive and driven to seek the wealth that gives power. What therefore needs to be discussed is the nature of the opportunity that was given to William, his family and his followers.

In 1066 William exercised a very great authority, both within Normandy and beyond its borders, an authority which was not entirely personal. Though its roots must have lain in the tenth century, it is very difficult to show how it had developed owing to the very small amount of significant evidence that has survived from that time. Even before the conquest of England,

---

[1] A.-S.C., 1087, E (p. 164); 'and loved greediness above all'.

his power and authority in Normandy had been scarcely less than royal. The rights he asserted over forests, coinage, and castles, his power to call out the *arrière-ban* and to collect taxes of a public character have seemed to be best explained by saying that Rollo and his early successors must have taken over the powers and functions of Carolingian counts in the *pagi* or parts of *pagi* that were granted to them or which they conquered, and, since they also exercised (for example) the powers which the king would normally have had over bishoprics and monasteries, the pre-eminent rights of the Frankish monarchy there as well.[1] It has to be assumed, if this explanation is accepted, that at the beginning of the tenth century these powers were relatively intact still in the hands of the counts who administered the lands that became Normandy, and that Rollo and his successors somehow found the means to keep them intact or to recover them. Some evidence for this has indeed been found (beyond the correspondence between the later authority of the dukes in Normandy and that of a Carolingian count) in the indications that a count of Exmes was functioning in the year 900 and a count of Rouen as late as 905,[2] in the fact that the chronicler Flodoard usually (though not always) describes the cession of territory to the Northmen in terms of *pagi* or groups of *pagi*,[3] and in the fact that the *pagi* survived as local units longer in Normandy than elsewhere in northern France.[4] It is as significant perhaps that although the 'dukes' did not adopt a consistent style before the middle of the twelfth century, 'count' was their usual title at least until the time of William the Conqueror, that no other counts are known in Normandy before the end of the tenth century, and that when these do appear they were kinsmen of the duke.[5] On this argument, the origin of ducal authority

[1] Above, pp. 5–10, 238–9, and references there given; Musset, 'Que peut-on savoir de la fiscalité publique en Normandie à l'époque ducale?'.

[2] *Recueil des actes de Charles III le Simple*, Nos. xxxv (p. 75), li (p. 112); Yver, 'Premières institutions', pp. 302–6; 'Musset, 'Ruine et reconstitution d'une administration: de la Neustrie franque à la Normandie ducale'.

[3] 911 ('maritimis quibusdam pagis', Flodoard, 'Historia Remensis Ecclesiae', p. 577); 924 ('Cinomannis et Baiocae . . . concessae', Flodoard, *Annales*, p. 24); but the 'grant' of 933 is otherwise described (ibid., p. 55). Cf. above, pp. 5–10, and Lemarignier, *Hommage en marche*, pp. 15–18, where perhaps a little too much is made of the evidence for this particular purpose; Yver, 'Premières institutions', pp. 309–11.

[4] Lemarignier, 'La dislocation du "pagus" et le problème des "consuetudines"', pp. 401–2, note 4.   [5] Above, pp. 232 n. 1, 258–9.

would lie in a situation in which Rollo and his successors were counts in plurality of all the *pagi* and parts of *pagi* that made up the Normandy of the tenth and eleventh centuries, preserving or reviving, and in any case appropriating to themselves throughout their territories, the delegated authority of a Carolingian count and much of the authority of a Carolingian king.

Such a process is difficult to visualize if the Normandy of William the Conqueror is thought of as being at least as much the product of war and conquest as of legitimate royal grants in 911, 924, and 933.[1] Yet the Scandinavian settlement in Normandy can only have been really substantial in a few quite restricted areas, mostly near the coast;[2] and there were large parts of the later duchy, particularly in the centre and the south, which were hardly colonized at all by the Northmen though dominated by them, where Frankish institutions could have survived, at least in memory, and from which they could have been restored to those parts where Scandinavian settlement was more intense. Most of the Northmen, particularly those settled in the Seine Valley, seem quickly to have adopted the religion and the language of the Frankish population,[3] and Norman law when it was formed was Frankish in character with few Scandinavian elements.[4] It is possible indeed that the two contrasting views of Norman origins, that which stresses the institutional continuity with Frankish Neustria[5] and that which emphasizes the Scandinavian renewal,[6] are not totally irreconcilable; for while the direct transmission of authority from king to Viking chieftain cannot be demonstrated and is hard to vizualize, a gradual assumption of powers from those parts of the future duchy where surviving Carolingian institu-

[1] As argued in chapter 1.

[2] Musset, 'Naissance de la Normandie', pp. 101–6; Adigard des Gautries, *Les Noms de personnes scandinaves en Normandie de 911 à 1066*, pp. 262–4.

[3] Musset, 'Naissance de la Normandie', pp. 119–20. If William Longsword sent his son Richard to learn Danish at Bayeux, as the story goes (Prentout, *Étude critique sur Dudon*, pp. 311, note 1, 347), it implies that the Northmen of the Seine were losing their Scandinavian language almost within a generation of the settlement; but it should be noted that the evidence for a rapid accommodation between the Northmen and the indigenous population applies almost entirely to the eastern part of the future duchy.

[4] Above, pp. 264–5.

[5] Works of Musset, Yver, etc.

[6] De Bouard, 'De la Neustrie carolingienne à la Normandie féodale'.

tions had been disrupted least, though it cannot be demonstrated either,[1] places less strain on the imagination. Nevertheless, since power and authority were not necessarily held together in the tenth and eleventh centuries, as the kings of West Francia must have been acutely aware, to offer a theory of the origin of ducal authority does not by itself explain the Normandy of William the Conqueror. The origin and sources of ducal power have still to be sought, for only ducal power could preserve and develop a possible inheritance of Frankish authority.

Whoever was the recipient of the 'grants' of 911, 924, and 933,[2] or who it was who led the raids into Flemish, 'French', or Breton territory during the half-century following the first agreement of the Northmen with King Charles the Simple,[3] Rollo and his successors can hardly have been the only possible leaders among the Northmen of the Seine; and though they must certainly have enjoyed all the authority and pre-eminence recognized in a Viking chieftain, this must have been questioned from time to time by subordinate or fellow chieftains and certainly by the leaders of independent settlements in Normandy. That there were such independent settlements is certain. Fresh bands of Northmen arrived in 942 (Sihtric),[4] possibly in 945 (Harold),[5] certainly in 962;[6] and there is evidence of an independent colonization of the Cotentin by people of Norse descent who had come by way of the Western Isles and the Irish Sea.[7] Sometimes, as in 962, these new arrivals may have come at the 'duke's' invitation; but however they

---

[1] One slight hint of this is the existence of mysterious units that appear fleetingly as *pagi* in the north of the Cotentin (a region heavily Scandinavianized) early in the eleventh century (Yver, 'Premières institutions', pp. 310–11), for they show that the term *pagus* could be applied, in Normandy, to units which had not existed, or which had not been *pagi*, in Frankish times; and this suggests that some of the *pagi* which appear in eleventh-century documents could be revivals as much as survivals. Certainly, if an administration was to be revived it must have survived sufficiently, and sufficiently near, for this to be possible.

[2] 911, 'Nordmannis' (Flodoard, 'Historia Remensis Ecclesiae', p. 577); 'Nortmannis Sequanensibus videlicet Rolloni suisque comitibus' (Diploma of King Charles the Simple, 918; *Recueil des actes de Charles III le Simple*, no. xcii, p. 211); 924, 'Nordmanni' (Flodoard, *Annales*, p. 24); 933, 'Willelmus princeps Nordmannorum' (ibid., p. 55).

[3] Above, pp. 5–8.   [4] Lauer, *Louis IV d'Outremer*, pp. 99–100.

[5] Ibid., pp. 131–3; Prentout, *Étude critique sur Dudon*, pp. 359–63.

[6] Prentout, *Étude critique sur Dudon*, pp. 385–8. On these independent Scandinavian forces, cf. Musset, 'Naissance de la Normandie', pp. 102–3.

[7] Musset, 'Aperçus sur la colonisation scandinave dans le nord du Cotentin'.

came they would not necessarily accept the authority of a 'count of Rouen' immediately. The confused events that followed the murder of William Longsword in 942 show that there were deep divisions and several independent-minded leaders among the Northmen of the Seine, as there had been in the English Danelaw until recently; and if King Louis d'Outre-mer had been an Edward the Elder or an Æthelstan, it is likely that nothing would ever have been heard of a 'duchy of Normandy'.[1] The process by which Rollo and his dynasty overcame their rivals is almost entirely hidden from us. No doubt it was accomplished by the suppression, from time to time, of revolts like that of 934;[2] and the great rebellion that William the Conqueror crushed at Val-ès-Dunes in 1047 was both a dynastic challenge and a last gesture of independence from the country west of the Orne towards a line of 'dukes' who had hitherto lived and moved, for the most part, east of the Risle.[3]

Many things may have contributed to the triumph of the early 'dukes' over internal rivals. The reality of their authority as Viking chieftains seems to be shown by the survival of an effective power of banishment (*ullac*), which they exercised freely well into the eleventh century.[4] A succession of strong personalities among the early 'dukes', the long reign of Richard I, and the apparent absence of disputes within the ruling family during the tenth century must have helped; and in moments of great crisis, during the minority of William the Conqueror and just after, perhaps also during the minority of Richard I, such power and authority as the king of West Francia possessed seem to have been exercised in their favour.[5]

However, their most conspicuous advantage was their wealth.

---

[1] Lauer, *Louis IV d'Outremer*, pp. 130–1; Musset, 'Relations et échanges d'influences', pp. 66–7.

[2] Prentout, *Étude critique sur Dudon*, pp. 292–6.

[3] De Bouard, *Guillaume le Conquérant*, pp. 22–8. On the late integration of the far west into the duchy, below, pp. 305–6.

[4] Musset, 'Naissance de la Normandie', pp. 108, 114. This writer thinks of ducal authority from 911 to the middle of the eleventh century as having two aspects, that of a 'jarl of Rouen' and that of a Frankish count or 'super-count' ('Relations et échanges d'influences', pp. 72–3; 'Gouvernés et gouvernants', pp. 453–60); but although the two must have co-existed in some measure throughout this time, the first must have been dominant at the beginning and the second at the end of it.

[5] Douglas, 'Rise of Normandy', pp. 109–10; *William the Conqueror*, pp. 44–51; Prentout, *Étude critique sur Dudon*, pp. 346–67.

The conditions created by the raiding and settlement, and the fighting that went on in and around Normandy during the first half of the tenth century enabled Rollo and his early successors to possess themselves of an enormous accumulation of land and treasure.[1] Whenever they can be traced, the ancient *fisci* and *villae regales* reappear in the hands of the duke, suggesting that in the territories granted to or seized by the Normans the royal lands were taken over by him, or at least passed through his hands. None of the Frankish monasteries in the territories that became Normandy has a continuous history through the troubles of the ninth and early tenth centuries, save perhaps Mont-Saint-Michel; and when the restoration of monastic life began in Normandy all the foundations and re-foundations that were made until the 1030s were made by the duke or members of his family, as if only they were in a position to do this at that time. In some cases, indeed, it can be shown that lands given to Norman monasteries in the tenth and eleventh centuries had formerly belonged to Frankish churches, suggesting that their properties also had come into the hands of Rollo and his successors.[2] Nor is it at all unlikely that they had profited by the long gaps that appear in the succession of bishops in the Norman dioceses, apart from Rouen, during the ninth and tenth centuries,[3] or that they had taken lands belonging to Frankish landowners who had perished or who had fled the country.[4] No doubt some of the vast landed wealth which the early 'dukes' acquired in this way had to be shared

[1] Cf. Musset, 'Naissance de la Normandie', pp. 107–8, 118–19.

[2] Musset, 'Les domaines de l'époque franque', pp. 42–52; 'Les destins de la propriété monastique'; 'Ruine et reconstitution d'une administration: de la Neustrie franque à la Normandie ducale'; 'Les premiers temps de l'abbaye d'Almenèches'; Douglas, *William the Conqueror*, pp. 109–10. Not all the destruction of churches was the work of the Northmen. Saint Évroult seems to have survived until attacked by troops of Hugh the Great, Duke of the Franks, in the 940s (Orderic Vitalis, *H.E.* (ed. Le Prévost), iii. 89–99; (ed. Chibnall), iii, pp. xvii–xviii, 308–18). For Mont-Saint-Michel, Hourlier, 'Le Mont-Saint-Michel avant 966'.

[3] Above, p. 12. A continuous succession at Évreux seems just possible but unlikely (*Gallia Christiana*, xi. col. 570). There may also have been a continuous succession of bishops of Coutances, but they resided at Rouen for over a century (Le Patourel, 'Geoffrey of Montbray', pp. 134–5).

[4] For the destruction of the higher ranks of the Frankish aristocracy in the territory that became Normandy, Yver, 'Premières institutions', pp. 306–7; Musset, 'Naissance de la Normandie', pp. 100, 122; but there seems to be no more than general probability that any considerable part of their property came into the hands of the dukes.

with companions in arms and subordinate or allied leaders. Dudo de Saint-Quentin says specifically that this was done;[1] but we may be sure that the lion's share remained to the ducal family, as a similar share of the portable loot must have done[2]— and all this in addition to the profits of justice and the taxes and tolls which the dukes were able to levy, in large part as successors to Frankish royalty.[3]

This exceptional wealth of the Norman dukes was of great importance when a feudal aristocracy began to develop in the duchy. As Normandy turned away from its remaining ties with Scandinavia and took its place among the territorial principalities of Western Francia,[4] it was inevitable that some form of feudal society would develop there as elsewhere; but his landed wealth presented the ruler of Normandy with opportunities which came to few contemporary princes. It has recently been argued that the Norman aristocracy of 1066 was largely composed of 'new men', men whose families had risen to prominence in at most two or three generations.[5] In fact the ancestry of few families of this aristocracy can be traced beyond the year 1000.[6] This, it is true, could be due to lack of surviving evidence, for Norman documents of the tenth century are certainly not plentiful; but there are some positive indications from the eleventh century that these families were indeed 'new'. Some had come from neighbouring lands, especially Brittany,[7] and from further afield, even Germany;[8] and since these 'immi-

---

[1] 'Securitatem omnibus gentibus in sua terra manere cupientibus fecit [Rollo]. Illam terram suis fidelibus funiculo divisit . . ., atque de suis militibus advenisque gentibus refertam restruxit'; Dudo, *De Moribus*, p. 171; cf. Musset, 'Les Domaines de l'époque franque', pp. 10–12.

[2] A danegeld was levied in France in 924 and again in 926: Joranson, *Danegeld in France*, pp. 163–74.

[3] Yver, 'Premières institutions', pp. 337–63.   [4] Above, pp. 13–14.

[5] On the 'new aristocracy' in Normandy, Douglas, 'Rise of Normandy', pp. 115–20; *William the Conqueror*, pp. 84–104; Musset, 'Aux origines de la féodalité normande'; 'Observations sur la classe aristocratique normande au XIe siècle'; 'Naissance de la Normandie', pp. 122–4.

[6] Two very rare exceptions are Tosny (Douglas, *William the Conqueror*, pp. 85–6; Musset, 'Naissance de la Normandie', *Documents*, pp. 90–4; and Bellême (White, 'The First House of Bellême'). But both originated beyond the bounds of Normandy.

[7] Musset, 'Aux origines de la féodalité normande'. For the family of Giroy as an example, Orderic Vitalis, *H.E.* (ed. Le Prévost), ii. 22; (ed. Chibnall), ii. 22.

[8] e.g. Baldric 'the German' and Viger his brother who came to Normandy to serve Duke Richard founded a family and received great possessions (Orderic Vitalis, *H.E.* (ed. Le Prévost), ii. 75–7; (ed. Chibnall), ii. 82–4).

grants' had become vassals of the duke, he must have accepted them and they may even have come at his invitation. Some others seem to have owed their advancement to personal service rendered to him;[1] but many of the most distinguished claimed kinship with him.[2] Of these last the highest in rank were those who bore the title of count, a small inner group, partly noble, partly official, which also first appeared about the year 1000.[3]

The evidence may not be quite sufficient, perhaps, to say positively that this new aristocracy had been deliberately created by the duke, to form a military élite attached to him personally and to provide a force which would enable him to control the lands he ruled, to beat down rivals at home and hold his own with neighbouring princes; but there are strong indications that this was so to a very large extent.[4] That so many of its members claimed kinship and that some others seem to have been brought in from beyond the bounds of the duchy already suggests this; but it can also be shown that some were endowed, at least in part, from the ducal domain, that is from ducal wealth;[5] and when a family enriched itself, as some clearly did, at the expense of churches founded or refounded by the ducal family, this cannot always have been without the duke's knowledge and consent.[6] The duke himself seems to have felt free to take land from the church to support his lay following, certainly until the middle of the eleventh century,[7] as he could take lands from those who proved unfaithful and give it to others whom he could trust.[8] At all events, if the military aristocracy in Normandy at the time of the conquest of England, a small and

---

[1] e.g. Warenne, Montgomery, fitzOsbern (Le Patourel, *Norman Barons*, pp. 5–7, 9, 17–18).

[2] Below, pp. 335–6.   [3] Above, pp. 258–9.

[4] Cf. Douglas, *William the Conqueror*, pp. 98–100, 137–8; Musset, 'Naissance de la Normandie', pp. 123–4.

[5] Douglas, *William the Conqueror*, pp. 89–90. The ducal domain, it is true, may well have suffered from the depredations of the magnates at times of political difficulty, as at Duke Robert's accession or during the minority of William the Conqueror (ibid., pp. 32, 39–40); but this would hardly account for all the ducal domain that came into their hands during the first half of the eleventh century.

[6] Douglas, ibid., pp. 90–1.

[7] Musset, 'Une nouvelle charte de Robert le Magnifique pour Fécamp', pp. 145–50. William the Conqueror gave (or restored) to Ranulf fitzAnquetil (*vicomte* of Bayeux) the half of Guernsey which his father, Duke Robert, had given to Mont-Saint-Michel (Fauroux, *Recueil*, Nos. 73, 111, pp. 212, 272).

[8] As at the beginning of the career of William I de Warenne (Douglas, *William the Conqueror*, pp. 99–100).

closely interrelated group,[1] was not entirely the creation of the duke, it almost certainly was so to a greater extent than the similar aristocracies of neighbouring principalities were the creation of their rulers; it owed its wealth and its prospects largely to him and it was entirely at his service.

In all the *comtés* and groups of *comtés* that were being hammered into territorial principalities during the eleventh century, the ruler had to have a body of *fideles* who would provide at least the nucleus of the armed force he would need to maintain and extend his authority. For this purpose he not only had to have a reputation for fearless and profitable leadership;[2] he had to have an almost inexhaustible supply of land and treasure with which to keep the loyalty of his vassals and add to their number,[3] for in practice his following could only be maintained by endowing its members with land on a tenure that was normally if not yet rigidly hereditary. For this purpose, no amount of land that a ruler might have at his disposal would last for ever, and sooner or later he would be driven to resuming lands within his own territories, or attempting to do so,[4] and looking beyond them for more. Thus counts and dukes were in competition with one another both for territories and for the vassals with which to secure and hold them. In this way the count of Anjou and the duke of Normandy were rivals for control of the intervening *comté* of Maine; at the least, neither could allow the other to establish a firm suzerainty over the chief landowners there or in the adjacent parts of Brittany. Hence the reaction which the gradual

---

[1] Below, pp. 335–8.

[2] William's invasion army in 1066 is a good example of the attractive power of competent leadership and the prospect of gain. Orderic Vitalis described him as one 'whom the divine hand protected' (*H.E.* (ed. Le Prévost), ii. 103–4; (ed. Chibnall), ii. 118). Cf. his remarks on William Rufus's campaign in Maine: 'Franci ergo et Burgundiones, Morini et Britones, aliaeque vicinae gentes ad liberalem patricium concurrerunt et phalanges ejus multipliciter auxerunt' (ed. Le Prévost, iv. 45).

[3] e.g. the complaint of Robert Curthose to his father, as reported by Orderic Vitalis: 'Aliquando rem familiarem volo habere, ut mihi famulantibus digna possim stipendia retribuere' (*H.E.* (ed. Le Prévost), ii. 378; (ed. Chibnall), iii. 98).

[4] e.g. after the revolt of 1047, Duke William confiscated the lands both of Nigel de Saint-Sauveur, *vicomte* of the Cotentin, and of Ranulf fitzAnquetil, *vicomte* of Bayeux; and Nigel, certainly, spent some years in exile; but both recovered their estates and honours, or the greater part of them. On Saint-Sauveur, Delisle, *Histoire du château de Saint-Sauveur-le-Vicomte*, pp. 19–21; and for Ranulf, Douglas, *William the Conqueror*, p. 93.

fastening of the suzerainty of the count of Anjou over Maine produced in Normandy,[1] and William's interest in building up a clientage among the barons of eastern Brittany as an answer to the efforts of the counts of Anjou and of Blois to dominate the *comtés* of Nantes and of Rennes.[2]

In this universal competition of the proto-feudal world, the Norman dukes had a clear advantage. For in the countries bordering on Normandy to the south, and elsewhere, men in the higher ranks of the aristocracy could generally trace their ancestry to the great families of Carolingian times and their local powers and authority to the continuance or usurpation of functions derived from Carolingian administration—or so it is now thought. They were in fact the slightly less successful members of the same class as the counts themselves, who therefore had to compete with them for vassals and ultimately bend them to their authority (in practice bring them into their vassalage and make that relationship effective) as well as competing with one another in the process of creating princi-palities out of Carolingian counties. Whatever the dukes of Normandy had managed to carry over or revive of Carolingian powers and authority, they did not have this particular dis-advantage of a Carolingian inheritance to face; for it seems that the upper ranks of the Frankish aristocracy in the land that became Normandy had been substantially destroyed or driven out at the time of the Viking raids and settlement.[3] Since so many of the greater Norman barons of the mid eleventh century claimed kinship (real or supposed) with the duke, it is clear that he, and not ancient lineage, was the source of honour and 'nobility' in the duchy. For all the internal troubles that the dukes did have to face, there was less fundamental conflict of interest between them and their aristocracy than between count and barons in neighbouring principalities.[4]

The competitiveness of the duke and neighbouring rulers was

---

[1] Above, pp. 17–18.   [2] Above, p. 92.   [3] Above, p. 285.

[4] The idea which this paragraph tries to express is based on G. Duby, 'Une enquête à poursuivre: la noblesse dans la France médiévale', and Boussard, 'L'origine des familles seigneuriales dans la région de la Loire moyenne'. The difference between Normandy and its neighbours in this respect clearly needs further investigation. For a survey of the literature on the question whether or to what extent the nobility of the later eleventh and twelfth centuries in Western Francia generally owed its power and authority ultimately to a commission of 'public' authority in Carolingian times, Guillot, *Le Comte d'Anjou*, i., introduction.

reproduced in the lower levels of what was rapidly becoming a feudal hierarchy. As each baronial dynasty built up its estates it began to form its own clientage in competition with its neighbours,[1] since some form of 'subinfeudation' was often the only practicable method of exploiting extensive lands; and under the conditions of the eleventh century a body of military vassals was as necessary to a baron at his level as it was to the duke at his. For this, a family would not only strive to add to its properties by marriage, purchase, and violence; it would look to the duke for support and favour as well as for leadership in profitable enterprises, involving its interests and ambitions with his. Such an aristocratic society was not yet feudal in the sense in which that word could be used of twelfth-century conditions,[2] but it was by its nature competitive, acquisitive, and aggressive. There could be no stability, for a position could only be held by further expansion. Thus the domination of neighbouring lands was part of the same process as the formation of a military aristocracy in Normandy, which was itself a big part in the process which was creating a territorial principality of the eleventh-century kind out of the Viking robber-state of the century before.

Thus one source, perhaps the main source, of the dynamic that produced Henry's great complex of lands and lordships was the pressures created by feudalism in the early stages of its development. Because of their wealth and because of other conditions created by the Viking settlement in Normandy, the Norman dukes of the eleventh century were in an unusually favourable position to exploit those pressures in their own interest, and each conquest improved that position. For them and their royal successors this meant not only the conquest of the 'kingdom of the English' but the assertion of claims to lordship over the Welsh and the Scots and the conversion of those claims into feudal form and language. This would lead on to an attempted conquest of Ireland which William the Conqueror himself is said to have considered.[3] It meant that the

---

[1] Douglas, *William the Conqueror*, pp. 95–7.

[2] Haskins argued that systematic feudalism already existed in Normandy in 1066 (*Norman Institutions*, pp. 5 ff.). This view has been criticized by Strayer ('On the Early Norman Charters', pp. 40–3), Douglas (*William the Conqueror*, pp. 96–104), Musset ('Naissance de la Normandie', pp. 123–5), etc.

[3] A.-S.C., 1087, E (p. 164); cf. Southern, *Saint Anselm and his Biographer*, pp. 133–5.

overlordships already established on the Continent must be defended at the least, intensified and extended where possible. In the *comté* of Maine and in the Vexin it had to be defended; in Brittany, Boulogne, and even in Flanders it could be intensified; along the southern frontier of Normandy it could be extended. William Rufus is said to have planned to acquire Aquitaine by the same means as he had acquired Normandy and to have aspired to the throne of France;[1] while Henry, by marrying his daughter and heiress to the heir of the county of Anjou, was preparing the way, as he would have seen it, for the absorption into the Norman complex of all the lands and lordships that the counts of Anjou had been accumulating. Personal ambition and response to social and political pressures clearly pointed in the same direction.

The working of these pressures can also be seen in the way that William and his successors treated the conquered kingdom of England. Notwithstanding his claim to be the lawful successor of Edward the Confessor, William seems to have joined in the plundering of the moveable wealth of England during the early years after Hastings, if he did not lead it. Treasure was urgently needed to pay mercenaries, to reward allies who did not wish to accept grants of land in England, to refill coffers that must have been seriously depleted by the expense of mounting the campaign, to repay spiritual debts to Norman churches which had prayed for a divine blessing on his enterprise, and to provide the display which his royal dignity demanded. Most of his vassals and fellow conquistadors, however, must have expected something more than treasure, and to the lands they had inherited or lately acquired in Normandy were added extensive lands in England so that, from the king's point of view, they might enlarge the services they could render, now in England as well as in Normandy; while many who had had small landed possessions or none in Normandy before 1066 now entered the ranks of the Norman military aristocracy by accepting fiefs in England. In this respect the effect of the Conquest was to enlarge William's vassalage

---

[1] Orderic Vitalis, *H.E.* (ed. Le Prévost), iv. 80; Suger, *Vita Ludovici Grossi Regis*, pp. 10–12. Odo of Bayeux, his uncle, is said to have thought of making a bid for the papacy (Orderic Vitalis, *H.E.* (ed. Le Prévost), iii. 188–90; (ed. Chibnall), iv. 38–40).

enormously; and if it increased his military commitment, it certainly increased his military potential. For the time at least it put him way ahead of his immediate rivals.

At their level the Norman baronial families were as ambitious as the Norman dukes and kings. In a few cases the build-up of a great Normanno-English baronial estate can be traced to what seem to be its beginnings in Normandy and followed in its extension to England and beyond, and the various elements in the rise of these families observed. This can be done particularly well in the case of the Montgomery family,[1] whose first traceable member, Roger I, laid the foundations of its fortunes by marrying into the ducal family and by holding ducal office as *vicomte* of the Hiémois. Whether his tenure of this office was cause or effect, it is certainly connected with his acquisition of lands in that region which had belonged to destroyed monasteries, lands which the duke probably had in his custody if not in his possession, as well as lands belonging to the ducal monasteries of Bernay, Jumièges, and Fécamp, adding them to the estate from which he took his name. His son, Roger II, third in order of birth though the eldest son to survive, succeeded to his lands and, after a few years, to the *vicomté*. He first appears as a young man, with William fitzOsbern, in the army that Duke William took to Domfront and Alençon in 1051-2,[2] and clearly in the duke's most intimate confidence. The family property was eventually enormously increased by his marriage to Mabel de Bellême who brought the huge inheritance of her family in 'France', Maine, and Normandy.[3] Though his service in 1066 consisted in assisting the Duchess Matilda in her custody of Normandy during her lord's absence rather than in the army that went to England, he was one of the first to secure large properties across the Channel, Arundel and Chichester

    [1] Musset, 'Une nouvelle charte de Robert le Magnifique pour Fécamp', pp. 146–9; 'Les premiers temps de l'abbaye d'Almenèches', pp. 19–29; 'Les Fiefs de deux familles vicomtales de l'Hiémois au xie siècle, Les Goz et les Montgommery'; *Complete Peerage*, xi. 682–97; Mason, 'Roger de Montgomery and his sons (1067–1102)'; Douglas, *William the Conqueror*, pp. 91–5, 98–9, etc.; Lloyd, *History of Wales*, ii. 388–90, 400–14; Brunel, *Recueil des actes des comtes de Pontieu* pp. iv–v.
    [2] William de Poitiers, *Gesta*, pp. 38–40. For the date, Douglas, *William the Conqueror*, pp. 383–90.
    [3] White, 'The First House of Bellême'; Boussard, 'La seigneurie de Bellême aux xe et xie siècles'.

most probably in 1067, and the lands of the earldom of Shropshire in 1071. On these last he is known to have settled men who were already his vassals for lands in Normandy, and with them he and his sons were able to extend their possessions by conquest far into Wales. All this, apart from some of the Welsh lands, descended eventually to Roger's eldest son Robert de Bellême (so called, no doubt, because he had succeeded to his mother's lands when she died some fifteen years before his father); and he, not satisfied with this, added the *comté* of Pontieu in France by marriage and the great honour of Tickhill-Blyth in England by buying the king's recognition of a rather remote claim. Such possessions, stretching from the Somme Estuary, through southern Normandy and the adjacent lands beyond the frontier, through southern and midland England into Wales, could not be held without the service of many trustworthy vassals and must have induced an enormous sense of power. His brother Arnulf, who held much of modern Pembrokeshire together with Holderness in Yorkshire, even had visions of a kingdom in Ireland.[1] It is true that this vast accumulation proved ephemeral owing to a political miscalculation on the part of Robert de Bellême; but the rise of the family from quite small beginnings, so far as we know, to such wealth and power in the space of some sixty years shows what was possible in Norman society during the eleventh century.

Similar 'family biographies' could be compiled[2] for Warenne,[3] 'Beaumont',[4] Montfort (sur Risle),[5] Tosny,[6] the families of

[1] For his marriage to a daughter of Muircartach, 'king of Ireland', *Brut y Tywysogion, Peniarth MS. 20, Translation*, p. 24.

[2] In general, Douglas, *William the Conqueror*, chs. 4 and 11; Le Patourel, *Norman Barons*.

[3] Loyd, 'The Origin of the Family of Warenne'; *E.Y.C.*, viii (*Honour of Warenne*), 1–13 and *passim*; *Complete Peerage*, ix, App., pp. 3–7; xii (1), 491–7.

[4] Douglas, *William the Conbueror*, pp. 86–7 etc.; *Complete Peerage*, ii. 68–9; vii. 520–30, 737–8; xii (2), 357–62, 829–37, App. pp. 2–6; Houth, 'Galeran II, comte de Meulan'; White, 'King Stephen's Earldoms', pp. 56–72 and 'The Career of Waleran, Count of Meulan and Earl of Worcester (1104–66)'.

[5] Douglas, *William the Conqueror*, pp. 88, 291, etc.; *Domesday Monachorum*, pp. 65–70; *Complete Peerage*, ix. 120.

[6] Douglas, *William the Conqueror*, pp. 85–6, 88, 95–6, 270; *Complete Peerage*, xii (1), 168–9, 753–64. The progress of this family is also described by Musset in 'Naissance de la Normandie', *Documents*, pp. 90–4, but it seems that the Berengar who was tenant-in-chief in Yorkshire, Leicestershire (Belvoir), etc. at the time of Domesday belonged to a junior branch of the family and was not a brother of Ralph 'of Flamstead' and Robert 'of Stafford' (Ellis, 'Biographical Notes', *Y.A.J.*,

William fitzOsbern,[1] of the earls of Chester,[2] and many others. They would show how origin within the ducal family itself or kinship with it, personal service to the duke in a military or official capacity, enterprise and good fortune and no doubt a personal compatibility with the ruling duke, the opportunities which the internal condition of Normandy in the early eleventh century offered, and the working of the principle that wealth begets wealth[3] enabled the more successful to build up an accumulation of lands and lordships which, if they could have been concentrated, would have amounted to a principality and might take a family to the verge of royalty.[4] They would show how Duke William and his immediate predecessors were able to harness the energy and the ambition of this new aristocracy to their own, and how ambition grew with the enlargement of Norman dominion which their leadership and vigour achieved, from Normandy to England and from England into Wales and Scotland;[5] while those from France beyond the duchy who

iv, 135–7; Clay, *Early Yorkshire Families*, pp. 20–1 (s.v. 'Clere'); *Manuscripts of the Duke of Rutland at Belvoir Castle*, iv. 106).

[1] *Complete Peerage*, vi. 447–51; vii. 529–30; Douglas, 'The Ancestors of William fitzOsbern'; Wightman, 'The Palatine Earldom of William fitzOsbern'; Round, *Studies in Peerage*, pp. 181–206; and, for William de Breteuil, David, *Robert Curthose*, pp. 144–5, etc.

[2] Musset, 'Les plus anciennes chartes du prieuré de Saint-Gabriel', pp. 124–9; 'Les origines et le patrimoine de l'abbaye de Saint-Sever'; 'Naissance de la Normandie', *Documents*, pp. 94–8; *Complete Peerage*, iii. 164–7; Barraclough, 'The Earldom and County Palatine of Chester', pp. 25–33. The estates of this family like those of Montgomery can be traced to small beginnings in Normandy and shown spreading across the duchy before they spread likewise across England and Wales. They dispel once and for all any idea that William the Conqueror can have had any conscious policy of dispersing the lands of his tenants-in-chief. Such estates grew bit by bit as opportunity presented itself. They were dispersed already in Normandy before 1066; and the larger Anglo-Saxon estates which the Normans took over were often themselves dispersed.

[3] Perhaps only a Robert de Bellême could offer the sums which would induce William Rufus to sanction his succession to the vast lands of his deceased younger brother and his remote kinsman Roger de Bully, and only a family such as his could establish the monasteries, *bourgs*, boroughs, and markets from which the cash could be obtained.

[4] Besides Arnulf de Montgomery, lord of Pembroke and Holderness, who aspired to a kingdom in Ireland, William II de Warenne first tried to marry Edith (Matilda), daughter of the king of Scots and eventually King Henry I's queen, then an illegitimate daughter of King Henry himself, and ultimately married Isobel, widow of Robert 'de Beaumont' and granddaughter of King Henry I of France.

[5] e.g. the Montgomery build-up outlined above. Gilbert fitzRichard (de Clare) added Ceredigion to his lands in Kent and East Anglia; his second son Gilbert, who inherited the Norman lands of his uncle Walter, received the rape of Pevensey

acquired lands in Normandy or in England might carry Norman influence and interests back to their own lands.[1] Duke or king could not survive, still less advance, without the co-operation of his *fideles*, vassals or barons (as the nomenclature and to some extent the relationship changed), while they for their part had everything to gain from loyalty to a leader as long as he was competent and enterprising. The fate of families which were destroyed or reduced for disloyalty[2] would have made this as plain then as it is now, for there must always have been men ready to fall on a fellow baron who had incurred the king's enmity. Duke, king, and barons had embarked upon a vast joint enterprise for the increase of their wealth, their power, and their position in the world. Even the manner of their living must have been so similar as to be indistinguishable, apart from the manifestations of royalty. Although it would be difficult to write anything that could be regarded as a biography of a lay member of the aristocracy at this time, it is clear that such men, dividing their time between the king's affairs and their own, found themselves involved as much in a life of continual movement as he was, and for much the same reasons.[3]

and the earldom of Pembroke from King Stephen, and this younger Gilbert's son Richard ('Strongbow') momentarily added a kingdom in Ireland, won with the aid of his vassals in South Wales (*Complete Peerage*, iii. 242–4; vi. 498–501; x. 348–57; Ward, 'The Estates of the Clare Family, 1066–1317'). Robert fitzHamon held lands in Normandy and England before he took possession of Morgannwg (Nelson, *Normans in South Wales*, pp. 94–101). Although it is hard at present to be specific, it seems most likely that families like Brus, Moreville, and de Sules still retained interests in France in addition to their broad lands in England when they accepted fiefs in southern Scotland (above, pp. 11–12).

[1] e.g. the counts of Boulogne, the Montfort l'Amaury and Bellême families, the counts of Brittany/earls of Richmond, etc.

[2] e.g. fitzOsbern, de Gael, Montgomery, Grandmesnil, etc.; Davis, 'What happened in Stephen's reign', pp. 6–7, for examples.

[3] William II de Warenne, second earl of Surrey, is a good example. Little is known of his early life or his immediate reaction to the accession of Henry Beau-clerc to the throne of England in 1100; but he supported Robert Curthose when the issue of the succession was raised and declared for him when he invaded England in July 1101. After the 'Treaty of Alton' he was in attendance on the king (September), though he crossed to Normandy with Robert later in the autumn and apparently stayed there until 1103 when he was reconciled with Henry on Robert's intercession, and recovered his English lands. Thereafter he was loyal to Henry. He commanded a division in Henry's army at Tinchebrai and may therefore have been in attendance on him through much of his stay in Normandy during 1106–7, presumably securing his Norman lands at the same time. He seems to have been in England for the next three or four years, but thereafter there is every indication that he was in Normandy at some time in all the periods that the king spent in the

Such a society had the instincts and the outlook of men who had found riches and power very quickly, reinforced perhaps by the general development of patrimonial succession and dynastic sentiment. Some of its members could indeed boast two or three generations of wealth and consequence in Normandy, but no more than that, and they were few. More characteristic were men like William I de Warenne who, from being the younger son of a comfortable though by no means outstandingly wealthy father in Normandy, acquired enormous possessions on both sides of the Channel; or the Lacy brothers, whose original lands in Normandy may not have been negligible but certainly bore no relation as to size and value with the vast estates they held in the north and west of England at the time of Domesday.[1] Even under Henry Beauclerc, Orderic could still speak scornfully of some of the most powerful men of his day as 'raised from the dust'.[2] Men who had had the opportunity to rise so quickly would feel, if they thought about it, that there was no limit to the heights which they and their families might attain. They would take lands wherever they might be situated, hoping that a remote possession might grow into a new centre of power and influence or, if this did not happen, could at least be traded for others that seemed more promising. There must have been a continual jostling of pressure-groups in the king's court, ready at any moment to put in a claim or a bribe to secure lands or treasure taken in a campaign or in the suppression of a rebellion or confiscated more or less judicially.

Moreover, the aggressiveness of this Norman lay society and

duchy (1111–13, 1114–15, 1116–20, 1123–6, 1127–9, 1130–1, 1133–5) and in England likewise during the intervening periods. Naturally it is impossible to say that the distribution of his time between England and Normandy corresponded exactly with that of the king, or what proportion of each period he spent at court in either country; but from 1111–35 he made at least as many transfretations as the king, and charters of his survive relating both to his Norman and to his English lands. He was in attendance at Henry's death-bed at Lyons-la-Forêt in 1135, attended 'councils' at Nottingham (1109) and Northampton (1131), commanded a division at the battle of Brémule (1119), and on Henry's death was put in charge of Rouen and the Pays de Caux by the baronial council which governed Normandy for the time being. Nevertheless he was soon back in England after Stephen's coronation and attended the Easter court of 1136. He died probably in May 1138 (*E.Y.C.*, viii (*Honour of Warenne*), 7–10, 62–81; *Complete Peerage*, xii (1), 495–6; *Regesta*, ii, iii, *passim*. Cf. above, pp. 190–5.

[1] Wightman, *Lacy Family*, chs. 1, 4, 7, and 8.
[2] Orderic Vitalis, *H.E.* (ed. Le Prévost), iv. 164–7.

its leaders was supported, perhaps even encouraged, by the Church in Normandy.[1] There is an extraordinarily close parallel between the ecclesiastical regeneration of Normandy before 1066 and the formation of the Norman military aristocracy. The Church as well as the aristocracy was 'new' in 1066. The destruction of the Frankish monasteries in the lands that were to be Normandy and the gaps in the succession of bishops were such that all was to be built up anew, diocesan organization as well as monastic life; and the best part of a century elapsed after the settlement of the Northmen in the Seine Valley before that reconstruction could be said to be under way.

As far as the monasteries were concerned, those that were set going before William the Conqueror's accession in 1035 (Saint-Ouen, Jumièges, Fontanelles-Saint-Wandrille, Mont-Saint-Michel, Fécamp, Bernay, Cérisy, Montivilliers, Sainte-Trinité-de-Rouen, and Sainte-Amand-de-Rouen) owed the impetus of their foundation or refoundation to the ducal family and all, or nearly all, of their material endowment as well. After that date the Norman aristocracy took a hand in the founding and refounding of monasteries, and once started went into it with enthusiasm. It is from this time, or a little before, that the monastic movement in Normandy took on its characteristic features. In the thirty years or so between 1035 and 1066 no less than twenty-five monasteries and nunneries and at least half a dozen colleges of secular canons were founded or refounded in the duchy, all the monasteries save the two great foundations at Caen and all the colleges save Cherbourg by baronial families.[2] It was a prodigious effort, made the more remarkable by the fact that the two western dioceses were still hardly touched before 1066, so that the territory immediately involved was a good deal less than the whole of the duchy. While there is evidence that some lands of the destroyed Frankish monasteries found their way back to their successors of the

---

[1] What follows on the part of the Church in the Norman dynamic is almost entirely derived from Knowles, *Monastic Order*, ch. v and App. v; Douglas, 'The Norman Episcopate before the Norman Conquest', and *William the Conqueror*, ch. 5 —though these writers might not always approve of the emphasis laid upon certain aspects of it here.

[2] On the secular colleges, Musset, 'Recherches sur les communautés de clercs séculiers'. An average of at least one religious community founded each year over thirty years in a country the size of Normandy is certainly remarkable.

eleventh century,[1] this can have been no more than a small proportion of the total required to support the new and revived establishments; and it is hardly surprising that the men who acquired great possessions in England generally thought of the monasteries struggling into existence back home before considering the foundation of new monasteries on their newly acquired lands across the Channel, or that the Norman monasteries themselves should welcome gifts which might be as difficult to exploit as they were far away.[2] It may even have been becoming hard to find lands to support new monasteries in some parts of Normandy at the time. One quite important element in the Norman colonization of England, therefore, the lands and churches acquired by Norman cathedrals and monasteries,[3] owed something to the 'newness' of the monastic establishment in Normandy at the time of the Conquest.

It may well be that a genuine religious enthusiasm was the chief conscious motive of the Norman aristocracy in producing this extraordinary spate of monastic foundations, but this was not incompatible with some more material advantages that were to be gained from it. There can be no doubt that flourishing monasteries conferred prestige upon their founders and patrons, among whom there would certainly be an element of competition in this activity,[4] an emulation which would not be discouraged by the monks themselves. Thus Humphrey de Vieilles had founded a monastery and a nunnery at Préaux, William fitzOsbern two monasteries (Cormeilles and Lire), and Roger de Montgomery no less than three houses (Saint-Martin-de-Séez, Saint-Martin-de-Troarn, Almenèches) before they and their successors were able to continue the good work in England. Many of the transfers of property which, in the surviving documents, look like free gifts, were in fact sales; and both this and the functions which the monasteries gradually developed as safe deposits and sources of credit[5] enabled many

[1] Above, p. 304 n. 2.

[2] Above, pp. 37–8, 44–5; cf. Malmesbury, *Gesta Regum*, ii. 334.

[3] The colleges, already going out of fashion, characteristically obtained very little in this way: Musset, 'Recherches sur les communautés de clercs séculiers', pp. 16–19, 23.

[4] e.g. Orderic Vitalis, *H.E.* (ed. Le Prévost), ii. 11–12; (ed. Chibnall), ii. 10; quoted by Douglas, *William the Conqueror*, p. 112.

[5] Delisle, *Études sur la classe agricole en Normandie*, pp. 195–219; Génestal, *Rôle des monastères comme établissements de crédit*, pp. 1–86; Musset, 'La vie économique de

a baron to turn a part of his landed wealth into cash when that was needed for military purposes, or to secure a succession, to round off or extend existing possessions, or finance a pilgrimage or crusade, as well as providing him with spiritual services and hospitality. The foundation of churches might also serve to establish or strengthen an interest in some desirable locality.[1] The monastic movement of the mid eleventh century in Normandy thus contributed to the rise of the military aristocracy as well as benefiting from it. The two were certainly completely bound up together, the monasteries, like the bishops, being involved even in the military organization of the duchy.[2]

Yet, though material resources were a condition precedent to any monastic development, endowments were far from being all that the revived and the new monasteries of Normandy needed. There being no ecclesiastical tradition in the country after the Viking settlement, ideas of monastic observance and ritual, of the plan and character of monastic buildings, all had to be sought abroad; and here again it was the duke who took the initiative. The communities which recolonized ancient sites in the tenth century came from Flanders and brought customs ultimately derived from Lotharingia; but these early revivals (few, in any case) showed little vigour. It was not until Duke Richard II's insistence brought William da Volpiano from Dijon in 1001 to the ducal foundation at Fécamp that Normandy found its real monastic inspiration. This was derived from Cluny, but with differences that may perhaps be traced to St. William's own intellect and character—notably an interest in learning and education rather than the ceaseless ritual of Cluny itself. Manuscripts were imported to be copied and to lay the foundations of libraries, some of them coming from

l'abbaye de Fécamp sous l'abbatiat de Jean de Ravenne', pp. 69–76. William of Malmesbury praised Earl Robert of Gloucester for not exploiting his foundation at Tewkesbury and indicated that his restraint was exceptional at the time (Malmesbury, *Gesta Regum*, ii. 520).

[1] Chibnall, 'Ecclesiastical Patronage and the Growth of Feudal Estates at the Time of the Norman Conquest'. For further examples and qualifications, Yver, 'Autour de l'absence d'avouerie en Normandie', pp. 201–13.

[2] Haskins, *Norman Institutions*, pp. 8–22. But cf. Douglas, *William the Conqueror*, pp. 101–4, and Strayer, 'On the Early Norman Charters', pp. 41–2. Even if knight service was not so fully organized in Normandy before 1066 as Haskins thought, it seems that 'contractual military service had been imposed on all the older Norman monasteries and on most if not all the Norman bishops' (Douglas).

England;[1] the plans and the style of the buildings must have come, like the rules of observance, ultimately from Cluny.[2]

Since so many new monasteries were being founded in such quick succession on so restricted a territory, and since each foundation drew its customs, its first abbot, and often a nucleus of monks from an existing house in the duchy, they naturally acquired the sense of forming a distinct group among the monasteries of western Christendom; and their intimate relationship with the duke and the aristocracy led to ready identification with the duchy.[3] To the enthusiasm and the headlong expansion of this group was added the brilliance of Le Bec. The fortunate chance which produced a Herluin, and the original variation on the monastic practices of the time that he was able to work out such as would attract the teaching and the organizing ability of a Lanfranc[4] and the intellect and the deep spirituality of an Anselm, gave to the Norman monks a feeling of distinction and a sense of mission that associated easily with the ambitions of the duke and the aristocracy.

The reconstruction of diocesan organization was slower, more traditional, and shows no such spectacular leap forward as the monasteries made between about 1035 and 1065. It is likely that the duke had had a part in the re-establishment of the bishoprics analogous to that which he played in setting the monasteries going again, though this cannot be demonstrated. By 990 all seven bishoprics had bishops, though the bishops of Coutances still resided at Rouen and did little, if anything, in what had been their diocese. A suggestion of ducal initiative is contained

---

[1] Above, pp. 23 n. 6, 250–2.

[2] Clapham, *Romanesque Architecture in Western Europe*, pp. 138–40. The partly restored abbey church at Bernay, one of the earliest of such buildings to survive in Normandy, seems to the non-technical eye to owe a great deal to Cluniac inspiration.

[3] Musset notes a tendency of the Norman monasteries, from the beginning of the eleventh century until the conquest of England, to accept endowments only within the duchy; whereas before the end of the tenth century, both before and after the destructions of the Viking wars, the monasteries on what came to be the land of Normandy had possessed estates in almost all parts of Gaul: 'Les destins de la propriété monastique durant les invasions normandes'; cf. Yver, 'Autour de l'absence d'avourie en Normandie', p. 210.

[4] Lanfranc's part in the negotiation of Duke William's reconciliation with the papacy and in the controversy over the ideas of Berengar of Tours must have contributed substantially to the prestige of the Church in Normandy; Prentout, *Histoire de Guillaume le Conquérant*, pp. 98–101; Macdonald, *Lanfranc*, pp. 41–55; Southern, 'Lanfranc of Bec and Berengar of Tours'.

in the story which credits Duke Richard I with an attempt, premature as it proved to be, to re-establish the cathedral body at Coutances and, presumably, to persuade the bishop to reside in his cathedral city.[1]

The Norman bishops of the early eleventh century, taken as a body, had little to commend them as religious leaders. They were drawn mainly from the military aristocracy that was growing up in Normandy or from the ducal family itself;[2] they shared the assumptions and the instincts of that class and represent, indeed, one of the means by which it kept a hand on the property of the Church. Given that the duke had a very large part in the election of abbots as well as bishops, it is remarkable that there should be such a contrast, speaking generally, between the men chosen for the two offices. Yet if the level of spirituality was low among the bishops, they did not lack organizing ability. The constitution of the cathedral chapters and the structure of diocesan administration (particularly in the development of the office of archdeacon and of a routine of diocesan synods) seems to date from the middle of the eleventh century,[3] some of the financial resources being drawn from Norman conquests in South Italy and later in England,[4] and a vigorous and indigenous effort at reform was set on foot. This reform was pursued in a series of councils of the ecclesiastical province of Rouen, legislating on matters of organization and discipline; and the duke's part in them was such that it could almost be said that they owed what effectiveness they might have to him, certainly from the time that William the Conqueror achieved full control of his duchy.[5]

The duke had given much to the Church in Normandy, perhaps not entirely disinterestedly; the Church could give much in return—also, perhaps, not entirely disinterestedly. The duke's part in its regeneration undoubtedly increased his authority in the duchy and his standing among contemporary

---

[1] *Gallia Christiana*, instrumenta, col. 218; Fauroux, *Recueil*, p. 23 (No. 15); Nos. 6 (pp. 76–7), 28 (p. 116).

[2] Above, p. 249.

[3] Douglas, 'Norman Episcopate', pp. 107–14. For the example of Coutances, Le Patourel, 'Geoffrey of Montbray', pp. 141–2. Musset has, however, published a text which suggests at least the possibility that there was some organization at Coutances before the bishops returned from Rouen to reside in their cathedral city: 'Les origines du prieuré de Saint-Fromond', pp. 479–80, 484.

[4] Below, pp. 331–2.   [5] Above, p. 246 n. 5.

rulers, giving him all but the full dignity of royalty.[1] His record would certainly stand him in good stead when William appealed to the pope to recognize the justice of his cause in the matter of the succession to the kingdom of the English; while the gift of a papal banner conferred upon his invasion something of the aura of a crusade. It was about this time, moreover, that the Church at large (with Norman help) was beginning to develop the idea of the Holy War, an idea which, it must be said, less scrupulous minds could use to justify almost any aggression.[2]

It is not necessary to believe all that the Normans said about the Old English Church,[3] conscious as they must have been that they were occupying positions which, but for the Conquest, would have been held by men of English birth, or even that the ecclesiastical changes which they made in England after the Conquest were for the better in any absolute sense; but it is important to see that to enthusiastic and self-confident Norman churchmen the English Church would have seemed to need a great deal of reform and invigoration. The penetration of Normans into England during the reign of Edward the Confessor must have provided them with all the information they needed on its condition—and the opportunities it offered. English monasteries would have seemed to them old-fashioned and lethargic at best, and thin on the ground;[4] the administration of the secular Church backward and amorphous;[5] and the whole damned in 1066 by the perjured king and schismatic archbishop of Canterbury at its head. Those with ambition must have noted what happened when Edward the Confessor, having lived long in Normandy, succeeded to the throne of

---

[1] Cf. above, pp. 238–9, 246.

[2] Douglas, *The Norman Achievement*, ch. v (esp. pp. 102–9).

[3] e.g. Malmesbury's strictures in *Gesta Pontificum*, pp. 70–1, and *Gesta Regum*, ii. 304–5; and Lanfranc's views on English saints and English customs (Macdonald, *Lanfranc*, pp. 187–9). Cf. however, Darlington, 'Ecclesiastical Reform in the Late Old English Period', pp. 402–3.

[4] At the time of the Conquest there are reckoned to have been thirty-five Benedictine monasteries for men in England, between twenty-six and twenty-eight in Normandy (Knowles, *Monastic Order*, pp. 85–6, 100, 701–2). Although there were none in England north of Burton-on-Trent this represents a far higher density, area for area, in Normandy than in England.

[5] Above, pp. 249–50. There is much that could be said in defence of the Old English Church (cf. Darlington, ubi supra, *passim*), but in this context the Norman attitude, determined largely by circumstances, is more important than the facts; and that attitude can be inferred from the changes they made.

England,[1] or when Norman suzerainty was substituted for Angevin in the *comté* of Maine.[2] Even the Norman monasteries had reason to think that victory for William in England would be very much to their advantage, as indeed it proved to be.[3]

It may not be necessary to look further for the dynamic which produced the conquests in Britain and in northern France, and the political structure which the Normans built out of those conquests. The need for expansion inherent in a developing feudal society, especially one in which the leading families had acquired their wealth and standing so quickly, the peculiar conditions of the formation of Normandy which allowed for the creation of a personal relationship of a particular kind between the ducal family and the aristocracy, and the circumstances, intimately bound up with these, which enabled William and his sons to draw on neighbouring lands for men and money and to win the co-operation of the Church which could not only influence opinion decisively but contribute moral and even physical support, were sufficient in themselves. But a dynamic force needs an instrument. Although it is possible that the Norman armies were organized and disciplined in a way hardly to be found in the armies they had to meet, they were not invincible. We shall never know, perhaps, how much William owed to luck or to Harold's mistakes at Hastings; but he had to withdraw from Dol in 1076 when the king of France brought up his army; neither he nor his son William Rufus was able to recover the small territory of the Vexin Français, and Henry was soon hard pressed even in what he must have known to be the strategically vital area of the Vexin Normand. In any case, it was neither the victory at Hastings nor the success of the campaigns in the west and the north of England that, by themselves, enabled the Normans to conquer England as William conquered it. Campaigns and battles were followed up by a detailed taking possession of every part of the country and the fastening of a direct and physical hold upon it. It was this that gave the Norman conquest of England its special character and it was achieved, it seems, principally by the castle and the way in which the Normans used the castle.

---

[1] Above, pp. 22–3.   [2] Above, p. 38.

[3] For the possessions of the Norman monasteries in England before 1066, Matthew, *Norman Monasteries and their English Possessions*, ch. 1.

A castle is essentially a defensive work; directly, it can only defend itself and the people who are in it, at least until the development of long-range artillery.[1] Nevertheless, since it can serve as a base and a refuge for men operating in country which has been penetrated but not yet conquered as well as a stronghold in country to be defended as one's own, it could be used as an instrument of conquest and colonization. This was shown very clearly by the manner in which the counts of Anjou, Fulk Nerra and his son Geoffrey Martel, conquered the Touraine from the counts of Blois. By planting castles at Langeais, Montrichard, Montbazon, Montboyau, and the rest, they so undermined the authority of the count of Blois that when he met with a defeat in the field in 1044 he had no alternative but to surrender almost all that remained to him in the *comté*.[2] Likewise William the Conqueror, some years before he embarked upon a deliberate conquest of the *comté* of Maine, garrisoned (if he did not found) a castle at Ambrières, on the way from Caen and Domfront to Mayenne. The chief lord of the region, Geoffrey de Mayenne, appealed to the count of Anjou for help; but when the count and his allies laid siege to the place, William brought up a relieving force which beat off the attackers, captured Geoffrey de Mayenne, and forced him to do homage.[3] Since William's objective in Maine, or at least what he achieved there, was the transference of the allegiance of the barons of Maine from the count of Anjou to himself,[4] this can be regarded as a significant first step.

On the eve of the conquest of England the Normans were certainly quite familiar with castles in their own country, although the total number of such structures there may not have been so great at that time as has sometimes been ima-

---

[1] e.g. the castles of the north of England were unable to prevent the forces of King William the Lion from penetrating deep into the country in 1173 and 1174 (Brown, *English Medieval Castles*, pp. 164–7); and in 1346 the very powerful castle at Caen could do nothing to prevent Edward III from capturing the town which it seems to dominate (Prentout, 'La prise de Caen par Édouard III, 1346', esp. pp. 41–2). Many of the problems relating to castles in England and Normandy during the eleventh and twelfth centuries are well discussed by Brown in *The Normans and the Norman Conquest*, pp. 43–5, 234–9.

[2] Halphen, *Comté d'Anjou*, pp. 26–48; illustrative map in Southern, *Making of the Middle Ages*, p. 84.

[3] Halphen, *Comté d'Anjou*, p. 78; Latouche, *Maine*, pp. 31–2, 61; Douglas *William the Conqueror*, pp. 70–2.

[4] Above, p. 18.

gined.[1] The most ancient of them, and perhaps still the majority, were of ducal foundation and were placed generally in the custody of the counts and the *vicomtes*. Naturally, the effective control which the duke could exercise over these castles depended on the degree of fidelity accorded to him by such officers; and the distinction between a private castle and a ducal castle in the hands of a potentially rebellious or obstructive castellan might be quite theoretical; but there were certainly seigniorial castles, constructed by the greater families on their own lands and for their own purposes as well. It seems clear, however, that castles in Normandy were already of many different sorts, varying from considerable structures of stone to affairs of earth and timber which could be thrown up in quite a short time and would afford only a limited protection.[2] It is also clear that William the Conqueror, though he may have lost control of the castles or some of them from time to time and certainly during a part of his minority, recovered that control during the course of his reign.[3]

For the most part the construction of these castles can be related to the need for fortified residences and administrative centres, felt by duke and barons alike, and the maintenance of garrisons in outlying parts of the duchy; but one group may have been intended for a rather more active function. At the beginning of the eleventh century the extreme west of the duchy was almost a land apart. It had been overrun and partly settled by Bretons as well as Northmen;[4] the northern part of the Cotentin seems to have been colonized independently by Norse people coming via Ireland and the western parts of Britain,[5] the whole western peninsula may still have been largely pagan,[6] and as the dukes had hitherto resided almost wholly in the east of the duchy their authority can have been exercised only spasmodically west of the Orne.[7] The foundation of Falaise in the Hiémois,[8]

---

[1] On castles in Normandy at this time, Yver, 'Châteaux forts en Normandie', pp. 28–63.

[2] e.g. de Bouard, 'Petites enceintes circulaires d'origine médiévale en Normandie'; Decaens, 'Enceintes d'Urville et Bretteville-sur-Laize'.

[3] 'Consuetudines et Justicie', Haskins, *Norman Institutions*, p. 282 (para. 4): Yver, 'Châteaux forts en Normandie', pp. 60–3.   [4] Above, p. 6.

[5] Musset, 'Aperçus sur la colonisation scandinave dans le nord du Cotentin'.

[6] Le Patourel, 'Geoffrey of Montbray', pp. 134–5.

[7] De Bouard, 'De la Neustrie carolingienne à la Normandie féodale', pp. 10–11; *Guillaume le Conquérant*, pp. 23–5.

[8] Yver, 'Châteaux forts en Normandie', pp. 38–9.

Cherbourg, Le Homme (L'Isle-Marie), and Brix in the Cotentin, all most probably by Duke Richard II,[1] Cherrueix beyond the Couesnon by Robert I,[2] Saint-James-de-Beuvron by William the Conqueror, and the fortification of Caen also probably by William,[3] look like the framework of security for a campaign of colonization and development which would integrate the west with the remainder of the duchy and establish ducal authority there on a much firmer basis. Evidence for such development may be found in the *bourgs* formed at Caen, Cherbourg, and Saint-James, the development of Saint-Lô and Coutances, and the appearance of *hospites* in the Channel Islands and elsewhere.[4]

Castles were used by the Normans during the first phase of military conquest in England. The very first thing that William did when he had disembarked on the Sussex coast was to contrive a fortification in the remains of the old Roman fort at Pevensey and throw up a castle at Hastings. He added to whatever fortifications there were already at Dover as he passed through on his way to London; and as soon as he had possession of London he ordered the construction of castles there. Castles were founded at Exeter in the course of his campaign in the south-west early in 1068; at Warwick, Nottingham, and York on his way to the North later in the same year, and at Lincoln, Huntingdon, and Cambridge on his way back; a second castle was planted at York in 1069, and castles at Chester and Stafford in 1070.[5] When William left England in the spring of 1067 for his triumphal tour of Normandy, he left the continuing work of conquest to William fitzOsbern and Odo bishop of Bayeux, supported by other prominent Norman barons. According to Florence of Worcester he gave orders that they should build

---

[1] Ibid.; Fauroux, *Recueil*, No. 58 (p. 182).

[2] Above, p. 9 n. 6.

[3] Yver, 'Châteaux forts en Normandie', pp. 58–9.

[4] In general, de Bouard, 'De la Neustrie carolingienne à la Normandie féodale', pp. 11–12 and *Guillaume le Conquérant*, pp. 58–60. For the *bourgs* at Caen, Cherbourg, Saint-James-de-Beuvron, etc., Legras, *Bourgage de Caen*, pp. 34–59, etc. (with plan) and Musset, 'Peuplement en bourgage et bourgs ruraux en Normandie du Xe au XIIIe siècle', esp. pp. 183–9. For Saint-Lô and Coutances, Le Patourel, 'Geoffrey of Montbray', p. 138; and for the *hospites*, Le Patourel, 'Early History of St. Peter Port', pp. 175–8, 200–1, and Delisle, *Études sur la classe agricole en Normandie*, pp. 8–14.

[5] Brown, Colvin, and Taylor, *King's works*, i. 20–1.

castles in suitable places; MS. D of the Anglo-Saxon Chronicle records that the order was carried out.[1] It may be that there were already fortifications of various sorts in England;[2] but sieges are notably absent from the accounts we have of the military phase of the conquest (the short siege of Exeter city in 1068 is a rare exception), and Orderic explicitly attributes the weak resistance of the English to the very small number of 'fortifications which the French call castles' in their country.[3] There had already been two or three long sieges of castles in Normandy.[4]

At this stage, castles were built to maintain Norman garrisons at certain Channel ports, to overawe the chief city of the realm, along important lines of communication, and in exposed or distant parts of the country where they might hold a counter-attack until a relieving force could be brought up[5] or at least give the alarm before too much was lost. This was still the first phase of the conquest, when 'key points' in the country were being seized; but there is evidence to show that castles were also used in later phases when the Normans took possession of the country in detail and colonized it. This evidence is to be found in the structure of certain baronial estates as they are described in Domesday Book; and the inferences that may be drawn from the descriptions of them can be illustrated and in some measure substantiated in one case where the process of conquest and colonization can be observed in action.

It has often been noted that the estates of the greater barons, as they appear in Domesday and later, were generally scattered and intermingled with one another often over a very wide area.

[1] Florence of Worcester, *Chronicon*, ii. 1; A.-S.C., 1066, D (p. 145). Cf. Orderic Vitalis, *H.E.* (ed. Le Prévost), ii. 165–7; (ed. Chibnall), ii. 194–6.

[2] Apart from the fortified towns and residences (burhs, boroughs, burys), the question of the existence in England of castles in a stricter sense before 1066 has been reopened, Davison, 'The Origins of the Castle in England'. Cf. Stenton, *Norman London*, pp. 15–16.

[3] 'Munitiones enim, quas castella Galli nuncupant, Anglicis provinciis paucissime fuerunt; et ob hoc Angli, licet bellicosi fuerint et audaces, ad resistendum tamen inimicis extiterant debiliores' (Orderic Vitalis, *H.E.* (ed. Le Prévost), ii. 184; (ed. Chibnall), ii. 218). It is perhaps worth emphasizing that Orderic does not say that there were no castles in England before 1066, but that there were very few.

[4] Yver, 'Châteaux forts en Normandie', p. 50.

[5] As at Shrewsbury and Exeter in 1069, and as they failed to do at York (Orderic Vitalis, *H.E.* (ed. Le Prévost), ii. 192–4; (ed. Chibnall), ii. 226–8).

Indeed, if the whole estate of a baron is considered, this is true of nearly all of them.[1] There are several reasons for this. Large estates were usually built up piecemeal, as opportunity served and land became available in different parts of the country.[2] There is a suggestive correlation, for example, between the two great groups of estates held by the bishop of Coutances in 1086 and the two areas in which he took a leading part in the suppression of revolts in 1069 and 1075.[3] It often happened that a Norman lord took over the entire estate of one or more English landowners, and such estates were often dispersed already,[4] as indeed were the estates they possessed in Normandy.[5] Few Normans seemed unwilling to take over any lands that they could get, wherever they might be situated or however far they might be from their chief possessions. But the discrete estates so formed often included compact blocks of territory under a single lordship. On the largest scale, Hugh d'Avranches held most of the county of Cheshire, though he held much besides;[6] Roger de Montgomery held Shropshire in the same way,[7] William fitzOsbern had held Herefordshire similarly, probably with much of Gloucestershire and Worcestershire as well,[8] and Alan de Bretagne held Richmondshire together with a vast estate stretching disjointedly down the eastern half of England.[9] Likewise the bishop of Bayeux held most of Kent,[10] Brian de Bretagne and later Robert de Mortain had most of Cornwall,[11] and Roger 'de Poitou' what would eventually be Lancashire.[12] On a medium scale, there were the rapes of Sussex and the Isle of Wight (as William fitzOsbern had held it)

[1] In general, Lennard, *Rural England*, pp. 28–30, 33 ff.; and for compact estates, ibid., pp. 30–3.

[2] As in the build-up of the Montgomery or Warenne estates in England (above, pp. 292–3).

[3] Le Patourel, 'Geoffrey of Montbray', p. 152.

[4] Lennard, *Rural England*, pp. 29–30.

[5] e.g. the estates of Roger de Montgomery or Hugh d'Avranches in Normandy (above, pp. 292, 294, notes).

[6] Tait, *Domesday Survey of Cheshire*, pp. 26, 30–44; Barraclough, 'Earldom and County Palatine of Chester', pp. 30–3.

[7] Mason, 'Roger de Montgomery and his sons', pp. 2–10.

[8] Wightman, 'The Palatine Earldom of William fitzOsbern'.

[9] *E.Y.C.*, iv, v (*Honour of Richmond*) *passim*; Jeulin, 'Un grand "Honneur" anglais'; Stenton, *English Feudalism*, pp. 194–5.

[10] *V.C.H. Kent*, iii. 188–90.

[11] *V.C.H. Cornwall*, ii, part 8, pp. 57–8.

[12] Tait, *Medieval Manchester*, pp. 151–63.

in the south;[1] the honours or castleries of Pontefract (Lacy),[2] Conisborough-Wakefield (Warenne),[3] Tickhill-Blyth (Bully),[4] and Holderness (Drew de la Beuvrière)[5] in the north; and the Midland blocks about Henry de Ferrers's castle of Tutbury,[6] William Peveril's castle in the Peak,[7] or the castle of William fitzAnsculf at Dudley.[8] Those on the smallest scale were of a somewhat different character. They consisted of a group of very small sub-tenancies in the vicinity of a castle or seigniorial residence.[9] Examples have been noted at Carisbrooke and Montacute in the south, Clifford and Ewyas Harold in the west, and Belvoir in the East Midlands,[10] and there were others. These small sub-tenancies generally supported or helped to support knights (who in the eleventh century did not necessarily have the social status they later acquired), apparently in a stage midway between full maintenance in their lord's household and enfeoffment with lands sufficient for a more independent life.[11]

The structure of these compact blocks of different sizes needs more comparative study, but some of their characteristics are clear. They were all related to a great baronial castle or residence. The term 'castlery' which was sometimes applied to them is an indication of this relationship;[12] but connection with

[1] *V.C.H. Hampshire*, i. 406–10; Mason, *William the First and the Sussex Rapes*, pp. 4–7. There were similar concentrations about Saltwood and Tonbridge castles (*V.C.H. Kent*, iii. 187–8, 190–1). Cf. Stenton, *English Feudalism*, p. 195.

[2] Wightman, *Lacy Family*, esp. pp. 17–20; Stenton, *English Feudalism*, pp. 195–6.

[3] Wightman, *Lacy Family*, p. 20; *E.Y.C.*, viii (*Honour of Warenne*), 137–40, 178–81, etc.

[4] Wightman, ibid.; *V.C.H. Nottinghamshire*, i. 223–6; *V.C.H. Yorkshire*, ii. 165–7 (cf. Timson, 'Edition of Blyth Cartulary').

[5] *V.C.H. Yorkshire*, ii. 171–2. This is an interesting case, for the complaints of the canons of Beverley may reflect the effort of the lord to make his hold on the area exclusive.

[6] *V.C.H. Staffordshire*, iv. 29–30; Stenton, *English Feudalism*, p. 196; Lennard, *Rural England*, pp. 32–3.

[7] *V.C.H. Derbyshire*, i. 303–4; *V.C.H. Nottinghamshire*, i. 227–30.

[8] Stenton, *English Feudalism*, p. 195; Lennard, *Rural England*, pp. 30–1.

[9] Stenton, *English Feudalism*, pp. 144–5, 195; *V.C.H. Herefordshire*, i. 272–4 (Round).

[10] *V.C.H. Hampshire*, i. 408–9; Round, 'The Origin of Belvoir Castle'; Wightman, *Lacy Family*, pp. 132–3; and for Montacute, *V.C.H. Somerset*, i. 411–12.

[11] Stenton, *English Feudalism*, pp. 144–5.

[12] Stenton, ibid., pp. 194–6, where the castlery is described as 'a well-defined district within which the whole arrangement of tenancies was primarily designed for the maintenance of the castle', with the accompanying characteristic that the

a castle can be shown in every case, whether or not the term 'castlery' is actually found. They were certainly of post-Conquest creation (although it is possible that in a few cases the Normans may have adapted earlier estates), the English estates from which they were constructed having been re-organized in the process;[1] and only in the case of these blocks was King William prepared to grant or to acquiesce in the taking of what had been royal land.[2] The only possible reason for the construction of such blocks, since it is clear that it needed some effort to bring them into existence, must be that they enabled a baron to concentrate his knights and his vassals with their lands about one of his castles.

Since many of these territorial blocks are found near the coast, by the Welsh Border, or in the north of England, it has generally been thought that William created them for the defence of his kingdom. This interpretation, however, has to meet certain objections. Some of the blocks were not on any frontier. Tutbury, Dudley, the Peak, even Tickhill, certainly Belvoir or Montacute, were well behind the lines. If such blocks were for the defence of the kingdom, it might be expected that the king would go to some trouble to keep them in being; yet the Isle of Wight and the Herefordshire blocks were broken up after the forfeiture of Roger de Breteuil in 1075, the position of the bishop of Bayeux in Kent was not perpetuated after his exile in 1088, nor that of Robert de Bellême in Shropshire after 1102, the Sussex rapes did not endure as units of property,[3] and it has been observed that the interests of the earls of Chester seemed to turn away from North Wales after the disaster of 1098.[4]

This suggests that the purpose of these tenurial blocks was immediate rather than long-term, associated with the period of conquest and not so much defensive as offensive; that they might indeed represent the fighting units in the Norman armies[5]

lord of the castle was the lord of all or nearly all the manors within the district. Mason, in *William the First and the Sussex Rapes* (pp. 6–7), suggests that the compactness and exclusiveness of these blocks were relative, an important point.

[1] e.g. Wightman, *Lacy Family*, pp. 43–50; *V.C.H. Shropshire*, i. 299; Tait, *Domesday Survey of Cheshire*, pp. 58–62.

[2] Mason, *William the First and the Sussex Rapes*, pp. 4–6; Wightman, 'The Palatine Earldom of William fitzOsbern', pp. 7–12.   [3] Mason, ubi supra, pp. 20–2.

[4] Barraclough, 'Earldom and County Palatine of Chester', pp. 32–4.

[5] Above, pp. 34–5.

taking up positions for further advance.[1] While it is not possible in every case to identify the sub-tenants as men who had already been their lord's tenants in Normandy, it is clear that this was so to a large extent in Shropshire; and there is some evidence that it was so in Cheshire, Herefordshire, Richmond, Holderness, and the rape of Hastings.[2] Their strategic purpose and their part in the business of conquest would be clearer if the chronology of the Norman occupation and settlement of England were better known; but there is much to suggest that the blocks in the south (the Isle of Wight, the rapes of Sussex, Cornwall, Kent) were formed very early,[3] that the Midland blocks (Hereford, Cheshire, Shrewsbury, Peak, Tutbury, etc.) belong to the 1070s,[4] and those in the north (Pontefract, Richmond, Tickhill-Blyth, etc.) were mostly later.[5]

If this chronology bears any relation to the facts, it too would indicate that these territorial blocks centred on castles were created, not so much for the defence of a conquered kingdom, but as part of the actual process of conquest. Such tenurial concentrations, which could readily be formed in the early stages of the conquest of an area, would be very difficult to put together later on when several men had already staked their claims there. The king, likewise, would have no need to keep them in being after they had served their initial purpose, as in fact he did not; though it might not be wise to try to break them

[1] This at any rate is how some of them are described by Orderic Vitalis (*H.E.* (ed. Le Prévost), ii. 218–24; (ed. Chibnall), ii. 260–6). Note especially the passage 'Willelmo dapifero Normanniae . . . aliosque plures prostravit' (in the editions respectively, pp. 218–19, 260). On the supposed defensive functions of the marcher lords in Wales, cf. Edwards, 'The Normans and the Welsh March', p. 175.

[2] Above, pp. 32–5; *V.C.H. Shropshire*, i. 296–301 (cf. Orderic Vitalis, *H.E.* (ed. Le Prévost), ii. 220–1; (ed. Chibnall), ii. 262; Douglas, *William the Conqueror*, pp. 95, 270); Tait, *Domesday Survey of Cheshire*, pp. 44–59; *V.C.H. Herefordshire*, i. 274–80. For Richmond and Holderness, above, pp. 32–3. For Hastings, *V.C.H. Sussex*, i. 377.

[3] The Isle of Wight certainly before 1071, the year of William fitzOsbern's death; most probably 1067 when he was based on Winchester. For the rapes of Sussex, Mason, *William the First and the Sussex Rapes*, pp. 7–9. Brian de Bretagne must have been established in Cornwall by 1069 (Douglas, *William the Conqueror*, p. 267) and the bishop of Bayeux in Kent probably in 1067.

[4] For Hereford, Cheshire, Shrewsbury, above, p. 41. For Peak, *V.C.H. Derbyshire*, i. 303; Tutbury, *V.C.H. Staffordshire*, iv. 25 and Orderic Vitalis, *H.E.* (ed. Le Prévost), ii. 222; (ed. Chibnall), ii. 264. Orderic describes the distribution of lands, mainly in the Midlands, as taking place after the death of Earl Edwin and the imprisonment of Earl Morcar (ibid., respectively, pp. 218, 260).

[5] Above, pp. 41–2.

up if they persisted by a natural succession. That they could in fact be used as part of the process of conquest and colonization is evident from the history of Norman aggression in Wales generally; while the methods used, and the place of the castle in those methods, are shown very clearly in the series of campaigns conducted in North Wales, where they are relatively well recorded, where the chronology of the successive phases is reasonably secure, and where the process was interrupted before it was completed, giving a kind of archaeological section of an operation of this kind still in progress, uncomplicated by later events and later records.

The campaigns began with the foundation of Chester Castle by King William in 1070[1] and its commitment, a little later, to Hugh d'Avranches.[2] Hugh had an able vassal and lieutenant in his kinsman Robert 'of Rhuddlan'[3] who, by 1073, had established himself in the place from which he took his name[4] and had doubtless begun the construction of the castle there. He was soon raiding deep into Gwynedd. By 1086 the country between Chester and Rhuddlan had been partly colonized by Norman vassals of Hugh d'Avranches, including Robert 'of Rhuddlan' himself. The hundred of Atiscross (that is, the northern part of the later county of Flint) east of Wat's Dyke had already been distributed among the earl's Norman vassals; west of the Dyke the earl had organized the manor of Bistre and distributed sub-tenancies similarly, but in the manor of Rhuddlan (which seems to have occupied the remainder of north-west Atiscross or Tegeingl) only the borough had been established with its eighteen burgesses.[5] Robert, meanwhile, had moved on. He had founded the castle of Degannwy,[6] perhaps as early as 1075–6,[7]

[1] Orderic Vitalis, *H.E.* (ed. Le Prévost), ii. 199; (ed. Chibnall), ii. 236.

[2] Date uncertain, probably 1071 (Barraclough, 'Earldom and County Palatine of Chester', pp. 26–7). It is irrelevant to this discussion that there should be no certain evidence of his holding the title of earl before 1077 (*Handbook of British Chronology*, p. 420).

[3] On Robert's career generally, Orderic Vitalis, *H.E.* (ed. Le Prévost), iii. 280–9; (ed. Chibnall), iv. 134–46; Loyd, *Anglo-Norman Families*, p. 85.

[4] For the date, Lloyd, *History of Wales*, ii. 382, note 80; and for the campaign generally, ibid., pp. 378–92, 403–11, and Davies, *Episcopal Acts*, i. 79–83, 86–7, 91–7.

[5] D.B., i. 268 b 2, 269 a; Tait, *Domesday Survey of Cheshire*, pp. 22–6, 224–43 and map. Cf. Lloyd, *History of Wales*, ii. 366, 385–7.

[6] Orderic Vitalis, *H.E.* (ed. Le Prévost), iii. 283–4; (ed. Chibnall), iv. 138: 'fines suos dilatauit, et in monte Dagannoth qui mari contiguus est fortissimum castellum condidit'.   [7] Davies, *Episcopal Acts*, i. 79.

and had taken possession of the cantreds of Rhos and Rhufoniog, that is the country between Rhuddlan and Degannwy, for in Domesday it is stated that he held them of the king in fee; but there is no indication that there was any degree of Norman settlement there as yet.[1] In 1086 he also held 'Nort Wales' (by which the kingdom of Gwynedd west of the Conwy seems to be meant), minus the lands belonging to the bishopric of Bangor, for a farm of £40 a year.[2] Though he is not recorded as having done more than raid Gwynedd, he already knew enough about the country to enter a claim to the detached cantred of Arwystli and to produce witnesses to say that it belonged to 'Nortwalis'.

Robert was killed near Degannwy in 1088.[3] His work was taken up by his lord, the earl of Chester, who planted castles at Bangor and Caernarvon in Arfon, Aberlleiniog in Anglesey, and at some unknown place in Meirionydd; and this had given him sufficient hold on the country to secure the appointment of the Breton Hervé to the bishopric of Bangor and to give land in Anglesey to his new foundation of St. Werburgh in Chester. This was in 1092–3; but it was all swept away by the great Welsh counter-attack of 1094, and campaigns by William Rufus and then by the earls of Chester and Shrewsbury together failed to restore the position. In course of time Gruffydd ap Cynan and his sons won back nearly all that the Welsh had lost.[4]

This narrative clearly shows the technique. In the advance from Chester to the west a castle had first been built at Rhuddlan. By 1086 Atiscross hundred, the country between Chester and Rhuddlan, had been conquered and colonization was well advanced. By that time also a castle had been established at Degannwy, and the country between Rhuddlan and Degannwy apparently conquered; but there was little sign of colonization there as yet. Further west, Gwynedd had been raided; and a year or two later a serious attempt was made to conquer the country. Castles were planted there and a French bishop

[1] D.B., i. 269 a 2. The borough at Degannwy was founded in the thirteenth century (Beresford, *New Towns*, pp. 546–7).

[2] D.B., i. 269 a 2; cf. above, pp. 40, 211–12.

[3] Lloyd, *History of Wales*, ii. 390–1. This chronology has been criticized by Mrs. Chibnall in the introduction to her edition of Orderic Vitalis, vol. iv (pp. xxxiv–xxxviii). She proposes 1093 as the date of Robert of Rhuddlan's death, with consequent adjustments to the narrative; but this redating would hardly affect the point of the story as related above.

[4] Lloyd, *History of Wales*, ii. 403–11, 462–9.

installed at Bangor—this last a preliminary move, no doubt, in the process of colonization, but it was premature. The first stage was to raid the country; the second, to plant one or more castles well in advance, and then to do the work of systematic conquest and subsequently of colonization under the protection that a castle could afford to those engaged in these operations. When sufficient progress had been made, the next convenient stretch of country was raided, another castle or castles built some way further on, and the process repeated. How often a formal royal grant was obtained either before or in the course of the operation, as Robert 'of Rhuddlan' may have done in respect of 'Nort Wales', it is impossible to say. Grants of land 'to be conquered' were well known in fourteenth-century France. The technique can also be seen, though not perhaps so clearly, in the campaigns led by the earl of Shrewsbury and his sons which took them as far as Pembroke, where they founded a castle and a priory;[1] and Pembroke further shows how a well-sited castle, courageously held, could survive a native counter-attack and facilitate the return of the invaders when they came to recover what had been temporarily lost.[2]

If this technique or something like it was also used by the Normans in England, the significance of those concentrations of small knightly estates about a castle and the concentration of vassals in larger castleries becomes plain. It might be objected that there was a difference between Wales and England in this respect, in that the Welsh princes were generally in possession when the Normans attacked, whereas a great many English landowners must have lost their lives or their liberty or fled the country in the course of the fighting from 1066 to 1071, or later. It does not follow, however, that even in such cases the new Norman lord would meet with no resistance when he came to take possession; he would certainly have been wise to make preparation for it. If the castles at Rhuddlan and (in intention) Degannwy, and the men who used them, were partly a cover for settlement in progress to the rear and partly a base for further advance, then the foundation of the castle at Chester and the great concentrated estate about it that was given to Hugh d'Avranches should be regarded as a first step not only to

---

[1] Lloyd, ibid., pp. 388–90, 400–1; Davies, *Episcopal Acts*, i. 81–2, 108–9.

[2] Lloyd, ibid., pp. 401, 406–8; Davies, ibid., pp. 114–15.

conquest and colonization in North Wales but also in that part of north-west England. This is how Carlisle was used by William Rufus in the conquest and colonization of Cumbria;[1] how the counts of Anjou had used their castles in Touraine;[2] how the Norman dukes had used them in the western part of their duchy, and how, for that matter, King Edward the Elder and Æthelflæd of Mercia had used their boroughs to conquer the Danelaw.[3]

But the castle, once established, was more than a military instrument. It soon became the occasional residence of its lord. Not all barons, even in the early phases of the colonization, seem to have made their chief residence in a castle;[4] but most castles became residences, at least from time to time, and many eventually served as the centre from which a great estate was administered and exploited for its lord. There is little direct evidence of the non-military functions of the castle in the early years, save in the ecclesiastical and other settlements that so often went with them; but as accompanying instruments of domination and colonization these settlements were very important.

A number of people must have been associated with each castle from the first. Religious provision had to be made for them, and there seems indeed to have been a chapel in most castles of any importance. The natural 'staffing' for such a chapel at that time would be a group of clerks,[5] as originally at Arundel[6] or Clare,[7] or more permanently at Pontefract[8] and Richmond.[9] But the century following the Norman Conquest was the age of the monks. In some cases, as again at Arundel and

---

[1] Above, p. 69.

[2] Above, p. 304. The count of Anjou dispossessed a number of the tenants of the count of Blois in the Touraine and put in his own men (Boussard, 'L'éviction des tenants de Thibaud de Blois par Geoffroy Martel, comte d'Anjou, en 1044'). This in effect is what the Normans were to do on a vastly greater scale in England. Castles, likewise, must have been an important element in the build-up of the great frontier lordship of Bellême (Yver, 'Châteaux forts en Normandie', pp. 39–40).   [3] A.-S.C., 912–21 (pp. 62–8).

[4] Stenton, *English Feudalism*, pp. 63–4.

[5] For the castle colleges in Normandy, Yver, 'Autour de l'absence d'avouerie en Normandie', pp. 195–201.   [6] Matthew, *Norman Monasteries*, p. 55.

[7] Knowles and Hadcock, *Religious Houses*, p. 87.

[8] Wightman, *Lacy Family*, pp. 24, 38, 61; and similarly at Clitheroe, ibid., p. 63.

[9] *E.Y.C.*, iv (*Honour of Richmond*, i), 8–9, 147. For the castle-chapels more generally, Denton, *English Royal Free Chapels*, ch. v.

Clare, the college was converted into a priory;[1] in others, a monastery was founded in the first place, either within or in very close proximity to the castle. In many cases the original nucleus of monks was brought from a Norman or French monastery, as at Chester[2] or Shrewsbury,[3] or the convent was both colonized from and permanently subjected to a Norman or French monastery, as at Bramber, Eye, Tutbury, Blyth, Lancaster, Pembroke, Carisbrooke, and many others.[4] In Wales this was normal; and whether the 'mother' house was an abbey in France or a Normanized monastery in England, the monks were equally 'foreign' in the Welsh countryside.[5]

The people of the castle also had to be provisioned. For their needs, in the first place, a settlement was often established beside the castle. Such settlements were not necessarily urban to begin with. The word used in contemporary records is *burgus*, and their founders may well have had a French *bourg* in mind rather than an English borough. A *bourg* could be quite rural;[6] nevertheless there was a good chance that trade or industry would develop in these foundations if circumstances were generally favourable, for the requirements of the castle would provide the starting-point.[7] Some of the earliest of these foundations were made on the borders of Wales, where towns had been few before 1066. William fitzOsbern, who was killed in 1071, had founded boroughs beside his castles at Wigmore and Clifford,[8] and very probably at Chepstow and Monmouth[9] as well. In time such boroughs grew up or were deliberately planted beside most of the major castles in South Wales and the

---

[1] Knowles and Hadcock, *Religious Houses*, pp. 86–7. For this and the castle priories generally, Matthew, *Norman Monasteries*, pp. 55–8.

[2] Tait, *Chartulary of the Abbey of St. Werburgh, Chester*, pp. xxiii–xxv.

[3] Knowles and Hadcock, ubi supra, p. 76; Orderic Vitalis, *H.E.* (ed. Le Prévost), ii. 415–23; (ed. Chibnall), iii. 142–8.

[4] Matthews, *Norman Monasteries*, pp. 38, 46, 47, 48, 50, 55–8.

[5] Above, p. 66.

[6] At least it could be so in Normandy: Musset, 'Peuplement en bourgage et bourgs ruraux en Normandie'. Cf. Miller, 'Medieval New Towns'.

[7] William Malet founded a market beside his castle at Eye (Suffolk), but not, apparently, a borough (Beresford, *New Towns*, p. 334; Loyn, *Anglo-Saxon England and the Norman Conquest*, p. 370; Armitage, *Early Norman Castles*, pp. 155–6). This suggests that the essential need was to provide a means of getting supplies to the garrison and the people of the castle in normal times, a need that would favour the development of any borough founded beside a castle.

[8] D.B., i. 183 b 1, 183 a 2.

[9] Beresford, *New Towns*, pp. 559–60; Lloyd, *History of Wales*, ii. 375.

March. But the same is generally true of England as well during the period of conquest and colonization. Castles were either built in existing towns, as at London, Winchester, York, Exeter, Cambridge, and so on, or boroughs were founded beside the castle, as at Barnard Castle, Richmond, Pontefract, and Newcastle in the north,[1] Penwortham,[2] Ludlow, Bridgnorth, and Okehampton in the west,[3] or Arundel, Hastings, New Windsor, Belvoir, Montacute, and Tutbury[4] in other parts of the country. When a castle was built in an existing town, Domesday often records the presence of French burgesses there.[5] Some of the small castle-boroughs of Wales and the Border country were given the 'laws of Breteuil' which were the customs of a castle-borough in Normandy. Domesday states that the burgesses of the castle-borough of Rhuddlan had been granted 'the laws and customs which are in Hereford and Breteuil';[6] and there were French burgesses in Hereford. Though it might be difficult to produce specific evidence to show that the early settlers in the castle-boroughs, or some of them, were French, it would be hard to believe that none of them were.[7]

More than the castle itself, it was the combination of castle, monastery, and borough, or of two of these elements, that formed one of the chief instruments of Norman colonization in Britain. The conjunction was already known in Normandy.[8] Among the castles which the early eleventh-century dukes of Normandy had founded in the west of their duchy, there was a ducal *bourg* and two monasteries, each with its own *bourg*, at Caen;[9] a castle, a *bourg*, and a college of canons at Cherbourg.[10]

[1] Beresford, *New Towns*, pp. 432, 518, 525–6, 473–4, respectively.
[2] D.B. i., 270 a 1.
[3] Beresford, *New Towns*, pp. 481–2, 479–80, 425, respectively.
[4] Ibid., pp. 492, 494, 395–6, 461–2, 483, 486. For Arundel see also Round, 'Castles of the Conquest', pp. 331–3; and for Belvoir, the same writer's note, 'The Origin of Belvoir Castle'.
[5] All the cities and boroughs in which French burgesses are mentioned in Domesday, and those in which they can be inferred, had early Norman castles (above, pp. 38–9).
[6] D.B. i., 269 a. One Frenchman is mentioned in a berewick of Rhuddlan.
[7] Above, p. 39.
[8] Musset, 'Peuplement en bourgage et bourgs ruraux en Normandie', pp. 186–95. [9] Legras, *Bourgage de Caen*, pp. 39–42 and plan.
[10] Fauroux, *Recueil*, No. 224 (pp. 428–9); Yver, 'Châteaux forts en Normandie', p. 39.

Roger de Montgomery built a castle beside his nunnery or founded a nunnery beside his castle at Almenèches, and apparently a *bourg* there as well.[1] Duke William had founded a castle at Breteuil on his frontier over against the royal domain and had given custody of it to William fitzOsbern, who founded the *bourg* and very probably the priory there,[2] as he founded the priory and most probably the borough by his own castle at Chepstow.[3] It was at Fécamp, beside the ducal castle-palace, that Duke Richard II made his most successful move towards reviving the monastic life in Normandy; and there seems to have been a *bourg* there also by 1040.[4] Examples of this same conjunction may be found in Anjou[5] and elsewhere.

In Normandy, the castle–*bourg*–monastery complex seems to have served as a means of mutually interdependent feudal, economic, and ecclesiastical development, the castle for physical and the monastery for spiritual protection with the *bourg* as 'un petit foyer de peuplement aggloméré',[6] a form of 'internal colonization'. Across the Channel, however, since it was part of a process of conquest and colonization from outside, a fortified centre with Norman knights, Norman monks or canons and often Norman burgesses would have seemed a formidable instrument of domination and exploitation to the surviving English or Welsh people, for the 'Frenchmen' had been put there by the Norman king or baron to maintain his hold upon the land and upon his large share of its products.

---

[1] Musset, 'Les premiers temps de l'abbaye d'Almenèches', pp. 22–3. The earliest evidence of the *bourg* is, however, much later.

[2] Yver, 'Châteaux forts en Normandie', p. 58; Génestal, *Tenure en bourgage*, pp. 237–9; *Abbayes et prieurés*, p. 183. The *bourg* received the customs of Cormeilles, where fitzOsbern was lord of the *bourg* and founder of the monastery; and the priory was a dependency of Lire, fitzOsbern's other monastic foundation in Normandy.

[3] Castle: Armitage, *Early Norman Castles*, pp. 125–6; borough: Beresford, *New Towns*, p. 559; the priory depended on fitzOsbern's foundation at Cormeilles (Knowles and Hadcock, *Religious Houses*, pp. 53, 62).

[4] Fauroux, *Recueil*, No. 94 (pp. 245–7); Yver, 'Châteaux forts en Normandie', p. 34.

[5] Halphen, *Comté d'Anjou*, pp. 88–96.

[6] Musset, 'Peuplement en bourgage et bourgs ruraux en Normandie', p. 193.

9. Intimations of Empire

THE argument of this book has been that the spread of Norman domination in northern France and in Britain was a continuous and consistent process. Beginning with the first settlements of the Vikings in the lower Seine Valley and along the coast towards Brittany, the Northmen may have extended the area of their settlements a little during the course of the tenth and early eleventh centuries but they certainly extended the range of their domination a great deal, not only over the land that eventually became the duchy of Normandy, but in Brittany and elsewhere. As the social structure and the distribution of wealth in Normandy became more characteristically feudal in form this domination took the form of feudal lordship. Taken as a whole, both within Normandy and beyond its borders, this was an aristocratic domination rather than a mass settlement of Scandinavian peoples on Gallic soil; and this aristocracy did not limit its ambitions to the continental mainland. Even in Viking days, the raiding and settlement of the lands on either side of the English Channel had been very closely related; but from the time of the marriage of Emma, the sister of Duke Richard II, to Æthelred king of the English, the relationship began to take the form of an aristocratic penetration of England; and this, after Duke William's conquest of the kingdom, became an overwhelming aristocratic and ecclesiastical colonization. From England, colonization spread to Scotland and conquest and colonization into Wales; and overlordship was strengthened and even extended in northern France. In the early twelfth century there must have seemed to be no limit to the lands which the Norman kings and their barons might not dominate in one way or another.

At the same time as it was thus extended, this aristocratic domination was organized into a political structure. The duke of the Normans made himself also the king of the English, and governed the two lands directly by dividing his time between them, crossing the sea frequently from one to the other and

journeying constantly through the length and breadth of each.
Though his royal status was never formally extended to Normandy by any act or ceremony, his power and authority were
effectively no less kingly there and no more restricted in principle than they were in England. King, household, and court were
common to the two countries; men drawn from the household,
or at least holding the titles of household offices and rejoining
the king's entourage from time to time, were employed on
judicial and administrative work in both countries; and the
activity of the king's court was increasing constantly, setting
limits to all other jurisdictions. This activity so increased, indeed, that it was necessary to delegate certain financial and
judicial work on a regular basis to commissions of auditors and
commissions of justices, as well as to justices exercising royal
justice in commission regionally or by itineration. Although, in
retrospect, it can be seen that these commissions ultimately
formed the basis of a complete administration proper to each
country, with differences in detail between them arising partly
out of native customs and institutions, in Norman times they
were scarcely as yet distinguished from the itinerant household
and court or from one another, either in membership or function, and the men concerned were drawn from and returned
to the central body which was common to the two countries.
That there was no intention under the Norman kings to form
complete and distinct administrations, one for each country,
even to the extent that this was done under their Angevin
successors, seems to be shown by the degree to which there was
assimilation in law and institutions and in other respects. The
measure of unity and integration between Normandy and England which such governmental development produced was also
manifested in the attitude of the royal family, which regarded
all its lands, rights, and prerogatives as an indivisible inheritance, and by the nature of the interests which the aristocracy
and the higher churchmen had in both countries and which
depended in the last resort on their continuing union.

Beyond Normandy and England, the Norman kings translated the old superiority of the kings of the English over the
kings of the Scots and the Welsh princes into feudal overlordship, and retained their suzerainty over those of their vassals
who acquired fiefs in Scotland or conquered principalities in

Wales. On the Continent, likewise, earlier attempts to dominate Brittany were transmuted into feudal suzerainty over the count or duke of the Bretons and directly over some of his barons; the relationship with the counts of Flanders was given feudal form; suzerainty over the count of Maine (and sometimes directly over his barons) was imposed, if insecurely held, and a similar domination fastened rather more firmly over the counts of Boulogne and of Pontieu. Along the Norman border, particularly to the south-east, families which held lands or were acquiring lands on either side of a hardening frontier were being drawn more and more into Norman overlordship. Though the intensity of this lordship over such families and over the native rulers of neighbouring principalities changed and fluctuated, speaking generally it was increasing; and even though such overlordships tended to overlap with one another, as was characteristic of the eleventh century, so that a count of Flanders could be simultaneously the vassal in some sense of the emperor and of the king of France as well as of the Norman king, and there was at least potentially a dual allegiance in all the Norman king's continental lands and lordships, the whole, lands ruled directly and lands subjected to some form of overlordship, formed a single coherent political structure, though naturally very different from any modern sovereign state. Indeed, to speak of 'lands ruled directly and lands subjected to some degree of overlordship' is probably to make too great a distinction. The Norman king's rights over the king of Scots, the Welsh princes, the duke of Brittany, and so on were clearly limited; but his rights over the barons, knights, religious institutions, and even the peasantry within Normandy and England, were also limited, to a greater or lesser extent, by their various rights and liberties. There was no generalized concept of subjection or citizenship; to the king it must have seemed that he possessed a bundle of rights and grades of authority which could differ widely as from one region, institution, or person to another; yet this was the basis of the political entity over which he ruled.

Certainly, it was the power which he derived from all his lands and lordships together that confronted a prince who was beyond the range of his domination, just as it was the whole of the lands and the varying degrees of suzerainty and traditional

authority which the king of the Franks exercised in his kingdom
that constituted his power; and this totality of the lands and
lordships of the Norman kings (rather than the kingdom of the
English, for instance) was as much the political reality of its
day as the kingdom of the Franks, effectively more so. No doubt
if it had lasted longer or developed further a name would have
been found for it in its own day;[1] but as this did not happen
the historian who recognizes its existence while it did last must
provide it with one, for convenience if nothing else. Up to this
point the non-committal phrase 'the Norman lands and lordships' has been used in this book; but this is clumsy as well as
non-committal and hardly expresses what seems to have been
the political reality. The search for a more compendious term
naturally raises the whole question of its political character and
the possibility of classifying it into one or other of the recognized
categories of states. It is at least worth considering whether
'The Norman Empire' might be appropriate as well as simpler
and more specific.

It will at once be objected that the Norman lands and lordships did not constitute an empire in any sense normally used
by modern historians when writing of the Middle Ages or by
medieval writers themselves. There was no emperor. The Norman kings made no pretence that their authority was in any
way related to that of the ancient Roman emperors, nor did
they claim the special qualities attributed to the rulers of the
'Roman Empire' of their time. If it is held that the only true
empires in Christendom during the Middle Ages were the
Roman empires of East and West, and that the term should be
reserved for those empires and the ideas they embodied, then
to speak of a 'Norman Empire' could only be a misuse of words.
Even though the nature and the extent of the Norman kings'
dominion could readily be compared with that of some more
or less contemporary Spanish kings, or that of the West-
Saxon kings of the tenth and early eleventh centuries, to whom
imperial or quasi-imperial titles were attributed, and even
though William the Conqueror or those who served him did not
entirely abandon the idea behind such titles, particularly in

---

[1] The Hyde chronicler speaks of a 'regnum Norman-Anglorum' (*Liber Monasterii
de Hyda*, p. 300) and uses other expressions suggesting the idea of a cross-Channel
state; but his use of these terms seems to be idiosyncratic (above, pp. 231–2).

their coronation ceremonial, the titles themselves are not to be found on the seals or the coins of the Norman kings, nor on such of their written acts as can be identified as composed by their own clerks.[1]

If, on the other hand, the word 'empire' is used in its modern and more general sense, there is much more to be said for applying it retrospectively to the Norman complex in northern France and Britain. In this sense the term has been used of political structures whose head did not take an imperial title and even of those which existed before the Roman idea of empire was conceived. Though qualifications may have to be made, the characteristics which have been used to identify such empires[2] are also found in the Norman complex. Relative to its neighbours and indeed to most contemporary states in western Europe, it was a 'great power', more powerful certainly than the kingdom of the Western Franks, the Scandinavian kingdoms, the kingdom of the Scots, or the Welsh and Irish kingdoms and principalities. There was one clear centre of power, which was sovereign in the sense that the ruler acknowledged no higher secular authority in any of his lands or overlordships.[3] The

---

[1] For imperial titles attributed to Spanish and Anglo-Saxon kings, Folz, *L'idée d'empire en Occident*, pp. 49–54; above, pp. 58–9, and cf. Barlow, *Edward the Confessor*, pp. 135–8. The extent to which Anglo-Saxon usage in this respect persisted under William the Conqueror is shown by Schramm, *History of the English Coronation*, p. 30; and that this was not entirely foreign to Norman ideas is illustrated by comparisons between William and Julius Caesar (e.g. William de Poitiers, *Gesta*, pp. 246–56; *Carmen de Hastingae Proelio*, vv. 32, 350–4) and some of the formulae included in the post-Conquest *Laudes* (Douglas, *William the Conqueror*, p. 250). The titles of the Norman kings are discussed above, pp. 231–6. Even among those of their acts that were written, so far as we can see, by clerks employed by the beneficiaries, the title 'victoriosus Anglorum basileus' attributed to William the Conqueror in an Exeter diploma of 1069 (*Regesta*, i, No. 28; Chaplais, 'Authenticity of the Royal Anglo-Saxon Diplomas of Exeter', pp. 31–3) seems quite exceptional.

[2] These characteristics are described in *Grands Empires* (Société Jean Bodin, xxxi). See especially ch. xxiii, 'La notion d'empire dans l'histoire universelle', by John Gilissen, where, at p. 863, empires other than those of the sub-class 'grands empires' are recognized as such 'quand [ils] sont au moins une grande puissance dans le cadre régional et que, dans ce cadre, [ils] possèdent les autres qualités requises: État souverain, concentration de pouvoir, composition complexe, tendance à l'hégémonie, au moins régionale, territoire plus vaste que les autres États, durée relativement longue.'

[3] The treaty of 1101 recognized that the suzerainty of King Philip limited the obligations of the count of Flanders to King Henry (*Diplomatic Documents*, i. 1); but Henry would have regarded Philip's suzerainty as equal to his own, not superior. Otherwise the statement is certainly true in practical terms; and if the

complex was composite in character, including several ethnic, political, and quasi-political groups of people. It showed a striving for hegemony and certain of its rulers were credited with ambitions extending far beyond the principalities which actually fell under their rule or overlordship. Certainly its territorial extent could not be compared with that of many of the great empires of the world's history; but if to Normandy and England are added the vassal principalities, the whole amounts to no inconsiderable stretch of country, particularly in relation to the effective political units of its time; and it lasted for about three-quarters of a century, longer than some of the empires to which the title could not be denied.

The qualifications that have to be made concern chiefly the extent to which feudal relationships entered into the structure of the Norman complex, for the idea of feudalism may well be regarded as the antithesis of the idea of empire. Certainly, if feudalism is conceived of as a state of affairs in which political power and authority are disintegrating, where the ruler has to share them with magnates and institutions in his realm because he can no longer exercise them himself, then the idea of a 'feudal empire' makes little sense.[1] But when a ruler is personally strong, capable of inspiring loyalty, and possessed of great wealth, and at the same time is building institutions for the fuller exercise of his authority, the feudal relationship may be a positive source of strength, may even be made into one of the chief bonds holding such a complex together. It could hardly be maintained that the feudalization of the relationships between the chief men in Normandy and their duke made William the Conqueror any less powerful than his ancestors; while the translation into feudal form of the ancient superiority of the kings of the English over the kings of the Scots certainly strengthened that relationship to the advantage of the king of the

implications of Henry's refusal to do homage to King Louis VI are pressed to their logical conclusion, a legalistic argument could be constructed to show, for example, that when Louis ceded to Henry 'Belismum et Cenomanensium comitatum, totamque . . . Britanniam' (Orderic Vitalis, *H.E.* (ed. Le Prévost), iv. 307–8) those countries were, at least in feudal terms, completely detached from his kingdom of France.

[1] *Grands Empires*, pp. 769–70, 809–11, 843–4. To say that 'les empires féodaux n'ont guère de cadres administratifs' may be true of feudal states in general, but it would be a very hard judgement on England and Normandy under the rule of the Norman kings.

English. Even so, the extent to which all such relationships were contractual, whether between the king and his vassals in kingdom and duchy or between the king and the princes ruling beyond either, naturally raises doubts about the propriety of calling a political structure depending in large measure (though not wholly) on these relationships an empire, although the suzerain's part in these relationships seemed to be growing stronger all the time,[1] at least until Stephen's reign.

The force of such qualifications is in any case more than compensated for by other considerations. The Norman kings were more than kings. In addition to their kingdom, and to a duchy in which they were scarcely less than kings, they were overlords of other kings. For such a complex as they ruled, a word that describes a political structure of higher status than a kingdom seems not inappropriate. It included a number of *regna*, at least in the contemporary sense of that term; and even though imperial or quasi-imperial titles were not given to the Norman kings themselves, this is the sense in which they were attributed to Spanish and West-Saxon kings. Besides, if the word 'empire' is used in its more modern sense, and is associated with the implications of its derivatives 'imperialism' or 'empire-building', it appears all the more fitting, for these implications extend the notion of hegemony to exploitation, which is not hard to find in the Norman lands. Indeed, the centre of power, the agent and beneficiary of that exploitation, can perhaps be identified more precisely than it has been hitherto; and, if it were, this would give the Norman lands and lordships the appearance of an empire in the modern if not the medieval sense.

It can certainly be said that the Normans made full use of the resources of England, the land which they conquered and colonized. Naturally the statistics on which it would be possible to say positively that this amounted to exploitation in the pejorative sense do not exist; but such evidence as there is suggests a great deal. It was ultimately the wealth of England that raised the Norman dukes to the position of power and magnificence held by a William the Conqueror or a Henry Beauclerc, as it raised many a baronial family from a position in Normandy which was outstanding only by provincial standards to one which, in terms of wealth, could be compared with that

[1] Save, perhaps, to the extent that fiefs were becoming more securely hereditary.

of many territorial princes on the Continent; and the fact that their lands were not concentrated in one region was not necessarily a source of weakness. The conquest of England also vastly increased the opportunities of attaining high office that were open to Norman churchmen.[1] Englishmen were prominent in the armies assembled by the Norman kings for the defence of their lands; and whether or not they had to bear a disproportionate burden of service in this respect, or whether indeed they regarded it as a burden, it is at least clear that they were used in operations that related to the defence of the Norman lands and lordships as a whole rather than to that of England alone.[2]

Military strength was, however, at least as much a matter of money as of men, even in the eleventh century.[3] Normandy was a wealthy country already in 1066 and the duke was able to exploit this wealth.[4] The invasion army with its high proportion of mercenary and quasi-mercenary troops could hardly have been enlisted, mobilized, concentrated, and conveyed across the Channel wholly on the basis of services owed and promises. It may be that after the dukes had built up their military aristocracy in Normandy and taken their share in the refoundation of monasteries and cathedrals in the duchy, and also after the disorders of William the Conqueror's minority, the ducal demesne was less extensive than it had been;[5] if so this would have been a reason for seeking to make good such losses beyond the duchy—though the duke must have had the means of recovery within it, if more slowly, without recourse to foreign conquest.[6]

But the indications are that England was wealthier still.[7] The West-Saxon kings had found ways to exploit this wealth, and the circumstances of the Conquest made it easy for William and his sons to exploit it still more fully. Edward the Confessor had had a large demesne: William, after all that he had distributed to his barons, still possessed in 1086 a demesne which was quite

[1] Above, pp. 35-7, 44, 49-51, 195, 248-9.
[2] Above, pp. 201-6.　　　　　　　　　　　　　[3] Above, esp. pp. 202-3.
[4] Musset, 'Conditions financières d'une réussite architecturale', pp. 312-13, and earlier works of the same author there cited; Brown, *Normans and the Norman Conquest*, pp. 51-3.
[5] As Musset suggests, 'Naissance de la Normandie', pp. 118-19.
[6] Above, pp. 145-8.　　　　　　　　　　　　　[7] Above, pp. 29-30.

twice as large as Edward's and was made to yield proportionately more.[1] William took over his predecessors' profitable management of the coinage, a far more efficient organization than he had in Normandy,[2] and, of even greater importance, he kept in being the machinery for levying the geld. This was a general tax upon land; and though its assessment was complex and variable, its incidence could be adjusted to the king's needs and at his will.[3] William the Conqueror is thought to have imposed a geld upon the country quite frequently, perhaps almost annually and at a greatly enhanced rate towards the end of his reign.[4] He was followed in this by William Rufus and Henry Beauclerc.[5] In addition, there was the plundering of England by the Normans in the years immediately after 1066 and the more or less arbitrary levies made later on.[6]

Nor, when William or his sons gave lands in England to their barons and ministers, did they lose all the benefits they might have derived from them. The fiefs which were thus created were hereditary in the sense that a direct heir would normally succeed his ancestor; but the king could exploit all the uncertainties that still hung over indirect successions, could exact more or less arbitrary reliefs from heirs who did succeed to their heritages, and could confiscate for disloyalty or rebellion.[7] Moreover the services which were an essential part of feudal tenures, military or other, performed in person or commuted for a money payment, were certainly of value; and the king could demand huge fines and bribes for favours of all kinds— such as the £3,000 which Robert de Bellême is said to have paid William Rufus for the inheritance of his younger brother Hugh, or the 'large sum' he paid to King Henry for the honour of Tickhill-Blyth, the inheritance of 'his relative' Roger

---

[1] Corbett, 'The Development of the Duchy of Normandy and the Norman Conquest of England', pp. 508–9; Hoyt, *Royal Demesne*, pp. 5, 75–81, and *passim*.

[2] Above, pp. 235, 261.

[3] Stenton, *A.-S.E.*, pp. 636–40; Loyn, *Anglo-Saxon England and the Norman Conquest*, pp. 305–14.

[4] Galbraith, 'The Date of the Geld Rolls in Exon Domesday', pp. 14–17; *Making of Domesday Book*, pp. 95–8.

[5] Poole, *Domesday Book to Magna Carta*, pp. 110–11; Prestwich, 'War and Finance' pp. 30, 37.

[6] Above, pp. 29–30; Prestwich, *ubi supra*, pp. 36–7 and, e.g., Stephenson *Borough and Town*, pp. 160–2.

[7] Above, pp. 107, 149. On reliefs, Pollock and Maitland, *H.E.L.*, i. 308–14.

de Bully.[1] In some instances a proportion of this money may have come ultimately from lands and interests across the Channel; but the bulk of it must have been raised on the English estates of a baron if only because, generally speaking, these were relatively so much larger than those in Normandy. Payments of this order must mean that the king was levying, in effect, a very considerable tax on the revenue that his barons derived from their estates and his servants from their offices; and this was the more easily and effectively done in England for some time after 1066 because the Norman kings were conquerors, grants were recent, and the conditions attached to them fresh in the memory.[2] Churchmen suffered as well as laymen, for the king's rights over churches were very profitable even when they were not misused as Rufus is said to have misused them.[3]

It is not very hard, therefore, to find justification for the strictures which the author of MS. E of the Anglo-Saxon Chronicle at that point wrote into his obituary of King William:

The king and the chief men loved gain much and over-much— gold and silver—and did not care how sinfully it was obtained provided it came to them. The king sold his land on very hard terms—as hard as he could. Then came somebody else, and offered more than the other had given, and the king let it go to the man who had offered him more. Then came a third and offered still more . . .

> The king was so very stark
> And deprived his underlings of many a mark
> Of gold and more hundreds of pounds of silver,
> That he took by weight and with great injustice
> From his people . . .[4]

The chronicler in his emotional and simplistic way, attributes

---

[1] Orderic Vitalis, *H.E.* (ed. Le Prévost), iv. 32–3. Other examples quoted by Prestwich, ubi supra, and by Southern, *Medieval Humanism*, pp. 215–17.

[2] Assessments to knight-service, for example, were relatively higher in England than in Normandy (Stenton, *A.-S.E.*, p. 550).

[3] e.g. Makower, *Constitutional History of the Church of England*, pp. 314–16; Poole, *Domesday Book to Magna Carta*, pp. 169–70.

[4] A.-S.C., 1087, E (pp. 163–4). William Rufus, likewise, 'was always harrassing this nation with military service and excessive taxes' (ibid., 1100, E, p. 176). Cf. Malmesbury, *Gesta Regum*, ii. 335–6, quoted by Prestwich, ubi supra, pp. 23–4. On the exploitation of England in particular and in this way, the testimony of Orderic Vitalis is quoted above, p. 47. Add, e.g., A.-S.C., 1097, E (p. 175).

this exploitation (which can only refer to England) to personal avarice. King William would no doubt have replied that these were the revenues needed for the maintenance of his dignity and his government; but England was not taxed for the government of England alone, but for the maintenance of Norman rule wherever it could be established. This is shown by the recurrent refrain in the Anglo-Saxon Chronicle, 'In this year . . . the king went overseas into Normandy . . . and the people . . . were often severely oppressed by the taxes the king took';[1] and even more directly in such incidents as the agreement which King Henry made with the count of Flanders in March 1101.[2] By this agreement the count undertook to provide a substantial body of knights for service in England, Normandy, or Maine, when called upon to do so, in return for an annual payment of £500. Although it is hard to find direct evidence that the payment was actually made or the service rendered[3] (the contract was renewed in 1110, *c.* 1128 and again in 1163), the money for the payment could only have been raised in England at the time when the agreement was first made because at that time Henry was king of England only, and within a few months had undertaken to give up almost all the lands he still held in Normandy. England could be exploited in this way because the Norman kings were able to superimpose levies and dues which can be described as feudal upon the sophisticated financial administration which the Anglo-Saxon kings had already constructed in the country, and they were not entirely without experience of levying direct taxes in their own duchy.

England could also be exploited, or at least made use of, directly through her land. The activities of the marchers in Wales were based largely upon the lands they held more securely in England;[4] while the lands which the Scottish kings came to hold in England, particularly the earldom of Huntingdon which King David acquired before he became king and on which he had lived the life of a great Anglo-Norman baron, not only assisted the process of assimilating the Scottish

---

[1] Above, p. 203.   [2] Above, pp. 79–80.   [3] Above, p. 80 n. 2.

[4] As shown, for example, by the Lacy honour of Weobley, Wightman, *Lacy Family*, pp. 118–19, 142–5, 150–1, 165–6; cf. Barraclough, 'Earldom and County Palatine of Chester', pp. 30–2, and the careers of men like William fitzOsbern, Roger de Montgomery and his sons, and Robert fitzHamon (above, pp. 292–4, 312–14).

monarchy to that of the Norman kings but furthered the suzerainty which these were establishing over the kings of Scots.[1] Tenure of the English lands which formed the honour of Boulogne made the count unquestionably the vassal of the Norman kings and gave them the opportunity to exercise some authority over him even in his strategically important *comté* across the Channel.[2] Though many of the Breton lords who received lands in England seem to have abandoned their holdings after the rebellion of 1075, they certainly did not all do so; and the allegiance which those who remained owed to the king for their English lands served to strengthen his interests in Brittany and indirectly his suzerainty over the duke.[3]

Yet although the Norman kings used English men, English money, and English land to defend what they had won and to extend their conquests and their influence wherever it was possible to do so, Normandy nevertheless remained the centre of their interests, not only sentimentally as their patrimony and their country of origin, but also in practical ways. The kings themselves spent rather more of their time, for example, in Normandy and the neighbouring lands than in Britain. This is certainly true of William Rufus after he had taken possession of the duchy in 1096 and of Henry after Tinchebrai;[4] and though it is not possible to be so sure about William the Conqueror, impressions for what they may be worth certainly suggest that he was in Normandy or on its borders for at least half his time between Christmas 1066 and September 1087, and very probably rather more.[5] Such a distribution of their time might reflect many things, the incidence of internal disorder, trouble on the frontiers, or even personal preference;

---

[1] Above, pp. 69–73, 207–10.   [2] Above, pp. 76–7, 214–15.
[3] Above, pp. 215–16.

[4] A rough calculation based on *Handbook of British Chronology*, pp. 31–2, gives Rufus about 28 months in France out of the 47 between September 1096 and August 1100, and for Henry about 210 out of the 350 between September 1106 and December 1135 (cf. above, pp. 175–6).

[5] 'His itinerary cannot be reconstructed, but it is clear that between 1072 and 1084 he spent at least a part of each year in Normandy, and that he was absent from England for nearly three consecutive years between 1077 and 1080' (Stenton, *A.-S.E.*, p. 601). 'From the end of 1067 to 1072 he was primarily engaged in suppressing English rebellions, and establishing his power. From 1073 to 1085 he spent most of his time in Normandy' (Douglas, *William the Conqueror*, p. 211). He was also in Normandy from the summer of 1086 until his death near Rouen on 9 September 1087.

but it must also suggest an order of priority, and whatever qualifications may be made it still remains a remarkable fact that the Norman kings should devote less than half their time, when they were ruling both, to the larger and the richer of their lands. As for the barons, it is unlikely that the movements of any of them could be known in sufficient detail to give an idea of the relative amount of time and attention that they gave to their continental lands and their English estates, or to the king's business in either country.[1] The English lands were normally so much more extensive and, in the early years after 1066, needed so much organization, that it might well be expected that they would require more attention than those on the Continent. Yet a survey would probably produce several instances like that of the two branches of the Lacy family which clung to their relatively small Norman inheritance when, to a modern way of thinking, it would seem so much more convenient and economical to have concentrated their estates in the north and the west of England; and it is hard to see why they should have acted as they did if they did not retain a certain regard for their stake in Normandy.[2]

There are, moreover, clear indications that the Normans used some of their new-found wealth, not only to support and extend their conquests and their influence, but for the direct enrichment of Normandy itself. Although the plundering of treasure in England that took place immediately after the Conquest, and the transfer of some of this treasure to Norman churches, did not continue on anything like such a scale or as violently, it nevertheless did go on. The simultaneous building of the two great abbeys at Caen, for instance, was an enormous undertaking for the age, and it almost certainly required English as well as Norman money. There are indications that William Rufus was still plundering Waltham on their behalf when he was king.[3] The bishops of Séez and Coutances both

[1] The example of William de Warenne quoted above, p. 295 n. 2, suggests that the greater magnates at least were moving from one country to the other much as the king did.

[2] Wightman, *Lacy Family*, ch. 7. Many other examples could be given of what seems a relatively small estate in Normandy tenaciously maintained, e.g. the Bassets and Geoffrey of Clinton (below, p. 347), or the families of Percy (*Complete Peerage*, x. 435–6, note b, 441, note a), Bigod (ibid., ix. 577, 580, note c) and d'Aubigny (earls of Arundel, below, p. 341).

[3] Musset, 'Conditions financières d'une réussite architecturale', pp. 309–10.

paid visits to southern Italy, collecting money from their compatriots there for the building of their new cathedrals;[1] and
Geoffrey de Montbrai, the bishop of Coutances, must have been
able to add quite considerably to the sums realized by this
fund-raising tour from his vast possessions in England, not only
for building but for the re-establishment of the cathedral staff
and the diocesan organization.[2] Bishop Odo's building and his
patronage of art and learning at Bayeux can hardly be dis-
sociated from the landed wealth he acquired in England,[3] and
Abbot Mainier of Saint-Évroult made a very successful journey
to England in order to collect gifts of money, churches, and
lands from King William and his barons.[4]

Perhaps the most striking example of a 'transfer' of money
from England to Normandy was involved in the crusade of
Robert Curthose. The cash required for the undertaking was
raised in England by William Rufus and lent to Robert on the
security of the duchy of Normandy.[5] It was presumably spent
on preparations in Normandy as well as on the journey to the
East and on Robert's crusading activity there. On his way back
Robert paused in South Italy, married Sybil da Conversano,
and raised the money to redeem his duchy from his father-in-
law and other friends in the peninsula.[6] When he finally returned he found that William Rufus was dead and Henry was
still securing his position in England. The money did not have
to be repaid; and whether Robert dissipated it frivolously in
a few days, as William of Malmesbury says he did, or used

---

[1] Ibid., pp. 310–11; Musset, 'A-t-il existé en Normandie au xie siècle une
aristocratie d'argent?', pp. 286–7; Le Patourel, 'Geoffrey of Montbray', pp.
136–7.

[2] Le Patourel, ibid., pp. 155–6 and *passim*. The tract 'De statu Constantiensis
Ecclesie makes it clear that although Bishop Geoffrey was already contributing
generously to the needs of his cathedral before his wealth was dramatically enlarged after 1066 and that the value of his possessions in Normandy was also
growing rapidly, nevertheless the lands he obtained in England enabled him to
operate on a very much larger scale in Coutances (*Gallia Christiana*, xi, instrumenta,
cols. 219–22).

[3] Nicholl, *Thurstan Archbishop of York*, pp. 3–7; Gleason, *Ecclesiastical Barony*, pp.
13–15; Douglas 'Norman Episcopate', pp. 105, 112; Vallery-Radot, *Cathédrale de
Bayeux*, pp. 10–11.

[4] Orderic Vitalis, *H.E.* (ed. Le Prévost), iii. 18–32; (ed. Chibnall), iii. 232–42.
Saint-Évroult was also obtaining funds from Italy, ibid. (ed. Le Prévost), ii. 56–60;
(ed. Chibnall) ii. 58–64.

[5] David, *Robert Curthose*, pp. 91–2.

[6] Ibid., pp. 117–18, 123–4.

part of it to win over certain barons as Orderic has it,[1] the money was still presumably spent in Normandy. In effect England had provided 10,000 marks of silver for a Norman adventure; and the money had been spent, some of it twice over, in Normandy. Even in Henry's day there is Orderic's well-known picture of Richard Basset 'returning to his native village in Normandy "bursting with the wealth of England", building a stone castle and attempting to overawe his humble equals by the magnitude of his operations'.[2] Another way of putting it would be to say that he was investing in his home property some of the fortune he had made in what was then the land of opportunity which he and his compatriots were colonizing, as many have done in different parts of the world since his time.

But as with the continuing exploitation of England's moveable wealth, the land itself went on contributing to the resources of Normandy even after the distribution as recorded in Domesday Book. It is certainly true that after the 'conquest generation' Norman barons put more of their wealth into the religious institutions they were founding in England and proportionately less into the monasteries founded by their fathers and grandfathers in Normandy; yet Norman houses continued to receive support from English lands. For not only were the lands and churches in England that were given to them given in perpetuity, so that rents and other dues would go on being paid indefinitely, at least in principle, but the flow of such endowments certainly did not cease with the end of the eleventh century. It has already been suggested that those monasteries which were being founded in Normandy at the time of the conquest of England would have been glad to receive even such distant and potentially troublesome gifts;[3] but there were others being founded or refounded in Henry's time, such as Aumale and Saint-Georges-de-Boscherville, which received endowments in England; and, in the case of Saint-Georges, such gifts must have helped to build the astonishing church that still graces what was quite a modest foundation.[4] In addition,

---

[1] Malmesbury, *Gesta Regum*, ii. 461; Orderic Vitalis, *H.E.* (ed. Le Prévost), iv. 103–5. [2] Southern, *Medieval Humanism*, pp. 218–19; below, p. 347.
[3] Above, pp. 37–8, 44–5, 298.
[4] Above, p. 45 n. 1. Both were earlier collegiate foundations, but were refounded as Benedictine monasteries in 1120 and 1114 respectively and do not appear to have received their English properties until then (*Abbayes et prieurés*, pp. 34,

gifts of property in England were still being made to established monasteries in Normandy;[1] and in all this the most important point surely is that this wealth was flowing in one direction only, both before 1100 and after. For all that the monasteries and cathedrals of Normandy obtained in this way, it is very hard to find examples of English churches acquiring property in Normandy.[2]

Similarly those families, like the Paynels of Hambye, which had possessed extensive estates in England and yet chose to stand by their Norman rather than their English lands in 1204 and so to identify themselves finally with the duchy, had derived much of their wealth and consequence from England during the twelfth century.[3] If it was northern France, a region which included Normandy though it included much besides, that took the lead in art and architecture, learning and literature, at the end of the twelfth century, perhaps the great clerical civilization of the thirteenth century owed something to the wealth of an England exploited by Normans for Normandy.

One may speak in general terms of 'the Normans' exploiting England for Normandy or for their wider ambitions; but it is perhaps possible to define the exploiting group more precisely. If this reveals a concentration of wealth and power in a small ruling minority closely bound up with the royal family, it would suggest a situation which, in modern phraseology, is often described as 'imperialistic'.

49–50). Zarnecki says that one capital in Saint-Georges 'is practically a copy' of one at Steyning in Sussex ('1066 and Architectural Sculpture', p. 101), which suggests that the abbey may have obtained masons as well as money from England.

[1] e.g., *Cal. Docs. France*, Nos. 369, 427 (1), 469, 568, 723, 921–2. It is true that at all times lands in England might be used to endow a conventual priory there dependent upon a Norman monastery, and that the payments made to the mother house might eventually be little more than nominal; but it seems that most grants of lands in England to continental houses were intended to add to their revenues, and did so, rather than to found such priories (Chibnall, 'Some Aspects of the Norman Monastic Plantation in England', pp. 402–7; Matthew, *Norman Monasteries and their English Possessions*, pp. 27–65). For the economic value of their English possessions to some Norman monasteries, Matthew, ibid., pp. 65–70.

[2] No systematic search has been made, but only one or two examples of an English monastery obtaining properties in Normandy before 1144 have turned up. William de Moion (Mohun) gave lands and churches in the Cotentin to his priory at Bruton in Somerset; but this was as late as 1142 (*Complete Peerage*, xii (1), 38–9, note i). Merton Priory obtained the priory of Cahagnes in Normandy at some date (Matthew, ubi supra, p. 102, note 5).

[3] *E.Y.C.*, vi (*Paynel Fee*), esp. pp. 24–7.

We may begin with Orderic's short list of the most distinguished men in Normandy when the decision to invade England was being taken.[1] First he names the Norman bishops who were in office at that date; then thirteen laymen who, he says, 'inherited the warlike courage of their ancestors and excelled in judgement and wise counsel'. These laymen were Richard count of Évreux, Robert count of Eu, Robert count of Mortain, Ralph de Conches (Tosny), William fitzOsbern, William de Warenne, Hugh d'Ivry,[2] Hugh de Grandmesnil, Roger de Montbrai, Roger 'de Beaumont', Roger de Montgomery, Richard fitzGilbert (de Brionne), and Baldwin de Meules his brother. This list is based on a similar list which William de Poitiers gives in the same context,[3] though Orderic's list is longer. It includes all the names that William de Poitiers gives save one, whom William mentions simply as 'Hugh vicecomes' but who is most probably Hugh, *vicomte* of Avranches and the future earl of Chester.[4]

However much these lists of outstanding men in Normandy may owe to their compilers' knowledge of later events,[5] they would not be very different from any list that could now be made of the leading members of Duke William's 'new aristocracy' at that time, men who were closely associated with him in terms both of kinship and vassalage. Odo de Bayeux (named by Orderic among the bishops) and Robert de Mortain were William's half-brothers; and no less than nine others (Richard d'Évreux, Robert d'Eu, William fitzOsbern, William de Warenne, Roger 'de Beaumont', Roger de Montgomery, Richard fitzGilbert, Baldwin de Meules, and Hugh d'Avranches),[6] together with

---

[1] Orderic Vitalis, *H.E.* (ed. Le Prévost), ii. 121–2; (ed. Chibnall), ii. 140.

[2] For the identification of 'Hugo Pincerna' with Hugh d'Ivry, see Round, *King's Serjeants*, pp. 140–1.   [3] William de Poitiers, *Gesta*, p. 148.

[4] Hugh's father, Richard Goz, who was *vicomte* of Avranches, was living as late as 1082 (*Complete Peerage*, iii. 165); but Hugh may well have held the *vicomté* some time before his father's death. A 'Hugo vicecomes' attests charters relating to Avranches and the Avranchin before 1066 (Fauroux, *Recueil*, Nos. 73, 110, 145, 229; pp. 214, 271, 326, 440).

[5] Against this suggestion it could be argued that both lists include Richard count of Évreux, who died in 1067; and Orderic includes Hugh d'Ivry who, if he was not unprovided for, did not acquire spectacular possessions in England or make himself famous; and the bishops of Avranches and Séez do not appear to have received anything either in their personal or their official capacity.

[6] For Richard count of Évreux, Robert count of Eu, William fitzOsbern, Richard fitzGilbert, and Baldwin de Meules, cf. Douglas, *William the Conqueror*,

the bishops of Lisieux and Avranches,[1] could be regarded as kinsmen in some degree. Besides this, William fitzOsbern was a seneschal, Hugh d'Ivry a butler, Richard d'Évreux and Robert d'Eu were counts, Richard fitzGilbert and Baldwin de Meules the sons of a count, Hugh d'Avranches and Roger de Montgomery were *vicomtes* and Ralph de Conches was 'the standard-bearer of the Normans'.[2]

In the great share-out of England after 1066, this small group obtained quite a disproportionate amount of the spoils. Taking Corbett's figures as an indication, and bearing in mind all the limitations they must have,[3] King William, his queen, and his two half-brothers took lands to the value of about 18,000 pounds a year out of a total theoretical value of the whole country put on the same basis at 73,000 pounds, that is about a quarter. Five of Orderic's distinguished laymen (William fitzOsbern, William de Warenne, Roger de Montgomery, Hugh d'Avranches and Richard fitzGilbert) obtained estates in England of the highest order of magnitude (Corbett's 'Class A'), that is worth more than 750 pounds a year, and the others or their sons received estates in the higher categories—all except Hugh d'Ivry, and he was not unprovided for.[4] Of the four others who, in Corbett's classification, obtained estates in England of the largest size, Eustace de Boulogne and Alan de Bretagne were not on Orderic's list of distinguished Norman laymen because they were not Normans, though both were kinsmen of King

pp. 417–26, pedigrees Nos. 1, 5, 6 and 8; for William de Warenne, *Complete Peerage*, xii (1), 491–3; Roger 'de Beaumont', ibid., vii. 521, note c, 522; Roger de Montgomery, ibid., xi. 683 and note c. Maud the sister of Hugh d'Avranches married Ranulf II, *vicomte* of Bayeux, who was a grandson of Duke Richard III (Douglas, *William the Conqueror*, p. 93). In some cases the relationship between these men and Duke William was remote; and, in so far as our knowledge of it depends upon the genealogies which Robert de Torigni inserted into the work of William de Jumièges (*Gesta*, pp. 320–9), may be scarcely historical (see however White, 'The Sisters and Nieces of Gunnor, Duchess of Normandy'); but there can be no doubt that kinship with the ducal family, real or supposed, was of great significance in the rise of a Norman family. One could almost speak of a 'ruling clan'.

[1] Douglas, 'Norman Episcopate', p. 103. Count Rudolf, father of Bishop John of Avranches, was a son of William Longsword; Bishop Hugh of Lisieux was son of William count of Eu and so grandson of Duke Richard I (Le Patourel, *Norman Barons*, p. 6; Douglas, *William the Conqueror*, pedigree No. 5).

[2] For Ralph de Tosny, or 'de Conches', Orderic Vitalis, *H.E.* (ed. Le Prévost), ii. 121; (ed. Chibnall), ii. 140.

[3] Above, p. 32.

[4] Round, *King's Serjeants*, p. 141.

William;[1] Geoffrey de Montbrai, the bishop of Coutances, was put among the bishops;[2] only Geoffrey de Mandeville was ignored by Orderic, and his origins and relationships are certainly obscure.[3] By the time of William the Conqueror's death, the concentration of wealth in the king, his immediate family, and a very small group (the bishops of Bayeux and Coutances, Orderic's thirteen distinguished Norman laymen, with the count of Boulogne, Alan de Bretagne, and Geoffrey de Mandeville) is unmistakable. Together they held well over half the land of England;[4] and it would be necessary only to add the lands of the Church (by 1087 nearly all the bishops and most of the abbots of the greater monasteries were of Norman origin) and hardly more than 150 holders of estates of moderate size (who were also of continental origin) to account for almost the whole country.[5]

The members of this group, moreover, were closely related, not only to the ruling family but to one another.[6] Richard fitz-Gilbert (de Brionne or 'de Clare') and Baldwin de Meules were brothers;[7] so were Robert and Henry 'de Beaumont';[8] the two Alans and Brian de Bretagne (Penthièvre);[9] Ralph and Robert de Tosny (with their relations Robert and Berengar de Tosny

---

[1] For Eustace, Douglas, *William the Conqueror*, pedigrees Nos. 3 and 4, and for the estates he obtained in England, Round, *Studies in Peerage*, pp. 153–6, etc. It is certainly remarkable that Eustace should have obtained or retained one of the largest estates in England after his escapade of 1067—an example perhaps of the strength of the ties of kinship or of the importance to William of having some hold over the count of Boulogne. Corbett unaccountably omitted Alan de Bretagne. Mason ('The "Honour of Richmond" in 1086') pointed out that his should be included among the very largest Domesday estates in England. For his kinship with William, *E.Y.C.*, iv (*Honour of Richmond*, i), 84–6.

[2] Le Patourel, 'Geoffrey of Montbray', pp. 152–4.

[3] Loyd, *Anglo-Norman Families*, p. 57; *Complete Peerage*, v. 113–16; Hollister, 'The Misfortunes of the Mandevilles', pp. 18–19; Clay, *Early Yorkshire Families*, p. 56.

[4] Douglas, *William the Conqueror*, pp. 269–70.

[5] Corbett ('The Development of the Duchy of Normandy and the Norman Conquest of England', p. 508, cf. Lennard, *Rural England*, pp. 24–5) estimated that some dozen pre-Conquest landowners still held lands to the total value of 4000 pounds a year, or about 5½%, in 1086. To these should probably be added the smaller monasteries not, or not yet, 'Normanized'; but not many English landowners of any consequence retained possession for long after 1086—a few perhaps in the larger towns.

[6] Cf. Stenton, *A.-S.E.*, pp. 622–3; Douglas, *William the Conqueror*, pp. 85–8, 95–6, 270, etc.

[7] Pedigrees in Round, *Feudal England*, facing p. 473; Douglas, *William the Conqueror*, pedigree No. 5.

[8] *Complete Peerage*, vii. 520.   [9] *E.Y.C.*, iv (*Honour of Richmond*, i), 84.

who were father and son);[1] Ilbert and Walter de Lacy.[2] Moreover such men characteristically married the daughters of their peers. Richard fitzGilbert married a daughter of Walter Giffard the elder; his brother, Baldwin de Meules married a cousin or niece of William the Conqueror; William fitzOsbern married a daughter of Roger de Tosny, the standard-bearer; Robert 'de Beaumont' married Isobel, who was the daughter of the count of Vermandois and a granddaughter of King Henry of France, while she married, secondly, William II de Warenne; and the son and successor of Henry 'de Beaumont' married a daughter of this same William II de Warenne.[3] These are only examples and much longer lists could be made. Ties of kinship and family interest were strengthened by ties of homage. There are many instances in Domesday Book of men who were tenants-in-chief, often of great eminence, who held some of their estates as sub-tenants of other tenants-in-chief.[4] In some instances this might be a relic of earlier days when they had needed a powerful patron;[5] or such a tenancy might have been sought to round off an estate[6] or to acquire an interest or a base in some particular area;[7] but however these sub-tenancies came into being, one important effect of them could only have been to reinforce the cohesion of this very compact and closely interrelated group.

In their way, the men who took the higher positions in the English Church also formed a compact group. Before the Conquest, the bishops of Normandy had been drawn almost entirely from the same aristocratic group as took the land of England; and some such men were appointed to English bishoprics after 1066, though they were in a minority. Some were related by ties of kinship among themselves. There were

---

[1] Above, p. 293 n. 6.   [2] Wightman, *Lacy Family*, pp. 55–6, and *passim*.

[3] Respectively, *Complete Peerage*, iii. 242; iv. 309; vi. 448; vii. 526; xii (1), 496; xii (2), 362.

[4] e.g., *V.C.H. Oxfordshire*, i. 380, 385; *V.C.H. Surrey*, i. 280. For some Yorkshire examples, Ellis, 'Biographical Notes, ii. The Under-tenants' (*Y.A.J.*, v), pp. 289, 291, 314–17, 322–4, etc.

[5] This might explain the estates which Ilbert de Lacy still held of the bishop of Bayeux in Oxfordshire and Lincolnshire at the time of Domesday (Wightman, *Lacy Family*, pp. 31–5).

[6] e.g. the same Ilbert's tenancy of the manor of Warmfield, held of the archbishop of York (ibid., pp. 29–30), or Roger de Lacy's tenure of Holme Lacy of the canons of Hereford (ibid., pp. 127–31).

[7] e.g. several Lacy estates on the Welsh border, ibid., pp. 131–4.

several pairs of brothers: Archbishop Thomas I of York and Bishop Samson of Worcester; Thomas II of York and Richard of Bayeux (these two were the sons of Bishop Samson); Thurstan of York and Audoen of Évreux; Walkelin of Winchester and Simeon abbot of Ely (Gerard of Hereford and York was their nephew); Ralph d'Écure of Rochester and Canterbury and Seffrid of Chichester were half-brothers. Archbishop Anselm and his namesake, the abbot of Bury St. Edmunds and elect of London, were uncle and nephew. But the chief link between them was the fact that so many had been ducal or royal clerks. During their service in the royal chapel they must have made one another's acquaintance as well as the king's, suggesting association of a quasi-professional kind;[1] and to this it may be added that Archbishop Lanfranc secured bishoprics for two of his pupils, Arnost and Gundulf of Rochester, and the abbey of St. Albans for his nephew Paul; while Archbishop Thomas I of York and Bishop Samson of Worcester owed the cost of their education and something no doubt of their promotion to Bishop Odo of Bayeux. The Norman abbots of the more important English houses mostly came from a small group of monasteries in Normandy: Jumièges, Caen, Le Bec, Mont-Saint-Michel, and Fécamp;[2] and there is evidence of something like a 'Le Bec colony' at Canterbury.[3] These relationships made it possible to extend much of the self-conscious compactness of the Norman Church to England, and to reproduce among the more important prelates that monopoly of the positions of authority and of wealth by a small and closely associated group that was characteristic of the lay aristocracy—with a close connection between hierarchy and aristocracy.[4]

This general situation, in which wealth and power in England was concentrated in the hands of a relatively small group of men, most of whom had important though not easily measured lands and interests in Normandy and were of social and

---

[1] Above, pp. 49–51, 348–9. There was even a hereditary element among the royal chaplains, Bethell, 'English Black Monks and Episcopal Elections in the 1120s', pp. 674–5.

[2] Knowles, *Monastic Order*, p. 704. Of the bishops, Remigius and Herbert Losinga had held office at Fécamp; Arnost, Gundulf, and possibly Herfast, as well as Archbishops Lanfranc and Anselm, had been monks at Le Bec.

[3] Dodwell, *Canterbury School of Illumination*, pp. 7–8.

[4] Cf. above, pp. 296–301.

political eminence in both countries, persisted throughout the time of the Norman kings. The special conditions of Normandy in the mid eleventh century and the conquest of England had given William the Conqueror an almost unique opportunity to create his own aristocracy and to control the distribution of wealth among the people of the lands he ruled—however much he may have had to yield, on occasion, to the pressure of those with claims upon him. William Rufus, and still more Henry Beauclerc, had to work within a relatively more settled society and with families already established in positions of wealth and influence. They therefore had to find their means of control in somewhat different ways. Henry, it is true, as a result of the conflict with his brother Robert Curthose between 1101 and 1106, had the disposal of a considerable amount of confiscated land in England (the accumulation of the Montgomery family alone was enormous),[1] and later in Normandy; but this, even with the power still left him to manipulate the succession to fiefs in certain circumstances, never gave him the vast opportunity his father had enjoyed. Yet, though there is no second edition of Domesday Book to provide the basis even for such calculations as Corbett was able to make for the later part of the Conqueror's reign,[2] such evidence as there is suggests strongly that there was still quite a small group of wealthy men 'at the top' in Henry's time; the only difference being that this group included a number of men whose position derived partly, and in some cases primarily, from the manipulation of the administrative and judicial processes in the king's service under his protection and favour,[3] as well as those who owed their importance to inherited wealth and military potential.

The two wealthiest men after the king in the Norman lands of Henry's later years were his favoured nephew Stephen de Blois and his illegitimate son Robert de Caen, or 'of Gloucester'.

[1] For an estimate of the extent and value of this confiscated land, or some of it, Hollister, 'The Anglo-Norman Civil War: 1101', pp. 317–18, 320–1.

[2] Some deductions can be drawn from the Pipe Roll of 1130—the work that some men did as justices and sheriffs, something of the price they paid for office and favour, and, from the record of exemptions from Danegeld, some idea of the distribution of their demesne lands (e.g. Southern, *Medieval Humanism*, pp. 214–20; Davis, *King Stephen*, pp. 8–9). Otherwise historians have been reduced to basing their conclusions on the values given in Domesday (e.g. Hollister, ubi supra, p. 320).

[3] In general, Southern, ubi supra, pp. 206–33.

Both owed their wealth almost wholly to Henry; both must have received their lands after Henry became king; and for both the great bulk of those lands lay in England though both had interests on the Continent.[1] There were many other men of wealth whose fortunes were made, by whatever means, while Henry was king; but there is much to suggest that a great number of those who prospered outstandingly under his rule had already attached themselves to him before 1100 and had performed services then that would ensure his favour later on. Like his father, Henry had been able to recruit to his service the greater part of those who would later form his aristocracy before he became king.

About three-quarters of a century ago J. H. Round remarked, in his characteristic phraseology: 'It would seem, indeed, although the fact has been hitherto overlooked, that a group of families whom Henry had known when lord of the Cotentin were endowed by him with fiefs in England.'[2] He instanced, 'in addition to Alan fitzFlaald, founder of the house of Stewart,[3] and to Richard de Reviers, ancestor of the earls of Devon,[4] the Hayes of Haye-du-Puits were given the honour of Halnaker (Sussex),[5] the Aubignys, afterwards earls of Arundel, obtained from him a fief in Norfolk;[6] the two St. John brothers, from St. Jean-le-Thomas, were granted lands in Oxfordshire and Sussex and founded another famous house;[7] while the family

---

[1] Davis, *King Stephen*, pp. 7–10, 14–15; Patterson, 'William of Malmesbury's Robert of Gloucester', p. 994, note 41, and *Earldom of Gloucester Charters*, pp. 3–4; *Complete Peerage*, v. 683–6.

[2] Round, *Studies in Peerage*, pp. 124–5.

[3] From Dol-de-Bretagne, ibid., pp. 115–16, 120–4.

[4] Richard took his name from Reviers in the Bessin; but his two principal fiefs were at Vernon in the Vexin Normand and Néhou in the Cotentin, *Complete Peerage*, iv. 309–11; Loyd, *Anglo-Norman Families*, p. 85.

[5] References for the de la Haye family are collected in Le Patourel, *Normandy and England*, pp. 34–5.

[6] There were two d'Aubigny brothers, William d'Aubigny *pincerna*, whose son was the first earl of Arundel (*Complete Peerage*, i. 233–5; ix. 366–7) and Nigel d'Aubigny who founded the second Mowbray family with a huge estate in Normandy and England which was put together wholly in Henry's reign (ibid., ix. 367–9; Greenway, *Charters of the Honour of Mowbray*, pp. xvii–xxv, and *passim*). They took the name d'Aubigny from Saint-Martin d'Aubigny, a little to the north of Coutances, and Mowbray ultimately from Montbrai, a little to the south of the same city (Loyd, *Anglo-Norman Families*, pp. 7, 71).

[7] Saint-Jean-le-Thomas, near Avranches. For the family, Round, 'The Families of St. John and of Port'; Loyd, *Anglo-Norman Families*, pp. 89–90.

of Paynel also, sprung from the Cotentin, owed to Henry lands in England.'[1]

Round took the point no further, save to add the name of Geoffrey of Clinton to his short list;[2] nor did he offer any evidence that these men or their families were in contact with Henry before 1100, though clearly they could have been. It is not difficult, however, to show that Henry's interest in western Normandy, as well as in the duchy generally and in Brittany, and his activities there, were much greater during the 1090s than Round suggested;[3] and also that the list of families who did well in his time and were identified in some way with western Normandy or Brittany could be lengthened very considerably. These two points by themselves would offer no more than a long coincidence; but enough evidence can be found of actual contact at this time between Henry and those who achieved predominance in his lands to suggest rather more.

In 1088 Henry had bought the Cotentin from his brother Robert Curthose (or perhaps had taken it as pledge for a loan), drawing no doubt on his father's legacy for the purpose.[4] It seems that this made him 'count of the Cotentin', a position which gave him possession of ducal lands and rights (including castles), with suzerainty over the duke's vassals who had fiefs there so that, in fact, the ducal administration in the Cotentin now functioned under his authority.[5] Orderic adds that he re-

---

[1] The Paynels held Les Moutiers-Hubert south of Lisieux and Hambye near Coutances. Though the second gave them important interests in the Cotentin, it is not certain that they originated there and they were already established in England by 1086—*E.Y.C.*, vi (*Paynel Fee*), 1–2; Clay, *Early Yorkshire Families*, pp. 68–70; Loyd, *Anglo-Norman Families*, p. 77.

[2] Round, 'A Great Marriage Settlement'.

[3] Henry's activity in Normandy between 1087 and 1100 can be put together in general terms from references in Freeman, *William Rufus*, and David, *Robert Curthose*.

[4] 'Robertus . . . dedit illi comitatum Constantiniensem vel, ut alii dicunt, invadiavit' (William de Jumièges, *Gesta*, interp. Torigni, p. 269); 'Henrico duci tria milia librarum argenti erogavit, et ab eo totum Constantinum pagum . . . recepit' (Orderic Vitalis, *H.E.* (ed. Le Prévost), iii. 267; (ed. Chibnall), iv. 120). For Henry's legacy, ibid. (ed. Le Prévost), iii. 244; (ed. Chibnall), iv. 94–6; William de Jumièges, *Gesta* (interp. Torigni), pp. 268–9. Cf. Malmesbury, *Gesta Regum*, ii. 337, 468; Huntingdon, *Historia Anglorum*, p. 211; A.-S.C., 1087, E (p. 163).

[5] Orderic Vitalis, *H.E.* (ed. Le Prévost), iii. 350–1, 378; (ed. Chibnall), iv. 220, 250. Orderic at one point styles him *Constantiniensis comes* and at another says that he ruled the people of the Cotentin 'strenue' (ed. Le Prévost, iii. 291, 350; ed. Chibnall, iv. 148, 220). The nuns of Caen complained that 'comes Henricus

ceived in addition the whole fief (*totum feodum*) in Normandy of Hugh, *vicomte* of Avranches and earl of Chester, and Mont-Saint-Michel.[1] This must have meant suzerainty over Earl Hugh rather than possession of his lands, for he remained Henry's loyal supporter, with ducal rights over the abbey and its lands—and the Mount served Henry as a final stronghold in 1091. Besides all this, it appears from other evidence that he had the ducal rights over the bishop of Avranches as well as (in principle) over the bishop of Coutances, and other rights and property in the Avranchin.[2] It is very likely that he did homage to Robert

pedagium accepit de Chetelhulmo et de omni Constantino et super hoc facit [*sic*] operari homines Sancte Trinitatis de eadem villa et patria ad castella suorum hominum' (Haskins, *Norman Institutions*, p. 63). Among the additions to a charter of Néel, *vicomte* of the Cotentin, to the abbey of Saint-Sauveur is the item 'Ecclesiam de Tornebusc cum uno vavassore, et decimam totius parrochie dedit Eudo vicecomes, concessu Henrici comitis'—Eudes was brother and successor of Néel as *vicomte* of the Cotentin (Delisle, *Histoire du Château de Saint-Sauveur-le-Vicomte*, p. 27 and pièces justificatives, p. 53). Cf. the passage in 'De statu Constantiensis ecclesie' quoted below). It seems that Henry owed his title *comes* to his position in the Cotentin rather than to his membership in the royal family, for it does not appear to have been the custom in the Norman ducal family to give the title to the duke's sons as such, as it was in the Breton ruling family (Fauroux, *Recueil*, pp. 58–9, references given in notes 215, 219, 221, 222; *E.Y.C.*, iv (*Honour of Richmond*, i), 97–101). In his father's charters Henry usually appears as 'filius regis' and in those of William Rufus as 'frater regis'.

[1] 'Sic Henricus Abrincas et Constantiam Montemque Sancti Michaelis in periculo maris, totumque feodum Hugonis Cestrensis consulis quod in Neustria possidebat primitus optinebat' (Orderic Vitalis, *H.E.* (ed. Le Prévost), iii. 267; (ed. Chibnall), iv. 120). In addition to their possessions in England, the lands of Earl Hugh stretched right across Normandy and those of Mont-Saint-Michel through the western part of the duchy and into neighbouring principalities (above, p. 294, note 2; Dubois, 'Les dépendances de l'abbaye du Mont Saint-Michel', map p. 623).

[2] The tract 'De statu Constantiensis ecclesie' (*Gallia Christiana*, xi. instrumenta, col. 221) has an important reference to Henry's position. 'Ea igitur tempestate [i.e. 1087–8] praedictus Robertus dedit minori fratri suo Henrico comiti omnem pagum Constantiensem simul et Abrincatensem, necnon et episcopatus nunc et usque. Cum ergo Abrincensis episcopus dominatum praedicti principis suscepisset, Gaufridus Constantiensis funditus abnuit, ecclesiamque Constantiensem, cujus erat minister in vita sua, neminem habere dominum, nisi quem Rotomagensis haberet ecclesia, verbo edixit et opere complevit . . .' (cf. Le Patourel, 'Geoffrey of Montbray', pp. 146–8). It is clear that Henry had important interests in the Avranchin for, apart from his rights over the Norman fief of Hugh earl of Chester, the *vicomte* of Avranches, and over the abbey and the lands of Mont-Saint-Michel, and Orderic's statement which included Avranches among his possessions (preceding note), he was also able to give the castle of Saint-James-de-Beuvron to Earl Hugh in recognition of his services (William de Jumièges, *Gesta*, interp. Torigni, pp. 271–2); but it seems unlikely that he had the *comitatus* of the Avranchin as well as of the Cotentin, for there was a count of Mortain as well as a *vicomte* of Avranches

for his share in what almost amounted to a partition of Normandy between them.[1]

In 1091 his brothers drove Henry out of these lands;[2] but in the next year he obtained the *oppidum* of Domfront from which he was able to recover what he had lost—with the approval, it is said, of William Rufus.[3] Thereafter he and Rufus co-operated against their elder brother. Rufus put Henry in charge of his campaign of 1095 in Normandy, with a liberal supply of treasure;[4] and when he took possesson of the duchy in 1096 he granted to Henry the Bessin (except for Bayeux and Caen) and the Cotentin, both 'ex integro', though in the case of the Cotentin this could only be a confirmation of the position Henry already held there.[5] It is possible that Henry had some part in the first construction of Rufus's new castle at Gisors; he was certainly one of Rufus's commanders in the campaign of 1097 in the Vexin Français.[6]

It is easy to see that Henry's position in Normandy and his activities there gave him enormous opportunities. Orderic speaks as though he controlled almost as much of the duchy as Rufus did just before Rufus took it in pawn in 1096.[7] He had the

at the time. Geoffrey of Coutances may have come round in the end, for he died peacefully in his cathedral city early in 1093; though it is not quite certain that Henry had recovered the Cotentin as early as that after his dispossession in 1091.

[1] There is no mention of homage for the western lands in 1088; but Robert released Henry from his homage in the agreement of 1101, and the most likely occasion for this homage was when Henry received the Cotentin from him (David, *Robert Curthose*, p. 134). William of Malmesbury says that Henry held the Tower of Rouen 'in ejus fidelitatem' in 1088 (Malmesbury, *Gesta Regum*, ii. 468); but that phrase is not perhaps unambiguous.

[2] Orderic Vitalis, *H.E.* (ed. Le Prévost), iii. 377–9; (ed. Chibnall), iv. 250–2; William de Jumièges, *Gesta* (interp. Torigni), pp. 270–1; Malmesbury, *Gesta Regum*, ii. 363–5; Florence of Worcester, *Chronicon*, ii. 27.

[3] Orderic Vitalis, *H.E.* (ed. Le Prévost), iii. 384–6; (ed. Chibnall), iv. 256–60; William de Jumièges, *Gesta* (interp. Torigni), pp. 271–2.

[4] David, *Robert Curthose*, p. 87.

[5] William de Jumièges, *Gesta* (interp. Torigni), p. 275.

[6] 'Hoc tempore predictus rex Willelmus fecit quoddam castellum, nomine Gisors, in confinio Normanniae et Franciae, quod sepe nominatus frater ejus Henricus, qui ei divina dispositione successit, menibus ambitum et turribus excelsis inexpugnabile reddidit' (ibid.). This sentence is ambiguous, for it could mean that Henry was working on Gisors Castle 'hoc tempore' or after he had succeeded Rufus as king. The archaeological evidence seems to suggest that the first stage of construction included all the essential parts of the castle as it still exists, motte, donjon, 'chemise', and curtain wall to its present dimensions (Pépin, *Gisors et la vallée de l'Epte*, pp. 28–31). For the 1097 campaign in the Vexin, Orderic Vitalis, *H.E.* (ed. Le Prévost), iv. 19–24.   [7] *H.E.* (ed. Le Prévost), iii. 475–6.

revenues of his extensive lands there, possibly something still of his father's legacy, and the use at times of Rufus's treasure. He had friends in Brittany and hired mercenaries there (Orderic says directly that he had military assistance from Brittany in the critical year 1091 and ultimately took refuge there),[1] and at one time or another he could make contact with almost anyone he wished in Normandy. As far as the barons were concerned, this meant anyone of any importance; for although William Rufus seems to have taken care that Henry should possess no lands in England while he was king,[2] Henry was in fact in the country on several occasions between 1087 and 1100. Moreover the greater Norman barons of the time maintained their estates in Normandy, however small they might be in relation to their lands in England, and in the troubled times of Robert's rule in Normandy would certainly wish to keep an eye on them. Those with possessions in the regions that Henry controlled would have to have some understanding with him.

It is this which gives significance to Round's list of families which had interests in the western parts of Normandy and which prospered in England after Henry had made himself king, and to the additions that can be made to it—Brian fitzCount, for instance, who acknowledged that he owed his fortune to Henry, was an illegitimate son of Alan Fergent, duke of Brittany;[3] Ranulf le Meschin, *vicomte* of the Bessin, who was permitted by Henry to add the earldom of Chester and the *vicomté* of Avranches to his Norman inheritance, and his

---

[1] Ibid. (ed. Le Prévost), iii. 378–9; (ed. Chibnall), iv. 250. Cf. Malmesbury, *Gesta Regum*, ii. 468, 478; Prestwich, 'War and Finance', p. 32.

[2] Malmesbury indicates that Henry inherited his mother's lands (*Gesta Regum*, ii. 337, 468), which certainly included lands in England (e.g., Ellis, *General Introduction to Domesday Book*, i. 6, 452). Apparently he had not received possession by 1087, and in the next year he applied to Rufus for them (David, *Robert Curthose*, p. 52); but Rufus gave them to Robert fitzHamon (Orderic Vitalis, *H.E.* (ed. Le Prévost), iii. 350; (ed. Chibnall), iv. 220; *Complete Peerage*, v. 683). If the story is true, it is remarkable that this did not estrange Henry from Robert fitzHamon, or if it did the estrangement can have been no more than momentary. Henry was also in England possibly in 1091, through the winter of 1094–5 (including a few weeks while Rufus was still in Normandy), and he was in the fatal hunting-party in the New Forest on 2 August 1100 (David, *Robert Curthose*, pp. 65–6, 87, 120–1. The evidence for the 1091 visit is somewhat weakened by Offler, *Durham Episcopal Charters*, pp. 48–53).

[3] Southern, *Medieval Humanism*, p. 220; above, p. 42.

younger brother William, who received the barony of Copeland in Cumberland and married the heiress of the honour of Skipton.[1] The families which were beginning to take fiefs in Scotland, while Henry was king and overlord of the king of Scots, traced their origin with suspicious regularity to some place in the Cotentin peninsula or on the Breton border.[2] Three men are expressly mentioned as rendering noteworthy assistance to Henry in the Cotentin, particularly when he was recovering his position there after the disaster of 1091, Hugh of Avranches and Chester, Richard de Reviers (or 'Redvers', one of Round's examples), and Roger de Mandeville.[3] Earl Hugh did not live to receive his full reward, for he died in 1101; but his son was a ward of the king, married one of the royal nieces and no doubt would have achieved and acquired great things if he had not perished in the White Ship.[4] Richard de Reviers found his fortune in the West Country[5] and Roger de Mandeville, who was not of the family which rose to the earldom of Essex but took his name from Magneville, only a mile or two from the Reviers seat at Néhou in the Cotentin, obtained lands in Devon and Wiltshire.[6]

Besides these, many of Henry's ministers who prospered greatly in the royal service had interests in western Normandy and could have entered his service, or at least made his acquaintance, while he was still count of the Cotentin. We can be certain of this in the case of the most important of all, Roger of Salisbury, whom William of Malmesbury describes as Henry's steward or treasurer before 1100 and who was described as '[a] priest of Avranches' at the time of his election to the bishopric of Salisbury in 1103.[7] The man who later held the same position in Normandy as Roger had in England, John

---

[1] *Complete Peerage*, iii. 166; *E.Y.C.*, vii (*Honour of Skipton*), 4–6.

[2] Barrow, *Kingdom of the Scots*, pp. 320–7.

[3] William de Jumièges, *Gesta* (interp. Torigni), pp. 271–2; Orderic Vitalis, *H.E.* (ed. Le Prévost), iii. 350–1; (ed. Chibnall), iv. 220.

[4] *Complete Peerage*, iii. 164–6; Malmesbury, *Gesta Regum*, ii. 474.

[5] *Complete Peerage*, iv. 309–12.

[6] Loyd, *Anglo-Norman Families*, pp. 57–8; Sanders, *English Baronies*, p. 42.

[7] 'Insinuatus est primo comiti Henrico, qui postmodum rex fuit, pro prudentia res domesticas administrandi, et luxum familie cohibendi' (Malmesbury, *Historia Novella*, p. 37). Le Patourel, *Normandy and England*, pp. 35–6; Kealey, *Roger of Salisbury*, pp. 4–5, 96–8, 277; Ker, *English Manuscripts in the Century after the Norman Conquest*, plate 9a. Above, pp. 51 n. 10, 142–3.

bishop of Lisieux, is said to have been known to Henry already when he came to the court as a refugee in 1103; and this is not unlikely, for he had been brought up among the clerks of the cathedral at Séez, not very far from Henry's stronghold of Domfront which Henry had freed from the tyranny of Robert of Bellême, the oppressor of Séez.[1] Others are only possibilities: Aubrey II de Vere, Henry's chamberlain, a justice, and sheriff or joint-sheriff in some dozen counties, whose family took its name from Ver south of Coutances, had interests in Brittany and acquired lands in England that formed the basis of the earldom of Oxford;[2] Geoffrey of Clinton who was a treasurer and a justice, amassing a huge estate in the southern Midlands in the course of his career, still held the family castle at Semilly near Saint-Lô and other lands in the Cotentin;[3] Ralph and Richard Basset, among the most prominent of Henry's justices and who also acquired a large estate in the Midlands, still held their castle of Montreuil-au-Houlme between Argentan and Domfront;[4] the brothers Payn and Eustace fitzJohn, whose services to Henry seem to have been less specialized and whose family, so far as it can be traced, had property in Caen and in the Avranchin, accumulated their fortune in the west and in the north of England respectively.[5]

This is already beginning to suggest that Henry had been using his resources in the 1090s to build up a party of supporters, and the nucleus of a body of royal ministers, in anticipation of any greater opportunities that might come his way. In looking for his men, however, he had not been restricted to western Normandy and the Breton borderland. Among the most wealthy and influential families of his reign were the 'Beaumonts', represented then by the brothers Robert and Earl Henry of Warwick.[6] They are not known to have had any interests whatever in western Normandy, the family estates being in the Risle Valley, from Pontaudemer upstream, and they were already well established in England; but Robert inherited the

---

[1] Orderic Vitalis, *H.E.* (ed. Le Prévost), iv. 273–5 (cf. ibid., ed. Le Prévost, iii. 384–5; ed. Chibnall, iv. 256–8); Le Patourel, *Normandy and England*, pp. 32–3.
[2] Le Patourel, ibid., pp. 11 note 25, 30.
[3] Southern, *Medieval Humanism*, pp. 214–18; Round, 'A Great Marriage Settlement'; Le Patourel, ubi supra, pp. 30–1. [4] Le Patourel, ibid., p. 33.
[5] *Complete Peerage*, xii (2), 268–74 and Appendix B; Clay, *Early Yorkshire Families*, p. 99 and genealogy. [6] Above, p. 293 n. 4.

comté of Meulan in the Vexin Français from his mother, he is known to have co-operated with Rufus's forces in the campaigns there of 1097 and 1098, and at that time if no other must have made contact with Henry who was one of the commanders in the earlier campaign.[1] Robert is specifically mentioned by William of Malmesbury as one of Henry's supporters against Robert Curthose in 1101;[2] while his brother Earl Henry is spoken of then as a friend of Henry's of long standing.[3] Robert was subsequently put by Henry in the way of acquiring the lands which formed the basis of the earldom of Leicester;[4] Earl Henry obtained the Gower peninsula which carried the family's interests into Wales;[5] and both were among the most powerful and influential barons of King Henry's reign.

In the nature of things, Henry could hardly hope to draw all the greater barons of the Norman lands to his cause before he made his bid for the kingdom, and those who were not already in some relation with him had to decide what their attitude was going to be when faced with the situation created by his *coup* and Robert's safe return to Normandy a few weeks later. The magnates who decided immediately or later to support Robert may have done so from feelings of personal loyalty, from some idea of legitimacy, or simply from a calculation of where their own interests lay; but they may also have felt that Henry's supporters (whom in modern terminology they may well have thought of as 'Henry's gang') were a threat to the position they had established for themselves under the two Williams. To this extent the struggle between Henry and Robert was also a struggle between two rival groups of magnates, with interests likewise both in Normandy and in England; and it may be that for this reason alone any real accommodation between the two brothers was ultimately impossible. Some of Henry's opponents were intransigent or were relentlessly hunted down by him;[6] some came to terms;[7] some

[1] Orderic Vitalis, *H.E.* (ed. Le Prévost), iv. 20–1.

[2] Malmesbury, *Gesta Regum*, p. 471. [3] Ibid., p. 470.

[4] *Complete Peerage*, vii. 524–5. [5] Ibid., xii (2), 359.

[6] Not always directly by reason of their support for Robert in 1101, Hollister, 'The Anglo-Norman Civil War: 1101', pp. 330–2. The most notable were Robert de Bellême with his brothers and William de Mortain (*Complete Peerage*, xi. 692–6; iii. 428–9 and, e.g., Mason, 'Roger de Montgomery and his Sons', pp. 14–24).

[7] William II de Warenne was deprived of his English lands in 1101, but they were restored to him in 1103 (*Complete Peerage*, xii (1), 495). Walter I Giffard is

may have avoided the necessity of declaring themselves until it was clear which side would win;[1] but when Henry had secured Normandy and things had settled down, the old situation was restored—wealth and power in the Norman lands concentrated into the hands of the king and perhaps a couple of dozen great magnates[2] and prelates, or so it seems. This dominant minority had been very largely re-fashioned since 1086. Some of William the Conqueror's magnates or their sons had lost their position for rebellion in the ordinary sense, some by supporting the losing side in the disputes over the succession. Rufus had raised up 'new men', though not many; while Henry had recruited a following while he was still a count in Normandy and it was this following, with those of the older-established families who came over to him, that constituted his aristocracy, his dominant and exploiting minority.

It is probable that such a concentration of wealth, and the power and the exploitation involved in it, were inherent in the system we call feudalism, as it is in some other economic and social structures. Certainly one of the essential qualifications for successful rule as king or duke in the eleventh and twelfth centuries was the ability to attract a sufficient number of likely men to one's service and to hold them in the only ways then possible, by grants of land and then more land or, as was coming to be practicable in Henry's time, by appointment to offices from which profit could be made and invested in land (or which gave opportunities to acquire land directly); and the accumulation of offices by individuals whom Henry favoured was as

named by Orderic as one of Robert's supporters (*H.E.*, ed. Le Prévost, iv. 103–4); he died in 1102 but his son seems to have succeeded to his lands (*Complete Peerage*, ii. 386–7).

[1] Stephen, lord of Richmond and of vast lands in Brittany, and the members of the 'Clare' family are outstanding people not mentioned as taking part either in Robert's invasion or Henry's resistance, and they continued to prosper (*Complete Peerage*, x. 786–7; iii. 242–3; vi. 498–9; x. 348–9. Cf. Hollister, 'The Anglo-Norman Civil War: 1101', pp. 320–1).

[2] 'There could never at any one time have been more than about twenty such men at the top, pushing the interests of themselves and their families, and succeeding in varying degrees in their struggle for social eminence' (Southern, *Medieval Humanism*, p. 225). The writer was probably thinking primarily of England when he made this estimate; but though there might be a great disparity between the extent of a baron's lands on either side of the Channel, there was only one Norman baronage and the big men in England were the big men in Normandy and in the overlordships beyond both.

characteristic as the accumulation of estates in land.[1] In terms of land at any rate this is what William the Conqueror had done; but if Orderic's story is anywhere near the truth William had done his best to prevent his sons from forming their *clientelae* during his lifetime,[2] whatever his motives may have been. Rufus was fortunate in that he could allege his father's deathbed dispositions, persuade the archbishop of Canterbury to recognize him as his father's heir in England, and get possession of his father's treasuries there. For him that was a sufficient basis. The contrast is striking between his and Henry's success and Robert's ineffectual attempts to form an adequate following, even with what the king of France had put at his disposal before 1087,[3] with command of his father's treasury at Rouen and the resources of Normandy after that date;[4] or later on the basis of the money he had collected in South Italy for the redemption of Normandy[5] or by exploiting the hostility which some of the established barons felt towards Henry's men.

Whatever Henry's prospects may have seemed to be in 1087 or later (his father's prophecy that he would eventually possess all the inheritance was written into Orderic's *History* long after

[1] e.g., Southern, ubi supra, pp. 214–20, for the accumulations of Geoffrey of Clinton, the Bassets, and others of the 'administrative barons'; and Le Patourel, *Norman Barons*, pp. 9–16, 23–4 for those of William II de Warenne, the Beaumonts, and Ranulf le Meschin as examples of barons of the more traditional kind.

[2] Orderic Vitalis, *H.E.* (ed. Le Prévost), ii. 377–81; (ed. Chibnall), iii. 96–102. That the formation of such a *clientela* was thought by Orderic to be very much on Robert's mind and what was to be expected, is indicated by the despairing cry put into Robert's mouth, 'Quid ergo faciam, uel quid meis clientibus tribuam?' It is also implied by Robert's demand for Normandy which all chroniclers mention in one form or another. Nevertheless, still according to Orderic, several important magnates accompanied him when he left Normandy. Cf. above, p. 137 n. 1.

[3] David, *Robert Curthose*, pp. 23–8.

[4] Robert de Torigni in his interpolations to William de Jumièges (*Gesta*, p. 268) speaks of Robert as being based in Pontieu at the time of his father's death, with a number of young nobles from Normandy who hoped that he would be their future lord. Immediately he heard the news he went straight to Rouen (as Rufus made straight for Winchester) and took possession of the city, presumably with his father's treasury there, and of the duchy. How far the withdrawal of Henry's 5,000 pounds of silver had depleted the treasury (Orderic Vitalis, *H.E.* (ed. Le Prévost), iii. 244; (ed. Chibnall), iv. 94–6) it is impossible to say; but Orderic indicates that Robert had the money to pay a number of young knights and tiros for a while, though it was soon exhausted and Robert then had to approach Henry (ibid., ed. Le Prévost, iii. 266–7; ed. Chibnall, iv. 118).

[5] Malmesbury says that he dissipated this money (*Gesta Regum*, ii. 461); Orderic that he gave large sums to certain magnates promising more if he became king (*H.E.*, ed. Le Prévost, iv. 103–5).

it had been fulfilled), and whatever his part may or may not have been in his brother's death in the New Forest,[1] Henry had methodically prepared for his opportunity when it should come. To do this he had had to gather a number of supporters, men of established position and 'new men'; and when he 'succeeded', these men naturally took a leading share in the government and the wealth of his empire, as William's men had done after 1066. Whether they exploited England for Normandy or both for themselves—and all of them seem to have had both insular and continental interests—this domination by a small governing class, bound together among themselves by ties of kinship and vassalage and monopolizing a disproportionate amount of the wealth of the lands they ruled, was imperialism of at least one kind.

Some expression of it can be seen in their buildings. The Norman kings and their barons spent a good deal of their wealth on building and strengthening castles, for however much labour could be forced out of the neighbouring peasantry,[2] technicians and materials cost money.[3] William constructed a network of castles in England;[4] Rufus and Henry fortified the frontier of Normandy on a vast scale.[5] But castles were often residences, even 'palaces', as well as strongholds, and they could be built for display as much as for security. The Conqueror built a new palace at Winchester and perhaps at Gloucester too;[6] his surviving Tower of London and the keep at Colchester take military architecture to the point of magnificence.[7] William Rufus built Westminster Hall, a vast structure for its age,[8] and Henry transformed his father's works at Caen.[9] The sheer

---

[1] Most recently discussed, with full references to the literature, by Hollister in 'The Strange Death of William Rufus'.

[2] Brown, Colvin, and Taylor, *King's Works*, i. 24–6.

[3] Ibid., i. 26–9. The castle which Gundulf built at Rochester apparently cost £60.

[4] In general, ibid., i. 20–4. There were at least fifty castles in existence in England by 1087; but the difficulties of calculating the exact number at any given time are indicated by Brown in *Normans and Norman Conquest*, pp. 234–9 (235, note 155).

[5] Brown, Colvin, and Taylor, *King's Works*, i. 35; Pépin, *Gisors et la vallée de l'Epte*, pp. 13–17; William de Jumièges, *Gesta* (interp. Torigni), pp. 309–10.

[6] Brown, Colvin, and Taylor, *King's Works*, i. 42–5.

[7] Ibid., pp. 29–32.

[8] Ibid., 45–7. This building certainly made an impression when it was built, and its dimensions are impressive enough even today.

[9] De Bouard and Merlet, 'Le château de Caen'.

domineering size of these buildings must have done much to reinforce the menace latent in them.

Their churches also, built generally on a scale much greater than those of other parts of Europe at that time, are an enduring memorial to this form of 'imperialism'.[1] The fact that some of those in Normandy, such as Jumièges and the two abbey-churches at Caen, were planned and at least partly built before 1066 only reinforces the conclusion that the conquest of England, though the greatest single operation in Norman 'expansion', was nevertheless only one of several such operations; for it is unlikely that so many buildings on such a scale could have been put up in so short a time on the resources of Normandy alone.[2] Yet some of the churches they built in England were vaster still,[3] buildings which were sometimes, as at St. Albans, clearly designed with more of an eye to overwhelming size than to good craftsmanship.[4] How fearfully impressive they, like the palaces and the great tower-keeps of the castles, must have seemed to those accustomed to the scale of Anglo-Saxon churches[5] and halls[6] can only be imagined; but it is hard to

---

[1] 'Perspectives grandioses, presque impériales'; 'une architecture de prestige': Musset, 'Conditions financières d'une réussite architecturale', pp. 307, 313.

[2] Michon and Martin du Gard, *L'Abbaye de Jumièges*, pp. 19–23. Cf. Musset, ubi supra, pp. 307–9, 310–11. Musset remarks, 'Tout au long du xie siècle, les églises normandes purent compter sur des ressources très supérieures à celles que le duché pouvait normalement mettre à leur disposition.'

[3] e.g. Winchester, St. Albans, Bury St. Edmunds, St. Paul's, Norwich, York Minster, etc.

[4] St. Albans, even in its eleventh-century form, was huge and very plain, its plainness due no doubt to the use of materials that could be obtained easily and cheaply on the spot, Roman brick and Roman tiles and flint. Such decoration as was given to it was provided by re-used baluster shafts from the pre-Norman church and paint. The presbytery was showing signs of collapse in the thirteenth century and part of the nave actually fell early in the fourteenth—*V.C.H. Hertfordshire*, ii. 486; Clapham, *English Romanesque Architecture: After the Conquest*, pp. 22–4, 38–9. Winchester central tower fell within a few years of its erection.

[5] The dimensions of the Saxon Church at Peterborough may be compared with those of its Norman successor in *V.C.H. Northamptonshire*, ii, plan facing p. 440; and those of the Saxon cathedral at North Elmham with its ultimate successor at Norwich (Clapham, *English Romanesque Architecture: Before the Conquest*, p. 89; *After the Conquest*, plan facing p. 35). Even more impressive is the contrast between the Saxon and the Norman cathedrals at Winchester, Biddle, 'Excavations at Winchester, 1970', p. 116.

[6] e.g. plans of the royal sites at Yeavering and Cheddar in Brown, Colvin, and Taylor, *King's Works*, i. 2–6 and Rahtz, 'The Saxon and Medieval Palaces at Cheddar', pp. 56, 58. Traces of thegns' halls have been found at Sulgrave, Northamptonshire (Davison, 'Sulgrave') and Goltho, Lincolnshire (Beresford, 'Goltho').

resist the idea that one reason for their size and splendour was to impress in this way, as in the imperial cities of earlier and later times.

Expressions of imperialist sentiment in words have not survived in any very great number; but even though they generally include Norman exploits in the Mediterranean lands in their celebration, they nevertheless express the Normans' concept of the political edifice they had constructed in Britain and France and its destiny. In a well-known poem of the late 1140s the poet likens Rouen to Rome, for 'has not the Norman people indeed chosen Rouen for its capital, whence it has reduced to tribute Brittany and England, Scotland and Wales?'[1] The speech which Henry of Huntingdon attributes to the bishop of Orkney, before the battle of the Standard, begins: 'Great nobles of England, sons of Normandy, when you are about to join battle you should remember your name and your lineage, and consider who you are, where you are and against whom you wage war. For no one resists you with impunity. Brave France tried but gave up; fierce England lay conquered before you; rich Apulia flourished anew under your rule; renowned Jerusalem and noble Antioch both submitted to you. Now Scotia, which is rightly yours, tries to throw you back'.[2] Such sentiments are developed in the harangue which Ailred of Rievaulx puts into the mouth of Walter Espec for the same occasion: 'Why should we despair of victory when victory has been given to our race by the Most High as it were in fee? For did not our ancestors invade the greater part of Gaul with a small force and erase the very name from the country and the people? How often has an army of the Franks melted before them? How often have a few of them won victory from hordes of Manceaux, Angevins, or Aquitanians? Our fathers and we brought this island to our obedience and under our laws in but a little time, when the all-conquering Caesar scarcely achieved this with huge forces and heavy losses . . . Who conquered Apulia, Sicily, Calabria but your Normans? . . . These [Scots] are they

---

[1] The poem is printed in Richard, *Notice sur l'ancienne bibliothèque des échevins de la ville de Rouen*, p. 37; partly reprinted by Haskins in *Norman Institutions*, p. 144 (note 72). The quotation above is taken from the paraphrase in Jamison, 'The Sicilian Norman Kingdom in the Mind of Anglo-Norman Contemporaries', pp. 249–50.

[2] Huntingdon, *Historia Anglorum*, p. 262.

who thought only of surrender, not resistance, when William, the conqueror of England, advanced through Lothian, Calatria, and Scotia to Abernethy, where the warlike King Malcolm submitted to us.'[1]

Clearly such notions can be attributed directly only to the men who wrote them; but that they were committed to writing by men like Henry of Huntingdon and Ailred of Rievaulx must mean that they were current among the higher Norman aristocracy, the 'dominant and exploiting group', and represent their attitude to what has been described as 'the Norman achievement'. The idea that the Normans held assurance of victory as a fief of the Deity is quite extraordinary, and perhaps more astonishing still is the fact that the words in which it was expressed were chosen by St. Ailred of Rievaulx. These sentiments, and those expressed in the poem about Rouen, which significantly puts the domination of Brittany, England, Scotland, and Wales from that city into a context different from that of King Roger's rule over Mediterranean lands, were also imperialism of a kind. With other manifestations of the spirit of conquest and exploitation, which the Normans certainly exhibited and which has so often lain at the root of imperialist ideas in other lands and other ages, these sentiments go some way to justify the use of the term 'Norman Empire' to describe the complex of dominion and lordship which William the Conqueror and Henry Beauclerc, with their vassals and ministers, built up on either side of the English Channel.

[1] 'Relatio de Standardo', pp. 185–6.

BIBLIOGRAPHY

This bibliography is intended to do no more than to identify the works cited, for all are given in more or less abbreviated form in the footnotes. Where a reference has been greatly abbreviated and might not be easily recognizable, the shortened form is here given before the full reference. Entries have been alphabetized in accordance with the form used in the footnotes. Place of publication is given only where it might assist the identification of a work.

Abbayes et prieurés de l'ancienne France, vii. *Province ecclésiastique de Rouen*, by Dom J.-M. Besse (Archives de la France monastique, Ligugé, Paris), 1914.

Actus Pontificum Cenomannis in urbe degentium, edd. G. Busson and A. Ledru (Société des Archives historiques du Maine: Archives historiques du Maine, ii), 1901.

ADIGARD DES GAUTRIES, J., 'Les noms de lieux de l'Eure attestés de 911 à 1066', *Annales de Normandie*, iv (1954), 39–59, 237–55; v (1955), 15–33.

   Les Noms de personnes scandinaves en Normandie de 911 à 1066, 1954.

ALEXANDER, J. J. G., *Norman Illumination at Mont St Michel, 966–1100*, 1970.

ANDERSON, A. O., *Early Sources of Scottish History, A.D. 500 to 1286*, 1922.

   Scottish Annals from English Chroniclers, A.D. 500 to 1286, 1908.

Annales Monastici, ed. H. R. Luard (Rolls Series), 1864–9.

Anselmi (S.) Cantuariensis Archiepiscopi Opera Omnia, ed. F. S. Schmitt, 1938–61.

ARMITAGE, E. S., *The Early Norman Castles of the British Isles*, 1912.

A.-S.C.: Anglo-Saxon Chronicle. References are given by correct year and manuscript (where a particular MS. is quoted) as in *The Anglo-Saxon Chronicle. A Revised Translation*, ed. D. Whitelock with D. C. Douglas and S. I. Tucker (1961), with page reference to that edition. *The Anglo-Saxon Chronicle*, newly translated by E. E. C. Gomme (1909), has also been quoted.

ASTON, T. H., 'The Origins of the Manor in England', *T.R.H.S.*, 5th series, viii (1958), 59–83.

BARLOW, F., *Edward the Confessor*, 1970.

   'Edward the Confessor's Early Life, Character and Attitudes', *E.H.R.*, lxxx (1965), 225–51.

   The English Church, 1000–1066, a Constitutional History, 1963.

'Guenta' (Appendix to Biddle, M., 'Excavations at Winchester, 1962–3'), *Antiquaries Journal*, xliv (1964), 217–19.

BARRACLOUGH, G., 'The Earldom and County Palatine of Chester', *Transactions of the Historic Society of Lancashire and Cheshire*, ciii (1952 for 1951), 23–57, and, separately, Oxford, 1953. References are given to *Transactions*.

BARROW, G. W. S., *Feudal Britain. The Completion of the Medieval Kingdom. 1066–1314*, 1956.

'King David I and the Honour of Lancaster', *E.H.R.*, lxx (1955), 85–9.

The Kingdom of the Scots: Government, Church and Society from the eleventh to the fourteenth century, 1973.

Robert Bruce and the Community of the Realm of Scotland, 1965.

BATESON, M., 'The Laws of Breteuil', *E.H.R.*, xv (1900), 73–8, 302–18, 496–523, 754–7; xvi (1901), 92–110, 332–45.

Bayeux Tapestry: The Bayeux Tapestry, a Comprehensive Survey. General editor, F. M. (Sir Frank) Stenton, 1957.

BAZELEY, M. L., 'The Extent of the English Forest in the Thirteenth Century', *T.R.H.S.*, 4th series, iv (1921), 140–72.

B.É.C.: *Bibliothèque de l'École des Chartes*. Paris, 1839– .

BECKERMAN, J. S., 'Succession in Normandy, 1087, and in England, 1066: the Role of Testamentary Custom', *Speculum*, xlvii (1972), 258–60.

B.É.H.É.: *Bibliothèque de l'École des Hautes Études*. Paris, 1869– .

BERESFORD, G., 'Goltho', *Archaeological Excavations 1973* (Department of the Environment, London, 1974), pp. 86–7.

BERESFORD, M., *New Towns of the Middle Ages. Town Plantation in England, Wales and Gascony*, 1967.

BESNIER, R., *La Coutume de Normandie: histoire externe*, 1935.

BETHELL, D. L., 'English Black Monks and Episcopal Elections in the 1120s', *E.H.R.*, lxxxiv (1969), 673–98.

'William of Corbeil and the Canterbury York Dispute', *Journal of Ecclesiastical History*, xix (1968), 145–59.

BIDDLE, M. 'Excavations at Winchester, 1970: Ninth Interim Report', *Antiquaries Journal*, lii (1972), 93–131.

B.I.H.R.: *Bulletin of the Institute of Historical Research*. London, 1923– .

BINNS, A. L., 'Sun Navigation in the Viking Age, and the Canterbury Portable Sundial', *Acta Archaeologica* (Copenhagen), xlii (1971), 23–34.

BISHOP, T. A. M., *Scriptores Regis*, 1961.

BISHOP, T. A. M., and CHAPLAIS, P. (edd.), *Facsimiles of English Royal Writs to A.D. 1100. Presented to Vivian Hunter Galbraith*, 1957.

BLAIR, P. HUNTER, *An Introduction to Anglo-Saxon England*, 1956 (reprint, 1960).

BLANCHET, A., and DIEUDONNÉ, A., *Manuel de numismatique française*, 1912–36.

BOUSSARD, J., 'Le comté de Mortain au xie siècle', *Le Moyen Age*, lviii (1952), 253–79.

'Les destinées de la Neustrie du ixe au xie siècle', *Cahiers de civilisation médiévale, X^e–XIIe siècles* (Poitiers), xi (1968), 15–28.

'L'éviction des tenants de Thibaud de Blois par Geoffroy Martel, comte d'Anjou, en 1044', *Le Moyen Age*, lxix (1963), 141–9.

'L'origine des familles seigneuriales dans la région de la Loire moyenne', *Cahiers de civilisation médiévale, X^e–XIIe siècles* (Poitiers), v (1962), 303–22.

'La seigneurie de Bellême aux xe et xie siècles', *Mélanges Louis Halphen*, 1951, pp. 43–54.

BROOKE, C. N. L., 'The Composition of the Chapter of St. Paul's, 1086–1163', *Cambridge Historical Journal*, x (1950–2), 111–32.

'Continental Influence on English Cathedral Chapters in the XIth and XIIth Centuries', *XIe Congrès international des sciences historiques. Résumés des communications* (Stockholm), 1960, pp. 120–1.

BROOKE, Z. N., *The English Church and the Papacy. From the Conquest to the Reign of John*, 1931.

BROWN, R. ALLEN, *English Medieval Castles* (New Heritage Series), 1954.

The Normans and the Norman Conquest, 1969 (reprint, 1973).

'The Norman Conquest', *T.R.H.S.*, 5th series, xvii (1967), 109–30.

BROWN, COLVIN, and TAYLOR, *King's Works*: R. Allen Brown, H. M. Colvin, and A. J. Taylor, *The History of the King's Works. The Middle Ages*, 1963.

BRUNEL, Cl., *Recueil des actes des comtes de Pontieu (1026–1279)* (Collection de documents inédits, Paris), 1930.

Brut y Tywysogion: Brut y Tywysogion, Peniarth MS. 20, 1941; *Brut y Tywysogion or The Chronicle of the Princes, Peniarth MS. 20 Version, Translated . . .*, 1952; *Brut y Tywysogion or The Chronicle of the Princes, Red Book of Hergest Version*, 1955. Ed. and trans., Thomas Jones (Board of Celtic Studies, University of Wales; History and Law Series, Nos. 6, 11, and 16).

B.S.A.N.: *Bulletin de la Société des Antiquaires de Normandie*, Caen, 1860– .

BULLOUGH, D. A., 'Anglo-Saxon Institutions and Early English Society', *Annali della Fondazione Italiana per la Storia Amministrativa*, Milan, ii (1965), pp. 647–59.

Cal. Docs. France: *Calendar of Documents preserved in France illustrative of the history of Great Britain and Ireland*, i. *A.D. 918–1216*, ed. J. H. Round, 1899.

CAMDEN: *Publications of the Camden Society* (London). Old Series, i–cv (1838–72); New Series, i–lxii (1871–1901); Third Series, i–xciv (1900–63); Fourth Series, i– (1964–). From N.S. lviii (1898), published by R.H.S.

Carmen de Hastingae Proelio of Guy Bishop of Amiens, [The], edd. C. Morton and H. Muntz (Oxford Medieval Texts), 1972.

Cazel, F. A., Jr., 'Norman and Wessex Charters of the Roumare Family', in *A Medieval Miscellany for Doris Mary Stenton*, edd. P. M. Barnes and C. F. Slade (Pipe Roll Society, N.S. xxxvi, 1962 for 1960), pp. 77–88.

Chambers, R. W., 'The Continuity of English Prose', in *The Life and Death of Sʳ Thomas Moore, Knight . . . by N. Harpsfield*, ed. E. V. Hitchcock (Early English Text Society, Original Series No. 186), 1932 for 1931.

Chanteux, H., 'Le toponyme "Bretteville" en Normandie et son origine', *Recueil Brunel*, i. 248–54.

Chaplais, P., 'The Anglo-Saxon Chancery: from the Diploma to the Writ', *Journal of the Society of Archivists*, iii (1965–9), 160–76. Reprinted in *Prisca Munimenta. Studies . . . presented to Dr. A. E. J. Hollaender*, ed. F. Ranger (1973), pp. 43–62. Page references given to the *Journal*.

'The Authenticity of the Royal Anglo-Saxon Diplomas of Exeter', *B.I.H.R.*, xxxix (1966), 1–34.

'Une charte originale de Guillaume le Conquérant pour l'abbaye de Fécamp: la donation de Steyning et de Bury (1085)', *L'Abbaye bénédictine de Fécamp*, i (Fécamp, 1959), 93–104, 355–7.

English Royal Documents. King John–Henry VI. 1199–1461, 1971.

'Henry II's Reissue of the Canons of the Council of Lillebonne of Whitsun 1080 (? 25 February 1162)', *Journal of the Society of Archivists*, iv (1970–3), 627–32.

'The Seals and Original Charters of Henry I', *E.H.R.*, lxxv (1960), 260–75.

'La souveraineté du roi de France et le pouvoir législatif en Guyenne au début du xivᵉ siècle', *Le Moyen Age*, lxix (1963, Livre Jubilaire), 449–69.

Chartrou, *L'Anjou*: J. Chartrou, *L'Anjou de 1109 à 1151. Foulque de Jérusalem et Geoffroi Plantegenêt*, [1928].

Cheney, M., 'The Compromise of Avranches of 1172 and the Spread of Canon Law in England', *E.H.R.*, lvi (1941), 177–97.

Chibnall, M., 'Ecclesiastical Patronage and the Growth of Feudal Estates at the Time of the Norman Conquest', *Annales de Normandie*, viii (1958), 103–18.

'Some Aspects of the Norman Monastic Plantation in England', *La Normandie bénédictine au temps de Guillaume le Conquérant (XIᵉ siècle)* (Lille, Facultés catholiques, 1967), pp. 399–415.

Chrimes, S. B., *An Introduction to the Administrative History of Mediæval England*, Studies in Medieval History, vii (1952).

Chronicon Monasterii de Abingdon, ed. J. Stevenson (Rolls Series), 1858.

Chroniques des comtes d'Anjou et des seigneurs d'Amboise, edd. L. Halphen and R. Poupardin (Collection de textes pour servir à l'étude et à l'enseignement de l'histoire, Paris), 1913.

Chron. Nantes: La Chronique de Nantes, ed. R. Merlet (Collection de textes pour servir à l'étude et à l'enseignement de l'histoire, Paris), 1896.

CLAPHAM, A. W., *English Romanesque Architecture*, i. *Before the Conquest*, ii. *After the Conquest*, 1930 (reprint, 1964).

   Romanesque Architecture in Western Europe, 1936.

   'Sompting Church', *The Archaeological Journal*, xcii (1936 for 1935), 405–9.

CLAY, C. T. (Sir Charles). For volumes in *Early Yorkshire Charters*, edited by Sir Charles Clay, see *E.Y.C.*

   'The Early Treasurers of York', *Y.A.J.*, xxxv (1943), 7–34.

   Early Yorkshire Families, with illustrative documents edited by D. E. Greenway (Y.A.S., Record Series, cxxxv), 1973.

   'Notes on the Chronology of the Early Deans of York', *Y.A.J.* xxxiv (1939), 361–78.

Complete Peerage: The Complete Peerage of England, Scotland, Ireland, Great Britain and the United Kingdom, by G.E.C. New edition by the Hon. Vicary Gibbs, 13 vols. in 14, 1910–59.

Concilia Scotiae: Ecclesiae Scoticanae statuta tam provincialia quam synodalia quae supersunt, MCCXXV–MDLIX, ed. Joseph Robertson (The Bannatyne Club, Edinburgh), 1866.

CORBETT, W. J., 'The Development of the Duchy of Normandy and the Norman Conquest of England'. *The Cambridge Medieval History*, edd. J. R. Tanner, C. W. Prévité-Orton, and Z. N. Brooke, v (1926), 481–520.

CRONNE, H. A., 'The Office of Local Justiciar in England under the Norman Kings', *University of Birmingham Historical Journal*, vi (1957–8), 18–38.

   'Ranulf de Gernons, Earl of Chester, 1129–1153', *T.R.H.S.*, 4th series, xx (1937), 103–34.

   The Reign of King Stephen, 1135–54. Anarchy in England, 1970.

   'The Royal Forest in the Reign of Henry I', *Essays in British and Irish History in Honour of James Eadie Todd*, edd. H. A. Cronne, T. W. Moody, and D. B. Quinn (1949), pp. 1–23.

CRUMLIN-PEDERSEN, O., 'The Viking Ships of Roskilde' in *Aspects of the History of Wooden Shipbuilding* (Maritime Monographs and Reports, No. 1, National Maritime Museum, Greenwich, 1970), pp. 7–11.

Curia Regis Rolls of the reigns of Richard I and John preserved in the Public Record Office (H.M.S.O., London), 1922– .

DARLINGTON, R. R., *Anglo-Norman Historians. An Inaugural Lecture* (Birkbeck College, University of London), 1947.

   'Ecclesiastical Reform in the Late Old English Period', *E.H.R.*, li (1936), 385–428.

(ed.), *The Vita Wulfstani of William of Malmesbury* (Camden Third Series, xl), 1928.

DAVID, C. W., *Robert Curthose, Duke of Normandy* (Harvard Historical Studies, xxv), 1920.

DAVIES, *Episcopal Acts*: J. Conway Davies, *Episcopal Acts and Cognate Documents relating to Welsh Dioceses 1066–1272* (Historical Society of the Church in Wales, Nos. 1, 3–4), 1946–8.

DAVIS, H. W. C., 'The Battle of Tinchebrai: A Correction', *E.H.R.*, xxv (1910), 295–6.

'Henry of Blois and Brian fitzCount', *E.H.R.*, xxv (1910), 297–303.

DAVIS, R. H. C., *King Stephen*, 1967.

'King Stephen and the Earl of Chester Revised', *E.H.R.*, lxxv (1960), 654–60.

'The Norman Conquest', *History*, li (1966), 279–86.

'What happened in Stephen's Reign', *History*, xlix (1964), 1–12.

DAVISON, B. K., 'The Origins of the Castle in England. The Institute's Research Project', *Archaeological Journal*, cxxiv (1968 for 1967), 202–11.

'Sulgrave', *Current Archaeology*, ii (No. 12, 1969), 19–22.

D.B.: Domesday Book. Printed in 'facsimile', 1783 (2 vols.); reissued with two additional volumes, *Indices* and *Additamenta*, by the Record Commission, 1811–16. References to vol. i are given as in Galbraith, *Making of Domesday Book*, p. vii.

DEANESLY, M., 'Roman Traditionalist Influence among the Anglo-Saxons', *E.H.R.*, lviii (1943), 129–46.

DE BOUARD, M., *Guillaume le Conquérant* (Coll. Que sais-je?), 1958.

'De la Neustrie carolingienne à la Normandie féodale: continuité ou discontinuité?', *B.I.H.R.*, xxviii (1955), 1–14.

'Sur les origines de la trève de Dieu en Normandie', *Annales de Normandie*, ix (1959), 169–89.

'Les petites enceintes circulaires d'origine médiévale en Normandie', *Château Gaillard. Études de Castellologie européenne*, i, *Colloque des Andelys* (Université de Caen, 1964), 23–33.

DE BOUARD, M., and MERLET, J., 'Le château de Caen', *Les Monuments historiques de la France*, N.S., viii (1962), 1–17.

DECAENS, J., 'Les enceintes d'Urville et de Bretteville-sur-Laize (Calvados)', *Annales de Normandie*, xviii (1968), 311–75.

DECK, S., 'Les marchands de Rouen sous les ducs', *Annales de Normandie*, vi (1956), 245–54.

DE LA BORDERIE, A. le Moyne, *Histoire de Bretagne*, iii, 1899.

DELISLE, L., *Études sur la condition de la classe agricole et l'état de l'agriculture en Normandie au moyen âge*, 1851.

Histoire du château et des sires de Saint-Sauveur-le-Vicomte, suivie de pièces justificatives, 1867.

Recueil de jugements de l'échiquier de Normandie au XIIIe siècle (Paris), 1864.

'Des revenus publics en Normandie au douzième siècle', *B.É.C.*, x (1848–9), 173–210, 257–89; xi (1849), 400–51; xiii (1852), 105–35.

DELISLE–BERGER, *Recueil*: L. Delisle, and E. Berger, *Recueil des actes de Henri II* . . . *concernant les provinces françaises et les affaires de France,* 1909–27.

DENTON, J. H., *English Royal Free Chapels, 1100–1300. A Constitutional Study,* 1970.

DEPT, G. G., *Les influences anglaise et française dans le comté de Flandre au début du XIIIe siècle* (Université de Gand, Recueil de travaux publiés par la Faculté de Philosophie et Lettres, fasc. 59), 1928.

'Les marchands flamands et le roi d'Angleterre (1154–1216)', *Revue du Nord,* xii (1926), 303–24.

DHONDT, J. *Études sur la naissance des principautés territoriales en France (IXe–Xe siècle)* (Rijksuniversiteit te Gent, Werken uitgegeven door de Faculteit van de Wijsbegeerte en Letteren, 102), 1948.

Les origines de la Flandre et de l'Artois (Centre d'Études régionales du Pas-de-Calais, Arras), 1944.

'Les relations entre la France et la Normandie sous Henri Ier', *Normannia* (Caen), xii (1939), 465–86.

'Les seigneuries du ixe au xiiie siècle', in *Histoire des territoires ayant formé le département du Pas-de-Calais* (Commission départementale des monuments historiques du Pas-de-Calais, dir. M. l'Abbé Lestocquoy, Arras 1946), pp. 34–83.

Dialogus: The Course of the Exchequer (Dialogus de Scaccario), by Richard, son of Nigel, ed. and trans. C. Johnson (Medieval Classics), 1950. Other editions noted ibid., pp. xii–xiii.

DICKINSON, W. C., *Scotland from the Earliest Times to 1603 (A New History of Scotland,* i), 1961.

DIEUDONNÉ, A., 'La numismatique normande: les monnaies féodales', *B.S.A.N.,* xxxvi (1926 for 1924–5), 337–44.

Diplomatic Documents: Diplomatic Documents preserved in the Public Record Office (ed. P. Chaplais), i. *1101–1272* (1964).

D.N.B.: Dictionary of National Biography, edd. L. Stephen and S. Lee (London), 1885–1901; (reprinted Oxford) 1921–2.

DODWELL, B., 'The Foundation of Norwich Cathedral', *T.R.H.S.,* 5th series, vii (1957), 1–18.

DODWELL, C. R., *The Canterbury School of Illumination, 1066–1200,* 1954.

Painting in Europe, 800–1200 (Pelican History of Art), 1971.

DOLLEY, R. H. M., *The Norman Conquest and the English Coinage* (London), 1966.

DOLLEY, R. H. M., and METCALF, D. M., 'The Reform of the English Coinage under Eadgar', in *Anglo-Saxon Coins. Studies presented to F. M. Stenton on the Occasion of his 80th Birthday*, ed. R. H. M. Dolley (1961), pp. 136–68.

DOLLEY, R. H. M., and YVON, J., 'A Group of Tenth-Century Coins found at Mont Saint-Michel', *British Numismatic Journal*, xl (1972 for 1971), 1–16 and plate vi.

Domesday Monachorum: *The Domesday Monachorum of Christ Church Canterbury*, ed. D. C. Douglas (R.H.S.), 1944.

DOUGLAS, D. C., 'The Ancestors of William fitzOsbern', *E.H.R.*, lix (1944), 62–79.

' "Companions of the Conqueror",' *History*, xxviii (1943), 129–47.

'The Earliest Norman Counts', *E.H.R.*, lxi (1946), 129–56.

'Edward the Confessor, Duke William of Normandy, and the English Succession', *E.H.R.*, lxviii (1953), 526–45.

The Norman Achievement, 1050–1100, 1969.

'The Norman Conquest and English Feudalism', *Economic History Review*, ix (1938–9), 128–43.

'The Norman Episcopate before the Norman Conquest', *Cambridge Historical Journal*, xiii (1957), 101–15.

'Odo, Lanfranc, and the Domesday Survey', *Historical Essays in Honour of James Tait*, edd. J. G. Edwards, V. H. Galbraith, and E. F. Jacob (1933), pp. 47–57.

'The Rise of Normandy', *Proceedings of the British Academy*, xxxiii (1947), 101–130.

'Rollo of Normandy', *E.H.R.*, lvii (1942), 417–36.

William the Conqueror: The Norman Impact upon England, 1964.

DUBOIS, DOM J., 'Les dépendances de l'abbaye du Mont Saint-Michel et la vie monastique dans les prieurés', *Millénaire monastique du Mont Saint-Michel*, i (dir. Dom J. Laporte: Bibliothèque d'Histoire et d'Archéologie chrétiennes, Paris), 1966, pp. 619–76.

DUBY, G., 'Une Enquête à poursuivre : la noblesse dans la France médiévale', *Revue historique*, ccxxvi (1961), 1–22.

DUDO, *De Moribus*: *De Moribus et actis primorum Normanniae Ducum auctore Dudone Sancti Quintini Decano*, ed. J. Lair, 1865.

DUMAS, A., 'Encore la question, "Fidèles ou vassaux?" ', *Nouvelle Revue historique de droit français et étranger*, xliv (1920), 159–229, 347–90.

DUMAS-DUBOURG, F., *Le Trésor de Fécamp et le monnayage en Francie occidentale pendant la seconde moitié du Xe siècle* (Bibliothèque nationale: Ministère de l'Éducation nationale, Comité des Travaux historiques et scientifiques, Mémoires de la section d'archéologie, i), 1971 (1972).

DUNCAN, A. A. M., 'The Earliest Scottish Charters', *Scottish Historical Review*, xxxvii (1958), 103–35.

DURTELLE DE SAINT-SAUVEUR, E., *Histoire de Bretagne des origines à nos jours*, 3rd edn., 1946.

EADMER, *Historia Novorum*: *Eadmeri Historia Novorum in Anglia* . . . ed. M. Rule (Rolls Series), 1884.

EARLE, J., and PLUMMER, C., *Two of the Saxon Chronicles Parallel*, 1892–9.

EASSON, D. E., *Medieval Religious Houses, Scotland*, 1957.

Ecclesiastical Documents, ed. J. Hunter (Camden, viii), 1840.

EDWARDS, J. G. (Sir Goronwy), *Littere Wallie preserved in Liber A in the Public Record Office* (University of Wales, Board of Celtic Studies, History and Law Series, No. 5), 1940.

'The Normans and the Welsh March', *Proceedings of the British Academy*, xlii (1956), 155–77.

EDWARDS, K., *The English Secular Cathedrals in the Middle Ages. A Constitutional Study with Special Reference to the Fourteenth Century*, 2nd edn., 1967.

E.H.R.: *English Historical Review* (London), 1886– .

ELLIS, A. S., 'Biographical Notes on Yorkshire Tenants named in Domesday Book', *Y.A.J.*, iv (1877), 114–57, 214–48, 384–415; v (1879), 289–330.

ELLIS, H. (Sir Henry), *A General Introduction to Domesday Book* (Record Commission, London), 1833 (reprint, 1971).

ENGELS, L. J., 'De obitu Willelmi ducis Normannorum regisque Anglorum: Texte, modèles, valeur et origine', *Mélanges Christine Mohrmann: Nouveau recueil offert par ses anciens élèves*, 1973, pp. 209–55.

English Historical Documents, i. *c. 500–1042*, ed. D. Whitelock, 1955; ii. *1042–1189*, edd. D. C. Douglas and G. W. Greenaway, 1953.

E.Y.C.: *Early Yorkshire Charters*. Vols. i–iii, ed. W. Farrer, 1914–16; vols. iv–xii, ed. C. T. (Sir Charles) Clay, Y.A.S., Record Series, Extra Series, i–x (with Index to vols. i–iii by C. T. Clay and E. M. Clay, as vol. iv), 1935–65.

FARRER, W., 'An Outline Itinerary of King Henry the First', *E.H.R.*, xxxiv (1919), 303–82, 505–79 (reprinted separately, 1920).

FAUROUX, *Recueil*: M. Fauroux, *Recueil des actes des ducs de Normandie (911–1066)* (Mémoires de la Société des Antiquaires de Normandie, Caen, xxxvi), 1961.

FINBERG, H. P. R., 'Sherborne, Glastonbury, and the Expansion of Wessex', *T.R.H.S.*, 5th series, iii (1953), 101–24.

FISHER, D. J. V., 'The Anti-Monastic Reaction in the Reign of Edward the Martyr', *Cambridge Historical Journal*, x (1950–2), 254–70.

FLEURIOT, L., 'Breton et cornique à la fin du moyen âge', *Annales de Bretagne*, lxxvi (1969), 705–24.

FLODOARD, *Annales*: *Les Annales de Flodoard*, ed. Ph. Lauer (Collection de textes pour servir à l'étude et à l'enseignement de l'histoire, Paris), 1906.

FLODOARD, 'Historia Remensis Ecclesiae', edd. J. Heller and G. Waitz in *Monumenta Germaniae historica*, Scriptores, xiii (1881), 405–599.

FLORENCE OF WORCESTER, *Chronicon*: *Florentii Wigorniensis monachi, Chronicon ex chronicis* . . . , ed. B. Thorpe (English Historical Society, London), 1848–9.

FLOWER, C. T., *Introduction to the Curia Regis Rolls, 1199–1230 A.D.* (Selden Society, lxii), 1944 for 1943.

FOLZ, R., *L'idée d'empire en occident du Ve au XIVe siècle* (1953).

FOREVILLE, R., 'Le Synode de la province de Rouen aux XIe et XIIe siècles,' *R.H.D.*, li (1973), 566–7.

FREEMAN, *Norman Conquest*: Freeman, E. A., *The History of the Norman Conquest of England, its causes and its results*. Edition cited: vols. i and ii, 3rd 1877; iii and iv, 2nd 1875–6; v, 1876, vi; 1879.

FREEMAN, E. A., *The Reign of William Rufus and the Accession of Henry the First*, 1882.

GALBERT DE BRUGES, *Histoire du meurtre de Charles le Bon, comte de Flandre (1127–1128)*, ed. H. Pirenne (Collection de textes pour servir à l'étude et à l'enseignement de l'histoire, Paris), 1891.

The Murder of Charles the Good, Count of Flanders, trans. etc. J. B. Ross (Records of Civilization, Sources and Studies), 1959 (revised ed. 1967).

GALBRAITH, V. H., 'The Date of the Geld Rolls in Exon Domesday', *E.H.R.*, lxv (1950), 1–17.

'Girard the Chancellor', *E.H.R.*, xlvi (1931), 77–9.

The Making of Domesday Book, 1961.

Gallia Christiana in provincias ecclesiasticas distributa, xi. *Provincia Rotomagensis*, ed. Paul Piolin, 1874.

GANSHOF, F. L., 'Charlemagne et les institutions de la monarchie franque', in *Karl der Grosse*, i. *Persönlichkeit und Geschichte*, ed. H. Beumann, 1965, pp. 349–93.

Feudalism, trans. P. Grierson, 1952 (*Qu'est-ce que la féodalité?*, 2nd edn., 1947).

'Note sur le premier traité anglo-flamand de Douvres', *Revue du Nord*, xl (1958), 245–57.

'Les relations féodo-vassaliques aux temps post-carolingiens', *I Problemi comuni dell'Europa post-carolingia* (Centro Italiano di Studi sull'Alto Medioevo, Settimana ii, 1954, Spoleto), 1955, pp. 67–114.

GARAUD, M., *Les Châtelains de Poitou et l'avènement du régime féodal: XIe et XIIe siècles* (Mémoires de la Société des Antiquaires de l'Ouest, 4e serie, viii), 1964.

GÉNESTAL, R., 'La formation et le développement de la Coutume de Normandie', *Travaux de la Semaine d'histoire du droit normand tenue à Guernesey . . . 1927* (Université de Caen, Faculté de Droit), 1928, pp. 37–55.

'La formation du droit d'aînesse dans la Coutume de Normandie', *Normannia* (Caen), i (1928), 157–79.

Du rôle des monastères comme établissements de crédit, étudié en Normandie du XIe à la fin du XIIIe siècle, 1901.

La Tenure en bourgage dans les pays régis par la coutume de Normandie (Université de Paris, Faculté de Droit), 1900.

GEORGE, R. H., 'The Contribution of Flanders to the Conquest of England', *Revue belge de philologie et d'histoire*, v (1926), 81–99.

Gesta Henrici: Gesta Regis Henrici Secundi . . ., ed. W. Stubbs (Rolls Series), 1867.

Gesta Stephani: The Deeds of Stephen, trans. etc. K. R. Potter (Medieval Texts), 1955, to which references have been given. Also printed in *Chronicles of the Reigns of Stephen, Henry II, and Richard I*, iii, ed. R. Howlett (Rolls Series), 1886, 3–136.

GIBBS, M., *Early Charters of the Cathedral Church of St. Paul, London* (Camden, 3rd series, lviii), 1939.

GLANVILL, *Tractatus: Tractatus de legibus et consuetudinibus regni Anglie qui Glanvill vocatur*, ed. G. D. G. Hall (Medieval Texts), 1965.

GLEASON, S. E., *An Ecclesiastical Barony of the Middle Ages: The Bishopric of Bayeux, 1066–1204* (Harvard Historical Monographs, x), 1936.

Grands Empires (Les), Recueils de la Société Jean Bodin pour l'histoire comparative des institutions, xxxi (Brussels), 1973.

GREENWAY, D. E. (ed.), *Charters of the Honour of Mowbray, 1107–1191* (British Academy, Records of Social and Economical History, New Series, i), 1972.

GRIERSON, P., 'The Relations between England and Flanders before the Norman Conquest', *T.R.H.S.*, 4th series, xxiii (1941), 71–112.

GUILLOT, O., *Le Comte d'Anjou et son entourage au XIe siècle*, 1972.

HALPHEN, L., *Le Comté d'Anjou au XIe siècle*, 1906.

Handbook of British Chronology, edd. F. M. (Sir Maurice) Powicke and E. B. Fryde (R.H.S., Guides and Handbooks, No. 2. 2nd edn.), 1961.

HARVEY, S., 'Domesday Book and its Predecessors', *E.H.R.*, lxxxvi (1971), 753–73.

HASKINS, C. H., *Norman Institutions* (Harvard Historical Studies, xxiv), 1918.

Heads (The) of Religious Houses, England and Wales, 940–1216, edd. D. Knowles, C. N. L. Brooke and V.C.M. London, 1972.

HEMMEON, M. de W., *Burgage Tenure in Mediaeval England* (Harvard Historical Studies, xx), 1914.

HENCKEN, H. O'N., *The Archaeology of Cornwall and Scilly* (The County Archaeologies), 1932.

Historiens de la France: *Recueil des Historiens des Gaules et de la France* . . . *par* Dom Martin Bouquet, nouvelle édition publiée sous la direction de M. Léopold Delisle, 1869– .

History: *History. The (Quarterly) Journal of the Historical Association.* New Series, 1916– .

HODGKIN, R. H., *A History of the Anglo-Saxons*, 2nd edn., 1939.

HOLLISTER, C. WARREN, 'The Anglo-Norman Civil War: 1101', *E.H.R.*, lxxxviii (1973), 315–34.

    (with KEEFE, T. K.) 'The Making of the Angevin Empire', *Journal of British Studies* (Hartford, Connecticut), xii (1973), 1–25.

    The Military Organization of Norman England, 1965.

    'The Misfortunes of the Mandevilles', *History*, lviii (1973), 18–28.

    'The Strange Death of William Rufus', *Speculum*, xlviii (1973), 637–53.

HOLT, J. C., 'The Assizes of Henry II: The Texts', in *The Study of Medieval Records: Essays in honour of Kathleen Major*, edd. D. A. Bullough and R. L. Storey, 1971, pp. 85–106.

    The Northerners. A Study in the Reign of King John, 1961.

    'Politics and Property in Early Medieval England', *Past and Present*, 57 (Nov. 1972), pp. 3–52.

HOURLIER, Dom J., 'Le Mont Saint-Michel avant 1066', *Millénaire monastique du Mont Saint-Michel*, i (dir. Dom J. Laporte: Bibliothèque d'Histoire et d'Archéologie chrétiennes, Paris), 1966, pp. 13–28.

HOUTH, E., 'Galeran II, comte de Meulan: catalogue de ses actes précédé d'une étude biographique', *Bulletin philologique et historique (jusqu'à 1610)* (Ministère de l'Éducation nationale, Comité des Travaux historiques et scientifiques), 1961 for 1960 (ii), pp. 627–82.

HOYT, R. S., *The Royal Demesne in English Constitutional History: 1066–1272*, 1950.

HUDSON, W. H., and TINGEY, J. C., *The Records of the City of Norwich*, 1906–10.

HUGH THE CHANTOR, *The History of the Church of York, 1066–1127*, ed. and trans. C. Johnson (Medieval Texts), 1961, to which references are given. Also published in *Historians of the Church of York and its Archbishops*, ed. J. Raine (Rolls Series), 1879–94, ii. 98–227.

HUNTINGDON, *Historia Anglorum*: *The History of the English by Henry, Archdeacon of Huntingdon*, ed. T. Arnold, (Rolls Series), 1879.

JAMISON, E., 'The Sicilian Norman Kingdom in the Mind of Anglo-Norman Contemporaries', *Proceedings of the British Academy*, xxiv (1938), 237–85.

JEAN DE MARMOUTIER, 'Historia Gaufredi ducis Normannorum et comitis Andegavorum', *Chroniques des comtes d'Anjou et des seigneurs d'Amboise*, edd.

L. Halphen and R. Poupardin (Collection de textes pour servir à l'étude et à l'enseignement de l'histoire, 1913), pp. 172–231.

JEULIN, P., 'Un grand "Honneur" anglais. Aperçus sur le "comté" de Richmond en Angleterre, possession des ducs de Bretagne (1069/71–1398)', *Annales de Bretagne*, xlii (1935), 265–302.

'L'hommage de Bretagne en droit et dans les faits', *Annales de Bretagne*, xli (1934), 380–473.

JOHN, E., *Orbis Britanniae and other studies* (Studies in Early English History, 4), 1966.

JOLLIFFE, J. E. A., *The Constitutional History of Medieval England, from the English Settlement to 1485*, 1937.

JONES, M. C. E., *Ducal Brittany, 1364–1399. Relations with England and France during the reign of Duke John IV* (Oxford Historical Monographs), 1970.

JORANSON, E., *The Danegeld in France* (Augustana Library Publications, 10, Rock Island, Illinois), 1923.

JOÜON DES LONGRAIS, F., *Henry II and his Justiciars, Had they a Political Plan in their Reforms about Seisin?*, Lecture delivered at Gonville and Caius College, Cambridge, 19 September 1961 (Imp. Bontemps, Limoges), 1962.

KANTOROWICZ, E. H., *Laudes Regiae. A Study in Liturgical Acclamations and Medieval Ruler Worship*, 1958.

KEALEY, E. J., *Roger of Salisbury, Viceroy of England*, 1972.

KER, N. R., *English Manuscripts in the Century after the Norman Conquest. The Lyell Lectures, 1952–3*, 1960.

KING, E., 'King Stephen and the Anglo-Norman Aristocracy', *History*, lix (1974), 180–94.

KLIMRATH, H., *Études sur les coutumes* (1867). Reprinted from *Revue de législation et de jurisprudence*, vi (1837), 107–35, 161–214, 321–93. Page references are given to the reprint, but the map only appears in the *Revue* (British Library).

KNOWLES, D., *The Episcopal Colleagues of Archbishop Thomas Becket* (Ford Lectures, University of Oxford, 1949), 1951.

The Monastic Constitutions of Lanfranc (Medieval Classics), 1951.

The Monastic Order in England: a History of its Development from the Times of St. Dunstan to the Fourth Lateran Council, 943–1216, 1940 (2nd edn., 1963, preserves pagination of first edn.).

KNOWLES, D., and HADCOCK, R. N., *Medieval Religious Houses: England and Wales*, 2nd edn., 1971 (first edn., 1953).

KÖRNER, S., *The Battle of Hastings, England, and Europe: 1035–66* (Bibliotheca Historica Lundensis, xiv), 1966.

LAMB, H. H., *The Changing Climate: selected papers*, 1966.

LAMBERT D'ARDRE, *Chronicon*: *Chroniques de Guines et d'Ardre par Lambert curé d'Ardre*, ed. le Marquis de Godefroy Menilglaise (Société des Antiquaires de la Morinie), 1855.

LANDON, E., 'Everard Bishop of Norwich', *Proceedings of the Suffolk Institute of Archaeology and Natural History*, xx (1930), 186–98.

LARSON, L. M., *The King's Household in England before the Norman Conquest* (Bulletin of the University of Wisconsin, No. 100), 1904.

LATOUCHE, R., *Histoire du comté du Maine pendant le Xe et le XIe siècle*, 1910.

LAUER, PH., *Le règne de Louis IV d'Outremer* (B.É.H.É., fasc. 127), 1900.

 Robert Ier et Raoul de Bourgogne (923–936) (B.É.H.É., fasc. 188), 1910.

LAWRIE, A. C. (Sir Archibald), *Early Scottish Charters prior to A.D. 1153*, 1905.

Leges Henrici Primi, ed. with translation and commentary by L. J. Downer, 1972.

LEGG, J. Wickham, *Three Coronation Orders* (Henry Bradshaw Society, xix), 1900.

LEGG, L. G. Wickham, *English Coronation Records*, 1901.

LEGGE, M. Dominica, 'Anglo-Norman and the Historian', *History*, xxvi (1941), 163–75.

 'La précocité de la littérature anglo-normande', *Cahiers de civilisation médiévale, X^e–XIIe siècles* (Poitiers), viii (1965), 327–49.

LEGRAS, H., *Le Bourgage de Caen. Tenure à cens et tenure à rente (XIe–XVe siècles)*, 1911.

LEMARIGNIER, J.-F., 'La dislocation du *pagus* et le problème des *Consuetudines* (x^e–xie siècles)', *Mélanges Louis Halphen* (1951), pp. 401–10.

 Étude sur les privilèges d'exemption et de juridiction ecclésiastique des abbayes normandes depuis les origines jusqu'en 1140, 1937.

 'Les fidèles du roi de France (936–987)', *Recueil Brunel*, ii. 138–62.

 Hommage en marche: Recherches sur l'hommage en marche et les frontières féodales (Travaux et Mémoires de l'Université de Lille, N.S., Droit et Lettres, xxiv), 1945.

LE NEVE, *Fasti 1066–1300*: *John Le Neve, Fasti Ecclesiae Anglicanae, 1066–1300*, i. *St. Paul's London* (1968); ii. *Monastic Cathedrals* (1971), compiled by D. E. Greenway.

LENNARD, R., *Rural England, 1086–1135. A Study of Social and Agrarian Conditions*, 1959.

LE PATOUREL, J., 'The Authorship of the Grand Coutumier de Normandie', *E.H.R.*, lvi (1941), 292–300.

 'The Early History of St. Peter Port', La Société Guernésiaise, *Report and Transactions*, xii (1933–6), 171–208.

 'Geoffrey of Montbray, Bishop of Coutances, 1049–1093', *E.H.R.*, lix (1944), 129–61.

The Medieval Administration of the Channel Islands, 1199–1399 (Oxford Historical Series), 1937.

Norman Barons (The Historical Association, Hastings and Bexhill Branch), 1966 (reprinted by the Historical Association, 1971).

'The Norman Colonization of Britain', *I Normanni e la loro espansione in Europa nell'alto medioevo* (Centro Italiano di Studi sull'Alto Medioevo, Settimana xvi, 1968, Spoleto), 1969, pp. 409–38.

Normandy and England, 1066–1144 (Stenton Lecture, 1970, University of Reading), 1971.

'The Norman Succession, 996–1135', *E.H.R.*, lxxxvi (1971), 225–50.

'The Origins of the War', in *The Hundred Years War*, ed. K. Fowler (Problems in Focus Series), 1971, pp. 28–50.

'The Plantagenet Dominions', *History*, 1 (1965), 289–308.

'The Reports of the Trial on Penenden Heath' in *Studies in Medieval History presented to Frederick Maurice Powicke*, edd. R. W. Hunt, W. A. Pantin, and R. W. Southern, 1948, pp. 15–26.

'What did not happen in Stephen's Reign', *History*, lviii (1973), 1–17.

Letters of John of Salisbury, edd. W. J. Millor, H. E. Butler, and C. N. L. Brooke (Medieval Texts), i, 1955.

LEX, L., 'Eudes comte de Blois, de Tours, de Chartres, de Troyes, et de Meaux (995–1037) et Thibaut son frère (995–1004)', *Mémoires de la Société académique d'Agriculture etc. du département de l'Aube*, lv (Troyes), 1891.

Liber Eliensis, ed. E. O. Blake (Camden 3rd series, xcii), 1962.

Liber Monasterii de Hyda, ed. Edward Edwards (Rolls Series), 1866.

LLOYD, *History of Wales*: J. E. (Sir John) Lloyd, *A History of Wales from the Earliest Times to the Edwardian Conquest* (3rd edn.), 1939.

'Wales and the Coming of the Normans', *Transactions of the Honourable Society of Cymmrodorion*, Session 1899–1900 (1901), pp. 122–79.

LONGNON, A., *Atlas historique de la France depuis César jusqu'à nos jours. Première partie, de 58 avant J.-C. à 1380 après J.-C.: Atlas*, 1885–9; *Texte explicatif des planches*, 1907.

LOT, F., *Les Derniers Carolingiens: Lothaire, Louis V, Charles de Lorraine (954–991)* (B.É.H.É., fasc. 87), 1891.

Études critiques sur l'abbaye de Saint-Wandrille (B.É.H.É., fasc. 204), 1913.

Fidèles ou vassaux? Essai sur la nature juridique du lien qui unissait les grands vassaux à la royauté depuis le milieu du IXe siècle à la fin du XIIe siècle, 1904.

LOT, F., and FAWTIER, R., *Histoire des institutions françaises au moyen age*: i. *Institutions seigneuriales* (1957); ii. *Institutions royales* (1958); *Institutions ecclésiastiques* (1962).

LOT, F., PFISTER, C., and GANSHOF, F.-L., *Les Destinées de l'Empire en Occident de 395 à 888* (Histoire générale: Histoire du Moyen Age, ed. G. Glotz), edition of 1940–1.

LOYD, L. C., 'The Origin of the Family of Warenne', *Y.A.J.*, xxxi (1934), 97–113.

The Origins of Some Anglo-Norman Families, edd. C. T. Clay and D. C. Douglas (Publications of the Harleian Society, ciii), 1951.

LOYN, H. R., *Anglo-Saxon England and the Norman Conquest* (Social and Economic History of England, i), 1962.

'The Imperial Style of the Tenth Century Anglo-Saxon Kings', *History*, xl (1955), 111–15.

LUCAS, H. S., *The Low Countries and the Hundred Years' War, 1326–1347* (University of Michigan Publications, History and Political Science, viii), 1929.

LUCHAIRE, A., *Louis VI le Gros. Annales de sa vie et de son règne (1081–1137), avec une introduction historique*, 1890.

LYON, B. D., *From Fief to Indenture. The Transition from Feudal to Non-Feudal Contract in Western Europe* (Harvard Historical Studies, lxviii), 1957.

LYON, B., and VERHULST, A., *Medieval Finance. A Comparison of Financial Institutions in Northwestern Europe* (Rijksuniversiteit te Gent, Werken uitgegeven door de Faculteit van de Letteren en Wijsbegeerte, 143), 1967.

Magni Rotuli Scaccarii Normanniae sub Regibus Angliae, ed. T. Stapleton (Society of Antiquaries of London), 1840–4.

MAKOWER, F., *The Constitutional History and Constitution of the Church of England*, 1895.

MALMESBURY, *Gesta Pontificum*: Willelmi Malmesbiriensis Monachi, De Gestis Pontificum Anglorum libri quinque, ed. N.E.S.A. Hamilton (Rolls Series), 1870.

MALMESBURY, *Gesta Regum*: Willelmi Malmesbiriensis Monachi, De Gestis Regum Anglorum libri quinque, ed. W. Stubbs (Rolls Series), 1887–9.

MALMESBURY, *Historia Novella*: The Historia Novella by William of Malmesbury, trans. etc. by K. R. Potter (Medieval Texts), 1955, to which references are given in this book. It is also printed in Malmesbury, *Gesta Regum*, ii. 523–96.

Manuscripts (The) of His Grace the Duke of Rutland, K.G., preserved at Belvoir Castle, iv (Historical Manuscripts Commission), 1905.

MASON, J. F. A., 'The "Honour of Richmond" in 1086', *E.H.R.*, lxxviii (1963), 703–4.

'Roger de Montgomery and his sons (1067–1102)', *T.R.H.S.*, 5th series, xiii (1963), 1–28.

William the First and the Sussex Rapes (The Hastings and Bexhill Branch of the Historical Association), 1966. (Reprinted 1967, revised 1972; The Historical Association).

Materials for the History of Thomas Becket, Archbishop of Canterbury, edd. J. C. Robertson and J. B. Sheppard (Rolls Series), 1875–85.

MATTHEW, D., *The Norman Monasteries and their English Possessions* (Oxford Historical Series, 2nd series), 1962.

MAYR-HARTING, H., *The Bishops of Chichester, 1075–1207: Biographical Notes and Problems* (The Chichester Papers, No. 40, published by Chichester City Council), 1963.

Mélanges Louis Halphen: *Mélanges d'histoire du moyen âge dédiés à la mémoire de Louis Halphen*, Préface de C.-E. Perrin, 1951.

Memoranda Roll (The) for the Michaelmas Term of the First Year of the reign of King John (1199–1200), with an introduction by H. G. Richardson (Pipe Roll Society, N.S., xxi), 1943.

MICHON, L.-M., and MARTIN DU GARD, R., *L'Abbaye de Jumièges* (Petites monographies des grands édifices de la France), 1935.

MILLER, E., 'Medieval New Towns', *Northern History* (Leeds), iii (1968), 192–7.

MOORE, M. F., *The Lands of the Scottish Kings in England* (Studies in Economics and Political Science, No. 43), 1915.

MORRIS, C., 'William I and the Church Courts', *E.H.R.*, lxxxii (1967), 449–63.

MORRIS, W. A., *The Medieval English Sheriff to 1300* (Publications of the University of Manchester, Historical Series), 1927.

MURRAY, K. M. E., *The Constitutional History of the Cinque Ports* (Publications of the University of Manchester, Historical Series), 1935.

MUSSET, L., *Les Actes de Guillaume le Conquérant et de la reine Mathilde pour les abbayes caennaises* (Mémoires de la Société des Antiquaires de Normandie, xxxvii), 1967.

'Aperçus sur la colonisation scandinave dans le nord du Cotentin', *Annuaire des cinq départements de la Normandie* (Caen), cvii (année 121, 1953), 34–7. Title only in off-print.

'Les conditions financières d'une réussite architecturale: les grandes églises romanes de Normandie', *Mélanges offerts à René Crozet*, edd. P. Gallais and Y.-J. Riou, i (1966), 307–13.

'Les destins de la propriété monastique durant les invasions normandes (ixe–xie s.). L'exemple de Jumièges'. *Jumièges. Congrès scientifique du XIIIe centenaire* (Rouen, 1955), i. 49–55.

'Les domaines de l'époque franque et les destinées du régime domanial du ixe au xie siècle', *B.S.A.N.*, xlix (1946 for 1942–5), 7–97.

'A-t-il existé en Normandie au xie siècle une aristocratie d'argent?' *Annales de Normandie*, ix (1959), 285–99.

'Les fiefs de deux familles vicomtales de l'Hiémois au xie siècle, Les Goz et les Montgommery', *R.H.D.*, xlviii (1970), 342–3.

'Gouvernés et gouvernants dans le monde scandinave et dans le monde normand (xie–xiie siècles)'. *Gouvernés et gouvernants*, ii, Recueils de la Société Jean Bodin, xxiii (Brussels), 1968, 439–68.

'Sur les mutations de la monnaie ducale normande au xie siècle: deux documents inédits', *Revue numismatique*, 6e série. xi (1969), 291–3.

'Naissance de la Normandie (v^e–xie siècles)', in *Histoire de la Normandie*, pp. 75–130; *Documents de l'histoire de la Normandie*, pp. 59–98. Publiés sous la direction de M. de Bouard (Coll. 'Univers de la France et des pays francophones'), 1970, 1972.

Normandie romane, i. *La Basse Normandie* (Zodiaque), 1967.

'Une nouvelle charte de Robert le Magnifique pour Fécamp' ('Actes inédits du xie siècle', 2), *B.S.A.N.*, lii (1955 for 1952–4), 142–53.

'Observations sur l'histoire et la signification de la frontière normande (x^e–xiie siècles)', *R.H.D.*, xli (1963), 545–6.

'Observations sur la classe aristocratique normande au xie siècle', *R.H.D.*, xxxvi (1958), 142–3.

'Aux origines de la féodalité normande: l'installation par les ducs de leurs vassaux normands et bretons dans le comté d'Avranches (xie siècle)', *R.H.D.*, xxix (1951), 150.

'Les origines et le patrimoine de l'abbaye de Saint-Sever', *La Normandie bénédictine au temps de Guillaume le Conquérant (XIe siècle)* (Lille, Facultés catholiques, 1967), pp. 357–67.

'Les origines du prieuré de Saint-Fromond: un acte négligé de Richard II', *B.S.A.N.*, liii (1957 for 1955–6), 475–89.

'Peuplement en bourgage et bourgs ruraux en Normandie du xe au xiiie siècle', *Cahiers de civilisation médiévale, x^e–xiie siècles* (Poitiers), ix (1966), 177–208.

'La place de la Normandie dans la géographie coutumière de l'ancienne France', *Annales de Normandie*, xviii (1968), 186–7 (review of J. Yver, *Égalité entre héritiers et exclusion des enfants dotés*, 1966).

'Les plus anciennes chartes normandes de l'abbaye de Bourgueil' ('Actes inédits du xie siècle', 3), *B.S.A.N.*, liv (1959 for 1957–8), 15–54.

'Les plus anciennes chartes du prieuré de Saint-Gabriel (Calvados)', ('Actes inédits du xie siècle', 1), *B.S.A.N.*, lii (1955 for 1952–4), 117–41.

'Les premiers temps de l'abbaye d'Almenèches, des origines au xiie siècle', *L'Abbaye d'Almenèches-Argentan et Sainte Opportune. Sa vie et son culte*, dir. Dom Y. Chaussy (Bibliothèque d'histoire et d'archéologie chrétiennes, Paris), 1970, pp. 11–36.

'Que peut-on savoir de la fiscalité publique en Normandie à l'époque ducale?', *R.H.D.*, xxxviii (1960), 483–4.

'Recherches sur les communautés de clercs séculiers en Normandie au xie siècle', *B.S.A.N.*, lv (1961 for 1959–60), 5–38.

'Recherches sur quelques survivances de la fiscalité ducale', *B.S.A.N.*. lv (1961 for 1959–60), 317–25, 420–35, 525–30.

'Réflexions d'un historien sur les origines du droit normand', *R.H.D.*, xlii (1964), 363–4.

'Relations et échanges d'influences dans l'Europe du Nord-Ouest (xᵉ–xıᵉ siècles)', *Cahiers de civilisation médiévale, Xᵉ–XIIᵉ siècles* (Poitiers), i (1958), 63–82.

'Ruine et reconstitution d'une administration: de la Neustrie franque à la Normandie ducale', *R.H.D.*, xxx (1952), 275.

'La vie économique de l'abbaye de Fécamp sous l'abbatiat de Jean de Ravenne (1028–1078)', *L'Abbaye bénédictine de Fécamp*, i (Fécamp, 1959), 67–79, 345–9.

NEILSON, N., 'Custom and the Common Law in Kent', *Harvard Law Review*, xxxviii (1924–5), 482–98.

NELSON, L. H., *The Normans in South Wales, 1070–1171*, 1966.

NICHOLL, D., *Thurstan Archbishop of York (1114–1140)*, 1964.

NORTH, J. J., *English Hammered Coinage*, 1960–3.

OFFLER, H. S., *Durham Episcopal Charters, 1071–1152* (Surtees Society, clxxix), 1968 for 1964.

OLESON, T. J., 'Edward the Confessor's Promise of the Throne to Duke William of Normandy', *E.H.R.*, lxxii (1957), 221–8.

OLSEN, O., and CRUMLIN-PEDERSEN, O., 'The Skuldelev Ships', *Acta Archaeologica* (Copenhagen), xxix (1958), 161–75; xxxviii (1967), 73–174.

ORDERIC VITALIS, *H.E.*: Orderic Vitalis, *Historia Ecclesiastica*; ed. A. Le Prévost (Société de l'Histoire de France, Paris), 1838–55; ed. M. Chibnall (Oxford Medieval Texts), ii–iv, 1969–73. *The Ecclesiastical History of England and Normandy* by Ordericus Vitalis, trans. T. Forester (Bohn's Antiquarian Library), 1853–6.

PAGE, W., *London, its Origin and Early Development*, 1923.

PATTERSON, R. B. (ed.), *Earldom of Gloucester Charters. The Charters and Scribes of the Earls and Countesses of Gloucester to A.D. 1217*, 1973.

'William of Malmesbury's Robert of Gloucester: a Re-evaluation of the *Historia Novella*', *American Historical Review*, lxx (1965), 983–97.

PÉPIN, E., *Gisors et la Vallée de l'Epte* (Petites monographies des grands édifices de la France, Paris), 1939.

PETIT-DUTAILLIS, Ch., *Étude sur la vie et le règne de Louis VIII*, 1894.

Studies and Notes Supplementary to Stubbs' Constitutional History, trans. W. E. Rhodes and W. T. Waugh (Publications of the University of Manchester, Historical Studies), 1908–29 (ed. 1923 of vols. i–ii quoted).

Pipe Roll 31 Henry I: *The Pipe Roll of 31 Henry I. Michaelmas 1130*, 1929 (Facsimile reproduction of *Magnum Rotulum Scaccarii vel Magnum Rotulum Pipae* ..., ed. J. Hunter (Record Commission), 1833.

PIRENNE, H., *Histoire de Belgique*, i (5th edn.), 1929.

PLUCKNETT, T. F. T., *A Concise History of the Common Law* (4th edn.), 1948.

POCQUET DU HAUT-JUSSÉ, B.A., 'Les Plantagenets et la Bretagne', *Annales de Bretagne*, liii (1946), 1–27.

'Le plus ancien rôle des comptes du duché, 1262', *Mémoires de la Société d'Histoire et d'Archéologie de Bretagne*, xxvi (1946), 49–68.

POEY D'AVANT, F., *Monnaies féodales de France*, 1858–62 (reprint, 1961).

POLLOCK and MAITLAND, *H.E.L.*: F. (Sir Frederick) Pollock, and F. W. Maitland, *The History of English Law before the time of Edward I* (2nd edn.), 1898. Second edition reissued with introduction by S. F. C. Milsom, 1968.

POOLE, A. L., *From Domesday Book to Magna Carta, 1087–1216* (The Oxford History of England, iii), 2nd edn., 1955.

'Henry Plantagenet's Early Visits to England', *E.H.R.*, xlvii (1932), 447–52.

POOLE, R. L., 'The Appointment and Deprivation of St William, Archbishop of York', *E.H.R.*, xlv (1930), 273–81.

The Exchequer in the Twelfth Century (The Ford Lectures delivered in the University of Oxford in Michaelmas Term, 1911), 1912.

POPE, M. K., *The Anglo-Norman Element in our Vocabulary: its Significance for our Civilization* (Manchester University Lectures Series, xxxvii), 1944.

POUMARÈDE, J., *Les successions dans le sud-ouest de la France au moyen âge* (Publications de l'Université des Sciences Sociales de Toulouse; Centre d'histoire juridique, Série historique, 1), 1972.

POWICKE, F. M. (Sir Maurice), *The Loss of Normandy, 1189–1204*, 1913. References are given to the second edition, 1961.

PRENTOUT, H., *Étude critique sur Dudon de Saint-Quentin et son Histoire des premiers ducs Normands* (Mémoires de l'Académie Nationale des Sciences, Arts et Belles-Lettres de Caen), 1915.

Histoire de Guillaume le Conquérant, i. *Le duc de Normandie* (Mémoires de l'Académie Nationale . . . de Caen, N.S. viii), 1936.

'La prise de Caen par Édouard III, 1346. Étude critique' (Mémoires de l'Académie Nationale . . . de Caen, 1904), 3–73.

PRESCOTT, J. E. (ed.), *The Register of the Priory of Wetherhal* (Cumberland and Westmorland Antiquarian Society, Record Series), 1897.

PRESTWICH, J. O., 'War and Finance in the Anglo-Norman State', *T.R.H.S.*, 5th series, iv (1954), 19–43.

RAFTIS, J. A., *The Estates of Ramsey Abbey: A Study in Economic Growth and Organization* (Pontifical Institute of Medieval Studies, Toronto; Texts and Studies, 3), 1957.

RAHTZ, P., 'The Saxon and Medieval Palaces at Cheddar, Somerset—An Interim Report of Excavations in 1960–62', *Medieval Archaeology: Journal of the Society for Medieval Archaeology* (London), vi–vii (1964 for 1962–3), 53–66.

RALPH DE DICETO, *Ymagines Historiarum*: *Radulfi de Diceto Decani Londoniensis, Opera historia. The Historical Works of Master Ralph de Diceto*, ed. W. Stubbs (Rolls Series), 1876.

RAMSAY, *Foundations*: J. H. (Sir James) Ramsay, *The Foundations of England, or Twelve Centuries of British History* (*B.C. 55–A.D. 1154*), 1898.

Recueil Brunel: *Recueil de travaux offert à M. Clovis Brunel . . . par ses amis, collègues et élèves* (Mémoires et Documents publiés par la Société de l'École des Chartes, xii), 1955.

Recueil des actes de Charles III le Simple, roi de France, ed. Ph. Lauer (Chartes et Diplômes relatifs à l'histoire de France, publiés par les soins de l'Académie des inscriptions et belles-lettres, Paris, 7bis), i, 1940.

REES, W., *South Wales and the March, 1284–1415. A Social and Agrarian Study*, 1924.

Regesta: *Regesta Regum Anglo-Normannorum*, i. *1066–1100*, edd. H. W. C. Davis and R. J. Whitwell (1913); ii. *1100–35*, edd. C. Johnson and H. A. Cronne (1956); iii. *1135–54*, edd. H. A. Cronne and R. H. C. Davis (1968); iv. *Facsimiles of Original Charters and Writs of King Stephen, the Empress Matilda and Dukes Geoffrey and Henry, 1135–54*, edd. H. A. Cronne and R. H. C. Davis (1969).

Regesta Regum Scottorum, i. *The Acts of Malcolm IV King of Scots, 1153–1165*, ed. G. W. S. Barrow, 1960.

Regularis Concordia: *The Monastic Agreement of the Monks and Nuns of the English Nation*, trans. and ed. Dom Thomas Symons (Medieval Classics), 1953.

'Relatio de Standardo', *Chronicles of the Reigns of Stephen, Henry II, and Richard I*, iii, ed. R. Howlett (Rolls Series), 1886, pp. 181–99.

RENOUARD, Y., 'Essai sur le rôle de l'empire angevin dans la formation de la France et de la civilisation française aux XIIe et XIIIe siècles', *Revue historique*, cxcv (1945), 289–304.

R.H.D.: *Revue historique de droit français et étranger*, 4e série (Paris), 1922– .

RHEIN, A., *La Seigneurie de Montfort-en-Iveline, depuis son origine jusqu'à son union au duché de Bretagne* (Mémoires de la Société Archéologique de Rambouillet, xxi, Versailles), 1910.

R.H.S.: Royal Historical Society, London.

RICHARD, A., *Histoire de comtes de Poitou, 778–1204*, 1903.

RICHARD, CH., *Notice sur l'ancienne bibliothèque des échevins de la ville de Rouen* (Rouen), 1845.

RICHARD, J., *Les Ducs de Bourgogne et la formation du duché du XIe au XIVe siècle* (Publications de l'Université de Dijon, xii), 1954.

RICHARDSON, H. G., *The English Jewry under Angevin Kings*, 1960.

RICHARDSON, H. G., and SAYLES, G. O., *The Governance of Medieval England from the Conquest to Magna Carta* (Edinburgh University Publications, History, Philosophy and Economics, No. 16), 1963.

RICHER, *Historiae*: Richer, *Histoire de France (888–995)*, ed. R. Latouche (Les Classiques de l'Histoire de France au Moyen Âge, Paris),1930–37.

RITCHIE, R. L. Graeme, *The Normans in England before Edward the Confessor* (Inaugural Lecture, University College of the South West, Exeter), 1948.

    The Normans in Scotland (Edinburgh University Publications, History, Philosophy and Economics, No. 4), 1954.

ROBERT DE TORIGNI, *Chronica*: *The Chronicle of Robert de Torigni, Abbot of the Monastery of St. Michael-in-Peril-of-the-Sea*, ed. R. Howlett, *Chronicles of the Reigns of Stephen, Henry II, and Richard I*, iv (Rolls Series), 1889.

ROBERTSON, *Laws*: *The Laws of the Kings of England from Edmund to Henry I*, ed. A. J. Robertson, 1925.

ROGER OF HOWDEN, *Chronica*: *Chronica Magistri Rogeri de Houedene*, ed. W. Stubbs (Rolls Series), 1868–71.

Rolls Series: *Rerum Britannicarum Medii Aevi Scriptores, or Chronicles and Memorials of Great Britain and Ireland during the Middle Ages*, published under the direction of the Master of the Rolls, London, 1858–96.

ROTH, C., *A History of the Jews in England*, 3rd edn., 1964.

Rotuli de Liberate ac de misis et praestitis, regnante Johanne, ed. T. D. Hardy (Record Commission), 1844.

Rotuli Litterarum Clausarum in turri Londinensi asservati, ed. T. D. Hardy (Record Commission), 1833–44.

Rotuli Normanniae in turri Londinensi asservati, Johanne et Henrico Quinto Angliae Regibus, i (all published), ed. T. D. Hardy (Record Commission), 1835.

Rotuli de Oblatis et Finibus in turri Londinensi asservati, tempore Regis Johannis, ed. T. D. Hardy (Record Commission), 1835.

ROUND, J. H., 'Bernard the King's Scribe', *E.H.R.*, xiv (1899), 417–430.

    'The Castles of the Conquest', *Archaeologia*, lviii (1) (1902), 313–40.

    The Commune of London and other studies, 1899.

    Geoffrey de Mandeville. A Study of the Anarchy, 1892.

    'A Great Marriage Settlement', *The Ancestor*, No. 11 (1904), pp. 153–7.

    'The Families of St. John and of Port', *The Genealogist*, N.S., xvi (1899), 1–13.

    Feudal England: Historical Studies on the XIth and XIIth Centuries, 1909.

    The King's Serjeants and Officers of State with their Coronation Services, 1911.

    'The Origin of Belvoir Castle', *E.H.R.*, xxii (1907), 508–10.

    Studies in Peerage and Family History, 1901 (reprint, 1970).

SALTMAN, A., 'John II, Bishop of Rochester', *E.H.R.*, lxvi (1951), 71–5.

    Theobald Archbishop of Canterbury, 1956.

SANDERS, I. J., *English Baronies. A Study of their Origin and Descent, 1086–1327*, 1960.

SAWYER, P. H., *The Age of the Vikings* (2nd edn.), 1971.

'The Wealth of England in the Eleventh Century', *T.R.H.S.*, 5th series, xv (1965), 145–64.

SCHRAMM, P. E. (trans. L. G. Wickham Legg), *A History of the English Coronation*, 1937.

SIMEON OF DURHAM, *Opera: Symeonis monachi opera omnia*, ed. T. Arnold (Rolls Series), 1882–5.

SIMPSON, A. W. B., *An Introduction to the History of the Land Law*, 1961.

Sir Christopher Hatton's Book of Seals, edd. L. C. Loyd and D. M. Stenton, 1950.

SOMERVILLE, R., 'Lanfranc's Canonical Collection and Exeter', *B.I.H.R.*, xlv (1972), 303–6.

SOUTHERN, R. W. (Sir Richard), 'Lanfranc of Bec and Berengar of Tours', *Studies in Medieval History presented to Frederick Maurice Powicke*, edd. R. W. Hunt, W. A. Pantin, and R. W. Southern, 1948, pp. 27–48.

The Making of the Middle Ages (1953).

Medieval Humanism and Other Studies, 1970.

Saint Anselm and his Biographer. A Study of Monastic Life and Thought, 1059–c. 1130, 1963.

STENTON, D. M., *English Justice between the Norman Conquest and the Great Charter, 1066–1215*. Jayne Lectures for 1963 (American Philosophical Society), 1965.

STENTON, *A.-S.E.*: F. M. (Sir Frank) Stenton, *Anglo-Saxon England* (The Oxford History of England, ii), 2nd edn., 1947.

'The Danes in England', *Proceedings of the British Academy*, xiii (1927), 203–46.

'English Families and the Norman Conquest', *T.R.H.S.*, 4th series, xxvi (1944), 1–12.

STENTON, *English Feudalism*: F. M. (Sir Frank) Stenton, *The First Century of English Feudalism, 1066–1166*, 2nd edn., 1961.

Norman London. An Essay. (Historical Association, London. Leaflet Nos. 93, 94), 1934.

'The Scandinavian Colonies in England and Normandy', *T.R.H.S.*, 4th series, xxvii (1945), 1–12.

William the Conqueror and the Rule of the Normans ('Heroes of the Nations'), 1908 (reprint, 1928).

STEPHENSON, C., *Borough and Town: a Study of Urban Origins in England* (Monographs of the Mediaeval Academy of America, No. 7), 1933.

(STEVENSON, W. H.), *Records of the Borough of Nottingham; being a Series of Extracts from the Archives of the Corporation of Nottingham*, published under the authority of the Corporation of Nottingham, 1882–1956.

STEWART, I. H., *The Scottish Coinage. With Supplement*. 1967.

STONES, E. L. G., ed. and trans., *Anglo-Scottish Relations 1174–1328. Some Selected Documents* (Medieval Texts), 1965.

STRAYER, J. R., *The Administration of Normandy under Saint Louis* (Monographs of the Mediaeval Academy of America, No. 6), 1932.

'On the Early Norman Charters, 911–1066'; J. R. Strayer, *Medieval Statecraft and the Perspectives of History*, 1971, pp. 39–43 (reprint of review of Fauroux, *Recueil*, in *Speculum*, xxxvii, 1962, 607–10).

STUBBS, W., *Select Charters and other illustrations of English Constitutional History* (ed. H. W. C. Davis, 1929).

SUGER, *Vita Ludovici Grossi Regis*: Suger, *Vie de Louis VI le Gros*, ed. and trans. H. Waquet (Les Classiques de l'histoire de France au Moyen Age), 1929.

TAIT, J., *The Chartulary or Register of the Abbey of St. Werburgh, Chester*, Part 1 (Chetham Society, Manchester), N.S. lxxix (1920).

The Domesday Survey of Cheshire (Chetham Society, Manchester), N.S. lxxv (1916).

Mediæval Manchester and the Beginnings of Lancashire (University of Manchester Publications, Historical Series), 1904.

TAYLOR, H. M. and J., *Anglo-Saxon Architecture*, i and ii, 1965.

TAYLOR, Thomas, *The Celtic Christianity of Cornwall, Divers Sketches and Studies*, 1916.

THORNE, S. E., 'English Feudalism and estates in land', *Cambridge Law Journal*, 1959, pp. 193–209.

TIMSON, R. T., 'Edition of Blyth Cartulary' (summary of Ph.D. thesis), *B.I.H.R.*, xxxviii (1965), 223–4.

TOUT, T. F., *Chapters in the Administrative History of Medieval England: The Wardrobe, the Chamber and the Small Seals* (Publications of the University of Manchester, Historical Series), 1920–33.

Très Ancienne Coutume de Bretagne (La), ed. M. Planiol (Bibliothèque bretonne armoricaine; publiée par la Faculté des Lettres de Rennes, fasc. ii), 1896.

Très Ancien Coutumier de Normandie (Le), ed. E.-J. Tardif. *Coutumiers de Normandie*, i. 1ère partie, *Texte latin*, 1881; 2ème partie, *Textes français et normand*, 1903.

T.R.H.S.: *Transactions of the Royal Historical Society* (London), 1871– .

TUCOO-CHALA, P., *La Vicomté de Béarn et le problème de sa souveraineté, des origines à 1620*, 1961.

VALIN, L., *Le Duc de Normandie et sa cour (912–1204). Étude d'histoire juridique*, 1910.

VALLERY-RADOT, J., *La Cathédrale de Bayeux* (Petites Monographies des grands édifices de la France, Paris), [1922].

VAN CAENEGEM, R. C., *The Birth of the English Common Law*, 1973.

Royal Writs in England from the Conquest to Glanvill (Selden Society, lxxvii), 1959 for 1958–9.

V.C.H.: *The Victoria County History of the Counties of England*, 1900– . (References given in the form, *V.C.H. Hampshire*, etc.).

VERCAUTEREN-DE SMET, L., 'Étude sur les rapports politiques de l'Angleterre et de la Flandre sous le règne du comte Robert II (1093–1111)', *Études d'Histoire dédiées à la mémoire de Henri Pirenne par ses anciens élèves* (preface signed by F. L. Ganshof, E. Sabbe, F. Vercauteren) (Brussels, 1937), pp. 413–23.

VERLINDEN, C., *Robert Ier le Frison, Comte de Flandre. Étude d'histoire politique.* (Universiteit te Gent, Werken uitgegeven door de Faculteit der Wijsbegeerte en Letteren, 72), 1935.

VISING, J., *Anglo-Norman Language and Literature*, 1923.

Vita Edwardi: The Life of King Edward who rests at Westminster, ed. and trans. F. Barlow (Medieval Texts), 1962.

WAINWRIGHT, F. T. 'Æthelflæd Lady of the Mercians', *The Anglo-Saxons: Studies in Some Aspects of their History and Culture presented to Bruce Dickins*, ed. P. Clemoes, 1959, pp. 53–69.

WALTER MAP, *De Nugis Curialium*, ed. M. R. James (Anecdota Oxoniensia, Medieval and Modern series, part xiv), 1914. Translated by M. R. James (Cymmrodorion Record Series, ix), 1923.

WAQUET, H., *Histoire de la Bretagne* (Coll. 'Que sais-je?'), 1948 (1943).

WARD, J. C., 'The Estates of the Clare Family, 1066–1317'. Unpublished London Ph.D. thesis, 1962. Summary in *B.I.H.R.*, xxxvii (1964), 114–17.

WEBB, C. C. J., *John of Salisbury* ('Great Medieval Churchmen'), 1932.

WEST, F., *The Justiciarship in England, 1066–1232* (Cambridge Studies in Medieval Life and Thought, N.S., xii), 1966.

WHITE, G. H., 'The Career of Waleran, Count of Meulan and Earl of Worcester (1104–1166)', *T.R.H.S.*, 4th series, xvii (1934), 19–48.

'Constables under the Norman Kings', *The Genealogist*, N.S., xxxviii (1922), 113–27.

'Financial Administration under Henry I', *T.R.H.S.*, 4th series, viii (1925), 56–78.

'The First House of Bellême', *T.R.H.S.*, 4th series, xxii (1940), 67–99.

'The Household of the Norman Kings', *T.R.H.S.*, 4th series, xxx (1948), 127–55.

'King Stephen's Earldoms', *T.R.H.S.*, 4th series, xiii (1930), 51–82.

'The Sisters and Nieces of Gunnor, Duchess of Normandy', *The Genealogist*, N.S., xxxvii (1920), 57–65, 128–32.

'Treasurers in Normandy under Henry I', *Notes and Queries*, cl (1926), 59–60.

WHITELOCK, D., 'The Dealings of the Kings of England with Northumbria in the Tenth and Eleventh Centuries', *The Anglo-Saxons: Studies in Some Aspects of their History and Culture presented to Bruce Dickins*, ed. P. Clemoes, 1959, pp. 70–88.

WIGHTMAN, W. E., 'Henry I and the Foundation of Nostell Priory', *Y.A.J.*, xli (1966), 57–60.

The Lacy Family in England and Normandy, 1066–1194, 1966.

'The Palatine Earldom of William fitzOsbern in Gloucestershire and Worcestershire (1066–1071)', *E.H.R.*, lxxvii (1962), 6–17.

WILLIAM DE JUMIÈGES, *Gesta Normannorum Ducum*, ed. J. Marx (Société de l'Histoire de Normandie, Rouen, Paris), 1914.

WILLIAM OF NEWBURGH, *Historia*: *The Historia Rerum Anglicarum of William of Newburgh*, ed. R. Howlett. *Chronicles of the Reigns of Stephen, Henry II, and Richard I*, i and ii (Rolls Series), 1884–5.

WILLIAM DE POITIERS, *Gesta Guillelmi ducis Normannorum et regis Anglorum*, ed. R. Foreville (Les Classiques de l'histoire de France au Moyen Age, Paris), 1952.

WILLIAMS, A. H., *An Introduction to the History of Wales*, 1941–8.

WILLIAMS, G. H., *The Norman Anonymous of 1100 A.D.* (Harvard Theological Studies, xviii), 1951.

WILLIAMSON, E. W., *The Letters of Osbert of Clare, Prior of Westminster*, 1929.

WILSON, R. M., 'English and French in England, 1100–1300', *History*, xxviii (1943), 37–60.

WOOD, C. T., 'Regnum Francie: A Problem in Capetian administrative usage', *Traditio*, xxiii (1967), 117–47.

WORMALD, F., 'An Eleventh-Century Copy of the Norman *Laudes Regiae*', *B.I.H.R.*, xxxvii (1964), 73–6.

'The Survival of Anglo-Saxon Illumination after the Norman Conquest', *Proceedings of the British Academy*, xxx (1944), 127–45.

Y.A.J.: *Yorkshire Archaeological and Topographical Journal*, i–xi (1870–91); *Yorkshire Archaeological Journal*, xii– (1893–).

Y.A.S.: Yorkshire Archaeological Society.

YVER, J., 'Autour de l'absence d'avouerie en Normandie', *B.S.A.N.*, lvii (1965 for 1963–4), 189–283.

'Le bref anglo-normand', *Revue d'histoire du droit: Tijdschrift voor Rechtsgeschiedenis* (Groningen, Brussels, The Hague), xxix (1961), 313–30.

'Les caractères originaux de la coutume de Normandie', *Mémoires de l'Académie des Sciences, Arts et Belles-Lettres de Caen*, N.S., xii (1952), 307–56.

'Les caractères originaux du groupe de coutumes de l'ouest de la France', *R.H.D.*, xxx (1952), 18–79.

'Les châteaux forts en Normandie jusqu'au milieu du xIIᵉ siècle. Contribution à l'étude du pouvoir ducal', *B.S.A.N.*, liii (1957 for 1955–6), 28–115, 604–9.

'Contribution à l'étude du développement de la compétence ducale en Normandie', *Annales de Normandie*, viii (1958), 139–83.

'Le développement du pouvoir ducal en Normandie de l'avènement de Guillaume le Conquérant à la mort d'Henri I, 1035–1135', *Atti del Convegno Internazionale di Studi Ruggeriani* (Palermo, 1955), pp. 183–204.

'Les premières institutions du duché de Normandie', *I Normanni e la loro espansione in Europa nell'alto medioevo* (Centro Italiano di Studi sull'Alto Medioevo; Settimana xvi, 1968; Spoleto), 1969, pp. 299–366.

'Le "Très Ancien Coutumier" de Normandie, miroir de la législation ducale?', *Revue d'histoire du droit: Tijdschrift voor rechtsgeschiedenis* (Groningen, Brussels, The Hague), xxxix (1971), 333–74.

ZARNECKI, G., *English Romanesque Sculpture, 1066–1140*, 1951.

Romanesque Sculpture at Lincoln Cathedral (Lincoln Minster Pamphlets, 2nd series, 2), [1963].

'1066 and Architectural Sculpture', *Proceedings of the British Academy*, lii (1967 for 1966), 87–104.

OUTLINE GENEALOGY OF THE
NORMAN DUKES AND KINGS

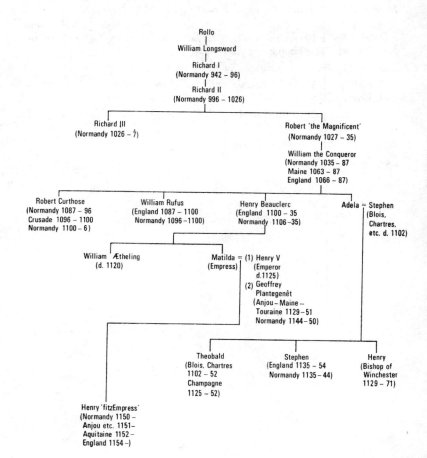

Rollo
|
William Longsword
|
Richard I
(Normandy 942 – 96)
|
Richard II
(Normandy 996 – 1026)

Richard III
(Normandy 1026 – ?)

Robert 'the Magnificent'
(Normandy 1027 – 35)
|
William the Conqueror
(Normandy 1035 – 87
Maine 1063 – 87
England 1066 – 87)

Robert Curthose
(Normandy 1087 – 96
Crusade 1096 – 1100
Normandy 1100 – 6)

William Rufus
(England 1087 – 1100
Normandy 1096 –1100)

Henry Beauclerc
(England 1100 – 35
Normandy 1106 –35)

Adela = Stephen
(Blois,
Chartres,
etc. d. 1102)

William Ætheling
(d. 1120)

Matilda = (1) Henry V
(Empress)   (Emperor
              d.1125)
         (2) Geoffrey
             Plantegenêt
             (Anjou – Maine –
             Touraine 1129 – 51
             Normandy 1144 – 50)

Theobald
(Blois. Chartres
1102 – 52
Champagne
1125 – 52)

Stephen
(England 1135 – 54
Normandy 1135 – 44)

Henry
(Bishop of
Winchester
1129 – 71)

Henry 'fitzEmpress'
(Normandy 1150 –
Anjou etc. 1151–
Aquitaine 1152 –
England 1154 –)

O

MAP 1. THE NORMAN EMPIRE

This map is designed to show the territories over which King Henry Beauclerc exercised dominion in some degree and those with which he was in constant and direct contact. It also gives some idea of the range of his itinerary. The ports known to have been used for royal transfretations from 1067 until 1144 are marked. Names of places at which Henry issued charters and writs dated 'in transfretatione' or 'in transitu' have been italicized. No attempt has been made to mark all the places that figure in Henry's known itinerary, and to do so might well give a misleading impression; but the places marked in Normandy indicate the extent of his movement there. The only considerable area in the duchy which he does not appear to have visited after Tinchebrai is made up of the Avranchin with the southern parts of the dioceses of Coutances and Bayeux, though he must have known this region well.

Area in which King Henry spent most of his time while in England

0 20 40 60 80 100 miles
0   40   80   120   160 km

KINGDOM
OF THE
SCOTS

•Carlisle
Durham•

York•

GWYNEDD

POWYS

Nottingham•

Norwich•

Northampton• •Huntingdon
Brampton

MARCHER
LORDS
Gloucester• Woodstock•
•Oxford Dunstable•

Bath• •Westminster London•

Winchester Canterbury•
Salisbury• Bishops Waltham •Dover
Romsey• Fareham Winchelsea•
Eling• Arundel• •Wissant
Westbourne Hastings•
Southampton• Pevensey FLANDERS
Portsmouth BOULOGNE
ST. POL

ENGLISH CHANNEL
St. Valéry
Le Tréport PONTHIEU
Dieppe• •Eu AMIENS
Barfleur• Arques BEAUVAIS
St. Vaast VEXIN
la Hougue Rouen• FRANÇAIS
Caen• Touques• Gisors•
VEXIN
NORMAND Seine
Falaise• DREUX Paris•
Verneuil•
THIMERAIS MONTFORT
PERCHE L'AMAURY
Alençon• MAINE
BRITTANY Le Mans•
Rennes• VENDÔME Orleans•

Angers• Tours•
Nantes• ANJOU Loire
TOURAINE

Severn
Trent
Thames
Itch
Southampton
NORMANDY
BLOIS CHARTRES
ROYAL DOMAIN

MAP 2. NORMANDY IN THE ELEVENTH AND EARLY TWELFTH CENTURIES

This map has been prepared to illustrate the problem of the Norman frontier in the time of the Norman dukes and kings, by showing the degree of coincidence or non-coincidence of the boundaries of the Carolingian *pagi*, the medieval dioceses and the territory within which the *Coutume de Normandie* eventually 'crystallized'. To this has been added the position of the cathedral cities, religious houses established by 1135 and the principal castles known from literary evidence to have been in existence by that date. Other places within the boundaries of the *coutume* and of the Norman dioceses, and places beyond those boundaries, have been marked only where there seemed to be some particular reason for doing so.

The boundaries of the *pagi*, as in the tenth century, are based on Longnon, *Atlas historique de la France*, pl. VII, and *Texte*, pp. 93–210; those of the dioceses on the map printed in *Magni Rotuli Scaccarii Normanniae* (ed. Stapleton) and reprinted in Powicke, *Loss of Normandy*. It should be noted that later ecclesiastical boundaries are often the principal evidence for the earlier limits of the *pagi*. The boundary of the *coutume* is based on Lemarignier, *Hommage en marche*, ch. 2 (with works referred to there and the sketch map at the end of the volume, 'Frontières de la Normandie') and Klimrath, *Études sur les coutumes*. The limits of the *coutume* could be defined very much more closely, even to parish boundaries; but such precision and the research that would be needed for it have not been attempted in a map on this scale. For the 'Conquêts Hue de Gournay' (24 parishes in the Beauvaisis annexed to Normandy but preserving many customs of the Beauvaisis), Lemarignier, *Hommage en marche*, pp. 20–2. The religious houses (those certainly or probably established by 1066 with their names italicized) have been identified from *Abbayes et prieurés de l'ancienne France* and Knowles, *Monastic Order in England*, pp. 701–2; the castles from Yver, 'Châteaux forts en Normandie'. Yver included only those castles that are attested by the evidence of the chronicles. Archaeological evidence and general probability have not been taken into account and places such as Bricquebec, La Haye-du-Puits, and Montbrai in the Cotentin, for example, have not been marked on the map, though it could be taken as virtually certain that they had a castle of some sort by 1135. Yver also remarks, 'Une carte détaillée de la fortification normande aux environs de 1130 exigerait assurément de bien autres recherches que celles que j'ai pu faire.' Castles are represented on this map with the same reserve.

INDEX

Names and subjects in footnotes, including medieval and modern texts and authorities, have not been indexed when they are mentioned in the main text above them on the page, save exceptionally. Place-names have been located by department in France and by historic county in England (i.e. as before the changes of 1974 and other changes of recent years), except where the name of the county simply adds the suffix '-shire' to the name of a town. Bibliography, genealogy, and maps have not been indexed.

king of, relationship with, 11–12, 218–21, 239, 242; Frankish royal and monastic lands, seizure of, 285; kinship with aristocracy, 287–9, 292, 294, 335–6; itineration of, 123; jurisdiction of, 265–7 (delegation of, 266); revenues of, 146–7, 154, 203, 222–3, 286, 329; royal attributes of, 238–9, 270, 281, 289, 320; style and titles of, *see* Titles; wealth and power, origin of, 283–92, 297; *see* Henry II, Henry Beauclerc, Richard I, Richard II, Richard III, Robert I, Rollo, William the Conqueror, William Longsword, (William Rufus)

Enrichment of, after 1066, 29, 149, 331–4; 'feudal phase' of, 14, 21; formation of duchy, 3–27; frontier of, 4, 8–9, 10–12, 81, 83, 101, 216–17, 258; law and custom of as in 1066, 264; rebellions in, 81–2; '*regnum*' of, 231; royal government in after 1066, 239–43; seneschal of, 116, 274, 277; separation from England (1144–54), 95–6; 'Viking phase', 13–14, 21, 286, 290, 319; wealth of, 145–6, 203, 326; writs, used in, 244–5

Northampton, 124; assize of, 275 n; council at, 295–6 n

Northamptonshire, 68 n, 72

North Elmham (Norfolk), *see* Elmham

Northmen (Danes, Norse, Vikings, etc.), 3–5, etc.; adopt Frankish language and religion, 13, 282

Agreement between King Charles the Simple and Rollo, 911 (Treaty of Saint-Clair-sur-Epte), 3, 5, 8, 11–12, 16, 218, 283; 'grant' by King Rudolf, 924 (Bessin, Hiémois ?), 3, 5–6, 11, 283; 'grant' by King Rudolf, 933 (Cotentin, Avranchin ?), 3, 5–7, 11, 283

Leaders of, 283; their authority, 283–4

Raids and destruction by, in Brittany, 6–8, 14; in England, 21, 146; in Normandy and northern France, 3, 5–6, 12–13, 285, 289, 297

Settlements in Britain, 52–7; in the Loire Valley and Brittany, 5, 7, 9;

in Normandy, 3, 5–9, 11–13, 218, 282–4, 290, 297, 299, 304, 319

Northumberland, 102; earls of, *see* Robert de Montbrai, Henry of Scotland

Northumbria, earldom of, 25, 55–6, 97; earls of, 56; *see* Morcar, Siward, Tostig; kingdom of, 53, 55, 57, 60, 123; magnates of, 56

North Wales, 98–9; Norman campaigns in, 204, 310, 312–14; 'Nort Wales', 62, 211, 313–14; *see* Gwynedd

Norway, 55, 122; kings of, 25

Norwich (Norfolk), 45; bishops of (Elmham–Thetford–Norwich), *see* Everard, Herbert Losinga, Herfast, William de Beaufour; cathedral church of, 352 n

Nostell (Yorkshire, West Riding), priory, 49 n

Nottingham, 45; castle, 306; council at, 295–6 n

Novel Disseisin, writ of, 273

Noyon (Oise), 6

Odo, bishop of Bayeux, 29–30 n, 332, 337, 339; castle-building, 144 n, 306–7; earl of Kent, 259 n, 310; lands in England, 32–5, 37, 44 n, 47, 291 n, 308, 311 n, 332, 335–6, 338; regent, 141–2

Offa's Dyke, 32

Oger 'the Breton', 74

Oise, river, 16, 83, 95

Okehampton (Devon), castle, borough, 317

Orbec (Calvados), 33

Ordeal, 268–9

Orderic Vitalis, 18–19, 27, 33–4, 39, 42, 47, 76, 90, 144, 165, 182, 187, 189, 197, 200, 202–3, 228, 237, 239, 240, 296, 303, 335–7, 342–3, 350; on castles in England before 1066, 307 n; on the White Ship disaster, 177–8

Orival (Seine-Maritime), 51 n

Orkney, bishop of, 353

Orne, river, 284, 305

Osbern, father of Osbern and William fitzOsbern, seneschal, 136 n

Osbern fitzOsbern, bishop of Exeter, 22, 24 n, 50, 249 n

DATE DUE